Blueprints for thinking

Blueprints for thinking

The role of planning
in cognitive development

Edited by

SARAH L. FRIEDMAN
National Institute of Child Health and Human Development

ELLIN KOFSKY SCHOLNICK
University of Maryland, College Park

RODNEY R. COCKING
University of Delaware

The right of the
University of Cambridge
to print and sell
all manner of books
was granted by
Henry VIII in 1534.
The University has printed
and published continuously
since 1584.

CAMBRIDGE UNIVERSITY PRESS
Cambridge
London   New York   New Rochelle
Melbourne   Sydney

Published by the Press Syndicate of the University of Cambridge
The Pitt Building, Trumpington Street, Cambridge CB2 1RP
32 East 57th Street, New York, NY 10022, USA
10 Stamford Road, Oakleigh, Melbourne 3166, Australia

First published 1987

Printed in the United States of America

Library of Congress Cataloging-in-Publication Data
Blueprints for thinking.
Includes indexes.
1. Cognition in children.   2. Planning in children.
I. Friedman, Sarah L.   II. Scholnick, Ellin Kofsky.
III. Cocking, Rodney R.   [DNLM: 1. Child Development.
2. Cognition–in infancy & childhood.   3. Planning
Technics.   4. Psychology, Educational.   WS 105.5.C7 B658]
BF723.C5B53   1987   155.4′13   86-21640

British Library Cataloguing in Publication Data
Blueprints for thinking : the role of planning
in cognitive development.
1. Decision-making
I. Friedman, Sarah L.   II. Scholnick,
Ellin Kofsky   III. Cocking, Rodney R.
153.8′3   BF441

ISBN 0 521 25605 4

To the people who figure in our plans,
especially to Myron, Moshe, Daphne,
and Matthew

Contents

vii

Contributors

Rodney R. Cocking, Educational Development, University of Delaware, Newark

Carol E. Copple, 7503 Palmer Lane, Takoma Park, Maryland

Martin V. Covington, Psychology Department, University of California, Berkeley

Richard De Lisi, Graduate School of Education, Rutgers University, New Brunswick, New Jersey

Michael Dreher, University of Munich, Munich, West Germany

Janice Flaugher, Educational Testing Service, Princeton, New Jersey

Sarah L. Friedman, National Institute of Child Health and Human Development, Bethesda, Maryland

William Gardner, Department of Psychology, University of Virginia, Charlottesville

Mary Gauvain, Department of Psychology, University of Pennsylvania, Philadelphia

Jacqueline J. Goodnow, Macquarie University, North Ryde, N.S.W., Australia

Jan Hawkins, Bank Street College of Education, New York City

Hans Kreitler, Department of Psychology, Tel Aviv University, Ramat Aviv, Israel

Shulamith Kreitler, Department of Psychology, Tel Aviv University, Ramat Aviv, Israel

Ann McGillicuddy-De Lisi, Psychology Department, Lafayette College, Easton, Pennsylvania

Rolf Oerter, University of Munich, Munich, West Germany

Louis Oppenheimer, University of Amsterdam, Amsterdam, The Netherlands

Roy D. Pea, School of Education, Communication and Technology, New York University, New York City

Robert A. Randall, Department of Anthropology, University of Houston

Barbara Rogoff, Psychology Department, University of Utah, Salt Lake City

Ellin Kofsky Scholnick, Psychology Department, University of Maryland, College Park

Irving E. Sigel, Educational Testing Service, Princeton, New Jersey

Foreword

In the *Leviathan*, Thomas Hobbes noted:

From Desire, ariseth the Thought of some means we have seen produce the like of that which we ayme at; . . . because the End, by the greatnesse of the impression, comes often to mind, in case our thoughts begin to wander, they are quickly again reduced into the way: . . . in all your actions, look often upon what you would have, as a thing that directs all your thoughts in the way to attain it.

Although the human capacity for choice and planning was recognized clearly by pre-Enlightenment scholars, twentieth-century behavioral scientists have to be reminded of the importance of these functions because of a continued tension that seeks to minimize human thought. The desire to eliminate mental products from explanations of behavior was enhanced after World War I by the philosophy of logical empiricism and is sustained, in part, by the promise of proponents of artificial intelligence that programs might simulate cognition without extensive subroutines for future options to possible frustrations. It is useful, therefore, to be reminded that a theory of human behavior without a set of constructs that refers to plans is simply not possible. Clark Hull had to invent the anticipatory goal response in order to explain the running behavior of rats; Tolman posited the notion of cognitive map; and social learning theorists continue to rely on the idea of expectancy. In one sense, Erik Erikson's developmental stages can be viewed as implying ontogenetic changes in the content of plans because growth is accompanied by a rearrangement of the hierarchy of goals. It is also obvious that John Flavell's research on metamemory owes some of its reception to the consensual notion that psychology requires a construct referring to an executive function that monitors the elementary cognitive processes. Thus, few contemporary behavioral scientists would quarrel with the necessity of a family of concepts that deals with the ability to generate cognitive structures representing possible outcomes – a phrase that captures the sense meaning of planning. There is debate, however, over the referential meanings of this term and, therefore, disagreement over what we have learned.

xi

The child's disposition to generate plans varies with the specific context – its familiarity, of course, but also its motivational relevance at the moment. Every observer has seen a two-year-old playing with toys suddenly stop and search for a particular toy in an action so directed it would be difficult to deny the prior generation of a plan. Yet we know that this child might not behave in a planful way in many of the experimental contexts a psychologist might impose in the laboratory. That is why it is useful to regard the development of planning competences as an S-shaped function, with the ordinate representing the proportion of relevant contexts in which evidence of planning appears, and the abscissa representing age.

As this welcome volume makes clear, we must parse the concept of planning into a family of talents specified by context, as we parse economies into categories defined by historical era and geographical location. Planning is not a mental essence, but a conventional superordinate for a series of related phenomena that include sailing skills, writing, and the making of mud pies. Once the child completes the transition into early childhood, between the second and third birthdays, he or she is potentially capable of organizing a great many future actions. The task for psychologists is to determine the conditions under which these processes will or will not be activated, as psycholinguists ask for children who have begun to speak about the conditions that will lead to syntactically correct or incorrect utterances.

The editors and I share the conviction that in the seamless sequence between thought and action, planning usually refers to the former function, even though it occurs during the execution of a long and complex problem-solving sequence. There is, however, an occasional confusion between subjective and objective descriptions of planning. Some psychologists use the term "planning" to refer to an individual's conscious awareness of a planned sequence, whereas others use the same term in the objective frame of the scientist. Because the information that defines each of the frames has a different source, the two perspectives are complementary and need not be consistent. Scientists cannot know the mental states of animals; hence, these states are ignored in objectively framed descriptions and explanations of animal behavior. Karl Von Frisch did not assume that honeybees plan their dance after returning from a source of pollen. And if all the pigeons generating data affirming the laws of scheduled reinforcement were able to tell us that they were not pecking at the key in order to obtain food, the confession would not weaken the validity of the objectively framed theoretical statements that link the occurrence of operant responses to the schedule of food delivery.

Human beings, however, have a private awareness of their intentions, beliefs, and feeling states. Although these states have primacy in the conduct of our personal lives, an objectively framed explanation of a person's behavior need not be consistent with the subjective frame, nor with the terms particular persons may use to describe their beliefs or conscious plans. We have learned from elegant experiments that people do not have access to their own mental processes when they solve problems, and there is often no relation between a person's report of a motive state and an objective index of that motive. As the philosopher Churchland noted, "Our private judgements, when used as data for objectively framed propositions, have no epistemic clout: As measuring instruments humans stand rather badly in need of wholesale recalibration" (1979, p. 41).

No serious epistemological consequences follow from the suggestion that the subjective meaning of a child's report of conscious planning is different from the meaning ascribed to the same information in the objective frame of the investigator. It is not necessary to decide whether subjective or objective meaning is more valid, or whether scientists should judge each meaning of planfulness with reference to some third, ideal frame. The subjective and objective meanings of planfulness simply generate concepts with different meanings because they have different sources. Hilary Putnam has noted, "To grant that there is more than one true version of reality is not to deny that some versions are false" (1983, p. 19). I suggest that progress will be made if investigators agree that the concept of planning as now used is in the objective frame and that another word should be invented to refer to a child's conscious awareness of being planful.

As mechanistic, biological explanations of behavior become more credible and powerful, citizens and scientists are losing their faith in the nineteenth-century concept of will, and some are ready to believe that the human species is so closely related to dogs, lions, and baboons that our biology is able to subdue each person's sense of what is right. If we are only hairless versions of gorillas, then it will become easier to excuse violent acts of aggression by sane adolescents who were overcome by their impulses. These papers on planning are important, for they remind us that the human will has not been dissolved by neurotransmitters or captured by neural nets. Although I do not doubt the essential correctness of modern evolutionary theory, some scientists have become too accepting of Darwin's view that "Man still bares in his bodily frame the indelible stamp of his lowly origin." An uncritical attitude toward that assumption could make it a self-fulfilling prophecy. Hidden between the lines of this timely book is the hope that if the next generation is tutored more consciously in the utility and value of planning, adolescent muggings and terrorist murders might decrease and the future might be a little less dangerous. Thus this volume fills two important needs: It enhances our understanding of the human mind, and acts as an antidote to an addiction that tempts us to surrender too easily to biological determinism.

Jerome Kagan

References

Churchland, P. M. (1979). *Scientific realism and the plasticity of mind.* Cambridge: Cambridge University Press.
Putnam, H. (1983). *Realism and reason. Philosophical Papers* (Vol. 3). Cambridge: Cambridge University Press.

Acknowledgments

The editors' work on this volume was encouraged by Drs. Susan F. Chipman, Lois-ellen Datta and Shirley Jackson who, like the editors, were employed by the National Institute of Education at the time that the volume was planned. The editors wish to thank these individuals for facilitating the work on this book. Special appreciation goes to Dr. Marian Radke-Yarrow, chief of the Laboratory of Developmental Psychology at the National Institute of Mental Health and to the Department of Psychology of the University of Maryland at College Park. Rodney Cocking wishes to acknowledge the support he received while he was a visiting professor at the University of Delaware and to thank Dean F. B. Murray. The ideas presented in the volume do not necessarily represent the views of the institutions in which the editors have been employed while preparing the volume.

Part I

The prevalence of planning

1 The planning construct in the psychological literature

Ellin Kofsky Scholnick and Sarah L. Friedman

I. The problem of planning

The philosopher Wittgenstein (1953) noted that there are so many definitions of the word "game" that it is difficult to describe what they all have in common. He could just as well have chosen as his example, "planning." Cognitive scientists have described problem solving as planful behavior and even labeled one problem-solving heuristic as "planning" (e.g., Newell & Simon, 1972). Comprehension of narratives is thought to be based on detection of characters' plans (e.g., Schank & Abelson, 1977). Discussions of planning enter into analyses of behavioral control and intention. Plans are the subject of theories of behavioral attribution (Schmidt, 1976). Analyses of metacognitive activities, with their focus on executive monitoring and control strategies, also emphasize planning. Memory development (e.g., Brown, Bransford, Ferrara, & Campione, 1983) has been attributed to acquistion of planning skills, which enable the learner to treat each memory task as a problem overcome by shrewd tactics.

Planning has been used to account for so many diverse facets of functioning that the definition of the term has become vague. Two theorists who use the term may not share the same focus. Miller, Galanter, and Pribram (1960) define planning as execution of a behavior that matches a scheme, whereas Hayes-Roth and Hayes-Roth (1979) include anticipating a course of action as well.

No wonder there is such confusion. Planning is a set of complex conceptual activities that anticipate and regulate behavior. Planning relies on representation of the environment, anticipation of solutions to problems, and then monitoring of strategies to see whether they meet the problem and follow the plan. To plan is to act simultaneously on three levels: in the reality of a problem, in accordance with an imagined scheme, and in the role of mediator between the scheme and the behavior. The variety

3

of definitions of planning may result from emphasis on one of the three levels of planning activity; in turn, the vagueness may reflect a failure to specify which of the levels is being referred to or how the levels are integrated. An adequate theory of planning has to be very comprehensive and to encompass every level of cognition.

Second, planning has been treated from two frameworks, as a general cognitive skill or as a context-specific activity. Many theories of problem solving emphasize the general structure of planning activity, whereas in the study of memory and conversation the focus is on context-specific strategies, which are regarded as the same as plans. Because plans for conversation may have little to do with plans to reconstruct the Tower of Hanoi, it is hard for the reader to arrive at a definition of planning.

Yet a third source of confusion arises because in some theories, such as in the realm of problem solving, planning is a mandatory activity and little attention is devoted to the factors that prompt the person to plan in the first place. However, planning may be optional and the decision whether or not to plan may be determined by individual differences on dimensions such as cultural or personal norms about the desirability of plans, familiarity with the context in which planning is called for, and the cognitive and motivational status of the individual. Theories that regard planning as mandatory focus on the construction of the plan to the neglect of motivational aspects, whereas theories that recognize that planning does not always take place may concentrate on explaining why people plan and thus may deemphasize the mechanisms of planning. A fourth reason for the diversity is that some theories attempt to account for individual differences in planning efficiency in terms of the number of planning components present and the speed of their execution. Others stress stylistic variations in approaches to planning dependent on contextual cues. The stylistic variations may reflect qualitative differences in performance.

Yet a fifth reason why discussions of planning seem so diffuse is that planning not only takes place on many levels but also involves many different activities, each reflecting a facet of goal-directed action. Different analyses of planning emphasize different aspects of the course of goal-directed behavior, leading to the confusion. The aim of this chapter is to analyze which aspects of goal-directed action are captured by different theories of planning. We will even show that dictionary definitions of planning do the same, and focus on different aspects of motivated behavior. We hope that this framework will serve as a basis for understanding the chapters in this volume and the larger field as well.

II. A plan for the discussion of plans

There is a difference between the action of Halley's comet and the behavior of the director of the Office of Management and Budget. Only the director is planful. Plans are the expression of goal-directed behavior, and more specifically, of behavior that is voluntary, self-conscious, and intended (e.g., Chapman, 1984; Kreitler & Kreitler, 1976). Goal-directed behavior has many components. Understanding a behavior requires knowledge of how individuals represent the environment and the problems that arise, decide on a goal that solves their problem, formulate a set of strategies to reach the goal, execute the strategies they have chosen, monitor and repair their strategic decisions and actions, and evaluate the outcome of actions and the schemes that guided them (e.g., Hayes, 1981). It is our contention that theories of planning tend to single out one or more of these components of goal-directed action and use them as the basis for their models of planning. Our discussion of plans will emphasize these structural components, but we shall also examine how these components are influenced by developmental and cultural differences. When presenting the structural components of planning, we will describe how these were treated in the existing psychological literature on planning as a general cognitive skill and in specific domains such as writing or story grammars. We will also deal with individual differences, and speculate where developmental changes are to be expected. Information about the development of planning receives additional consideration at the end of the chapter, where we draw together analyses of the origins of planning. Thus the plan for this chapter is to present a framework for viewing theories of planning and its developmental prerequisites.

III. The components of goal-directed action

A. Representation

In the *Oxford English Dictionary* (1971, p. 2195) one definition of "plan" was the inspiration for the title of this book, *Blueprints for thinking*. A "plan" is a "diagram, table or program indicating the relations of some set of objects or the times or places of some intended proceedings." This definition has two important implications. First, "plan" is not an action but an entity, such as a "map." Second, the definition emphasizes a crucial prerequisite for planning – the availability of a mental representation of the spatial and causal structure of particular events. Action always takes place in an environment, but that environment is not always a direct copy of the stimulus world. Instead people mentally recreate the stimulus world to reflect their understanding of how, when, and where individuals and objects function. This representation of the environment constrains definitions of problems, goals, and means to solution. Consequently, plans and the actions they inspire reflect people's representations of the setting for a problem. Whereas few planning theorists only describe the model of the environment that people use in creating plans, several planning theorists claim that the content of plans is determined by a person's model of physical and psychological causation.

Discussions of representation in planning vary on two dimensions. First, some planning theorists argue that the planner's representation is a relatively faithful model of the problem space, although it may be incomplete. We will call these "veridical" models. Other theories note the existence of biases towards selecting aspects of the environment due to "idiosyncratic" personal experiences. Failures in problem solving reflect distortions in representation, not gaps. Those distortions are most apparent in problems that have open-ended solutions. Thus the first contrast is between verdical versus idiosyncratic representations. Second, some discussions of representation in planning attempt to account for particular problem-solving tasks, whereas others attempt to account for a general representation of the environment that would enable planning of any type to occur.

1. Veridical–general plans. Emphasis on the importance of initial representations is apparent in many discussions of text comprehension and problem solving. Because they postulate grammars or normative analyses of events, we discuss their content here. Story grammars, which relate the course of intentional behavior, begin with the setting that defines the framework for the plot (e.g., Rumelhart, 1977; Stein & Glenn, 1979). According to Newell and Simon (1972), problem solving starts with an analysis of the subject's representation of the initial parameters of the task because that initial state is a key determinant of performance. In Schank and Abelson's theory, a normative representation of goal-directed behavior is the basis for an entire theory of planning.

Schank and Abelson's description of plans arose from their attempts to write a computer simulation of text comprehension. Although they were concerned with the objective structure of narratives, their theory is meant to account for representation of any goal-directed behavior. They define plan as a repository for general information that will connect events . . . made up of general information about how actors achieve goals. A plan explains how a given state or event was prerequisite for, or derivative of another state or event. (Schank & Abelson, 1977, p. 70)

The content of a plan as representation goes well beyond our earlier definition of representation of the initial problem state. Plans include representation of the goal and knowledge of the methods that would enable reaching it. The methods or plan boxes include knowledge of the properties and location of the goal object, ways to gain control over it, and preparations to use the object once it is obtained. Readers who possess such a comprehensive representation can determine whether each component is present in a text. If components are missing, they can note how story characters attempt to produce the necessary preconditions.

From this perspective, plans reflect theories or abstractions about the structure of the social and physical environment (e.g., Brown, Collins, & Harris, 1978; Bruce, 1980; Kagan, 1984). Therefore, examination of plans provides a window into the nature of representation. The content of plans may also vary with age and cultural setting. Two- and 3-year olds can already recognize when an object, an event, or a behavior deviates from a standard (i.e., representation) they have abstracted (Kagan, 1984). Yet because they are ignorant of the meaning of an action, its preconditions, and usual consequences, they may have difficulty generating adequate plans. Because plans tap expectations of normative behaviors and motives associated with particular situations, there are bound to be differences among cultures in the content, if not the structure of plans.

Two chapters in this volume describe the development of planning in terms of general representational skills. De Lisi suggests that advances in planning result from advances in representational skill. Cocking and Copple search for the origins of representational skills by examining several representational media such as play and art.

2. Veridical–specific plans. Schank and Abelson discussed the general structure of plans, but plans are often tailored to specific circumstances. The Hayes-Roths' (Hayes-Roth & Hayes-Roth, 1979) description of errand planning includes among the components of planning a knowledge base that contains situation-specific data. When the plan is to eat at a restaurant, the knowledge base provides data on specific routes and other information useful for testing the viability of the plan. Even if people had general spatial and causal knowledge, a plan would be inadequate without knowledge of the local environment. The Hayes-Roths' model stresses the importance of translating abstract plans into tactics consistent with local conditions.

These verdical models of planning suggest that an essential component of planning is a representation of the environment that contains both the general causal and spatial networks that underlie interactions and the local conditions for generating and executing particular plans. From the cognitive science viewpoint, planners need a richly structured knowledge base. Developmental differences in planning often reflect differences in knowledge. As in any domain of problem solving, the child will appear more expert when the plans to be generated deal with familiar circumstances. When we look at the origin of plans, the question is not merely the quantity of knowledge entering a representation, but the emergence of symbolic skills toward the end of the first year of life.

3.   Idiosyncratic–specific plans.   John Bowlby (1969) and Hans and Shulamith Kreitler (1976) suggest that the specific information and global world view that people incorporate into their representation of reality and therefore into their plans may be biased by idiosyncratic personal experiences. In trying to account for individual differences in attachment behavior, Bowlby attributes one source of variation to the person's model of the interpersonal and physical environment in which attachments are created.

> During his second and third [year] when he acquires the powerful and extraordinary gift of language, a child is busy constructing working models of how the physical world may be expected to behave, how he himself may be expected to behave, and how each interacts with all the others. Within the framework of these working models he evaluates the situation and makes his plans. How these models are built up and thenceforth bias perception and evaluation, how adequate and effective for planning they become, how distorted as representations they are and what conditions help or hinder their development, all of these are matters of great consequence for understanding. (Bowlby, 1969, p. 304)

For Bowlby, the origin of planning is toddlers' growing awareness of their own intentions and the intentions of their attachment figures. The discovery of differences between the two sets of intentions leads to plans to make them agree. These interpersonal plans are shaped by the child's concepts of the self and others as loving and lovable as well as the complexity and adequacy of the child's working model of the world.

4.   Idiosyncratic–general plans.   The Kreitlers (e.g., Kreitler & Kreitler, 1976) who are contributors to this volume, also stress the role of personal meanings in constructing a representational model in which planning can take place. However, their model extends to all domains of planning, and they are more specific about the constituents of planning. They suggest that one of the first steps in formulating a plan is stimulus interpretation. People impose meaning dimensions on events, and individual differences in behavior are predictable from knowledge of the availability and frequency of use of those dimensions. The Kreitlers describe four kinds of meaning variables: (a) contents (such as temporal, sensory, or emotional); (b) logical form of the relation between meaning and object (such as negation); (c) type of relation (such as similarity or comparison); and (d) relation to other objects in the representational or semantic field. Of greatest interest are the content dimensions that are conducive to and may even be prerequisites for planning. Because planning takes place in space and time, attention to these dimensions fosters planning. People who are interested in how things work are probably going to devise effective plans. Plans involve both contingent and causal relations so that the tendency to analyze sequences and notice antecedents and consequences sets the stage for planning. Sensitivity to the range of situations in which particular relations hold may also facilitate plan construction. Because novel plans often develop through noticing analogies to similar circumstances, the tendency to engage in comparisons may also foster planning.

The salience of these meaning variables may predict general planning skills. Moreover, people may be more prone to construct or use plans that incorporate particular content if that content is more prominent in their meaning network. A popular planning task, the Tower of Hanoi (Anzai & Simon, 1979; Klahr, 1978), sets the problem of transferring rings stacked on a pole in increasing size order to another pole without violating the size order. Someone who is conscious of size differences may be more successful on the Tower task than someone else who is highly attuned to feelings and who in turn may excel in planning resolutions to interpersonal dilemmas (Spivack & Shure, 1974).

The Kreitlers have devoted most of their attention to analyzing the sources of individal differences in "cognitive orientation" and to the implications of such differences for the content and adequacy of plans. They have extended their analyses of individual variations beyond the content of plans to the goals plans are intended to fulfill. Yet the Kreitlers' list of meaning variables is also a rich source for a developmental analysis of the cognitive prerequisites for planning. Planning frequently requires awareness of the spatial, temporal, causal, and enablement relations in an environment (see also Brown, Collins & Harris, 1978; Pea, 1982; Wilensky, 1981a, 1981b). If the child does not have these meaning dimensions available or if they are available in an incomplete form, those gaps will

handicap planning. Attempts to teach interpersonal planning to children
(e.g., Spivack & Shure, 1974) incorporate lessons on these same conceptual prerequisites. Similarly, Piaget (e.g., 1978) noted that thorough
understanding of the mechanisms of causation is a prerequisite for anticipatory planning.

B. Choosing a goal

Knowledge of the environment is insufficient for forming a plan because
the planner must also know how to define and evaluate goals. So we turn
to the next step in planning. This facet of intentional behavior is the basis
for one dictionary definition of a plan as "a project or definite purpose"
(Stein, 1975 p. 1015). The amount of attention the process of goal definition receives in a theory of planning seems to depend upon the kinds
of tasks to be accounted for and the model of the planner. Some problems
have well-defined goals or "final states" (Newell & Simon, 1972) which
people are presumed to know in advance and to maintain intact during
problem solving as a guide to behavior. Alternatively, some problems like
essay writing are ill defined (Flower & Hayes, 1981). Often, even when
the goals are clear, people prefer to work opportunistically, refining and
redefining goals as they learn more about the task and the outcomes of
initial actions (e.g., Hayes-Roth & Hayes-Roth, 1979). Fluid goals may
also characterize planners who are inexperienced or who have multiple,
conflicting aims (e.g., Bruce & Newman, 1978; Wilensky, 1981a, 1981b).
Theories that account for problem solving in ill-defined domains and for
planners who are opportunistic, inexpert, or conflicted often include elaborate descriptions of the mechanics of goal selection. In contrast, discussion of the process of goal definition is skeletal in analyses of performance
on tasks with well-defined end states (e.g., Newell & Simon, 1972). When
a problem is defined by the experimenter and understood by the planner,
the leap from problem representation to specification of the nature of an
appropriate solution may be so rapid that the appeal to elaborate goal
detection mechanisms may be unnecessary.

1. Detection.   Cognitive science models of planning or plan comprehension discuss three aspects of defining a goal: detection, monitoring,
and evaluation. In accounting for story comprehension and demanding
problem solving, Anderson (1983) and Greeno, Riley, and Gelman
(1984) invoke a pattern recognition device. The device scans situations
to detect the conditions that invoke certain learned problem-solving procedures with their associated goals. Algebraic equations may immediately
elicit the goal of placing the unknowns on one side of the equation (e.g.,

Brown, Collins, & Harris, 1978). Goal detection is inherent in the situation and is managed automatically by production statements. In the problem-solving strategy of means–end analyses, where the goal is well defined, individuals analyze the preconditions for solution and then choose subgoals to realize those preconditions.

Both Schank and Abelson (1977) and Schmidt (1976) have posited a motivation analyzer or detector that scans people's actions and infers from them the goals that motivated them. Those inferences are based on a model of universal motivations or standard goals such as fulfillment of biological needs and self-preservation and a set of role stereotypes about the kinds of motives particular people like stockbrokers might possess. Failure to detect the goal results in inappropriate plans and problem-solving strategies. One prevalent explanation of young children's poor performance on Piagetian tasks is that they do not share the same view of the task and do not have the same goals as the experimenter (e.g., Donaldson, 1979) and hence do not create adequate problem-solving plans.

2. Monitoring. Schank and Abelson suggest a second role for the system which deals with goals: monitoring their fate during the execution of a planned action. Goals may be changed in midstream; one goal may be substituted for another or abandoned. Sometimes completion of one goal is interrupted until another more pressing goal is satisfied. The monitor keeps track of every goal so that the problem solver can return to it when disrupted or can explain why goals have been cast aside.

3. Evaluation. Wilensky (1981a, 1981b) adds evaluation to the other functions of the goal system because he tries to account for situations in which multiple goals arise. He proposes a "goal detector" that will eventually generate goals to be handed on to the rest of the system, which will then create and execute plans. The goal detector often works simultaneously on many overlapping or conflicting goals. On the basis of evaluative criteria, the "generator" selects the goals to be used in forming plans. The generator is aided by a "noticer," which monitors the person's internal states (such as hunger) and external conditions (e.g., the presence of an ice-cream vendor) for changes of interest to the system. This input helps the evaluation of the importance and feasibility of realizing particular past and present goals. Thus the noticer detects needs, opportunities, and potential dangers, which form the basis for evaluation.

4. Selection. Intertwined with the formation, monitoring, and evaluation of goals is the process of goal selection. In explanations of planning in well-defined problems, goal selection is a mechanical property of the system. In Anderson's (1983) analysis, goals are stacked by recency, situational fit, and past success. Schank and Abelson (1977) propose that goals are stacked in terms of their availability, feasibility, cost, and effort in attaining them. But who does the computation, and how does the system learn to adopt those criteria? Greeno and his colleagues (1984) contend that problem solvers themselves evaluate the goals they detect to see if the prerequisite and corequisite conditions for goal attainment exist. For example, when the goal is to attend a wedding in a distant city, the potential guest checks the availability of money, a local airport, and a convenient flight schedule. In both Wilensky's and the Hayes-Roths' theory, decision making is assigned to a particular specialist. The noticer in Wilensky's system prioritizes according to a fixed set of instructions. Some instructions eliminate goals that are unfeasible, difficult, or impossible to achieve. Similarly, like Schank and Abelson, Wilensky claims that some instructions incorporate a cost–benefit analysis. The noticer is instructed to choose the goal that is the most valuable and least costly in terms of time and effort. Other instructions describe ways to combine goals for multiple plans so as to conserve resources. The metaplan in the Hayes-Roths' model actually constructs task-specific decision criteria.

Wilensky's model assumes that all planners use the same criteria with the same weightings to set goals and that planners have the knowledge germane to those decisions as well as the competence to calculate those weightings. Both developmental and cross-cultural researchers are wary of these assumptions. Children may not know what is realizable because of inadequate evaluation of their own ability. They may value efficiency less and consider any solution adequate. Hayes-Roth (1980) contends that young children may be less prone to evaluate consciously their goal choices, and even adults may not set appropriate priorities during planning because they misconstrue the task constraints and their own resources. As we shall see in the next section, people may also decide that it is too costly to analyze goals. They would prefer to devote their effort to action rather than to goal choice and planning. Finally, people possess different values. Dreher and Oerter in this volume (also Oerter, 1978) note that Western societies value highly economy of effort and delegation of responsibility. Each value dictates the necessity of planning as well as the contents of plans. The Kreitlers (1976) argue that a theory of goal choice also assumes a theory about what the person wants to attain, thinks others attain, and thinks are general standards for goal attainment. People actually work with *several* theories of goal evaluation which may be difficult to reconcile.

In summary, planning involves goal choice. Few theories of planning discuss solely goal selection, but it is central to Wilensky's analysis. As in our analysis of representation, this component in planning is very complicated, requiring an elaborate model of decision making. Developmental psychologists are particularly interested in the origin of priorities and growth in skills in weighing and computing such priorities.

C. Deciding to plan

The elaborate analysis of goals assumes a reflective problem solver using a set of criteria to evaluate goals and then proceeding to be equally reflective in devising a plan for goal satisfaction. In reality, vast individual differences exist in the extent to which people deliberate when choosing means to satisfy goals. We capture this aspect of planning in the adjective "planful."

Although many cognitive science models of planning assume that once a goal is chosen, the individual automatically stops to plan an attack, many developmental and personality theorists have speculated about the origins of planfulness, the kinds of situations that evoke planning, and the kinds of persons who plan. Often young children, and impulsive, hyperactive, and distractible individuals do not plan, so there have been several theories that emphasize planfulness and many programs that attempt to remediate deficiencies in planfulness. Those analyses stress one or more of the following components underlying planfulness: (a) a set of beliefs about the self and the task; (b) sensitivity to the situations that warrant planning; (c) the status of the strategy to be activated by a plan; and, most importantly (d) the level of the person's self-control.

1. Planning beliefs. European Action Theory, which inspired the research of Oppenheimer and Dreher and Oerter in this volume, addresses the beliefs that underlie planfulness. Skinner and Chapman (1984) suggest that how and whether the individual plans depends on a constellation of three beliefs. The raw material for planning, as we have stated in the section on representation, comes from the individual's beliefs about the causal structure of the physical environment in which planning occurs. A second set of environmental beliefs about control also affects planning. Assumptions that factors such as fate, chance, the forces of nature, or an unresponsive government completely determine the outcome of events hamper willingness to plan. Often the elderly and impoverished fail to plan because they feel themselves at the mercy of uncontrollable forces. Thus European Action Theory includes the same factors found in American theories of locus of control and social attribution and specifically applies them to the decision to plan. As in those theories, an additional set of beliefs about the self also influences decisions to plan.

Skinner and Chapman call those beliefs "agency," whereas Bandura (1981) has labeled them "self-efficacy." Planners must believe they can reach a goal by their own efforts. People who deem themselves incompetent may fail to plan because they think they are incapable of carrying an action through to its conclusion.

Skinner and Chapman suggest that this triad of beliefs has a social origin because cultures transmit opinions about people's ability to control events in general and beliefs about the ages at which mastery is likely to arise and to diminish. They differentiate occupations and educational levels on the basis of the extent to which they require planning. Dreher and Oerter's data on planning in this volume support this view. Moreoever, social interactions provide information about personal competencies. The chapter by McGillicuddy-De Lisi and her colleagues describes how a handicapped child affects parental expectations of planning.

2. *Knowing when to plan.* General beliefs about one's ability to affect a malleable environment are often supplemented by knowledge of situations where plans would be helpful. The most extensive discussions of situations that lend themselves to planning appears in the metacognitive literature. In examining research on use of mnemonic strategies and communication skills (e.g., Flavell, 1977; Patterson & Roberts, 1982), it became apparent that children may understand the goal of a task but that they are ineffective problem solvers because they do not know they *need* to step back from the problem to plot a solution that capitalizes on what they know about themselves and the problem-solving environment. De Lisi in this volume suggests that awareness of the need to plan characterizes one of the most mature forms of planning.

As in other aspects of planning, there is controversy over the nature of the need to be planful. The debate lies between those who use a general problem-solving approach versus those who analyze situation-specific cues prompting planfulness. The general approach stems from work with impulsive children, which demonstrated that teaching specific plans had little impact on behavior. Numerous researchers tried to hand children ready-made strategies and plans, but once prompts to use plans ceased, the children ceased using them (e.g., Borkowski, 1985). Knowing when and why a strategy is useful facilitates deliberation in children. Similarly, training programs for children whose impulsivity and distractibility makes them poor planners have often handed children plans of action that specify when the child is to act and what is to be done, but the child used the plan only in the setting in which it was taught unless he or she was specifically told why a plan was effective (Pressley, 1979; Urbain & Kendall, 1980).

Consequently Meichenbaum, a cognitive behavioral therapist, instructs children to approach each task with questions such as "Did I stop to think? What plans can I try? Am I using the plan? How did it work out?" (e.g., Meichenbaum, 1977; Meichenbaum & Asarnow, 1979; Meichenbaum, Burland, Gruson, & Cameron, 1985). These queries are thought to be helpful because they provide an emphasis on planning that is relevant to any situation and also provide the child with data that will enable decisions about the particular planning tactics for different classes of situations. The questions require the child to be aware of the need to insert steps between problem presentation and action, which we designate as planfulness.

Although teaching planfulness is not the primary aim of programs teaching critical thinking to elementary school children, Covington, in this volume, discusses how metacognitive awareness of the appropriateness of plans and the necessity for planning can result from programs teaching critical thinking skills. He provides a taxonomy of problem situations that require differences in the quality and quantity of planning. The more open-ended the problem-solving task, the more planning must go into problem representations, goal definition, and the search for solution strategies. Unlike Meichenbaum, he claims that in teaching planning, the program must strike a balance between some weak but general awareness of the need to plan and some strong but situation-specific skills which stipulate the amount of planning appropriate for particular circumstances. Both Covington, and Rogoff and colleagues in this volume discuss some of the cases where children need to devote effort in planning. Covington ties his discussion to his problem taxonomy, whereas Rogoff and associates talk about external demands for efficiency.

Discussion of the appropriateness of planning also arises in the Kreitlers' theory. Instead of stressing the external properties of the problem, they emphasize belief systems. Before planning, the individual pulls together beliefs about whether people, and peers in particular, plan, whether he or she ought to plan, and whether the planner him- or herself usually plans in this situation. These norms are combined to decide whether a particular situation warrants planning. Goodnow's chapter suggests the content of some of those norms, which are based on situations where one should be spontaneous or passionate rather than planful versus situations where there is a need to husband resources. In addition, problem-solving plans are based on a perception that certain facets of the environment can be moved around to produce conditions more conducive to goal attainment. When the pieces of the environment are people, there are strong constraints on whether they can be manipulated easily and therefore whether one should plan a problem-solving strategy.

In every perspective, the person knows something about whether people usually plan, and the individual differences in engaging in plans reflect social norms and accumulated knowledge about the appropriateness and efficacy of planning.

According to Vygotsky (1978; Wertsch, 1979a, 1979b, 1980) this knowledge is acquired through social interactions with planful adults. Parents act as models who analyze tasks, engage in planning, and demonstrate solution strategies which children will incorporate into their own repertoires. In conversations, the child learns what and when adults plan, specific typical plans, and the use of planning aids such as charts, maps, and diagrams. Vygotsky's analysis of the socialization of planfulness inspired four chapters in this volume: two on parental influence, by McGillicuddy–De Lisi and her colleagues and by Goodnow, and two on peer influences in planning, by Rogoff and colleagues and by Cocking and Copple.

3. Plan availability. Individual differences in planfulness may also reflect the status of the strategy that will be incorporated in planning. Planning is often absent at two extremes of learning. Some problems and the behaviors needed to solve them are so routine that their solution is achieved without much expenditure of attention and effort. In fact, response to a situation is so stereotyped that it is hard to alter the action and insert a new plan. When driving to work, one need not plan the well-practiced route. Consequently, one often drives oblivious of any decision making and sometimes even unaware of the details of a particular trip (Langer, 1985). At the other extreme, when the strategy to be incorporated in a plan is effortful or the act of strategy choice is onerous, the individual may simply fail to plan because the act of planning may be more troublesome than making mistakes during problem solving. When the child lacks a strategy to use in planning or when the use of a strategy is demanding, the child may not plan at all. That is why children are often handed plans and drilled on them so that they can perform effectively without the added problem of figuring out what to do. Perhaps that also accounts for the Kreitlers' report in this volume of an intriguing finding: Children first plan aspects of well-known routines like laying out clothes at night in preparation for getting ready for school the next day. Vygotsky specifically acknowledges that children may be poor planners because they cannot simultaneously define a problem, choose a plan, and execute it when the planned strategy is new. Therefore, parents act as scaffolds for chlidren's efforts by controlling elements of the task that are beyond the child's capacity so that the child can concentrate on those aspects that lie within their competence. Adults help abstract the skeletal structure of a task so that the child may match a plan to it. As more aspects of the problem-solving situation are mastered by the child, then the child has a model for and the capacity for taking charge of personal planning.

4. Self-control. The motivation to plan has to be coupled with the capacity for self -control and self-regulation if planning is to occur. There is an extensive theoretical and empirical literature on individual differ-neces and developmental changes in the ability to control the impulse to act without delay in order to plan. Two major theoretical traditions, the psychoanalytic and the Russian, have dealt with the origins of planfulness.

Freud (1959, 1963) called attention to the inevitable gaps between arousal of any desire for a goal and the availability of resources to satisfy the desire. The ego arises to bridge the gap by imposing tolerance for delay, while the individual plans and executes instrumental actions that should realistically achieve goals. Eventually, the superego provides another source of self-regulation: evaluation of the ethics of actions. For Freud, plans are both the means by which people achieve self-control, and an index of intentional and deliberate behavior.

Mischel and his colleagues (e.g., Carter, Patterson, & Quasebarth, 1979; Mischel, 1983; Mischel & Patterson, 1976, 1978) have incorporated the emphases on plans as both a means of control and as a product of control in their research. In that research, children get an attractive reward if they can wait for it or if they persist in a boring task despite temptation. Har-riet Mischel (1984) has suggested that delay capacity actually reflects two processes: The first is the choice to delay, which we discussed in the pre-ceding section. It is determined by the subjective value of the delayed reward and the child's belief that the reward will still be available after the delay. The second is the ability to handle the delay based on the avail-ability of strategies to redirect attention, to transform the goal object into something that is temporarily less desirable, and to engage in self-moni-toring. Between the ages of 5 and 10 years, children not only discover delay strategies, but also shift from sole reliance on physical ploys such as covering up a tempting object to mental ones such as thinking about something else or claiming that the hotly desired reward may be over-rated. At about age 10, children also begin to understand that there is a difference between planning a self-control tactic and actually carrying out the tactic. At that age, children's knowledge of delay plans begins to be correlated with sustaining a delay. Walter Mischel (1983) finds a similar link between knowledge of delay plans and the ability to exert self-control. Teachers describe children who are more successful in delaying gratification as more planful, reflective, and more able to concentrate.

Some children have the self-control that enables them to pause before embarking on a task. These "reflective" children set goals and devise strategies before they start acting. Other children are "impulsive" and fail to pause before acting (e.g., Kagan & Kogan, 1983). Several psychologists have tried to help impulsive children by teaching them plans to slow down, analyze percepts, focus attention, and generate solution strategies (see reviews by Kopp, Krakow, & Vaughn, 1983; Pressley, 1979; Urbain & Kendall, 1980). Four- and 5-year-olds can prolong self-control when given explicit instructions. However, even when handed plans, nursery school children may not use them because they do not know when to ' implement the plan. Older children do not need to be cued (Carter, Patterson, & Quasebarth, 1979). Thus self-regulation needs to be coupled with the other component we have discussed: knowledge of when planning helps.

Luria (1976; Zivin, 1979), a Soviet psychologist, also emphasizes the role of self-regulation in the development of self-control. Like the research just reported, Luria has charted the ontogeny of deliberation and self-control, as well as specified the mechanisms by which tactics for self-control have an impact on self-regulation and planfulness. The major influences on self-regulation are verbalization and social control, which create a barrier against headlong action and a guide for performance.

Children are first the targets of directions that serve to motivate and then later in development to inhibit actions. The child who is first commanded by adults eventually utters self-commands and then internalizes those directives as plans for actions. Speech works to organize activity and to slow it down. The way it organizes activity changes with age. Initially speech helps by calling attention to an action and creating a regular rhythm to segment acts and control the flow, much as the predictable cadence of commands set to music helps in learning an aerobic activity. Later, the syntax of sentences will organize actions. Clauses beginning with the word "if" or "before," clarify the contingencies and sequence of actions. For the older child, the semantics of speech or its representational content becomes important. Speech can serve to remind the child of the goal, while acting (see also Fuson, 1979; Meacham, 1979).

So far, we have been describing the role of speech as an accompaniment of action. But speech also serves to evaluate a plan after its completion. Eventually speech that is used during the act as a form of self-control moves toward creation of the next step in our series, a precursor of actions. The child uses the rich network of semantic connections to generate strategies and anticipate their consequences. Speech moves from permitting planfulness to providing the content of a plan. Luria has also speculated on the mechanisms by which speech acts to retard actions, which he attributes to more rapid conduction of speech signals on neural pathways, allowing blockage of motor activities.

In summary, the decision to formulate a course of action aimed at achieving a goal is an important link in the chain of cognitive events that constitute planning and that allows the person to reach the goal. The extent to which individuals engage in this step of planning is determined by a complex interaction of beliefs, personality, and cognitive skills of planners and the situations in which they find themselves.

D. Formulating a plan

In motivated, reflective individuals who are aware of the value of thinking before acting and who lack a ready-made strategy, the choice of a goal will be followed by the formulation and execution of a course of action. This phase of goal-directed actions appears in dictionary definitions of plans such as "any method of thinking out acts and purposes beforehand" (Stein, 1975, p. 1014), "to project a scheme for work" or "the way it is proposed to carry out some proceeding" (O.E.D., 1971, p. 2195), and in the Hayes-Roths' discussion of planning as "the predetermination of a course of action aimed at achieving some goal" (Hayes-Roth & Hayes-Roth, 1979, pp. 275–276).

There have been two contrasting approaches to anticipatory planning. One kind of model (Byrne, 1977; Newell & Simon, 1972; Sacerdoti, 1977) sets up an ordered set of procedures – planning heuristics or algorithms – by which a single processor solves the problem. The planning process is driven by the processor's understanding of the problem. Often the processing is serial and constrained by the planner's formal analysis of the problem domain. Proficient planners think out the entire plan before acting. These are anticipatory plans.

In contrast, some approaches to planning blur the distinction between covert planning and overt problem-solving strategies because in many cases there is a constant flow between imagining a strategy, executing it, and then revising ideas as unpredictable outcomes arise. Additionally, once a plan is devised, it may become a problem-solving strategy. To compound the confusion, Newell and Simon (1972) even referred to one method of problem solving that involved simplification of the problem space by excising variables, as "planning." Models that mix thinking and acting are called *opportunistic* or *transactional*. Not surprisingly the anticipatory model is most often involved when the goal is well defined, familiar, and simple whereas the opportunistic model lends itself to accounts of ill-defined tasks and immature or inexpert problem-solvers.

1. Anticipatory plans.   Greeno, Riley, and Gelman (1984) have developed an anticipatory planning model which incorporates a developmental perspective. They consider planning skill the central organizer of the cognitive system. In every task, children apply their understanding of structure of a particular domain *(conceptual competence)* and of the specific task setting *(utilizational competence)*. The link between general knowledge and the particular task where that knowledge is relevant is forged by *procedural competence* or planning. It consists of:

the procedures that recognize goals of different types during planning, that search for action schemata with consequences that match goals that have been recognized, and that determine when planning is successfully completed. Procedural competence also includes theorem proving methods that search for features of the task-setting that can be used to prove that conditions will be satisfied and additional planning heuristics that use these theorem-proving methods when they are needed. (Greeno, Riley, & Gelman, 1984, p. 99)

A planning net takes a goal and searches through available schemes to find consequences that match it. Next it generates from its knowledge of the world, actions that will produce the desired consequences. Choice of an action leads to determining the conditions that must be present while an action is being performed and predictions of what must happen after the action is performed. When the prerequisites and corequisites are unavailable, a plan is devised for supplying the missing requisites. As a result, the planner constructs a sequence of actions to reach a goal. If there are several plans, the planner will select the most viable and efficient. Thus competence depends on the child's repertoire of concepts and procedures that provide the basis for plans and the child's ability to manipulate ideas prior to acting upon them.

2. Opportunistic planning.   It may not be feasible to plan an entire course of action in advance because the environment is constantly changing, or the goal is ill defined, or parts of the task are delegated to many individuals. Often the planner mixes goal-guided and data-based decisions. The Hayes-Roths (1979) have developed a model of plan formation that is opportunistic and multidirectional, to account for situations

Table 1.1. *The five parts of the planning blackboard*

Executive	Metaplan	
Priorities	Problem definition	
Attention focus	Problem-solving model	
Schedule	Policies	
	Solution criteria	
Plan abstraction	Knowledge base	Plan
Intentions	Errands	Outcomes
Schemes	Layout	Designs
Strategies	Locations	Procedures
Tactics	Routes	Operations

where top-down, serial processing by an individual problem solver is inappropriate. We will discuss this model extensively because it has inspired the work by Pea and Hawkins, Dreher and Oerter, and Rogoff, Gauvain, and Gardner in this volume.

The model resembles a management team rather than a solitary problem solver. Although their definition of planning stresses anticipation, the Hayes Roths claim we do not "preplan" but plan in action. Thus their description mixes problem representation, goal definition, anticipation, action, and evaluation in a free-flowing, multidirectional sequence. The lack of a single direction of decision making and a single source of data dictate a different organizing device than Greeno's. Planning takes place on a blackboard. Specialists scan sections of the board and create new data on the basis of what they have read. The new information, in turn, may be of use to other specialists or to a central executive who decides the next action. The model specifies the origin and organization of information used in planning and the specialists who generate and transfer information.

The blackboard is divided into planes or windows, which in turn have subdivisions. Specialists carry information from one plane to another or use data on one plane to produce further data useful on another part of the blackboard. The partitioning of the blackboard was originally devised to account for how students planned to schedule errands in a downtown area with fixed locations for the errands and time constraints on the length of stay and hours of operation of some facilities.

Table 1.1 shows the blackboard model and its five planes. The *executive* plane, similar to the executive control system in contemporary information processing models (Anderson, 1983), determines and monitors allocation of resources during planning. It operates at three levels to record general *priorities, attentional focus,* or the specific part of the blackboard to be worked on next, and the *schedule* of the specific content in the attended area, that is important at a given moment.

The *metaplan* plane embodies knowledge of the essentials of planning, such as *problem definition* or the information on the goal, available resources, possible actions and constraints, the *problem-solving model* or knowledge of modes of attack, *policies* enabling choice among strategies based on cost, and *solution criteria* allowing calculation of risk.

The first two planes of the blackboard set the framework for the problem and manage resources, whereas the other three do the actual problem solving. Each is subdivided into parts differing in abstraction. At each level of abstraction the *plan abstraction* plane lists the general directive; the *knowledge base* provides information relevant to the directives; and the *plan* plane combines the two sources of information into actions.

The most abstract level on each of the three working planes sets the framework for actions. A priority set by the metaplan plane, "Do the most important errands," inspires the plan abstraction plane to generate an *intention,* which singles out errands that must be done today, whereas the knowledge base supplies the deadlines for the *errands,* and the plan plane lists the *outcome* candidates.

These three abstract sections – the plan abstraction, knowledge base, and plan plane – tell what to do, but the next, more specific level of the three planes organizes the actions. The *scheme* section of the plan abstraction plane may suggest looking for errands clustered near one another; the knowledge base provides a *layout* to judge proximity; whereas the *design* division of the plan plane selects promising clusters for further analysis.

Even more detail is provided at a more specific level of the plan, knowledge base, and plan abstraction plane. This level lists some general methods for the goal of visiting errands clusters. The plan abstraction plane provides a *strategy* ("go to the closest cluster"); the knowledge base contributes its *location*; whereas the plan plane chooses the *procedure* that tells the store to visit. The actual movements are planned on the most specific level. The plan abstraction plane lists the *tactics* consistent with the decision to visit the nearest store ("Choose the shortest way"); the knowledge base supplies the shortest *route,* whereas the plan lists the *operations* needed to follow the route.

The formulation of a plan does not necessarily proceed from the general to the specific. A person may roam about one section of town, notice the proximity of many errands, and evolve a strategy. When that information is put onto the blackboard, specialists who have been assigned to that area read it, translate it, and spread it to other areas of the black-board, sparking activity in the specialists who reside there.

The specialists, despite their anthropomorphic titles, are not little men inhabiting the planner's head. They are production statements in a computer program. When a condition arises on the blackboard that matches a particular production statement in the planner's repertoire, the corresponding action is retrieved. The action translates the condition into new information. Should new information trigger several production statements, the executive plane decides which one to attend to. Importance and recency are the usual basis for allocating attentional resources.

Goldin and Hayes-Roth (1980) scored the plans of five college students for spatial efficiency, temporal realism, and sensitivity to the importance of errands. The highest-scoring planner also used most the two black-board planes that regulate planning, the executive and metaplan plane, and was more flexible than the others in switching between areas of the blackboard. Even within the three working planes of plan abstraction, knowledge base, and plan, the best planner stayed on the more abstract subdivisions more often. However, the best planner did not devise procedures devoid of details because such a plan is inadequate. The bulk of planning takes place at a low level. It is also worth noting that even the best planner was unrealistic about time constraints.

Hayes-Roth, Cammarata, Goldin, Hayes-Roth, Rosenschein, and Thorndyke (1980) have also spotted potential sources of difficulty for the young planner. A multidimensional, parallel processing model demands a large working memory and flexible attentional strategies. The orchestration of plans, like the management of a business, requires good administration and good judgment (metacognition) as well as sufficient knowledge to translate decisions into action. Although the Hayes-Roths have worked with just one type of plan, their diagnoses of difficulty have wide implications.

The Kreitlers do not use the language of cognitive science, but their planning model overlaps with that of the Hayes-Roths. In their model, after a behavioral intent to reach a goal has been formulated, the individual devises a *program*. Part of that program corresponds to the plan abstraction and metaplan planes of the opportunistic planning model. A *program scheme* provides a major outline of the sequence of actions required to reach a goal and the conditions necessary for plan execution. Another facet of the program generates the actual *operations* by filling in spatial and temporal details.

These descriptions have one striking limitation. Planning is equated with individual problem solving. Yet plans are often shared and their contents are negotiated. To use the language of the Hayes-Roths, who governs writing on different planes of the blackboard? When the partners in planning are adults and children, we also learn about the origin of the program schemes and procedures discussed by each theory. Research inspired by Vygotsky (e.g., Wertsch, 1979b, 1980; Wood, Bruner, & Ross, 1976; Zaporozhets, Zinchenko, & Elkonin, 1971) demonstrates how parents both model the components of planning and take over parts of the planning problem so as to help the child until such time as the child can manage all the burdens of the task. Anne McGillicuddy-De Lisi and her colleagues (this volume) describe shared planning in pairs in which one child was language disabled and the other was not. The more competent partner assumed responsibility for the metaplan and executive planes. Even for equally competent partners (see Oppenheimer, this volume), plan formulation involving two people is different from individual planning because the planners must negotiate between themselves, and they can share the role of creator and monitor. Existing formulations of planning need to be expanded to account for collaborative planning.

E.   Executing and monitoring plans

Opportunistic models of planning mix anticipation of a course of action with the next two steps, executing the act and monitoring the execution (e.g., Hayes-Roth & Hayes-Roth, 1979; Kreitler & Kreitler, 1976). In this section we focus on the execution and monitoring. Often planning is equated with carrying out a strategy that has been decided on, or the actual "method of action or procedure" (Stein, 1977, p. 1014). Study strategies are described as plans although all we see is the overt action (e.g., Rogoff, Newcombe, & Kagan, 1974). Because a description of execution would simply deteriorate into a catalog of the strategies the child has available, we will integrate our discussion of execution and monitoring. Although strategies may be performed without any consideration of their impact, monitoring ensures that a strategy accomplishes its planned purpose and enables repair when the strategy fails to accomplish its purpose. Many descriptions of strategy execution combine both monitoring and repair. For example, Wilensky (1981a) divides the job of planning among a goal detector, a planner, and an executor. The planner suggests plans, tests them, and revises them if there are goal conflicts, whereas the executor carries out plans and debugs them if unforeseen circumstances arise.

1.   Monitoring.   Miller, Galanter, and Pribram (1960) consider execution of a strategy under the guidance of a scheme to be the most essential aspect of planning. A plan is a template for action which initiates, shapes, and stops behavior. They describe a plan as a hierarchical process like a computer program that controls the order in which a sequence of operations can be performed. Each step stipulates what the individual must achieve. Failure to meet those standards leads to revision of strategies or problem solving. After meeting the standard, action then switches to the next step in the sequence. Miller and his colleagues were interested in demonstrating that a wide variety of behaviors could be described in the language of planning, but their model could apply just as well to the operation of a thermostat as to a human plan. For example, a thermostat tests the match between the external temperature and its setting. When the temperature is colder than the setting, then the furnace is tested. If it is off, it is turned on until the temperature approaches the desired warmth, and then the system is at rest. Warmer temperatures would produce the opposite strategy, testing the furnace to turn it off. Thus planning is described as a series of TOTE units where the individual *tests* to see if a goal is satisfied, *operates* to achieve the goal, *tests* the efficacy of the operation and, when the goal is satisfied, *exits*.

Miller and his colleagues have suggested that there are several important ways plans differ which may affect the monitoring process. They may differ in detail, flexibility, and the specificity of stop orders. In addition they differ in scope in that some are short-range whereas others long-range. These dimensions might differentiate inexpert from expert planners. Frese and Stewart (1984) have elaborated on this analysis and have suggested four levels of planning which differ in the degree of abstraction, in the amount of monitoring each requires, and in the flexibility of behavior each plan permits. The first level of their taxonomy resembles the sensorimotor plans described by De Lisi in this volume. The most primitive plans are a set of highly automatized actions that tend to be executed regardless of environmental conditions. Well-learned skills like typing fit this grouping. In learning a skill, plans become more specific; less effort is taken to execute them; less feedback is needed from the environment to guide plan execution, and planning is reduced to execution of a tactic with little monitoring. The plans are useful because so little effort is expended in monitoring, and the strategy is highly accessible in appropriate circumstances, but there is a loss in flexibility. At the next level up, the person has a tactic usable in a particular situation, but that tactic is modifiable and one tactic can be exchanged for another if the first one fails. At a higher level, there are more general skills applicable across a wider range of situations, such as how to study for a history test rather than how to review for an examination on the Civil War. At the most abstract level, the metacognitive, lies the person's knowledge of general problem-solving strategies which would enable a person to generate a plan in any area. General problem-solving heuristics are metacognitive plans. Skilled individuals will choose the level of self-regulation or plans appropriate to a given task. Often there are cultural expectations about the level at which planning is done. For example, managers may be thought to use abstract plans, whereas assembly line workers may use automated skills. It is possible, as De Lisi argues, that with development children's plans become more abstract or the process of education prompts acquisition of more general problem-solving strategies.

Although Miller, Galanter, and Pribram (1960) emphasize monitoring, they do not specify many details about how it is done. However, there are some descriptions of strategy use that provide more information because the planned strategy is complex, the cues to its effectiveness are subtle, and the user is inept. Ann Brown and her co-workers (Brown, Bransford, Ferrara, & Campione, 1983; Brown, Campione, & Barclay, 1979; Brown & De Loache, 1978) noted that young children execute strategies inefficiently because of failure to monitor each step and to evaluate the effect of the strategy. The failures arise from unfamiliarity with the task, problems with introspection, and processing overload. Children may find it hard to use one internal process (e.g., monitoring) to control another (e.g., memory). When children must encode a problem, choose a strategy, and then execute it, they may be unable to do the additional chore of checking strategy effectiveness. There are grave consequences. Strategies are often executed inefficiently. Even when adults help children to make strategies work, children may not learn much from their use unless they engage in monitoring. Brown, like Piaget, argues that strategy monitoring is the origin of planning. When children evaluate what works and why, they are in a better position to form anticipatory plans because the principles that underlie a domain become evident. Note the contrast between this position and that of Newell and Simon, who claim that today's anticipatory plan becomes tomorrow's strategy. Brown and Piaget argue that today's monitoring of a strategy produces tomorrow's anticipatory plan. Their emphasis on monitoring resembles Meichenbaum's. Brown asserts that the development of memory skills reflects more than growth in capacity, speed of processing, and the knowledge base. A tripartite executive system develops which (a) schedules strategies and anticipates outcomes, (b) checks for strategy efficiency and effectiveness, and (c) revises.

Empirical support for the young child's difficulty in monitoring appears in both the research on memorization strategies and in Markman's (1977, 1979) studies of text comprehension. She presented young children with instructions and expository material in which there were obvious contradictions that were not detected. These failures may reflect unfamiliarity with the subject matter, the subtlety of the contradiction, or the irrelevance of the contradiction to the main thread of the text (Baker, 1984). Markman suggests that two processing variables may also underlie children's failure to monitor their own comprehension. Monitoring a story line or set of instructions requires anticipation of what comes next, but children may not often make spontaneous predictions. Children may also use inadequate standards when they monitor. They may use recognition memory tests to judge whether they are ready to recall material or may test comprehension by examining their ability to decode single words rather than their grasp of a story line. Hence their failures in checking may reflect inappropriate standards, not inaction. Thus, monitoring a plan is as complicated as plan construction and seems to depend on some of the same abilities.

2. *Debugging.* During the course of monitoring, it may become apparent that the plan does not accomplish its intended purpose. The planner may then decide to make revisions. In domains in which ready-made plans are not useful or in which plans are very complex, the process of revision becomes central. Writing is a good example (Flower & Hayes, 1981). There are many reasons why revision is so difficult even for expert writers (Bereiter & Scardamalia, 1982; Burtis, Bereiter, Scardamalia, & Tetroe, 1983; Flower & Hayes, 1981; Scardamalia & Bereiter, 1983, 1985; Scardamalia, Bereiter, Woodruff, Burtis, & Turkish, 1983; Tetroe, 1981). The final product represents many lines of thought and many pieces of information which must be integrated into a coherent whole. Some goals in writing – transmitting knowledge and intriguing an audience – may seem incompatible. Because of the difficulty of writing, authors may devote so much effort to generating text that little is left for the revision process.

Revision is, therefore, a complicated skill involving many steps. Bereiter and Scardamalia suggest that the initial steps in the process may use up so many resources that the later ones are performed inadequately. Four steps precede actual revision: authors plan a representation of the intended message and then produce the actual text; then they must compare the two and diagnose where mismatches occur. Monitoring of the execution of intentions may then instigate repair processes which bring the text in conformity with the intended plan. Alternatively, the individual may change the plan itself. This leads to more specific revision processes such as elaboration, deletion, reorganization, etc. Failure to revise may occur because the writer (a) does not plan, (b) does not compare plan and output, (c) uses inappropriate standards to judge the plan or output or (d) uses inappropriate repair procedures. Because writing usually requires extensive planning and revision, it is an excellent source of data on both processes.

Often children are ignorant of the qualities necessary for a good essay and of appropriate revision strategies. Because the task of writing overloads the novice writer's processing capacities, Bereiter and his colleagues have used two tactics to help them revise. Either they ask children to wait to revise until they have finished composing, or they have provided written reminders to compare, diagnose, and revise while they compose. The reminders do not always work because revision requires highly developed metacognitive knowledge. Even experienced adult writers find it hard to be dispassionate and objective about their own productions. A major problem in editing is knowing when failures of communication occur. Markman's work documented that early school age children are poor judges of text clarity. Depending on the text, by sixth to eighth grade, children can detect logical inconsistencies and poor wording, but they do not know how to repair their productions. It is ironic that in many areas, novices' lack of knowledge leads to many errors and their ignorance also deprives them of appropriate repair strategies. In writing, a "least effort" rule often predominates. Children make local repairs such as adding or deleting a word. Few recast a sentence or reorganize a paragraph (e.g., Brown, Day, & Jones, 1983). Recasting or reorganizing text, of course, requires keeping the goal and plan in mind, as well as former solutions, while trying out new ones. These analyses of rewriting are similar to descriptions of young children's attempts to revise failed verbal messages (e.g., Peterson, Danner, & Flavell, 1972). Children simply repeat themselves before realizing the necessity of paraphrasing their remarks. Children's difficulties with revision of a completed product suggest that they may also find it hard to revise during the phase of anticipatory planning when the child must actually simulate outcomes.

F.   Learning from plans

Perhaps the least discussed aspect of planning is the aftermath of plan execution, when the planner judges that the goal has been reached. One possibility is that when a plan leads to execution of a successful strategy, that strategy may enter the planner's repertoire (e.g., Newell & Simon, 1972). Thus the person does not learn to plan but simply learns a specific plan. Another possibility is that the person also learns more general planning skills (Brown et al., 1983; Meichenbaum & Asarnow, 1979). These skills are generally harder to acquire because strategy implementation gives direct information about the strategy but only indirect information about the wisdom of planful strategy choice. However, each time a strategy is used, it becomes less effortful, and this may enable the individual to devote more attention to examining its consequences, to fine-tuning the plan and evaluating the efficacy of the planning process itself. Moreover, as noted earlier, consciousness of monitoring and repair processes leads to awareness of the temporal and causal constraints that underlie actions (e.g., Schank & Abelson, 1977). Thus the evaluation of a strategy may lead to crucial abstractions about a domain and these, in turn, may facilitate planning in other domains, too.

IV. The origins and development of planning

Plans and planning have been described as a set of complex conceptual abilities that reflect knowledge, the ability to represent it flexibly and abstractly, the ability to recognize or set goals, strategic skill, and skills in monitoring, evaluating, and repairing strategies. The origins of this fascinating repertoire have been discussed by many theorists, and often their speculations have been woven into the text. Now we would like to draw together explicit and implicit assumptions about what develops and how. Five different aspects of planning skills have been the focus of developmental analyses of planning: representation, self-control, strategies, orchestration skills, and metacognition.

The Soviets, and also Freud and Kagan, link the development of planning to representation of goals and strategies for self-control. Those representations are used to monitor and evaluate behavior. Kagan, who places issues of self-control within the context of the emergence, acquisition, and maintenance of morality, has asked, "When do children gain a representation of some goal state that they can achieve, and what are the sources of these representations?" He claims that

around the world, two- and three-year-olds begin to reflect on the correctness, the competence and the appropriateness of their actions before, during and after execution. They compare their behavior, thoughts and feelings against the standard and try to keep in close accord with the standard, as a space vehicle's program corrects its course in flight. (Kagan, 1984, pp. 129–130)

Kagan distinguishes between general standards that are innate, such as mastery and behaving morally, and specific standards that are prescribed by the society in which the child lives. Early in life, the child acquires standards through abstraction of norms, recognition of the deviation from norms, and empathy with others. Later this process becomes more complex because the individual has a need for cognitive consistency among beliefs, actions, and the perceived demands of reality. Although the process of acquiring standards and acting upon them through planned behavior is in part biologically driven, it is also mediated by social agents who encourage or discourage specific behaviors and who serve as role models with whom the growing child identifies.

A similar focus on the development of planning in the context of the emergence of representational skills that enable self-control is pervasive in psychoanalytic writing. For Freud (1959, 1963), the growth of ego skills to handle the frustration that occurs when goals are unfulfilled provides the means to delay, such as defenses; the imagination to plot ways to achieve goals; and the standards of practicality by which to judge goals. The impetus to development is largely maturational, although development is shaped by the frustrations and conflicts society presents to the child and the superego standards the child incorporates from parents.

Similarly, Soviet theories attribute the origins of planning to verbal skill, which enables both the development of representation and self-control. However, they differ from Freud in emphasizing how verbal control is transmitted socially. For Luria (1976) the first step in the development of planning is the emergence of self-control. The tool for self-control is parental directives, which organize the child's actions and slow them down. Incorporation of those directives enables the child to exercise self-control. In addition, the conscious decision making that is required in forming a sentence may provide a prototype of self-control which is carried over into the realm of behavior. During the process of incorporation, the child becomes able to use the content of directives as a means of thinking through problems and solving them. The child moves from being self-controlled to planful.

Luria's theory mixes two mechanisms for change. First, change is due to socialization. Parents provide the contents of plans and teach the child to be planful. Additionally, the acquisition of language, or what Soviets call the second signal system, has a physiological impact which provides the foundation for planfulness. Because transmission of linguistic information is faster than transmission of motor data, language can serve to inhibit motor activity and orchestrate it. Thus language enables the child to plan. Because linguistic information also generalizes more rapidly than learned actions, the child can begin to anticipate the behaviors that will solve problems instead of solving problems by trial and error.

Vygotsky (1962) also stressed the crucial role of language in planning, but he emphasized the way in which language is used to represent a problem, a goal and the potential means of attaining it. Language is essential to problem solving because its abstraction frees the child from the present situation to deal with possibilities and hence to plan. Vygotsky, like Luria, has emphasized how parents influence language development. Conversations with the child become conversations that are carried out with the self overtly and then covertly. The internalization of language produces the thinking skills that are necessary for planning. His theory also refers to three other roles for parental influence. First, parents transmit the tools for planning, and second, they provide information about where planning is appropriate. They are the source of strategy and metacognitive information on the use of strategies. Third, Vygotsky is one of the few theorists to discuss the origin of orchestration skills. We have repeatedly stressed the complexity of planning, which operates on three levels: the plane of thought, of action, and of self-guidance. Parents model each of those functions by defining problems for their toddlers, suggesting strategies, and commenting on their execution and the outcome. Until the child can manage all these complex activities, the parent assumes some of the roles and then gradually relinquishes them to the child. They are both mentors and managers.

Miller, Galanter, and Pribram (1960) focus primarily on acquisition of strategies and heuristics for problem solving and some general problem-solving skills, a topic discussed by the Soviets. Their learning theory also overlaps with the Soviets'. New plans arise either from revisions of old ones or from imitations of plans observed in others. The acquisition of language enables individuals to learn by listening to others talk about the appropriateness of planning. Language also provides a means to monitor plan execution. Once acquired, refinement of a plan depends on environmental feedback.

Similarly, the Kreitlers (1976) have speculated on the acquisition of strategies. Once a behavioral intent to reach a goal has been formulated, the individual devises a program. Some of these programs are innate, some are learned, and others are constructed through inferential processes. During development, there is a switch from reliance on innate to learned and then to creatively constructed plans. Because the Kreitlers have a comprehensive theory of planning, their developmental emphases are not confined to plan execution. Particularly in chapter 6 in this volume, they discuss other components of planning such as the development of a meaning system which represents the environment in a way conducive to planning and the development of a set of attitudes toward planning. The latter motivational component is strongly influenced by acculturation, whereas the development of a meaning system reflects the cognitive development of the individual.

We have neglected a description of planning that equates that process with the development of representational skills. For Piaget (1976, 1978), planning is an inevitable outgrowth of two facets of cognitive development, the growth of representation and understanding of causal and logical mechanisms. As the child moves from trying to deal practically with problems, the child tries to figure out why particular actions work under some local conditions but not others. The integration of knowledge leads to a theory of a domain which forms the basis of anticipations. In Piaget's theory of equilibration, there is an inevitable push toward the theory building and self-reflection that produces planning. The construction of an adequate representation of the environment created by children's reflections on the outcomes of their actions produces planning. This viewpoint is shared by De Lisi.

Finally, there are many cognitive science models of planning which specify what must be known in order to plan. Like Piaget, and Bowlby, each of these theorists builds planning upon the individual's ability to represent and organize the essentials of the problem space. The coherent organization typical of experts makes it easier for them to plan. However, planning is a context-specific skill because few people have comprehensive knowledge and familiarity with every situation. Comments on the acquisition of strategies echo standard learning theory. However, just as conceptual knowledge of a domain gets organized, so, too, does procedural or strategic knowledge. Therefore, when a strategy is well known, it can be taken apart for repair and one strategy can be substituted for another. With the exception of Vygotsky, these theories have the most to say about the processes of management of plans. The burden in planning comes in resource management and allocation of attention between the demands of planning, acting, and monitoring. As components of planning become more practiced, they require less effort and they free resources from action, for planning and self-evaluation. Thus an important source of the growth of planning skills is mastery of the materials and actions that form the content of plans. From this view, exemplified in the literature on cognitive behavior modification and writing, progress occurs when one provides the component skills and external aids toward managing them.

Flavell and Wellman, who are developmentalists, emphasize yet another source of development, "metacognition" (Flavell & Wellman, 1977). The term includes what Greeno and colleagues (1984) call procedural knowledge, skill in matching concepts and strategies to particular, local conditions for problem solving. Growing accessibility may reflect breadth of experience in problem solving. Additionally, Flavell and Wellman suggest that metacognition also includes sensitivity to one's own capacities and skills in general and while executing a particular task. Perhaps these sensitivites are also shaped by external feedback and modeling.

V. Conclusion

Our discussions of planning are based on componential analysis. Planning consists of a sequence of activities, and different theorists have highlighted different facets of the steps in goal-directed behavior. But which are the most important facets? Perhaps an example of actual planning will be revealing.

There is a computer game, "Snooper Troops," that requires planning. It begins with a crime. Someone had been harassing the Kims, leading up to the night when an intruder made ghostly noises, shut off their electricity, and stole their valuable Siamese cat. The object of the game is to identify the culprit in the shortest time by the most efficient route. In order to figure out which of the eight suspects had the motive, opportunity, and knowledge of the Kim household to carry out the crime, the player must decide how to gather the information. The suspects live in different parts of town, and the snooper must determine the location of their residences by constructing a street map. They are available for questioning at home on specified weekdays, and when they are absent, the detective can sneak into their houses and look for clues without being caught. The sleuth's travel should be based on a consideration of the availability of the suspects, their location, and the accumulation of information about them.

Cracking this case calls upon the same abilities used to select and prepare dinner menus (Byrne, 1977), schedule shopping expeditions (Hayes-Roth & Hayes-Roth, 1979), or rebuild the Tower of Hanoi (Klahr, 1978). In solving the mystery, the snooper must learn the facts surrounding the theft so as to represent the problem. The detective must recognize the goal of finding the criminal expeditiously, devise means to gain necessary data, organize a search consistent with geographical and temporal constraints, monitor the results of search activities, build a case through logical inference, and decide when the list of suspects has been narrowed sufficiently to implicate the criminal. Moreover, there are embedded strategies. The snooper's task is to devise a strategy for discovering how a suspect devised a way to break into the Kims' residence.

We hope that this chapter has helped the reader to identify all the components of planning that must be exercised by the Snooper Trooper.

Investigators of planning, however, have not so far agreed on which facets of goal-directed action should be singled out for discussion and investigation. They have used the term "planning" to describe different parts of goal-directed action. Because the aspects emphasized dictate theories of the function of plans and speculations about development, we have decided to include all aspects in this review chapter. By doing so, perhaps we have provided the readers of this chapter with the tools to evaluate the contributions each chapter makes to our understanding of the various aspects of planning. Although our analysis has distinguished the various parts of the process, it may also lead to the conclusion that planning is not merely the sum of all its parts. In planning, the same representational requirements enter into understanding of the problem domain, then into construction of a plan, simulation of its operation, and revision and evaluation of actions. There are multiple evaluation points – of the goal, the plan, adequacy of its execution and of the outcome – which may be governed by the same criteria. Motivation to define a goal surely affects motivation to plan the action. Planning is an important skill because it requires integration of all the components and, in fact, is the means by which we integrate problem solving.

References

Anderson, J. R. (1983). *The architecture of cognition.* Cambridge, MA: Harvard University Press.

Anzai, Y., & Simon, H. (1979). The theory of learning by doing. *Psychological Review, 86,* 124–140.

Baker, L. (1984). Spontaneous versus instructed use of multiple standards for evaluating comprehension: Effects of age, reading proficiency, and type of standard. *Journal of Experimental Child Psychology, 38,* 289–311.

Bandura, A. (1981). Self-referent thought: A developmental analysis of self-efficacy. In J. H. Flavell & L. Ross (Eds.), *Social cognitive development: Frontiers and possible futures* (pp. 200–239). New York: Cambridge University Press.

Bereiter, C., & Scardamalia, M. (1982). From conversation to composition: The role of instruction in a developmental process. In R. Glaser (Ed.), *Advances in instructional psychology* (Vol. 2, pp. 1–64). Hillsdale, NJ: Erlbaum.

Borkowski, J. G. (1985). Signs of intelligence: Strategy generalization and metacognition. In S. Yussen (Ed.), *The growth of reflection* (pp. 105–144). New York: Academic Press.

Bowlby, J. (1969). *Attachment and loss: Vol. 1. Attachment.* New York: Basic Books.

Brown, A. L., Bransford, J. D., Ferrara, R. A., & Campione, J. C. (1983). Learning, remembering and understanding. In P. H. Mussen (Ed.), *Handbook of child psychology* (4th ed.) (Vol. 3, pp. 77–166). New York: Wiley.

Brown, A. L., Campione, J. C., & Barclay, C. R. (1979). Training self-checking routines for estimating test readiness: Generalization from list learning to prose recall *Child Development, 50,* 501–512.

Brown, A. L., Day, J. D., & Jones, R. S. (1983). The development of plans for summarizing texts. *Child Development, 54,* 968–979.

Brown, A. L., & DeLoache, J. S. (1978). Skills, plans, and self-regulation. In R. S. Siegler (Ed.), *Children's thinking: What develops?* (pp. 3–35). Hillsdale, NJ: Erlbaum.

Brown, J. S., Collins, A., & Harris, G. (1978). Artificial intelligence and learning strategies. In H. F. O'Neil (Ed.), *Learning strategies* (pp. 107–139). New York: Academic Press.

Bruce, B. C. (1980). Plans and social actions. In R. J. Spiro, B. C. Bruce, & W. F. Brewer (Eds.), *Theoretical issues in reading comprehension* (pp. 367–384). Hillsdale, NJ: Erlbaum.

Bruce, B., & Newman, D. (1978). Interacting plans. *Cognitive Science, 2,* 195–233.

Burtis, P. J., Bereiter, C., Scardamalia, M., & Tetroe, J. (1983). The development of planning in writing. In C. G. Wells & B. Kroll (Eds.), *Exploration of children's development in writing* (pp. 153–174). Chichester, England: Wiley.

Byrne, R. (1977). Planning meals: Problem-solving on a real data-base. *Cognition, 5,* 287–332.

Carter, D. B., Patterson, C. J., & Quasebarth, S. J. (1979). Development of children's use of plans for self-control. *Cognitive Therapy and Research, 4,* 407–413.

Chapman, M. (1984). Intentional action as a paradigm for developmental psychology: A symposium. *Human Development, 27,* 113–114.

Donaldson, M. (1978). *Children's minds.* New York: Norton.

Flavell, J. H. (1977). *Cognitive development.* Englewood Cliffs, NJ: Prentice-Hall.

Flavell, J. H., & Wellman, H. (1977). Metamemory. In R. V. Kail, Jr., & J. W. Hagen (Eds.), *Perspectives on the development of memory and cognition* (pp. 3–34). Hillsdale, NJ: Erlbaum.

Flower, L., & Hayes, J. R. (1981). Plans that guide the composing process. In C. H. Fredericksen & J. F. Dominic (Eds.), *Writing: The nature, development and teaching of written communication* (Vol. 2, pp. 39–58). Hillsdale, NJ: Erlbaum.

Frese, M., & Stewart, J. (1984). Skill-learning as a concept in life-span developmental psychology: An action–theoretic approach. *Human Development, 27,* 145–162.

Freud, S. (1959). Formulations regarding the two principles in mental functioning. In *Collected papers* (Vol. 4). New York: Basic Books.

Freud, S. (1963). Introductory lectures on psychoanalysis. In J. Strachey (Ed.), *The standard edition of the complete psychological works of Sigmund Freud* (Vols. 15 & 16). London: Hogarth.

Fuson, K. C. (1979). The development of self-regulating aspects of private speech: A review. In G. Zivin (Ed.), *The development of self-regulation through private speech* (pp. 135–217). New York: Academic Press.

Goldin, S. E., & Hayes-Roth, B. (1980). *Individual differences in planning processes* (Rand Note N-1488-ONR). Santa Monica, CA: Rand Corp.

Greeno, J., Riley, M. S., & Gelman, R. (1984). Conceptual competence and children's counting. *Cognitive Psychology, 16,* 94–143.

Hayes-Roth, B. (1980). *Estimation of time requirements during planning: Interactions between motivation and cognition* (Rand Note N 1581-ONR). Santa Monica, CA: Rand Corp.

Hayes-Roth, B., Cammarata, S., Goldin, S. E., Hayes-Roth, F., Rosenschein, S., & Thorndyke, P. W. (1980). *Human planning processes* (Rand Note R-2670-ONR). Santa Monica, CA: Rand Corp.

Hayes-Roth, B., & Hayes-Roth, F. (1979). A cognitive model of planning. *Cognitive Science, 3,* 275–310.

Hayes, J. R. (1981). *The complete problem solver.* Philadelphia: Franklin Institute.

Kagan, J. (1984). *The nature of the child.* New York: Basic Books.

Kagan, J., & Kogan, N. (1983). Individual variation in cognitive processes. In P. H. Mussen (Ed.), *Handbook of child psychology* (4th ed., Vol. 2, pp. 1273–1365). New York: Wiley.

Klahr, D. (1978). Goal formation: Planning and learning by preschool problem solvers: or "My socks are in the dryer." In R. S. Siegler (Ed.), *Children's thinking: What develops?* (pp. 181–212). Hillsdale, NJ: Erlbaum.

Kopp, C. B., Krakow, J. B., & Vaughn, B. (1983). Patterns of self-control in young handicapped children. In M. Perlmutter (Ed.),*The Minnesota Symposia on Child Psychology* (Vol. 16, pp. 93–128). Minneapolis: University of Minnesota Press.

Kreitler, H., & Kreitler, S. (1976). *Cognitive orientation and behavior.* New York: Springer.

Langer, E. J. (1985). Playing the middle against both ends: The usefulness of adult cognitive activity as a model for cognitive activity in childhood and old age. In S. Yussen (Ed.), *The growth of reflection* (pp. 267–285). New York: Academic Press.

Luria, A. R. (1976). *Cognitive development: Its cultural and social foundations.* Cambridge, MA: Harvard University Press.

Markman, E. M. (1977). Realizing you don't understand: A preliminary investigation. *Child Development, 46,* 986–992.

Markman, E. M. (1979). Realizing you don't understand: Elementary school children's awareness of inconsistencies. *Child Development, 50,* 643–655.

Meacham, J. A. (1979). The role of verbal activity in remembering the goals of action. In G. Zivin (Ed.), *The development of self-regulation through private speech* (pp. 237–263). New York: Wiley.

Meichenbaum, D. (1977). *Cognitive behavior modification.* New York: Plenum.

Meichenbaum, D., & Asarnow, J. (1979). Cognitive–behavioral modification and metacognitive development. Implications for the classroom. In P. Kendall & S. Hollon (Eds.), *Cognitive–behavioral interventions: Theory, research and procedures* (pp. 11–35). New York: Academic Press.

Meichenbaum, D., Burland, S., Gruson, L., & Cameron, R. (1985). Metacognitive assessment. In S. R. Yussen (Ed.), *The growth of reflection* (pp. 1–30). New York: Academic Press.

Miller, G. A., Galanter, E., & Pribram, K. (1960). *Plans and the structure of behavior.* New York: Holt, Rinehart & Winston.

Mischel, H. N. (1984). From intention to action: The role of knowledge in the development of self-regulation. *Human Development, 27,* 124–128.

Mischel, W. (1983). The role of knowledge and ideation in the development of delay capacity. In L. S. Liben (Ed.), *Piaget and the foundations of knowledge* (pp. 201–230). Hillsdale, NJ: Erlbaum.

Mischel, W., & Patterson, C. J. (1976). Substantive and structural elements of effective plans for self-control. *Journal of Personality and Social Psychology, 34,* 942–950.

Mischel, W., & Patterson, C. J. (1978). Effective plans for self-control in children. In W. A. Collins (Ed.), *Minnesota Symposia on Child Psychology* (Vol. 11, pp. 199–230). Hillsdale, NJ: Erlbaum.

Newell, A., & Simon, H. (1972). *Human problem solving.* Englewood Cliffs, NJ: Prentice-Hall.

Oerter, R. (1978). The influence of environmental structure on cognitive development during adolescence: A theoretical model and empirical testing. In A. M. Lesgold, J. W. Fokkema, & R. Glaser (Eds.), *Cognitive psychology and instruction.* (pp. 375–388). New York: Plenum.

Oxford English Dictionary. (1971). (compact ed.). New York: Oxford University Press.

Patterson, C. J., & Roberts, R. J., Jr. (1982). Planning and the development of communication skills. In D. L. Forbes & M. T. Greenberg (Eds.), *Children's planning strategies: New directions for child development* (Vol. 18, pp. 29–46). San Francisco: Jossey-Bass.

Pea, R. D. (1982). What is planning development the development of? In D. L. Forbes & M. T. Greenberg (Eds.), *Children's planning strategies: New directions for child development* (Vol. 18, pp. 5–27). San Francisco: Jossey-Bass.

Peterson, C. L., Danner, F. W., & Flavell, J. H. (1972). Developmental changes in children's responses to three indications of communicative failure. *Child Development, 43,* 1463–1468.

Piaget, J. (1976). *The grasp of consciousness: Action and concept in the young child.* Cambridge, MA: Harvard University Press.

Piaget, J. (1978). *Success and understanding.* Cambridge, MA: Harvard University Press.

Pressley, M. (1979). Increasing children's self-control through cognitive interventions. *Review of Educational Research, 49,* 319–370.

Rogoff, B., Newcombe, N., & Kagan, J. (1974). Planfulness and recognition memory. *Child Development, 45,* 972–977.

Rumelhart, D. E. (1977). Understanding and summarizing brief stories. In D. Laberge & S. J. Samuels (Eds.), *Basic processes in reading: Perception and comprehension.* Hillsdale, NJ: Erlbaum.

Sacerdoti, E. D., (1977). *A structure for plans and behavior.* Amsterdam: Elsevier.

Scardamalia, M., & Bereiter, C. (1983). The development of evaluative, diagnostic and remedial capabilities in children's compositions. In M. Martlew (Ed.), *The psychology of written language: A developmental approach* (pp. 67–95). London: Wiley.

Scardamalia, M., & Bereiter, C. (1985). Fostering the development of self-regulation in children's knowledge processing. In S. Chipman, J. Segal, & R. Glaser (Eds.), *Thinking and learning skills: Current research and open questions* (pp. 563–577). Hillsdale, NJ: Erlbaum.

Scardamalia, M., Bereiter, C., Woodruff, E., Burtis, J., & Turkish, L. (1983). The effects of modelling and cuing on high level planning. Unpublished manuscript.

Schank, R. C., & Abelson, R. P. (1977). *Scripts, plans, goals, and understanding.* Hillsdale, NJ: Erlbaum.

Schmidt, C. F. (1976). Understanding human action: Recognizing the plans and motives of other persons. In J. S. Carroll & W. S. Payne (Eds.), *Cognition and social behavior* (pp. 47–67). Hillsdale, NJ: Erlbaum.

Skinner, E., & Chapman, M. (1984). Control beliefs in an action perspective. *Human Development, 27,* 129–133.

Spivack, G., & Shure, M. B. (1974). *Social adjustment of young children: A cognitive approach to solving real-life problems.* San Francisco: Jossey-Bass.

Stein, J. (1975). *The Random House college dictionary.* New York: Random House.

Stein, N. L., & Glenn, C. G. (1979). An analysis of story comprehension in elementary school children. In R. O. Freedle (Ed.), *New directions in discourse processing* (Vol. 2, pp. 53–120). Norwood, NJ: Ablex.

Tetroe, J. (1981). The effect of planning on children's writing. Unpublished manuscript.

Urbain, E. S., & Kendall, R. C. (1980). Review of social–cognitive problem-solving interventions with children. *Psychological Bulletin, 88,* 109–143.

Vygotsky, L. S. (1962). *Thought and language.* Cambridge, MA: MIT Press.

Vygotsky, L. S. (1978). *Mind in society: The development of higher psychological processes.* Cambridge, MA: Harvard University Press.

Wertsch, J. V. (1979a). A state of the art review of Soviet research in cognitive psychology. Unpublished manuscript.

Wertsch, J. V. (1979b). From social interaction to higher psychological processes: A clarification and application of Vygotsky's theory. *Human Development, 22,* 1–22.

Wertsch, J. V. (1980). Semiotic mechanisms in joint cognitive activity. Paper presented at a conference on the theory of activity. USSR Acadamy of Sciences, Moscow.

Wilensky, R. (1981a). Metaplanning: Representing and using knowledge about planning in problem solving and natural language understanding. *Cognitive Science, 5,* 197–233.

Wilensky, R. (1981b). A model for planning in everyday situations. Paper presented at the third annual meeting of the Cognitive Science Society. Berkeley, CA.

Wittgenstein, L. (1953). *Philosophical investigations.* New York: Macmillan.

Wood, D., Bruner, J. S., & Ross, G. (1976). The role of tutoring in problem-solving. *Journal of Psychology and Psychiatry, 17,* 89–100.

Zaporozhets, A.V., Zinchenko, V. P., & Elkonin, D. B. (1971). Development of thinking. In A. V. Zaporozhets & D. B. Elkonin (Eds.), *The psychology of preschool children* (pp. 186–254). Cambridge, MA: MIT Press.

Zivin, G. (1979). Removing common confusions about egocentric speech, private speech, and self-regulation. In G. Zivin (Ed.), *The development of self-regulation through private speech* (pp. 13–50). New York: Wiley.

2   Planning in cross-cultural settings

Robert A. Randall

This chapter characterizes the prevalence and importance of plans and planning skills in cross-cultural settings mainly by surveying the ethnographic literature. Much of relevant cognitive science research has treated "planning" as a type of problem solving, and "plans" as sequences of action categories that may become well learned (cf. Greeno, 1974; Hayes-Roth & Hayes-Roth, 1979). The relatively small group of ethnographers who have studied, in other cultures, processes and schemata that are similar to planning and plans, have developed data and theory that are compatible with this view (Quinn, 1975; Randall, 1977), but for several reasons, there has been a significant difference in research focus and therefore, in methodology.

In particular, cognitive ethnographers have been concerned not just with plans that have been routinized, but with ones that through processes of cultural transmission are found in similar form throughout a segment of society (D'Andrade, 1981). Ethnographers have, accordingly, not evidenced much interest in novel plans and their planning, so they have not generally acquired verbal protocols in order to gain insight into the process and its results (Wallace, 1965). Rather, they have focused their efforts on obtaining an accurate representation of plans *routinely* used by people in the process of performing *socially significant* acts. In turn, this focus has spawned considerable interest in (a) interviewing strategies for studying routines (Spradley, 1979); (b) quantitative methods for verifying the actual use of hypothesized routine plans by groups of individuals; and (c) the information processing structure of such routines.

As a result, there now exist models of enough routine plans in enough cultures so that certain types of inference about plan structure and plan use are becoming possible. Specifically, we are now in a position to hypothesize how daily activities are integrated into and controlled by more abstract and complex long-range plans, and we now know something about how routine sequences of hundreds of activities and activity alternatives might be recalled from long-term memory.

Briefly, such complex routines display a demonstrable patterning in the sequential and hierarchical organization of goals. In the one case where this organization has been described in sufficient depth (our 1977 research on Philippine Samal fishers[1]), insight has been gained both into the process of routinization of plans and into the problem-solving rules underlying culturally transmitted routines. Because hypotheses about the organization of goals in non-Western social contexts have, in addition, much in common with "standard" cognitive science explanations of problem solving in Western, mainly laboratory contexts (cf. Newell & Simon, 1972), there is reason to believe that a truly general problem-solving theory of planning may be feasible.

This chapter is divided into three parts. The first and largest part is a discussion of the routine selection plan and its structure as cognitive ethnographers view it. The second part is a brief discussion of the implication of ethnographic studies for our understanding of planning and plan modification. And finally, the chapter closes with an even shorter summary of present ethnographic knowledge of plan development in children. Although ethnographers have long been concerned with cognitive development, they have in only one case concerned themselves with plan development, and in that study, the youngest subjects were adolescents. My remarks consider this study, some more speculative data of my own on the relation between adult socialization norms and the development of plans, and some questions that ethnographic theories of plans and planning raise about the development of planning skills.

I. The routine selection plan

A. The development of the concept of plans for selecting routines

Ethnographic interest in planned behavior was renewed during the 1950s and 1960s by developments in structural semantics, in cognitive psychology, and in cognitive approaches to ethnography. Initially, research took two distinct paths. One approach attempted to specify in a psycholinguistically accurate manner the hierarchically organized sequential structure of complex routines for primitive agriculture (Conklin, 1954, 1957), religious rituals (Frake, 1964), weddings (Metzger & Williams, 1963), imprisonment (Spradley, 1970), drug dealing (Agar, 1975), and so forth. A second line of research attempted to determine empirically through a technique known as "componential analysis," the sets of "attributes of meaning" associated with numerous alternative terms in a semantic domain.

At first, the componential analysis research problem was viewed as one of determining in various languages which attributes go with particular names for kin (Goodenough, 1956; Lounsbury, 1956). It soon became obvious, however, that the kin terms used are determined not only by the attributes of the relative, but also by aspects of the *situation* in which they were used (Frake, 1960; Tyler, 1969). Geoghegan, in his research on the similar problem of providing a description of address terminology semantics for Philippine Bisayan (1966, 1971a), was the first ethnographer to realize that such an approach was compatible with the planning literature (Miller, Gallanter, & Pribram, 1960). He thus began to use flow charts to describe "output selection routines" for processing numerous "situational assessments" relevant to selection. Rather than merely associating various attributes of meaning with particular names conventionally used to address others, Geoghegan characterized the process as "plans for selecting an address term."

This approach led, as we shall see, to several important advances. Ultimately, it proved necessary to combine this approach with the hierarchical model pioneered by Conklin (Randall, 1977), but before the motivation for integrating the two can be fully appreciated, a more detailed summary of the selection plan research will prove informative.

In Geoghegan's approach, the various possible addresses a person might use to another (e.g., English: *Margaret, Mom, Madam, Girl, Ms., Misez, Pumpkin,* etc.) were treated as contrasting alternative *selections.* But in contrast to the traditional approach, the attributes routinely associated with a particular address term – such as "respected," "adult," and "male" for *Sir* – were said not to be elements of meaning because a speaker is not attempting to communicate such facts to an addressee. Rather, in routine situations, a speaker is merely communicating the name of the addressee. The attributes of *Sir* are thus not elements of meaning, but rather are more accurately understood as situational considerations or assessments used to select an alternative term of address.

Subsequent Geoghegan research on address terminology among Philippine Samal (1971b, 1973a) demonstrated that plans for selecting address terms were very complex indeed. Samal, and probably all peoples, select an *address form type* (ff. 1973a, p. 336). For the Samal, depending on the situation, this would consist of a sequence of between one and three name classes such as kin terms, honorifics, religious or governmental titles, and either personal names or personal name substitutes.

Once an address form type is selected, the Samal selects appropriate name realizations for the various categories of names required by the address form type. Once this is done, the address term might be subjected to still further selection procedures. The personal name selected might be classified as a "true name" or might be selected by a speaker simply because a "true name" was the name *habitually* used to address the person in question. But in the *unusual* event that the individual wanted to communicate affection, a nickname would be used and, if, further, he or she wanted to communicate respect, then a nickname substitute would be used. This, in turn would be selected by considering situational information such as the addressee's 'stage in the life cycle,' 'relative age,' 'size,' and 'sex.'[2]

Geoghegan and several of his Stanford colleagues (Fjellman, H. Gladwin, Keesing, Quinn) subsequently generalized this approach. A routine plan for selecting among alternatives can be seen as an ethnographic hypothesis that can be tested quantitatively. A statement of the sort, "if conditions X, Y, and Z prevail, then alternative Q will be selected," amounts to an empirically confirmable hypothesis. Geoghegan, in several widely circulated and quoted papers (e.g., 1969, 1971c), showed that the distribution of living arrangements on one island in the Southern Philippines could be situationally predicted with greater than 90% accuracy if one knew both the situations Samal saw themselves in and the plan they used to routinely select a living arrangement in a particular situation. This finding was subsequently confirmed with residence selection plans of other Samal, and in a repetition of research on the same village six years later.[3]

Since the early residence selection and address term selection studies, numerous papers have appeared that describe selection plans employed for various purposes in the Soloman Islands, Kenya, Ghana, Mexico, and the Philippines (Fjellman, 1976; Geoghegan, 1973b; C. Gladwin 1976, 1977; H. Gladwin, 1971; H. Gladwin & C. Gladwin, 1971; cf. Keesing, 1967; ff. Randall, 1977, p. 166; Quinn, 1976; Young, 1980, 1981).

In the United States, there have also been numerous similar selection plan studies, and these encompass an equally wide range of tasks (C. Gladwin, 1979a, 1979b, 1980, 1983; C. Gladwin & Butler 1984; C. Gladwin & Downie, 1979, 1982; H. Gladwin & Murtaugh, 1980, 1984; Mukhopadhyay, 1980, 1984; Pittman, 1983, 1985, 1986). The studies have attempted to describe cultural knowledge with constructs that can be assigned a cognitive interpretation consistent with available psychological evidence concerning cognitive capacities. Such "cognitive ethnography" has been used to answer questions of interest to ethnologists, agricultural economists, transportation planners, and educators of teachers.

Despite their topical diversity, however, these studies have much in common because the class of cognitive structures posited are similar and because those that have been tested quantitatively typically predict about 90% of alternative–selection observations.

B. Obligatory sequences in routine plans

Cross-cultural research on the structure of routine plans is consistent with the general hierarchical list-structure view of artificial intelligence proposed by Newell, Shaw, and Simon (1958; Newell & Simon, 1972), and assumed in most recent cognitive science research (cf. Abelson, 1981; McDermot, 1978; Schank & Abelson, 1977). Put simply, routine plans consist of sequences of categories. Each of these may, in principle, contain subsequences of categories, and these subcategories may contain sub-subsequences of categories, and so forth. Each category is a goal, together with a routine for selecting among activities that could realize the goal. A routine plan can thus be described as a large hierarchical structure which partitions a very long sequence of motor activities into shorter sequences of more abstract categories (Table 2.1).

Rituals and a few other activities may be performed in fixed sequence, but such invariant strings of categorized activity are rare among routines. More typically, routines contain numerous branching points where what is done next depends not only on what was done last (Simon & Kotovsky, 1963; Simon & Sumner, 1968), but also, as we have seen from the address term study, on processed input from various types of situational information. In the cognitive science literature, analogous routines have frequently been referred to as "production systems" (Klahr, 1976; Newell & Simon, 1972) or as "action rules" (Abelson, 1981).

Cross-cultural research agrees with Schank and Abelson's hypothesis that such situational information is either *obligatorily* processed or is *exceptionally* processed (Geoghegan, 1971b; Randall, 1977). Processing is "obligatory" in the sense that a person, in order to execute a plan *competently,* must acquire the necessary information before continuing. Exceptionally processed situational information need not, by contrast, be considered before selecting a subsequent action. Rather, a person may operate on a set of expectations about the correct sequence of actions. Only if, in the appropriate context, the individual "happens" to become aware that some significant situational variable differs from what one would usually expect to be the case, is a different course of action selected.

There are three sorts of situations in which information must be obligatorily procesed before a subsequent activity can be competently performed. In some cases, people must *search* the state of some environ-

Table 2.1. *A portion of Samal scad fishing routine*

SELECT 'Do anchored scad fishing at Sapan Shoal (UNLESS there might be a storm):
REPLACE SELECT 'Do anchored scad fishing at Sonoy Shoal.'

11000 Get the tackle ready. (UNLESS there are other equipment problems): INSERT 'get
      the other equipment ready.'

12000 'Get everything ready.'

13000 'Depart.'

14000 'Continue to paddle until reaching a good spot at Sapan Shoal.'

15000 'Anchor the canoe.' (UNLESS have no anchor):
      REPLACE Tie on to an anchored canoe.
  15100 Drop the anchor.
    15110 nil (UNLESS anchor line and tackle are twisted): INSERT Untangle them.
    15120 Go to the front of the canoe.
      15121 nil (UNLESS it's crowded in front):
          INSERT Put lantern raft in the rear of the canoe.
        151211 'Get the raft.'
        151212 'Put the raft in the rear.'
      15122 'Crawl to the bow' (UNLESS lantern raft is in rear):
          REPLACE 'Slowly go to the front.'
    15130 'Get the anchor.'
      15131 nil (UNLESS the anchor is stuck on the canoe's anchor rest): INSERT 'Free
        the anchor.'
      15132 'Grab the anchor.'
      15133 'Hold anchor firmly.'
      15134 'Move anchor over the sea beside the canoe.'
    15140 Drop the anchor in the sea.
      15141 'Hold the anchor line.'
      15142 'Let go of anchor.'
      15143 Sit at the rear (UNLESS the lantern raft is in the rear):
          REORDER 15143, 15144 to 15144, 15143.
      15144 Continue to let out the anchor line until the anchor line stays below on the
        bottom.
  15200 Continue to feed the anchor line until the anchor bites in.
    15210 Continue to wait until the current is going straight by the canoe.
    15220 Jiggle the line toward the rear.
  15300 Let the anchor line out somewhat.
    15310 SEARCH How strong is the current?
    15320 (weak): Put it about 5 fathoms out.
    15330 (average): Put it about 10 fathoms out.
    15340 (strong): Put it about 15 fathoms out.
  15400 Tie the anchor line (UNLESS the line has been used up):
      REPLACE Wrap the anchor line around the outrigger spreader.

Source: Randall (1977).

mental variable or variables before a subsequent activity may be competently selected. In other cases, a subsequent activity may not be competently implemented until *monitoring* indicates that a *start cue* has occurred. In still others, a subsequent activity may not be implemented until monitoring indicates that *a stop cue* has occurred. In common traffic situations, for example, one might back out of a driveway, then *wait* while monitoring the road for "no more traffic." When cues that warrant this inference occur, one *starts* driving. Once on the road, one might *search* "What time is it?" and then select Main Street as a route appropriate to rush hour. Finally, one might drive down Main Street until monitoring indicates that the stop cue "Southmore Street" occurs. At this point, driving along Main Street should stop, and a turn should be made.

Since Geoghegan drew ethnographic attention to searching, and developed an axiomatic theory of such searching (1973a), it has become evident that searches are exceedingly common in routine plans. Essentially, when a routine plan requires one or more searches, the person must, before continuing to implement a plan, deliberately acquire information concerning some relevant situational variable or variables. This can be accomplished by looking, listening, touching, or asking questions; by enacting possibly complex action sequences that make it possible to get such sense data; or by merely searching memory.

For example, in Table 2.1, a Philippine scad fisherman may wish to prevent an anchor point from coming out of the sand on the sea bottom. To do this, it is necessary to put the anchor line at an angle with the bottom and to keep the line taut. Routinely, a fisherman realizes this goal by searching the strength of the current and letting the line out '5, 10, or 15 fathoms' depending on whether 'the current is weak, average, or strong.'

By contrast, start cue monitoring may or may not incorporate a deliberate search. Start cue monitoring is typically described by Samal as 'continuing to wait *until* X,' where "X" is an event that justifies the beginning of some activity. Quite possibly, the waiting is not actually continuous, but Samal apparently believe that 'waiting' is and should be continuous. In any case, Samal fishermen in the Southern Philippines say they should 'continue to wait *until* a certain star sets over the Point' in order to begin the yearly 'Southern Monsoon fishing'; they should 'continue to wait *until* the nineteenth night of the lunar month' to begin the monthly lantern fishing; they should 'continue to wait *until* the sun sets or others light their lanterns' in order to begin nightly anchor fishing, and, as in the table, they should 'continue to wait *until* the current is going straight by the canoe,' in order to let out the anchor line.

Stop cue monitoring (Miller, Gallanter, & Pribram, 1960; cf. Randall, 1977) differs from start cue monitoring in that the stop cue terminates activity and the start cue initiates activity. However, superficially, the two types of processing have much in common. In both cases, one should 'continue to do something *until*' an anticipated event occurs. Southern Philippine fishermen 'continue to do Southern Monsoon fishing *until* the season of forceful night ebb currents,' and they 'continue to do lantern fishing *until* the monthly time of the full moon,' and, as in Table 2.1, they 'continue to feed an anchor line *until* it bites into the sand.'

Yet there are important differences between start cue and stop cue processing as well. In start cue monitoring, one 'continues to wait.' Such 'waiting' may be realized by executing a fairly wide range of other tasks, by thinking over the routine to be performed, or by merely resting. What is done while waiting is frequently of no consequence to competent plan execution so long as the person knows when the anticipated start cue event occurs. The occurrence of the start cue event is, therefore, typically unrelated to whatever one was doing while one was waiting.

By contrast, stop cue processing involves repeatedly doing a specified sequence of activities until the stop cue occurs. Sometimes, such a stop cue event may occur whether or not the activity was performed competently. Thus, the 3:15 p.m. school bell ends class. Similarly, dawn ends the Philippine fisherman's lantern fishing, and acquisition activity is replaced by sleep, whether or not anything has been accomplished. But such "time limit" monitoring is a relatively rare constituent of the routines we observe in field conditions.

Rather, more commonly, the stop cue event can occur only when the activity sequence has been performed competently a sufficient number of times. This is because stop cue events can occur only when the goal of the activity has been accomplished, or when it seems likely that the goal of the activity cannot be achieved despite the performance of the planned sequence of activities. Accordingly, Samal fishermen 'continue to jiggle their scad line at 15 fathoms' either 'until the scad bite' or 'until one thinks they won't bite.' In the latter case, after 'the time of about two smokes' has elapsed, they adjust their line to 17 fathoms and begin again.

With both start cue monitoring and stop cue monitoring, however, searching may or may not be employed to acquire the cue. From Samal reports on their monitoring and considerable observation of fishing, it seems generally true that a Samal's monitoring will be casual and irregular well before the cue is expected, and only occasionally at this point, will a deliberate and conscious search for the cue occur. Later, as goal realization approaches, or the time of starting or stopping approaches, monitoring behavior changes. Then searching may become more delib-erate and frequent, depending on whether (a) the cue can be easily missed, (b) the consequences of missing the cue are considered serious, and (c) the cue's appearance can be easily "noticed," or must be con-sciously and deliberately searched for. In any event, this monitoring is not, as has sometimes been suggested (Miller, Gallanter, & Pribram 1960, p. 36; Newell & Simon, 1972, p. 32), part of a fixed sequence of activities being performed prior to cue occurrence. Typically, searching can occur *at any point while* the person is waiting for the start cue or *while* the per-son is executing an activity designed to achieve a goal completion stop cue.

Searching, start cue, and stop cue monitoring all oblige the person to acquire certain types of information before proceeding with the perfor-mance of a subsequent activity. Searches, for example, require one to dis-cover which of several equiprobable states a situational variable is in before a subsequent activity can be selected and executed (Geoghegan, 1973a:279). But if, as is far more frequently the case, the states of a situ-ational variable are not thought to have equiprobable occurrence, then it is more efficient to ignore the less frequent states of the variable, and assume that the *usual* state of the variable will be in effect.

C. Exceptions and optional information processing

Optional information processing occurs when an unusual, but relevant item of information impinges on awareness. Even though such infor-mation is not searched, it nevertheless is routinely used to select acti-vity sequences when unusual circumstances prevail. Geoghegan (ff. 1973a:266) was the first to understand the ethnographic importance of such processing when he made use of the well-known worldwide linguis-tic phenomenon known as "marking" (Greenberg, 1966; Jakobson, 1941). In languages, words that reference culturally important items are also more frequently used, are simpler in linguistic form, and are usually acquired earlier by children (Greenberg, 1966). These are termed "unmarked." They contrast with the less important, less often used, more complex "marked" forms acquired later by children. Geoghegan argued that unusually processed address terms were marked, and connected to unmarked address terms by "marking rules." As was shown earlier in the discussion of address term selection (section I.A), usual address terms communicate far less than those which are unusual in the context. Geoghegan, however, realized that marking is not a particularly linguistic process at all, but rather is essentially a cognitive process which often appears both in communicative and noncommunicative plans.

Geoghegan's marking rule research drew attention to the fact that much information relevant to routine plan selection is simply *noticed*. That is, people regularly classify certain items of unusual situational information as "relevant" and may select an unusual routine even though they made no conscious attempt to acquire the information. Philippine fishermen, for example, usually head for Sapan Shoal *unless* 'word strikes' that 'the scad are really biting at the Little Island'; and they usually buy No. 24 hooks *unless* they 'happen to hear' there are No. 25 hooks in stock (Randall, 1977).

In subsequent research, however, it has been pointed out that *noticing* probably results from what Neisser (1967) has referred to as "preattentive awareness" (Gladwin & Murtaugh, 1980). It seems likely, for example, that Philippine fishermen have some out-of-awareness processing mechanism for monitoring the state of rarely changing, but situationally important variables. Thus, 'gossip' about productive shoals or about the availability of a better hook would be distinguished from the abundant irrelevent "noise" typically impinging on the senses, and some process would bring the exceptional information to the fisher's attention at the appropriate moment.

No ethnographic research has attempted either to learn how such out-of-awareness processes develop, nor which sorts of information are most likely to be so processed. From the Philippine fishing data, however, it would appear that there are at least three mechanisms for becoming aware of exceptional information. Probably, some unusual situations are of such importance for the competent execution of a plan, that they are routinely monitored by an out-of-awareness process. Other unusual information, such as a gunshot, may be recognized immediately and be directed to attention because it is associated with highly disturbing stimuli. Still other information, such as indications of major equipment malfunction, may sometimes come to attention only when routine plan execution produces incompetent results.

Routine exceptions are easily elicited from Samal. In interviewing, one typically asks a person the native language equivalent of 'If you do X, what is the first thing you usually do?' This is then followed with 'And then what do you usually do?' Questioning of this type is then pursued until the person terminates the sequence or indicates that 'it depends.' When the latter occurs, one asks 'It usually depends on what?' The answer provides a situational variable to be searched. Proper questioning will then determine what the person sees both as possible alternative states of the variable and as possible sequences of activity to be selected for each state of the variable.

Once the usual routine has been established, it becomes important, both for accuracy and for reasons that will become apparent in section II, to discover as many routine exceptions as possible. One does this by systematically taking each 'usual' activity in the sequence, and asking the person 'why do you sometimes not do (the usual) *Y,* after you do *X?*' Persistence with this type of questioning will typically discover numerous exceptions to almost every 'usual' activity.

A study of exceptional processing by Philippine scad fishermen (Randall, 1977) shows that exceptions result either in *deleting* a usual sequence, *inserting* one, *replacing* one (i.e., deleting then inserting), or *reordering* a routine sequence (i.e., deleting an activity and inserting it either previously or subsequently). These processes are, of course, well known both as transformations within generative grammar theory, and within computer programming, so it is not surprising that we find that usual sequences within Philippine fishing plans are subject to each of these exceptional branching processes as well.

By contrast, if one attempts to explain why, for example, routines contain deletions in some circumstances and additions in others, there is much that is new and somewhat surprising. A careful analysis of 101 exceptions in a Philippine scad fishing routine, reveals a very marked *patterning* in the routine. The logic underlying this patterning is better discussed in section II, but here it is important to consider certain regularities in the function of exceptions. These regularities are determined by the goal being pursued and the person's preference ranking for activities that can realize the goal. In practice, one determines what goal a person (or set of people) has by asking why he or she (or they) engage in a certain activity. They normally are aware what preferred change of state the activity is meant *directly* to realize (cf. Dowty, 1972; Randall, 1977; Simon, 1967; Wright, 1963), and in most cases, one can easily obtain goal data from Samal fishers (Table 2.2).

Deletion exceptions almost always occur when some usually encountered *obstacle*[4] is for some reason not encountered, or when some *material means* that is usually made available in order to execute the plan, is, for some reason already available. Thus, a Philippine fisherman must usually 'get duck feathers' as one of several material means necessary for 'making feather lures' for a scad line; but, if for some reason sufficient duck feathers have been saved, this act is of course deleted. Analogously, when leaving the fishing shoal, the rattan container used to keep fish fresh must usually be lifted into the boat, so that the drag from the night's fish

Table 2.2. *A portion of the anchoring routine illustrating the goal structure*

15000 GOAL Prevent what prevents the canoe and other means from being available for use at a good spot at Sapan shoal.
   REALIZATION SELECT 'Anchor the canoe.'
   15100 GOAL Cause the anchor location to change to place of use at the bottom of the sea.
      REALIZATION SELECT 'Drop the anchor.'
   15110 GOAL Prevent what prevents 'Drop the anchor.'
      REALIZATION SELECT nil (UNLESS anchor line and scad line are twisted):
      SELECT INSERT 'Untangle them.'
   15120 GOAL Cause a change in the location of the labor from stern to anchor.
      REALIZATION SELECT 'Go to the front of the canoe.'
      15121 GOAL Prevent what prevents 'Go to the front of the canoe.'
         REALIZATION SELECT nil (UNLESS 'It's crowded in the front of the canoe'):
         SELECT REPLACE 'Put lantern raft at rear.'
         151211 GOAL Cause change in location of hand to lantern raft.
            REALIZATION SELECT 'Get the raft.'
         151212 GOAL etc.
   15130 GOAL Cause location of anchor to change to one's hand.
      REALIZATION SELECT 'Get the anchor.'
      15131 GOAL Prevent what prevents 'Get the anchor.'
         REALIZATION SELECT nil (UNLESS anchor is stuck in anchor rest):
         INSERT SELECT 'Free the anchor.'
      15132 GOAL Change location of anchor to one's hand.
         REALIZATION SELECT 'Pick up anchor.'
         151321 GOAL Prevent what prevents a change of location of anchor from hand.
            REALIZATION SELECT 'Grasp anchor firmly.'
   15140 GOAL Cause location of anchor to change to the bottom of the sea.
      REALIZATION SELECT 'Drop the anchor.'
      15141 GOAL Prevent change from possession of anchor to nonpossession.
         REALIZATION SELECT 'Hold on to anchor line.'
      15142 GOAL Prevent what prevents 'Drop the anchor.'
         REALIZATION SELECT 'Let go of anchor.'
      15143 GOAL Cause a change in location of labor to 'drop anchor' from bow to stern.

catch will not prevent rapid and easy transport to the shore. If there has been so little catch that the container has never been lowered into the sea, however, the container is not an obstacle to transport, and so the usual lifting operation is deleted.

Lest the above seem a lesson in the obvious, let me make explicit the implications of this finding. People do not just memorize by rote long sequences of activities, together with an even larger number of exceptional sequences. Rather, usual activities are actually the performative realizations of goals designed to achieve means availability, obstacle removal, and the like. The deletion exception applies, in certain unusual circumstances, to any activity whose associated goal can be realized without activity. Quite obviously, if such means availability or lack of obstacle should become usual, then the routine would be altered so as to assume the new usual circumstances.

Insertion exceptions function inversely to deletion exceptions (Randall, 1977, p. 136). Material means that are usually available need not be made available except in the unusual case where they are not available. Fishermen insert routines for repairing canoes in the unusual case where a canoe leaks; and they insert routines for borrowing a pressure lantern when their own does not function. As well, when fishermen encounter an unusual obstacle, they characteristically insert subroutines for overcoming them. Samal fishermen circumnavigate enormous logs floating in the water; they hang fish out of the reach of cats; they fight off marine bandits who attack; and, as in Table 2.2, they free an anchor stuck on an anchor rest.

Deletion exceptions then, occur because there *is* an unusual means available or because there *is not* a usual obstacle to overcome; insertion exceptions, by contrast, occur because there *is not* a usual means available or there *is* an unusual obstacle to overcome.

In certain well-defined situations, replacement exceptions occur instead of deletions or insertions. People typically list numerous other sequences which could serve as alternative methods for realizing the goal. An urban resident might, for instance, usually get to work by car, but could walk or (in some places) use a subway, taxi, bus, or bicycle. A fisherman might usually buy line at a particular store, but he could buy it at other stores, or 'ask for' some from a relative, or steal some, or use any of several other culturally categorized means acquisition activities. As well, Samal replace usual address terms with marked ones.

Once a goal realization preference ranking is established, certain characteristic types of replacement exceptions appear. Routinely, a Samal will insert an alternative that is expected to overcome the usual obstacles to goal achievement in the usual way, or will make available in the usual way the material means necessary for goal achievement. If, on occasion, the typical obstacles to goal achievement will probably be hard to overcome or the usually available means will probably not be easily available,

Samal are less likely to insert subroutines to overcome the obstacle or make the means available. Rather than insert an activity that might fail, they typically select a less preferred, but less risky exceptional strategy for goal attainment (cf. Simon, 1957).

Thus, an American might replace "drive to work" with "take the bus," rather than count on a mechanic to repair a car in time for work. Similarly, a Philippine fisherman, upon noticing 'storm clouds' in the west, will replace the night's fishing location. A shoal upwind from land is selected over the usual downwind shoal because, should a storm hit, it would be difficult and dangerous to go upwind to shore.

Another type of exceptional replacement process occurs when highly preferred goal-realizations that are ordinarily very difficult to perform because of obstacles or lack of means, suddenly can be performed because the obstacles can be easily overcome or because the means can be easily made available. In such cases, the usual routine will be replaced by the more preferred one, at least if the fisherman behaves competently and is aware of the unusual situation.

There are numerous examples of this sort of thing in fishing and other Samal planning data, but the following can serve as illustrations: A fisherman readily prefers a certain type of motorized daytime net fishing to the usual nighttime hook-and-line fishing. The cost of net and motor boat is so high, however, that the former fishing technique can only rarely be performed. Yet, several times during my 15-month field investigations, when visitors arrived with net fishing equipment, fishermen who were asked to participate, readily selected and performed net fishing.

Replacement exceptions occur, however, not just because there is an unusual opportunity or an unusual lack of opportunity. Replacement exceptions also occur because preference orders among alternatives may routinely vary according to the situation (cf. Agar, 1975). For various reasons, an alternative that ordinarily poorly achieves a goal, may in unusual circumstances be expected to do a superior job of achieving a goal. When people have reason to expect such unusual success, they of course replace the usual with an alternative expected to get better results.

Southern Philippine fishermen, for example, fish mainly to acquire money. The techniques they routinely use, typically acquire money in greater quantity than a large number of easily executed but normally less productive techniques. In unusual cases, however, where gossip tells a fisherman that 'frigate mackerel have been really biting,' he replaces the usual techniques with this temporarily preferred frigate mackerel trolling alternative. A similar sort of thing occurs when a fisherman finds that the usual fishing depth is unproductive, and therefore tries a possibly more productive one; or when a fisherman hears that a certain motorized fish carrier is leaving for market very early, and therefore replaces their usual (trusted) fish carrier with one that can be expected to return a higher market price.

A special case of the replacement exception is the reordering exception. In situations such as those described above, where changes in the presence or absence of means and obstacles make usually impractical but more preferred sequences practical, or less preferred sequences necessary, it is sometimes possible to replace the usual goal-realization routine with a different sequence of the same activity categories.

As we will see in section II, the sequential ordering of some activities is fixed obligatorily, but other sequences are routine simply for reasons of preference. One does X before Y because it is easier, or because it is less likely to result in failure or because it is less likely to be criticized by others. In Table 2.1, for example, it is shown that a fisherman usually moves to the rear of the canoe after dropping the anchor and before 'letting out the anchor line.' This is because the anchor works by sticking a point in the sand and then setting up resistance to being pulled across the bottom by the current. By moving to the rear of the canoe, an angle is formed with the vertical, which helps keep the point in the sand. When equipment is in the rear, however, a fisherman will avoid this obstacle by letting out the line first, then removing the blocking equipment, and then moving to the rear. Although letting out the line while in the front of the canoe allows less of an angle to be formed with the vertical and therefore a less fast anchorage, it is preferred because it avoids risking equipment spillage.

If, by contrast, one expects an obstacle to be *temporary,* or one expects the means to soon become available, one can replace the usual ordering of activities with one that exploits the more favorable conditions expected in the near future. A fisherman, for example, routinely 'packs his boat after eating the sunfall meal,' but if the meal is late and has not yet become available for eating, then he 'packs his boat and then returns home to eat.' In such a situation, one could not substitute an entirely new sequence because there is no alternative to packing the boat and no good alternative to eating a meal. One could perhaps keep to the usual sequence by inserting an activity to make dinner available, but such activities might lead to domestic squabbles, and in any case would probably not be successful. The best alternative, therefore, is to pack the boat and then eat the meal. In doing so, one needs to make one extra trip between boat and house, and one risks having something stolen from the boat while the meal is being eaten. But even so, the reordering replacement is preferred.

Reorderings may also occur when unusual opportunities present themselves. A fisherman usually ties 30–40 flies for his line before he melts lead to make lead sinkers. This is because fly tying is by far the more time consuming, and, if necessary, sinkers of an inferior sort can be fashioned in a few minutes. By contrast, if the previous night's fishing line can be easily repaired by adding a few flies, most fishermen prefer first to do the more time-consuming task of making high-quality sinkers. They thus select preferred reorderings when the risks of doing so can be minimized.

In sum, the sequential performance of a routine depends significantly upon environmental variation, and upon exceptional rules for selecting alternatives that are sensitive to this variation. There are several cognitive processes whereby exceptional information may be noticed, and exceptions may perform several different functions in altering usual sequences. There are three types of replacement exceptions, two types of deletions, two types of insertions, and reordering exceptions. Analysis of very large routines such as the very long Philippine Samal scad fishing routine (Randall, 1977, pp. 318–345; cf. the illustration in Table 2.1), shows that such exception types occur in highly predictable contexts. The occurrence of obstacles and the availability of means, in particular, have major effects not only on whether the sequences selected will be usual or unusual, but also on which functional types of exceptions will be selected.

We do not know very much, however, about the acquisition of exceptional routines, about the development of capacities to process the requisite information or to use a range of exceptions, nor do we know much about the causes of differences among individuals either in exception routine inventory or in exception routine type. Presumably, replacements, deletions, and insertions are generated from preference-ordered goal realizations. We do not know at what point children develop this generative ability, however, nor do we know much about how the preference orders are learned. The Philippine study indicates that many goal-realization preferences are learned from others. But there are undoubtedly more active discovery processes at work as well: Adult fishermen have, at several points, been forced, through the unavailability of routine means (such as certain sinkers or shoals) to try previously unknown means. These turned out to be improvements, and subsequently became routine among all fishermen. As well, one would expect that fishermen must, on occasion, employ metaphorical schemata (cf. Schön, 1979) to generate goal realization preference rankings, but these need to be more carefully studied in both adults and children.

D. Exceptions and their correct placement in plan hierarchies

From the discussion above, it might be assumed that the task of modeling a routine action plan is fairly easy. One need simply elicit a sequential list of goals and their routine realization, and then amend it with all possible routine exceptions. When one does this carefully, however, it very soon becomes obvious that some exceptions are widely applicable to numerous routines, whereas others apply uniquely to a particular routine. This fact has important implications for research on planning.

In Southern Philippine fishing, for example, it is common practice to light a kerosene pressure lantern in order to attract fish. If, at the time that the lantern is being lit, a strong wind is blowing and thus *preventing* the match from remaining lit, fishermen insert the exception 'move the lantern to the floor of the canoe near one's legs' and then perform the usual activity of 'light the match near the lantern.' In this way, the exceptional insertion overcomes the exceptional obstacle.

An informant, if pressed to name other exceptions to 'lighting a match' in the usual way, is highly likely to name unusual circumstances that are in no way particular to match lighting. If waves are temporarily choppy, the way match lighting will be accomplished might be changed, but so too would nearly every other task the fisher attempts. If the weather gets bad, or looks as if it soon will do so, fishers and everyone else in small craft head for land. Fishers, in such circumstances, have special techniques for reeling line in quickly and freeing themselves of stuck anchors, but the fact remains, bad weather is a potential exception to virtually any marine activity they might do. Still more global exceptions exist: Fishers typically mention a variety of 'dangers' (such as 'sickness' and 'violence') as reasons why nearly all routines may be performed in unusual ways.

These more global exceptional circumstances, however, are commonly found in routine plans that have been studied in many parts of the world (e.g., Ghanaian marketing, Gladwin & Gladwin, 1971; Philippine house entering, Frake, 1975; Philippine living arrangement selection, Geoghegan, 1969; U.S. heroin buying, Agar, 1975). Violence, in particular, is treated as a 'very serious' offense by first-grade teachers, and handled differently from other 'off-task' behaviors (Pittman, 1986). How then are such global exceptions to be described in a cognitively accurate description of routine plans?

In Randall (1977), it was argued that it would be highly redundant to model routine plans by listing all exceptions potentially applicable to each activity. Rather, if one tries to merely describe routines (and not their creation), one should describe routines as subordinate parts of more inclusive routines. At each hierarchically more dominant goal realization, one would list just those exceptions that apply to all subordinate goal realizations, and that do not apply to superordinate goal realizations. Thus, for example, 'bad weather' (and any number of environmental cues that allow such an inference) might be considered an exception to 'getting things at sea' (to use the indigenous idiom), and so would therefore be used to replace more than 70 fishing techniques, and all of the sequences used to implement these. Accordingly, bad weather might affect even the lighting of a match, or the twitching of finger muscles used to accomplish this minor goal. In formal logical terms then, exceptions satisfy the distributive law of algebra. Exceptions to two or more activities are exceptions to the combination of all such activities: $aX + aY = A(X + Y)$.

This observation, though, suggests far more questions than answers. Anchored scad fishing, for example, often takes 14 hours to complete, yet clearly is but one of several alternative methods of realizing a more general plan to 'get fish from the sea.' By asking a standard question of the sort, "Why do you get fish from the sea?" one learns it is done either to 'acquire something to sell' or to 'acquire something to eat.' There are of course alternative ways to get something to sell, and 'getting fish from the sea' is just one. Something to sell, in turn, is acquired in order to obtain money, and money is of course acquired to obtain a wide variety of items which, in many cases, can also be obtained in alternative ways. Many such items are purchased in order to 'help maintain the family,' and this goal itself is part of still more basic goals related to 'being happy,' 'having help when one needs it,' and so forth.

The point of the above, however, is not to attempt description of the extraordinarily complex 'family maintenance' routine Philippine fishermen seem engaged in. Rather, it is to make the point that even the most mundane behavior is affected by the more basic goals such behavior is designed to affect. A sudden death of a spouse, for example, changes the family structure significantly, thus changing monetary requirements, and therefore fishing behavior. Samal frequently regard such altered behavior as appropriate for people in such circumstances, so our models of plans must somehow take the hierarchical structure of such facts into account.

As the cognitive science literature makes clear (cf. Schank & Abelson 1977, p. 106), and the above makes obvious, some goals function to facilitate more basic goals. There is, therefore, a system of *priorities* built into routine plans, and these serve to guide both the routine and novel selection of alternatives when unusual circumstances emerge. As a general rule, a person assigns greater priority to achieving preconditions for major goals, and assigns lesser priority to achieving subgoals hierarchically subordinate in the plan. A fisher, for instance, who is in the act of dropping a line, but who also realizes that a loose anchor is allowing the canoe to drift, uses the hierarchical routine to determine that the canoe must be anchored again before the line can be used. He will therefore interrupt the act of line dropping in order to satisfy a prerequisite to the hierarchically dominant goal of remaining where the fish are located. By the same token, neither of these exceptional circumstances would be of much consequence, if other circumstances jeopardized the achievement of more basic goals involving prosperity, health, and happiness.

All this may seem obvious enough, but if so, it should be pointed out that virtually all cross-cultural studies of plans and planning have taken for granted the hierarchically more basic goals for which most activities are carried out. This oversight unfortunately occurs in much of the systematic efforts at task description in the psychological and artificial intelligence literature as well. The traditional disinterest in hierarchically more dominant goals is not just the result of deemphasizing the role of exceptions in plans. In the early stages of plan research, it may have been productive to study tightly bounded problems such as nail hammering, chess playing, address terminology, or restaurant eating. But if we want to explain planning as we actually observe it, then models must be developed that incorporate the full hierarchy of goals people actually use.

How, for example, would an artificial intelligence chess-playing program model a human who makes a bad play in order to end the game in order to go meet someone? Or how would Schank and Abelson's script processor (1977) interpret a "restaurant story" in which a medical intern "looked at her watch, and then got up without finishing the soup, left the money on the table, and hurriedly left"? Probably, such artificial intelligence models would have difficulty with such material, because they require knowledge of priorities that are not part of a program specific to chess playing or restaurant eating. Yet if cross-cultural data are to be believed, hierarchically dominant goals greatly affect the nature of actual behavior. Models that ignore the full hierarchical structure of behavior fail to predict accurately. And perhaps most importantly, they ignore a central feature of planning competence: the ability to know when and how to interrupt minor activities when they become counterproductive to basic goals.

To confirm that a hypothesized plan is actually used, it is thus necessary to describe extremely large and complex routines that operate at abstract levels and are designed to achieve major life goals. In practice, description in enough detail to predict is an ambitious project, and so far, has never been successfully achieved. Nevertheless, much can be learned about the cognitive processes involved from an analysis of what has so far been described. In particular, one can do as the linguists do: infer from the structure of observed sequences the planning rules generating the sequences.

II. Inferences about planning processes

Up to this point, we have been surveying the cross-cultural literature on the structure of plans, and have largely ignored the more interesting issue of how plans are fashioned in the first place. In part, this is because there is a marked paucity of cross-cultural materials on the subject. More importantly, though, the discussion of planning has been postponed because most of what ethnographers have learned about planning is the result of inference from description of routine plans.

In particular, we now know that (a) planning routines are highly sensitive to environmental conditions; (b) that this requires the processing of information regarding events, means availability, and obstacles relevant not only to the immediate goals of motor activity, but also to major life goals; and (c) that the routine selection of alternatives is determined by the outcome of this processing. In order to predict behavior, we must thus infer the existence of extremely large and complicated plans and so question whether such routines could be directly memorized.

A.   Are routine plans directly memorized?

As it happens, there is considerable evidence that large routines are not directly memorized. Once routine plans are described along the lines suggested by Schank and Abelson (1977) and Randall (1977) as hierarchically organized sequences of goals together with the activity selection routines designed to realize them, it becomes obvious that during long routines such as scad fishing, certain substantive goal category sequences are repeated numerous times. The most likely reason for this pronounced patterning of forms is that fishers use very general problem-solving rules together with regularly monitored information about environmental and resource conditions to construct and reconstruct activity sequences.

Except for Randall (1977), there have been no attempts in the cross-cultural ethnographic literature to explain how people might recall their routine selection plans. This omission is almost certainly due to a persistent failure to recognize both the exceedingly large number of exceptions potentially affecting the selection process and the exceedingly ramified hierarchical plan structure such exceptions imply. If one can assume that plans are short, and affected by little circumstantial information, then one can also tacitly assume that such plans are memorized by rote much as one might learn a telephone number.

If, on the other hand, one attempts to explain the recall of plans such as those used in Philippine fishing routines, where there are usual sequences of several hundred activities together with exceptional sequences containing several hundred more activities, it becomes obvious that people would not be determining a "next" activity to be executed simply by "reading" conditional inputs and the "last" activity performed from some sequential list in memory (cf. Newell & Simon, 1972). Rather, it would be far more efficient to generate or regenerate the sequence through the use of problem-solving rules.

As it happens, there are several types of evidence which suggest that this latter type of plan recall occurs. First, even in routines that have been repeated thousands of times, there are subsequences that are not in the least routine. Philippine scad fishing, for example, contains numerous subsequences involving speech, and, as is well known, speech has a characteristically novel content (cf. Chomsky, 1965).

As well, in some scad fishing activities, a wide range in possible sequencing is allowed. A fisher should, for example, 'hang an alcohol can on his pressure lantern' sometime after he buys the alcohol and before he launches the canoe. Before alcohol is bought, there is nothing to hang; and after the canoe is launched, the alcohol could spill if placed elsewhere. But in the hour or so between these activities, it makes no difference when one hangs the alcohol can on the lantern, and thus fishermen tend to do it 'when it is convenient' or 'when they think of it.' The point here is that in the midst of even the most routine plans, fishermen must choose the sequencing of some activities by considering preconditions and goals.

The cognitive form that the information processing of relevant circumstantial information takes is variable as well. In Section I, it was argued that obligatory routine information searches occur when two or more environmental conditions relevant to activity selection are assumed by the person to be more-or-less equally probable, and that exceptions are found in routines when it is assumed that a particular situation will be unusual. Although these observations are cognitively significant, they tell us little about the storage of information processing instructions in routines.

Careful study of routine plans reveals numerous instances where the same situational variable must be obligatorily searched before continued execution at one point in the sequence, and simply noticed, if the person becomes preattentively aware, at another point. Thus, for example, a fisher arriving at a shoal will select an anchor line length and a fishing line length by searching 'whether the current is strong or weak'; but later, the fisherman will lengthen the lines if the current is noticed to have become stronger, or will shorten the lines if the current is noticed to have become weaker.

It is possible, in principle, to *describe* such a routine as a sequence, but it seems unlikely that such a sequence is *directly* stored in memory. Rather, the fisherman knows that the lines should be short when the current is weak and longer when it is strong, and also knows generally that one should search for information when one cannot assume answers, but should preattentively notice changes in important variables when the consequences of failing to notice are minor and the status quo can be assumed.

There are, in addition, several other types of evidence against the idea that people simply execute very long, directly memorized lists. Some of these have been explained in the necessary detail elsewhere (Randall, 1977, pp. 112–130), but one, in particular, provides insight into the planning process. Samal reports of their routines show a characteristic patterning quite different from what one would expect from someone recalling a directly memorized list of activities. Fishers, for example, if asked how to do 'mackerel net fishing,' start the description with the pursuit of the mackerel school. Yet this is hardly where the fisher starts the activity. Fishers first learn how to do mackerel netting. Then they must acquire the equipment. Then, on the night in question, they must get a partner, prepare the equipment, and select a proper time and direction. Net fishers thus "forget" to mention parts of the sequence that they never forget to implement in practice. Similarly, when asked to describe in detail how to drop an anchor, fishers *uniformly* neglect to mention that they get up and crawl forward in the canoe to get to the anchor line.

Why, if such a list of activities is directly memorized, would such an overlearned sequence be so poorly described by Samal? In some contexts, fishermen might omit discussion of activities they assume the listener already knows. Given the obvious ignorance of the listener in the cases described above, however, such an explanation for these answers seems doubtful. Perhaps, instead, the fisher assumed the listener would be uninterested in the preliminary details of these activities and so omitted them, but if so, what is it about preliminary activities that consistently makes them uninteresting? Another possible explanation for the omission of preliminary activities is that for some reason the act of anchor dropping is conscious, whereas the preliminary crawling activities are not. If so, then why would the former activity be conscious and the latter not? Certainly, there is no reason to suppose one phase of the sequence is any more "overlearned" or "difficult" than the other.

Rather, it seems more likely that fishers fail to mention certain parts of the routine because they assume that anyone can *deduce* these parts. They can assume this, because, in executing the plan themselves, they consciously or unconsciously use very general problem-solving rules as mnemonics in recalling what must be done next. Because the fisherman is obviously the labor means, and the anchor is obviously the equipment means employed, and because prior to use, means must be located where they can be used, the listener can easily "figure out" what precedes anchor dropping. Hence, nothing need be said about it.

One further type of evidence suggests that rural Samal, and quite possibly urban Westerners as well, use goal sequences to deduce subsequent activities to be executed. In complex routine fishing plans, certain activities appear repeatedly in the sequences. 'Buy', 'carry,' and 'repair,' for example occur more than 30 times in the plan for scad fishing, and these, as well as 'drop,' 'put,' 'paddle,' and others, are found repeatedly throughout more than 70 other fishing plans as well. It would be highly inefficient for a memory to store separate subplans for buying each and every item that might be bought, or separate subplans for carrying different items, or for paddling to different locations. Presumably then, subplans for performing these activities are stored "centrally," and then modified when used in particular routines in particular contexts.

But how is such recall and modification achieved? Not much is known about the modification of frequently used routines, possibly because researchers have preferred to study particular routines in detail, rather than groups of related routines. Recall of frequently used subplans, however, is almost certainly accomplished through the use of very general planning rules.

B. *Planning rules and planning*

Careful examination of goal sequences shows that there are potentially three subgoals that must be attained in order to achieve a desired state of affairs. These take the form of problem-solving rules for plan generation (ff. Randall 1977, p. 131). First, the fisher must overcome any obstacles *preventing* a change to the desired state of affairs; then the fisher must cause a change to the desired state of affairs; and then, as Wright (1963, 1967) has noted, the fisher must prevent events that might change the desired state of affairs to a less desirable state. With respect to any particular desired state, the order of these subgoal sequences seems to be fixed.

This ordering, however, is not always obvious or even overt in the routine selection plan structure. Frequently, for example, the three sequential subgoals are interspersed with activities designed to achieve other goals. Moreover, it is also commonplace to find that some subgoals are realized by no activity at all. A person who is trying to create a plan to accomplish some goal might create a plan with subgoals for overcoming obstacles, or preventing reversion to an undesirable state; but if there are no obstacles expected to interfere with changing to and maintaining a desired state of affairs, there would be no need to realize these subgoals with activities. Similarly, in some circumstances, a person might achieve a desired change of state of affairs with minimal or no effort (cf. Wright, 1963). Fishers, for example, can sometimes change their location simply by waiting until a current is running in the proper direction.

None of the above subgoals can be realized, however, without the prior realization of *implementing* goals. One cannot overcome some obstacle, cause a change to some desired state, or prevent changes from these states without first *selecting an activity to realize the goal,* and then *causing the availability of the means to implement the activity* (Randall, 1977. p. 131).

Problem-solving rules such as those mentioned above are used to identify goals that must be realized. In routine plans, once such goals are identified and recalled, the selection of an appropriate activity to realize the goal is relatively straightforward. When routinely relevant situational conditions are subjectively unpredictable, a person routinely searches the relevant condition or conditions, and then recalls from memory the goal realization routinely assigned to the set of conditions determined; but when situationally relevant conditions are more predictable, the person simply recalls the usual goal realization from memory unless exceptional circumstances are "noticed." In newly constructed plans, by contrast, a more active search selection process would be required for activities capable of realizing generated goals.

Whether routine or more novel, activity selections require the prior availability of means, and for any given activity, there are potentially numerous means that must be made available for use prior to execution. It is commonplace both in economics and in the ethnographic literature to claim that any human activity potentially requires labor, equipment, supplies, and resources. Cross-cultural data give ample evidence that people the world over use these types of means in implementing their plans, but there is little systematic evidence that they categorize means thus. Philippine fishermen make a categorical distinction between material means that are expended during the activity (supplies), and means that are more durable (equipment). They also realize that there must be 'people who know how to do it,' but there is no general category corresponding to "labor" or to "resources."

Causing a material means to become available for use, potentially entails the accomplishment of three subgoals: causing the means to be in a usable location, causing it to be in usable condition, and causing the rights to its use to be assigned to those doing the labor (Randall, 1977, p. 143; cf. Schank & Abelson, 1977, p. 12–13). Each such subgoal is then achieved by recursively applying the rules discussed above. To locate means, to make them usable, or to obtain the rights to them, it may be necessary to overcome obstacles, to make the desired changes, and then to prevent changes that would make the particular means unavailable. In turn, such subgoals would require that activities be selected to realize them, and that the means be made available to achieve them.

For example, once a fisherman has acquired the rights to a lantern in usable condition by 'leasing it for a share of the catch' *(nambi?)*, he will select and perform numerous activities designed to prevent the lantern from becoming unusable while he is performing dozens of lantern fishing subplans. He will set the lantern well away from the edge of the table in order to prevent its falling, he will tie it to a lantern stand in the canoe in order to prevent its loss in the sea, and he will prevent salt water from marking the glass shade and obscuring the illumination, by covering the lantern with a cloth until shortly before it is lit.

The result of applying these rules recursively then, is the highly ramified, extensive hierarchically organized list structure we know from studies of routine plans (Tables 2.1 and 2.2). Clearly, in the rare cases where such lengthy sequences are newly planned, the planning process must involve what Simon and his colleagues have called "backward chaining" (Newell & Simon, 1972), or what has been termed "left branching" in generative linguistics (Chomsky, 1965). In most cases, one would expect people to begin with goals they would like to achieve, and then consider those activities that might realize them and those means that would be necessary to implement these activities. Then, possibly standard routines for preventing equipment from becoming unusable would have to be inserted as the equipment is moved from one location to another. There is some evidence to support this view (Randall, 1977, p. 303), but unfortunately, there is insufficient cross-cultural research to make any worthwhile generalizations.

Table 2.3. *Problem solving rules underlying Samal fishing*

---

100 Cause the preferred state ^{a} of item X. →
  110 Cause the preliminary facilitating state of item X.
  120 Realize: Prevent obstacles that prevent change to the preferred state.
  130 Realize: Change item X to the preferred state.
  140 Realize: Prevent a change of item X to a less preferred state.

200 Realize: Goal →
    (where goal equals any of the accomplishments to right of realize in 120–140).
  210 Select a plan to realize the goal.
  220 Cause the preferred state: The means to do the plan is available for use by the
     laborers.
  230 Execute the plan.

300 the means →
  310 the labor means →
    311 labor means a, 312 labor means b, etc.
  320 & the supplies →
    321 supply a, 322 supply b, etc.
  330 & the equipment →
    331 equipment a, 332 equipment b, etc.
  340 & the resources →
    341 resource a, 342 resource b, etc.

400 is available for use by the laborers →
  410 means is located at place of use
  420 & means is in usable condition at place of use
  430 & means is rightfully usable by laborers at place of use.

---

^{a}Examples of preferred states: X is nice looking; X is feeling good; X is available for use by the laborers.

In short, Samal routine selection plans are structured by very general problem-solving rules (Table 2.3). Although these generative recursive rules have not been reported elsewhere, they employ categories that have been widely researched, and information processing mechanisms that are well known in the cognitive science literature. The Samal data strongly suggest that such problem-solving processes play an active role not only in the construction of novel plans, but also in the recall and use of culturally standard routines.

III. Developmental implications of ethnographic plan research

It might be interesting to speculate about novel planning in children by making inferences from the planning rules discussed above, from data on the modification of plans, and from case studies of their novel construction (ff. Randall, 1977, p. 296), but because no observations are available before late adolescence, nothing can be said on the topic here. Rather, it seems more worthwhile to summarize what we do know about the development of routine plans, and then consider what implications ethnographic inferences about planning have for development research.

A. The development of routine plans

Although there has been significant interest among ethnographers in cognition (cf. Lave, 1977; Reed & Lave, 1979), there has been no systematic research either on the development of planning rules or on the development of routine plans, apart from Geoghegan's Samal address term study more than a decade ago (1971b, 1973a). Even Geoghegan's study takes the abilities of 14-year-olds as a starting point for formal theorizing, so it is not very informative about the development of plans in children. Geoghegan's generalizations are supported, however, by our own less systematic observations on the development of Samal fishing plans in children, and accords reasonably well with some cognitive science theorizing on the development of routines in Americans, so it seems useful to review Geoghegan's findings in some detail here.

Geoghegan's systematic longitudinal data (1973a:184–205, 322–335) concern the development of routines for selecting the name substitutes described earlier (section I.A). He describes routines for individual Samal, aged 14–58 years, and provides less formal data for children and numerous adults.

Generally, the picture that emerges is one of increasing complexity in the selection process both with respect to the number of usual and exceptional alternatives selected among, and with respect to types of information potentially relevant to such selection. Routines used late in adulthood, can, moreover, potentially deal with a much wider range of communicative situations than do the less developed routines. Partly, this is the result of additions to the selection routines. But also, older adults seem to make selections at more abstract levels in the plan. One might expect that as people age, selections would become more routine, that there would be less evaluation of alternatives, and that the selection process would therefore be simplified. However, age also confers more authority and responsibility, so that older people are often permitted a wider range of alternatives, and are held responsible for the accomplishment of more basic goals. The result, therefore, is that despite routinization, the complexity of the selection process may increase with age.

Geoghegan argues that the earliest address routine requires the child to search for a distinction between 'adults' and 'children' and to assign them appropriate pronames accordingly. Later, the 'adult' category is narrowed: Those who have been married are known as 'adults,' whereas those who have not, but who have reached puberty, are given distinct pronames depending on the outcome of a second information search for their 'gender.'

The gender criterion is also relevant to addressing children, so that a competent child (perhaps at age six) would have five alternative pronames: two for children of each gender, two for adolescents of each gender, and one for adults. Still later, Samal begin to distinguish children who are older from children who are younger. A 'relative age' search is thus added to gender in selecting a proname for children, so that the child eventually acquires pronames for younger children of each gender, older children of each gender, 'bachelors,' 'maidens,' and adults.

As puberty approaches, fewer 'older children' will be encountered. Geoghegan's data show that in children around the age of 12 years, the 'relative age' search gradually becomes an exceptional consideration, and then disappears from the routine entirely. Once the child becomes recognized as an adolescent, a new search emerges: Children of each gender are given distinct pronames depending on whether they are 'big' or 'small,' or whether they 'can walk' or 'cannot yet walk.'

This search gradually becomes a three-way size distinction, so that, depending on size and gender, there are six proname address terms for children. Also, as adults age, they begin to encounter younger adults, and so distinguish younger, older, and same-age adults of each gender. The relative age search thus reemerges in the new context. The adult thus acquires a routine which, by searching age, gender, and in some contexts either size or relative age, distinguishes 14 pronames.

As was mentioned earlier, Samal personal names come in three types: 'true names,' 'nicknames,' and 'pet names' (such as English *Dear*). Pronames may substitute for each of these, and there is as well a class of 'honorific' pronames, so altogether there are seven classes of names that a Samal might select a realization for. However, Samal children usually use the nickname or the nickname substitute if they do not know the personal nickname. They select the pronickname by the procedures discussed above.

At least by age 14, there are exceptions where nicknames are not selected. If Samal wish to communicate negative feelings, they select a 'true name' or 'true name substitute,' much as an angry American might say *Barbara!* rather than *Barbie*. By contrast, if Samal want to communicate positive feelings, they use a 'pet name' substitute.

With age, the routine grows (see Figure 2.1). As can be seen in the figure, there is a gradual development in the routine for selecting a class of

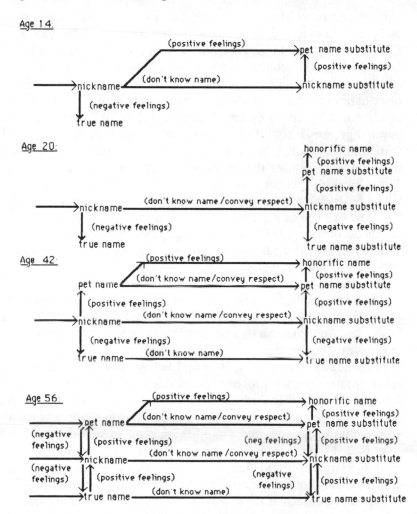

Figure 2.1. The development of Samal exceptional proname address (from Geoghegan, 1973a.)

names until Samal are nearly 60 years of age. At that point, however, more than one name class may be used to select a usual name for an individual. This, in turn, creates possibilities for communicating very negative or very positive feelings by using a true name instead of a usual pet name, or by using a pet name instead of a usual true name.

More generally still, Geoghegan's data seem to suggest that at the earlier stages, children and adolescents mainly learn routines for selecting names. The more abstract routines for selecting classes of names obviously come later, and are apparently modified until the Samal is well advanced in years. In Geoghegan's sample, only one person in her late fifties had options concerning the name type to be habitually used on another. All others were required to use nicknames or nickname substitutes habitually. Samal address development therefore exhibits the tendency noted by others (Anzai & Simon, 1979) for routines to be incorporated progressively into more comprehensive routines.

It would be foolish to make too much of this one study, but some of these findings parallel the development of Samal fishing plans as well. The majority of Samal children do not go to school. Girls mainly help with housework and sometimes gather mollusks; boys are 'instructed' to 'fish.' By the age of six, children know that labor is divided within the family according to the same criteria used in address selection: 'age' and 'sex.' Also, as with address terminology, Samal children at about 6 years of age know few alternative fishing techniques.

For boys, there is initially only one form of fishing permitted: 'quasi-fishing' from the beach. The goal is 'to have fun,' but in bad weather the technique may provide table fish. No detailed studies of this technique have been attempted, so it is not possible at present to compare the information processing capabilities required by this technique, with those used by adults. Later, when the child is 'big' (about 9 years), there is a rudimentary selection process: If it is safe (daytime, good weather), and if the canoe and other means are available, 'simple hooking' is permitted not far from shore. If these conditions are not met, the less productive and therefore less preferred shore fishing is pursued.

With age, and, as the Samal put it, with 'strength' and 'knowledge,' activities are permitted that are more difficult, more dangerous, more expensive, further from shore, and that potentially produce more income. The usual approach is for a 'soon to be adolescent' to accompany older relatives in the same canoe. At first, this is in the daytime, but later it occurs at night. Initially, the accompanying relative provides visual and some verbal information about goals, means, obstacles, alternative realizations of goals, and conditions for selecting one goal over another. But adults claim that the main reason for such supervision is the danger of nighttime fishing – particulary the difficulty a young boy would have in saving himself or his expensive equipment in a sudden storm.

Gradually, the situations in which an elder is required declines. As the boy learns, he begins to use a separate canoe and ties himself to the canoe of an adult. In early adolescence, income and fish are still turned over to the family 'in order to help.' A boy, at this point might know 20 or more types of fishing, but at this stage, if he has a resident father, he will select whatever type of fishing his father 'instructs' him to. Thus, the more basic goals remain his father's concern. Later, when he begins to court and save for marriage, and is therefore working for his own future family, rather than his natal family, he gains some independence from his father's directions. With marriage, or whenever full financial responsibility for a family is assumed, the fishing technique selection routine reaches its greatest complexity: Up to 56 alternatives may be selected, depending on means available, expertise, probable fish behavior, likely obstacles, and financial goals (Randall, 1985). Although fishermen, at this stage, typically continue to select and perform the same techniques they used through adolescence, they do so with considerable increase in conscious planning. Rather than merely do whatever 'Father' says, the newly married fisherman now considers his own preferences, those of his wife, the new household's financial situation, and the resources available through a new set of in-laws.

In general, Samal parents think that young children's fishing plans should involve techniques that require less knowledge and strength, require cheap and easily constructed means, are much less lengthy and dangerous, and initially require no responsibility for results. Samal males are thus expected to learn how to perform the routines long before they are expected to understand the hierarchically more dominant goals fishing is designed to accomplish. Knowledge of the basic goals of fishing, of means to achieving these goals, and of obstacles that could prevent their achievement are probably well understood by adolescence, but it is only later, with decline in parental influence, that such issues enter a Samal's fishing technique selection plan on a daily basis, and it is only at this point that individuals are actually permitted to integrate basic goals with their fishing behavior.

A comparison of development of address term selection and fishing strategy selection shows incremental growth in the numbers of alternatives considered and in the situations where they may be selected. In both types of development, the hierarchically more basic plans which develop last, function to permit a less socially controlled articulation between basic goals and routines. The present data support the view that more general routines are built from previously learned hierarchically subordinate routines (Anzai & Simon, 1979), but the cause of this growth is not so obviously the result of cognitive processes such as familiarization and chunking. Rather, in both fishing and address selection, Samal begin to make hierarchically more dominant selections once others in their society think it appropriate for someone of the person's status to pursue self-selected goals.

At this point, there is no reason to doubt that age-related memory limitations have an effect on plan development, and there may, as well, be age-related changes in the processing of exceptional information, but as yet, there have been no cross-cultural studies designed to study such development.

B. The development of planning skills

Despite the quite general nature of the problem-solving rules for planning and their seeming universal plausibility, there is, as yet, no systematic evidence that such rules are universal. There is, though, considerable evidence that the posited concepts are linguistic universals (cf. Fillmore, 1968; Dowty, 1972), and of course, there is considerable supporting cognitive science research on spatial goals, means, and the like (Schank & Abelson, 1977). Research on the development of planning skills thus first needs to confirm the wider existence of the planning rules in adults and in children.

Whether or not such planning rules are universal, ethnographic theories argue for research first into the development of routines, and then into the planning skills such routines imply. The Samal research would also argue for investigation of how the following develop: (a) the ability to distinguish alternative goal realizations and the conditions that make their selection appropriate; (b) the ability to delete, insert, replace, and so on, and its relation to means, obstacles, and preferences; (c) the ability to interrupt low-level routines when higher-level exceptions of various types become applicable.

It would also be useful to know how children develop a knowledge of necessary means, and methods appropriate for the acquisition of means. Initially, the child expects means to be provided, but how does an older child learn to do the providing? Obviously, the older child must learn to categorize specific means into more general types, must learn something about property rights, and must learn the culture's standard plans for the appropriate transfer of these rights. Adult Samal, for example, have significantly different acquisition categories than do Americans (Randall, 1984), and different ideas about situations where particular acquisitions are appropriate. Thus, for example, it is fairly common for 10-year-old Samal 'to ask for a share' when someone 'who loves them' has 'a lot.' To make such acquisitions possible, Samal adults, and quite possibly Samal children deliberately pursue loving relations with distant relatives. What, if any, such cultural differences have upon the development of planning skills is, of course, unknown, but given the centrality of means acquisition to all planning, it would not be surprising if such cultural differences affect cognitive processes and even planning capabilities.

IV. Conclusion

From the foregoing, it should be obvious that Samal fishers and many other peoples create, modify, and implement hierarchically complex and lengthy plans by processes which, as Miller, Galanter, and Pribram suggested decades ago, are probably quite general. What these processes are, and how they are best studied, however, are not so clearly understood. We know very little cross-culturally about actual planning processes because most of the socially significant plans we observe in field conditions are routine solutions to old and frequently discussed problems. Ethnographic studies have therefore mainly attempted to describe plans that can be proved to be in regular use. These studies are of use to researchers seeking to know how experts operate, or to researchers who want to evaluate human response to policy, but they also provide significant data that any theory of planning, or theory of the development of planning must address. How are the routines we observe created, and once created, how are they recalled?

Although there are admittedly no certainties in this matter, the ethnographic work that has been done strongly suggests a generative version of the Schank–Abelson script hypotheses. To be generative, it appears that certain goal states must play an especially privileged role in the planning process. Among these are obligatorily ordered goals designed to overcome obstacles, to bring about desired changes expected to promote the accomplishment of high priority goals, and to prevent reversion to less desired states. As well, there must be goals designed to cause the availability of means to achieve these goals such as goals for causing means to be acquired, for causing means to be in good condition, and for causing means to be located where usable. Yet even if this general perspective should turn out to be universal, we will, unless the pace of cross-cultural planning research greatly accelerates, continue to know very little about the conceptualization and organization of these privileged goals either in adults or in children.

Notes

1. In this paper, the designation "Samal" refers to the Northern Sinama-speaking peoples of the Basilan Strait researched mainly in 1971–72 and in 1980. The research was sponsored by the National Science Foundation, the University of Houston, and the University of California School of International Studies.
2. As is commonplace in linguistic tradition, single quotes are used to represent English *glosses* of expressions in other languauges. These are to be understood not as exact translations, but as rough approximations useful to nonspeakers as mnemonics.
3. Geoghegan sometimes referred to his models as "decision rules," but Quinn (1975) has

pointed out that the term "decision" should be reserved for selections that involve an *evaluation* or *judgment* about the correct course of action. For this reason, it seems more appropriate to refer to schemata in which one of two or more alternatives is routinely selected as "routine selection plans" (cf. Randall, 1977).
4. The term "obstacle" is used here in a different sense from Schank and Abelson (1977, p. 53). They define an obstacle as the absence of an enablement for a script action. Here, the term never refers to the absence of means, even though such absence would make a goal realization impossible. Rather, the term is used to designate agents or objects that block or prevent actions (cf. Schank & Abelson, 1977, pp. 115–116).

References

Abelson, Robert P. (1981). Psychological status of the script concept. *American Psychologist, 36,* 715–729.
Agar, Michael. (1975). Selecting a dealer. *American Ethnologist, 2,* 47–60.
Anzai, Y., & Simon, Herbert A. (1979). A theory of learning by doing. *Psychological Review, 86,* 124–140.
Chomsky, Noam. (1965). *Aspects of the theory of syntax.* Cambridge, MA: MIT Press.
Conklin, Harold. (1954). *The relation of Hanunoo culture to the plant world.* Ph.D. dissertation, Yale University. (Ann Arbor: University Microfilms 67–4119, 1954).
Conklin, Harold. (1957). *Hanunoo agriculture, a report on an integral system of shifting cultivation in the Philippines.* Rome: FAO Forestry Development Paper No. 12. (Ann Arbor: University Microfilms).
D'Andrade, Roy G. (1981). The cultural part of cognition. *Cognitive Science, 5,* 179–195.
Dowty, David. (1972). On the syntax and semantics of the atomic predicate CAUSE. *Chicago Linguistic Society Papers, 8,* 62–73.
Fillmore, Charles (1968). The case for case. In E. Bach & R. Harms (Eds.), *Universals in linguistic theory.* New York: Holt, Rinehart & Winston.
Fjellman, Steve. (1976). Talking about 'talking about residence': The Akamba Case. *American Ethnologist, 3,* 671–682.
Frake, Charles. (1960). The Eastern Subanun of Mindanao. In George P. Murdock (Ed.), *Social structure in Southeast Asia.* Chicago: Quadrangle Books.
Frake, Charles. (1964). A structural description of Subanun "religious behavior." In Ward Goodenough (Ed.), *Explorations in cultural anthropology.* New York: McGraw-Hill.
Frake, Charles. (1975) How to enter a Yakan house. In M. Sanchez and B. Blount (Eds.), *Sociocultural dimensions of language use.* New York: Academic Press.
Geoghegan, William. (1966). Information processing systems in culture. Paper presented at AAAS Meetings (Section H) Symposium on Mathematical Anthropology. Berkeley, CA.
Geoghegan, William. (1969). Decision-making and residence on Tagtabon Island. Working Paper 17. Language Behavior Research Laboratory. Berkeley, CA: ERIC Microfiche Files.
Geoghegan, William. (1971a). Information processing systems in culture. In Paul Kay (Eds.), *Explorations in mathematical anthropology.* Cambridge: MIT Press.
Geoghegan, William, (1971b). *Natural information processing rules.* Ph.D. dissertation, Stanford University. (Republished as 1973a).
Geoghegan, William. (1971c). Residential decision-making among the Eastern Samal. Paper, Department of Anthropology, University of California, Berkeley. (ERIC Microfiche Files).
Geoghegan, William. (1973a). Natural information processing rules. Monographs of the

Language Behavior Research Laboratory, University of California, Berkeley. (ERIC Microfiche Files)

Geoghegan, William. (1973b). Decision making in a complex environment: Selecting a drift route in Samal lantern fishing. Paper presented at American Anthropological Association Annual Meeting, Mexico City.

Gladwin, Christina. (1976). A view of the plan Puebla: An application of hierarchical decision models. *American Journal of Agricultural Economics, 58,* 881–887.

Gladwin, Christina. (1977). *A model of farmers' decisions to adopt the recommendations of plan Puebla.* Ph.D. dissertation, Stanford University.

Gladwin, Christina (1979a). Cognitive strategies and adoption decisions: A case study of nonadoption of an agronomic recommendation. *Economic Development and Cultural Change, 28*(1), 155–173.

Gladwin, Christina. (1979b). Production functions and decision models: Complementary models. *American Ethnologist, 6,* 653–674.

Gladwin, Christina. (1980). A theory of real-life choice: Applications to agricultural decisions. In Peggy Barlett (Ed.), *Agricultural decision making: Anthropological contributions to rural development* (pp. 45–85). New York: Academic Press.

Gladwin, Christina. (1983). Contributions of decision-tree methodology to a farming systems program. *Human Organization, 42,* 146–157.

Gladwin, Christina, & Butler, John. (1984). Is gardening an adaptive strategy for Florida family farmers? *Human Organization, 43,* 208–216.

Gladwin, Christina, & Downie, Masuma. (1979). *The future of corn production in the Altiplano of Western Guatemala: How do farmers decide?* Guatemala: Informe del Instituto de Cienica y Technologia Agricolas (ICTA).

Gladwin, Christina, & Downie, Masuma. (1982). The complementary role of Florida farm wives: How they help the family farm survive. Paper presented at Annual Meeting, Society for Economic Anthropology. Athens, GA.

Gladwin, Hugh. (1971). *Decision making in the Cape Coast (Fante) fishing and fish marketing system.* Ph.D. dissertation, Stanford University, CA.

Gladwin, Hugh, & Gladwin, Christina. (1971). Estimating market conditions and profit expectations of fish sellers at Cape Coast, Ghana. In George Dalton (Ed.), *Studies in economic anthropology, anthropological studies* (Vol. 7). Washington, DC: American Anthropological Association.

Gladwin, Hugh, & Murtaugh, Michael. (1980). The attentive–preattentive distinction in agricultural decision making. In P. Barlett (Ed.), *Agricultural decision making.* New York: Academic Press.

Gladwin, Hugh, & Murtaugh, Michael. (1984). Test of a hierarchical model of auto choice on data from the national transportation survey. *Human Organization, 43,* 217–226.

Goodenough, Ward. (1956). Componential analysis and the study of meaning. *Language, 32,* 195–216.

Greenberg, Joseph. (1966). *Language universals with special reference to feature hierarchies.* The Hague: Mouton.

Greeno, James. (1974). Hobbits and orcs: Acquisition of a sequential concept. *Cognitive Psychology, 6,* 270–292.

Hayes-Roth, Barbara, & Hayes-Roth, Frederick. (1979). A cognitive model of planning. *Cognitive Science, 3,* 275–310.

Jakobson, Roman. (1941). *Kindersprache, Aphasie, und allgemeine Lautgesetze.* Uppsala: Almquist & Wiksell. (Parts published in *Selected writings: word and language.* The Hague: Mouton, 1971).

Keesing, Roger. (1967). Structural and decision models of Social Structure: A Kwaio case. *Ethnology, 6,* 1–16.

Klahr, David. (1976). *Cognitive development: An information processing view.* Hillsdale, NJ: Erlbaum.

Lave, Jean. (1977). Cognitive consequences of traditional apprenticeship training in West Africa. *Anthropology & Education Quarterly, 8*(3), 177–180.

Lounsbury, Floyd. (1956). A semantic analysis of Pawnee kinship usage. *Language, 32,* 158–194.

McDermot, Drew. (1978). Planning and acting. *Cognitive Science, 2,* 71–109.

Metzger, Duane, & Williams, Gerald. (1963). A formal ethnographic analysis of Tenejapa Ladino weddings. *American Anthropologist, 65,* 1072–1101.

Miller, George, Galanter, E. & Pribram, K. (1960). *Plans and the structure of behavior.* New York: Holt, Rinehart.

Mukhopadhyay, Carol Chapnick (1980). *The sexual division of labor in the family: A decision making approach.* Ph.D. dissertation, University of California at Riverside.

Mukhopadhyay, Carol Chapnick. (1984). Testing a decision process model of the sexual division of labor in the family. *Human Organization 43,* 227–251.

Neisser, Ulric. (1967). *Cognitive psychology.* New York: Appleton-Century-Crofts.

Newell, Allen, Shaw, J. C., & Simon, Herbert. (1958). Elements of a theory of human problem solving. *Psychological Review, 65,* 151–166.

Newell, Allen, & Simon, Herbert A. (1972). *Human problem solving.* Englewood Cliffs, NJ: Prentice-Hall.

Pittman, Sherry. (1983). A cognitive ethnography and quantification of a first grade teacher's selections of strategies to manage students. Presented at Annual Meeting, Southwest Educational Research Assoc., January 27–29. (ERIC Microfiche ED 225-967).

Pittman, Sherry. (1985). A cognitive ethnography and quantification of a first-grade teacher's selection routines for classroom management. *The Elementary School Journal 85,* 541–558.

Pittman, Sherry I. (1986). Verifiable ethnographic models of teachers' routine plans for managing first-grade students during reading seatwork. Ed.D. dissertation. University of Houston, University Park. (Ann Arbor: University Microfilms).

Quinn, Naomi. (1975). Decision models of social structure. *American Ethnologist, 2,* 19–45.

Quinn, Naomi. (1976). A natural system used in Mfantse litigation settlement. *American Ethnologist, 3,* 331–351.

Randall, Robert A. (1977). *Change and variation in Samal fishing: Making plans to 'make a living' in the Southern Philippines.* Ph.D. dissertation, University of California at Berkeley. (Ann Arbor: University Microfilms 77-31511).

Randall, Robert A. (1984). The Sinama acquisition lexicon in problem solving and problem setting. Unpublished manuscript.

Randall, Robert A. (1985). Steps toward an ethnosemantics of verbs: Complex fishing technique scripts and the 'unsaid' in listener identification. In J. W. D. Dougherty (Ed.), *Directions in cognitive anthropology.* Urbana, IL: University of Illinois Press.

Reed, H. J., & Lave, Jean. (1979). Arithmetic as a tool for investigating relations between culture and cognition. *American Ethnologist, 6,* 568–582.

Schank, Roger, & Abelson, Robert. (1977). *Scripts, plans, goals, and understanding.* Hillsdale, NJ: Erlbaum.

Schön, Donald A. (1979). Generative metaphor: A perspective on problem-setting in social policy. In A. Ortony (Ed.), *Metaphor and thought.* Cambridge: Cambridge University Press.

Simon, Herbert A. (1957). *Models of man, social and rational.* New York: Wiley.

Simon, Herbert A. (1967). The logic of heuristic decision making. In N. Rescher (Ed.), *The logic of decision and action.* Pittsburgh: Pittsburgh Press.

Simon, Herbert, & Kotovsky, K. (1963). Human acquisition of concepts for sequential patterns. *Psychological Review, 70,* 534–546.

Simon, Herbert, & Sumner, R. (1968). Pattern in music. In B. Kleinmuntz (Ed.), *Formal representation in human judgment.* New York: Wiley.

Spradley, James. (1970). *You owe yourself a drunk.* Boston: Little, Brown.

Spradley, James. (1979). *The ethnographic interview.* New York: Holt, Rinehart & Winston.

Tyler, Stephen. (1969). Context and variation in Koya kinship terminology. In Stephen Tyler (Ed.), *Cognitive anthropology.* New York: Holt, Rinehart, & Winston.

Wallace, Anthony. (1965). Driving to work. In Melford Spiro (Ed.), *Context and meaning in cultural anthropology.* New York: Macmillan.

Wright, Georg H. von. (1963). *Norm and action.* New York: The Humanities Press.

Wright, Georg H. von (1967). The logic of action – a sketch. In N. Rescher (Ed.), *The logic of decision and action.* Pittsburgh: Pittsburgh University Press.

Young, James. (1980). A model of illness treatment decisions in a Tarascan town. *American Ethnologist, 7,* 106–131.

Young, James. (1981). *Medical choice in a Mexican village.* New Brunswick, NJ: Rutgers University Press.

Part II

Models and conceptions of planning

3   A cognitive–developmental model of planning

Richard De Lisi

I. Introduction

The media of modern Western culture is replete with "plans." Radio and television advertisements admonish listeners to plan for such future events as their retirements from the world of work, or their children's college educations by taking advantage of high-interest-bearing savings accounts, by investing in the financial markets, or by opening up individual retirement accounts (IRAs). Bookstores contain dozens of "how to" publications which provide readers with plans to lose weight (diet books), to become more physically fit (health/exercise books), to become wealthy (money management books), and so on. Finally, newspapers inform their readers of a politician's plan for reducing a budget deficit, a city's plan for urban renewal, or a governmental agency's plan for evacuation of thousands of residents in case of a nuclear power plant malfunction. This cursory survey suggests that a consumer of our culture's media is well aware that planning is deemed so important for modern living that many earn a living by devising plans for other people. When thought of as intended actions, plans are based on socially shared meanings and expectations that can be communicated (Meacham, 1984).

Not to be outdone by the lay media, the current psychological literature has turned its attention to planning. Cognitive psychologists have offered descriptions of the human mind, which assert that *plans* are units of procedural knowledge that coexist with propositions, which are units of declarative knowledge (Wickelgren, 1981). *Procedural knowledge* refers to "knowing how" whereas *declarative knowledge* refers to "knowing

Thanks are due to Edith Neimark for her constructive critiques of preliminary drafts of this manuscript. Edith's comments, as well as those of the editors, helped to sharpen the presentation of ideas as they appear in the final version of the chapter. Author's address: Richard De Lisi, Ph.D., Department of Educational Psychology, Graduate School of Education, Rutgers, The State University of New Jersey, New Brunswick, New Jersey, 08903.

that" (Anderson, 1980). When considered to be units of the mind, plans serve to interpret and explain perceived events (Schank & Abelson, 1977) and to generate a temporal sequence of internal or external events directed at goal attainment (Case, 1984; Hayes-Roth & Hayes-Roth, 1979).

The latter sense of the term "plan" has received more empirical investigation than the former sense of the term. Thus, in treating "plan" as a psychological construct, psychologists have focused on the role of plans in individual problem-solving settings. In this type of research, the assumption is made that problem-solving behavior is guided by a plan. The psychologist seeks to describe a subject's behavior (overt, and verbally reported) with some kind of model, and thereby describe the underlying plan. Such cognitive models of plans are then tested via efforts at reproduction of human performance with computer program simulations. The problem-solving behaviors that have been examined usually have well-defined initial and end states such as chess or Tower of Hanoi puzzles, scheduling a series of errands in a hypothetical town, and so on (Hayes-Roth & Hayes-Roth, 1979; Klahr, 1978; Klahr & Robinson, 1981). The models seek to capture a subject's inner representation of the "problem space," subgoals, and depth of search for projected moves through the problem space toward the final objective (Spitz, Webster, & Borys, 1982).

Current cognitive models of plans differ in several respects such as whether planning is described as hierarchical or heterarchical, and in terms of the number and nature of the "mental demons" attributed to the working, problem-solving mind (Boden, 1983; Brown, Bransford, Ferrara, & Campione, 1982). Despite such differences, the objective of cognitive models of planning remains the same: to describe what occurs in the mind of a problem solver from the time a problem is posed until it is solved or abandoned.

Although cognitive models of planning are quite complex, the notion that individuals plan their moves in a game of chess, or carefully sequence a neighborhood trip to the supermarket, bank, and dry cleaners, will probably strike the layperson as eminently reasonable. What might seem less reasonable, however, are extensions of the cognitive approach to subhuman species. Such extensions have been made by Boden (1983) and Griffin (reported by Webster, 1984), who each used artificial intelligence (AI) theories to support the claim that many animals can and do plan. For example, Boden argued:

The lesson of AI is that many animals must have both representations and symbolic languages enabling them to interpret stimulus information sensibly in widely different contexts and to take appropriate action accordingly. The more flexible the action, the more complex must be the computational resources for monitoring, planning, and scheduling different types of activity. . . . This is true whether or not the animal is able to communicate with its conspecifics. . . . And it is true whether or not the animal is able, like humans, to employ syntactically structured public language, using units of meaning whose semantic import is determined by social conventions rather than by fixed genetic mechanisms. (Boden, 1983, p. 13)

As noted in the article by Webster (1984) on Griffin's work in cognitive ethology, such attribution of plans and conscious intentions to animals is rejected by large segments of the scientific community.

Is planning a uniquely human activity? From what has been said so far, we know that (human) adults plan both alone and in concert with others. This raises a problem for scientific attempts to study planning in human and subhuman organisms: Namely, the scientist may fall prey to anthropomorphism or "adultomorphism" (Piaget, 1927). In each case there is the danger of attributing one's own cognitive competencies to organisms who do not yet, or perhaps never will, possess them. Literary license will excuse Burns's attribution of plans to mice, but it will not do for scientific anthropomorphic attributions. The converse side of this problem is a kind of adult chauvinism in which the investigator assumes that cognitive activities such as planning are present only in those organisms considered to be conspecifics.

This issue is as old as psychology itself. Does one follow Tolman and analyze behavior at the molar level and speak of cognitive maps and plans in mice as they move through a maze, or does one side with Hull and the molecular level of fractional anticipatory goal responses? Are the computer programs that simulate human problem solving running in the working memory of the human as well as in the machine? This issue of the attribution of plans to living organisms, like so many others in psychology, is largely a matter of philosophy, theoretical orientation, and their consequent definitions and terminology. It is possible to define planning in such a way that any behavior that we (adults) see as goal-directed may be said to be guided by a plan (as suggested by Boden, 1983). Such an approach would characterize plans as procedural knowledge and correctly note that plans are evident in both human and subhuman behavior. On the other hand, a definition of planning might require the ability to communicate an awareness of goals, planning activities, and intended actions (as suggested by Meacham, 1984). In the latter case, only subjects whose psyches approached those of mature adults would be said to be capable of planning. This approach would not deny that plans are units of procedural knowledge. It would add, however, to the characterization of plans, the fact that they are also units of declarative knowledge at least for some persons. In other words, in the case of mature human planning, it seems correct to argue that we *know that* we *know how* to plan (see examples in the opening paragraph of this chapter).

II. A cognitive–developmental approach

Given the importance of planning for everyday living as well as the current interest in the topic in the psychological literature, it would seem fruitful to have a framework that could accommodate the above-mentioned and other definitional possibilities. The remainder of this chapter presents such a framework with a taxonomy of plans that highlights the cognitive components of different types of plans as evidenced by humans across the life-span and by subhuman organisms. The taxonomy characterizes plans in the twofold sense of being both procedural and declarative knowledge.

The taxonomy was not constructed in a theoretically neutral fashion. Instead, it is based on ideas and principles derived from traditional cognitive–developmental psychology. This approach has a somewhat different objective from that of cognitive psychology as characterized above. Although the nature of cognition during problem solving is of interest to the cognitive developmentalist, there is a fundamental assumption that efforts to describe planning at one point in time will have greater psychological validity if they take explicit account of the ontogenesis of plans. The present taxonomy, then, does not seek to describe and/or model any one specific plan, per se. Rather, the numbered taxonomy is suggestive of a developmental progression and change in plans and planning.

In accordance with theorists such as Piaget and Vygotsky, it is assumed that planning undergoes qualitative changes as a consequence of the course of both evolution and human cognitive development. This will not necessarily deny the existence of plans in subhuman species or young children, but it will lead to a search for transformations in plans such as increasing differentiation and integration of plans and their components (Werner, 1948).

An important theme in any cognitive–developmental analysis, and invoked here, is an attempt to account for behavior from the organism's perspective. An example will illustrate what is at issue. Consider an action such as an adult driving an automobile over a familiar route, as in a daily commute from home to office. Drivers frequently report having made such trips with an "automatic pilot," that is, they have no recollection of the trip just completed or of the act of driving itself. Daily commutes are often made without the driver's being aware of following a "plan" either at a *molar level* (no conscious representation of the route home) or a *molecular level* (no awareness of various acts performed while operating the vehicle).

Note, however, that to an outside observer, the commuter's behavior would appear to be extremely planful. For example, the driver could be observed to slow down and signal well before actually making a turn (molecular level), and to have taken the most efficient route home in terms of time and distance traveled (molar level). We appear to have a paradox in which the observer would describe the commuter's actions as planful whereas the driver would not use such an adjective to describe the basis of his or her actions.

This does not imply that all instances of adult (or "expert") driving are made "on automatic pilot." Suppose the commuter discovers a detour on the usual route due to road construction. The commuter might then form an explicit cognitive map or representation of several possible routes and select an alternative pathway. While traversing this new route, the driver not only attends to the route in a deliberate fashion (e.g., looks for signs that indicate when the next turn is coming), but also attends to the mechanics of driving itself rather deliberatively (e.g., silently directs the self to slow down and be careful because of uncertainty as to the nature of pedestrian and vehicular traffic patterns on this new way home).

In these two examples of commuter behavior, we have the same overt behavior, namely driving, and we have the same "goal" or objective, to get from home to office. Despite these similarities, it will be argued that there is a difference between the plans that serve to guide the usual versus alternate trips home. The fact that in the second instance the driver was explicitly aware of the underlying representation of the route and also aware of the need for a plan, serves to distinguish between types of plans in the present cognitive–developmental taxonomy.

III. Definition of terms

In everyday usage, the term "plan" has two major connotations. A plan may be defined as a drawing or diagram such as a map of a town's roads or an architect's blueprint for a building. Alternatively, a method of doing something, a procedure, or a detailed program of action, may constitute a definition of a plan. The first definition emphasizes the representational–entity aspects of a plan that might be communicated from one person to another. The second definition highlights the functional–behavioral aspects of a plan, that is, organization and control of behavior.

Implicit in both definitions is the notion of a goal and goal attainment. When used in the functional, procedural sense of the term, a sequence of actions is properly labeled as based on a plan when it seeks to achieve an objective. For example, the behaviors performed by a robin that result in the construction of a nest might be said to exemplify a plan in the functional sense of the term. In contrast, the ritualistic and repetitive pacing of a caged lioness would not be properly labeled as based on a plan even though there is a definite sequence of behaviors. What is (apparently) missing in the latter instance is a goal toward which the behaviors are directed. The representational–entity sense of plan also has the implicit notion of a goal. For example, blueprints or "plans" for a building are generated because of a desire to have such a building constructed at some point in the future. Thus, goal attainment is a salient feature of a plan regardless of whether the functional or representational meaning is emphasized.

Psychological investigations of planning have often merged the two aforementioned senses of the term. A plan is defined as some kind of entity that serves to organize, control, and direct behavior. For example, in their seminal book, *Plans and the Structure of Behavior,* Miller, Galanter, and Pribram (1960) define "plan" as "any hierarchical process in the organism that can control the order in which a sequence of operations is to be performed" (p. 16). They introduce the notion of "TOTE" – test, operate, test, exit – a feedback loop, as the unit of analysis of plans. One example is a plan for hammering nails, that is, a directing organization which controls the ongoing behavior without the status of conscious activity. Later on in the book, Miller et al. refer to human speech as an important basis for directing behavior and imply that speech is our special, human "planner."

Subsequent analyses of plans have also focused on control and organization of behavior but have posited that the underlying entity is some kind of *symbolic representation* of possible actions in various settings (see quote from Boden, 1983 above; Hayes-Roth & Hayes-Roth, 1979; Sacerdoti, 1977; Wilensky, 1981). As was suggested earlier in this chapter, such approaches may be problematical in that they seem to deny the existence of differences between the bases of animal and human behaviors, and between different kinds of human activities (such as driving home versus making preparations for evacuation in case of a flood). For if all goal-directed behaviors are said to be based on plans that consist of symbolic representations and mental computations, then what differentiates one from the other? From the organism's perspective, is there not a difference between possession of a "planful" procedure in the behavioral repertoire versus *knowing* that one possesses a repertoire that contains such a procedure? In regard to this issue, Miller et al. (1960) speculated that humans are capable of higher levels of plans, even for motor behaviors, owing to their linguistic–speech capabilities.

It is precisely on this issue that traditional cognitive–developmental approaches can be useful. Theories of human intelligence proposed by Piaget (1960) and Vygotsky (1978) make a distinction between practical, overt behaviors directed toward goals, and "theoretical," internal behaviors directed toward goals. The latter were said to be based on mental operations and *symbolic representations* of the environment, whereas the former were not based on representations. Although Piaget and Vygotsky differed in their treatment of the nature of human representation, they agreed that it was not a cognitive given but instead, a cognitive *construction*. Specifically, the ability to *evoke absent realities* (Piaget's [1962] definition of symbolic representation) was described as a slow-to-develop, step-by-step process during the first several years of life.

In accordance with these views, a distinction can be made between encoding of stimulus information which is present to the senses (an ongoing perceptual "representation") and a subsequent re-presentation of this same stimulus information without environmental impingement on the senses (a symbolic representation or evocation of absent realities). The assumption will be made that the latter ability develops during the course of human ontogenesis and is perfected in humans to a degree far greater than is found in any member of the animal kingdom. See Furth (1981) for a discussion of the development of symbolic representation.

Given this definition of symbolic representation, the cornerstone of the present treatment of plans is a careful analysis of the relationship between functional and representational components. Specifically, it is assumed that this relationship is dynamic rather than static, in the main because of developmental changes in representational abilities. In lower-level types of plans, functional components take precedence over representational components, whereas the opposite relationship exists in higher-level types of plans. In the latter instance, for example, consider that blueprints for a building do not specify the steps that are necessary if the structure is to be realized. Similarly, governmental agencies, academic units, and the like, are often charged with the task of devising a plan with full knowledge that implementation is unlikely. The goal in this type of situation is not so much to plot a course of action, but instead to communicate a rationale for choosing one of several possible courses of action. In other words, construction of a plan becomes a goal unto itself. In cases such as these, there can exist a complete separation between functional and representational components such that the latter is dominant over the former. This type of plan is probably unique to human beings and is designated as the highest level of plan (an end state) in the present taxonomy.

The assumption of a dynamic relation between functional and representational components of plans is one theme that underlies the present taxonomy. A second theme is the relationship between plans and the process of planning. *Planning* refers to the generation of plans and consists of three phases: (a) recognition of the need for a plan, (b) formation of a plan, and (c) plan execution or implementation. Plan execution includes monitoring progress toward goals such that modifications in behavior and/or subgoals can be made. More will be said about the planning process in a subsequent section. It will be argued that the phases of planning are undifferentiated in the simplest type of plan and emerge as subjectively experienced distinct entities as more complex types of plans become possible.

IV. A developmental taxonomy of plans

A. A preliminary model

Figure 3.1 presents a preliminary model of a plan and of planning which will serve as a basis for presentation of the taxonomy. The lower part of the figure depicts a general model of a *plan* consisting of functional and representational components. As previously noted, the functional component is the organizational–directing aspect of a plan, whereas the representational component is the "entity" aspect of a plan. The dynamic relation between these two components is such that one or the other may not exist in certain instances of a plan.

The upper half of Figure 3.1 presents a general model of the planning process. As depicted in Figure 3.1, planning is considered to be a cognitive or metacognitive (Flavell, 1979) activity based on a self- or other-imposed monitor. The flow of the phases of planning, each of which may be minimally evidenced by a temporary interruption of ongoing behavior, is indicated by the arrows of the figure. When a goal is perceived (arrow a), a person recognizes the need for a plan and (eventually or immediately) generates one to achieve the goal (arrow b). This subsequently results in behavior (arrow c), which is monitored in terms of its success at goal attainment (arrow d). The broken arrow (e) going from the monitor to the goal represents those instances in which a goal is modified or abandoned as a consequence of plan formation or execution.

The ability to engage in planning, as well as the nature of the relationships among the phases of planning, is assumed to develop and change

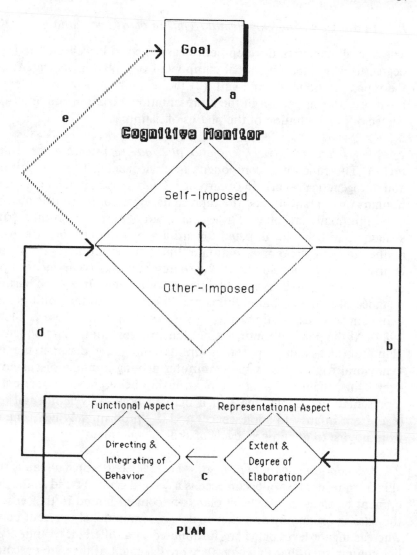

Figure 3.1. A preliminary model of a plan and planning.

during the course of ontogenesis. Thus, just as certain types of plans may lack either a functional or a representational component, in some cases the formation and execution phases of planning may be more salient than the recognition phase, whereas in other instances, recognition and formation may have a primacy over execution.

B. An overview of developmental trends in plans and planning

The overall course of development is assumed to be reflected in (1) the degree to which the functional component of a plan is dependent upon the representational component, (2) the relation of plan to context, (3) the degree of elaboration of the representational component, and (4) the degree of differentiation of the phases of planning.

1. The relation between functional and representational components. The functional component is phylogenetically more primitive and ontogenetically early in occurrence. For example, in the plans of subhumans or human infants, the representational component is absent or only minimally at play. These plans are "pure" function, that is, sequences of behavior directed toward a goal without a preexisting and deliberate symbolic representation of the to-be-performed actions. In the course of human development, the representational component of plans arises and serves to direct the functional component. In a given particular instance of human planning, this would continue to the point at which behavior becomes routinized as in skill development (Frese & Stewart, 1984). At the point of routinization, the representational component of a plan diminishes in importance unless something disrupts the usual behavioral routine (as in the commuter driving example discussed earlier). Thus, there is a dynamic relationship between the functional and representational components of a plan in both "developmental" time (e.g., from infancy to adolescence) and in "problem solving" time (e.g., from novice to nonnovice levels of skill development).

2. The relation of plan to context. The degree to which a plan is separable from its context of occurrence is a second general trend in the development of plans. Lower-level plans are context bound in the sense that they are instigated by and executed in an immediately present context, whereas higher-level plans are formulated in a different, temporally earlier context than that in which they are executed, if they are executed at all.

Lower-level plans are characterized by a predominance of functional over representational components, which necessitates a lack of differentiation between plan and context. The presence of a representational component, however, does not ensure a complete differentiation of a plan from its context of occurrence. Instead, this separation occurs gradually and may be said to exist on a continuum. At one end of the continuum are plans that cannot be separated from their contexts of occurrence (such as when a 10-month-old baby crawls across a room to retrieve a favorite toy which has just rolled under a piece of furniture). At the other end of the continuum are plans that are so fully differentiated from context that the contexts themselves are hypothetical rather than real (such as when a governmental agency devises a plan to evacuate a city in case of a nuclear power plant malfunction.)

Progress from one end of this continuum to the other end occurs during the course of human ontogenesis, because of development of *3. the degree of elaboration of the representational component of a plan*. Much of the literature in cognitive–developmental psychology has addressed the cognitive underpinnings of human representation such as logical structure, mental anticipation, knowledge base, and memory. In some instances, such discussions have been linked to plans directly. For example, one criterion used by Inhelder and Piaget (1958) to distinguish between formal operational and concrete operational approaches to scientific problem solving (such as determining which of four factors affects the frequency of oscillation of a pendulum) was the presence of a systematic plan to isolate variables. In this instance, change in logical structure (from multiple classification to a complete combinatorial system) was linked to the ability to represent more adequately a problem situation that resulted in a more adequate plan for problem solving. In a similar vein, Spitz et al. (1982) discussed the role of depth of search (a mental anticipation of possible moves) in Tower of Hanoi problem solving. Younger children as well as mentally retarded adolescents were found to search less deeply, which hindered their ability to represent possible moves and construct subgoals. As a consequence, these subjects performed less well than older children of normal intelligence. In this example, increased depth of search was said to result in representation of a greater number of moves such that the child is planning in more of a symbolic rather than an immediate context.

4. Degree of differentiation of planning phases. This final component of the development of plans refers to the extent to which plan recognition, formation, and execution are temporally and functionally differentiated. In the simplest type of plan, the three phases are part of one, undifferentiated entity. At intermediate levels, plan formation emerges as a subjectively experienced separate phase which becomes increasingly separate from its execution in overt conduct. At higher levels, recognition of the need for a plan becomes salient and eventually (rather than immediately) leads to deliberate plan formation, which is so fully separate from execution that the latter need not occur at all.

Table 3.1. *A developmental taxonomy of plans and planning*

Plan type	General description	Phases of planning	Goals	Examples
1 "Plan in action"	A sequence of behaviors that is performed to achieve an objective. Nonsymbolic representation of situations in which behaviors are performed. Subject is aware of success or failure at goal attainment but is not aware of planning in any of its phases.	Planning phases occur simultaneously as one undifferentiated entity. Subject does not recognize the need for a plan; plan formation and execution are undifferentiated. The facilitations or hindrances provided by others are post hoc and fortuitous.	Goals are imposed or triggered by circumstances. Plan is oriented to the immediate context.	Sensorimotor means–ends behavior. Instinctual behaviors. Habitual behaviors.
2 "Plan of action"	A deliberate sequencing of behaviors designed to facilitate goal attainment. Representation of situations in which behaviors are performed is symbolic. Subject is aware of plan formation prior to execution.	Plan formation and execution are differentiated but temporally contiguous. Another person may recognize the need for a plan and communicate this to the subject. This same person might assist with plan formation and monitor execution.	Goals are anticipated in thought. Plans are oriented to real (not hypothetical), short-term contexts.	Novice playing chess. Adult direction of child problem solving. Skill acquisition in adults.

3 "Plan as a strategic representation"	A deliberate, strategic representation of anticipated future states of the environment and behavior sequences designed to deal with them. Subject is aware of each phase of planning, and represents relationships among formulations, executions, and goals.	Subject now recognizes that plans are needed and useful. Such recognition leads to plan formation. Plan formation and execution are fully differentiated such that execution is no longer temporally contiguous with formation.	Goals are future oriented and hypothetical. Plans are not restricted to immediate contexts.	Expert playing chess. Making arrangements for a vacation next summer.
4 "Plan as an end unto itself"	A subjective or collective deliberate effort to devise a plan. Recognition of the need for a plan is salient. Subject forms a plan with full awareness that execution may never occur.	Recognition of the need for a plan is fully differentiated from plan formation and assumes a primacy such that recognition may be the only phase to reach completion.	Plan formation is the goal and occurs in the service of recognition of need for a plan.	A government agency makes plans for evacuation in case of a nuclear power plant failure.

This differentiation of planning phases is due in large part to an increasing human capacity for self-regulation and cognitive monitoring. Developmental descriptions of self-regulation have as their anchor points, an initial period of automatic, nonconscious regulation; and an end state of deliberate, conscious regulation. For a discussion of these two types of self-regulation as well as intermediate types of regulation, see Brown et al. (1982) and Frese and Stewart (1984). For the present purposes, it will suffice to indicate that a person capable of deliberate self-regulation recognizes the need for a plan to a greater degree than a person capable of only lower levels of self-regulation. In other words, there is a difference between *having* one's behavior guided by a plan and *knowing* that one's behavior is being guided by a plan. In the latter instance, plans themselves, not only goals and subgoals with their attendant courses of action, are objects of knowledge and (perhaps) discussion.

C. Types of plans

The previous section has summarized developmental trends in the progress of plans and planning. These trends will serve as foci for discussion in the following four-part taxonomy of plans. Table 3.1 presents an overview of the taxonomy. Each of the four types is discussed below and related to previous analyses of planning.

1. Type 1 plans. A "type 1 plan" is defined as a sequence of overt behaviors performed to achieve an objective. From the subject's perspective, the underlying entity that orchestrates the sequence is purely functional and operates in a nonconscious, automatically regulating fashion. There is no representational component to a type 1 plan in that courses of action are not mentally evoked prior to overt conduct. The subject is aware of goals, anticipates goal attainment, and is aware of the plan's resultant success or failure at realization of its objective. In a type 1 plan, the three phases of planning occur together simultaneously as one undifferentiated entity as the subject strives to attain a goal in an immediate context. The subject may be able to convey what its objective is, but cannot communicate the plan or intended course of action per se. The latter can be evidenced only in behavior. To summarize, using terminology of current cognitive psychology, a type 1 plan is procedural (not declarative) knowledge.

Type 1 plans may be dichotomized as involuntary or voluntary. The prototype exemplar of an involuntary plan is an instinct in which the underlying controlling entity is inherited and fixed whereas the particular behaviors are not inherited and are subject to modification (Miller et al., 1960). Another example of an involuntary type 1 plan is a posthypnotic suggestion in which a subject is "programmed" to perform certain acts in a specified context without the subject being aware of the underlying basis for conduct.

Voluntary type 1 plans include sensorimotor means–ends behaviors (Piaget, 1952) which initially operate in a trial-and-error fashion. Such plans can be thought of as forms of practical (as opposed to conceptual) problem solving. Examples include using one object to retrieve another object, and locomotion through a space by reading cues along the way (rather than by following a preconceived route). A third class of type 1 plan, which lies midway between involuntary instincts and voluntary practical problem solving, is a habit or skilled motor sequence, as in driving an automobile, touch typing, or playing a piece of music on an instrument by rote memory.

In each of the above varieties and instances of type 1 plans, the subject is aware of a goal and seeks to attain it by performing a sequence of behaviors without prior specification to the self or to others of the actual steps to be taken. Two familiar models of type 1 plans are Piaget's (1952) analysis of sensorimotor schemes and the test–operate–test–exit (TOTE) unit proposed by Miller et al. (1960). These two models of type 1 plans are depicted in Figures 3.2a and 3.2b, respectively. In each case, the model depicts the idea of an underlying, directing organization of overt behavior without having attained the status of conscious, deliberate representation of behavior and its regulation.

The issue of the origins of voluntary type 1 plans has been the subject of much debate. Nativistic, empiricistic, developmental, and cognitive theories of voluntary, goal-directed movement sequences have been proposed during this century (see Adams, 1984, for a review of these approaches). Most theorists have posited that feedback from attempts at goal attainment serve to modify the underlying plan and thereby overt behavior, but again, the issue of how feedback (e.g., knowledge of results) operates is far from settled. (See Salmoni, Schmidt, & Walter, 1984, for a review of the motor learning and knowledge of results literature.)

For purposes of the present analysis, it will suffice to indicate two general classes of origin of type 1 plans in human behavior. For children and adults capable of generating higher levels of plans (described below), one important source of habitual, type 1 plans is a higher-level plan. For example, in acquiring a skill, there is often an initial phase of deliberate self- or other-guided instruction. This instruction uses explicit symbolic descriptions of projected courses of action. In cases such as these, conduct

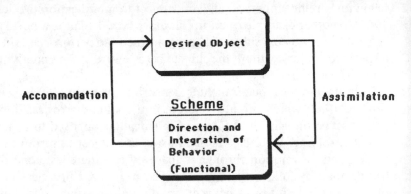

a. A sensory-motor scheme

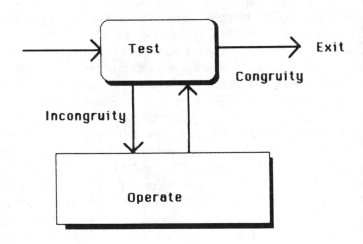

b. A TOTE sequence

Figure 3.2. Models of type 1 plans. Part *b* reprinted with permission from Miller et al., *Plans and the Structure of Behavior* (New York: Holt, Rinehart & Winston, 1960), p. 26.

is first guided by higher levels of planning, but the overall objective is to form a habitual, type 1 plan such that prior representation of courses of action is not needed. The conduct of daily activities is facilitated by formation of such plans. The original representational basis becomes apparent only when the usual routine is blocked or ineffective owing to a change in present circumstances not noted or known at the outset of plan execution (Vygotsky, 1978). Thus, the capacity to plan at higher levels in no way precludes planning at lower levels.

But what of infants and young children, who may be capable of only type 1 levels of plans? The origins of their voluntary attempts at practical problem solving begin with the onset of intentional behavior during the first year of life. Piaget (1952) maintained that at first, intent derives from action (repetition or "exercise" of schemes) rather than instigating and directing it. That is, the infant's actions often result in a fortuitous consequence which the infant tries to replicate. In Piaget's analysis of sensorimotor intelligence, substage 4 was identified as the origin of true intentional behavior, that is, the point at which intentions precede and serve to initiate movements toward goals. (See Bruner, 1973, and Harding, 1982, for further discussions of intentionality in infancy.) As infants become increasingly mobile and skillful at manipulation of objects in the environment, parental attempts to block, modify, or displace their movements in, and manipulations of, the environment also become more frequent (for reasons of safety, convenience, and so on). Such experiences of having their plans in action modified or displaced by others lead infants to discover that their plans can, and must be, coordinated with those of other persons. Frustrations in plan execution are an important class of experience which incline the young child to anticipate behavioral outcomes prior to their execution. Such experiences contribute to the development of type 2 plans in early childhood.

2. *Type 2 plans.*   A "type 2 plan" is defined as a deliberate sequencing of overt behaviors designed to facilitate goal attainment. Type 2 plans are similar to type 1 plans in that they are directly expressed in overt conduct. However, instead of courses of action being triggered by and directly linked to circumstances as in type 1 plans, type 2 plans are characterized by having goals *and* behavioral sequences anticipated in thought prior to action.

The new feature of a type 2 plan is a representational component which serves to anticipate goals and formulate courses of action prior to their execution. This anticipation may be performed by the self or by another individual. In the latter instance, the plan must be communicated to the subject. The representational component (whether self- or other-generated) augments the functional component, which continues to direct and integrate actual, overt conduct. The emergence of a representational component with type 2 plans has two major consequences: (a) It makes it possible for the plan itself, not only its goal, to be communicated from one person to another; and (b) plan formation is now differentiated from

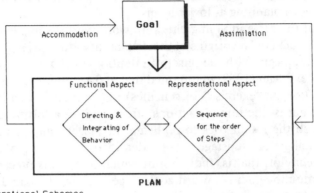

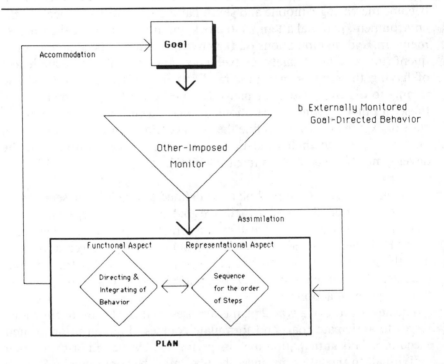

Figure 3.3. Models of type 2 plans.

plan execution, rather than being bound together in a functional unit as is characteristic of type 1 plans.

Despite these advances, there are limitations inherent in type 2 plans. Although the formation phase of planning is differentiated from the execution phase, the two phases remain temporally contiguous because type

2 plans are oriented to goals in immediate, short-term contexts. In addition, recognition of the need for a plan is not yet a phase of planning fully distinct from formation. The type 2 planner is thinking about what her next steps or courses of action will be, but her behavior is not cognitively strategic. In other words, although a representation of a course of action is generated, it (the representation) is not monitored, checked, or evaluated in terms of its overall effectiveness vis-à-vis other possible means of goal attainment. Oversight of the planning process, especially recognition of the need for a plan and for evaluation of same prior to execution, occurs only if a more competent other person acts as a monitor. The type 2 planner is not able to engage in deliberate, conscious, self-reflective regulation of behavior on his own.

Figures 3.3a and 3.3b present schematic models of type 2 plans. Each of these builds upon the type 1 plan depicted in Figure 3.2a with the addition of a representational component. Figures 3.3a and 3.3b differ in that 3a does not include a monitoring component whereas 3b does. The latter model covers those instances in which another person recognizes that a (better) plan is needed and communicates this fact to the subject. This same other person may assist with plan formation (by making suggestions, providing feedback, etc.) and help monitor execution (via verbal instruction, direct modeling, etc.). The family research project which employed a paper-folding task described in the chapter by McGillicuddy-De Lisi et al. (this volume) provides an example of a type 2 plan. Without someone such as a parent to provide monitoring, type 2 plans require execution with its attendant feedback from obtained results in order for modifications in the plan to occur (Figure 3.3a).

An article by Brown, Day, and Jones (1983) contained another example of type 2 plans as described above. These investigators compared the ability of students at four grade levels to create written summaries of stories previously memorized to a specified criterion. The students were provided with scratch paper and subtly encouraged to make rough drafts of their 40-word summaries prior to handing in their final drafts. Creation of, and revisions in, rough drafts versus creation of a final product directly, was used as index of "planning" versus "not planning," respectively. College students and eleventh graders were significantly more likely to "plan" their summaries than were fifth and seventh graders. Younger nonplanners were more likely to run out of room and thereby include fewer important units in their summaries for the second halves of stories. Younger planners and older subjects were all equally adept at summarizing both halves of stories.

Rather than label these two types of students as "plan" versus "no plan," the present taxonomy would characterize the difference between younger subjects who did not sketch out a rough draft and those who did, as engaging in type 2 versus type 3 planning. It seems likely that all students used symbolic representations of the stories to develop their written summaries (and, as it turned out, these representations were accurate for the first halves of the stories). Younger students, however, were less likely to recognize the need for a plan, that is, to create a first draft which could be checked for its length and comprehensiveness. These characteristics – goal-directed behavior based on a prior representation that is not spontaneously evaluated by the subject prior to execution, but instead is more or less directly expressed in overt conduct – are the salient defining features of type 2 plans (as depicted in Figure 3.3a).

Brown et al.'s (1983) study suggests that there exists an age-related trend in progression from type 2 to type 3 plans (the latter are described below). Their results also indicate the advantage of the higher type of plan on this kind of task. Those few younger students who did revise a rough draft beforehand performed as well as their older counterparts. Level of planning can override age differences in terms of being predictive of written, scholastic performance (Brown et al., 1983).

The onset of type 2 plans during early childhood follows the construction of the symbolic function during the first two years of life (Piaget, 1962). This cognitive achievement allows the child both to follow the symbolic suggestions of others and to mentally formulate courses of action on her own prior to their execution. This is not to say that all instances of symbolic behavior are also instances of type 2 plans. Instead, when this newly developed capacity to evoke absent realities serves as a basis to represent means toward ends and goals, then the representation comprises part of a plan (see Figure 3.3).

McCune-Nicolich (1981) described several levels in the development of children's symbolic play during the period of 1 to 3 years of age. Her highest level, "internally directed symbolic games," provides examples of type 2 plans in early childhood. The structure of such symbolic play was characterized as hierarchical by McCune-Nicolich:

... requiring the coordination of at least two representational structures, a covert mental transformation or intention which directs a separate but related pretend behavior. There is first an intention to act, indicated by verbalization, search, or both. This intention directs the subsequent pretend act. For example, the child might encounter a baby doll, say "drink," find a cup, and give the doll a drink. (McCune-Nicolich, 1981, p. 787)

Other examples of type 2 plans include those instances in which another person maps out a course of action for the subject, who follows directives without evaluating the quality of the plan ahead of time. This is often typical of novices as they attempt to learn a new task or procedure (Brown & DeLoache, 1978). School teachers and their pupils are frequently engaged in such type 2 planning activities. In some instances, the overall objective of such type 2 plans is the eventual mastery of the procedure by the student such that a type 1 plan can subsequently control behavioral sequencing. In this way, motor and cognitive skills become "automatic"; this frees up room in working memory for additional representations to occur (Case, 1978, 1984). For example, a child who has followed a teacher's plan for learning number facts and has successfully mastered the necessary associations, is in a better position to plan solutions for mathematical problems in subsequent parts of the curriculum.

In other instances of type 2 plans in which a person maps out a course of action for another, the overall objective is to get the subject to recognize the need for a plan and for evaluation of the plan prior to its execution. For example, by requiring pupils to revise drafts of their written compositions prior to submitting final drafts, a teacher seeks not only to provide a technique that improves the quality of writing, but also to teach the importance of self-monitoring of one's own work. The latter characteristic is the salient defining attribute of type 3 plans. The fact that experiences of being guided by another can lead to an internalization (or self-control) of the monitoring aspect of planning was first discussed by Vygotsky (1962, 1978). The chapter by McGillicuddy De Lisi et al. (this volume) summarizes this aspect of Vygotsky's theory.

3. Type 3 plans. A "type 3 plan" is defined as a deliberate representation and strategic evaluation of anticipated future states of one's experiential world and behavior sequences designed to deal with them. In a type 3 plan, the individual is fully aware of each phase of the planning process. Specifically, recognition of the need for a plan is differentiated from plan formation, which in turn is no longer temporally contiguous with plan execution. Along with recognition of the need for a plan that initiates the planning process, there is a strategic evaluation and comparison of formulated plans prior to execution. Such mental checking can lead to revision in a particular plan as need be, based upon anticipated contingencies arising from execution.

Two features serve to distinguish type 3 from type 2 plans. First, there is an increased symbolic complexity to the representational component of the plan. Multiple courses of action are fully elaborated and compared, rather than conduct being determined by a single, global, preconceived course of action. Often, such complex plan formation entails the use of external aids such as notes, lists, diagrams, or computations, and the

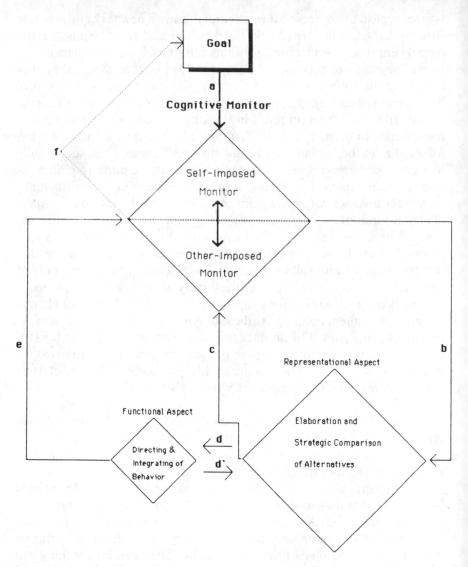

Figure 3.4. Model of a type 3 plan.

obtaining of relevant facts, such as costs, availability, advantages, disadvantages, and so on. Such increased representational complexity makes type 3 plans more detached from their contexts of occurrence than type 2 plans.

The second distinguishing feature of type 3 plans is the fact that the subject (not another person) now initiates and monitors the planning process in each of its successive phases. These features were exemplified by the students labeled "planners" in the Brown et al. (1983) study of written summarizations discussed earlier. These student (type 3) planners recognized the need for a plan (i.e., created a first draft), evaluated the plan (i.e., made written revisions), and only then executed it (i.e., created their final drafts). This illustrates both increased symbolic complexity and self-controlled oversight of goal-directed behavior, which are the salient features of type 3 plans.

Figure 3.4 presents a schematic model of a type 3 plan. Its central and identifying feature is a self-imposed cognitive monitor which serves to recognize the need for a plan and to oversee its formulation and execution. (Because another person may still assist with the oversight of the planning process, the other-imposed component of cognitive monitoring is retained in Figure 3.4.) The flow of the planning process is depicted by the arrows of Figure 3.4. Once a goal is perceived or generated, the type 3 planner recognizes the need for a plan (arrow a); this recognition leads to plan formation (arrow b), which can be mentally executed and checked (arrow c). At some later point, the plan is actually executed if possible (arrow d) or revised if not (arrow d'), and, once executed, is again monitored in terms of its approximation to the goal (arrow e). The broken arrow (f) going from the monitor to the goal represents those instances in which a goal is abandoned or modified as a consequence of monitoring plan formation or execution (arrows c and f). The representational component of the plan depicted in Figure 3.4 now involves more than anticipation of a goal and a means of attainment. It also involves an elaboration of alternative means along with weightings based upon costs, benefits, and likelihoods of successful completion. These weightings, in turn, draw upon stored knowledge from past experience as well as new information collected for the purpose of plan formation. At this level, it is expected that the subject has a repertoire of plans which can be consciously invoked as the need arises. The fact of increased differentiation between the representational and functional components in type 3 plans is indicated in Figure 3.4 by removal of the solid rectangle which housed these two components at the previous level (cf. Figure 3.3).

Before presenting the last type of plan in the taxonomy, a few more examples of type 3 plans will be mentioned. Strategic behaviors such as those required to solve problems arising in games like chess or contract bridge are instances of type 3 plans. Except for novices who are unfamiliar with the rules and purpose of the game, chess, for example, is played by deliberately anticipating and mentally evoking a series of projected moves by each side in turn. The various sequences are compared and evaluated in order to determine the best next move. An actual move is made only after such a mental procedure is conducted. If the opponent makes one of several anticipated responses, the plan may be continued. If the opponent makes an unexpected response, further planning may ensue before a second actual move is made. Limitations on the generation and monitoring phases of chess planning, that is, a never ending hierarchy of preconceived possible moves, come not only from the limitations of human memory, but also from the rules of the game itself. In chess, each player has a clock with a predetermined total of minutes allocated for each side to complete the game. If time runs out on a player, he loses regardless of the position at that moment. Time per move can be distributed by a player in any fashion, which makes chess planning additionally complex. For example, the serious player might take the time to read books and memorize standard chess openings so that the first five to ten moves can be made quickly, almost without thought (type 2 or even type 1 planning). This will reserve precious time and mental energy for strategic planning during middle- and end-game positions. These features of chess performance were noted by Byrne (1984) in his analysis of the 1984 world chess championship's first game. Psychological studies have indicated that with increased expertise, the ability to encode and manipulate representations of chess positions increases, making the plans of experts superior to those of nonexperts (Chi, Glaser, & Rees, 1982).

Other familiar examples of type 3 plans include planning a vacation, wedding ceremony, or other social occasions such as a dinner party. In planning a vacation, for example, the phases of planning are fully differentiated. The decision to take a family vacation is typically made with consideration of the need for a plan; that is, questions such as the following must be resolved at the outset: Do family members have similar times off from work and school? Are airline seats and hotel reservations available? Is the range of possible activities sufficient for each member of the family to have a good time? Once questions such as these are satisfactorily resolved, the decision to take a vacation is made, and a plan must be formulated. Additional questions arise. Is the money saved by car travel worth the loss of time sacrificed by foregoing air travel? Which "package deal" is truly advantageous? Plan formation also entails the actual purchase of airline tickets and securing of hotel reservations, arranging for overlapping times off, and so on. Once formed, the plan may be executed, usually at a much later date such as 3 to 12 months in the future. Failures or frustrations during any phase of the process might lead to "better" planning in the future. For example, a family that decides to travel from New York City to Orlando, Florida during the last two weeks of December but does not begin to formulate the plan until December 10, will probably have difficulty completing plan formation. Because this route is heavily traveled during this time period, the family might well be unable to secure travel and/or lodging accommodations. In such an instance, the family's disappointment would have stemmed from a failure to recognize the need for a plan well in advance of plan formation.

4. Type 4 plans. A "type 4 plan" is defined as an individual or collective deliberate effort to devise a plan; that is, construction of an acceptable plan is now an end unto itself rather than serving as a means toward a goal. A type 3 plan is a strategic attempt to solve a problem in an immediate or future context. When not only contexts, but problems themselves become hypothetical, there is a shift from type 3 to type 4 planning. If the person engaged in type 3 planning may be said to be a problem *solver,* the person engaged in type 4 planning may be called a problem *finder.* As such, type 4 plans are more strategic or metacognitive than type 3 plans. The phases of type 4 planning are now fully differentiated such that (a) recognition of the need for a plan need not lead to immediate formation of a plan; and (b) plan formation occurs with the explicit understanding that many, if not all, of the envisioned alternatives might never be executed. In other words, because the "problems" which they seek to address are hypothetical, type 4 plans are more detached from context than type 3 plans. In type 4 planning, a person envisions a future scenario and realizes that an adequate plan to address anticipated occurrences does not exist. Recognition of the need for a plan is salient. If the assistance of others is needed in order for planning to continue, they will have to be persuaded that the "problem" is "real" in the dual sense that it *could* occur and, if it did, that adequate means to address it were not presently at hand. Thus in type 4 planning, it is often necessary to communicate a convincing rationale for the need for a plan. For this reason, the representational component of type 4 plans may be elaborated in great detail with consideration of possible states of the world, attendant courses of action, computation of potential costs and benefits, and so on.

Figure 3.5 presents a model of a type 4 plan. Note that the functional component of a plan has dropped out so that type 4 plans are purely representational and metacognitive. (In contrast, recall that type 1 plans were purely functional, nonrepresentational, and not monitored.) Of course, one of the alternatives generated by type 4 planning may come to be executed and serve to direct and integrate overt conduct. At this point, the individual would be said to have shifted from type 4 to type 3 planning.

The decision to write a will provides an example of type 4 planning. Oftentimes a person recognizes the need for a will but takes several months or even years to act on that recognition. Obviously, the plan is

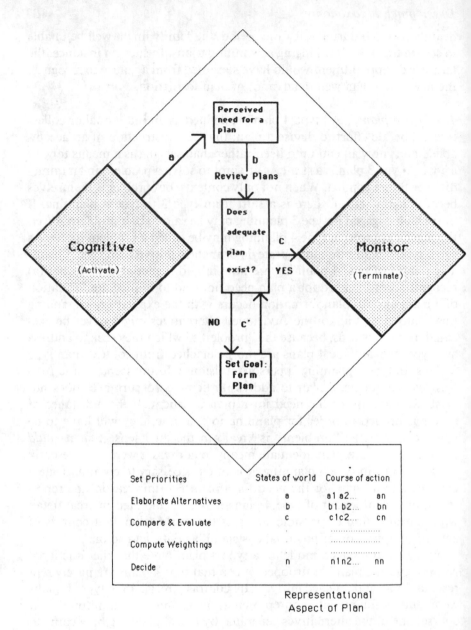

Figure 3.5. Model of a type 4 plan.

formed (a will is devised in accordance with state laws) with full awareness that the person (will writer) will not see it executed.

Because type 4 plans are usually created for significant anticipated states with far-reaching impact, such as death, averting catastrophe, allocation of limited resources, and so on, the responsibility for such planning is rarely assigned to a single individual. Societal institutions often constitute the specific agency for creation of type 4 plans (e.g., planning boards, boards of directors, trustees of education, chiefs of staff, etc.). The following self-explanatory quote from an article in the February 23, 1983 edition of the *New York Times* illustrates this feature of type 4 plans.

New York State, New Jersey, Pennsylvania, Delaware and New York City today reached agreement on a plan to enlarge four reservoirs to increase regional water supplies. The 39-page plan, designed to help the region cope better with future droughts, was negotiated over the last four years and was announced by the Delaware River Basin Commission. It bears the signatures of the Governors of the four states and of Mayor Koch. The commission, created in 1916 to regulate use of the river's water, will hold public hearings on the plan before deciding whether to adopt it. . . . Development of today's agreement followed a 1975 decision by the commission to drop plans for a proposed Tocks Island Dam across the Delaware five miles north of the Delaware Water Gap near Stroudsburg, PA. The proposed huge Tocks Reservoir had been intended to meet the basin's water supply needs by creating a 12,000-acre, 37-mile lake. Environmentalists objected that the lake would become polluted and, during drawdowns, expose ugly mud flats and mar the natural beauty of the area.

This is a good illustration of type 4 plan in that (a) the plan was formed over a number of years by a governmental agency to (b) replace a prior plan now thought to be inadequate even though the first plan was never executed; and (c) formation of the new plan was fully separate from execution in that those who formed the new plan knew that it, too, might never be carried out pending (d) their ability to communicate a rationale for this particular course of action at a public hearing.

V. Summary and review

A four-part taxonomy of plans was presented. The taxonomy was constructed with the assumption that a plan is some kind of underlying "entity" that serves to organize and direct behavior toward goal attainment. In type 1 plans, the entity is purely functional, as the organism is directed toward ends without a deliberate representation or preconception of means. Instinctual and habitual behaviors are examples of conduct based on type 1 plans. Examples of psychological models of type 1 plans include Miller et al.'s (1960) TOTE concept and Piaget's (1952) discussion of sensorimotor schemes.

In type 2 plans, the organism represents means prior to their realization in behavior. These plans are not fully strategic in the sense that they are not evaluated and compared with other possible courses of action, but instead are more or less directly executed. If such monitoring does occur, it is conducted by another person. This type of plan was first discussed by Vygotsky in the 1920s and 1930s (Vygotsky, 1978). Vygotsky maintained that adults use speech to direct the problem-solving behaviors of children. In time, children internalize this function of speech and become monitors of their own behaviors. Thus, Vygotsky provided an early account of a developmental shift in plans (from type 2 to type 3) which relied heavily on human speech not only to represent courses of action but also to oversee the planning process itself. The present taxonomy does not limit the representational basis of type 2 plans to speech alone.

Type 3 plans are more strategic in that the planner is fully aware of the need for a plan, to generate and evaluate several courses of action (which makes for increased representational complexity), and of the importance of monitoring both formation and execution. In previous discussions of this sense of the term "plan," the latter aspects have sometimes been called "metaplanning" (e.g., Pea, 1982); alternatively, "planning" is seen as step 1 of problem solving, whereas "control" is viewed as step 2 (e.g., Hayes-Roth & Hayes-Roth, 1979). The present taxonomy is similar in intent but explicitly distinguishes between instances in which behavior is based on a plan (type 2) and instances in which a person *knows* that behavior is based upon a plan (type 3). Observational studies of young children's play and speech behavior indicate that type 2 plans may be identified in children as young as 18–36 months (Bretherton & Beeghly, 1982; McCune-Nicolich, 1981), and perhaps at even younger ages (Gopnik, 1981). Interviews with children indicate that by ages 8–9 years, children are aware of the importance and scope of type 3 plans (Pea, 1982); however, on specific tasks it may be several years until this level of planning serves to guide their behavior (e.g., the written summarization task studied by Brown et al.,1983).

The final level of planning, type 4, covers those instances in which formation of a plan is itself an objective. Such an activity is driven by metacognitive awareness that an adequate plan is, or may be, needed to cover anticipated future events or contingencies. Because not every anticipated contingency will occur, type 4 plans are formed with the knowledge that execution may never occur. Unlike type 3 plans, which are constructed to solve problems, type 4 plans are constructed for their own sakes. Such plans are objects of knowledge to be discussed, debated, and communicated among individuals or institutions. The social contexts and demands of many occupational tasks require that type 4 plans be generated during the long span of the adult years.

VI. Concluding integration

Given the importance of planning, psychological research on this construct will no doubt flourish for some years to come. The present taxonomy should be of assistance to both theoreticians and practitioners alike, as they continue to investigate the formation, execution, and monitoring of plans. In this chapter, it has been suggested that planning be considered from the perspective of the subject or subjects involved. Specifically, the cognitive components of various types of plans have been identified. This information should be of interest to those who are charged with the daily supervision of another person's conduct (e.g., supervisors with staff members, teachers with pupils, etc.). Such supervisory personnel often seek to encourage others to adopt more planful approaches to tasks at hand. A useful start is careful consideration of what is "lacking" in the "nonplanner." One nonplanner might lack knowledge of the task at hand, which results in an impoverished representation of the problem situation. A second nonplanner may need assistance with self-monitoring of the planning process itself. A third nonplanner might need assistance with both aspects of planning. In short, by highlighting what it is that develops in the ability to plan, the present taxonomy can be useful in attempts to teach others to plan.

A related concern that pertains to planning instruction is the need for "planning instructors" to be clear as to their own objectives vis-à-vis "planning learners." For example, those who write diet books, exercise books, and so on, are engaging in type 4 planning with respect to themselves. Their books, in contrast, are meant to be type 2 plans for their respective audiences (e.g., the book says I should do this now, so I will). The purpose of such programs is often to change the reader's daily routine, that is, create new type 1 plans in the reader. This is usually the case in books that present diets and exercise programs. Financial planning guides, in contrast, seek to build up sufficient knowledge and predispositions in the reader such that the reader may eventually assume control of the financial planning process itself; that is, the book seeks to develop type 3 plans in its readers. Given these different objectives, type 2 plans must be constructed with an eye toward their ultimate objective vis-à-vis the person being guided. In educational settings such as classrooms, this distinction is crucial. Drill and practice programs may be sufficient to build "basic skills" in pupils (e.g., mastery of number facts) but may fall far short in developing "thinking skills" in these same pupils (e.g., mathematical problem solving). In the language of the present taxonomy, carefully constructed drill sequences may be sufficient to develop type 1 plans in students, but may leave these same students very limited in their ability to see the need for thoughtful approaches to problems in which the student assumes responsibility for oversight of the problem-solving situation (type 3 planning). If the present taxonomy can be of assistance to researchers who are interested in investigating issues such as those concerning the nature of human planning, it will have served a useful purpose.

References

Adams, J. A. (1984). Learning of movement sequences. *Psychological Bulletin, 96*, 2–28.

Anderson, J. R. (1980). *Cognitive psychology and its implications.* San Francisco: Freeman.

Boden, M. A. (1983). Artificial intelligence and animal psychology. *New Ideas in Psychology, 1*, 11–33.

Bretherton, I., & Beeghly, M. (1982). Talking about internal states: The acquisition of an explicit theory of mind. *Developmental Psychology, 18*, 906–921.

Brown, A. L., Bransford, J. D., Ferrara, R. A., & Campione, J. C. (1982). *Learning, remembering and understanding.* Technical Report No. 244. University of Illinois at Urbana-Champaign.

Brown, A. L., Day, J. D., & Jones, R. S. (1983). The development of plans for summarizing texts. *Child Development, 54*, 968–979.

Brown, A. L., & DeLoache, J. S. (1978). Skills, plans, and self-regulation. In R. S. Siegler (Ed.), *Children's thinking: What develops?* (pp. 3–35). Hillsdale, NJ: Erlbaum.

Bruner, J. S. (1973). Organization of early skilled action. *Child Development, 44*, 1–11.

Byrne, R. (1984, September 12). Match for chess title: An aggressive opening. *The New York Times*, p. C22.

Case, R. (1978). Intellectual development from birth to adulthood: A neo-Piagetian interpretation. In R. S. Siegler (Ed.), *Children's thinking: What develops?* (pp. 37–72). Hillsdale, NJ: Erlbaum.

Case, R. (1984). The process of stage transition: A neo-Piagetian view. In R. J. Sternberg (Ed.), *Mechanisms of cognitive development* (pp. 19–44). New York: Freeman.

Chi, M. T. H., Glaser, R., & Rees, E. (1982). Expertise in problem solving. In R. J. Sternberg (Ed.), *Advances in the psychology of human intelligence*, Vol. 1 (pp. 7–75). Hillsdale, NJ: Erlbaum.

Flavell, J. H. (1979). Metacognition and cognitive monitoring: A new area of cognitive developmental inquiry. *American Psychologist, 34*, 906–911.

Frese, M., & Stewart, J. (1984). Skill learning as a concept in life-span developmental psychology: An action theoretic analysis. *Human Development, 27*, 145–162.

Furth, H. G. (1981). *Piaget and knowledge. Theoretical foundations* (2nd ed.). Chicago: University of Chicago Press.

Gopnik, A. (1981). Words and plans: Early language and the development of intelligent action. *Journal of Child Language, 9*, 303–318.

Harding, C. G. (1982). Development of the intention to communicate. *Human Development, 25*, 140–151.

Hayes-Roth, B., & Hayes-Roth, F. (1979). A cognitive model of planning. *Cognitive Science, 3,* 275–310.

Inhelder, B., & Piaget, J. (1958). *The growth of logical thinking from childhood to adolescence.* New York: Basic Books.

Klahr, D. (1978). Goal formation, planning and learning by preschool problem solvers. In R. S. Siegler (Ed.), *Children's thinking: What develops?* (pp. 181–212). Hillsdale, NJ: Erlbaum.

Klahr, D., & Robinson, M. (1981). Formal assessment of problem-solving and planning processes in preschool children. *Cognitive Psychology, 13,* 113–147.

McCune-Nicolich, L. (1981). Toward symbolic functioning: Structure of early pretend games and potential parallels with language. *Child Development, 52,* 785–797.

Meacham, J. A. (1984). The social basis of intentional action. *Human Development, 27,* 119–124.

Miller, G. A., Galanter, E., & Pribram, K. H. (1960). *Plans and the structure of behavior.* New York: Holt, Rinehart & Winston.

Pea, R. D. (1982). What is planning development the development of? In D. L. Forbes & M. T. Greenberg (Eds.), *Children's planning strategies* (pp. 5–27). San Francisco: Jossey-Bass.

Piaget, J. (1927). The first year of life of the child. Paper presented at the British Psychological Society, March 1927. Reprinted in H. Gruber & J. J. Voneche (Eds.) (1977). *The essential Piaget.* New York: Basic Books.

Piaget, J. (1952). *The origins of intelligence in children.* New York: Norton.

Piaget, J. (1960). *The psychology of intelligence.* Totowa, NJ: Littlefield, Adams, & Co.

Piaget, J. (1962). *Plays, dreams, and imitation in childhood.* New York: Norton.

Sacerdoti, E. D. (1977). *A structure for plans and behavior.* North-Holland, Amsterdam: Elsevier.

Salmoni, A. W., Schmidt, R. A., & Walter, C. B. (1984). Knowledge of results and motor learning: A review and critical appraisal. *Psychological Bulletin, 95,* 355–386.

Schank, R. C., & Abelson, R. P. (1977). *Scripts, plans, goals and understanding.* Hillsdale, NJ: Erlbaum.

Spitz, H. H., Webster, N. A., & Borys, S. V. (1982). Further studies of the Tower of Hanoi problem-solving performance of retarded young adults and non-retarded children. *Developmental Psychology, 18,* 922–930.

Vygotsky, L. S. (1962). *Thought and language.* Cambridge, MA: MIT Press.

Vygotsky, L. S. (1978). *Mind in society.* Cambridge, MA: Harvard University Press.

Webster, B. (1984, March, 13). Do animals have the capacity to plan? *The New York Times,* pp. C1, C6.

Werner, H. (1948). *Comparative psychology of mental development.* New York: International Universities Press.

Wickelgren, W. A. (1981). Human learning and memory. In M. R. Rosenzweig & L. W. Porter (Eds.), *Annual Review of Psychology* (Vol. 32, pp. 21–52). Palo Alto, CA: Annual Reviews Inc.

Wilensky, R. (1981). Meta-planning: Representing and using knowledge about planning in problem solving and natural language understanding. *Cognitive Psychology, 5,* 197–233.

4 Plans and planning: their motivational and cognitive antecedents

Shulamith Kreitler and Hans Kreitler

I. Introduction: intent and plan of this chapter

The concept of plan was a latecomer on the scene of modern psychology. Notwithstanding Head's (1920) and Bartlett's (1932) extensive discussions of schemata and their function, the idea did not catch on until 1960, the year of publication of the still so prominent book by Miller, Galanter, and Pribram, *Plans and the Structure of Behavior*. Since then, the concept has gained ground and has been used, though under different names, in various domains of psychology, as for instance, understanding of texts (Schank & Abelson, 1977), problem-solving (Newell & Simon, 1972), language (Allport, 1980), motor behavior (Eccles, 1972; Fowler & Turvey, 1978; Newell, 1978), social behavior (Sacks, Schegloff, & Jefferson, 1974), and so on. However, not only did Miller et al. succeed in introducing the plan concept, in spite of the still prominent behavioristic attitude (Harvey & Greer, 1980); they also seem to have influenced the manner in which the concept is used. Their book contains extensive discussions about the diverse functions of plans but virtually nothing about the origin of plans besides the suggestion that new plans – that is, plans that were neither inherited nor learned – are formed by using plans for plan construction. It was probably the deterring impact of this reductio ad infinitum that convinced many psychologists to focus their attention foremost on plans and their behavioral results. Thus planning, as well as the motivational and cognitive determinants of planning and the selection of plans, have been largely neglected in psychological research.

Considering this state of affairs, it becomes immediately apparent that an extensive and comprehensive research program would be required for studying the many hitherto unknown aspects of planning. In the present

Thanks are due to the experimenters and mainly to Miss Mihal Rieck, all of whom have helped in data collection, and to all the children, teachers, and principals who have cooperated in making the study possible.

110

chapter, we address ourselves only to two of these aspects, the motivational determinants and the cognitive antecedents of planning.

Like problem solving, conceiving a poem, or imagining the social order of an extraterrestrial state, planning is a voluntary cognitive activity. Being voluntary, the occurrence and elaboration of planning are influenced by factors as, for instance, whether one considers planning to be important, whether one believes in the usefulness of careful planning, whether one thinks one will function more efficiently if there remains a broad margin for spontaneity, and so on. We regard these factors as falling within the domain of cognitive motivation: *cognitive,* because they appear in the form of beliefs; *motivational,* because they determine the direction and intensity of action (see Section II.A). However, even if one believes without any reservation in the personal and general benefits of planning and intends to plan as carefully and thoughtfully as possible, the result may still be disappointingly poor if the planner lacks one or more of the cognitive abilities required for devising an adequate plan. It is unlikely that an individual could plan adequately without having well-developed notions of sequential ordering, hierarchical integration, time, and place, or without being able to think of causes, consequences, alternatives, and so on. Planning probably requires these as well as many other factors, all of which have to be determined by empirical research.

Our well-founded conviction that these two groups of factors fall within the broad domain of cognition and even interact with each other should not blur their necessary distinction. The first group of factors *(cognitive motivation)* are dealt with by our theory of cognitive orientation, and, on the basis of previous findings in regard to other behaviors, may be expected to be predicted by means of particular belief structures specified by this theory. The second group of factors *(cognitive abilities)* are dealt with by our psychosemantic theory of cognition, and, on the basis of previous findings in regard to other cognitive acts, may be expected to be correlated with particular meaning variables. Thus, in this chapter we will discuss planning from the motivational and cognitive viewpoints, separately as well as jointly. Hence, our approach may best be characterized as the motivational–cognitive approach to planning.

Accordingly, we will first outline the theory of cognitive orientation (sections II.A and II.B) and present an experiment that demonstrates its contribution to the understanding of major motivational aspects of planning (section II.C). Then we will discuss our theory of meaning (section III.A) and show empirically its predictive power in regard to planning (section III.B). Finally, we will combine the predictive power of both approaches (section IV.A) and discuss the results (section IV.B).

II. The motivational determinants of planning

A. The theory of cognitive orientation (CO theory)

Whereas theories of motivation in general try to illuminate and explain the forces and conditions that cause the behavior of living organisms, psychological theories of motivation attempt to answer the question as to why a human or a group of humans acts in a particular manner. Because psychology is the empirical science of human functioning, psychological theories should adhere not only to the general requirements of theories (e.g., explanatory power, logical coherence, etc.), but also to the methodological requirements of empirical sciences, especially the requirement to prove their hypotheses by successful predictions and, if a causal claim is made, by experimental modification with a predicted outcome, thus satisfying Popper's falsification criterion.

In the field of human molar behavior and its motivational determinants, our theory of cognitive orientation (Kreitler & Kreitler, 1976, 1982) was shown to fulfill these requirements. The theory is based on the assumption that human molar behavior above the level of spinal reflexes is initiated and guided by *cognitive contents,* that is: (a) meanings the subject assigns to external or internal stimulation for the sake of their identification and elaboration, as well as (b) more complex meaning structures, usually called *beliefs,* that by virtue of their orientative aspects determine the course of output behavior. This assumption has three important methodological implications:

1. Information about the relevant meaning structures (i.e., beliefs) must yield reliable behavior predictions.
2. Experimental modification of the predicting belief clusters must bring about a modification of behavior in line with the modification.
3. The theory has to present a coherent description of the major processes involved in input identification, input elaboration, and shaping of output behavior.

In line with implications (1) and (2), the CO theory has been successfully applied in more than 40 studies for predicting various molar behaviors, such as achievement, persevering or giving up after success or failure, pain tolerance, coming late to meetings (Kreitler & Kreitler, 1976), curiosity behaviors (Kreitler, Kreitler, & Zigler, 1974), quitting smoking after behavior therapy (Kreitler, Shahar, & Kreitler, 1976), orderliness and assertiveness (Lobel, 1982), and so on. Studies of experimental behavior modification were carried out in domains such as decrease or increase of pain tolerance, increasing curiosity behaviors in children

(Kreitler & Kreitler, 1976), or decreasing impulsiveness (Zakay, Bar-El, & Kreitler, 1984).[1] In the present context, a short summary of the CO theory may suffice for understanding the motivational determinants of planning as revealed by our experiment (section II.C) as well as the place of planning in a general theory of human molar behavior.

The CO theory can best be described as an unfolding sequence of stages. The first stage is triggered by external or internal stimulation that, because of its mismatch with immediately preceding stimulation, is subjected to a procedure of primary input identification (called "meaning action"). The procedure can be regarded as an attempt to answer the metaphorical question "What is it?" It consists in assigning to the input a limited number of meaning values in a relatively fixed order (S. Kreitler & Kreitler, 1983a) (called "initial meaning"), and may result in identifying the input, (a) as a signal for defensive, adaptive or conditioned response, or (b) as a signal for molar action, or (c) as irrelevant in the present situation, or (d) as new or particularly significant, and hence as a signal for an orienting response. The particular identifications are implemented by innate programs underlying unconditioned, conditioned, or orienting reflexes (alternatives a and b, respectively).

The second stage is set in operaton when (a) the input has not been identified sufficiently to inhibit the orienting response, or (b) the input has been identified as a signal for molar action from the very beginning, or (c) the evoked unconditioned or conditioned responses proved to be insufficient for coping with the input. This stage (called "meaning generation") is focused on the metaphorical question "What does it mean, and what does it mean for me?" It consists in elaborating the meaning of the input in personal and interpersonal modes (see Table 4.4), in a manner affected by personal preferences and traits, using a greater variety of meaning variables and more complex meaning structures, mainly particular beliefs. The meaning elaboration continues until either one or more beliefs indicate the need for action or some specific action which initiates the next stage, or the beliefs indicate no need for action, which terminates the sequence.

The third stage is focused on the metaphorical question "What will I do?" and consists in further elaborating the meaning of the course of action in terms of four types of beliefs:

1. *Beliefs about Goals,* expressing states, events, or acts desired by the self (e.g., I want to be rich; I want to avoid temptations).
2. *Beliefs about Norms,* expressing moral, social, esthetic, practical, or arbitrary rules and standards concerning states, events, or acts (e.g., One should drive on ice carefully; A person should not boast).

3. *Beliefs about Self,* describing one's own habits, tendencies, traits, acts, etc. in the past, present, or the future (e.g., I don't like music; I am fairly lazy).
4. *General Beliefs,* describing other people, events, states, objects, and acts of the environment (e.g., Most people don't plan; Effort pays).

The meaning elaboration involves matchings and interactions between beliefs ("belief clustering"), based on clarifying the orientativeness of the beliefs (i.e., the extent to which they support or do not support the indicated course of action). If the majority of beliefs of a certain type support the action, that belief type is considered as positively oriented in regard to that action; alternately, it may be negatively oriented or may lack orientativeness. If all four belief types support the indicated action, or at least three support it, whereas the fourth is neutral, a cluster of beliefs (called *CO Cluster*) orienting toward a particular act will result. Thus, a unified oriented tendency emerges. It is called *Behavioral Intent* (BI) and constitutes the answer to the question "What will I do?" (see Kreitler & Kreitler, 1982, about other alternatives including the retrieval of an almost complete CO cluster, the emergence of incomplete CO clusters and of inoperable clusters orienting toward daydreaming etc., or the formation of conflicts due to two CO clusters generating two incompatible BIs).

The fourth stage is focused on the metaphorical question "How will I do it?" It consists in implementing the BI by a behavioral program. Different programs are involved in executing an overt molar act, an act of fantasy, conflict resolution, etc. It is convenient to classify behavioral programs into four kinds in line with their origin. One kind consists of innately determined programs, such as those controlling reflexes or tropisms. A second kind consists of programs determined both innately and through learning, such as those controlling instinctive sequences (Dilger, 1960, 1962; Tinbergen, 1951), linguistic behaviors (McNeill, 1970), and probably defense mechanisms (Kreitler & Kreitler, 1972). The third kind includes programs that have been acquired only through learning, such as those controlling all culturally shaped behaviors (e.g., forms of greeting, peacemaking, conducting a conversation, running political elections and religious ceremonies) and personally formed habits (e.g., modes of preparing an examination, of relaxing, working, taking revenge). The fourth kind includes programs that have been constructed by the individual; these we propose to call plans (see section II.B).

Implementation of a BI by a behavioral program requires selection of a program, its retrieval, and often its adaptation to prevailing circumstances before it can be set into operation. More complex processes are invoked in case there arises a program conflict, that is, when two different programs appear to be equally adequate for implementing a BI or when a present program cannot be set into operation so long as another program is being enacted.

Behavior itself consists in the performance of the programmed action. Even when the behavior is noncognitive, the realization of the program is under cognitive control in which cognitive contents and processes are involved (Kelso & Wallace, 1978; Vorberg & Hambuch, 1978). The act is considered as completed when feedback indicates fulfillment in line with the program criteria; it is, however, considered as successful when feedback indicates fulfillment in line with the BI.

Figure 4.1 is a flowchart summary of the major processes of the CO theory. Figure 4.1 and the above brief account of the CO theory indicate that the major constructs to be considered in studies of predicting and changing behavior are the meaning assigned by the subject to the situation, the CO cluster concerning the particular act, and the availability of an adequate program for performing the act. In order to obtain the most accurate prediction or change of behavior, all three factors are to be assessed or changed in the case of each individual subject, though in practice one may often focus on the CO cluster while taking the chance of concluding from pretest subjects about the meaning likely to be assigned to the situation or of assuming the availability of common programs.

According to the CO theory, it is clear that though a program is indispensable for the occurrence of behavior, it is a necessary but by no means a sufficient condition for behavior. Behavior is evoked when there is a BI orienting toward that behavior *and* an adequate program. More concretely, if there is a program but no BI, no action will occur; when there is a BI, but no program, again no action should occur. But there is a difference between the two cases. Although a program may not trigger the generation of the adequate BI, it is likely that a BI will eventuate in the generation of an adequate program. The reason for this is probably that a new behavioral program may often be constructed quite easily out of other familiar programs. Studies dealing with changing pain tolerance in adults (Kreitler & Kreitler, 1976, pp. 253–271) and impulsiveness in 10- to 11-year-old children (Zakay, Bar-El, & Kreitler, 1984) showed that teaching the subjects a new program (for controlling pain or solving problems reflectively) without changing their CO cluster so that the cluster orients toward the behavior did not result in changed behavior; in contrast, changing the subjects' CO cluster so that it orients toward the behavior resulted in changed behavior, even when no new program was taught, but to a greater extent when a program was taught. These exper-

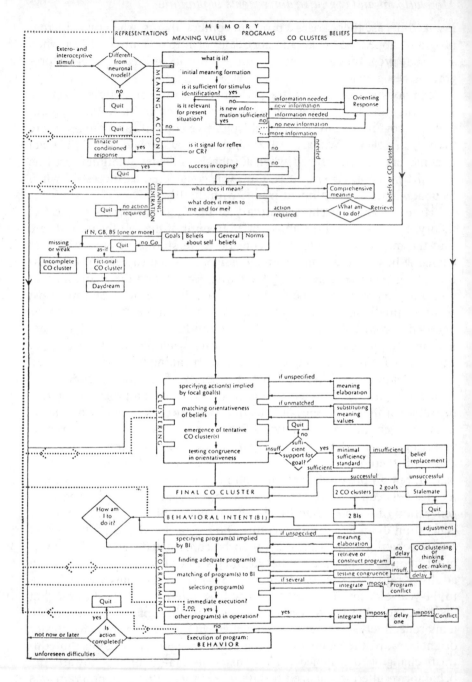

Figure 4.1. Overview of the main processes of the CO theory. (From H. Kreitler & S. Kreitler, 1976, with permission by Springer Publishing Company, Inc., New York.)

iments highlighted the importance of considering programs in studying or modifying behaviors.

When predicting behaviors, it is necessary to check whether the subjects have the programs corresponding to their motivational tendencies, this being the case less often in children than in adults, and less often in unusual behaviors than in regular and usual behaviors. When changing behaviors in an experimental or therapeutic setup, it is necessary to check whether the subjects have the programs corresponding to their new motivational tendencies, which is by no means always the case. However, because programs are the external overt aspect of behavior, it is often tempting to infer from it the underlying motivational matrix or trend; yet this is no more warranted than to infer from motivational tendencies (CO clusters and BIs) the characteristics of programs. This fact is of importance when, for example, consistency of behavior is at stake. All too often, absence of external similarity in behaviors on two or more occasions is taken as a sign for behavioral inconsistency, whereas it should be construed merely as evidence for changed programs (S. Kreitler & Kreitler, 1983b).

Accordingly, the motivational role of programs is that they constitute the tools with which BIs are implemented. By providing the bridge between the BI and actual behavior, they set the limits for the manifestations of motivational tendencies in behavior, define the particular domains in which these tendencies will be realized, and lend them their particular form which upon recurrence may become characteristic for the individual.

B. Programs and plans

Plans resemble programs in several respects. Both plans and programs may serve the implementation of a behavioral intent; both may be stored and then retrieved at some later point in time in order to be applied in circumstances similar to or even different from those characterizing the original conditions of their acquisition or formation; both are sequentially structured and may contain alternative subroutines; also, both are hierarchically organized and may be analyzed profitably in terms of two kinds of levels: the level of the relatively more general instructions (originally designated in the CO theory as "program scheme") and the level of the relatively more detailed instructions (originally designated in the CO theory as "operational program"), the former representing the more holistic and flexible aspects of action, the latter the relatively more rigidly determined aspects (Gallistel, 1980; Pribram, 1971). However, programs and plans differ markedly when considered from the point of view of a

general theory of behavior, particularly the CO theory. Indeed, the difference is so important that it suggests the use of two different semantic
labels.

Like problem solving, planning is a cognitive activity requiring so
much attention that it is rarely if ever performed concomitantly with
input elaboration and the shaping of output behavior. The saying "sit
back and plan" contains more than a grain of psychological insight. One
"sits back" and starts to plan or considers planning when it becomes
apparent that an intended action cannot be performed because one does
not know, or does not know for sure, how to perform it. In terms of the
CO theory, programs are retrieved, adjusted, and executed adjacent to the
emergence of a behavioral intent. If no suitable behavioral program is
available, the behavioral sequence is interrupted. The interruption elicits
a signal indicating the need for elaborating this stalemate situation
according to the processes constituting stage 2 and stage 3 (section II.A).
Sometimes, owing to prior experience, the feedback signal for renewed
elaboraton may be triggered off by a rudimentary program indicating the
need for planning or problem solving. In practice, both cases are equivalent in the sense that processes of prior stages are set into motion
whereas for the time being, the behavioral intent is stored in long-term
memory. Thus, neither the lack of an adequate program nor the direct
request for planning leads automatically to planning. If a New Yorker
wants to spend a weekend in the country but does not know where to go
and how to arrange it, he or she may decide to stay at home instead of
scanning the long list of newspaper advertisements and plotting the
details of the trip. In other words, the lack of a behavioral program is a
necessary but not a sufficient condition for planning.

According to the CO theory, there are some other shorter sequences
leading up to the planning. The most common of these culminates in
stage 2 (see section II.A) by the evocation of a goal belief that, on the one
hand, indicates the need or the possibility of planning but, on the other
hand, is too illusory, too fictional to induce an elaborate CO clustering.
Take the case of a person who, while driving down Sunset Boulevard,
sees a nice mansion with a tasteless yard in front of it. Being a fan of
refined gardening, the driver may at once start to plan a more beautiful
design for this front yard, notwithstanding the fact that he or she may
have no wish whatsoever to purchase or possess this particular villa.
Many people find planning to be a very enjoyable activity, whereas others
detest it, either because of its cognitive requirements or, more frequently
because they cherish spontaneous improvisations. The former are likely
to have a stored CO cluster orienting toward planning; the latter may

have a stored CO cluster negating planning or one orienting toward ad hoc improvisations, or even both kinds of CO clusters. Hence, the fictional driver in our example has perhaps a stored proplanning CO cluster that may have been activated by a norm belief (e.g., "A garden should be designed nicely"), a general belief (e.g., "This garden is ugly"), or a goal belief ("I would like to design this garden"), and so on. In case she or he had a weaker proplanning CO cluster, our driver may have merely thought: "These people should engage a better gardener."

Accordingly, it is evident that the difference between programs and plans is mainly functional. Whereas a program serves to implement immediately a behavioral intent, a plan is devised in order to serve at an earlier or later date as a behavioral program. Further, whereas program is an indispensable element if the sequence from input to output is to culminate in behavior, plan is an optional element that may be initiated by the lack of an adequate behavioral program but nevertheless requires a new loop in the sequence.

In sum, we regard planning as a cognitive function in its own right with its own specific motivational determinants and cognitive antecedents. Frequently, it becomes a subroutine, automatically set in motion whenever, in the course of shaping molar behavior, an adequate behavioral program is missing. Thus it may be codetermined by the strength of the behavioral intent whose execution has to be planned. But even in this case the impact of the motivational determinants and cognitive abilities concerned with planning per se will predominate. Therefore the CO theory can be expected to reveal the cognitive motivations promoting or hampering planning as well as to enable predicting the occurrence of planning and the intensity or devotion to planning mirrored by the resulting plans. Those cognitive aspects of planning that are not dependent on the belief structures (i.e., CO cluster) of the planner are to be accounted for by specific cognitive abilities (see section III).

C. Study: the cognitive orientation of planning

1. Purpose and hypothesis. The purpose of section C is to present findings concerning the motivational determinants of planning in a developmental perspective. The basic assumption was that planning is an act (see section II.B). Therefore, we concluded that planning would have motivational determinants similar to other molar acts (Kreitler & Kreitler, 1982), and hence that it would depend on a characteristic CO cluster. Previous studies already showed that the CO cluster predicts acts in the sphere of cognition, that is, intolerance of ambiguities (in 17- to 18-year olds) (S. Kreitler, Maguen, & Kreitler, 1975), decision making (in adults) (Zakay, 1976), and choice of reflective strategies in problem solving (in 9- to 11-year olds) (Zakay, Bar-El, & Kreitler, 1984). Accordingly, the general hypothesis of the study was that planning would be predicted by means of a particular CO cluster of planning. More specifically, it was expected that each of a series of variables reflecting different aspects of planning – mainly aspects reflecting the intensity and complexity of planning – would be related positively to the CO score of planning. The hypotheses were tested in four age groups ranging from 5 to 11 years. In view of previous studies that showed the predictive power of CO clusters in regard to behaviors in children as young as 5 years (e.g., Kreitler, Kreitler, & Zigler, 1974; Marom, 1978), it was assumed that the CO cluster of planning would predict planning from the age of 5 years onward. The findings were expected to shed light on the developmental course of the motivational determinants of planning, which is a prerequisite for a successful educational intervention in the acquisition of planning.

2. *Method: subjects.* The total number of subjects who participated in the study was 120, 30 in each of the following age groups (years; months): kindergarten (range: 4;9–5;6 years, $\bar{X}$ = 5;3 years), second grade (range; 6;9–7;8 years, $\bar{X}$ = 7.4 years), fourth grade (range: 8;7–10;4 years, $\bar{X}$ = 9;6 years) and sixth grade (range: 10;7–11;8 years, $\bar{X}$ = 11;4 years). There were 15 boys and 15 girls in each group. The children of each age group were selected randomly from three different schools, 10 from each school. The means of the IQ (measured by the Peabody Picture Vocabulary Test) were 107.2, 110.4, 112.3, and 113.5 in the kindergarten, second-grade, fourth-grade, and sixth-grade groups, respectively (the differences between the groups are not significant). All the children were of medium socioeconomic status (SES) (as assessed by the index of Hollingshead & Redlich, 1958).

3. *Method: instruments and variables.* The instruments included a set of "planning situations," a CO questionnaire, and a questionnaire assessing meaning (which will be described only in section III.B.2).

    a. *Planning situations.* In order to make the task as meaningful for the subjects as possible, the planning situations were constructed mainly on the basis of children's responses in another study (see Kreitler & Kreitler, chapter 6, this volume, Study A) to questions about the domains to which planning applies and the antecedents of planning. To enable cross-age comparisons, only those situations mentioned in the previous study by at least 6% of the children in each age group were included. In addition, an attempt was made to include also situations based on at least two domains of planning mentioned frequently by children in the different age groups. The original pool consisted of 19 situations, which were presented for judgments of clarity and interest to further pretest subjects. Ten situations were finally selected (see Table 4.1), each of which posed a special planning problem. The problems differed in several characteristics:

a. The character who is assumed to devise the plan (in Planning Situations Nos. 1–3, 5, 8–10, the character is a child, whereas in the rest it is an adult).

b. The character for whom the plan is presumably designed (in Planning Situations Nos. 1, 3, 5 and 8, a child plans presumably for him- or herself; in Planning Situations Nos. 2, 4 and 10, a child plans presumably for adults; and in Planning Situations Nos. 6 and 7, an adult plans presumably for adults).

c. The necessity of requesting further information (in Planning Situations Nos. 1–3, 6, and 10, it is necessary to request further information, whereas in Planning Situations Nos. 4, 5, 7–9, it is not necessary), and who presumably provides such information (i.e., another child in Planning Situations Nos. 1 and 6, adults in Planning Situations Nos. 2, 3, and 10).

d. The general type of plan requested: search plan (Planning Situations Nos. 1 and 6), operation plan (Planning Situation No. 2), a road plan (Planning Situation No. 3), a trip plan (Planning Situation No. 4), a flight plan (Planning Situation No. 5), a fighting plan (Planning Situation No. 7), a plan for solving an interpersonal problem with a peer (Planning Situation No. 8) or with parents (Planning Situation No. 9), and a plan for a day's errands (Planning Situation No. 10).

The same Planning Situations were administered to subjects of all age groups (except for minor changes in Planning Situations Nos. 1, 3, and 9; see Table 4.2). The gender of the characters mentioned in the Planning Situations was changed in line with the subject's gender (the names were of boys when the subject was male, and of girls when the subject was female). The Planning Situations were presented in the form of games, including dramatic enactments implemented by toys and other objects (see Table 4.1). The subjects' responses were given verbally or in drawings and enactments. All responses were recorded. After each response the child was asked only once: "What else?"

The responses were evaluated in terms of variables reflecting various aspects of planning. The variables may be classified into three groups. Each group was coded by different experimenters. The first group included 10 measures of general planning skills. They were all based on

Table 4.1. *Planning situations and criteria for evaluation*

No.	Description of planning situation	Evaluative criteria[a]
1	Children A & B often play together (the commonest game for the given age group is mentioned). B has been playing, & A joins him/her. An item necessary for the game is missing. B does not know where it is. A wants to look for it. What questions should A ask B?	Qs concern the lost item directly or indirectly (details about it and antecedents of loss); Qs reveal an hypothesis about the item's place; alternative hypotheses; hypothesis is realistic (e.g., item is unlikely to be in another city); Qs consider described reality (e.g., B does not known where item is); elaborating details of search; considering alternate means for attaining subgoals.
2	C's parents have bought a new washing machine. The people from the store have just brought it and took it down from the truck. They have placed it in the drawing room and urge the family to ask all they want to know and say what they want to be done with the machine before they go away. They are in a hurry. (Toys representing the house, the street, the machine, the truck, the company people, & the buyer family incl. the child are shown, & the plot is enacted.) What should the parents ask the people to do, and what Qs should they pose?	Qs refer to manner of operation (e.g., function of knobs, adequate powder, load); Qs refer to conditions bound with proper operation (electricity, upkeep, repair); Qs consider function of machine (washing); no irrelevant Qs about machine or other themes; no Qs about unrealistic properties of machine.
3	D's mother asked D to go to her friend, where D has never been, in order to bring back a cooking form she had left there (for youngest Ss: D wants to visit his friend L whom he/she had never visited; mother agrees) (Toys of the house, the street, & D are used; D is shown standing in the house's entrance.) Now D is about to leave the house. Which Qs should D ask the mother?	Qs refer to address & the way; to possible difficulties of reaching the location (distance, crossing roads, getting lost) &/or of identifying the place; no irrelevant Qs about person to be visited, the object, D's mother during the visit, etc.; considering the given conditions (mother's permission or request, time for leaving, etc.); considering different possibilities for learning about the address; for reaching the place; considering duration of stay; time & manner of returning; possibilities of not meeting desired person; Qs are ordered chronologically.
4	A family (the child, two parents, a 3-year-old sister) plus a dog are about to go for a one-day trip to	Mentioning food & drink for adults; food & drink for children; food & drink for dog; clothing items; provision for

Table 4.1. *(cont.)*

No.	Description of planning situation	Evaluative criteria[a]
	the desert where there are no shops or kiosks and there is a lot of sun. (Toys representing the protagonists are shown and kept before the child as reminders.) What should they prepare and what should they take with them?	shadow; entertainment (reading, games, etc.); comfort & resting; hygiene; first-aid; gasoline; considering need for buying things earlier; no unrealistic items in terms of kinds & quantity; ordering items chronologically (order of buying or packing or consuming); mentioning alternative items; considering possibilities for damaged items or need for more; considering reality (i.e., desert, impossibility of buying).
5	The story of Jack & the Beanstalk was told and shown by means of "pop-ups" (paper-cut moving pictures) emphasizing the child's poverty, the giant's treasure, & details of the terrain, up to the point when the giant smells the child's presence and the child, who is hiding, must flee. (The situation is demonstrated in a picture.) What does the child think about? What will he/she do? What is his/her plan?	Considering the need to hide; plan considers possibility of fight with the giant; planning escape (vs. "he goes away"); escape plan realistic; escape plan has more than three steps; alternatives concerning escape or any of its subgoals; considers taking gold coins; considers taking treasure now or later; alternatives concerning the taking of coins or treasure; taking account of terrain details; escape plan enables reaching home; chronological ordering.
6	R's mother notices that R came back from the school without his/her jacket. She wants to go & look for it. What should she ask R in order to be able to look for the jacket?	Qs reveal hypothesis about jacket's location; alternative hypotheses; realistic hypotheses; Qs concern the item (identifying details); Qs concern antecedents of loss; considering details of attaining subgoals (e.g., entering the school); considering alternatives for latter; no irrelevant Qs; hypotheses likely to lead to finding the jacket.
7	One group of soldiers (the "blues") is guarding a certain structure in which they hold their treasure. The "yellows" are determined to conquer the citadel. Here is the commander of the "yellows." He/She has a plan. Can you guess what it is? (If not, what would be your plan if you were the commander?) (An alternative plan is asked for.) (Blue and yellow plastic soldiers & a plastic structure were used to demonstrate the situation.)	Attack plan realistic; specifying details for attaining subgoals (e.g., reaching a certain place); attack plan has more than two parts; considers if–then eventualities; independent alternative plans; alternatives for attaining subgoals in original plan; plan leads to required goals.

Table 4.1. *(cont.)*

No.	Description of planning situation	Evaluative criteria[a]
8	P wants to play with A. A plays so well, and P has never played with him/her. Now P sits at home thinking: What can be done so that A will want to play with me? What does P think? What will P do? (An alternative plan is asked for; then the S's opinion about two proposed plans is requested: (a) P would stand alone during the playing period; (b) P would stand near A and watch him/her playing.)	Plan realistic; plan enables attaining goal; plan has more than 2 parts; more than 6 details in elaborated plan; independent alternative plans suggested spontaneously; readiness to accept – or if not, to further elaborate – one of suggested alternatives; considers if–then eventualities; considers possibilities of failure in plan and alternate steps; execution of plan lasts over a day.
9	Now it is morning. U is at school. U knows that in the evening there will be guests, an uncle, & an aunt that U loves dearly. U wants to stay with them the whole evening (for two oldest age groups: U knows that there is a special late-night TV show that he/she wants to watch), but U's parents do not allow U to stay up so late. Now U thinks: What can be done to make my parents allow me to stay up so late? What does U think? What is U's plan? (An alternative plan is asked for after S's response.)	Plan realistic; plan enables attaining goal; plan has more than 2 parts; independent alternative plans; considers possibility of failure in plan and alternative steps; considers if–then eventualities.
10	Y lives with his/her family out of town, far away. They almost never come to town. Now they have decided to come to town for 1 day & want to do the following things: visit Aunt J who is very old and weak; visit Uncle F whom they have not seen for a year; go together to the zoo; buy a special cupboard that is now on sale in a specific store in town; go to a special store in order to buy fish for Y's aquarium. (Toys representing each of the errands were introduced and left before the child as reminders.) They have to do all these things in 1 day. Please make a plan for them. Maybe you	Asks when cupboard store opens & closes; when aquarium stores opens & closes; when zoo opens & closes; location of aunt; of uncle; of cupboard store; of aquarium shop; of zoo; duration of traveling betweeen locations; prepares at least 2 details beforehand (e.g., phoning aunt); considers where to store during the day the bought things; plan includes all required items in one day; plan realistic; considers if–then eventualities; alternative plans; alternatives for attaining subgoals; presents plan only after getting all necessary information; presents plan only after planning is completed; is able to draw itinerary; itinerary conforms to obtained information.

Table 4.1. *(cont.)*

No.	Description of planning situation	Evaluative criteria[a]
	need to know various things in order to make the plan. You can ask me, & I'll give you all the information. (The standard information, provided upon request, included a map of the city described verbally and graphically, the location of the mentioned places, the hours when the stores and the zoo open and close, expected duration of driving from one location to another and of visits, etc.) (After presentation of the plan, the S was asked to draw the itinerary as if it were actually enacted.)	

Note: Q = question; S = subject.
[a]All criteria are formulated positively (i.e., in support of planning) and are dichotomous. The global evaluation of planning in each Planning Situation is based on the number of positively checked criteria, increasing from the lowest to the highest level in a four-step scale. The numbers defining each step represent the quartiles of the distribution.

data summed across the 10 Planning Situations. The assessed planning skills were:

1. Number of alternative plans presented by the child (either spontaneously, usually preceded by a remark like "There is another possibility" or "Something else can be done," or in response to a direct request as indicated in Planning Situations Nos. 7–9).
2. Number of if–then eventualities considered explicitly in the plans.
3. Number of chronological orderings used in describing a plan or in asking for information while planning.
4. Number of different questions asked by the child while planning.
5. Number of items considered or referred to.
6. Number of different domains to which refer the questions (see Variable No. 4) or items (see Variable No. 5) ("domain" was defined as a category of specific contents, e.g., food, entertainment, clothing, hygiene, and health in the case of Planning Situation No. 4, or machine operation, placement of machine, care of machine, repairs, etc., in the case of Planning Situation No. 2, in line with the sorting of the responses by two independent judges).
7. Number of general labels used in presenting a plan or asking questions while planning ("general label" was defined as a relatively more abstract term summarizing *and* preceding a series of more detailed instances of

acts or items, e.g., "food" in the following response: "I'll take food, that is, meat for the dog, enough milk for the sister, a pile of sandwiches, etc.").

8. Mean number of steps included in plans presented as first and major ones ("step" was defined as a relatively independent act incorporated within a plan, e.g., running for shelter, taking a bus, going to bed).

9. Mean number of steps included in plans presented as alternatives to major ones ("step" was defined as in Variable No. 8).

10. Mean number of steps (defined as in Variable No. 8) included in all plans – major and alternative ones.

For the 10 general planning skills, the interjudge coding reliability between two independent judges (graduate psychology students) was $r = .94$ across all measures.

The second group of planning variables included global evaluations of the adequacy of planning. There were 11 evaluation measures – one for each of the 10 Planning Situations separately, and one "overall evaluation" measure based on the mean of the 10 separate measures. Each of the global measures relating to one of the 10 Planning Situations was based on specific criteria, set up mainly on the basis of pretests and opinions of experts (two developmental psychologists), and partly in view of previous studies (e.g., Byrne, 1977; Hayes-Roth & Hayes-Roth, 1979). Table 4.1 presents the full list for each Planning Situation. It shows that the number of criteria for each Planning Situation ranged from 5 to 19. In evaluating a child's response to any of the 10 Planning Situations, the coder had to check "yes" or "no" on each of the criteria specific to that Planning Situation. On the basis of pretests, we established separately for each Planning Situation the distribution of the number of criteria checked as positive for the responses of children of a given age group. The distribution for each Planning Situation was divided into four sections in line with the quartiles. This procedure made it possible to define a four-step scale for the global evaluation measure for each Planning Situation, comparable across the 10 Planning Situations. The number of positively scored criteria in the lowest quartile got the score of 1; the number in the next quartile, the score of 2; the number in the next quartile, the score of 3; and the number in the highest quartile, the score of 4. The interjudge coding reliability of the 10 Planning Situations, between two independent judges was $r = .96$ (for the number of positively scored criteria) and $r = .98$ (for the global evaluation measures).

The third group of planning variables included seven variables reflecting aspects of contents, i.e., interpretations and considerations used by the subjects in planning. The different domains of contents correspond to categories of contents defined later as meaning dimensions (see section

III.A; Table 4.4): Feelings and Emotions (e.g., the plan for Planning Situation No. 5 is based on the consideration that Jack is so scared that he cannot run quickly), Cognitive Qualities (e.g., the plan for Planning Situation No. 8 is based on the consideration that child R is clever and hence would be impressed by A's special competence in some game), Sensory Qualities (e.g., in Planning Situation No. 6. asking about the color of the lost jacket so as to facilitate the search), Possessions, etc. A particular domain of contents was coded only if the specific contents played a role in the plan and not when it was merely mentioned. The material was coded independently by two graduate students in accordance with strictly defined criteria concerning each domain of contents. The intercoder reliability was $r = .90$. Of all kinds of contents used by the subjects in planning, only the seven that were used in planning by at least 10% ($n = 3$) of the children in each age group were selected for the study: (1) Temporal qualities; (2) Locational Qualities; (3) Quantity and Number; (4) Sensory Qualities; (5) Feelings and Emotions; (6) Judgments and Evaluations; (7) Cognitive Qualities.

For the sake of coding the material on the three groups of variables described above, the responses of all children to the 10 Planning Situations were intermingled. It was expected that this procedure would eliminate the halo effect that might occur if a coder knew he or she was dealing with the 10 responses of one and the same child.

b. Cognitive orientation questionnaire of planning. The CO questionnaire for predicting planning was constructed according to the standard procedure (Kreitler & Kreitler, 1982, pp. 127–129). Briefly, the meaning of planning was examined in pretest subjects; the recurrent content elements, called "meaning values" (see section III.A) were used for constructing beliefs of the four types orienting for and against planning; the preliminary questionnaire was administered to pretest subjects ($n = 40$, in each age level), and then shortened in view of the item-analyses and reliability checks. The final questionnaire included 29 questions: 8 General Beliefs, 5 Beliefs about Self, 8 Beliefs about Goals, and 8 Beliefs about Norms (alpha coefficients for each type of belief in each age group were in the range of .80 to .98). The questions were grouped around four focal issues that were used in order to provide meaningful and concrete contexts for assessing the children's beliefs. The issues were: attending (or not) to a road on which one goes with a parent but would later often go alone; preparing (or not) all objects necessary for a game before starting to play; preparing (or not) one's personal belongings before spending the night with a friend or relative; planning (or not) the theme and structure of a drawing before starting to draw. The details of the roads or the games were adapted to the age level. For each issue, two specific children behaving in diametrically opposed ways in regard to planning were described. Then the subject was asked several questions relating to the described issue and the fictional children; these questions were designed to assess the subject's Beliefs about Norms, Beliefs about Goals, Beliefs about the Self, and General Beliefs. For example, the subject was asked in random order who of the two described children was a better boy (Norm Belief), whom of the two (s)he most resembled at present (Belief about Self), like whom of the two described children (s)he wanted to be (Goal Belief), who of the two will do better (e.g., will find the road, or produce a better painting), and whether his or her friends were like one or the other of the described children (General Beliefs).

Here is a partial example of one part of the questionnaire:

Gadi and Dani are two children. [For girls, female names were used.] Gadi likes to draw, and Dani likes to draw. Before Gadi starts drawing, he looks at the page and decides what he will draw. Now, say, he decided to draw a street. So he thinks where on the page he will draw the road, where he will put the houses and all the other things. Dani does it differently. He starts drawing; and he draws whatever comes out. Sometimes it looks like it is going to be, say, a street, so he will draw a street. He follows things as they turn up.

Question 1: Whom are you like? Are you like Gadi who thinks beforehand what to draw and where to draw each thing or are you like Dani who draws whatever comes out?

The questionnaire was administered orally, and the answers were written down verbatim by the experimenter. The answers were scored as 1 when they supported planning, or as 0 when they did not support planning, according to predetermined criteria established on the basis of the initial pretests. For example, if a subject answered that (s)he wanted to be like the child who noticed all the details of the road when going with the parent, the answer was coded as 1 for a Goal Belief. The scores were summed for answers pertaining to each belief type across the different issues mentioned in the questionnaire. Thus each subject got four scores, one for each type of beliefs. According to the standard procedure, these scores were transformed into 1 or 0, depending on whether they were above or below the age group's mean for that belief type. The sum of the four transformed scores yielded one CO score, which could range from 4 (when all four belief types oriented toward planning), to 0 (when none oriented toward planning).

4. Method: procedure. Each subject was interviewed individually four times: In one session the Peabody Picture Vocabulary Test was administered; in another, the Planning Situations (II.C.3); in a third, the Cognitive Orientation Questionnaire of Planning (II.C.3); and in a fourth, the Meaning Questionnaire (III.B.2). The interval between the sessions was three to seven days. The order of the sessions was fully randomized. In the case of some subjects ($n = 8$) on the lowest age level, a break of 1 to 3 hours had to be introduced in the session of Planning Situations in the interests of better concentration. The duration of the sessions varied from 20 (for the CO questionnaire) to 45 minutes (for the Planning Situations).

5. Results. a. Development of CO. Table 4.2 presents the data concerning CO scores and the scores in the four belief types in ages 5, 7, 9, and 11. The table (lower part) shows that there are no significant differences between the four age groups in the means of the belief types and in the means of the CO scores. Moreover, the means do not present a linear or quadratic trend. But an examination of the distribution of CO scores (Table 4.2, upper part) shows that although the four age groups do not differ in the frequency of the subjects with high CO scores (i.e., CO 3 or CO 4), they differ in the frequency of subjects with low (i.e., CO 0 or CO 1) or medium (i.e., CO 2) CO scores. In the younger age groups, the distribution of subjects with different CO scores is more even; indeed, the distribution does not deviate from chance. The situation is different in 9-year olds: No subjects received low CO scores, and 33% of the subjects got CO 2, which may indicate a conflict in regard to planning (the percentages expected by chance are 40% and 20%, respectively). In 11-year olds the scene shifts again: Sixty percent of the subjects received low CO scores, and no subjects got CO 2 (the percentages expected by chance are 40% and 20%, respectively). Thus, the observed changes in CO scores indicate that in the studied age range, there is no regular increase in the CO scores orienting toward planning. This is plausible because these CO scores assess the strength of the motivation to engage in planning, which may indeed be expected to exist to the same degree in younger and older subjects.

The results do not rule out the possibility of developmental changes in the cognitive abilities enabling the formation of the CO cluster. Previous studies (Kreitler & Kreitler, 1982, pp. 161–162) showed that prior to the age of 5 years, CO clusters develop gradually out of a nuclear grouping including Norm Beliefs and Goal Beliefs, pointing in orientatively incompatible directions. It is likely that after the age of 5 there is further development in the cognitive processes involved in clustering so that the CO cluster may become a richer and firmer structure, often retrievable in an almost complete state. Moreover, CO clusters may also develop on

Table 4.2. Distribution across CO scores and means of belief types in the four age groups

	No. of Ss[a] with CO scores			Means of belief types[b] and CO scores				
Age	0 or 1	2	3 or 4	Beliefs about Self	General Beliefs	Beliefs about Norms	Beliefs about Goals	CO scores
5	8	5	17	2.63	3.70	3.10	4.00	2.47
7	8	8	14	2.60	3.00	4.30	3.50	2.13
9	0	10	20	3.54	3.80	5.00	4.00	3.00
11	18	0	12	2.50	3.74	4.20	3.20	1.40
Significance:[c]								
χ^2 (df = 3)	12.57**	9.87*	2.33	2.07	2.01	2.01	2.04	2.45
F (betw. grps.)				1.24	1.53	1.19	1.12	1.03
F (linear)				.98	.76	.81	.71	.70
F (quadratic)								

[a] The exact number of subjects who got each of the five CO scores is mentioned in the column headings of Table 4.3.

[b] The number of beliefs in the questionnaires was: Beliefs about Self = 5, General Beliefs = 8, Beliefs about Norms = 8, Beliefs about Goals = 8.

[c] The chi-square values for the distribution of scores in each age group separately are 3.58 (df = 2), 2.29 (df = 2), 20.00 (df = 2; p < .001), and 9.00 (df = 2) for ages 5, 7, 9, and 11, respectively. Chi-square value for the total distribution by scores and ages = 31.38 (df = 6; p < .001).

* p < .05.
** p < .01.

the personal level so that, for example, a child who at a younger age had a low CO score for planning may have at an older age a higher CO score for planning or vice versa. Such developments cannot be read from Table 4.2. Yet, Table 4.2 shows that on the group level, although there is no development, there is a shift in the distribution of the CO scores, which indicates (a) the possibility for some degree of conflict (in 9-year olds), and (b) a tendency toward polarization of the sample between subjects with low and subjects with high CO scores (in 11-year olds).

b. CO scores and planning variables. Table 4.3 presents the major findings concerning the hypotheses of section II. It shows the results of the analyses of variance performed separately in each group, with CO scores as the independent variable and the planning measures as dependent variables, as well as the results of pairwise comparisons of means in case they were significant. The analyses of variance were based on the means of the whole range of CO scores available in a particular age group (which, however, varies across age groups). This provides a more complete image of the relations between CO scores and planning variables than mean comparisons of low versus high CO scorers would. Thus, the findings can be evaluated both in terms of the significance of the relation between CO scores and each of the dependent variables, and in terms of the ordering of the means of the dependent variable in correspondence with the order of the CO scores (i.e., the former should increase linearly when the latter increase from 0 to 4).

We will deal first with the general planning skills and the global evaluation measures. Table 4.3 shows that in 5-year olds, CO scores predicted the following variables of general planning skills: number of chronological orderings (Var. No. 3), number of domains to which the child referred (Var. No. 6), and the number of general labels the child has used (Var. No. 7). Two further variables (Var. No. 2 and Var. No. 5) were related to CO scores on the $p < .10$ level of significance. In addition, CO scores predicted 7 out of the 10 global evaluation measures referring to Planning Situations (i.e., those referring to Planning Situations Nos. 2–4, 6–9) and the overall mean of the 10 global evaluation measures.

In 7-year olds, CO scores predicted 7 of the 10 variables of general planning skills. These were: number of chronological orderings (Var. No. 3), number of domains (Var. No. 6), number of general labels (Var. No. 7), number of if–then considerations (Var. No. 2), number of items (Var. No. 5), number of questions (Var. No. 4), and number of steps in major plans (Var. No. 8). Notably, the first three variables were predicted also

Table 4.3. *Relations of CO scores to planning variables*

Planning variable[a]		Means of groups[b]					F	Significant group dif.[b].
		CO 0 (n = 4)	CO 1 (n = 4)	CO 2 (n = 5)	CO 3 (n = 8)	CO 4 (n = 9)		
Age 5								
Alternate	(P. 1)	2.00	2.00	2.00	3.00	3.10	.46	
If–then	(P. 2)	3.50	5.12	6.02	7.67	8.80	2.62 ($p < .10$)	a < b, c, d, e*/a < b*/c, d < e*
Chronol.	(P. 3)	2.00	3.50	5.40	5.60	7.00	12.97****	
Questions	(P. 4)	1.80	1.40	1.77	1.75	2.32	1.50	
Items	(P. 5)	3.87	4.00	4.78	5.80	6.00	2.64 ($p < .10$)	a < d*/a < e*/b < e*
Domains	(P. 6)	1.00	1.19	1.34	1.40	1.92	5.74**	a,b,c,d < e**
Gen. Labels	(P. 7)	1.00	1.00	1.37	2.80	3.00	9.56****	a,b,c < d,e**
Steps/1st	(P. 8)	2.60	2.89	3.00	3.10	3.00	.10	
Steps/alt.	(P. 9)	1.08	1.25	1.22	2.00	2.30	.56	
Steps/all	(P. 10)	3.68	4.14	4.22	5.10	5.30	1.13	
Overall eval.		.82	1.42	1.84	2.14	2.89	5.69**	a,b < d,e*/a < c*/c < e*
Sit. 1		1.00	1.00	1.56	2.20	2.00	1.54	
Sit. 2		1.00	2.25	2.89	3.00	3.60	4.85**	a < b*/c < e*/a < c,d,e**/b < d,e**
Sit. 3		1.00	1.10	2.25	2.56	3.20	4.57**	a,b < c,d,e**/c < e*
Sit. 4		1.00	2.00	2.12	2.22	3.85	7.00***	a,b,c,d < e**
Sit. 5		1.00	1.20	1.50	2.00	2.30	1.94	
Sit. 5		.04	1.78	2.00	2.10	4.00	24.58****	a < b,c,d < e**
Sit. 7		.33	1.00	1.10	1.12	2.00	4.64**	a < b,c,d*/a < e**/b,c,d, < e*
Sit. 8		.90	1.00	1.37	2.00	2.80	10.59****	a,b < d,e**/a < c*/c < d,e*
Sit. 9		1.00	1.55	2.00	2.25	2.90	3.03*	a,b < c,d,e**/c < e*
Sit. 10		1.00	1.37	1.60	2.00	2.30	1.82	
Time	(C. 1)	7.00	5.00	6.40	4.87	8.56	2.03	
Location	(C. 2)	5.00	4.00	8.00	9.87	8.44	1.08	
Quantity	(C. 3)	4.00	1.00	3.00	2.12	1.44	1.97	

Sensory Qual.	(C. 4)	.00	.62	1.00	5.00	3.40	56.36****	a,b,c < d,e**/e < d**
Emotions	(C. 5)	1.00	3.00	2.80	1.75	1.22	2.16
Judgments	(C. 6)	1.00	1.00	3.80	1.12	2.11	2.01
Cognitive Qual.	(C. 7)	.60	1.00	1.40	1.12	.66	1.46

Age 7

		CO 0 (n = 8)	CO 2 (n = 8)	CO 3 (n = 8)	CO 4 (n = 6)		
Alternate	(P. 1)	4.50	3.00	6.00	8.00	2.45	
If-then	(P. 2)	5.00	8.00	8.30	13.00	18.53****	a < b,c < d**
Chronol.	(P. 3)	5.75	6.50	7.00	13.50	36.96****	a,b,c < d**/a < c*
Questions	(P. 4)	3.40	4.20	5.00	6.10	30.48****	a,b < c,d**
Items	(P. 5)	5.00	7.00	8.50	10.50	30.13****	a < b,c < d**
Domains	(P. 6)	1.60	2.25	3.80	4.60	13.17**	a,b < c,d**/c < d*
Gen. Labels	(P. 7)	2.50	3.00	4.00	5.10	14.29****	a,b < c,d**/c < d*
Steps/1st	(P. 8)	2.80	3.50	3.60	4.80	13.00**	a < b,c < d**
Steps/alt.	(P. 9)	2.00	1.50	2.30	2.60	1.87	
Steps/all	(P. 10)	4.80	5.00	5.90	7.40	2.22	
Overall eval.		1.85	2.22	2.99	3.44	29.25****	a,b < c*/c < d*/a,b < d**
Sit. 1		2.00	2.50	3.00	3.50	28.42****	a,b < c,d**
Sit. 2		2.00	3.00	3.10	3.40	21.90****	a,b < d**/a < c*
Sit. 3		2.00	2.00	3.50	4.00	6.74**	a,b < c,d**
Sit. 4		2.00	2.90	3.00	3.80	8.66***	a < b,c,d**/b,c < d**
Sit. 5		1.00	1.50	3.00	3.00	26.92****	a,b < c,d**
Sit. 6		2.00	1.50	2.50	2.00	2.45	
Sit. 7		2.50	1.80	2.80	3.40	7.50**	b < a,c,d**/a,c < d*
Sit. 8		2.00	2.50	3.00	4.00	24.21****	a,b < c,d**/b < c*
Sit. 9		2.00	3.00	3.00	4.00	2.12	
Sit. 10		2.00	2.50	3.00	3.40	4.78**	a,b, < c,d**/b < c*
Time	(C. 1)	5.00	8.00	8.50	13.00	18.55****	a < b,c < d**
Location	(C. 2)	12.00	8.00	9.50	19.00	18.54****	b,c, < a < d**
Quantity	(C. 3)	2.50	3.60	3.20	4.10	6.33**	a < b,c,d**

Table 4.3. *(Cont.)*

Planning variable[a]		Means of groups[b]				F	Significant group dif.[b]
		CO 0 (n = 8)	CO 2 (n = 8)	CO 3 (n = 8)	CO 4 (n = 6)		
Sensory Qual.	(C. 4)	4.00	2.00	3.00	6.00	12.13****	a,b < c < d**
Emotions	(C. 5)	2.00	1.50	2.30	2.60	2.57	
Judgments	(C. 6)	1.80	1.00	4.00	3.10	6.58**	
Cognitive Qual.	(C. 7)	2.50	2.00	4.30	3.80	4.56**	a,b, < c,d**/c < d*

		CO 2 (n = 10)	CO 3 (n = 10)	CO 4 (n = 10)	F	Significant group dif.[b]
Age 9						
Alternate	(P. 1)	6.50	9.50	8.00	17.31****	a < b,c**
If-then	(P. 2)	9.00	11.00	14.00	11.35***	a < b < c**
Chronol.	(P. 3)	6.14	7.82	8.87	25.95****	a < b < c**
Questions	(P. 4)	3.60	6.20	7.80	52.40****	a < b < c**
Items	(P. 5)	4.50	11.00	14.00	37.65****	a < b < c**
Domains	(P. 6)	2.40	3.90	6.10	38.00****	a < b < c**
Gen. Labels	(P. 7)	2.85	4.50	5.80	12.20****	a < b < c**
Steps/1st	(P. 8)	2.90	3.80	5.70	34.02****	a < b*/a < c**/b < c**
Steps/alt.	(P. 9)	2.30	3.90	4.00	1.16	
Steps/all	(P. 10)	5.20	7.70	9.70	7.73**	a < b < c**
Overall eval.		1.73	2.58	3.65	16.00****	a < b < c**
Sit. 1		2.00	3.50	4.00	50.63****	a < b,c**
Sit. 2		1.50	3.00	3.50	56.70****	a < b < c**
Sit. 3		2.50	3.00	3.80	8.56**	a,b < c**
Sit. 4		1.80	2.20	3.70	21.60****	a,b < c**
Sit. 5		2.00	2.50	3.30	3.78*	a < b,c*
Sit. 6		1.00	2.80	3.70	12.18****	a < b < c**

		CO 0 (n = 18)	CO 3 (n = 6)	CO 4 (n = 6)	F	
Sit. 7		2.00	2.50	4.30	8.47**	a,b < c**
Sit. 8		2.00	2.30	3.70	24.30****	a,b < c**
Sit. 9		2.00	3.00	4.50	22.50****	a < b < c**
Sit. 10		2.50	3.00	4.00	20.45****	a < b < c**
Time	(C. 1)	13.00	11.00	13.00	2.42 ($p < .10$)	
Location	(C. 2)	19.00	20.50	15.00	2.88 ($p < .10$)	
Quantity	(C. 3)	3.00	6.50	2.50	18.30****	a,c < b**
Sensory Qual.	(C. 4)	1.50	2.00	2.00	2.09	
Emotions	(C. 5)	2.00	2.50	4.00	24.30****	a,b < c**
Judgments	(C. 6)	4.00	2.50	4.50	2.63 ($p < .10$)	
Cognitive Qual.	(C. 7)	3.00	2.50	1.80	2.25	
Age 11						
Alternate	(P. 1)	5.68	7.65	8.42	16.41****	a < b < c**
If-then	(P. 2)	7.43	8.65	14.50	8.81**	a < b*/a,b < c**
Chronol.	(P. 3)	7.33	8.00	9.00	3.52*	a,b < c*
Questions	(P. 4)	2.60	3.60	5.40	23.58****	a,b < c**
Items	(P. 5)	7.00	10.33	11.00	7.14**	a < b,c**
Domains	(P. 5)	4.80	7.57	10.85	23.46****	a < b < c**
Gen. Labels	(P. 7)	5.71	6.60	10.20	6.54**	a < b < c**
Steps/1st	(P. 8)	2.50	4.10	6.70	15.49****	a < b < c**
Steps/alt.	(P. 9)	2.18	3.89	5.10	13.48****	a < b < c**
Steps/all	(P. 10)	5.43	7.90	11.80	17.04****	a < b < c**
Overall eval.		2.81	3.40	3.84	26.30****	a < b < c**
Sit. 1		3.00	3.18	3.60	8.10**	a,b < c**
Sit. 2		2.80	3.42	3.67	13.14****	a < b < c**
Sit. 3		2.95	3.43	4.00	43.20****	a < b < c**
Sit. 4		2.75	3.50	3.86	6.75**	a < b < c**
Sit. 5		2.80	3.47	4.00	51.30****	a < b,c**
Sit. 6		2.45	3.39	3.87	21.65****	a < b < c**

135

Table 4.3. (Cont.)

Planning variable[a]		Means of groups[b]			F	Significant group dif.[b]
		CO 0 ($n = 18$)	CO 3 ($n = 6$)	CO 4 ($n = 6$)		
Sit. 7		2.68	3.34	3.80	9.64***	a < b**/b < c*
Sit. 8		2.10	3.59	3.82	32.00****	a < b,c**
Sit. 9		2.81	3.50	3.90	13.15****	a < b < c**
Sit. 10		2.85	3.16	3.85	3.94*	a,b < c**
Time	(C. 1)	11.00	10.00	16.67	13.44****	a,b < c**
Location	(C. 2)	10.00	15.00	17.00	9.20***	a < b < c**
Quantity	(C. 3)	4.80	9.00	4.50	3.42*	a,c < b**
Sensory Qual.	(C. 4)	1.60	2.00	2.50	2.06	
Emotions	(C. 5)	2.70	6.50	3.00	8.19**	a,c < b**
Judgments	(C. 6)	9.00	2.00	4.00	12.20***	a < c < b**
Cognitive Qual.	(C. 7)	2.41	6.33	3.80	18.25***	a < c < b**

[a]"P." variables are the measures of general planning skills; "Sit." variables are the global evaluation measures of plan adequacy in each Planning Situation separately; "C." variables are measures reflecting cognitive contents. See text for description of variables.

[b]Comparisons between pairs of means were done in accordance with the Newman–Keuls method. The letters "a–e" refer to the means in the groups of CO scores in their order of listing.

*$p < .05$.
**$p < .01$.
***$p < .001$.
****$p < .0001$.

136

in 5-year olds at least on the $p < .05$ level, the next two were predicted in 5-year olds only on the $p < .10$ level, and the last two were not at all predicted in 5-year olds. Thus, the list of general planning skills predicted in 7-year olds includes all the variables predicted in 5-year olds as well as those related to CO scores on the $p < .10$ level of significance, and additional variables (i.e., the number of questions and the number of steps in major plans). Further, CO scores predicted 8 out of the 10 global evaluation measures of plan adequacy in the specific Planning Situations (the two unpredicted Planning Situations are Nos. 6 and 9, but there is in addition an irregularity in the order of the means in Planning Situation No. 7), and the overall mean of the 10 global evaluation measures.

In the group of 9-year olds, CO scores predicted all the variables of general planning skills and the global evaluation measures of plan adequacy in the specific Planning Situations predicted in 5-year olds and 7-year olds, and in addition further variables, i.e., the number of steps in all presented plans (Var. No. 10), the number of alternatives (Var. No. 1; though the order of the means is irregular), and two further global evaluation measures of plan adequacy (in Planning Situations Nos. 6 and 9). Thus, in 9-year olds, CO scores predicted 9 out of the 10 variables of general planning skills (the only unpredicted measure was Var. No. 9) and all 10 global evaluation measures and their mean.

In the group of 11-year olds, CO scores predicted all the variables of general planning skills predicted in 5-, 7- and 9-year olds, including the number of alternate plans (Var. No. 1) with regularly ordered means, and in addition the number of steps in alternate plans (Var. No. 9). Also, CO scores predicted all the global evaluation measures and their mean, as in the group of 9-year olds. Thus, in 11-year olds all variables of general planning skills and all global evaluation measures and their mean were predicted by CO scores.

Concerning the planning variables that were unpredicted by CO scores in the different age groups, it is worthwhile to note that in about 80% of the cases their means are in the order of magnitude that corresponds to the CO scores. This indicates that even in regard to these variables, the distribution of scores is already not completely random.

Concerning the seven variables reflecting contents in planning, in 5-year olds, one (Sensory Qualities) was related significantly to CO scores, but the means were not regularly ordered; in 7-year olds, six variables (Temporal Qualities; Locational Qualities; Quantity; Sensory Qualities; Cognitive Qualities; Judgments and Evaluations) were related significantly to CO scores, but only in one case (Temporal Qualities) was the ordering of the means regular as expected; in 9-year olds, two variables

(Quantity; Feelings and Emotions) were related significantly to CO scores, but the ordering of means was regular only in the latter; and in 11-year olds, six variables (all except Sensory Qualities) were related significantly to CO scores, but only in one case (Locational Qualities) were the means ordered regularly.

6. *Conclusions and discussion.* The major findings concern the relations between CO scores and the variables assessing planning. The findings show that CO scores are related significantly and linearly in the expected order to the variables assessing the general planning skills and the global evaluation measures of the adequacy of planning in the specific Planning Situations (the content variables will be dealt with separately). These findings support the major hypothesis of this part of the study, which is that CO scores would be related to planning, conceived as a cognitive activity. Because CO scores are an index measure of beliefs, the findings indicate that the act of planning is a function of the specific beliefs one has. These include beliefs about oneself (e.g., "Before I go somewhere, I myself think about all the things I may need and do not leave the job only to my mother"); beliefs about the environment and other people, that is, General Beliefs (e.g., "If a child does not watch carefully the way to thc kindergarten, he will not be able to find it when he goes alone"); Beliefs about Norms ("Before you start playing a game, you have to prepare everything you may need for the game"); and Beliefs about Goals (e.g., "I want to be a child who does not start a drawing before she knows what kind of drawing it would be"). The specific beliefs mentioned above were found to be related to the act of planning because they are related to the meaning of planning (as established in pretests) and represent the four types of beliefs that guide behavior, i.e., beliefs about norms, about goals, about oneself, and general beliefs. In view of previous studies (Kreitler & Kreitler, 1982), it should be emphasized that only the four kinds of beliefs together are related to behavior and not one or two types of beliefs separately. Moreover, because it was previously shown that changing the relevant beliefs of the four kinds brings about a change in the behavior in line with the changed beliefs, we emphasize that the behavior is a function of the beliefs and that it may be predicted on the basis of the beliefs.

In the present study, CO scores were found to be related to planning variables on the different age levels, including the lowest age level of 5 years. As mentioned, this finding as such is not surprising in view of previous studies in which CO scores were related to behaviors in children as young as 5 years (see section II.C.1). However, the remarkable point about the findings in this study is that the relation of CO scores to planning spreads gradually from the lowest to the highest age level to an increasing number of the examined variables. Concerning the measures of general planning skills, in the group of 5-year olds, 30% of these measures were predicted by CO scores; in the group of 7-year olds, 70% were; in the group of 9-year olds, 90% were; and in the group of 11-year olds, 100% were. Moreover, the trend is completely regular: The variables predicted at a higher age level include all those predicted at a lower age level and several additional variables. Notably, variables that at a lower age level were related to CO scores only marginally (on the level of $p < .10$) become related to CO scores more firmly (on the level of at least $p < .05$) at the higher age level.

In our opinion, the regular spread of the predictive range of CO scores in regard to planning depends on the gradual development of planning itself. Because the CO score predicts planning variables in four age groups, it has to be regarded as an adequate predictor of planning. The failure of predicting a certain variable at an earlier age level may be due to the fact that the variable has not yet become a manifestation of planning. For example, it is likely that CO scores of planning did not predict the number of alternate plans in 5- and 7-year olds because younger children form few alternate plans, or in other words, their planning zeal is manifested in other ways such as chronological ordering (Var. No. 3) and considering different domains (Var. No. 6). Also in the field of curiosity it was found that a particular variable such as patterned alternation manifested curiosity in one age level but not in another (Kreitler, Zigler, & Kreitler, 1976, 1984).

The conclusion that the relation of CO scores to planning is affected by age is of particular importance in a developmental context. A variable that does not reflect planning on one age level may reflect planning on a more advanced age level. Thus the changing predictive range of CO scores sheds light on the developmental course of planning. Table 4.3 shows that the core variables manifesting planning from the age of 5 onward are the number of domains (Var. No. 6), the number of general labels (Var. No. 7), and the number of chronological orderings in the plans (Var. No. 3). It is likely that the number of considered domains reflects the breadth of the meaning assigned to the problem; that general labels are summary statements indicating the major foci of the plan, specifying the areas in which most of the planning activity is to be concentrated; whereas chronological ordering represents the nuclear scheme for a program sequence. On the level of 7-year olds, these core variables are complemented by the number of questions (Var. No. 4), the number of items (Var. No. 5), the number of steps in major plans (Var. No. 8), and the number of if–then considerations (Var. No. 2). Whereas the first two (Var. Nos. 4 and 5) probably reflect a specification of the number of domains (Var. No. 6) and hence an increased consideration of aspects involved in the problem, the latter two (Var. Nos. 8 and 2) represent an advance in the act of planning itself. The increase in the number of steps in the plan indicates that the plan becomes richer and more complex; whereas the growing number of if–then considerations suggests that a new principle has been introduced into planning, bringing about the evocation of new units to be incorporated into the plan and binding together different steps or even parts of the plan. Thus, there is evidence for an increase both in the richness and the complexity of the plan's organizational structure. On the level of 9-year olds, the further development in complexity is manifested not only in if–then considerations but also in the presentation of more full-fledged alternatives to the major plans (Var. No. 1) and in the tendency to elaborate them more fully (as reflected in the significant relation of CO scores to Var. No. 10). In 11-year olds, this latter tendency turns into a firm fact. On this age level, development encompasses the alternative plans that become as elaborate as the major plans (Var. No. 9). Thus, in 11-year olds the orbit has broadened to include all the studied general planning skills. Of course, this does not indicate that there is no further progress in planning. Even in the set of variables considered in this study, there is evidence for trends of future development: Plans may become more abstract and tightly organized (see the strengthened relation of CO scores with general labels in 11-year olds) and hence more generally applicable; or, planning may become more economical in meaning assignment (see the slightly weakened relation of CO scores to Var. No. 4 in 11-year olds) and thus faster and more efficient.

The developmental course may be considered also in terms of the number of global evaluations of plan adequacy predicted by CO scores. The findings show that the number of Planning Situations in which plan adequacy is predicted significantly by CO scores increases from 70% in 5-year olds, to 80% in 7-year olds, and then to 100% in 9- and 11-year olds. The overall mean of these 10 measures was predicted already from the age of 7 years on. These results suggest that the child tends early to enlarge the range of situations in which (s)he applies planning, and that this tendency is bound from the very beginning to motivations grounded in cognitive contents. The predictive range in 5-year olds may be so surprisingly high (70%!) perhaps because the planning situations were selected as particularly meaningful for children.

It may be recalled that the third group of variables reflects the use of different kinds of contents, that is, interpretations and considerations, in planning. The results show that CO scores were related significantly to 14.3% of these variables in 5-year olds, to 85.7% in 7-year olds, to 28.6% in 9-year olds, and to 85.7% in 11-year olds. The findings for contents variables differ from those for the other variables in (a) the overall mean percentage of variables predicted by CO scores across all age groups (53.4% versus 75% for the general planning skills and 84.1% for the global evaluations); (b) the low degree of regularity in the ordering of means in line with CO scores (10% of all cases in which CO scores were related to contents variables versus 97% in the other two groups of variables); and (c) the absence of a regular pattern of developmental progression in the number and kind of variables related to CO scores (in contrast to the progression identified in the case of the other two groups of variables). Accordingly, it seems plausible to conclude that the frequency with which interpretations and considerations of particular kinds of contents are used in planning represents an aspect of planning that is not predicted by CO scores to the same degree as other aspects of planning, mainly those reflected in the complexity, the richness, and the adequacy of plans.

III. The cognitive antecedents of planning

A. The general and specific contributions of meaning to planning

Within the framework of the motivational–cognitive approach to planning described in section I, it was assumed that planning is a complex phenomenon, some aspects of which are more amenable to study in motivational terms whereas others are more amenable to study in cognitive terms. In section II, we focused on the motivational facet, studying the relations of CO scores to different measures of planning (section II.C). The findings (sections II.C.5 & 6) showed that CO scores are correlated primarily with measures of planning, reflecting the complexity, richness, and adequacy of plans. Thus, CO scores predict the extent to which a child will apply him- or herself to the act of planning. Yet, because planning is essentially a cognitive act, the findings show that CO scores predict in fact the extent to which the child will use his or her cognitive resources in planning.

It is evident, however, that the cognitive quality of planning would differ across children in line with individual differences in the cognitive abilities necessary for planning. Hence, over and beyond the motivational impact, there is also the cognitive impact. Its importance was highlighted earlier in regard to the variables reflecting the frequency in planning of interpretations and considerations in particular domains of contents. These variables were not predicted by CO scores to the same high extent as the other planning variables, possibly because the use of these variables depends to a higher degree on purely cognitive processes and contents. Yet, there is every reason to expect that cognitive processes and contents affect also the planning variables of the other groups, for all planning variables have a cognitive facet, regardless of whether they are predicted by CO scores or not.

As mentioned in the introductory section (I), our approach to cognition is primarily content oriented and therefore psychosemantic. We regard cognition as the meaning processing system that combines and produces meanings by exploiting semantic implications (Kreitler & Kreitler, 1976, chap. 2; S. Kreitler & Kreitler, in press-a). We define "meaning" as a referent-centered pattern of meaning values. "Referent" may be any stimulus ranging from a sensory cue or a word, to a picture, a total situation, or even a whole historical period, whereas "meaning values" are contents that may differ in their mode of expression, veridicality, and interpersonal sharedness. A unit of meaning consists of a referent and at least one meaning value. Units of meaning are characterized in terms of the following four sets of variables: (a) *Meaning Dimensions,* which describe the contents of the meaning values (e.g., Material, Sensory Qualities); (b) *Types of Relation,* which describe the manner in which the meaning values are related to the referent (e.g., in an attributive or comparative manner); (c) *Forms of Relation,* which describe the formal–logical relations of the meaning values to the referent (e.g., positive assertion, conjunction); and (d) *Referent-Shift Variables,* which describe the relations between the present referent and the previous referent(s) or the input in the chain of responses given to one input (e.g., identity, association). The four sets of meaning variables comprise the meaning system. A complete list of the variables of the meaning system and their definitions appears in Table 4.4.

Meaning is assessed by means of a questionnaire in which the subject is requested to communicate the interpersonally shared and personal meanings of a standard set of terms and phrases to an hypothetical person of his or her own choice, using any means of expression considered adequate. The responses are coded in terms of the standard list of meaning variables, each unit being coded on one meaning dimension, one type of relation, one form of relation, and one referent shift variable. For example, for the term "table," a subject's response might be "It is made of metal, and it stands where the other furniture is." This response includes two meaning units, and both are coded. The first is in the meaning

Table 4.4. *Major variables of the meaning system*

Meaning variable	Definition
Meaning dimensions (Dim.)	
Dim. 1. Contextual Allocation	Superordinate concept or structure to which the referent belongs. Eye: an organ, part of the body.
Dim. 2a+b. Range of Inclusion	Items that the referent includes as parts (Dim. 2b) or members of the class(es) it designates (Dim. 2a). Plant: includes leaves, trees.
Dim. 3. Function, Purpose, & Role	Functions of the referent or uses to which it is often put. Clock: shows the time.
Dim. 4a+b. Action & Potentialities for Action	Actions that the referent does or could do (Dim. 4a), or that are done to it or with it (Dim. 4b). Man: works and dreams; is sent to fight.
Dim 5. Manner of Occurrence or Operation	Stages, processes, acts, instruments involved in the occurrence or operation of the referent. Eating: bringing food into the mouth, munching, swallowing.
Dim. 6. Antecedents & Causes	The necessary and/or sufficient conditions for the referent's existence or operation. Sleeping: tiredness.
Dim. 7. Consequences or Results	Direct or indirect consequences of the referent's existence or operation. Hunger: eating.
Dim. 8a+b. Domain of Application	The items to which the referent is usually applied, serving as subject (Dim. 8a) or object (Dim. 8b) for them. Love: People love; you can love animals.
Dim. 9. Material	The material of which the referent is made. Ring: metal.
Dim. 10. Structure	The referent's structure or organization. Society: has a hierarchical structure.
Dim. 11. State & Possible Changes in It	The referent's actual or potential state and changes that could occur in it. Man: can be healthy, strong, sick.
Dim. 12. Weight & Mass	The referent's estimated or measured weight. Letter: weighs about 5 grams.
Dim. 13. Size & Dimensionality	The referent's estimated or measured size and spatial dimensionality. Point: tiny, bidimensional.
Dim. 14. Quantity & Number	The referent's estimated or measured quantity. Children: more than 50% of the population.
Dim. 15. Locational Qualities	The referent's place in absolute or relative terms. Moon: closer to the earth than to the sun.
Dim. 16. Temporal Qualities	The time at which the referent exists or existed, its duration. Love: may last for a lifetime.
Dim. 17a+b. Possession & Belongingness	The referent's possession (Dim. 17a) and to whom it belongs (Dim. 17b). Mr. Z: poor; TV: owned by the state.
Dim. 18. Development	The referent's ontogenetic or phylogenetic development, its history, & forerunners. Mail: was once sent by pigeons.
Dim. 19a+b. Sensory Qualities	Sensory qualities characterizing the referent (Dim. 19a) or perceivable by the referent (Dim. 19b), incl. visual (form, color, brightness, transparency), auditory, olfactory, internal (temperature, pain, kinesthetic), etc.

Table 4.4. *(cont.)*

Meaning variable	Definition
Dim. 20a+b. Feelings & Emotions	Feelings and emotions evoked by the referent (Dim. 20a) or felt by the referent (Dim. 20b). Mr. C: scares children; is unable to love.
Dim. 21a+b. Judgments, Opinions, & Evaluations	Judgment, opinions, and evaluations concerning the referent (Dim. 21a) or held by the referent (Dim 21b). Mr. Z: is dangerous; believes in death penalty.
Dim. 22a+b. Cognitive Qualities	Cognitive qualities and actions of the referent (Dim. 22b) or evoked by it (Dim. 22a). Mrs. L: very clever; reminds me of Mrs. M.
Types of relation (TR)	
TR 1a+b. Attributive	Specifying certain attributes as qualities of the referent, related to it as qualities to a substance (TR 1a) or as actions to their agent/doer (TR 1b). Child: small; plays.
TR 2a+b+c+d. Comparative	The meaning values are related to the referent through the intermediation of another meaning value or referent, reflecting similarity (TR 2a), dissimilarity (TR 2b), complementariness (TR 2c), or relationality (TR 2d). Sea: like the sky; unlike the soil; smaller than the ocean.
TR 3a+b+c. Exemplifying–Illustrative	The meaning values are related to the referent as exemplifying instances (TR 3a), or as exemplifying situations (TR 3b), or as exemplifying scenes (TR 3c). Happiness: a parent going for a walk with his/her child.
TR 4a+b+c+d. Metaphoric–Symbolic	The meaning values are related to the referent in a mediated nonconventional manner, as interpretations (TR 4a), conventional metaphors (TR 4b), original metaphors (TR 4c), or symbols (i.e., complex metaphors solving a problem imaginally) (TR 4d). Life: produced by destruction; destroys by producing; like a river.
Modes of meaning	
Lex. Mode	Lexical mode; interpersonally shared meanings. Defined as the attributive and comparative types of relation.
Pers. Mode	Personal mode; personal–subjective meanings. Defined as the exemplifying–illustrative and the metaphoric–symbolic types of relation.
Forms of relation (FR)	
FR 1. Positive	The meaning value is related to the referent positively. Table: round.
FR 2. Negative	The meaning value is related to the referent negatively. Table: not big.
FR 3. Mixed Positive & Negative	It is emphasized that the meaning value characterizes the referent only sometimes, to some extent. Apple: sometimes red.
FR 4. Conjunctive	It is emphasized that two or more meaning values characterize the referent conjuctively. Life: wonderful *and* difficult.

Table 4.4. *(cont.)*

Meaning variable	Definition
FR 5. Disjunctive	It is emphasized that of two or more presented meaning values, only one applies. Sickness: either serious or nothing.
FR 6. Combined Positive & Negative	It is emphasized that of two stated meaning values, one does not apply whereas the other does apply. Loneliness: not physical aloneness but psychological solitude.
FR 7. Obligatory	The meaning value relates to the referent in an obligatory sense. Law: should be obeyed.
Shifts in referent (SR)	
SR 1. Identical	Referent is identical with previous (or presented) referent.
SR 2. Opposite	Referent is the opposite (or negation) of previous (or presented) referent. Presented referent is "to eat," and subject communicates the meaning of "not to eat."
SR 3. Partial	Referent is a part or a subspecies of the previous (or presented) referent. Previous referent was "car" and present referent is "Mercedes."
SR 4. Previous Meaning Value	Referent is the whole or part of a previous meaning value.
SR 5. Modified	Referent is the previous (or presented) referent combined with a previous meaning value.
SR 6. Higher-Level Referent	Referent is a combination of several previous meaning values.
SR 7. Associative	Referent is related to previous (or presented) referent only by some association.
SR 8. Grammatical Variation	Referent is a grammatical variation of previous (or presented) referent. Previous referent was "to love" and subject responds to "loving" or "loved."
SR 9. Linguistic Label	Referent is the previous (or presented) referent considered as a linguistic label; includes etymological or phonemic responses.
SR 10. Unrelated	Referent is not related in any obvious way to previous (or presented) referent.

dimension Material, its type of relation is attributive, its form of relation is positive, and its referent is identical to the input. The second meaning unit is in the meaning dimension Locational Qualities, its type of relation is comparative (subtype: similarity), its form of relation is positive, and its referent is identical to the input. Again, if the subject responded to the input "to eat" with "Not eating leads to death," the response includes one meaning value and is coded as using the meaning dimension Consequences and Results, the attributive type of relation, the positive form of relation, and a referent which is the opposite of the input.´

The total of coded units in a person's responses to the meaning questionnaire produces the person's "meaning profile," that is, a list of the frequencies with which each meaning variable was used by the person. In order to control for differences in the number of responses, for purposes of statistical analyses the raw frequencies are converted into proportions out of the total number of meaning units in the individual's questionnaire.

Previous research has shown that the relative frequency of usage of a meaning variable in an individual's meaning profile is indicative of the individual's preference for that meaning variable, that is, it is related to the frequency with which the individual uses the meaning variable in various cognitive tasks. For example, if Locational Qualities predominate in an individual's meaning profile, that individual would tend to use meaning values of Locational Qualities in various tasks and would perform well in a task like mazes, which draws on mastery of locational contents (S. Kreitler & Kreitler, in press-a).

Meaning variables can affect cognitive functioning in two complementary ways, as contents and as cognitive processes. A meaning value can be considered as a classification of the contents of meaning values or as a cognitive process underlying the elicitation of a specific kind of meaning values. The former viewpoint is more static, emphasizing the availability of specific cognitive contents, whereas the latter viewpoint is more dynamic, emphasizing the impact of particular meanings and meaning variables on specific cognitive processes. In some contexts (e.g., when retrieval from memory is at issue), it makes more sense to focus on the available contents of meaning, whereas in other contexts (e.g., when problem solving is at issue), it makes more sense to focus on the semantic implications of particular meaning values or the dynamizing impact of meaning dimensions like Antecedents and Causes, or Consequences and Results. Thus, in some tasks the impact of meaning variables is manifest more in the form of the particular cognitive contents used, whereas in other tasks, more in the form of specific cognitive processes.

In the case of planning, we expected both kinds of impact to be evident. Insofar as planning requires the evocation and application of specific cognitive contents, it promotes the manifestation of actual meaning values in the form of interpretations and considerations corresponding in contents to the different meaning dimensions. Indeed, meaning values singly (e.g., "red," "to the right") and in combinations in the form of images (e.g., a map) and beliefs (e.g., norm beliefs like "First one should lift the lid, then put in the clothes, etc.") constitute the raw materials of plans in particular and behavioral programs in general. Hence, it is to be expected that in devising a plan, subjects would use different kinds of contents corresponding to meaning dimensions. Yet, insofar as planning involves thinking and problem solving, it enables the manifestation of meaning variables as processes, in the form of, say, causal analysis, drawing of inferences, categorizing, and labeling or stating analogies corresponding to the meaning dimensions Antecedents and Causes, Consequences and Results, Contextual Allocation, and the comparative type of relation, respectively. The impact of meaning on the cognitive contents in plans is specific; that is, one expects a relation between the salience of the meaning variable in the individual's meaning profile and the frequency of usage of the *same* variable in planning. The impact of meaning on the cognitive processes in planning is of a more general kind; hence, one expects interrelations between a whole set of meaning variables in the individual's meaning profile and the individual's scores on particular measures of planning.

B. Study: investigating the relations of meaning to planning

1. Hypotheses. Two general hypotheses guided the investigation of the relations between meaning and planning (see section II.C). The first dealt with the specific impact of meaning variables on planning: The frequency of using, in planning, specific interpretations and considerations relating to contents and processes bound with particular meaning dimensions would be related positively with the frequency of use of these meaning dimensions in the individual's meaning profile. This general hypothesis served as framework for the set of 14 specific hypotheses summarized in Table 4.5. Hypotheses 1–7 deal with the relations between the frequency of use of some specific kind of contents in the planning activity of the subject (manifested in the form of particular contents and interpretations in all 10 Planning Situations) and the frequency of use of that same kind of contents in the subject's meaning profile (manifested in the form of meaning values along the meaning dimensions corresponding to those contents). The seven particular kinds of contents were selected because they were used in planning by at least 10% of the children in each age group. Hypotheses 8–10 deal with the relations of frequencies of use of meaning dimensions in the meaning profiles and particular measures of general planning skills. The latter were selected because they presumably capitalize on the use of a single dominant meaning dimension. The par-

Table 4.5. *Correlation coefficients between contents variables in planning and use of specific meaning dimensions in the individual's meaning profile*

No. of hypoth.	Planning variable	Meaning dimension[a]	Correlation coefficients[b] in group			
			5	7	9	11
1	Frequency of considerations concerning time in all 10 Planning Situations	Temporal Qual. Dim. 16	.19	.34*	.79***	.43*
2	Frequency of considerations concerning locations in all 10 Planning Situations	Locational Qual. Dim. 15	−.23	.71***	.73***	.62***
3	Frequency of considerations concerning quantities and numbers in all 10 Planning Situations	Quantity and Number Dim. 14	.37*	.29	−.48**	.36*
4	Frequency of considerations concerning sensations in all 10 Planning Situations	Sensory Qual. Dim. 19a	.35*	.27	.98***	.76***
		Dim. 19b	.15	−.05	.03	−.19
		Dim. 19a+b	.38*	−.30	.96***	.35*
5	Frequency of considerations concerning feelings and emotions in all 10 Planning Situations	Feelings & Emotions Dim 20a	.25	.47**	.35*	.54**
		Dim. 20b	.41*	.50*	.36*	.59***
		Dim. 20a+b	.48**	.60***	.81***	.59***
6	Frequency of considerations concerning cognitive properties in all 10 Planning Situations	Cognitive Qual. Dim. 22a	−.30	.51**	.36*	.62***
		Dim. 22b	.10	.14	−.02	.26
		Dim. 22a+b	−.30	.49**	.33	.40*
7	Frequency of considerations concerning judgments and evaluations in all 10 Planning Situations	Judgments & Eval. Dim. 21a	.56***	.99***	.96***	.85***
		Dim. 21b	.20	.95***	−.54**	−.23
		Dim. 21a+b	.59***	.96***	.81***	.93***

#	Planning variable	Meaning dimension				
8	Frequency of chronological orderings in all 10 Planning Situations (Var. 3, section II.B.3)	Temporal Qual. Dim. 16	.38*	.36*	.96***	.84***
9	Frequency of general labels in all 10 Planning Situations (Var. 3, section II.B.3)	Manner of Occurrence. Dim. 5	.52**	.88***	.36*	.99***
10	Frequency of if-then considerations in all 10 Planning Situations (Var. 2, section II.B.3)	Causes & Anteced. Dim. 6	.51**	.68***	.82***	.88***
11	Drawing route of program in Planning Situation No. 10 vs. not drawing it	Locational Qual. Dim. 15	.21	.66***	.68***	.49***
12	Asking about time (opening & closing of stores, visits and traveling) in Planning Situation No. 10 vs. not asking	Temporal Qual. Dim. 16	.40*	.71***	.48**	.53***
13	Asking about locations (of stores & people) or distances in Planning Situation No. 10 vs. not asking	Locational Qual. Dim. 15	.29	.74***	.82***	.37*
14	Planning for more than one day in Planning Situation No. 8 vs. less than one day	Temporal Qual. Dim. 16	.54**	.50**	.77***	.52**

[a] Each listed meaning dimension was hypothesized as relevant for the particular planning variable mentioned in the specific hypothesis. All predictions entail a positive relation between the frequency of use of the planning variable and the proportional frequency of use of the meaning dimension in the subject's meaning profile.

[b] Pearson's product–moment correlations were used in the case of hypotheses 1–10; point biserial correlations were used in the case of hypotheses 11–14.

*p < .05.
**p < .01.
***p < .001.

ticular expected relations are based on previous research (S. Kreitler & Kreitler, in press-a), which showed that individuals high in Temporal Qualities tend to arrange presented events sequentially more than those low in this meaning dimension; subjects with high use of Manner of Occurrence and Operation succeed in analyzing a sequence of events into a set of interrelated headings better than those with low use of this meaning dimension; and subjects who use Causes and Antedecents more frequently tend to draw conclusions and focus on implications more than people with a low frequency of use of this meaning dimension. Finally, hypotheses 11–14 deal with the relations between frequencies of use of meaning dimensions in the meaning profiles, and measures in specific Planning Situations that emphasize the use of particular meaning dimensions. The latter measures were selected in order to demonstrate that the individual's meaning profile affects specific measures in addition to the summative scores referred to in hypotheses 1–7. All hypotheses deal exclusively with meaning dimensions because they focus solely on cognitive contents.

The second general hypothesis was that planning, as manifested in the global evaluation of planning across the 10 Planning Situations (see section II.C.3) would be related to a particular set of meaning variables reflecting various cognitive processes involved in planning. The specific hypotheses pertinent to this second general hypothesis were based partly on previous research about the meaning of behavioral programs (Kreitler & Kreitler, 1976, pp. 322–331; also Ziv-Av, 1978) and partly on previous research about the relations of meaning variables to cognitive functioning (S. Kreitler & Kreitler, in press-a , in press-b). These specific hypotheses can be divided into four groups in line with the four sets of meaning variables. First, we expected that planning would be related positively to the following meaning dimensions: Actions (Dim. 4a), Manner of Occurrence and Operation (Dim. 5), Locational Qualities (Dim. 15), Temporal Qualities (Dim. 16), Domain of Application (Dim. 8), Contextual Allocation (Dim. 1), Antecedents and Causes (Dim. 6) and Consequences and Results (Dim. 7) because of the role the former five play in the meaning of behavioral programs and the latter three in problem solving. Second, we expected planning to be related positively to the types of relation reflecting interpersonally shared meaning (the attributive and comparative) and negatively to the types of relation reflecting personal meaning (the exemplifying–illustrative and metaphoric–symbolic) because efficient planning requires enhanced consideration of interpersonally shared reality. Third, we expected planning to be related positively to the complex forms of relation (i.e., conjunctive, disjunctive, sometimes, "not this but this") because of the importance of those logical connections in problem solving as described earlier in this section. And fourth, we expected planning to be related positively to referent shift variables, reflecting a medium degree of shifting away from the previous or presented referents, because this degree of shifting is optimal for thinking whereas sticking too closely to previous referents may limit thinking, and shifting too far away may reduce the efficiency of the solution.

2. The task and procedure. As stated in section II.C.4, all subjects of all age groups were administered the meaning questionnaire, which included 15 terms and phrases in random order (i.e., school, I, but, why, inside, happy, a child fell, went away in anger, bright red, a long way, to eat, wisdom, to love, heard a melody, fast). The subject was requested to communicate the meaning of the stimuli – that is, the interpersonally shared and the personal meaning – to an hypothetical person (not the experimenter), using any modality of expression the subject considered adequate (e.g., talking, drawing, enacting, describing drawings, etc.). The task was administered individually. The experimenter sat by the subject and wrote down the responses. After each response, (s)he asked only once: "Anything else?" The responses were coded independently by two graduate students in psychology. The mean intercoder reliability across all questionnaires was $r = .95$. In order to control for varying number of responses (i.e., meaning values), the frequency of usage of each meaning variable in each questionnaire was transformed into a proportion out of the total of responses in that questionnaire.

Concerning the subjects of the study, the Planning Situations, and the measures of planning, see sections II.C.2–4.

3. Results. a. Development of the meaning variables. Before examining the findings concerning the stated hypotheses, we studied the distribution of use of each meaning variable in each age group. Table 4.6 presents the mean percentages for each group of all the meaning variables mentioned in sections III and IV of this chapter. Table 4.6 presents two important kinds of information: (a) about development across groups, and (b) about relative frequencies within groups. The comparison of means among the four age groups showed that the changes across ages were significant in 93.7% of all meaning variables (i.e., in 74 out of 79 cases). The five variables in which there were no significant changes include three variables that were not used at all (i.e., Dim. 12, TR 4a, SR 7; for the code, see Table 4.4) and only two variables that actually did not change significantly (i.e., Dim. 19a, Dim. 19a+b; for the code, see Table

Table 4.6. *Mean percentages and comparisons of the meaning variables in the four age groups*

Meaning variables	Age groups				F	Developmental trend
	5	7	9	11		
Meaning dimensions						
Contextual Allocation (Dim. 1)	.62	1.15	2.01	3.84	18.198****	linear increase
R. of Inclusion (classes) (Dim. 2a)	.49	.46	.00	.59	3.349*	U pattern
R. of Inclusion (parts) (Dim. 2b)	.89	.86	1.16	.84	11.082****	irregular
R. of Inclusion (Dim. 2a+b)	1.38	1.32	1.16	1.43	8.365****	U pattern
Function (Dim. 3)	.51	1.68	3.38	2.73	31.479****	increase to 9
Actions (active) (Dim. 4a)	17.45	16.89	14.16	14.68	18.062****	U pattern
Actions (passive) (Dim. 4b)	12.74	10.92	10.61	8.43	32.413****	linear decrease
Actions (Dim. 4a+b)	30.19	27.81	24.77	23.10	48.485****	linear decrease
Manner of Occurrence (Dim. 5)	2.63	5.19	4.68	5.15	5.341***	irregular increase
Antecedents & Causes (Dim. 6)	4.19	6.27	7.63	7.76	13.105****	linear increase
Consequences & Results (Dim. 7)	2.83	2.77	3.36	9.99	10.328****	linear increase
Domain of Applic. (subj.) (Dim. 8a)	16.19	14.95	11.60	14.37	28.249****	U pattern
Domain of Applic. (obj.) (Dim. 8b)	15.29	10.61	11.20	11.65	8.006****	U pattern
Domain of Application (Dim. 8a+b)	31.48	25.55	22.80	26.03	24.085****	U pattern
Material (Dim. 9)	.00	.00	.00	.05	9.087****	irregular increase
Structure (Dim. 10)	.00	.13	.00	.30	7.695****	irregular increase
State (Dim. 11)	1.45	1.58	1.59	1.51	6.675****	increase to 9
Weight & Mass (Dim. 12)	.00	.00	.00	.00	—	none
Size (Dim. 13)	.48	.13	.54	1.03	9.532****	U pattern
Quantity & Number (Dim. 14)	1.17	1.37	1.56	1.89	4.013**	linear increase
Locational Qual. (Dim. 15)	6.48	5.03	4.76	4.31	2.897*	linear decrease
Temporal Qual. (Dim. 16)	3.61	4.45	4.67	4.00	2.599*	increase to 9
Possessions (Dim. 17a)	.36	.92	.81	.44	5.675***	inverted U pattern
Belongingness (Dim. 17b)	.54	.46	.00	.59	5.273***	U pattern
Possess. & Belong. (Dim. 17a+b)	.90	1.38	.81	1.03	6.016***	irregular
Development (Dim. 18)	.06	.00	.00	.20	5.986***	U pattern

Sensory Qual. (of referent) (Dim. 19a)	3.33	3.18	2.49	2.71	1.768	U pattern
Sensory Qual. (by referent) (Dim. 19b)	1.01	.77	1.40	1.01	3.247*	irregular
Sensory Qual. (Dim. 19a+b)	4.34	3.95	3.90	3.71	.658	linear decrease
Emotions (evoked by ref.) (Dim. 20a)	.23	.64	.92	.10	13.390****	increase to 9
Emotions (felt by ref.) (Dim. 20b)	3.71	4.14	5.21	5.50	9.262****	linear increase
Feelings & Emotions (Dim. 20a+b)	3.94	4.78	6.13	5.60	15.748****	increase to 9
Judgments (about ref.) (Dim. 21a)	1.52	2.02	3.19	2.22	23.081****	increase to 9
Judgments (of ref.) (Dim. 21b)	.09	.34	.41	.70	11.750****	linear increase
Judgments & Evaluations (Dim. 21a+b)	1.60	2.37	3.60	2.92	44.052****	increase to 9
Cognitive Qual. (of ref.) (Dim. 22a)	.27	.38	.57	1.43	50.077****	linear increase
Cognitive Qual. (by ref.) (Dim. 22b)	1.86	2.70	4.06	3.08	7.452****	increase to 9
Cognitive Qual. (Dim. 22a+b)	2.13	3.09	4.63	4.51	22.885****	increase to 9

Types of relation

Attributive (substantive) (TR 1a)	23.45	30.15	39.38	42.75	34.892****	linear increase
Attributive (agentive) (TR 1b)	11.19	10.26	18.40	13.76	11.323****	irregular increase
Attributive (TR 1a+b)	34.75	40.41	57.78	56.51	69.311****	increase to 9
Comparative (similar) (TR 2a)	1.24	1.91	2.32	.97	8.199****	increase to 9
Comparative (dissimilar) (TR 2b)	.85	.22	.16	.68	7.253****	U pattern
Comparative (complementary) (TR 2c)	.49	.27	.08	.12	4.601**	U pattern
Comparative (relational) (TR 2d)	.35	1.16	1.06	1.62	7.087****	irregular increase
Comparative (TR 2a+b+c+d)	2.94	3.55	3.62	3.39	12.625****	linear increase
Exemplifying (instance) (TR 3a)	38.13	37.44	26.55	30.08	41.924****	U pattern
Exemplifying (situation) (TR 3b)	7.11	12.77	6.07	5.56	19.627****	inverted U pattern
Exemplifying (scene) (TR 3c)	16.93	5.37	4.56	2.14	23.442****	linear decrease
Exemplifying (TR 3a+b+c)	62.17	55.58	37.18	37.79	96.773****	U pattern
Metaphoric (interpretation) (TR 4a)	.00	.00	.00	.00	——	none
Metaphoric (metaphor) (TR 4b+c)	.14	.18	1.04	1.64	16.379****	linear increase
Metaphoric (symbol) (TR 4d)	.00	.27	.38	.67	7.402****	linear increase
Metaphoric (TR 4a+b+c)	.14	.46	1.43	2.31	12.816****	linear increase

Modes of meaning

Lexical Mode	37.68	43.95	61.40	59.90	80.297****	increase to 9
Personal Mode	62.32	56.04	38.60	40.10	54.306****	U pattern

Table 4.6. (cont.)

Meaning variables	Age groups				F	Developmental trend
	5	7	9	11		
Forms of relation						
Positive (FR 1)	93.57	89.20	94.06	90.19	8.742****	irregular
Negative (FR 2)	3.04	4.13	3.19	6.12	12.370****	irregular increase
Mixed Pos. & Neg. (FR 3)	.80	1.84	.26	.77	10.611****	irregular
Conjunctive (FR 4)	1.47	2.09	1.65	.80	15.022****	inverted U pattern
Disjunctive (FR 5)	.88	.63	.00	1.22	5.740***	U pattern
Combined Pos. & Neg. (FR 6)	.24	.69	.15	.59	8.358****	irregular increase
Obligatory (FR 7)	.00	1.43	.69	.26	31.660****	inverted U pattern
Complex (FR 3+4+5+6)	3.39	4.63	2.06	3.38	9.865****	irregular
Positive (FR 1+3+4)	95.84	93.13	95.91	91.79	10.537****	irregular
Negative (FR 2+6)	3.28	4.82	3.34	6.71	13.821****	irregular increase
Shifts in referents						
Identical (SR 1)	33.60	18.88	28.32	25.34	10.617****	irregular
Opposite (SR 2)	.73	.26	.08	.48	8.086****	U pattern
Partial (SR 3)	3.43	4.12	5.73	4.20	10.474****	increase to 9
Previous Meaning Value (SR 4)	.96	4.97	2.82	1.48	61.209****	inverted U pattern
Modified (SR 5)	54.23	59.15	51.78	57.32	4.548**	irregular increase
Higher-level referent (SR 6)	.40	.78	1.62	.89	25.731****	increase to 9
Associative (SR 7)	.00	.00	.00	.00	—	none
Grammatical Variation (SR 8)	.19	2.59	3.33	1.90	22.423****	increase to 9
Linguistic Label (SR 9)	6.16	6.42	5.07	7.04	16.006****	irregular increase
Unrelated (SR 10)	.31	2.83	1.25	1.36	19.508****	irregular
Shift Close (SR 1+3+8)	37.22	25.59	37.38	31.44	15.682****	irregular
Shift Medium (SR 4+5+6)	55.58	64.90	56.21	59.69	20.129****	irregular increase
Shift Far (SR 2+7+9+10)	7.20	9.52	6.41	8.88	9.810****	irregular increase

Note: For the description of the variables, see Table 4.1
$*p < .05.$ $**p < .01.$ $***p < .001.$ $****p < .0001.$

4.4). Thus, change may be identified as a characteristic of meaning variables across ages 5 through 11. Without counting the three variables (3.8% of the variables) with no responses and hence no changes, five kinds of changes were identified:

1. In 49.37% of the variables, usage increased with age (a) linearly from 5 to 11 years (in 15.19% of the variables), or (b) linearly from 5 to 9 years with a slight decrease in 11 years (in 18.99% of the variables), or (c) irregularly so that there was a peak and a trough between the lowest level which was at age 5 and the highest level which was at age 11 (in 15.19% of the variables).
2. In 6.33% of the variables, usage decreased linearly with age, from 5 to 11 years.
3. In 25.32% of the variables, the change assumed the form of a U pattern; that is, there was a decrease in usage from the age of 5 to 9 years (in 22.75% of the variables) or from the age of 5 to 7 years (in 2.53% of the variables) followed by an increase.
4. In 6.33% of the variables, the change was in the form of an inverted U; that is, the initial increase in usage from 5 to 7 years was followed by a decrease in 9 years and further in 11 years.
5. In 11.39% of the variables, the changes were irregular; that is, there was more than one up-and-down cycle from the lowest to the highest levels of frequency, and these levels did not occur at the ages of 5 and 11 years, respectively.

An examination of the different developmental trends shows that the largest group of meaning variables (49.37%) increases in frequency from the lowest to the highest age group. This finding is consistent with the general principle that meaning expands with age; that is, both the number of meaning values in each meaning variable and the number of meaning variables used by each subject increase. Such expansion is expected in view of the gradual accumulation of knowledge and increased mastery of various cognitive processes.

Paradoxically, cognitive development is probably responsible also for declines in usage of some meaning variables across the whole developmental span of 5–11 years or at least a part of it. It is to be expected that cognitive development would lead, for example, to a decline in the use of meaning variables with concrete meaning values like actions (Dim. 4) or dramatizations (TR 3c). Such meaning variables either may remain low in frequency or may undergo a revival accompanied by increase in frequency, probably when the meaning values change. Thus, whereas dramatized exemplifications, akin to as–if fantasy games, decrease in frequency, the whole exemplifying–illustrative type of relation (TR 3a+b+ c) increases again in the older age groups, possibly because it is then used more specifically for communicating personal meanings, as is evident also from the increase in other meaning variables involved in the Personal Mode of Meaning (i.e., TR 3a, TR 4b, TR 4c, TR 4a+b+c, Personal Mode).

However, cognitive development is not the only principle governing the development of meaning. Another major factor is personality development, which may enhance the salience of individually preferred meaning assignment tendencies, singly and in patterns (S. Kreitler & Kreitler, 1983a, 1983b). This factor would lead to a selective promotion and increased differentiation of specific individually preferred meaning variables, sometimes accompanied by a deemphasis and relative weakening of other nonpreferred meaning variables. Accordingly, each child may be expected to increase to some personally determined extent the use of some meaning variables and to decrease the use of others. This development may account mainly for the irregular pattern of change observed in almost 27% of the variables [see irregular change in (5) and irregular increase in (1), in the list above].

As noted, the second important kind of information presented in Table 4.6 concerns relative frequencies of meaning variables within each age group. In regard to meaning dimensions, there is a remarkable homogeneity between the different age groups: In all groups the most frequent meaning dimensions are Actions (Dim. 4a, Dim. 4b, Dim. 4a+b) and Domain of Application (Dim. 8a, Dim. 8b, Dim. 8a+b), whereas the least frequent include Structure (Dim. 10), Material (Dim. 9), and Development (Dim. 18). The situation is different in regard to types of relation. Five- and 7-year olds use the exemplifying–illustrative type of relation more than the attributive one, whereas the reverse is true for 9- and 11-year olds. Correspondingly, in the younger age groups the Personal Mode of meaning is more frequent than the Lexical Mode, whereas in the older age groups the Lexical Mode is more frequent than the Personal Mode. Data of this kind suggest that when subjects get older, they become increasingly competent cognitively in coping with issues objectively, while considering both multiple aspects of the given situation and their individual preferences.

   b. *Meaning variables and measures of planning.*   Table 4.5 presents the data relevant for evaluating the hypotheses stated earlier (section II.B.1), that is, the relations obtained in each age group between particular planning measures concerning contents and the frequency of the corresponding meaning dimensions in the individual's meaning profile.

On the whole, the data support the hypotheses about the specific contribution of meaning to planning. Hypotheses Nos. 7 (see mainly correlations with Dim. 21a), 8, 9, 10, 12, and 14 were fully confirmed in all four age groups. Hypothesis No. 5 (concerning Emotions) was almost fully confirmed in all age groups, except for the nonsignificant correlation with one subdimension of Feelings and Emotions (Dim. 20a) in the youngest age group. Hypotheses Nos. 1, 2, 6, 11, and 13 were confirmed in 7-, 9-, and 11-year olds but not in 5-year olds. Finally, hypothesis No. 4 (concerning Sensory Qualities) was confirmed only in 5-, 9-, and 11-year olds but not in 7-year olds, whereas hypothesis No. 3 (concerning Quantities) was confirmed in 5- and 11-year olds but not in 7- and 9-year olds. In sum, out of the 56 examined relations (14 variables in four age groups) 47 (i.e., 83.9%) turned out fully as expected (the mentioned number does not include the somewhat blurred relation of emotional considerations to Feelings and Emotions in 5-year olds). The 9 relations that do not support the hypotheses include 7 relations concerning frequencies of specific contents across the 10 Planning Situations, and 2 relations concerning specific measures of planning in particular Planning Situations. Notably, out of these 9 relations, 6 (i.e., 66.6%) occurred in the youngest age group.

Table 4.7 presents data relevant to the second set of hypotheses. According to these hypotheses, planning as manifested in the global evaluation (i.e., the mean of plan adequacy evaluations in the 10 Planning Situations) would be related to the specific set of meaning variables reflecting various cognitive processes involved in planning. The table shows that the findings regarding meaning dimensions were mostly as expected: Locational Qualities was related to planning as expected in all age groups; Actions, Temporal Qualities, Manner of Occurrence and Operation, and Antecedents and Causes were related to planning as expected in the responses of 7-, 9-, and 11-year olds, but not 5-year olds; Domain of Application was related to planning as expected in 5-, 7-, and 9-year olds but not 11-year olds; and Consequences and Results was related to planning as expected only in 5- and 11-year olds, but not 7- and 9-year olds. Some findings were contrary to expectations, mainly the negative correlations of Actions and Consequences and Results with planning in some age groups. In addition, Table 4.7 shows that planning was related to many more meaning dimensions than expected (13 in 5-year olds, 20 in 7-year olds, 17 in 9-year olds, and 22 in 11-year olds). All these additional dimensions were related to planning in the same direction in two, three, or even four age groups (see Dim. 11).

Concerning Types of Relation, the hypothesis was confirmed partly: In all age groups the attributive and comparative types of relation were related positively to planning (except TR 2c in 11-year olds). However,

Table 4.7. *Pearson product–moment correlation coefficients between the global evaluation of planning and meaning variables*

Meaning Variables[a]	Age 5	Age 7	Age 9	Age 11
Meaning dimensions				
Dim. 1		.65***	.73***	.71***
Dim. 2a	.34*	−.52**		.75***
Dim. 2b		−.47**	−.64***	.79***
Dim. 3		.59***	.34*	.40*
Dim. 4a	−.34*	.42*	.79***	.94***
Dim. 4b	.73***	−.41*	.58***	.42*
Dim. 5		.75***	.35*	.46**
Dim. 6		.51**	.69***	.39*
Dim. 7	.47**	−.50**	−.47**	.64***
Dim. 8a	.73***	.58***	.42*	−.56***
Dim. 8b	.45**	.50**		
Dim. 9				.58***
Dim. 10		.89***		.42*
Dim. 11	−.72***		.50**	.84***
Dim. 13		.87***		.86***
Dim. 14			.40*	.75***
Dim. 15	.40*	.72***	.74***	.37*
Dim. 16		.67***	.36*	.38*
Dim. 17a		−.55**		.57***
Dim. 17b	−.45*	.97***		
Dim. 19a	.37*	.49**	−.63***	
Dim. 19b	−.41*			−.50**
Dim. 20a			.35*	.34*
Dim. 20b	−.72***	.34*	−.74***	
Dim. 21a	.74***	.51**		−..33*
Dim. 21b		.98***	.67***	.91***
Dim. 22b		.88***		.39*
Types of relation				
TR 1a	.36*	.46**	.36*	.90***
TR 1b		.35*	.46**	.76***
TR 1a+b		.49**	.39*	.85***
TR 2a	.33*	.63***		
TR 2b	.56***	.94***		.42*
TR 2c				−.33*
TR 2d			.62***	.37*
TR 2a+b+c+d		.56***	.36*	.53***
TR 3a		−.54**	−.40*	−.80***
TR 3b			.52**	−.91***
TR 3c		.42*	.58***	
TR 3a+b+c		−.61***		−.96***
TR 4b				.35*
TR 4c		−.54**		.96***
TR 4b+c		−.41*		.60***

Table 4.7. *(cont.)*

Meaning Variables[a]	Age 5	Age 7	Age 9	Age 11
Modes of meaning				
Lexical Mode		.67***	.38*	.96***
Personal Mode		−.71***	.36*	−.58***
Forms of Relation				
FR 1	−.67***	−.76***	−.73***	−.62***
FR 2	.54**		.49**	.33*
FR 3		.87***	.76***	.61***
FR 4		.83***		
FR 5	.54**	.96***		.67***
FR 6	.46*	.48**	.35*	.75***
FR 7		.87***	.46**	.78***
FR 3+4+5+6 (complex)	.50**	.95***	.37*	.74***
FR 1+3+4 (positive)	−.72***	−.34*	−.47**	−.62***
FR 2+6 (negative)	.64***		.40*	.47**
Referent-shift variables				
Shift close[b]	−.36*	−.43*		−.39*
Shift medium[c]	.37*	.62***	.47**	.58***
Shift far[d]		−.58***	−.76***	

[a]Concerning the code of the meaning variables, see Table 4.4. Only meaning variables correlated with the planning variable in at least one age group are mentioned in Table 4.8.
[b]Sum of Referent-Shift Variables Nos. 1, 3, & 8, see Table 4.4.
[c]Sum of Referent-Shift Variables Nos. 4, 5, & 6, see Table 4.4.
[d]Sum of Referent-Shift Variables Nos. 2, 7, 9 & 10, see Table 4.4.
 *$p < .05$.
 **$p < .01$.
 ***$p < .001$.

the trend was less clear concerning the types of relation of the Personal Mode: In the youngest age group they were unrelated to planning, in the second age group they were related mostly negatively, as expected, but in the third and fourth age groups they were related at least partly positively.

The expectation concerning Forms of Relation was borne out for the separate variables as well as for their sum insofar as 75% of the expected correlations (i.e., 15 of 20) actually turned out to be significant, thus indicating that complex forms of relation are related to planning. An unpredicted finding, consistent across age groups, was a negative correlation with the positive form of relation (FR 1).

Finally, concerning referent shifts the findings fully support the hypothesis: The medium referent shifts were correlated positively with planning.

The expectation was further reinforced by negative correlations in some age groups with smaller or larger referent shifts.

4. Conclusions and discussion.   Concerning the specific contribution of meaning to planning, the findings (Table 4.7) showed that in the majority of cases the use of particular contents in planning and even the choice of specific strategies (i.e., the use of if–then considerations, general labels and chronological arrangements) are related positively to the salience of the corresponding meaning dimension in the subject's meaning profile. Notably, the relations are highly specific, as shown by the correspondence of the contents in planning with the specific adequate subdimensions in Sensory Qualities (Dim. 19a but not Dim. 19b), Judgments and Evaluations (Dim. 21a but not always Dim. 21b) and Cognitive Qualities (Dim. 22a but not Dim. 22b). It is worth noting that in the case of the mentioned meaning dimensions, children, in planning, used almost exclusively meaning values referring to qualities (as reflected in the subdimensions 19a, 21a, 22a) rather than to actions (as reflected in the subdimensions 19b, 21b, 22b).

The conclusions about the specific contribution of meaning to planning hold in regard to 95% of the cases in the second, third, and fourth age groups, but in regard to only 50% of the cases in the youngest age group. Specifically, the hypothesized relations that were not confirmed in the youngest age group involve the following meaning dimensions: Locational Qualities, Feelings and Emotions (only in regard to the subdimension Dim. 20a, possibly because children may not yet distinguish sharply enough between the two subdimensions 20a and 20b), Cognitive Qualities, and Temporal Qualities (only in the case of one measure of planning). In regard to the latter two dimensions, the reason may be the relatively low frequency of usage (see Table 4.6). Previous studies (Kreitler & Kreitler, 1977) indicated that a meaning dimension is not manifested in cognitive tasks if it does not have a frequency above a certain minimal threshold in the individual's meaning profile.

Concerning the general contribution of meaning to planning, the findings (Table 4.7) showed that the global evaluation of planning is correlated with a large set of meaning variables, indeed, many more than expected. This fact as such indicates the intimate relation of planning to the contents and processes of meaning. The number of meaning variables related to planning is so large because they include:

1.   Meaning variables that affect directly the cognitive processes involved in planning (in line with the hypothesis, these are Manner of Occurrence and Operation, Temporal Qualities, Antecedents and Causes, Conse-

quences and Results, Contextual Allocation, the different types and forms of relation, and the medium-ranged referent shifts).

2. Meaning variables that affect the contents used in planning, and hence resemble rather the specific contribution of meaning to planning (i.e., Quantity and Number, State, Sensory Qualities, Judgments and Evaluations, Possessions, Cognitive Qualities, Feelings and Emotions, and Function).

The latter group of meaning dimensions is involved probably because planning was represented by a global evaluation measure summarizing the quality and contents of planning across the 10 Planning Situations. Yet, as noted (section III.A), the general and specific contributions of meaning to planning are not sharply distinguished because they are two modes of activation or manifestation of the same meaning variables. Hence, it should not be surprising that the list of meaning variables affecting the processes of planning (i.e., section 3.a) includes meaning variables (e.g., Temporal Qualities) dealt with earlier in terms of their impact on the contents of planning. Similarly, it should not be surprising that the list of meaning variables affecting the contents of planning includes variables (e.g., Judgments and Evaluations) that probably affect planning also as process. Indeed, any meaning dimension may be manifested either as contents or as process. Yet the common root of both contents and process in no way invalidates the utility of the distinction.

The findings show that in all age groups planning is steeped in a matrix of meaning variables. This indicates that cognitively planning is a highly complex activity, perhaps more than is usually assumed. This conclusion corresponds also to the findings of Berger, Guilford, and Christensen (1957), who showed that responses to a test assessing planning skills in adults were correlated with cognitive factors indicating particularly high degrees of complexity and ingenuity.

Our findings show that actually the whole spectrum of meaning is related to planning in some form. This does not indicate that in every act of planning all the individual's cognitive processes and contents are activated. Rather, it is more likely that only a sample of these cognitive processes and contents is brought to bear on the problem at hand. Two factors play a primary role in the selection of processes and contents that are actually activated: the input situation and the individual's meaning profile. For example, if the task requires planning a route, the "input" – that is, the meaning of the problem situation – activates processes and contents bound with Locational Qualities. Yet this analysis does not enable a prediction that such processes and contents would actually be activated in a given case. If the individual has a very low or nil mastery of the dimension Locational Qualities, he or she is unlikely to use locational aspects in planning the problem at hand. Such a child may do the job, if at all, by relying on contents of another kind. On the other hand, if Locational Qualities is a salient meaning dimension in a child's meaning profile, that child is likely to note locational aspects and rely on spatial considerations even if they are not a salient element of the input situation. Accordingly, it is not very enlightening to speak about the cognitive processes required by planning without considering the cognitive resources available in the planners, because the latter contribute to the salience of the former no less than the former contribute in the long run to the shaping of the latter. Thus, if we find that a certain set of meaning variables is related to planning mainly in a certain age group, this finding reflects not only the cognitive requirements of the inputs, that is, of the problems presented to the children, but no less also the cognitive potentialities of the children at that age level. Notably, although planning was related to meaning variables on all age levels, the wealth and breadth of the relations increase with age; for example, the exemplifying and metaphoric types of relation become involved with planning only in 9- and 11-year olds. This finding is to be expected in view of the age-bound development of meaning (III.B.3.a).

Thus, on the one hand, the input situation evokes multiple meaning variables, and on the other hand, planners have available an increasing number of meaning assignment abilities. One implication thereof is that whereas certain problems may require or evoke certain meaning variables more than others, different individuals are likely to cope with the problems by applying different meaning variables in line with their available resources, sometimes compensating for a weak meaning variable by one or more stronger ones.

However, if we consider those meaning variables that are related to planning in all or most age groups as manifested in high correlations in the same direction, it is likely that they reveal not only the cognitive processes available to the children but at least to some extent also the cognitive requirements of the act of planning. Accordingly, the findings indicate that planning in a broad range of situations is promoted by particular cognitive processes: abstracting, classifying and labeling (Dim. 1); thinking causally, that is, in terms of causes and effects or conditions under which particular things occur (Dim. 6); thinking dynamically, that is, in terms of the processes, means, stages, etc. involved in the occurrence and operation of things, events, etc. (Dim. 5); thinking teleologically, that is, in terms of the function, purpose or role of things, events, objects, etc. (Dim. 3); evaluating in terms of general and personal standards of utility, goals, opinions, or beliefs (Dim. 21); thinking locationally, that is, in terms of where people, objects, things, etc. are in general or at given times, in absolute terms or relative to each other or some framework, and how far they are in physical or even metaphoric senses (Dim. 15); and thinking temporally, that is, in terms of durations and temporal relations, such as simultaneity or succession (Dim. 16). In addition, planning involves a particular form of processing the major themes on which planning focuses, elaborating them sufficiently to reveal their meaningful relations within a broader context without, however, shifting so far from the point as to lose contact with the issue at hand (referent-shift variables: positive correlations with medium-range shifts, negative with close-range and far-range shifts). Further, planning requires particular forms of relating cognitive contents to one another, that is, considering alternatives (FR 5) and probabilities (FR 3), while sometimes also rejecting possibilities completely (FR 2) or in favor of other ideas (FR 6). Finally, planning involves also specific ways of relating cognitive contents to one another, that is, attributively and comparatively, thus focusing on the reality-bound interpersonally shared mode of processing information (TR 1 and TR 2, and their subtypes).

IV. Cognitive orientation and meaning in shaping planning: a combined measure and its implications

A. *Predicting planning on the basis of CO scores and meaning variables*

1. Hypotheses. Findings presented in section II showed that CO scores orienting toward planning are related positively to measures of general planning skills and evaluations of planning adequacy, and to some degree even to variables assessing the contents used in planning. Findings presented in section III showed that meaning variables in the individual's meaning profile are related to cognitive processes and contents applied in planning. There are compelling reasons for combining these two sets of findings. On theoretical grounds (see section I), CO and meaning are considered to interact in regard to meaning in a complementary way: whereas CO scores predispose toward planning, the meaning variables provide the cognitive skills and contents necessary for performing the planning. On methodological grounds, combining CO scores and meaning as two predictors of planning may be expected first, to raise the level of prediction beyond the level obtained through each set separately; second, to widen the range of prediction, because some variables of planning were predicted only by CO scores or meaning but not by both; and third, to enable estimation of the relative contribution of CO scores and meaning in predicting the different measures of planning.

Two general hypotheses guided the analyses that will be discussed (see section IV.A.3). First, it was hypothesized that with respect to predicting all planning variables (i.e., the three groups of variables), both CO scores and meaning variables would have contributions due to the impact of each independently and of the two in interaction. Second, it was hypothesized that with respect to predicting the measures of general planning skills and the evaluations of plan adequacy (i.e., the first and the second groups of planning variables), the contribution of CO scores would be relatively greater, whereas with respect to predicting the contents measures of specific interpretations and considerations (i.e., the third group of planning variables), the contribution of meaning variables would be relatively greater. The two hypotheses are based on the rationale that the performance of planning requires both motivation (assessed through CO scores) and cognitive abilities (assessed through the meaning profile). Whereas the former provides the motive, with a particular intensity and orientation – the behavioral intent, in terms of the CO theory – the latter provides the means of implementing the behavioral intent, that is, for carrying out the plan. A further assumption, underlying particularly the first hypothesis, was that motivational directionality and implementing means may interact, for example, by complementing each other so that the availability of particular means reinforces the motivational directionality. Another assumption, underlying in particular the second hypothesis, was that the relative importance of the implementing means rises in prediction when the focus is on specific elements in the plan: in the present case, considerations of particular contents that depend on the availability of the particular meaning values corresponding to these contents. Yet both hypotheses remain exploratory in nature insofar as existing information did not enable formulating more specific expectations about the particular planning measures and the relative contributions of the different kinds of meaning variables.

2. Method: statistical analyses. The subjects, tasks, measures, and procedure of the study were described previously in sections III.C.3–4 and III.B.2. The combination of CO scores and meaning variables as independent variables in the prediction of planning was done by applying a stepwise multiple regression analysis of variance with dummy variables (Kim & Kohout, 1975, pp. 273–283). The special advantages of this design for our problem are that in addition to providing information about the relative differential contribution of each independent variable as well as of the introduced interaction terms to the prediction of planning, it specifies the order in which the different predictors "enter" the equation (so that relative primacy in the predictive matrix may be estimated) and enables estimation of the optimal combinations of predictors.

The predictors entered into the analysis for the general planning skills and the evaluations of plan adequacy were defined as follows: CO scores were split into high (i.e., CO scores 4 and 3) versus low (i.e., CO scores 2, 1 or 0). The meaning variables were split into four groups: meaning dimensions, types of relation, forms of relation, and referent–shift variables. For each group of meaning variables in each age group, an index was established based on the specific meaning variables of that kind that were found in that age group to be correlated with the mean global evaluation of planning (see Table 4.7). The index was the sum of all the correlated meaning variables, whereby a positively correlated variable got a positive sign and a negatively correlated variable got a negative sign. These indices were split dichotomously into $+1$ scores if the index based on an individual's data was above the mean of that index in the individual's age group, and -1 scores if it was below that mean. Thus, each individual got a separate score for each of the four groups of meaning variables. In addition, two interaction terms were defined: one between the four scores of meaning variables, and one between all the meaning variables and the CO scores.

In regard to the variables representing specific contents in planning, the analysis included as predictors: CO scores (split into high versus low, as above), the single particular meaning dimension corresponding to the specific type of contents (split into high versus low in accordance with the mean of that meaning dimension in that age group), and the interaction between the CO scores and the meaning dimension.

3. Results and conclusions. The findings show that all *general planning skills* in all age groups are predicted significantly by CO scores and meaning variables jointly. The level of prediction is remarkably high. The mean amount of variance accounted for in the group of 5-year olds is 66% (range of R^2 is .46–.90); in the group of 7-year olds, 93.7% (range of R^2 is .85–.98); in the group of 9-year olds, 92.4% (range of R^2 is .81–.98); and in the group of 11-year olds, 82.1% (range of R^2 is .40–.98). The mean across all four age groups is 83.5%. Notably, in all 40 cases (i.e., 10 variables in four age groups) both CO scores and meaning variables are included as predictors in the equation, and in all except one case (i.e., No. of alternate plans, in 9-year olds) the CO scores were entered first as the primary term in the prediction equation. Thus, these findings lend sup-

Table 4.8. Results of multiple stepwise regression analyses of variance on all planning variables in the four age groups

Planning variables[a]		Predictors[b]	Multiple R	Overall F
Age 5				
Alternate	(P. 1)	CO, SR, Dim., TR, FR, Int(MN)	.86	11.01****
If-then	(P. 2)	CO, SR, Dim., TR, FR, Int(MN)	.85	9.73****
Chronol.	(P. 3)	CO, Dim., FR, SR, TR, Int(MN)	.95	34.67****
Questions	(P. 4)	CO, FR, TR, Dim., SR, Int(MN)	.77	5.50***
Items	(P. 5)	CO, Dim., TR, SR, FR, Int(MN)	.77	5.74***
Domains	(P. 6)	CO, FR, SR, TR, Dim., Int(MN)	.68	3.32*
Gen. Labels	(P. 7)	CO, SR, TR, FR, Dim., Int(MN)	.93	25.42****
Steps/1st	(P. 8)	CO, Dim., SR, FR, TR, Int(MN)	.69	3.51*
Steps/alt.	(P. 9)	CO, SR, FR, Dim., TR, Int(MN)	.88	12.78****
Steps/all	(P. 10)	CO, Dim., SR, FR, TR, Int(MN)	.68	3.38*
Overall eval.		CO, Dim., SR, TR, FR, Int(MN)	.76	5.31***
Sit. 1		CO, SR, FR, Dim., TR, Int(MN)	.82	8.00****
Sit. 2		CO, TR, SR, FR, Dim., Int(MN)	.92	21.88****
Sit. 3		CO, Dim., TR	.72	9.38****
Sit. 4		CO, Dim., SR, TR	.71	9.45****
Sit. 5		CO, SR	.67	10.95****
Sit. 6		CO, Dim., SR	.87	27.90****
Sit. 7		CO, Dim., FR, SR, TR, Int(MN)	.91	18.95****
Sit. 8		CO, FR, Dim., SR, TR, Int(MN)	.91	18.95****
Sit. 9		CO, SR, TR, Dim., Int(MN)	.75	6.37***
Sit. 10		CO, Dim., SR, TR, FR, Int(MN)	.90	16.17****
Time	(C. 1)	CO, Int(MC), Dim., Temporal Qual.	.17	.25
Location	(C. 2)	Int(MC)	.40	5.33*
Quantity	(C. 3)	Dim., Quantity & Number	.32	3.29 (p = .08)
Sensory Qual.	(C. 4)	CO, Dim., Sensory Qual.	.64	9.64***
Emotions	(C. 5)	Dim., Feelings & Emotions, CO, Int(MC)	.65	6.27**
Judgments	(C. 6)	Dim., Judgments & Evaluations	.34	1.83
Cognitive Qual.	(C. 7)	Int(MC)	.35	3.80 (p = .08)

166

Age 7

Alternate	(P. 1)	CO, TR, Dim., Int(MN)	.99	283.25****
If-then	(P. 2)	CO, TR, Dim., Int(MN)	.96	186.55****
Chronol.	(P. 3)	CO, TR, Dim., Int(MN)	.95	58.64****
Questions	(P. 4)	CO, Dim., TR, Int(MN)	.98	199.97****
Items	(P. 5)	CO, TR, Dim.	.92	52.00****
Domains	(P. 6)	CO, TR, Dim., Int(MN)	.97	91.23****
Gen. Labels	(P. 7)	CO, TR, Dim., Int(MN)	.98	39.35****
Steps/1st	(P. 8)	CO, Dim., TR, Int(MN)	.99	198.80****
Steps/alt.	(P. 9)	CO, TR	.95	115.46****
Steps/all	(P. 10)	CO, TR, Dim., Int(MN)	.99	116.99****
Overall eval.		CO, Dim., Int(MN)	.98	114.89****
Sit. 1		CO, TR, Dim.	.83	19.07****
Sit. 2		CO, TR	.43	3.04 ($p = .06$)
Sit. 3		CO, TR	.76	18.90****
Sit. 4		CO, Int(MC)	.71	13.50****
Sit. 5		Dim., CO	.92	81.00****
Sit. 6		CO, TR	.95	126.90****
Sit. 7		CO, TR	.41	2.70 ($p = .08$)
Sit. 8		CO, TR	.90	39.87****
Sit. 9		CO, TR	.80	24.30****
Sit. 10		CO, TR	.61	16.80****
Time		CO	.75	36.87****
Location		CO, Dim., Locational Qual., Int(MC)	.99	237.87****
Quantity		Int(MC), Dim., Quantity & Number, CO	.95	74.53****
Sensory Qual.		CO	.81	52.12****
Emotions		CO, Dim., Feelings & Emotions, Int(MC)	.99	222.24****
Judgments		CO, Dim., Judg. & Evaluations	.85	92.45****
Cognitive Qual.		CO, Int(MC)	.64	9.47***

Age 9

Alternate	(P. 1)	Dim., CO, SR, FR	.94	144.79****
If-then	(P. 2)	CO, Dim., SR	.90	49.51****
Chronol.	(P. 3)	CO, FR, Dim.	.93	60.67****
Questions	(P. 4)	CO, SR, FR, Dim.	.96	138.81****

Table 4.8. *(cont.)*

Planning variables[a]		Predictors[b]	Multiple R	Overall F
Items	(P. 5)	CO, FR, Dim., SR	.97	137.44****
Doma:ns	(P. 6)	CO, FR, Dim.	.96	98.94****
Gen. Labels	(P. 7)	CO, FR, SR	.99	147.00****
Steps/1st	(P. 8)	CO, FR, SR, Dim.	.99	144.77****
Steps/alt.	(P. 9)	CO, Dim., FR, SR	.99	95.87****
Steps/all	(P. 10)	CO, FR, Dim., SR	.98	162.28****
Overall eval.		CO, FR, SR	.96	169.42****
Sit. 1		CO, SR	.96	138.22****
Sit. 2		CO, FR, SR, Dim.	.98	101.10****
Sit. 3		CO, Dim., FR	.84	34.52****
Sit. 4		CO, Dim., FR, SR	.96	91.80****
Sit. 5		CO, Dim., SR	.97	51.30****
Sit. 5		CO, Dim., FR, SR	.95	32.10****
Sit. 7		CO, FR, SR, Dim.	.93	30.80****
Sit. 8		CO, FR, SR, Dim.	.93	30.80****
Sit. 9		CO, FR, Dim., SR	.97	78.12****
Sit. 10		CO, Dim., FR	.75	12.83***
Time	(C. 1)	Int(MC)	.56	12.78***
Location	(C. 2)	Int(MC)	.78	43.45****
Quantity	(C. 3)	CO	.39	4.98*
Sensory Qual.	(C. 4)	Dim., Sensory Qual., CO	.51	8.96**
Emotions	(C. 5)	Dim., Feelings & Emotions, CO	.87	43.20****
Judgments	(C. 6)	Dim., Judgments & Evaluations	.38	5.72*
Cognitive Qual.	(C. 7)	CO	.92	147.13****
Age 11				
Alternate	(P. 1)	CO, Dim., SR	.92	48.53****
If-then	(P. 2)	CO, Dim., SR	.99	134.80****
Chronol.	(P. 3)	CO, FR	.95	94.23****
Questions	(P. 4)	CO, Dim., SR	.95	86.56****

Variable		Predictors	R	F
Items	(P. 5)	CO, Dim., SR	.94	73.76****
Domains	(P. 6)	CO, FR	.85	35.02****
Gen. Labels	(P. 7)	CO, Dim., SR	.94	72.80****
Steps/1st	(P. 8)	CO, Dim., SR	.97	152.88****
Steps/alt.	(P. 9)	CO, Dim.	.63	8.86***
Steps/all	(P. 10)	CO, Dim., SR	.85	21.75****
Overall eval.		CO, SR	.93	36.81****
Sit. 1		CO, SR	.92	72.90****
Sit. 2		CO, SR	.92	78.30****
Sit. 3		CO, SR, Dim.	.91	39.87****
Sit. 4		CO, SR, Dim.	.98	68.41****
Sit. 5		CO, SR, Dim.	.98	137.70****
Sit. 6		CO, Dim.	.96	135.10****
Sit. 7		CO, Dim., SR	.95	109.20****
Sit. 8		CO, SR	.80	39.20****
Sit. 9		CO, Dim.	.61	16.80****
Sit. 10		CO, Dim.	.97	65.34****
Time	(C. 1)	CO, Int(MC)	.95	136.52****
Location	(C. 2)	CO, Int(MC)	.74	16.71****
Quantity	(C. 3)	CO	.44	6.91*
Sensory Qual.	(C. 4)	CO, Dim., Sensory Qual, Int(MC)	.25	.58
Emotions	(C. 5)	CO, Dim., Feelings & Emotions	.93	81.38****
Judgments	(C. 6)	CO, Judgments & Evaluations	.76	37.86****
Cognitive Qual.	(C. 7)	CO, Cognitive Qual.	.67	23.26****

[a]"P." variables are the measures of general planning skills; "Sit." variables are the global evaluation measures of plan adequacy in each planning situation separately; "C." variables are measures reflecting cognitive contents. See text for description of variables.

[b]The table includes all predictors assigned in the stepwise regression analysis to the prediction equation, in the order of their assignment. The specific information about the F value of each predictor separately and the changes in Multiple R and Overall F due to each additional predictor had to be deleted from the table because of space limitations; it can be obtained from the authors upon request. List of abbreviations: CO = Cognitive Orientation score; Dim. = Meaning Dimensions; TR = Types of Relation; FR = Forms of Relation; SR = Referent-Shift Variables; Int(MN) = Interaction among the four kinds of meaning variables; Int(MC) = Interaction between meaning variables and CO scores.

$*p < .05.$ $**p < .01.$ $***p < .001.$ $****p < .0001.$

169

port to the two hypotheses (section IV.A.1) insofar as the measures of the general planning skills are concerned.

Judging by the means of the variance accounted for across the four age groups, the two variables predicted at the relatively lowest level are No. of domains (mean $R^2 = .76$) and No. of steps in alternate plans (mean $R^2 = .76$), whereas the two variables predicted at the relatively highest level were No. of general labels (mean $R^2 = .93$) and No. of chronological orderings (mean $R^2 = .90$). Yet the findings show that the number and pattern of predictors change more in line with age groups than particular planning variables. Thus the mean number of predictors in the group of 5-year olds is 6; in the group of 7-year olds, 3.7; in the group of 9-year olds, 3.6; and in the group of 11-year olds, 2.7. The reason for the decrease in the number of predictors from the youngest to the oldest group is probably the growing interrelations among the predictors. Concerning the patterns of predictors, the relatively most often recurrent pattern in 5-year olds is, in descending order: CO scores, Meaning Dimensions, Referent-Shift Variables, Forms of Relation, Types of Relation, and the Interaction among meaning variables (3 times). In 7-year olds, it is: CO scores, Types of Relation, Meaning Dimensions, and the Interaction among meaning variables (7 times). In 9-year olds, the pattern is: CO scores, Forms of Relation, and Meaning Dimensions (2 times). In 11-year olds, the pattern is: CO scores, Meaning Dimensions, and Referent-Shift Variables (7 times). If, however, we concentrate on the predictors recurring most frequently in the first three positions, then we find CO scores occurring as first in all age groups, whereas in the second and third positions we find, in 5-year olds, Meaning Dimensions (6 times) and Referent-Shift Variables (7 times); in 7-year olds, Meaning Dimensions (9 times) and Types of Relation (10 times); in 9-year olds, Meaning Dimensions (7 times) and Forms of Relation (8 times); and in 11-year olds, Meaning Dimensions (8 times) and Referent-Shift Variables (7 times). Thus, in all age groups the major predictors of general planning skills are CO scores and Meaning Dimensions, in this order. By the same token, the least important predictors are the interaction between meaning variables and CO scores that was never included in the prediction equations and the interaction among kinds of meaning variables that occurred in the last positions in the two youngest groups and dropped out completely in the two older groups.

Concerning the *evaluations of plan adequacy* in each Planning Situation separately and their overall mean, Table 4.8 shows that all 44 measures (i.e., 11 measures in four age groups) were predicted significantly by CO scores and meaning variables (only in two cases, in 7-year olds, $p <$

.10). The mean amount of variance accounted for in the group of 5-year olds is 67.09% (range of R^2 is .32–.72); in the group of 7-year olds, 60.82% (range of R^2 is 0.3–.97); in the group of 9-year olds, 86.27% (range of R^2 is .31–.92); and in the group of 11-year olds, 82.3% (range of R^2 is .14–.92). The mean across all age groups is 76.05%. The amount of explained variance is here somewhat lower than in regard to the general planning skills (76% versus 83.5%) probably because in the case of particular situations highly specific content aspects are more likely to exert an impact. In regard to all evaluation measures, CO scores and meaning variables are included as predictors in the equation, and in all except one case (i.e., evaluation of Planning Situation No. 5 in 7-year olds) CO scores occurred as the primary term in the equation. Hence, the findings support the two hypotheses (section IV.A.1) also insofar as the measures of evaluation are concerned. In terms of the mean amount of variance accounted for across all four groups, the two measures predicted at the relatively lowest level were the evaluations of Planning Situation No. 3 (mean $R^2 = .61$) and No. 9 (mean $R^2 = .63$), whereas the two measures predicted at the relatively highest measure were the evaluation of Planning Situation No. 6 (mean $R^2 = .87$) and the mean evaluation across all Planning Situations (mean $R^2 = .83$). Again, as in the case of general planning skills, the number and pattern of predictors change more in line with age groups than specific dependent variables. The mean number of predictors across all age groups is lower than in the case of the general planning skills ($\bar{X} = 3.18$ vs. $\bar{X} = 4.00$), suggesting that plan adequacy in particular planning situations may depend on a more limited range of factors than planning skills manifested in a great variety of situations. Yet, as in regard to general planning skills, the number of predictors is higher in 5-year olds ($\bar{X} = 4.73$) than in 11-year olds ($\bar{X} = 2.36$). Concerning the patterns of predictors: In 5-year olds no pattern recurs more than once; in 7-year olds the most frequently recurrent pattern consists of CO scores in the first place and Types of Relation in the second (7 times); in 9-year olds the recurrent pattern was: CO scores, Meaning Dimensions, and Forms of Relation (2 times). In 11-year olds there were two recurrent patterns: CO scores, Referent-Shift Variables, and Meaning Dimensions (3 times) and CO scores and Referent-Shift Variables (4 times). An examination of the predictors occurring most frequently in the first three positions shows that CO scores occupy the first position in all age groups, whereas in the second and third positions the most frequently occurring predictors are, in 5-year olds, Referent-Shift Variables (8 times) and Meaning Dimensions (7 times); in 7-year olds, Types of Relation (7 times) and Meaning Dimensions (3 times); in 9-year olds, Forms of Relation (9 times) and

Referent-Shift Variables (6 times); and in 11-year olds, Referent-Shift Variables (8 times) and Meaning Dimensions (7 times). Thus, across all age groups the most important predictors of plan adequacy evaluations are CO scores in the first place and Referent-Shift Variables in the second place (not Meaning Dimensions, as in the case of general planning skills). The least important predictors are, as in regard to general planning skills, the interaction terms.

Concerning the variables reflecting the *frequencies of interpretations and considerations in specific content domains,* Table 4.8 shows that in five cases (four in 5-year olds, two of which were on the level of $p < .10$, and one in 11-year olds) the combination of variables did not produce a significant prediction. Notably, also the overall percentages of variance accounted for by the predictors were lower than in the other groups of planning variables: on the average, 19% in 5-year olds, 75% in 7-year olds, 44% in 9-year olds, and 51% in 11-year olds. The mean across all age groups is 47%. The content variables predicted relatively least well across all age groups were those that concerned "quantity" (mean $R^2 = .33$) and "sensory qualities" (mean $R^2 = .35$), whereas those that were predicted relatively best concerned "locations" (mean $R^2 = .56$) and "emotions" (mean $R^2 = .75$). As in the case of the other groups of variables, the number of predictors tended to be higher in the younger age groups ($\bar{X} = 2.43$ in 5-year olds, $\bar{X} = 2.71$ in 7-year olds) than in the older age groups ($\bar{X} = 1.71$ in 9-year olds, $\bar{X} = 2.29$ in 11-year olds). As expected in line with the second hypothesis, CO scores were here somewhat less prominent predictors than in regard to the other planning variables: They occurred in 75% of the prediction equations (as compared to 100% in the case of the other two groups of variables), and, in the first position, only in 56.14% of the equations (as compared with 99% in the case of the other variables). Yet CO scores are relatively still the most prominent predictor of the contents variables. Second in prominence is the meaning dimension corresponding to the particular contents (it occurred in the second or third position in 53.57% of the cases) and the Interaction between CO scores and meaning variables (it occurred in the second or third position in 32.14% of the cases). Thus, CO scores and meaning variables occur jointly as predictors in 57.14% of the cases, and CO scores alone in an additional 17.9% of the cases. These findings indicate that CO scores and meaning variables constitute the optimal combination for prediction in regard to contents variables, too.

In sum, the findings of the stepwise regression analyses show that CO scores and meaning variables jointly enable highly significant predictions of planning variables of the different kinds. The improvement in the level of prediction over that obtained when CO scores and meaning variables were each applied separately is particularly remarkable in regard to the general planning skills and the evaluations of plan adequacy in the 10 Planning Situations. The two kinds of predictors account for a large part of the variance that often amounts to above 90%. The improvement is less remarkable in regard to variables reflecting different contents. In predicting all three kinds of planning variables the combination of CO scores and meaning variables, in that order, turned out to be optimal. Developmentally, two important trends were revealed: First, the joint prediction through CO scores and meaning leads to the highly impressive findings particularly from the age of 7 onward; and second, in lower age groups more of predictors are necessary than in higher age groups.

B.   Planning from the viewpoints of CO and meaning: some general conclusions

We started with the general assumption that planning is a complex phenomenon with motivational and cognitive aspects (section I). Hence, we examined the relations of planning with the motivational matrix, as manifested in the CO cluster, and with the cognitive matrix, as manifested in the meaning profile. The findings presented in section II showed that CO scores orienting toward planning are related positively to general planning skills and evaluations of plan adequacy in different Planning Situations. Practically, this indicates that children who have specific beliefs about norms, about goals, about themselves, and about the environment or other people, that is, beliefs that support planning directly or indirectly, are likely to engage in planning and to plan their behaviors more than children who do not have such beliefs in all four or at least three belief types.

The findings presented in section III showed that the frequencies of meaning dimensions in the subject's meaning profile are related, as expected, to the frequency with which the subject uses, in planning, specific contents and considerations corresponding to the dimensions. For example, a child in whose meaning profile Locational Qualities is a salient dimension tends to apply locational considerations in planning more than a child in whose meaning profile this meaning dimension is not frequent. Hence, the former child will have a distinct advantage particularly when an issue requires locational considerations, such as finding a route in an unfamiliar place, or planning a trajectory or a trip. In addition, the findings showed that general processes of planning are related to particular meaning variables. If we focus on the cognitive processes implied by the meaning variables, the findings revealed that in all age groups, planning is promoted mainly through (a) classifying, which implies abstracting; (b) thinking causally; (c) thinking teleologically (about functions and purposes); (d) thinking dynamically (about processes, means and stages of occurrence); (e) thinking locationally and temporally; (f) elaborating the major referents to some extent but without shifting too far away; (g) considering probabilities and alternatives while rejecting some possibilities; and (h) assuming an overall realistic manner that capitalizes on the propositional and comparative approaches and guarantees the salience of an interpersonally shared set.

It is evident that a great number of meaning variables of all aspects of the meaning system (i.e., Meaning Dimensions, Forms of Relation, Types of Relation, and Referent-Shift Variables) were found to be potentially relevant for planning. The relevance is potential because only a sample of all processes and contents is brought to bear on any specific planning issue. The selection is probably dictated both by the requirements of the problem at hand and the resources available to the planning individual.

Thus, the separate approaches to planning from the two distinct viewpoints of CO and meaning have undoubtedly led to an improved understanding of planning. But the most impressive results were obtained when both CO and meaning were applied jointly to the prediction of planning. Together the two kinds of factors have enabled remarkably high predictions of the extent, complexity, and adequacy of planning. Notably, in most cases both CO scores and meaning variables have independent and significant contributions in the regression equation. Practically, this indicates that predicting the act of planning requires consideration of both motivational and cognitive determinants. Theoretically it suggests that though CO scores and meaning are both cognitive elements, the distinction between them is useful and important. In the act of planning itself, CO scores provide a measure for the strength and direction of the behavioral intent orienting toward planning, whereas the meaning variables provide a measure for the availability of the cognitive tools (processes and contents) necessary for performing the planning. Initially, the beliefs supporting planning and the meaning variables that enable planning may be assumed to develop independently of each other. Yet, in later stages, interactions are probably very frequent. An enduring strong motivational tendency toward planning, reflected in a stored CO cluster orienting toward planning, may spur improvement (through learning, training, and sheer experience) in the cognitive abilities and contents necessary for planning, as reflected in the salience of specific meaning variables (see the relations of CO scores to content variations, section II.C.5). Similarly, a high level of the abilities and contents necessary for planning may, in turn, induce an increase in the strength of the tendency to plan, if it were not high to begin with. However, this plausible mutual influence between the motivational and cognitive determinants should not make us overlook alternative possibilities. For example, an individual may have a strong stored CO cluster predisposing toward planning but may not have the cognitive resources required for good planning. Such an individual may be expected to engage in planning, though the produced plans will be largely inadequate or of poor quality. On the other hand, another individual may have the cognitive resources for good planning but no CO cluster predisposing for planning. This individual may be expected not to engage in planning if she or he can at all avoid it.

The findings of the study also have important educational implications. In the contemporary age marked by the beginnings of the postindustrial era, planning is a useful asset both for the individual and for society. If more individuals are indeed going to be responsible for the greater part of their working schedules, as some social critics (Toffler, 1981) predict, then they must be able to plan carefully in even more domains than they do now. By the same token, if adequate adaptation to the new order is to be secured and resultant human stress and suffering are to be minimized, not only must social changes be predicted but also adequate plans must be prepared for their implementation. Moreover, there is no psychological evidence to support the widespread prejudice as to the inhibiting impact of planning on creativity and the ability to act spontaneously. Quite on the contrary, there is a lot of anecdotal material suggesting that serendipity is the prize that one often gets, precisely when following a meticulously laid-out plan for action. The notebooks of Beethoven or the detailed preliminary sketches of Michelangelo are a forceful testimony to the utility of careful planning and to its reinforcing impact on creativity.

Hence, it appears advisable to train individuals for planning. The findings of this study indicate how the training can best be done. Although it may not be harmful to teach planning by having the student memorize a great variety of plans and learn different planning skills, it would be much more effective to train planning by strengthening the motivational and cognitive antecedents of planning revealed by this study. Accordingly, it would be advisable first to diagnose the extent to which the individual has a CO cluster of beliefs supporting planning and the degree to which the major meaning variables necessary for planning are salient in his or her meaning profile. The next step would be to strengthen the beliefs orienting toward planning and the meaning variables necessary for planning according to procedures described elsewhere (Kreitler & Kreitler, 1976; S. Kreitler & Kreitler, in press-b). Because the training of CO and of meaning separately has been done successfully in various other domains (Kreitler & Kreitler, 1976, 1977, 1982; S. Kreitler & Kreitler, 1986, in press-b; Zakay, Bar-El, & Kreitler, 1984), there is every reason to expect that a combined training of both CO and meaning, when properly planned, will lead to appreciable improvements in planning.

Notes

1. A detailed presentation of the CO theory can be found in our book *Cognitive Orientation and Behavior* (Kreitler & Kreitler, 1976, chaps. 1–6). For shorter outlines, see Kreitler & Kreitler, 1972, 1982.)

References

Allport, D. A. (1980). Patterns and actions: Cognitive mechanisms are content-specific. In G. Claxton (Ed.), *Cognitive psychology: New directions*. London: Routledge & Kegan Paul.

Bartlett, F. C. (1932). *Remembering*. Cambridge: Cambridge University Press.

Berger, R. M., Guilford, J. P., & Christensen, P. R. (1957). A factor-analytic study of planning. *Psychological Monographs*, No. 71 (whole No. 453).

Byrne, R. (1977). Planning meals: Problem-solving on a real data-base. *Cognition, 5*, 287–332.

Dilger, W. C. (1960). The ethology of the African parrot genus *Agapornus*. *Zeitschrift fuer Tierpsychologie, 17*, 649–685.

Dilger, W. C. (1962). The behavior of lovebirds. *Scientific American, 206* (No. 1), 88–99.

Eccles, J. C. (1972) *The understanding of the brain*. New York: McGraw-Hill.

Fowler, C. A., & Turvey, M. T. (1978). Skill acquistion: An event approach with special reference to searching for the optimum of a function with several variables. In G. E. Stelmach (Ed.), *Information processing in motor control and learning*. New York: Academic Press.

Gallistel, C. R. (1980). *The organization of action: A new synthesis*. Hillsdale, NJ: Erlbaum.

Harvey, N., & Greer, K. (1980), Action: The mechanisms of motor control. In G. Claxton (Ed.), *Cognitive psychology: New directions*. London: Routledge & Kegan Paul.

Hayes-Roth, B., & Hayes-Roth, F. (1979). A cognitive model of planning. *Cognitive Science, 3*, 275–310.

Head, H. (1920). *Studies in neurology* (Vol. 2). London: Hodder & Stoughton/Oxford University Press.

Hollingshead, A. B., & Redlich, F. C. (1958). *Social class and mental illness*. New York: Wiley.

Kelso, J. A. S., & Wallace, S. A. (1978). Conscious mechanisms in movement. In G. E. Stelmach (Ed.), *Information processing in motor control and learning*. New York: Academic Press.

Kim, J.-O., & Kohout, F. J. (1975). Special topics in general linear models. In N. H. Nie et al., *Statistical Package for the Social Sciences (SPSS)* (2nd ed.) New York: McGraw-Hill.

Kreitler, H., & Kreitler, S. (1972). The cognitive determinants of defensive behavior. *British Journal of Social and Clinical Psychology, 11,* 359–372.

Kreitler, H., & Kreitler, S. (1976). *Cognitive orientation and behavior.* New York: Springer.

Kreitler, H., & Kreitler, S. (1977). Cognitive habilitation by meaning of aphasic patients and imbecile children. Invited address, at the award of Ph.D. h.c. to the senior author by the Johannes Gutenberg University on the occasion of its 500th anniversary, Mainz, West Germany.

Kreitler, H., & Kreitler, S. (1982). The theory of cognitive orientation: Widening the scope of behavior prediction. In B. A. Maher & W. B. Maher (Eds.), *Progress in experimental personality research* (Vol. 11). New York: Academic Press.

Kreitler, S., & Kreitler, H. (1983a). Perception as a process of meaning assignment. In W. D. Froehlich, G. J. W. Smith, J. G. Draguns, & U. Henschel (Eds.), *Psychological processes in cognition and personality.* New York: Hemisphere/McGraw-Hill.

Kreitler, S., & Kreitler, H. (1983b). Traits and situations: A semantic reconciliation in the research of personality and behavior. In H. Bonarius, G. van Heck, & N. Smid (Eds.), *Personality psychology in Europe.* London: Erlbaum.

Kreitler, S., & Kreitler, H. (1986). Modifying anxiety by cognitive means. In R. Schwarzer, H. van der Ploeg, & C. D. Spielberger (Eds.), *Advances in test anxiety research,* Vol. 5. Lisse, the Netherlands: Swets & Zeitlinger.

Kreitler, S., & Kreitler, H. (in press -a). *The cognitive foundations of personality.* New York: Springer.

Kreitler, S., & Kreitler, H. (in press -b). Cognitive rehabilitation of the mentally retarded.

Kreitler, S., Kreitler, H., & Zigler, E. (1974) Cognitive orientation and curiosity. *British Journal of Psychology, 65,* 43–52.

Kreitler, S., Maguen, T., & Kreitler, H. (1975). The three faces of intolerance of ambiguity. *Achiv für Psychologie, 127,* 238–250.

Kreitler, S., Shahar, A., & Kreitler, H. (1976). Cognitive orientation, type of smoker and behavior therapy of smoking. *British Journal of Medical Psychology, 49,* 167–175.

Kreitler, S., Zigler, E., & Kreitler, H. (1976). CO of curiosity and probability learning. In H. Kreitler & S. Kreitler, *Cognitive orientation and behavior.* New York: Springer.

Kreitler, S., Zigler, E., & Kreitler, H. (1984). Curiosity and demographic factors as determinants of children's probability learning strategies. *Journal of General Psychology, 145,* 61–75.

Lobel, T. E. (1982). The prediction of behavior from different types of beliefs. *Journal of Social Psychology, 118,* 213–223.

Marom, S. (1978). *Examination of CO clusters in children based on the theory of cognitive orientation.* Master's thesis, Department of Psychology, Tel Aviv University. (Summarized in Kreitler & Kreitler, 1982)

McNeill, D. (1970). *The acquisition of language: The study of developmental psycholinguistics.* New York: Harper & Row.

Miller, G. A., Galanter, E., & Pribram, K. H. (1960). *Plans and the structure of behavior.* New York: Holt, Rinehart & Winston.

Newell, A., & Simon, H. A. (1972). *Human problem solving.* Englewood Cliffs, NJ: Prentice-Hall.

Newell, K. M. (1978). Some issues on action plans. In G. E. Stelmach (Ed.), *Information processing in motor control and learning.* New York: Academic Press.

Pribram, K. H. (1971). *Languages of the brain: Experimental paradoxes and principles in neuropsychology.* Englewood Cliffs, NJ: Prentice-Hall, 1971.

Sacks, H., Schegloff, E. A., & Jefferson, G. (1974). A simplest systematics for the organization of turn-taking for conversation. *Language, 50,* 696–735.

Schank, R. C., & Abelson, R. P. (1977). *Scripts, plans, goals and understanding.* Hillsdale, NJ: Erlbaum.

Tinbergen, N. (1951). *The study of instinct.* London: Oxford University Press.

Toffler, A. (1981). *The third wave.* New York: Bantam Books.

Vorberg, D., & Hambuch, R. (1978). On the temporal control of rhythmic performance. In J. Requin (Ed.), *Attention and performance, VII.* Hillsdale, NJ: Erlbaum.

Zakay, D. (1976). *Decision by meaning: A decision making model based on the theory of cognitive orientation.* Ph.D. thesis, Tel Aviv University. (In English) (summarized in Kreitler & Kreitler, 1982).

Zakay, D., Bar-El, Z., & Kreitler, S. (1984). Cognitive orientation and changing the impulsivity of children. *British Journal of Educational Psychology, 54,* 40–50.

Ziv-Av, Y. (1978). *Slowness in different types of actions as a function of cognitive structures and contents* (Abstract in English). Master's thesis, Department of Psychology, Tel-Aviv University (summarized in Kreitler & Kreitler, 1982).

5   Social aspects of planning

Jacqueline J. Goodnow

The current literature on planning is often marked by three assumptions. One is that the major barriers to effective planning are cognitive or heuristic: They have to do, for instance, with the ability to set objectives, combine goals, recognize means–end relationships, and coordinate actions. The second is that plans seldom involve people. The individual plans in a solitary state, rarely if ever faced with the need to coordinate his or her plans with those of other people. Moreover, the pieces to be moved around in one's planning – the errands to be run, the chores or paragraphs to be fitted together – have no intrinsic reluctance to being moved around and present no arguments against their deployment from one slot in the plan to another. The third assumption is that there are few if any penalties to planning. In general, advance planning is regarded as "a good thing," regularly approved of and socially desirable.

My concern is that these assumptions do not fit well with many situations in everyday life. They ignore what I shall call the social aspects of planning. In real life, planning often encounters not only the barriers of one's own limited skills but also barriers imposed by social constraints on what is feasible or proper. In real life also, planning usually involves other people: as coplanners, as resources one may draw upon, or as pieces to be moved on one's planning board. Finally, the activity of planning is not always regarded as socially acceptable and may attract penalties. Consider, for instance, some statements overheard in recent months: "He treats going to a restaurant like a military campaign"; "I know I'm late, but I'm going to a party, not catching a train"; "It's weird – she has this schedule she has to check to make sure she says three nice things a day to the kid." Each statement contains a note of disapproval for "too

This paper has benefited from several discussions with Jeanette Lawrence of Murdoch University, Perth, Australia. It was written while the author was at the Center for Advanced Study in the Behavioral Sciences, Stanford, California. The financial support of the Spencer Foundation is gratefully acknowledged.

179

much" forward planning and a reminder that part of our social learning has to do with noting the situations where overt detailed planning is regarded as appropriate, and where it is regarded as a less desirable mode of action.

To point out the social aspects of planning is one thing. To go further, we need to ask: In what kinds of situations do we need to take these social aspects into account? And does a concern with social aspects lead us toward pinpointing specific gaps in our knowledge and toward any particular views about the nature of planning in general?

I shall argue that they do so. The material related to that argument, and to the analysis of planning situations, is presented in three sections. The first covers a brief account of my developing concern with planning and of the way this led to two general propositions about the nature of planning: (a) Planning consists of the movement of pieces from one state to another, with a major factor being the perception of pieces as not movable or as movable only in restricted fashion; and (b) planning is one of a set of alternative actions, varying in their appropriateness to particular situations and in the degree of approval given to them.

I. Some background and two general propositions

The social aspects of planning are not always the first to catch one's attention. In my case, the activity of drawing provides an example. People usually follow a particular formula or blueprint, most often in the form of a core series of actions (e.g., drawing a person by placing down the head, torso, and legs of an upright figure) followed by a number of more variable and peripheral items (Goodnow, 1978). Striking to me in these situations was the way people responded when they had to vary their usual routine. When children were asked to draw a person picking up a ball from the floor, for instance, they tended first to nibble at the edges of the problem, altering the peripheral items and arriving only slowly at the change in the core – abandoning its upright stance – that the problem requires (Goodnow, 1977). This reluctance to revise particular parts of plans could be seen in many other situations: situations involving travel, work, bringing up children, or facing a change in one's life plan (Goodnow, in press). The problem with revising a plan at this stage seemed to be primarily in the extent to which it called for a "radical" change rather than some tinkering with peripheral pieces.

At this stage, the social aspects of planning were of no major concern to me, and I paid no attention to the fact that children often draw together and are influenced by each other's plans: a fact Cocking and Copple draw attention to in this volume.

The presence of other constraints on plans and their revision became something to be thought about in the course of analyzing children's comments on what they would change if they could change one thing in the morning, at school, or in the world for other children (Goodnow, 1986; Goodnow & Burns, 1985). These comments made me aware, first of all, that the demands for planning start early in life, as one may judge from a first grader's comment on a possible change in the morning: "I wish school didn't start until about a quarter to eleven, so we can make our beds, tidy our room, have a shower, clean our teeth, and have a good breakfast. Then you might have time to watch a little television and you don't have to rush" (Goodnow & Burns, 1985). Such comments suggested that young children have a clear sense of coordinated actions and of the fact that moving one piece in a series affects many others. Their planning skills seemed in general to be strong at an earlier age than the literature on planning suggested.

The observation was thought provoking. More provocative still, however, were two other features of the children's comments. One was the children's frequent reference to other people's involvement in his or her own plans. Even in first grade, children commented on the way other people can make difficult the completion of one's own plan: "They wake you up at the wrong time, stay too long in the bathroom, are not ready to leave when you are," and may even "squabble with you and make you late." The second was the way in which certain pieces emerged in the morning schedule as more available for a change in state than others were. One of these pieces was breakfast (it was the children's most frequent nomination for being moved in time, skipped altogether, or compressed in time; in contrast, the time when one woke up was carefully guarded from change). The other movable piece was one's mother. Mothers were mentioned as able to salvage a morning by "getting your breakfast," "finding your things," or "driving you to school" far more often than fathers were. Why breakfast, I began to ask, and, a more troubling question, why mothers?

I began at this point to think about the need for a different view of planning than I had encountered in the literature on drawing, running errands, or organizing essays and study practices. The problem was underlined again by the need, in the course of asking about the nature of environmental supports for development, to consider the questions: When do parents plan activities or instructions for their children rather than let them make unguided discoveries (Goodnow, Knight, & Cashmore, 1985)? When do they plan exposure to particular environments or particular groups of possible friends rather than let children find their own social niches (Goodnow, 1985)?

Two last prompts toward second thoughts about planning came from (a) a study with Susan Delaney on how children's household tasks are organized (I shall draw from this material in a later section and shall accordingly simply note now that it forced me to think about the way a mother's planning is restricted by constraints on who can be asked to do what), and (b) some data and observations from a study by Lawrence, Dodds, and Volet (1983) on the difference between adolescents and housewives on an errand-planning task. The housewives were more effective planners, but the difference seemed to have two sources. One was the greater experience of the housewives. The other was the greater attachment of the adolescents to the notion that an afternoon in town should contain some time for "loafing," "hanging around," and "seeing what happens." One had the feeling that all this activity (planning ahead so that the maximum number of errands could be fitted into the minimum time) was in their view a rather strange way to spend an afternoon, perhaps even a rather strange approach to life.

From these demands to look more carefully at the nature of planning, two general propositions evolved. One was that planning involves the movement of pieces from one state to another, with the degree and type of movement often restricted by subjective perceptions of what is fixed and what is available as an option. The other was that planning is one of a set of possible actions, ranging from blind leaps to plans that map all contingencies in advance, with each action appropriate for particular occasions and each given varying degrees of social approval in particular situations. A brief expansion of these propositions is in order.

A. Planning as the movement of pieces

Developing a plan calls for moving pieces from one state to another: altering their place in a sequence, compressing the time usually allotted, combining pieces usually separate, or using old pieces in novel ways, all with the aim of progressing effectively toward a goal or, as Wilensky (1981) pointed out, toward a "piggybacking" of goals. The pieces may be rings for the Tower of Hanoi, cannibals and missionaries to be moved from one side of a river to another, or people and activities that need to be juggled to meet deadlines in a householder's or executive's day.

That view of planning clearly overlaps with some accounts of problem solving, so let us clear the ground with a distinction between the two. They do have similarities. To ask someone to work out ways of fitting the maximum number of errands into a fixed amount of time is to ask that person to solve a problem. The term "planning" enters when the problem calls for the anticipation of a series of moves and their probable outcomes, and for the advance formulation of some principle, guiding rule, or "blueprint" that will cover more than a single move and perhaps cover all possible moves. The similarity to situations that are usually called "problem solving," however, is sufficient to encourage one to draw, as I shall, from the literature on problem solving to understand the nature of planning.

I shall start with the question, What represents an ideal state for planning? In an ideal world, all pieces are infinitely and equally movable: a state of affairs that creates the largest number of options and places the least demands on information processing. In real life, however, all pieces in a puzzle or plan are not equally movable. Some pieces may not be movable or changeable at all, or only with difficulty and under special circumstances.

What then gives rise to varying degrees or forms of "fixedness" or "stickiness"? We may find the answer in the objective features of one's pieces: Mountains are not moved by faith, water is turned into wine only by a miracle, money is difficult to draw from an empty account, a friend who lives at a distance and has no telephone cannot readily be asked to go to the bank for one or to provide advice on a pressing problem. Of particular interest to me, however, are the occasions when the answer lies in the planner's perception of movability and the perception does not fit with what others see as possible. An example comes from Oerter's (1981) study of children of various ages, fitting in as many errands as possible into a particular afternoon. Suggestions of delegating (e.g., "having someone else go to the library for you") were rare and appeared only among adolescents. Why, I asked, should this be so? In everyday life, children of all ages seem to have little hesitation about asking others to do things for them or remember things for them (Goodnow & Burns, 1985; Kreutzer, Leonard, & Flavell, 1982). Somehow, the task has become defined as one in which these normally movable pieces are not to be used.

This perception of "fixedness," as people interested in problem solving will recognize, is what Duncker (1945) regarded as a core difficulty in finding solutions to problems. Again and again, he asked: What gives rise to the perception of something as fixed when it is in fact movable or alterable? What conditions lead us to regard something as given in nature and beyond the bounds of change, when it is in fact an option?

To answer such questions, we might define "fixed" as referring to the perception that a piece must be present in a plan. A vacation must include going away from home; the dinner party must include X; the one errand that cannot be omitted is – . To account for perceptions of this kind of fixedness, the most helpful literature is probably that dealing with "scripts." Nelson (1983), for instance, distinguished between "fixed" and "optional" slots, using the former term to refer to pieces or units that must be present in a particular script. A visit to the dentist, for instance, must involve your going there. Optimal slots may or may not occur: One may or may not have cavities, have one's teeth painted with fluoride, be given a balloon, etc. In Nelson's (1983) analysis, one learns from repeated experience to abstract the fixed and optional slots and to build scripts around the core pieces. The accumulation of experience, then, is the basis for perceiving some pieces as having to be included.

This is not, however, the only way in which a piece may be defined as fixed. "Fixedness" can refer to the perception that an item cannot be altered, that is, cannot be moved forward or backward in time, varying its place in a sequence; or cannot be used in ways other than the usual ways. For the conditions that promote this form of fixedness or "stickiness" (the latter term, also from Duncker, 1945), the most helpful sources are Duncker (1945) and some follow-up work by Scheerer and Huling (1960).

In Duncker's (1945) studies and in those of Scheerer and Huling (1960), the pieces to be thought about are objects and their uses. For Duncker (1945), problem solving calls for seeing an object as usable for a purpose it normally does not serve. The perception of "functional fixedness" stems especially from a recent reminder of the usual function, making that function salient and downgrading the visibility of others. For Scheerer and Huling (1960), the source of difficulty again has to do with the perception of novel functions or movable pieces. For example, the subject needs to recognize that a piece of string holding up a calendar is precisely what one needs for another purpose, but using the string calls for detaching it from the calendar. The perception of "functional fixedness" or "stickiness" is seen as arising, however, not only from the reminders of recent experience but also from a number of general assumptions about the extent to which objects can legitimately be changed or taken apart. These assumptions Scheerer and Huling (1960) see as socially acquired. Middle-class students, for instance, seem to be restricted by their greater training in respect for property and in the principle of "each thing in its own place." All students are less likely to plan fluidly when the string holds up a picture that seems of value rather than holding up an old calendar, or when the departmental secretary hangs up a new calendar with the announcement that this is being hung at the request of the director of the laboratory. In these situations social constraints built into the notion of respect for other people's property are the conditions that place limits on the planner's ability to regard all pieces as infinitely and equally movable from one state to another.

Social constraints such as those highlighted by Scheerer and Huling (1960) are the constraints I wish to highlight. They are, I shall argue, the constraints we need to understand in any situation in which planning involves people; either as coplanners or as pieces to be moved in the course of forming or acting out a plan.

B. *Planning as one of a set of possible actions*

For this second proposition, I need to start by drawing attention to several ways in which plans may differ from one another. They may differ, for instance, in fluidity, in the number of steps or contingencies covered, in the extent to which they are worked out in "top-down" or "opportunistic" fashion (Hayes-Roth & Hayes-Roth, 1979), or in the extent to which they involve a particular heuristic such as working backward from the goal rather than forward from one's current position (Duncker, 1945).

Plans may also be distinguished in terms of their degree of appropriateness to a situation. It makes little sense, for instance, to engage in detailed advance planning in a world where the number of uncontrollable events is large and one has too little control to make the exercise worthwhile. Without some degree of access to resources and some control over the movable pieces, one might indeed do better to bend with the wind or flow with the tide, engaging only in opportunistic leaps or in short-term plans with multiple options left open.

Finally, plans may be distinguished in terms of the degree of social approval given to the activity of planning in a particular situation. I have already noted some examples at the level of conversation. It is easy to find others both in everyday comments and in novels. The widow of Galbraith *(Cheaper by the Dozen),* to take one instance, transferred the time-and-motion study skills she had learned from her husband to the task of making a number of social calls while visiting her mother. On her return, she reported with pride that she had fitted in 10 or so calls and asked, "Wasn't that efficient?" "Much too efficient" was the frosty reply, with the clear implication that time-and-motion analysis did not go with the making of social calls.

The problem is not to find examples but to ask, What are the features of situations that give rise to a low level of approval for overt advanced planning and even to penalties for planning? What are regarded as more appropriate forms of action in these situations? How do people come to acquire the belief that planning is a desirable activity and also the knowledge that it is not always so?

C. *Putting the general views to use*

I have proposed two general ideas about planning: (a) that it involves the movement of pieces and the perception of these as movable in various ways, and (b) that the activity of planning is one elective in a set of possible actions, and not always the most appropriate or socially acceptable. The presentation has been brief. More important, there have been few indications so far of how one can put these ideas to use in the analysis of planning situations and activities.

Their usefulness, I propose, lies in helping us make sense of situations not yet well covered in the literature on planning: situations in which plans involve people, and situations in which plans are open for comment and evoke varying degrees of approval for the activity of planning. The remaining parts of this chapter are concerned with these two kinds of situations. There is some overlap between the two (e.g., the likelihood of social disapproval is higher when plans involve people), but the overlap is far from complete, and the two will accordingly be treated separately.

II. Plans that involve people

Consider a situation often used to explore the extent of forward planning and the nature of opportunistic departures from a plan: namely, the task of fitting in as many errands as possible into a particular afternoon (e.g., Hayes-Roth & Hayes-Roth, 1979; Lawrence et al., 1983; Oerter, 1981). Apart from one possible action being that of meeting a friend for lunch, other people are not involved. It is one's own time and freedom of movement that are at issue. Other people do not enter as helping in the planning or as possible solutions to the crunch of time. Suggestions of delegating, as I noted earlier, are rare.

In what ways do people enter into plans? I shall distinguish between two major ways. In one, people plan together or need to coordinate plans. In the other, people become involved as potential pieces in a plan. The plan calls for substituting one person for another (e.g., replacing a salesperson, executive, or spouse) or for shifting an activity from one person to another (e.g., transferring the task of cooking from one family member to another on a short- or long-term basis).

A. Planning together

I raise the issue of planning together not only because such occasions form a critical part of planning in everyday life, but also because the analysis of any form of working together will help in the exploration of a neglected aspect of competence (to invent a label, "cocompetence"). Most analyses of development concentrate on individuals acting alone, solving problems "on their own," in a style often reminiscent of Rodin's "Thinker." Most analyses are also built upon data from situations where no other person is present or – especially odd – situations where another person is present and knows the solution but may not be asked even to give hints.

These particular ways of assessing competence have left us with a great dearth of information about the nature of skill in working with others. We are in sore need of information about how people use others as resources to balance their own shortages or deficiencies (e.g., Cole & Traupmann, 1980; Edgerton, 1967; McDermott, Cole, & Hood, 1978). We are also in sore need of information about how people come to develop skills in "coregulation" or in "collaborative" behavior (Fischer & Bullock, 1984; Goodnow, 1986, Valsiner, in press).

Most of the knowledge we have comes from two types of work. In one, peer groups combine to solve a problem, with the question in the investigator's mind usually being one of whether groups are more efficient than individuals. In these studies, attention is only slowly shifting to questions about the processes and skills involved in effective peer group work (e.g., Peterson, Wilkinson, & Hallinan, 1984). In the other type of study, the people working together possess uneven degrees of skill or expertise, and the one has the role of teaching the other. The goal is to move from a state where the more expert partner does all the work or provides maximal support, to a state where the less expert partner can operate alone. This type of study is often interpreted within a Vygotskian framework (e.g., Rogoff & Wertsch, 1984). The situations studied range from conversations (starting from a state where the mother carries both sides of the exchange, e.g., Kaye, 1982), to teaching children how to weave (Greenfield, 1984), how to remember systems for shelving groceries (Rogoff & Gardner, 1984), or how to feed themselves at mealtimes (Valsiner, 1984).

The latter type of study (combining parties with varying expertise) has so far yielded the greater amount of information about how people interact in the course of joint action. It could readily be extended to the analysis of how people plan together, an extension already planned by Rogoff (personal communication). In any extension, however, it would be well to note some limits to the yield so far from this line of work. First, the information is directed mainly toward the way in which the more expert partner phases in support or dismantles the "scaffolding" (Wood, Bruner, & Ross, 1976) that enables the less expert partner to proceed. The expectations, understanding, or moves by the less expert partner are far less clear. Second, the situations studied so far are predominantly occasions where one person is a willing teacher and the other an eager learner. Only in Valsiner's studies of young children at mealtimes (Valsiner, 1984) and when learning to walk or climb alone (Valsiner, 1983) does one see a clear interest in situations in which the learner may be reluctant to take on an activity or the teacher may be interested in curbing solo action rather than encouraging it – situations likely to occur often in everyday life.

Finally, a limit to what has been learned comes from the relative lack of attention up to this point, to a range of conditions that facilitate or inhibit particular forms of collaboration, coacting, help seeking, and divisions or delegations of labor. The conditions considered are usually of a particular type, concentrated on the ability of the expert partner to detect changes in the ability level of the less expert and, in Kaye's (1982) analysis of mother-infant interactions, her willingness and ability to alter her own course of behavior so that it fits well with the other's state. An analysis of conditions mainly in terms of "responsiveness," however, takes one only so far in any general analysis of coplanning. There must be other conditions that affect joint action. Their nature is not immediately obvious, but let me suggest some possibilities, all dealing with the appropriateness to any given social setting of dividing up work in particular ways. The conditions I suggest come from asking, What has gone wrong in situations in which people feel that a division of planning or an arrangement for coplanning has not worked out well?

One type of condition must surely deal with what are regarded as the two boundary conditions for joint action. At one extreme, one should avoid taking over to such an extent that the other person feels that one is "writing the script" for him or her and leaving no room for autonomy or satisfying participation. (I am assuming that both parties in this case wish to have a hand in the planning.) At the other extreme, one should avoid taking no part, letting people flounder unhappily on tasks that are too much for them. The optimal ground does appear to be the kind of arrangement, if one is the more expert party, that allows the junior party to engage in "guided reinvention" (Locke, 1980).

The critical dimension underlying these feelings about coaction appears to be one of "too much" versus "too little," gauged especially against each party's skills and wishes. There is as well, however, a dimension of right and wrong allocation that does not deal with amount but with what people should do if a sense of equity is to prevail. Equity calls, for instance, for an appropriate sharing of the pleasant and the dreary parts of planning. Equity also calls for each party doing the tasks that are properly "his" or "hers" and that should not be assigned to others. This latter form of equity, or of "proper" working together, with its expectations and assumptions about the "ownership" of tasks, strikes me as particularly worth exploring in situations of joint planning. It is certainly prominent in a number of other situations in which the pieces are *people,* even when there is no commitment to joint planning.

B. Plans with people as pieces

Take the concrete situation of household tasks. The parents' problem is one of seeing that a number of household tasks get done. The most efficient way to get them done is to move tasks around freely from one family member to another, allocating tasks to a family member as a point is reached where help can best be used, handing them out to whoever is capable and is available at that particular time. In a world where only efficiency counts, the same freedom for shifting a task from one person to another should also apply to siblings, with each sib able to swap tasks easily with another as the need arises.

Why do these job-shifts not always occur in practice? Susan Delaney and I have faced that question in an analysis of household tasks, especially in the analysis of answers to questions about whether a sib would do a particular task for another child (this target child is aged 9–11 years). The tasks we were interested in fall into two general categories. One we have labeled "self-care" (making one's own bed, putting dirty clothes in a laundry basket or area, ironing one's own clothes, tidying one's room, putting away toys or books one has used, putting away a school bag left elsewhere in the house). The other category we have labeled "beyond self-care" (setting or clearing the table for a family meal, taking out trash, feeding a pet, cleaning, ironing, bringing in clothes from a laundry line, cooking for someone other than one's self). The tasks in both categories are all pieces in a puzzle that a mother might well wish to shift around in order to get a total amount of work done efficiently and on schedule.

For a self-care task, 44% of the mothers saw as possible the shift of a task from one sib to another. For tasks beyond self-care, 93% saw it as possible. (In both categories, we asked the question with reference to whatever specific tasks a child did.) We need to account for the difference between these percentages, for any difficulty with a job-shift in either category, and finally for the fact that few shifts in the self-care category occur willingly, even when they do occur.

The difference between the two categories of tasks provides the key. Household activities are perceived as belonging in various degrees to particular people. They are *their* jobs. For a number of jobs, this ownership tag is an exclusive one. With a strong moral intonation, for instance, a number of mothers say they "wouldn't ask one child to make another child's bed" or to tidy up another's room. To use some succinct phrases: "It's Sharon's bed, Sharon makes it; Sharon does Sharon's work"; or "Mark sleeps in it, Mark makes it." The principle can be readily applied to whatever one has used. "To each of us," these mothers state, belongs the task of "cleaning up after ourselves." To expect one child to "clear up after" another child, for many of these mothers, is to "encourage laziness," "breed friction," and "let children fudge their responsibilities." Some mothers take the same stance toward their "own" tasks, drawing strict lines between what one can and cannot ask a child to do. They can "help, yes," in one mother's words, "but not take responsibility for housework." "You don't have children," says another, "to do your work for you."

How is it, then, that any self-care tasks are ever done by a sib, if mothers are reluctant to ask and sibs have learned the plea of "it's not my job"? The answer is that close to half the mothers in this group are willing to ask or insist "occasionally," justifying the special occasion on the grounds of need (e.g., "the boys will make her bed sometimes, but only if she's going out somewhere" and the mother is not prepared to leave it unmade), and presenting it as a favor to be reciprocated rather than as an additional activity (e.g., "she does it for you sometimes"). All told, there were only five cases (within 46 families) of willing job-shifts in the self-care category, and these were all initiated by the children themselves rather than imposed by a planning mother. The tie between owner and job, this suggests, is not only looser for some jobs than for others; it is also more readily untied by some people (in this case, the owner) than by others.

That pair of possibilities (a looser tie between person and activity, and the occurrence of lateral rather than top-down initiative) accounts also for the greater likelihood of job-shifts for tasks that are beyond self-care. These tasks do not fall under the restrictive rule: "Each person cleans up after himself or herself." That exemption loosens the ownership tag. These tasks are also often carried out "together," and job shifts are often initiated among the children themselves. The picture is still not always one of total willingness. For tasks beyond self-care, however, mothers are more willing to insist on a shift ("I just say, 'I don't care whose turn it is to feed the cat'"), and children seem to feel that there is less legitimacy to the pleas "it's not my turn" or "not my job" when a table has to be set or a pet fed than when a bed has to be made. It is not only that a bed can wait more readily than a pet can; it is also that the task does not carry the onus of "cleaning up after someone else" and therefore is their moral responsibility.

How could one account then for cases where even tasks beyond self-care are not seen as shiftable from one sib to another? In the subgroup of three families where no child does for a sib a job in the second category, ownership tags turn out to be as strong as they are for self-care tasks. Mealtime patterns in one family provide a sharp example. Each of the two children (boy aged 9, girl aged 7) looks after his or her own dishes. "After dinner at night they usually take out their own dessert plates and put them in the dishwasher. They're learning to cook their own breakfast, and cakes. They bring their own knives and forks in, and pour their own milk." In effect, in this household one's own dishes and utensils, clean or dirty, are treated as if they were one's own bed or clothes to be hung up. Each is responsible for his or her own and nobody else's, and moving one's "own" job to someone else becomes for this family close to unthinkable.

There are clearly individual differences in the way particular families view the ownership of various activities, and it is interesting to speculate how these arise. The differences, however, are my concern in this paper only as illustrations of the point that ownership and negotiability are tags attached to activities – tags important because they open or limit the possibility of shifting a task from one person to another and the freedom with which anyone may plan for moving tasks (pieces) around.

Note, however, that it is not simply the presence of an ownership tag that matters. We need to pay attention as well to the conditions under which a tag may be moved temporarily or permanently and to the conditions that lead people to resist being assigned a place or an activity that originally belonged to someone else. Among these, a condition of particular importance is the presence of any implications about social status. There are, for instance, strong implications of relative status when a job is shifted to you in the face of your reluctance, especially if the job is in the "self-care" category. In many ways, to be expected to clean up after someone else is to be placed in the role of a servant in the household –

an unpaid one at that, as many mothers were quick to point out in relation to their own picking up after children and spouses. Complicating the movability of pieces are issues not simply of efficiency and ownership but also of morality and exploitation.

1. Outside the household. I have been arguing that everyday plans often call for shifts that involve people: either substituting one person for another or moving an activity from one person to another. Household tasks have provided an example of the way such moves are restricted by a number of ideas about the ownership of tasks and about the circumstances under which transfers or exchanges are regarded as possible or proper. Are household tasks special cases, or do the features of ownership and negotiability have similar effects on job-shifts and the feasibility of particular plans in other settings as well?

Four pieces of evidence suggest that generalizability is the case. One comes from Fikes's (1982) analysis of office work. Fikes started with the expectation that work could be programmed in a relatively straightforward "computer" or "top-down" fashion. The reality he found was a network of job-shifts, "third parties," and exchanges of favors, initiated at the work-face level. These were exceedingly difficult to fit into any precise plan, especially because they were often worker initiated. His conclusion was that "simple program execution is . . . misleading as a metaphor for understanding the skills and knowledge needed by computers or people to do the work" (Fikes, 1982, p. 33). As an alternative, he proposed that plans should be described in terms of agreed-upon commitments (e.g., such and such a job to be finished by a particular time), leaving leeway for the several parties to work out for themselves the flow and the exchange of work in a series of "negotiated agreements."

The second piece of evidence comes from Joffe's (1977) analysis of interactions between parents and preschool or kindergarten teachers. The latter work at a disadvantage, Joffe argues. They would like to tag particular activities as exclusively theirs (e.g., "scientifically based" child care, first introduction to reading), using this uniqueness to legitimate their status as professional workers and distinguish themselves from parents. To many observers, however, the tasks of a preschool teacher do not seem very different from those of a parent and might be expected to be readily exchanged. In the face of this perception, the preschool teacher has to work especially hard at convincing people that some activities *are* exclusively hers. They require special training and cannot be shifted to any "untrained" person. Creating such a mystique of exclusive skills is far from unknown in many professions. One might in fact say that the bane of a manager whose plans call for fluid job-shifts is the worker who establishes a "hold" on certain tasks, making them his or her "specialty."

The third example of a context in which ideas about the movability or exchangeability of people are important comes from the literature on families. To what extent are people regarded as replaceable? To what extent can one be substituted for another? This aspect of shiftability is somewhat different from the shifting of a task from one parent to another. One now shifts a set of tasks, a role, or a relationship. Everyday comments suggest that we hold some definite expectations about "better" and "poorer" substitutions (varying from one social group to another but definite within each). Replacing a spouse, for instance, can readily raise a comment that the person should have chosen someone his or her own age or remarried "too soon" (especially if he or she only recently asserted that "no one could take the place" of the previous spouse). At a more formal level, it has been proposed that men differ from women in their response to the loss of a spouse, with the difference taking the form of men's readier interest in replacement, occasioned in part by their previous dependence on spouses for both household care and social networks (Rosenman & Shulman, 1983). More broadly, clinicians describe difficulties in family relationships as taking the form of inappropriate substitutions of people, for instance, treating a child as if it were a parent, or acting toward a child as if one were a sib or peer rather than a parent (Baszormeny-Nagy & Spark, 1973).

The last example of the usefulness of thinking in terms of the movability of people is in the form of comments on the president of a banking firm, "a president whom many partners thought . . . self-centered, haughty, unfeeling, uncaring." Contributing to this reputation was the way he "would call partners at all hours, summon them to ride uptown in his chauffeured Oldsmobile, and then ignore them as he talked on the telephone or scanned a memorandum." In the words of one of his admirers, " . . . He would set his mind on something and see nothing else. He would walk down the hall with a stack of letters, read the mail, write replies and just throw them over his shoulder, assuming someone would be there to pick them up" (*New York Times Magazine,* February 17, 1985, p. 34). There turned out to be a price for assuming that people would always follow in his wake and especially for treating his partners as pieces he could move readily and without regard for legitimizing the move. His staff did not warn this senior executive of impending trouble, and, in the face of a push from another contender for his post, he was supported by too few partners to resist the challenge. In effect, *he* became the movable piece.

III. Plans that evoke approval and disapproval

Are there situations in which detailed advance planning is not the best
action we can take? Suppose I turn that question into a more social form:
Are there situations in which actions other than the kind we usually call
"planning" (advance mapping of several steps and contingencies) are
highly approved of, or at least where action without planning is not disapproved? If so, what are the features of such situations?

Consider first a setting where action without planning is not treated
with disapproval. The example comes from a recent talk in which an
anthropologist commented on the prevalence in the Philippines of an
attitude and practice that greatly bothered many U.S. observers and co-
workers. The name of the anthropologist, alas, has dropped out of memory, but the name of the practice – *bahala na* – has not. Nor has its general meaning: a reference to "barging ahead" or "acting anyhow," even
when no favorable outcome seems likely. To use the anthopologist's
example, a photographer is expected to take photographs at a picnic. At
the last moment, shortly before the arrival of the bus he must take to the
picnic, he discovers he has no film. He cannot buy film on the way.
Bahala na is his response. He goes to the picnic anyway, with the camera.
There might or might not be someone there with film. He might or might
not take pictures. What he will do is make one move forward rather than
decide the whole project is hopeless and do nothing.

Bahala na is not a disapproved practice in the Philippines, certainly
not to the extent that it would be, say, in the United States. There may
even be a positive value attached to one's going ahead in the face of such
uncertainty – "giving it a bash," to use an Australian phrase. What does
such a positive view of "action anyway" say about the virtue of planning?
It is a reminder that the virtue of planning is linked to conditions of living
where the number of uncontrollable events is manageable and where
there is sufficient control over resources to make the exercise worthwhile.
Without some degree of access to resources and some control of the movable pieces, one might indeed do better to bend with the wind or flow
with the tide, engaging only in opportunistic leaps or in short-term plans
with multiple options left open.

Suppose, however, that planning is objectively feasible. Are there settings where limits to planning are viewed with approval? What features
of a setting give rise to such views?

One example comes from feminist analyses of the way people plan a
life course. Women, it has been argued, have often been taught not to lay
out a life plan in any detail, not to develop interests of such intensity that

further actions will be dictated by those interests. Instead, their life plans of employment, interest, or places to live should be left relatively fluid so that they can be adapted to the more precise and determined plans of their spouses. This preparation for being a movable piece emerges in the value given to occupations such as secretary or teacher. It emerges also in preparation for being a "corporate wife": preparation in the form of being relatively knowledgeable about a large number of areas so that one may fit readily into the interest of several possible spouses, being neither so empty-headed as to signal poor potential for further development nor so expert that one is threatening, nor so committed to one area as to seem excessively self-directed (Ardener & Callan, 1984). Neither the right nor the obligation to plan, it appears, is equally distributed among all people.

Some further examples apply to both men and women. In all three of these, overt and detailed advance planning is not regarded as completely *comme il faut*. Suppose we see what can be learned from each of these.

The first is the occasion of a holiday, when many of us like to set planning aside. Some of us may choose to proceed "as if we had all the time in the world" and may stop wearing a watch, whereas others enjoy the sensation of "having everything worked out" for them. Such holidays highlight the way in which the decision to plan is often based on an underlying sense that it is important to be efficient, to value the minimizing of "waste," and to avoid positions of no-return or slow recovery. This sense of a scarce resource or a valuable resource, we suggest, is one of the conditions that sustain the effort of planning and give it a particular value in most people's eyes. It also gives rise to a sense of anomaly when a person is careful and planful with a resource that is not scarce, for example, when someone on holiday "counts seconds," or when the truly rich keep track of small amounts of money.

The second type of example comes from occasions of love or intimacy. The prevailing belief is that such occasions should be marked by a certain degree of spontaneity. "Falling in love" or "being carried away" is appropriate, whereas a visibly planned seduction – by either party – is not. There are, it is true, cultures and subcultures in which marriage is an affair carefully planned by others for the two parties. Any culture with a tradition of romantic love, however, is likely to equate high feeling with a lack of careful planning, or with an "extravagant" ignoring of consequences even when these are anticipated. (The same may be true for any culture with a strong tradition of honor.) The cultures that sustain attention to planning are likely to be those that, in Habermas's (1971) terms, place a premium on technology and rationality. They are also likely to require the careful marking of exceptions from rationality and to show the use of particular justifications for "unplanned" behavior (being "overcome," "carried away," "swept off one's feet," "bewitched," "madly in love," etc.).

The third and last type of example is more homely. It arises again from the work by Susan Delaney and myself on mothers' accounts of why they assign household tasks to children and why they do so in particular ways. Of the 46 mothers interviewed, only a small number use a roster system. Given children's concern with issues of equity, why is a roster system – allowing a visible record to be made of who has done what and who will be doing what at certain times – not more popular in this group? Part of the answer is contained in one mother's comment that she "couldn't stand to use a roster. It wouldn't seem like a home, more like a jail or a school, or one of those motels with a long list on the door of things you can and can't do." This type of comment is echoed in another's statement that a roster could "solve fights," but that she "liked to be more creative than that."

More subtly, mothers who avoid rosters strike us as often having in mind a much longer-term plan than a short-term roster allows. They do keep track of who has done what and they do plan for equity. Whereas children may plan for equity in terms of days or weeks, however, mothers may have months and years in mind. The point is nicely expressed by the mother of a 16-year old: "Lisa doesn't do dishes any more. She *could* do them. But she's the oldest, and she's got years of washing up behind her. Let the others take her turns now." These long-term contracts and the avoidance of short-term planning may strike us at first as a little odd. It is interesting to find, however, that in law, contracts that contain precise plans are likely to be short-term contracts. The longer-term a contract is, the less it is likely to specify the details of who is to do what and when (Macaulay, 1977; Macneil, 1978, 1981). These "relational contracts," as they are termed, allow for the possibility that circumstances may change over the long term and for the expectation that the goodwill behind the long-term agreement will lead to a shift in plan acceptable to both parties. The "marriage contract" may be the ultimate example.

In short, one can make some headway with the interesting question: When is overt and precise planning regarded as appropriate and when gauche? The situations where visible planning is expected to be downplayed turn out to be situations containing a supply of resources that allows one to be lavish and tolerate some waste, or situations where the definition of proper interpersonal relationships calls for the suspension or limitation of planning (coments of love or honor) or for placing more reliance on goodwill than on advance agreements about all possible contingencies (long-term relational contracts). These situations, I suggest, prompt a continuing concern with locating the features of situations that give lesser approval than usual to planning, and with such questions as: What justifications are offered for a lesser degree of planning or for making less visible the planning one does? How is it that in modern culture planning usually is seen in such an unequivocably positive light?

IV. The nature of learning to plan

I wish to close this paper by raising one last question prompted by considering the social aspects of planning: What is the nature of learning to plan?

To the extent that the demands of planning are seen as predominantly cognitive or heuristic, one is encouraged to look at learning or development by way of exploring individual differences in, say, the extent to which people use a "top-down" or "bottom-up" approach or the extent to which they use a device such as working backward from a goal.

To the extent, however, that the demands of planning are seen also as the need to know about social constraints (and to examine them for false assumptions), one is encouraged to look at the nature of learning or development in a different light. When the pieces in a plan are people and their activities, learning must cover the social rules and regulations that underlie right and proper ways to treat people. It must cover also the implications of status that accompany a request for help or a transfer of tasks. When our planning is open to comment by others, one aspect of socialization must certainly concern learning how to make appropriate judgments and discriminations; judgments about the amount of visible planning regarded as appropriate, about the expected match between particular kinds of occasions and particular forms or degrees of planning.

There seem to be no direct accounts of such learning, although the behaviors involved would appear to fit Shweder's (1982) description of nonrational moral behaviors ("nonrational" in the sense of not being open to proof or disproof; "moral" in the sense of carrying a strong connotation of right and wrong). What is certain is that there is considerable force in some of this socialization. It can be a grave social error, for instance, to take literally all statements about an occasion being "nothing formal, just a little dinner with a few of us." The words may sound as if the occasion belongs in the category of spontaneous, unplanned activities, but that often turns out not to be the case. Equally grave is the occurrence of error in categorizing activities as "those you can ask someone else to do for you" as against "those you should do for yourself." It is critical to know what goes into the "do-for-yourself" category, if one wishes to avoid the reputation of being one of those people who "expect someone else to brush their teeth for them."

I have found so far little material that helps answer questions about the learning of social constraints or of the value to planning. Consider, however, a suggestion from the sociologists Berger, Berger, and Kellner (1974), dealing with the acquisition of positive views about planning. They draw attention to the emphasis on a particular type of planning in many parts of modern society, namely, planning one's life course. We are encouraged, they argue, to develop some sense of how one's life is likely to unfold and to work toward making it do so. As part of that planning, they continue, we are expected to learn how to create options (leaving a way to retreat from a move, creating alternative routes), and how to choose effectively among them. This life plan, to take their argument further, is the theme of many family discussions about "the future" and gives rise to a sense of where one should be by a certain age. It also gives rise to an extension in values, in the sense that the planning deemed so valuable in discussions of one's life course begins to acquire the connotation of being valuable for all activities. The virtues of planning, in effect, come to be taken as a given rather than something that has to be learned from direct and specific experience with the rewards of planning or the disasters of not doing so.

This proposal of learning by generalization is a contribution to describing how we become socialized into viewing planning as a positive step in most situations. It does not answer the question, How can we tell that this generalization has occurred? Berger et. al. (1974) proposed that one sign is the intrusion of a practice or a value (in their terms, an "aspect of consciousness") into areas where it is inappropriate. (One plans, for instance, to "fall in love".) One might add as well the discomfort felt by adults when in a situation where forward planning is not feasible. Roth (1963) provided a striking example. Restricted to a sanitorium for tuberculosis at a time when drug treatment was not available, he observed the effort patients put into creating "benchmarks," that is, interpreting any action by doctors and nurses as indicative of how their recovery would unfold and what its time course might be. Finally, one might ask about children's use of future-oriented statements. Children have certainly acquired some sense of a life plan when they say that the value of learning to cook while in primary school lies in the fact that "you will not need to eat out all the time when you have a job – That would be too dear," or that the value of going to school lies in "your being able to get a job when you are grown up" (Goodnow & Burns, 1985). Those examples deal only with one social aspect of planning (its being viewed with varying degrees of approval). One could ask similar questions and entertain similar hypotheses about how we come to learn that some particular moves in a plan are likely to encounter social constraints. My purpose at this point, however, is not to search for clues as to how this learning comes about, but rather to note once more the point that is the focus of this paper, namely, that when one begins to ask about the social aspects of planning, we are helped to perceive gaps in our knowledge, to ask new questions, and to form new views about the nature of planning and its development.

References

Ardener, S., & Callan, H. (Eds.). (1984). *The incorporated wife.* London: Croom Helm.

Baszormeny-Nagy, I., & Spark, G. (1973). *Invisible loyalties: Reciprocity in intergenerational family therapy.* New York: Harper & Row.

Berger, P. L., Berger, R., & Kellner, H. (1974). *The homeless mind.* Harmondsworth: Penguin.

Cole, M., & Traupmann, K. (1980). Comparative cognitive research: Learning from a learning disabled child. In W. A. Collins (Ed.), *Aspects of the development of competence, Minnesota Symposia on Child Development* (Vol. 12). Minneapolis: University of Minnesota Press.

Duncker, K. (1945). On problem-solving. *Psychological Monographs, 58,* No. 270.

Edgerton, R. B. (1967) *The cloak of competence: Stigma in the lives of the mentally retarded.* Berkeley: University of California Press.

Fikes, R. E. (1982). A commitment-based framework for describing informal cooperative work. *Cognitive Science, 6,* 331–348.

Fischer, K., & Bullock, D. (1984). Cognitive development in middle childhood. In W. A. Collins (Ed.), *Development during middle childhood.* Washington, DC: National Education Association.

Goodnow, J. J. (1977). *Children drawing.* Cambridge, MA: Harvard University Press.

Goodnow, J. J. (1978). Visible thinking: Cognitive aspects of change in drawing. *Child Development, 49,* 637–641.

Goodnow, J. J. (1985). *Parenting and processes of cultural transmission.* Paper presented at the Conference on Families and Processes of Cultural Transmission, Stanford Center for Advanced Study in the Behavioral Sciences, March, 1985.

Goodnow, J. J. (1986). Some lifelong everyday forms of intelligent behavior: Organizing and reorganizing. In R. Sternberg & R. Wagner (Eds.), *Practical intelligence: Origins of competence in the everyday world.* Hillsdale, NJ: Erlbaum.

Goodnow, J. J., & Burns, A. (1985). *Home and school: Child's eye view.* Sydney: Allen & Unwin.

Goodnow, J. J., Knight, R., & Cashmore, J. (1985). Adult social cognition: Implications of parents' ideas for approaches to development. In M. Perlmutter (Ed.), *Social cognition, Minnesota Symposia on Child Development* (Vol. 18). Hillsdale, NJ: Erlbaum.

Greenfield, P. M. (1984). A theory of the teacher in the learning activities of everyday life. In B. Rogoff & J. Lave (Eds.), *Everyday cognition: Its development in social context.* Cambridge: Cambridge University Press.

Habermas, J. (1971). *Toward a rational society.* Frankfurt: Schrkemp Verlag.

Hayes-Roth, B., & Hayes Roth, F. (1979). A cognitive model of planning. *Cognitive Science, 3*, 275–310.

Joffe, C. (1977). *Friendly intruders: Childcare professionals and family life.* Berkeley, CA: University of California Press.

Kaye, K. (1982). *The mental and social life of babies: How parents create persons.* Chicago: University of Chicago Press.

Kreutzer, M. A., Leonard, S. K., & Flavell J. H. (1982). Prospective remembering in children. In U. Neisser (Ed.), *Memory observed: Remembering in natural contexts.* San Francisco: W. H. Freeman.

Lawrence, J. A., Dodds, A., & Volet, S. (1983). An afternoon off: A comparative study of adults' and adolescents' planning activities. In *Proceedings of the Australian Association for Research in Education.* Canberra: A.A.R.E.

Locke, A. (1980). *Guided reinvention of language.* New York: Academic Press.

Macauley, S. (1977). Elegant models, empirical pictures, and the complexities of contract. *Law and Family Review, 11*, 507–528.

Macneil, I. R. (1978). Contract adjustments of long-term economic relations under classical, neoclassical, and relational contract law. *Northwestern University Law Review, 72*, 855–905.

Macneil, I. R. (1981). Economic analysis of contractual relations: Its shortfalls and the need for a "rich classificatory apparatus." *Northwestern University Law Review, 75*, 1018–1063.

McDermott, R. P., Cole, M., & Hood L. (1978). "Let's try to make it a good day" – not so simple ways. *Discourse Processes, 3*, 155–168.

Nelson, K. (1983). Social cognition in a script framework. In J. Flavell & L. Ross (Eds.), *Social cognitive development.* Cambridge: Cambridge University Press.

Oerter, R. (1981). Cognitive socialization during adolescence. *International Journal of Behavioural Development, 4*, 61–76.

Peterson, P. L., Wilkinson, L. C., & Hallinan, M. (Eds.) (1984). *The social content of instruction: Group organization and group process.* New York: Academic Press.

Rogoff, B., & Gardner, W. P. (1984). Adult guidance of cognitive development. In B. Rogoff & J. Lave (Eds.), *Everyday cognition: Its development in social context.* Cambridge, MA: Harvard University Press.

Rogoff, B., & Wertsch, J. (Eds.) (1984). *The zone of proximal development.* San Francisco: Jossey-Bass.

Rosenman, L., & Shulman, A. (1983). Sex differences in coping with widowhood. Unpublished paper presented at the annual meeting of the Australian Psychological Society, Sydney, Australia.

Roth, J. A. (1963). *Timetables: Structuring the passage of time in hospital treatment and other careers.* Indianapolis: Bobbs-Merrill.

Scheerer, M., & Huling, M. D. (1960). Cognitive embeddedness in problem solving: A theoretical and experimental analysis. In B. Kaplan & S. Wapner (Eds.), *Perspectives in psychological theory: Essays in honor of Heinz Werner.* New York: International Universities Press.

Shweder, R. A. (1982). Beyond self-constructed knowledge: The study of culture and morality. *Merrill-Palmer Quarterly, 28*, 41–69.

Valsiner, J. (1983). Parents' strategies for the organization of child–environment relationships in home settings. Paper presented at biennial meeting of the International Society for the Study of Behavioral Development, Munich, August 1983.

Valsiner, J. (1984). Construction of the zone of proximal development in adult–child joint action. In B. Rogoff & J. Wertsch (Eds.), *The zone of proximal development.* San Francisco: Jossey-Bass.

Valsiner, J. (Ed.). (in press). *The role of the individual subject in scientific psychology.* New York: Plenum.

Wilensky, R. (1981). Meta-planning: Representing and using knowledge about planning in problem solving and natural language understanding. *Cognitive Science, 5,* 197–283.

Wood, D. J., Bruner, J. S., & Ross, G. (1976). The role of tutoring in problem solving. *Journal of child psychology and psychiatry, 17,* 89–100.

Part III

Children's skills of planning

6 Conceptions and processes of planning: the developmental perspective

Shulamith Kreitler and Hans Kreitler

I. Introduction

A. *Planning in developmental psychology*

Planning is one of the commonest, most ubiquitous and most important activities of human beings. Every person plans, regardless of whether he or she is good at it or not. The daily life of adults is hardly conceivable without some degree of planning. We plan the big things of life – marriage, a career, vacations, or the budget, to mention some of the commonest items on the list – as well as the small, all important details of when to leave work, or what to wear for a party. People plan for themselves as well as for society at large – their community, country, and the world in the future. According to theorists of the most varied schools, the ability to plan is an integral characteristic of human behavior responsible for the adjustment, well-being, and smooth functioning of the normal adult. Planning is assumed to make possible purposeful behavior (James, 1890), transcending the immediate concrete context of action (Werner, 1948, chap. 7), attainment of preset goals (Bühler, 1930, chap. 5), delay of gratification (Freud, 1963), and voluntary behavior with the concomitant control over oneself and the environment (Luria, 1960; Zaporozhets, 1960). Hence, planning may be considered as a basic ability of human beings.

At first glance it appears incontestable that like all basic abilities, the ability to plan develops from young ages up to adulthood. Yet at second thought it seems that this expectation is not so self-evident. Planning is based on dealing with the hypothetical, with what is not yet present physically. This requires hypotheticodeductive reasoning abilities which do not appear before the age of 11–12 years (Piaget & Inhelder, 1958). Thus, when analyzed from the viewpoint of adult cognition, it may seem that planning may not be expected to start developing before adolescence. In contrast to this conclusion, there is a lot of anecdotal evidence that children engage in planning, often by talking about their behavior in events they expect to occur. Further, there is evidence that children perform acts that seem to us to presuppose planning, such as in a hide-and-seek game, running straight for a particular hiding spot when the signal for hiding is given. Again, many studies showed that children are able to execute learned plans (Urbain & Kendall, 1980). Hence, it is likely that planning is based on cognitive abilities that develop well before adolescence. The noted discrepancy between expectation and experience lends increased importance to studies about the development of planning. Yet, surprisingly little is known about this theme. Indeed, planning is not even mentioned in the standard textbooks on developmental psychology. The major direct source of data about planning in children is studies about children's application of plans for performing cognitive tasks like remembering (Brown & DeLoache, 1978), mapping an environment (Nagy & Baird, 1978), or communicating information to others who may have different perspectives (Flavell, Botkin, Fry, Wright, & Jarvis, 1975). Although cognitive problems may be an important domain for planning, they certainly do not constitute the major or most common sphere for the manifestations of planning in children. Further, the studies deal mainly with the execution of plans, especially of those learned previously, rather than with the actual generation of plans.

Moreover, there are almost no theoretical discussions of the development of planning. One reason for this may be the attitude of Miller, Galanter, and Pribram (1960), who have contributed more than any others to introducing plans into psychology. In their influential book they hardly mention the theme, and seem to assume that the development of planning is part of the problem of plan formation in adults ("children acquire their store of heuristic methods by listening to verbal suggestions and then trying to execute them," p. 184). The insightful remarks about plan development set forth by Schank and Abelson (1977) are a notable exception to the theoretical neglect of planning. Regrettably their data base is limited to very few observations of one subject 3–4 years old.

To be sure, a lot of indirect information about planning is available in psychology. As noted, some of this information appears in the form of studies about the development of behaviors that presuppose planning, for example, achievement behavior or play. However, because so many other factors besides planning enter into the determination of these behaviors, the studies do not allow for drawing any firm conclusions about planning itself. Further information could be derived from studies about the development of abilities that are prerequisites of planning or partial manifestations of planning, for example, setting of goals and sticking to them (Werner, 1948, p. 198); distinguishing between major goals and subgoals that serve as means to ends (Leontiev, 1959); casual thinking (Laurendeau & Pinard, 1962); delay of gratification (Mischel & Patterson, 1978); generation of hypotheses (Ingalls & Dickerson, 1969); time perspective (Lovell & Slater, 1960); voluntary behavior (Luria, 1960; Zaporozhets, 1960); differentiating between wish and reality, wanting and being (Gunn, 1964); integrating information (Wilkening, Becker, & Trabasso, 1980); and so on. However, the number of such constitutents of planning is fairly large, and their role in the total act of planning may differ in various contexts and may even change through interactions with one another. Moreover, there is no certainty that all or even most constituents of planning have been identified. Hence, integrating these findings about partial aspects of planning – eclectically or even according to some theoretical model – would not lead to information that can replace directly collected data about the development of planning.

B. A working definition of planning

Before we could devise the experiments described in sections II and III, it was necessary to define planning. Miller et al.'s commonly used definition of plan, as a hierarchical process controlling the performance order of a sequence of operations, turned out to be too limited. By listing "hierarchy" and "sequence" as criteria of plans, it excludes plans that are not yet hierarchically structured or sequentially ordered. Hence it cannot serve as a guide for studying the development of hierarchization and sequencing in planning. On the other hand, definitions inspired by cognitive science, based on the conception that plan is a problem solution attained in a particular manner (Hayes-Roth & Hayes-Roth, 1979; Sacerdoti, 1977), turned out to be too broad. By emphasizing the problem-solving aspect of planning, such definitions include as plans any sequence or strategy in the most diverse domains of cognitive functioning (see below, this section).

Steering a middle course, we settled on the following definition: "Planning" is a complex cognitive activity that occurs when no program able to regulate action is available. This definition assumes that every act of behavior is regulated by programs, i.e., hierarchical systems of instructions on different levels of inclusion (Gallistel, 1980; Kreitler & Kreitler, 1982). Some of these programs are innately acquired (e.g., reflexes), some are partly innate and partly learned (e.g., instincts, defense mechanisms), some are fully learned (e.g., ways of greeting, marrying, shopping in a department store), and some are constructed by the individual. It is these latter programs that we suggest to call "plans" because their construction involves actual planning on the part of the individual. In contrast, the other kinds of programs are not the result of the individual's planning but are inherited or learned by one of the usual methods, such as verbal instruction, modeling, conditioning, and so on. Plans differ from programs in their origin, even though the individual may use in planning information or partial programs acquired previously through learning. To be sure, after a plan has been constructed, it may be indistinguishable from programs of the other kinds. Thus, it may be stored and then retrieved and executed at some later point in time, it may undergo transfer to situations other than the original situation that gave rise to it, it may be combined with other plans or programs, and so on. Accordingly, planning is the cognitive activity that produces plans.

Our emphasis that planning is a cognitive activity also highlights the distinction between planning and action. Planning often precedes action, may culminate in action, or may even be deduced from one or more actions. Nevertheless, planning is not identical with action, for the execution of plans depends not only on the plan but also on processes different from those involved in planning.

As a cognitive activity, planning shares many characteristics with other cognitive activities, primarily problem solving. Like problem solving, it involves several cognitive processes, it proceeds in stages, and it may be initiated by a problem situation. Nevertheless, planning differs from problem solving, as commonly conceived, in three major respects: First, planning is a cognitive construction of one or more steps to be undertaken, whereas problem solving is a cognitive execution of plans, evaluation of their adequacy, and sometimes even a mere motor manipulation. Second, planning refers to a future action, whereas problem solving may deal with issues that are unrelated to action or the future. Third, planning is focused specifically on *how* to do or attain something (e.g.; how to get to a certain location, how to manage with limited resources, etc.), whereas problem solving may deal with other issues too, for instance, *why* something exists or acts the way it does, what are the *results* of some object or event, what is the *purpose* of a given occurrence, and so forth. These distinguishing features make for differences in at least some of the cognitive processes involved in planning, as opposed to those involved in problem solving.

Finally, we characterized the cognitive activity of planning as complex because a great number of different cognitive processes are involved in it, as shown in another study (Kreitler & Kreitler, chapter 4, this volume, section III). Indeed, even a relatively simple planning task such as planning a party requires, at the very least, thinking about time, place, causes, functions, consequences, manner of occurrence, and many other things, some of which are certain to be overlooked, not to mention the processes of evaluation, integration, and decision making interspersed all along the sequence.

C. Purpose and plan of the chapter

The major purpose of this chapter is to present data about different aspects of planning in children 5–11 years old that would provide information about the development of planning in this age group. Such information is important both theoretically, for the sake of improving understanding of mental health and cognitive competence, and practically, for the sake of enabling the training of planning. We focused on the age span of 5–11 years because it is the period during which the major cognitive tools for planning may be assumed to be acquired. Whereas before 5 years of age, action may not yet be sufficiently controlled to allow for enough experience with planning, after 11 years of age there are already so many stored plans and programs that action may proceed smoothly without too often resorting to planning unless the individual is particularly motivated to do so (Kreitler & Kreitler, chapter 4, this volume, section II).

In order to gain insight into an activity as complex and central as planning, it is advisable to study both the conceptions of children about this activity – that is, "metaplanning" – and its actual performance. This chapter deals with both.

Section II presents a study about children's conceptions of planning and the development of these conceptions from the age of 5 to 11 years. There are two main reasons for studying children's conceptions of planning. The first is theoretical. The ideas children have about planning – that is, about what constitutes planning, its antecedents, consequences, importance, difficulties, range of application, and so on – may be expected to be an important factor within the matrix of determinants guiding the acquisition and performance of planning. Just as the ideas children have about memory ("metamemory") were shown to affect the children's recall (e.g., Appel, Cooper, McCarrell, Sims-Knight, Yussen, & Flavell, 1972; Flavell & Wellman, 1977), the ideas children have about planning may be assumed to affect the manifestations of planning. Similarly, just as "metamemory" alone does not suffice to account for memory abilities (Brown & Barclay, 1976; Kelly, Scholnick, Travers, & Johnson, 1976; Paris, 1978; Salatas & Flavell, 1976), we do not expect "metaplanning" alone to account for planning skills, but rather to constitute one factor within a theory about the development of planning.

Children and adults have beliefs of different kinds – for example, beliefs about oneself, about one's goals, or about what should or should not be done. Clusters of such beliefs have a cognitive–motivational function in regard to behavior, that is, they enable the prediction and change of behaviors (Kreitler & Kreitler, 1982). A belief cluster of this type was shown to be related to the manifestations of planning in children (Kreitler & Kreitler, chapter 4, this volume). Some of the children's conceptions about planning probably function directly as beliefs within such a cluster. More importantly, the children's conceptions about planning play a primary role in regard to all beliefs in the cluster because they define the themes for the beliefs and thus determine which beliefs are likely to be at all relevant. For example, if children consider planning as designed to save time, it would be important to examine the children's beliefs about saving time (e.g., whether they want to save time, whether they view themselves as able to save time, whether they consider that time should be saved); likewise if it is found that children do *not* consider planning as diminishing spontaneity, children's beliefs about spontaneity would be irrelevant for predicting or changing planning in children. Accordingly, we consider metaplanning as forming the cognitive groundwork for the cognitive–motivational factors that play a role in the acquisition and manifestations of planning.

The second reason for studying "metaplanning" is of a more practical nature. Children's conceptions about planning define the sphere of planning and thus determine what is relevant to planning and what is not. Hence, these conceptions may be used for devising planning tasks that would not only require planning per se but would also be considered by the children themselves as requiring planning. Even in a questionnaire, responses given to items considered by the subjects as relevant to the theme of the study differ from those given to items judged as irrelevant (S. Kreitler & Kreitler, 1981). Thus, the use of tasks relevant for planning from the viewpoint of children is of great importance in the study of children's planning. For example, if children consider planning as appropriate mainly in regard to interpersonal situations, a situation involving motor activity may not be grasped by them as requiring at all planning. Accordingly, studying children's conceptions about planning was necessary also in order to construct the planning tasks used in the second study (see Section III). Thus, Study A dealt with the conceptions children 5–11 years old have about planning and its different aspects: reasons, purpose, results, domains to which planning applies, identity of planners, frequency of planning, and so on. A special emphasis was placed on examining the relation of planning to the concerns, motivations, and potentialities of the developing individual.

Performance of planning is as distinct from conceptions about planning as a sexual act is distinct from speculating about sex. As noted, the conceptions are no doubt related to the act, but in a most indirect manner through the intermediation of other cognitive contents and processes that cannot be deduced only from the conceptions. Hence, in order to learn about the development of actual planning, actual manifestations of planning have to be studied. This is the theme of the second and major study, described in section III. This study deals with development of planning in children 5–11 years old, as assessed on the basis of the children's responses to 10 tasks requiring actual planning. Although these tasks were constructed in view of the findings of the first study (II), the two studies (described in sections II and III) are completely independent of each other, and each can be understood without the other. The findings provided information about the development of planning skills (e.g., chronological ordering of plans, construction of alternate plans) (section III.C.1) and their clustering into more stable and comprehensive cognitive structures (factors of planning, e.g., gathering of information, structuring of plans) (section III.C.4), the development of plan formation as reflected in the evaluated adequacy of the specific plans constructed by children (section III.C.2) and in the clustering of these plans in particular domains (e.g., interpersonal relations with peers, managing of errands) (section III.C.5), and the development of the cognitive processes enabling the activity of planning (e.g., elaborating the meaning of the situation, selecting aspects of the problem about which hypotheses are generated, applying principles for gathering information about the problem) (section III.C.3). The relations of planning variables with IQ are examined in section III.C.6, mainly in order to establish whether developments in planning can be accounted for by developments in IQ.

Finally, in section IV the different parts of the data are integrated with the purpose of presenting, hopefully, a coherent conception of the development of planning. This attempt at integration is based on considering, on the one hand, the development from the various complementary viewpoints, and, on the other hand, the planning individual with his or her developing reality testing and increasingly complex conceptions of planning, motivations, and potentialities for action.

II. Study A: development of conceptions about planning

A. Purpose and hypotheses

This study deals with several aspects of the contents and structure of children's conceptions of planning and their changes in the course of the age span from 5 to 11 years. The main aspects examined included the domains to which planning applies, and the individuals who are regarded as engaging in planning, as well as the nature of the planning activity, its purpose, antecedents, consequences, difficulties, and importance. Thus, the major purpose was to obtain information about "metaplanning," that is, the conceptions of naïve subjects about planning, which is of primary importance for understanding the cognitive–motivational background of planning. A secondary purpose was to identify domains of planning mentioned by a certain percentage of children in all groups so as to serve as nuclei for the construction of planning tasks to be used in studying planning in children (this chapter, section III; Kreitler & Kreitler, chapter 4, this volume, sections II and III) (see section I.C).

In view of the scarcity of information about the development of planning and metaplanning, no specific hypotheses were set up beyond general expectations of the following kind: From the age of 5 to 11 years there will be an increase in the number of domains for which planning is considered as adequate, in the antecedents of planning, in the benefits attributed to planning, in the groups of individuals considered to plan, and so on.

B. Method

1. *Subjects.* The subjects were 200 children, 50 from each of the following age groups (years; months): 5–6 years (preschoolers; $\overline{X} = 5;4$ years), 7–8 years (second graders: $\overline{X} = 7;7$ years), 9–10 years (fourth graders; $\overline{X} = 9;6$ years) and 11–12 years (sixth graders; $\overline{X} = 11;5$ years). All the children were from families of middle socioeconomic status. The number of boys and girls was equal in each group. The children were sampled randomly from five schools in the Tel Aviv metropolitan area, 10 children of each age group (5 boys and 5 girls) from each school.

2. *Procedure.* The children were interviewed individually by one of three experimenters, in a separate room on the school grounds. Each session lasted for 15–25 minutes. The interviewer sat next to the subject so

as to minimize the effects of the experimenter's nonverbal behavior on the child's responses. Before beginning the interview, the experimenter explained that the subject would be asked several questions about planning because "we want to know what children think about it." Paper and pencils were provided in case the subject preferred to draw or to write down the responses. All the subjects' responses were written down by the experimenter in the child's presence "because we want to remember what you said and to think about it."

3. Materials and measures. The children were interviewed in accordance with a questionnaire which had two parts. The first part included only one question, which was always asked as the first question: "Imagine someone – you don't have to tell me who it is – who does not know what planning is. Try to explain to him or her what it means. Tell him or her what people in general mean when they use this word and also what this word means for you in particular. You may explain by talking or writing or drawing or enacting, etc." The second part administered immediately afterward included 13 questions, asked in random order, and introduced by the statement: "Now I would like to ask you some more questions about planning: What kinds of things are planned?/ When will you carry out the things you plan?/ Who plans: children, grown-ups?/ Are there many children or grown-ups who plan?/ How often is planning done?/ Why (under which circumstances) is planning done?/ What is the purpose of planning (what is it good for)?/ What are the results of planning?/ How is planning done?/ What does one feel when one plans?/ Is planning difficult or not?/ What are the difficulties in planning?/ Is planning important or not?"

All questions were formulated in line with the system of meaning (Kreitler & Kreitler, 1982; chapter 4, this volume, section III) which enables the characterization and coding of meanings in general and hence also of cognitive contents in any particular sphere of interest, such as planning. A major part of the system of meaning – and the only one applied in this study – is an empirically derived set of 22 general categories used for characterizing contents; these categories are called "meaning dimensions," for example, Sensory Qualities, Antecedents and Causes, Temporal Qualities, etc. Each meaning dimension defines a certain area of contents, so that different responses referring to this area can be coded as reflecting the particular meaning dimension. For example, references to time, such as "yesterday," "never," "every day," "during a month," are all considered as reflecting the meaning dimension Temporal Qualities.

Thus, the first question in the questionnaire was formulated in line with the standard instructions for the communication of meaning (see above). It was designed to assess the different aspects of contents to which children of the four age groups referred spontaneously and thus provide information about the meaning dimensions characteristic of the meaning of planning. In regard to the second part of the questionnaire, the role of the meaning dimensions was to serve as a guideline for formulating the different questions. Thus, each question corresponds to one meaning dimension, for example, the question about why planning is done corresponds to the dimension of Antecedents and Causes, whereas the question about what should be planned corresponds to the dimension Domain of Application. Because the meaning dimensions constitute a comprehensive set of kinds of contents, formulating the questions in correspondence to the dimensions guaranteed adequate representation of content areas in the questionnaire. The original list of 22 questions was reduced to 13 on the basis of pretests.

The responses to the first question were analyzed in terms of meaning dimensions. Those to the further 13 questions were analyzed in terms of response categories (see Tables 6.1 to 6.11) based on content analyses of the original answers. In all cases an attempt was made to avoid far-flung interpretations and to keep as closely as possible to the original responses that are often presented in the tables together with the heading of the response category under which they were classified. The data were coded by experimenters who did not know the interviewees' names or ages. Checks on the reliability of coding showed intercoder correlations in the range of .89–.98 across the different questions.

C. Results

Preliminary findings showed no significant differences between boys and girls in all except two response categories in one age group that can be attributed to chance. Hence the findings are presented together for the whole sample of each age group.

Table 6.1 presents information about the *frequency with which the different meaning dimensions were used* by the children in communicating the meaning of planning. In order to examine the development of the interpersonally shared aspects of the meaning of planning, we first looked for manifestations of such aspects in the 11-year olds because if they exist, they are more likely to be found in older than in younger children. Further, we assumed that responses given by at least 30% of the children reflect aspects of meaning shared by the children in that age group more than those given by fewer than 30%. Table 6.1 shows that in 11-year olds

Table 6.1. *Percentages of subjects in the four age groups who used the different meaning dimensions in communicating the meaning of planning*

Meaning dimensions	Age groups			
	5 years ($n = 50$)	7 years ($n = 50$)	9 years ($n = 50$)	11 years ($n = 50$)
Domain of Application	84	90	82	92
Antecedents and Causes	36	76	70	44
Consequences and Results	12	60	46	50
Function, Purpose, & Role	—	20	32	80
Manner of Occurrence & Operation	—	12	14	16
Temporal Qualities	2	8	6	10
Locational Qualities	—	12	8	18
Quantity and Number	—	—	6	10
Feelings & Emotions	—	2	14	6
Judgments & Evaluations	4	4	10	16

Note: The table summarizes the coded responses to Question No. 1 in the questionnaire. The percentages in each age group do not add up to 100% because some children used more than one meaning dimension in their responses.

there are four meaning dimensions used by more than 30% of the children: Domain of Application (i.e., specification of the domains that are planned); Antecedents and Causes (i.e., the circumstances that trigger planning); Function, Purpose, or Role (i.e., the goal of planning); and Consequences and Results (i.e., what follows planning or the absence of planning). In view of our above-stated criteria, it is plausible to consider tentatively these four dimensions as constituting the core of the shared meaning of planning in children. This assumption is supported by findings that show how this shared core develops gradually and systematically from the youngest to the oldest age group. In the responses of 5-year olds, only the first two meaning dimensions appear with a frequency above 30% (Domain of Application and Causes); in the responses of 7-year olds the first three dimensions already appear (Results is added); and in the responses of 9- and 11-year olds, all four meaning dimensions appear. Indeed, there are some deviations from linearity in the frequencies of these dimensions in the four age groups (e.g., the dimensions Causes and Results increase from the first to the second group and then decline again in the oldest group). But more important than these fluctuations are (a) the recurrence of the four meaning dimensions in all age groups and (b) the systematic increases in their frequencies. These findings strengthen the assumption that these dimensions probably constitute the core of the shared meaning of planning in children and thus define the semantic space characteristic for planning as conceived by children. One implication of these findings is that they enable comparisons between the meaning of planning and of other perhaps similar concepts, such as thinking or daydreaming, which can be operationalized in the same terms. A more practical implication is that in training planning or in teaching children specific plans, it is advisable to focus on information concerning content areas defined by the four meaning dimensions so that the training appears relevant to the subjects.

Table 6.2 presents the data concerning the *domains appropriate for planning*. It shows that from 5 to 11 years not only is there a steady increase in the number of domains considered as deserving of planning, but there are also changes in the nature of the mentioned domains. Characteristically, the younger children consider planning as applicable primarily in regard to regular daily actions (e.g., eating, going to bed, dressing in the morning) centered mostly on oneself. In 7-year olds there is a remarkable broadening in the range of mentioned domains. Attainment of control over others and over oneself seems to be the feature common to the different domains the 7-year olds mention, that is, manipulating parents or teachers so as to get more privileges (reflecting control over adults), using machines (reflecting control over tools), performance of daily chores, such as homework, doing errands or cleaning one's room, and avoidance of commitments and obligations, such as keeping promises or complying with requests (reflecting control over one's time), and determining one's health, emotions, thoughts, and dreams (reflecting control over one's body and internal life). As in 5-year olds the approach is still egocentric in the sense that planning is considered as applicable only if there are immediate benefits for the planner. In 9-year olds there are notable increases in the numbers of children who consider planning as applicable to interpersonal relations with peers (e.g., fighting or making up with someone, inviting or being invited by a member of the other gender), daily chores, and achievement. On the whole, the approach is more realistic and sociable: Fewer childen consider planning as useful for controlling one's mental life or for avoiding commitments. However, the most interesting phenomenon in 9-year olds is the frequent application of planning for dealing with imaginary eventualities (e.g., if a thief comes in the night, if the school is attacked and I am the only defender). This finding indicates a convergence between daydreaming and planning. It is in accord with Freud's (1962) claim that daydreaming, like thinking is often, "experimental action." The categories of the imaginary themes, that is, coping with fear situations, taking revenge, acts of heroism, great

Table 6.2. *Kinds and frequencies of domains requiring planning mentioned by children in the four age groups*

Domains	Age groups			
	5 years (n = 50)	7 years (n = 50)	9 years (n = 50)	11 years (n = 50)
Recurrent daily actions	64	10	—	—
Searching for lost items	12	18	16	28
Manipulating grown-ups	4	34	24	22
Avoidance of commitments & obligations	—	58	30	22
Avoidance of punishment	—	44	12	8
Performance of chores	—	20	74	80
Relations with peers	6	26	68	92
Using some machine or instrument	6	24	10	8
Controlling one's body	—	32	14	—
Controlling one's mental life	—	26	8	—
Fantasy and daydreams	2	12	46	10
Entertainment	6	10	24	38
Ways and roads	8	12	16	18
Traveling (to far places)	2	20	32	26
Achievement and success	—	8	50	76
Budget and finances	—	4	16	32
One's personal future	4	14	24	38
Economic & managerial events in which self is not involved	4	6	28	38
General social & political issues	—	—	12	34
Mean number of domains per subject	1.18	3.78	5.12	5.90

Note: The findings are based on the children's answers to the question "What kinds of things are planned?" The numbers represent percentages of children computed on the basis of the total number of children in the age group. The percentages do not add up to 100% because most children mentioned more than one domain.

successes, fights and battles, correspond closely to most of those found by Singer and his associates (Singer & Antrobus, 1972) in their groundbreaking studies on daydreaming. The increase of fantasy themes in planning is probably important also developmentally because it may prepare the ground for liberating planning from the sphere of one's immediate interests. This trend already appears in 9-year olds, who consider the need for planning impersonal occurrences, such as timetables of flights and trains, running a theater, opening a business, or supplying water and food to cities. But the actual step toward liberating planning from here-and-now

Table 6.3. *Range and frequency of time periods for which planning is envisaged by children of the four age groups*

	Age groups			
Time periods	5 years (*n* = 50)	7 years (*n* = 50)	9 years (*n* = 50)	11 years (*n* = 50)
Responses are scheduled to occur:				
In the immediate future (within minutes to a week)	80	66	34	21
In the near future (in one to four weeks)	12	18	49	41
In the far future (after one year or more)	8	16	17	38
Responses refer to:				
Only one time period (immediate, near or far future)	62	54	40	16
Two or three time periods	38	46	60	84

Note: The findings are based on the children's answers to the question "When is planning done?" The numbers are percentages computed out of the totals of responses for each age group. The chi-square value for the totals of the upper part of the table is 50.88 (df = 6, p < .001), and of the lower part of the table, 24.89 (df = 3, p < .001).

concerns becomes evident in 11-year olds. They consider planning as applicable to many domains related to their personal reality-bound goals for the present (e.g., avoiding chores, entertainment, achievement) and the future (e.g., studies, career, marriage, leaving parents' home); but in addition, as applicable also to domains of general concern for the nation, for society at large, and even for humanity both in the present and the future (e.g., peace, solving social problems, ecology, space flights, etc.).

Table 6.3 summarizes the answers to the question "When will you carry out the things you plan?" The findings show that the *range of time* for which planning is envisaged increases steadily from 5 to 11 years. At the level of 5 years, 80% of all mentioned plans concern acts expected to occur within the immediate future (defined as the time range of minutes to 6–7 days from the present), and only 8% concern acts of the far future (defined as the time range of 2–3 months to more than 1½ years from the present). Indeed, 40% of all 5-year olds mentioned plans designed to be implemented in the immediate future only (i.e., no later than the present week). At age 11, only 21% of all plans concern the immediate future whereas 38% concern the far future. The largest shift from plans for the immediate future to plans for the near future (defined as the time range of 6–7 days to 3–4 weeks from the present) occurs between 7 and 9 years of age, whereas the major development toward plans for the far future (i.e., for more than 2–3 months ahead) occurs between 9 and 11 years of age. Notably, the plans of the younger children (5 and 7 years old) tend to be concentrated within one period of time (i.e., the immediate or the near future), whereas those of the older children tend to be more evenly distributed, those of children 11 years old more than those of children 9 years old. This point is also evident from the finding that there is a steady increase in the percentage of children who consider plans for different points in time, from 38% in 5-year olds to 84% in 11-year olds. One of the implications of these findings is that in order to train children's ability to plan, one should first increase their time perspective.

Table 6.4 presents a summary of the *antecedents for planning* mentioned by children in the four age groups. In 5-year olds, the main antecedents are the demand for action as such, often bound with the need to recall things as done previously, for example, "to take off your clothes, put them on the chair, and take a shower, exactly as you were taught to do." Thus, planning seems to refer mainly to routine actions, probably those that have not yet been sufficiently mastered. In 7-year olds, only 14% of the mentioned antecedents for planning refer to routine actions, and the main emphasis is placed on the need to plan actions performed under special circumstances (e.g., time pressure, examination) or actions of a special kind (e.g., new, dangerous). In 9- and 11-year olds there are further increases in the class of antecedents emphasizing special external or task-bound circumstances, which comprise about 30% of all responses. However, in these age groups there are interesting shifts in references to states in which emotions or achievement are involved: in 9-year olds there is an increase in references to special emotional states, whereas in 11-year olds there is instead an increase in references to desire for success. If we regard the class of external or task-bound circumstances and the class of special kinds of actions as reflecting *environmental* conditions, and the classes of emotional states and achievement as reflecting *psychological* conditions, then the developmental trend of the antecedents for planning could be described roughly as follows: There is a shift from an initial emphasis on routine actions (88% in 5-year olds) to an emphasis on actions extraordinary in some respects; among the latter the frequency of environmental conditions increases only slightly from the age of 7 to 9 years (66% to 70%, respectively) and then declines again in 11-year olds (46%), whereas the frequency of references to special psychological con-

Table 6.4. *Summary of responses to questions about the antecedents for planning in the four age groups of children*

Response categories	Age groups			
	5 years (n = 50)	7 years (n = 50)	9 years (n = 50)	11 years (n = 50)
The need:				
To perform an action	52	10	4	—
To perform an action as it was done previously	36	14	—	—
To perform special kinds of actions:				
Dangerous	2	12	14	6
Difficult		4	12	2
New		12	8	6
Revenge			4	
Unallowed acts		18	2	4
Total	2	46	40	18
To perform acts under special external or task-bound circumstances				
Alone for the first time	4	2	6	2
An examination		6	14	10
Under threat of punishment	2	2		2
Time pressure		4	8	10
Many things have to be done		4	2	4
Under supervision				
Particular manner of performance		2		
Total	6	20	30	28
To act when special emotional states are involved:				
Sadness			4	
Fear	4	2	10	
Excitement			6	4
Longing				2
Lack of confidence		4		
Anger		2		6
Offense			1	2
Boredom			1	2
Total	4	8	22	16
To act when achievement is involved:				
Doing something important		2	2	10
Doing something in which you want to succeed			2	20
Doing something in which you must not fail				8
Total	—	2	4	38

Note: The numbers represent the percentage of children out of the total number of children in the age group. The chi-square value based on the totals of the different categories is 162.01 ($df = 15$, $p < .001$).

Table 6.5. *Summary of the subjects' responses to questions about the purpose and about the results of planning*

	Percentages of subjects in age groups			
Response categories	5 years ($n = 50$)	7 years ($n = 50$)	9 years ($n = 50$)	11 years ($n = 50$)
Question: purpose of planning				
None, don't know	24	4	—	—
Performing routine actions, familiar but not mastered	74	22	12	—
Knowing how to perform	—	40	20	24
Performing fast, saving time	—	14	16	10
Feeling good	2	10	32	12
Success in performance (correct, precise)	—	10	20	54
Question: results of planning				
Performance of action	78	28	2	—
Positive emotional state or avoidance of bad emot. state	2	8	30	16
Success in performance	10	14	14	22
Getting something you would not get otherwise (money, good grade, time)	—	20	30	32
Good evaluation from others	10	22	8	8
Negative emotional state	—	2	8	4
Less success in performance	—	6	8	18

ditions increases most dramatically from the age of 7 to the ages of 9 and 11 years (10%, 26%, 54%, respectively). One implication of the findings concerning the antecedents of planning is that training for planning should be based on emphasizing different antecedents for planning in different age groups. Another implication is that in teaching the concept of "special circumstances," environmental conditions are to be emphasized prior to psychological ones, and, within the latter, emotional prior to motivational.

Table 6.5 presents the data concerning the *purpose and results* of planning. The answers to these two questions are presented in one table because they lead to similar conclusions. Children 5 years old claim that the role of planning is mainly to enable the performance of routine actions, already familiar but not entirely mastered, for example: "It is good to plan how to go to bed if you did it alone only one or two times." Correspondingly, the mere performance of action is the major result of planning emphasized by 5-year olds (Table 6.5). In contrast, children from the age of 7 onward consider the purpose of planning to enable performance of a particular kind. The qualifications, however, differ with age. Notably, 7-year olds emphasize the function of planning in regard to knowing *how* to perform, suggesting thereby that planning applies mainly when the individual does not quite know how to act. Accordingly, they consider obtaining a good evaluation from others as a possible benefit of planning. Children 9 years old mention far less the orienting role of planning but refer more often to the emotional function and emotional results of planning. The typical answer of this kind was: "When you do something you planned, you feel good." These answers probably reflect the feeling of competence that derives from improved control. Children 11 years old consider the function of planning to be mainly the improvement of action in terms of correctness, precision, or speed. Correspondingly, success in performance is one of the results of planning that they consider. However, like 9-year olds, they are concerned with the possibility of attaining through planning something that one is unlikely to attain otherwise (e.g., saving time or money). These responses reveal awareness of the unique benefits of planning. More importantly, these older children already mention possible negative results of planning, for example: "You enjoy less the action," "It is boring when you know everything that will happen," "You think only of the plan and not of what there is," and so on. Statements of this kind (20% in 11-year olds) probably form the nuclei for the active resistance to planning that is rather common in adults. The findings also suggest that already on the level of children, when training for planning, it is advisable to consider not only the weakness of the cluster of beliefs orienting toward planning but also the strength of the cluster of beliefs antagonistic to planning.

Table 6.5 shows that with age there is an increase in the number of children who mention positive results of planning (the percentages for the four groups are 22%, 64%, 78%, and 78%, respectively) and there is also an increase in the number of children who mention negative results of planning (the percentages for the four groups are 0%, 8%, 16% and 22%, respectively). The *evaluation of the importance of planning* may depend on these opinions. Thus, the percentages of children in the four age groups who consider planning as highly important are 28%, 42%, 76%, and 56%, respectively, and the percentages of those who consider it to be of low importance are 46%, 38%, 10%, and 28%, respectively. If the children's evaluations of the importance of planning are scored as high ($= 3$ points), medium ($= 2$ points), and low ($= 1$ point) ($\chi^2 = 26.57$, $df = 6$, $p < .001$), the overall means for the four age groups are 3.64, 4.08, 5.32

Table 6.6. *Kinds and frequencies of children's conceptions about the manner in which planning is done*

Response categories	Age groups			
	5 years (n = 50)	7 years (n = 50)	9 years (n = 50)	11 years (n = 50)
Performance of action (You do things)	50	6	—	—
Recalling, remembering	20	10	2	—
Thinking in the head	20	40	10	16
Imagining, fantasy	10	20	46	4
Specification of cognitive processes (You consider, examine, figure it out, decide, compare, etc.)	—	22	34	60
Mentioning elements of plans for planning (You think what you need, you ask, arrange it in your mind, etc.)	—	2	8	20

Note. The findings are based on the children's answers to the question "How is planning done?" The numbers are percentages of children computed on the basis of the total number of children in the age groups.

and 4.56, respectively ($F = 2.70$, $df = 3/196$, $p < .05$). Thus the data show a deviation from linearity in 11-year olds. In this age group there is a decrease in the evaluation of planning as highly important and a complementary increase in the evaluation of planning as unimportant. As a result, the whole developmental trend is shaped in the form of an inverted U. It seems likely that the drop in evaluation in 11-year olds is due to their previously noted enhanced awareness of the possible negative results of planning.

Table 6.6 deals with the children's responses concerning the *manner* in which planning is performed. It shows that the majority of 5-year olds think that planning is simply an action; most 7-year olds characterize planning as a cognitive action but do not proceed very far in specifying the involved cognitive processes; 9-year olds go into greater detail in this respect, adding a characteristic emphasis on fantasy; 11-year olds make valiant efforts in listing cognitive processes, and, most importantly, 20% of them show evidence for rudiments of plans for planning. The findings reflect the increasing sensitivity of the children to psychological processes revealed through introspection. The manifestation of plans for planning from about 9 years is in accord with findings in another domain of cognitive activity. Bjorklund, Ornstein, and Haig (1977) showed that teach-

Table 6.7. *The conceptions of children in the four age groups on difficulties in planning*

Response categories	Age groups			
	5 years ($n = 50$)	7 years ($n = 50$)	9 years ($n = 50$)	11 years ($n = 50$)
Difficulties in planning				
To execute the plan	48	14	4	2
Memory: to recall all the relevant items	—	10	—	—
Memory: to remember the plan while planning goes on	—	16	8	14
Memory: to recall everything that could happen	—	14	42	78
Memory: to remember the plan	20	12	14	24
Information gathering (to find out, to ask, etc.)	—	36	34	48
Planning: to arrange the items in order, to know where each part belongs, etc.	—	18	24	42
Prob. solving: to know what to do	—	10	22	14
Decision making: to decide, make up your mind	—	—	32	26
Nothing	32	4	2	10
Mean No. of difficulties per subject	.68	1.30	1.42	2.48

Note: The findings are based on the children's answers to the question "What is difficult about planning?" The numbers represent percentages of subjects, computed out of the total number of children in the age group. The percentages do not always add up to 100% because some children mentioned more than one kind of difficulty.

ing a plan for memorizing first becomes effective for children 8 to 11 years old. Awareness of plans for cognitive activities in general may be one reason for these findings.

The responses of the children to the question, "Is planning difficult or not?" show that the percentages of children who evaluated planning as easy are 66%, 54%, 42%, and 26% in the 5-, 7-, 9-, and 11-year olds, respectively, whereas the percentages of those who evaluated it as difficult are 8%, 24%, 32% and 50%, respectively. If the children's evaluations of difficulty are scored as difficult ($= 3$ points), medium ($= 2$ points), and easy ($= 1$ point) ($\chi^2 = 25.60$, $df = 6$, $p < .001$), the means for the four age groups are 1.42, 1.70, 1.90, and 2.24, respectively ($F = 2.65$, $df = 3/196$, $p < .05$). Thus, the overall evaluation of difficulty shows a linear increase from the youngest to the oldest group. Correspondingly, also the mean number of difficulties mentioned by each child rises from .68 for 5-year olds to 2.4 difficulties per child for 11-year olds (Table 6.7).

Increased familiarity with the activity of planning seems to breed increased awareness of its difficulties particularly when there are also increased abilities for introspection and expression. Most 5-year olds seem to confuse planning with execution of the plan and hence note mainly the difficulties attendant upon executing the plan. From the age of 7 years onward, the kinds of the difficulties mentioned by the children remain fairly constant, but the frequencies of each kind in the four age groups differ. The difficulties may be grouped tentatively into five classes. The class with the highest frequencies includes references to difficulties of memory, focused mainly on "internal information gathering" (i.e., remembering the plan in the course of planning and later, recalling items and eventualities relevant for planning) (the means are .20, .52, .65, and 1.16 for the four age groups, respectively). The second class of difficulties could be called "external information gathering" because it includes items such as "asking people," "observing," "learning what you have to know," etc. (the means are .00, .36, .34, and .48 for the four age groups). The third class includes references to problem solving (i.e., hitting on the idea of what to do), but its frequencies are relatively low (the means are .00, .10, .22, .14 for the four age groups). The fourth class includes references to decision making, which similarly is of low frequency (the means are .00, .00, .32, and .26 for the four age groups). The fifth and last class could best be called "structuring the plan" because it includes items such as "arranging the things in order," "knowing when each thing should occur," and so on (the means are .00, .18, .24, and .42 for the four age groups).

In sum, the children of all age groups mention mainly difficulties concerning the first stages of planning that capitalize on skills of the divergent type (i.e., external and internal information gathering), rather than difficulties concerning the later stages that require more convergent skills (e.g., deciding and structuring the plan). There may be two reasons for this. One is that becoming aware of all the relevant aspects and keeping them in mind are actually the more difficult parts of planning. The other possible reason is that children may get bogged down in the first stages of planning and often do not reach the later stages so that they have more opportunities to be exposed to the difficulties of the first than those of the later stages. The fact that older children, more often than the younger, mention the difficulties of deciding and plan structuring lends a modicum of credibility to the second suggested reason. Be it as it may, these findings are of particular importance for shaping a program for training planning in children.

The children's descriptions of the feelings in the course of planning reveal the affective tone accompanying planning (Table 6.8). In terms of

Table 6.8. *Kinds and frequencies of children's conceptions about the feeling tone of planning*

	Age groups			
Feeling tone	5 years (n = 50)	7 years (n = 50)	9 years (n = 50)	11 years (n = 50)
Positive feelings	26	50	52	36
Neutral feeling tone	70	26	30	34
Negative feelings	4	24	18	30

Note: The findings are based on the children's answer to the question "What does one feel when one plans?" The numbers represent percentages of children computed on the basis of the total number of children in the age group [$\chi^2 = 30.71$ ($df = 6$), $p < .001$)].

a 3-step scale (1 = negative tone, 2 = neutral tone, 3 = positive tone), in all age groups the affective tone tends to be positive. It rises slightly from the age of 5 to 9, when it reaches its peak, and then declines to its lowest level in 11-year olds. One possibility for the relatively high peak at 9 years is that 9-year olds, more than others, equate planning with daydreaming (Table 6.2), which is essentially enjoyable. Another possibility is that 9-year olds are aware of many positive benefits of planning but, unlike 11-year olds, do not yet dwell to the same extent on the negative results of planning (see Table 6.5).

The children's answers to the question "Who plans: children, grown-ups?" indicate that with age, fewer subjects think that planning is an activity performed mainly by adults (the percentages are 64%, 38%, 20%, and 10% for the four age groups, respectively) and more subjects emphasize that it is done by both adults and children (the percentages are 18%, 42%, 68%, and 84%, respectively) ($\chi^2 = 53.69$, $df = 6$, $p < .001$). In fact, the percent of subjects who claim that children engage in planning is 36%, 62%, 80%, and 90% in the four groups, respectively. These responses indicate that planning is a meaningful activity for the majority of children from the age of 7 years onward and that they see other children as increasingly engaging in it.

The children's judgments about the quantitative aspects of planning lead to essentially similar conclusions. When asked whether there were many or few planners, the percentages of children who indicated that there were many planners increased from the age of 5 years to 11 years (they were 12%, 36%, 70%, and 96% for the four groups, respectively), whereas the percentages of those who indicated that there were few planners decreased (they were 30%, 24%, 10%, and 0% for the four groups, respectively). In terms of a 3-step scale constructed so that "many" was scored as 3 points, "some" as 2 points, and "few" as 1 point (χ^2 = 79.09, df = 6, p < .001), the mean evaluations of the frequency of planners are 1.82, 2.12, 2.60, and 2.96 for the four age groups, respectively (F = 2.60, df = 3/196, p < .10). Similarly, concerning the frequency of planning itself, the answers show a decrease in the percentages of those claiming that it is done infrequently (i.e., 1–2 times per week or per month: 64%, 24%, 4%, and 10% for the four groups, respectively) or rarely (i.e., once in 2–3 months or in 1–2 years: 30%, 26%, 0%, and 0% for the four groups, respectively), whereas there is an increase in the percentages of those claiming that it is done very often (i.e., several times a day or once in 1–2 days: 6%, 50%, 96%, and 90% for the four groups, respectively). In terms of a 3-step scale (whereby "very often" = 3 points, "seldom" = 2 points, and "rarely" = 1 point), the mean evaluations of the frequency of planning are 1.94, 2.24, 2.96, and 2.90 for the four groups, respectively (F = 2.51, df = 3/196, p < .10). In terms of all noted indices, the evaluation of frequency increases from the age of 5 to 9 years, whereas at the age of 11 years there is a tendency for a slight decrease, possibly due to the awareness of some of these children of the negative results of planning (see Table 6.5).

D. *Some conclusions*

All the findings of Study A refer to children's conceptions of planning. It was shown that with age there is a growing consensus concerning the structural aspects of the meaning of planning. It may therefore be expected that at least in some areas there is a sufficient similarity in the views of the children to allow for a meaningful summary. Nevertheless, any attempt to summarize such descriptive data must necessarily be highly selective. The major points of interest seem to us to be focused around four themes which, perhaps not accidentally, correspond to the four meaning dimensions that recur in the children's communications of the meaning of planning: the domains of application, the antecedents, the purpose, and the results of planning.

The findings show that 5-year olds consider planning mainly as contributing to the regular performance of short-range daily routine actions. Apparently, planning is initially conceived as an activity that helps in recalling how recurrent actions were previously performed. Hence, it seems justified to conclude that for 5-year olds, planning fulfills an important role in turning recurrent actions into routine automatic actions. At the age of 7 years, the potentialities of planning for controlling the environment for the sake of attaining egocentric goals in the immediate and near future have been discovered. Planning is no longer needed for mastering routine acts but is conceived as increasing one's mastery over actions of a specific kind or actions performed under special conditions, predominantly of an environmental kind. At this age some children assume that planning can help in controlling even one's body and thought. At the age of 9, there is evidence that planning – already conceived as a fairly complex cognitive activity – may improve performance of actions carried out under special conditions, predominantly of an emotional kind. Major domains considered as calling for planning are interpersonal relations with peers and imaginary occurrences bound with negative or positive emotions. At the age of 11 years, planning is expanded to further domains subserving not only personal ends in the near and far future but also goals of import for society and even humanity at large in the far future. Thus, the major developmental trends in the children's conceptions of planning seem to be the following: There is development in the domains to which planning is considered as applicable (regular routine actions to actions performed under special conditions); in the range of time for which planning is conceived (immediate future to far future); in the beneficiaries of planning (the planning individual to society and humanity at large); as well as in further aspects, such as the conceived dynamics and difficulties of planning (a fairly simple action to a complex cognitive activity requiring memory, information gathering, etc.), the evaluation of the importance of planning, and the extent of attributing planning also to children. Common to all noted developmental trends is the relation of the conceptions of planning to the gradually increasing range of interests, interest in mastery, and mastery over cognitive processes characteristic of children 5–11 years old.

The presented findings about the development of children's conceptions of planning may serve as basic data for the further study of planning and lend themselves to varied theoretical and practical uses. Primary among the latter are providing information necessary for devising planning tasks (see section III), teaching specific plans, or training planning skills in general.

III. Study B: development of planning

A. Purpose and goals

The study was designed to investigate the development of actual planning skills in children 5–11 years old. The scarcity of available data (see section I.A) and the centrality of this domain in children's lives (see sections

II.C & D) lend importance to a study of this kind. Before it is possible to study the correlates of planning variables in other domains in children of different ages, it is necessary to learn something about development in the planning variables themselves. The study was designed to provide developmental information both on the more general level, in terms of global summary variables assessing planning skills and evaluating the quality of plans, as well as on the more fine-grained level, in terms of specific responses to particular planning tasks. In addition, attempts to explore the organization of the domain of planning by means of factor analyses will be described. Although the study is focused mainly on investigating the measures of planning themselves rather than relations between them and extrinsic variables, one exception was made in regard to the IQ measure. Checking the relations of planning measures to IQ was designed to assess the extent to which planning as a predominantly cognitive activity is a function of the traditionally assessed cognitive skills. Thus, the relations of planning variables to IQ are important in order to clarify whether the development of planning reflects mainly developments in intelligence at large or mainly developments particular to the domain of planning. Hence, the findings may shed light on the issue whether planning is sufficiently autonomous to be considered as a distinct domain within the cognitive system.

B. Method

1. Subjects. The subjects were 240 children, 60 in each of the following groups (years; months): 5–6 years (preschoolers; $\overline{X}$ = 5;3 years), 7–8 years (second graders; $\overline{X}$ = 7;8 years), 9–10 years (fourth graders; $\overline{X}$ = 9;8 years), and 11–12 years (sixth graders; $\overline{X}$ = 11;7 years). All the children were of middle socioeconomic status. In each age group, the number of girls and boys was equal. The children were sampled randomly from four different schools in the Tel Aviv metropolitan area, 15 children of each age group (7 or 8 boys and 7 or 8 girls) from each school. None of the children of this study participated in Study A (see section II.A.1)[1]

2. Materials. Planning was studied by means of the children's responses to 10 Planning Situations.[2] In order to ensure that the planning tasks would be considered by the children as relevant to planning, the Planning Situations were constructed on the basis of children's responses in a previous study (see section II, this chapter) to questions about the domains to which planning applies and the antecedents of planning (see mainly Tables 6.2 and 6.4). In order to enable comparison of responses in different age groups, the situations referred to domains mentioned by at least some children (6%) in each age group. For the sake of enabling children to enact planning also in situations most congenial for them, an attempt was made to include at least two domains mentioned frequently by children of a particular age group. As will be seen below, the tasks were varied not only in contents but also in other characteristics, for example, whether the planner was assumed to be a child (e.g., Planning Situations Nos. 1, 3) or an adult (e.g., Planning Situations Nos. 2, 4), whether the plan was assumed to be for the planner (e.g., Planning Situations Nos. 1, 8), or for others (Planning Situations Nos. 2, 7), and whether it was stated that further information was needed (e.g., Planning Situation No. 10), or it was not stated (Planning Situations Nos. 5, 8). The tasks were presented as games, and in some of them actual toys were used so that the child would be drawn to role-play the planning. Concrete details were always specified, and, whenever necessary, adapted to the children's age (e.g., the game mentioned in the first situation varied from the sandbox to chess). For male subjects, boys' names were used, and for female subjects, girls' names.

The Planning Situations will be described briefly both because a brief description suffices for understanding the results and because a more detailed presentation is available elsewhere (Kreitler & Kreitler, chapter 4, this volume, Table 4.1):

1. Two children often play together. B was using an item necessary for the game, which is now missing. A is willing to go and look for it. What should A ask B in order to go search for the item? (The names of A and B, the game commonest at the given age group, and the particular item were specified.)

2. The parents of C bought a new washing machine which is being presently unloaded. The people urge the parents to ask *now* everything that they want to know about the machine or that they want to be done to the machine because it would be very difficult to get a repairman later. What should the parents ask the people to do or explain to them? (The scene is enacted with toys.)

3. D is going some place for the first time (for 5-year olds, to his/her own friend; and for older children, to the mother's friend to fetch something). Now that D is about to leave, what should (s)he ask the mother? (The scene is enacted with toys.)

4. A family of four plus a dog are going for a day's trip to the desert where there are no shops. What should they take along? (Toys are used as reminders of the protagonists.)

5. The story of Jack and the Beanstalk is told and shown by means of pop-ups up to the point when the giant detects the presence of Jack, who is hiding. Jack is scared and decides to flee. What is his plan?

6. R came back from school without his jacket. R's mother wants to go look for it. What should she ask R?
7. There are two groups of soldiers, one guarding a citadel with a treasure, the other determined to conquer it. Can you guess the plan of the commander of the attacking group? (An additional plan is later requested; the scene is enacted with toys.)
8. P wants to play with another child with whom he/she has never played. He/She devises a plan. What is it? (The subject is later asked to devise an additional plan and to evaluate two suggested plans.)
9. U wants to stay up late that night (for guests or a TV show). His/Her parents do not usually agree. What is U's plan? (An additional plan is later requested.)
10. Y comes with his/her family to town for one day in order to do five different things (specified and represented by means of toys). The subject is requested to prepare a plan, to ask for any information needed (all provided by the experimenter upon request), and finally to draw the itinerary.

3. Procedure. Each subject had two individual sessions, with an interval of 5–7 days. In one session the Peabody Picture Vocabulary Test (PPVT) was administered, in the other the Planning Situations. The order of the sessions was randomized, and the experimenters changed. The sessions lasted 30–45 minutes, with a break of 1–3 hours in the Planning Situations session for some of the 5-year olds who became too tired. In administering the Planning Situations, the experimenter sat near the child, wrote verbatim the child's responses and described the child's actions. After the completion of each response, the child was asked "What else?"

4. Variables. The child's responses to the Planning Situations were evaluated in terms of three groups of variables. The first group included *general planning skills,* assessed in terms of characteristics of planning manifested in the various Planning Situations. The second group included *plan adequacy,* assessed in terms of global evaluations of the plans formed in each of the Planning Situations. The third group included *techniques and procedures of planning,* assessed in terms of particular responses manifested within each Planning Situation. The first group of variables was designed to provide information about the availability of basic planning skills; the second, about the efficiency with which the different skills are combined within the framework of particular plans in view of specific situational requirements and conditions; and the third, about the dynamics of planning as it proceeds in concrete cases. The three groups of variables were expected to complement each other.

a. General planning skills. In this study 10 general planning skills were assessed. The measures used were the following:

1. Number of alternative plans presented (either spontaneously or in response to a direct request in Planning Situations Nos. 7–9).
2. Number of if–then eventualities considered explicitly in the plans.
3. Number of chronological orderings used in describing a plan or in asking for information while planning.
4. Number of different questions asked while planning.
5. Number of items considered or referred to.
6. Number of different domains to which refer the questions or items. (A "domain" was defined as an independent content category, e.g., food or entertainment in Planning Situation No. 4.)
7. Number of general labels used in presenting a plan or asking questions while planning. (A "general label" was defined as a relatively more abstract term summarizing and preceding a series of more detailed instances of acts or items, e.g., "guard the passage" in the following response: "I'll guard the passage, that is, I'll send soldiers to guard the entrance, I'll block all the access roads, I'll blow up the bridge, etc.")
8. Mean number of steps included in the plans presented as first and major ones. (A "step" was defined as a relatively independent act that forms part of a plan, e.g., taking a bus, going to bed.)
9. Mean number of steps included in plans presented as alternatives to the major plans. ("Step" was defined as in Variable No. 8.)
10. Mean number of steps included in all plans, major and alternative ones. ("Step" was defined as in Variable No. 8.)

It was assumed that these measures assessed degrees of differentiation and complexity in the information gathered or considered (Variables Nos. 4–7), in the structure of the plans (Variables Nos. 8, 10), in sequencing the elements of the plans (Variable No. 3), and in considering alternatives (Variables Nos. 1, 2, 9). The intercoder reliability between two independent judges was $r = .94$ across all measures.

b. Plan adequacy. Plan adequacy was assessed through global evaluations of plans. The subject's responses to each of the 10 Planning Situations separately were evaluated globally in terms of a 4-step scale. The evaluation was based on specific binary criteria defined for each Planning Situation separately, mainly on the basis of pretests and the opinions of experts asked to specify what would constitute good planning in each of the situations and to evaluate different plans provided by children. Thus, the criteria reflected positive aspects of planning, such as asking for specific relevant information, considering the described conditions, attempting to do something about the major problem of the situation (e.g., looking for the jacket in Planning Situation No. 7, staying up late at night in Planning Situation No. 9), preparing for unlikely yet possible eventualities, and so on (see the list in Kreitler & Kreitler, chapter 4, this volume, Table 4.1). The 4-step evaluation scale was produced by dividing the distribution of positively scored criteria for each Planning Situation in each age group into four parts in line with the quartiles. The number of positively scored criteria in the lowest quartile got the score of 1, and in the highest, the score of 4. This procedure made it possible to compare the evaluations across Planning Situations and across the four age groups. Averaging across the 10 situational evaluations produced an overall evaluation score of plans for each child.

The coders' task was to score each set of responses to a Planning Situation in line with the appropriate criteria. The sum of the positively scored criteria was then transformed into an evaluation score. The intercoder reliability for two independent coders was $r = .98$ for the evaluation measures across all 10 Planning Situations.

      c. Techniques and procedures of planning. In order to assess techniques and procedures of planning, several specific variables were defined for each Planning Situation. In selecting the variables, we focused on aspects of the children's responses that reflected the manner in which planning was actually performed. In defining the variables, we were also guided by the following considerations: The variables should be characteristic for the specific Planning Situation, they should not be redundant (i.e., not recur in the different Planning Situations), and they should differ from the basic skills of planning described above. We ended up with a list of 37 variables we called "responses," presented in Table 6.12. There are variables concerning each Planning Situation, but their number varies (from two for Planning Situation No. 9, to 10 for Planning Situation No. 5). Intercoder reliability (between two independent coders) was $r = .95$.

C. Results and discussion

Because preliminary checks showed no significant gender differences, the findings will be presented for the whole sample of each age group together. In view of the diversity of variables dealt with, the discussion of all results will not be assigned to one separate section; rather each subsection of results will include a brief discussion relevant for the presented findings.

1. Development in general planning skills. Preliminary analyses showed that the 10 measures used to assess general planning skills are unrelated to the Planning Situations. Out of the 40 chi-square comparisons (for each of the 10 variables in each of the four age groups), only one yielded significant results (Variable No. 4: Number of items, in 9-year olds). This represents less than 5% of all comparisons and can therefore be attributed to chance. Because the assessed aspects of planning do not tend to occur with a significantly higher or lower frequency in any of the Planning Situations, they can justifiably be considered as characteristic of planning rather than of responses to one or another planning task. This conclusion also supports our procedure to sum the frequencies of these variables across all Planning Situations.

Table 6.9 presents the means, standard deviations, and results of the one-way analyses of variance concerning each of the 10 cross-situational measures of general planning skills. In the last column, significant differences between pairs of specific group means are shown. Because in some cases the developmental trend deviates from linearity, F values for the linear term, deviations from linearity, and the quadratic term are also included.

The findings show that in all variables there are highly significant differences in the performance of children in the four age groups. As may be expected, in all 10 variables younger children have lower means than older children. Three distinct developmental patterns can be detected in the data:

1. A regular linear pattern (the deviation from linearity is nonsignificant) with means that increase from 5 years to 11 years (see Var. 6: No. of domains; and Var. 7: No. of general labels).
2. A nonliner pattern (the deviation from linearity is significant) that consists of a uniform increase from 5 years to 9 years, followed by a significant decrease from 9 years to 11 years, which still leaves the mean value for 11-year olds above the means of 5- and 7-year olds (except in the case of Var. 4) (see Var. 1: No. of alternative plans; Var. 2: No. of if–then considerations; Var. 4: No. of questions; and Var. 5: No. of items).
3. An essentially linear pattern (the deviation from linearity is nonsignificant) that consists of a uniform increase from 5 to 9 years, followed by slight nonsignificant fluctuations from 9 to 11 years (see Var. 3: No. of chronological orderings; Var. 8: No. of steps in major plans; and Var. 10: No. of steps in all plans).

In order to obtain an overall evaluation of the rate of development in all 10 variables of the general skills of planning, we computed for each variable the ratio of the difference between the means in two consecutive ages out of the total range of maximum difference between the highest and lowest means. These ratios were converted into percentages. The means of these percentages across the 10 variables were 47.3% improvement from the age of 5 years to 7 years, 42.2% improvement from the age of 7 years to 9 years, and 5.3% decline from the age of 9 to 11 years.

The findings about the developmental trends and the overall evalua-tion of change might produce the impression that planning develops only up to the age of 9 years and then stops developing or even declines in some respects. This impression is erroneous because the variables that decrease after 9 years may be considered as direct or indirect manifesta-tions of planning on a relatively low level. In contrast, those variables that continue to increase after 9 years – mainly references to general labels and to domains – are direct or indirect manifestations of planning on a relatively high level (they progress 50% from 9 years to 11 years but only 25% on the average from 5 years to 7 years and from 7 years to 9 years).

Moreover, these variables that increase after 9 years are the key to pro-gression from the relatively less advanced to the relatively more advanced level, because they represent conceptual units on a higher level than steps of plans or specific items of information. As units on a higher level they are more powerful in their inclusiveness, generality, and evoc-ative potential (Flavell, 1970, p. 988; Schroder, Driver, & Streufert, 1967, chap. 2). "General labels" are more powerful than steps of plans; for example, one general label such as "diverting the attention of the treasure guardians" (in Planning Situation No. 7) may stand for a long list of more specific steps implementing it, such as, "staging a sham attack," "pro-ducing a big noise," "retreating from the battlefield," and so on. Indeed, "general labels" may even stand for whole plans, including alternate plans; for example, a general label like "Pleasing mother" (in Planning Situation No. 9) may stand for a list of specific steps, such as "Come back home from school without tarrying on the way," "Eat everything mother offers without grumbling," "Tell mother about successes in school," "Take the garbage can out," "Clean my room" and so on, or, if the gar-bage and the room are already taken care of, "Suggest to go to the store to buy whatever is missing." Similarly, a reference to a domain (Var. 6) is a more powerful conceptual unit than items of information manifested directly in the number of items considered or referred to (Var. 5), or indi-rectly in the number of questions asked (Var. 4). For example, a "domain" like "food" (in Planning Situation No. 4) may stand for long lists of nutritive items. Hence, using "general labels" may replace speci-fying particular steps of plans, whereas using "domains" may replace list-ing particular items or specifically asking about them.

Nevertheless, the specific steps or items are not simply discarded. They are necessary constituents of plans. A plan that consists *only* of general statements that do not imply concrete steps or items is inoperable; indeed it is not a plan at all, but in the best case a blueprint for a plan and in the worst case a list of normative injunctions. "General labels" and

Table 6.9. *Comparison of the four age groups in terms of the general planning skills*

Planning variables	Means and SDs in age groups:				F values	Significant group dif.
	a. 5 yr ($n = 60$)	b. 7 yr ($n = 60$)	c. 9 yr ($n = 60$)	d. 11 yr ($n = 60$)		All pairs of means**
No. of alternatives	2.47	5.20	8.00	6.60	22.82****	
	1.78	1.97	1.70	1.65	19.40****	
					24.53****	
					20.45****	
No. of if-then considerations	7.63	8.50	11.40	9.20	5.50**	a < c**
	3.60	3.02	1.97	3.25	7.51**	a < d**
					4.50*	b < c**
					1.98	c > d**
No. of chronological orderings	5.78	7.90	8.00	8.09	26.42****	a < b**
	2.17	3.20	3.21	2.73	5.75**	a < c**
					1.94	a < d**
					3.22	
No. of questions	1.90	4.78	5.68	3.60	18.99****	a < b**
	.89	1.43	1.85	1.64	7.82**	a < c**
					12.99****	a < d**
					3.84*	b > d*
						c > d**
No. of items	5.03	7.75	9.69	8.60	15.43****	a < b**
	3.57	3.39	3.98	3.02	14.57****	a < c**
					12.36****	a < d**
					4.20**	b < c**
						b < d*
No. of domains	1.52	2.91	4.35	6.42	21.72****	a < b*
	.54	.89	.97	1.32	19.82****	a < c**

Measure	a	b	c	d	Group means F	Linear F	Deviation from linearity F	Quadratic F	Comparisons
(continued)							1.31	2.98	a < d** b < c** b < d** c < d**
No. of general labels	2.10 1.06	3.49 .76	4.20 1.11	7.12 1.23	21.08****	33.51****	2.90	3.39*	a < b** a < c** a < d** b < c* b < d** c < d**
No. of steps in first plan	2.85 1.32	3.57 1.08	4.20 1.04	4.15 .99	11.69****	12.31****	2.65	.98	a < b** a < c** a < d** b < c* b < d*
No. of steps in alternate plan(s)	1.60 .87	2.14 1.08	3.56 1.21	3.10 1.25	17.77****	11.86****	2.90	1.46	a < b* a < c** a < d** b < c** b < d*
No. of steps in all plans	4.45 1.12	5.71 1.07	7.76 1.14	7.25 1.13	23.56****	12.03****	2.89	2.21	a < b** a < c** a < d** b < c** b < d**

Note: In the columns for the four age groups, the first number denotes the mean, the second the SD. In the column of the F values, the numbers denote the F ratio of the difference between the group means, of the linear term, of the deviation from linearity, and of the quadratic term, in that order. The differences between the group means presented in the last column are based on the Newman–Keuls method.

$*p < .05.$
$**p < .01.$
$****p < .0001.$

"domains" differ from such vacuous statements in their evocative power. They imply the concrete steps and items as integral elements of their meaning. Thus, the concrete steps and items continue to be present in the plan but merely potentially, in an implied fashion rather than explicitly. Because "general labels" and "domains" introduce organization into the plethora of accumulating details, they render superfluous the further expansion of details. Had the numbers of alternatives (Var. 1), items (Var. 5), and questions (Var. 4) continued to expand after 9 years at the rate they do up to 9 years, the individual would find it hardly possible to master the mass of accumulating explicitly stated information so as to form a coherent plan. Hence the decrease in the number of alternatives, if–then considerations, items, questions, and steps of plans is in fact an indication for development in planning. Moreover, the decline in these variables is merely apparent, because general labels and domains are conceptually more inclusive than steps of plans or specific items of information.

It is evident that the increased use of "general labels" and "domains" in the process of planning is responsible also for bringing to a standstill the use of chronological order (Var. 3). Because "general labels" are more inclusive than particular plan steps, fewer direct references to specific sequences are necessary. For example, if one states in detail, "Jack opens the door, then he goes into the corridor, then he looks right and left, before he steps out" (in Planning Situation No. 5), there are three references to chronological order, but there would be none if the answer were, "Jack steps out carefully."

As noted, one advantage of using "general labels" and "domains" is greater concentration of information and hence an easier load on memory in the course of planning and also after it, when the plan has to be remembered or recalled. When children were asked about the difficulties of planning, they most frequently mentioned difficulties of memory (see section II, Table 6.7). Hence, greater economy and an easier load on memory are important both objectively, from the viewpoint of development, and subjectively, from the viewpoint of the individual engaging in planning.

Another advantage of using "general labels" and "domains" is enhanced flexibility and adaptability of the plan. A plan that consists *only* of particular steps referring to particular items is liable to be too concrete and too rigid to allow for necessary accommodation to shifting circumstances. What renders a plan flexible and adaptable is the relation of the particular steps and items to more inclusive conceptual units that enable the derivation of other steps and items, should the original ones prove inadequate for some reason.

Upon analysis, "general labels" and "domains" turn out to be major constituents of what in another context we call "program scheme," i.e., a kind of overall strategy or set of rules concerning the kind of elements necessary for attaining the specified goal. It was distinguished from "operational program," which consists of a sequence of detailed instructions and specifications necessary for implementation in action (Kreitler & Kreitler, 1976, chap. 6).

It is of great interest to find out how the development from particular steps and items to general labels and domains takes place. Certain studies in learning (Grice, 1965; Mandler, 1962) seem to suggest that the less inclusive terms are acquired at an earlier stage in the process of learning than the more inclusive terms, and that they constitute a necessary condition for them. Our observations indicate two points important from a developmental perspective. The first is that general labels and domains are not newcomers emerging suddenly at some specific stage of development. They are in fact used by 5-year olds, but older children simply use them three to four times more frequently (Table 6.9). The second point is that the more inclusive units are initially appended to a list of specific steps or items that gradually grows shorter. For example, a child 5 years old may say (in Planning Situation No. 10) "They will visit the animals in the zoo; first they will go to the lions, then they must see the elephant, who is also a big animal, and the tiger, and then they must not forget to see the small animals – the canary, the snake, the squirrel, the fish. . . ." An 11-year old child is likely to present the former plan in terms such as: "They will visit the zoo and see the big animals like the lions and the tiger and the small ones like the squirrel." However, one must not conclude that the older child does not know or does not care about the detailed list of steps or items. The list exists implicitly and is easily available. One proof we have for this is based on the data provided by the children's responses to the question "What else?" asked after each response (see section III.B.3). These responses may be analyzed into three categories: (1) no further additions (the percentages for the four groups are 35%, 23%, 12%, and 9%, respectively); (2) completely new additions, such as a new plan or a new item in a previous plan (the percentages for the four groups are 57%, 64%, 50%, and 26%, respectively); and (3) specifications of inclusive conceptual units (i.e., references to "domains" and "general labels") used in previous plan(s) (the percentages for the four groups are 8%, 13%, 38%, and 66%, respectively) ($\chi^2 = 52.96$, $df = 6$, $p < .001$). Thus, whereas younger children (5- and 7-year olds) provided either no responses or completely new elements, the older children (9- and 11-year olds) increasingly tended to elaborate their previous plan(s). Notable, the sharp drop in "new additions" and the steep rise in "speci-

Table 6.10. *Comparisons of the four age groups in terms of the global evaluations of plan adequacy*

Evaluations of plan adequacy	Means and SDs in age groups:				F values	Significant group dif.
	a. 5 yr (n = 60)	b. 7 yr (n = 60)	c. 9 yr (n = 60)	d. 11 yr (n = 60)		
Situation No. 1	1.63	2.60	3.40	3.35	20.02****	a < b**
	.36	.67	.54	.49	18.63****	a < c**
					2.23	a < d**
					1.90	b < c**
						b < d**
Situation No. 2	2.60	2.80	2.71	3.18	7.89**	a < d**
	.87	.92	.99	.68	6.54**	c < d*
					1.68	
					.47	
Situation No. 3	2.25	2.80	3.06	3.29	18.95****	a < b*
	.45	.32	.28	.53	13.78****	a < c**
					.85	a < d**
					.06	b < d*
Situation No. 4	2.33	3.15	2.60	3.20	10.68****	a < b*
	.68	.35	.79	.93	2.91	a < d**
					4.59**	c < d*
					1.02	b > c*
Situation No. 5	1.46	2.00	2.60	3.21	9.82****	a < b*
	.21	.43	.31	.36	15.74****	a < c**
					1.83	a < d**
					.97	b < c*
						b < d**
						c < d*
Situation No. 6	2.10	2.06	2.50	2.80	6.75**	a < c*
	.89	1.03	.64	.68	4.78**	a < d**

	Age group a (M, SD)	Age group b (M, SD)	Age group c (M, SD)	Age group d (M, SD)	F values	Newman–Keuls
(continued)					2.12; 1.47	b < c*; b < d**; c < d*
Situation No. 7	1.10, .23	2.45, .42	2.88, .31	3.24, .46	12.79****; 15.89****; .57; .92	a < b**; a < c**; a < d**; b < c*; b < d**; c < d**
Situation No. 8	1.64, .68	2.80, .97	2.90, .75	3.24, .46 → 2.80, .86	3.65*; 3.40*; 1.65; .35	a < b**; a < c**; a < d**
Situation No. 9	2.04, .23	2.85, .45	3.20, .38	3.50, .25	18.95****; 23.74****; .56; .36	a < b**; a < c**; a < d**; b < c**; b < d**; c < d*
Situation No. 10	1.67, .32	2.80, .31	3.12, .65	3.31, .53	19.46****; 24.06****; .74; 1.92	a < b**; a < c**; a < d**; b < c*; b < d**
Mean of all ten evaluations	2.00, .44	2.60, .35	2.70, .30	3.20, .47	23.76****; 16.94****; 1.25; 1.33	a < b*; a < c**; a < d**; b < d*; c < d*

Note: In the columns for the four age groups, the first number denotes the mean, the second the SD. In the column of the F values, the numbers denote the F ratio of the difference between the group means, of the linear term, of the deviation from linearity, and of the quadratic term, in that order. The differences between the group means presented in the last column are based on the Newman–Keuls method.

$*p < .05.$ $**p < .01.$ $****p < .0001.$

fications" from the age of 9 years to 11 years is reminiscent of the break in the developmental trend of Variables Nos. 1–5 and 8–10 in Table 6.9.

2. Development in plan adequacy. Table 6.10 presents the means, standard deviations, and results of one-way analyses of variance concerning each of the evaluations of planning in the 10 Planning Situations and of the overall mean of these 10 evaluations. It may be recalled that the range of the evaluations is limited to the values ranging from 1 (low) to 4 (high). In the last column, significant differences between pairs of specific group means are presented. Because in some cases the trend is irregular, F values for the linear term, deviations from linearity, and the quadratic terms are also included.

The findings show that in all variables, including the overall mean evaluation, the level of plan adequacy in the younger children (5- and 7-year olds) is lower than that of the older children (9- and 11-year olds). The rate of change between any two groups is, however, not uniform. The average difference between the means of the 7- and 5-year olds is .749, between the means of 9- and 7-year olds is .268, and between the means of 11- and 9-year olds is .321 ($F = 4.02$, $df = 2/7$, $p < .10$).

In order to obtain an overall estimate of the rate of development in all 10 variables of the situational evaluations of plan adequacy, we computed for each variable the ratio of the difference between the means in two consecutive ages out of the total range of maximum difference between the highest and lowest means for that variable. These ratios were converted into percentages. The means of these percentages across the 10 evaluations were 54.1% improvement from the age of 5 to 7 years, 16.3% improvement from the age of 7 to 9 years, and 29.7% improvement from the age of 9 to 11 years. A comparison of these findings to those obtained in regard to the general planning skills (section II.C.1) shows both similarities and differences. The major similarity is that in both cases the relatively largest spurt of development takes place between 5 and 7 years. The differences are that there seem to be less development from 7 to 9 years in overall plan adequacy (16.3%) than in the general planning skills (42.2%), and more development from 9 to 11 years in overall plan adequacy (29.7%) than in the general planning skills (−5.3%). The discrepancies could be due to the distorting effect of the limited range of the evaluation scale, but it is more likely that it derives from the different nature of the assessed variables.

Differences between global and analytic assessments of phenomena are not unknown in psychology, as for example, the discrepancy in the affective tone characterizing the overall evaluation of a particular past period in one's life and the specific memories one recalls of that period (Kreitler & Kreitler, 1968). In fact, there is no reason to expect specific aspects or skills of planning to develop at exactly the same rate as the shaping of an overall plan. The shaping of a plan requires evocation of multiple processes and their integration, which may be based on cognitive processes at least partly different from those involved in skills like considering if–then eventualities or asking informative questions. Indeed, it is plausible that a marked increase in some of the particular planning aspects or skills may retard or even lower temporarily the level of the overall plan; for example, asking too many questions, or recalling too many items may render the shaping of an overall plan more difficult and hence less efficient than fewer questions or items. Similarly, an increase in the use of general labels and references to domains may temporarily inhibit the further development of the shaping of overall plans. This is what we probably observe in the means of the groups in Table 6.14.

The trends of development in the evaluations of plan adequacy are completely linear only in five cases (Planning Situations Nos. 3, 5, 7, 9, and 10) and in the overall mean for the 10 evaluations. In four cases there are deviations from the linear trend, but they do not fall into a regular pattern (in Planning Situations Nos. 2 and 4, the deviation is a decrease from 7 to 9 years; in No. 6, it is a slight decrease from 5 to 7 years; and in No. 8, it is a slight decrease from 9 to 11 years). The fluctuations are significant only in the case of Planning Situation No. 4, which is also the only situation with a significant deviation from linearity.

Such irregularities between the evaluations of the plans suggest that in different situations children tend to form plans that are on different qualitative levels. This assumption is confirmed by the highly significant differences in planning performance across the 10 Planning Situations in each age group (Table 6.11). Disparities of this kind indicate that planning skills of children are largely bound to specific contexts. Hence, there is a low level of uniformity in cross-situational performance. However, there is evidence that cross-situational uniformity in the overall level of planning increases with age. The alpha values (reflecting the internal consistency between the evaluations) and the coefficients of concordance (reflecting correspondence between the rankings of the evaluations) rise linearly from the age of 5 to 11 years (Table 6.11). These findings show that with age, there is an increase in intraindividual integration of planning skills so that the contextual relativity is gradually transcended and replaced by a more stable planning competence characteristic of the child.

Table 6.11. *Analyses of variance (repeated measures) and coefficients of concordance and reliability in the four age groups with the situational global evaluations of planning as dependent variables*

Source of variation	df	5 yr		7 yr		9 yr		11 yr	
		MS	F	MS	F	MS	F	MS	F
Between subjects	59	1.20		3.05		.60		3.58	
Within subjects	540	.67		.71		.84		.55	
Within measures	9	2.67	35.76*	5.19	65.56*	7.68	82.28*	2.41*	39.57*
Residual	531	.60		.56		.60		.48	
Total	599	.72		.94		.82		.84	
Coefficient of concordance, W		.1111		.1663		.2829		.3286	
Reliability coefficient, alpha		.4980		.8173		.8548		.8648	

*$p < .001$.

3. Development in techniques and procedures of planning. The present section represents an attempt to gain insight into the cognitive dynamics of the development of planning by observing concrete and specific details in the children's responses to the different planning tasks. Table 6.12 presents the means and standard deviations of the variables representing specific techniques and procedures of planning in the four age groups as well as the results of the one-way analyses of variance and significant differences between pairs of specific group means.

The responses to Planning Situation No. 1 (Looking for a lost item of a game) reveal some major difficulties children have in forming an overall plan and processes involved in the emergence of the plan. The most frequent response of 5-year olds is asking directly where the lost item is (Response No. 1, Table 6.12). By doing so, they disregard the stated information that the other child does not know where the item is. Moreover, this question does not provide information that could lead to the formation of a plan. Thus, this procedure reveals that planning requires the ability to make a detour, that is, to look away from the goal and to proceed from it to other related themes. A first step in this direction is taken when the child concentrates on the lost item itself, asking about its color, size, and other identifying characteristics (Response No. 2). One pitfall of this procedure is evident in 7-year olds, who might veer off toward characteristics of the item irrelevant for the search. Hence, the difficulty consists not merely in detaching oneself from the immediate goal, but in doing so without losing sight of this goal which provides the criteria for distinguishing between relevant and irrelevant information or ideas. The next major step in detaching oneself from the goal consists in speculating about possible locations (Response No. 3), which increases notably in 9-year olds. Such speculations, which constitute the raw material for full-fledged plans, appear characteristically in the form of one or more general hypotheses; for example, the missing item could have been misplaced in the box of another game, it may be hidden under something that covers it, and so on. Then the child selects one of these hypotheses in line with some criterion. Initially the criteria tend to be irrelevant to the issue, for example, the first idea that popped up, or the last idea considered; then the criteria gradually become more adequate: First they are based on personal experiences (e.g., "This is what happened to me once . . . "), later on a broader data base (e.g., "This is what happens to other children . . . "). (Concerning selection criteria, see also Response No. 27 and No. 32 in Table 6.12 and their discussion in section III.C.4.) The selected hypothesis is then elaborated into a plan. When pressed with the question "What else?" some children proceed "in depth," further elaborating the

Table 6.12. *Comparison of the four age groups in terms of techniques and procedures of planning*

Techniques and procedures of planning	Means and SDs in the age groups				F value
	5 years (n = 60)	7 years (n = 60)	9 years (n = 60)	11 years (n = 60)	
Situation No. 1					
1. No. of direct questions about where the item is	2.10 .40	1.18 .27	.67 .10	.16 .02	25.78****
2. Concern with the properties of the lost item	.35 .05	1.89 .40	1.22 .17	.26 .03	32.46****
3. Hypotheses about the item's possible location	.56 .09	1.66 .30	2.98 .55	1.70 .27	21.08****
4. Concern with the target, i.e., finding the item, and its meaning	.00 .00	.35 .07	1.68 .30	1.90 .34	9.15***
Situation No. 2					
5. No. of items concerning the preparation of the machine for operation	1.13 .32	2.00 .41	2.85 .50	1.56 .36	14.46****
6. No. of items concerning the operation of the machine	2.30 .41	2.86 .47	5.20 .56	2.40 .37	17.93****
7. No. of items concerning the machine's upkeep	1.09 .28	1.86 .30	3.03 .45	1.85 .35	13.77****
8. No. of items concerning the people & the transfer of the machine (irrelevant)	3.01 .56	1.22 .25	.22 .04	.00 .00	12.73****

Item					
9. No. of shiftings between categories of responses (divided by total responses)	.75 / .10	.52 / .15	.19 / .04	.06 / .01	15.84****
Situation No. 3					
10. No. of items directly concerning the way	.76 / .14	3.00 / .32	4.20 / .39	2.40 / .28	10.86****
11. No. of items concerning the house, street, & person	.00 / .00	.58 / .06	2.21 / .43	2.45 / .41	7.24**
12. No. of additional parts to the plan	.00 / .00	.76 / .12	1.95 / .43	2.22 / .45	10.45****
Situation No. 4					
13. No. of chronological ordering, of items	.09 / .01	1.66 / .34	1.73 / .35	1.54 / .28	3.67*
14. No. of different principles in stating items	1.10 / .44	2.40 / .53	3.21 / .54	4.15 / .62	19.55****
15. No. of substitute items	.05 / .01	1.86 / .25	1.94 / .31	1.67 / .28	13.31***
16. No. of items for taking along	5.03 / .65	8.00 / .43	9.80 / .66	9.00 / .93	15.43****
Situation No. 5					
17. "No problem"	.60 / .06	.53 / .10	.13 / .01	.00 / .00	10.93****
18. Concern with hiding	.33 / .08	.48 / .11	1.00 / .16	1.78 / .23	8.54**
19. Concern with escaping	.60 / .12	.87 / .24	1.02 / .31	1.68 / .36	5.75**
20. Concern with taking the giant's gold	.00 / .00	.20 / .05	.65 / .14	1.05 / .21	12.08****

Table 6.12. (cont.)

Techniques and procedures of planning	Means and SDs in the age groups:				F value
	5 years (n = 60)	7 years (n = 60)	9 years (n = 60)	11 years (n = 60)	
21. Concern with fighting	.16 .04	.22 .02	.83 .16	1.53 .26	17.82****
22. Concern with "transportation" back home	.35 .12	.86 .32	1.62 .38	1.93 .42	13.31****
23. No. of themes (Response Nos. 18–22) coped with	1.23 .54	3.42 .89	3.86 .85	4.66 .91	24.27****
24. No. of connections between parts of the plan (divided by the number of parts)	.25 .06	.32 .08	.53 .09	.87 .07	10.33****
25. No. of items of fantasy	.90 .43	2.83 .67	3.26 .94	1.89 .86	12.08*****
26. No. of shifts between reality & fantasy (divided by total No. of items)	.87 .31	.73 .38	.61 .30	.01 .001	5.37
Situation No. 6					
27. No. of hypotheses included in the plan	.02 .003	.80 .16	1.83 .24	3.45 .27	9.73***
Situation No. 7					
28. Mean No. of plans leading to attainment of target	.20 .03	.86 .17	1.49 .21	2.80 .53	12.56***

248

Situation No. 8					
29. Plans for subtargets	.00 / .00	.32 / .07	.68 / .16	1.35 / .24	9.16***
30. Duration of plan (in days)	.70 / .45	2.65 / .65	4.56 / .67	5.86 / .96	14.58****
31. Acceptance of suggested plans (Accept. 1, reject. 0)	.08 / .02	.12 / .03	.80 / .12	.76 / .17	6.72**
Situation No. 9					
32. No. of different binding principles between plan parts	.00 / .00	.14 / .03	1.01 / .15	1.42 / .18	9.53***
33. Mean No. of redefinitions of target	.04 / .01	.05 / .02	1.23 / .14	1.34 / .19	7.04**
Situation No. 10					
34. No. of items whose information is forgotten	3.12 / .67	2.97 / .84	3.18 / .75	1.63 / .46	6.23**
35. No. of items imagined or assumed	2.56 / .76	1.90 / .57	2.05 / .86	.61 / .24	9.84***
36. No. of considered aspects of the problems	2.43 / .77	3.18 / .95	4.09 / .98	5.68 / 1.02	10.00****
37. No. of aspects of target attained before execution stopped for lack of information	.65 / .22	1.79 / .43	2.34 / .37	3.64 / .54	7.89**

*$p < .05$.
**$p < .01$.
***$p < .001$.
****$p < .0001$.

249

plan by adding loops and alternate routes, whereas others proceed "horizontally," elaborating another hypothesis into a plan. The next major step we observed in the framework of responses to this Planning Situation takes place when the planner goes back again to the stated target in order to evaluate it in view of more inclusive goals (Response No. 4), for example, "After all, we need this item only in order to play; maybe we can replace it or play another game" (see also Response No. 33 and its discussion in section III.C.4). Hence, elaborating the meaning of the target may lead to substitute targets, which in turn give rise to other hypotheses for planning.

The responses to Planning Situation No. 2 (Arrival of new washing machine) shed light on developments in the manner of organizing information. The categories of questions concerning relevant information (Responses Nos. 5–7) increase from 5 to 9 years and then decrease, probably because of the increased use of "general labels" and references to "domains" (section III.C.1). In contrast, the category of irrelevant questions decreases regularly with age. This indicates a strengthened focusing on the relevant aspects of the problem situation. Moreover, there is a growing separation between the four categories of questions: At the age of 5 years, questions of all four categories are asked one after another, whereas at later ages questions of each category are grouped together to a greater extent. Thus, the "index of shifting" (i.e., number of shifts between categories divided by the number of responses) decreases dramatically from the age of 5 to 11 years (Response No. 9). These observations suggest that planning improves when the child intensifies meaning elaboration of the target with the result that the irrelevant aspects are sifted out and the relevant ones are ordered into functional groups.

Responses to Planning Situation No. 3 (Going for a visit, unfamiliar way) reveal two procedures of elaborating plans. One procedure that appears mainly from the age of 9 years on, consists in devising one or more routes, in addition to the major straightforward one, that do not replace the major plan but rather increase its chances of success. Thus, because the target is to reach a certain location, the main straightforward questions refer to the way and the address (Response No. 10). The less obvious ones refer to characteristics of the house and the flat or features of the family or person to be visited so that the location may be identified even if the precise address is forgotten or mistaken (Response No. 11). These responses increase from 5 to 11 years. Again, this elaboration has its dangers. The child may veer off into details unrelated to the target (e.g., When did the lady start dyeing her hair?). Another procedure consists in extending the plan by adding to it new sections. This occurs by enlarging the span of time beyond the attainment of the target. Only 5-

year olds dealt merely with attaining the specified target. From the age of 7 years onward, children added new sections to the plan, referring first to coming back to the point of origin, and then inserting additional links between arrival at the desired location and returning home (e.g., staying to play with the children over there, going to a movie). At the age of 11, the number of such additional planning sections may become impressive: One child added 15! It is as if planning required first the formation of a framework that could then be filled in at will.

Responses to Planning Situation No. 4 (Picnic) reveal development in means undertaken to guarantee that the major necessary aspects have been considered. In mentioning the things that have to be taken along, children proceed initially by following a chronological course which represents analogically the event (e.g., things you need for the road, then things you need for the midmorning break, lunch, etc.) (Response No. 13). This principle is later amplified by other principles, mainly, needs of the different participants in the picnic, needs bound with the different goals of the picnic (e.g., to have fun, to introduce the children to the desert), needs derived from the characteristics of the environment (e.g., absence of shops or shadow), and needs bound with particular eventualities (e.g., catastrophes, meeting friends). Characteristically, children beyond 5 years apply sequentially several principles (Response No. 14). This increases not only the number of items considered for taking along but mainly the likelihood that nothing of importance has been overlooked (Response No. 16; concerning the decrease after 9 years, see Var. 4 and Var. 5, section II.C.1). This in turn contributes to enhancing the adequacy of the plan. In 7- to 9-year olds, the number of items (Response No. 16) is boosted also by the increased tendencies to cite substitutes (Response No. 15, e.g., for shade you may take a tent or an umbrella) and to associate freely without considering the conditions of the Planning Situation (e.g., when specifying clothes, one 7-year old mentioned "coats, boots, raincoats, five pairs of woolen socks," and so on, disregarding the constraints of the problem that called for clothes for a *one-day picnic* to the *desert*). The latter indicates that good planning requires integrating the meaning of a theme (e.g., clothes) with the meaning of the problem situation (e.g., one-day picnic in the desert) by forming a new focal referent (e.g., clothes for a one-day picnic in the desert), different from the two separate referents. The failure to perform this integration lies at the core of many incomplete or inadequate plans formed by 7- and even some 9-year olds.

Responses to Planning Situation No. 5 (Jack and the Beanstalk) reveal developments in three major domains. First, there is development in understanding the problem. Many 5-year olds and even some older children disregard directly stated aspects (e.g., the mentioned danger) or fail to conceive of implied difficulties (e.g., on the way back) and hence see "no problem" and consequently no need for a plan. "No problem" responses decline when the child analyzes the situation and identifies its different themes (Responses Nos. 18–22). The number of themes with which the child copes in the plan increases with age (Response No. 23). Second, there is development in integrating the different sections of the plan. At first the children focus on each theme in turn (Responses Nos. 18–22), forming a separate plan for each one of them. These "plans" are initially unrelated, presented as different plans or even as different alternate plans before they are combined as parts of one integrated plan (Response No. 24). Third, there is development in keeping fact and fantasy apart. Notably, reference to fantasy is warranted by the nature of the present Planning Situation (and also Planning Situation No. 7, but see also Response No. 35), and its occurrence reveals the children's sensitivity to the given context. Yet its increasing use (Response No. 9) produced initially a confusion between realistic and imaginary items that is almost completely overcome by 11 years (see the decline in the number of shifts, Response No. 26). The latter development is of particular importance because planning requires dealing with hypothetical possibilities.

Responses to Planning Situation No. 6 (Search for jacket) reveal development in selecting hypotheses as the core for a plan (see Response No. 3 and its discussion). One selection criterion applied by 9- and 11-year olds was comprehensiveness, that is, the possibility of combining in the plan more than one hypothesis (Response No. 27).

Responses to Planning Situation No. 7 (Fight for the treasure) reveal not only the difficulties of integrating separate parts into a complete plan, but also of combining the different parts in such a way that the target is attained. Response No. 28 indicates that at least in younger ages, children may forget not only situational constraints, but even the target, especially when engrossed in planning something as exciting as a battle.

Responses to Planning Situation No. 8 (Contact with another child) reveal developments in three domains. First, there is development in the structuring of plans. There is increasing use in turning a step within a plan into a target in regard to which several alternative plans are formed (Response No. 29). For example, the plan may include a major step like "invite the child to my home," which turns into a target for which two alternate plans are formed, one based on evoking the child's curiosity, the other on evoking the child's desire for competition. Second, there is development in the duration of the conceived plan, from hardly a day, to over 5 or 6 days (Response No. 30). And third, there is development in evaluating new plans designed to attain the same goal for which the child planned (Response No. 31). Characteristically, the younger subjects (5 years) rejected the plans, often indicating that one does not need more than one plan and that one's own plan was superior. The suggested plans do not fare much better with 7-year olds, although the rejection is now on other, more objective bases (e.g., "It cannot be done," "It is not good"). At the age of 9, there is greater readiness to accept the suggested plans, but characteristically they are either changed so that they come to resemble the child's original plan or they are incorporated into the child's plan. These procedures are less frequent at the age of 11 years.

Planning Situation No. 9 (Staying up late) was highly familiar to the children. Thus, they felt sufficiently informed about it so as, on the one hand, to reject the original target as unrealistic and redefine the goal (Response No. 33, e.g., "I'll stay up and watch from a hiding place"), and, on the other hand, to suggest many alternate plans, some based on personal experiences. Accordingly, the responses provide insight into the manner in which the children interrelated the alternatives. The more frequent principles were: "If plan a fails, then plan b"; "if plan c, then it is also possible to apply plan d" (for added strength); and "if plan e, then it is impossible to apply also plan f." The number of applied interrelating principles increases with age (Response No. 32).

Responses to Planning Situation No. 10 (A day's errands) reveal how children cope with a planning task that is in fact too complex for them from the viewpoint of the amount of information that has to be obtained and integrated. Possibly because the problem does not easily lend itself to a partitioning into sections, as, for example, Planning Situation No. 5 (Jack and the Beanstalk), they try from the very start to encompass the whole range of involved aspects. As a result, the children, especially those 5–9 years old, do not exploit the information they got as answers to their own questions (either because of confusion or increased memory load) (Response No. 34), and assume things without having obtained any information to that effect (e.g., that two stores are near to each other or open at noontime) (Response No. 35). Furthermore, they also tend to overlook different specified and emphasized aspects of the problem (e.g., that all errands have to be finished in one day, that there are five errands) (Response No. 36). Characteristically, the younger children tend to announce that they have a finished plan, but, when trying to enact it by drawing a trajectory, they get stuck very soon because of incomplete planning (Response No. 37). The judgment of older children is more realistic in this respect.

In sum, the review of the children's responses in the different Planning Situations revealed some of the complexity of the cognitive processes involved in planning. The major conclusions are that planning develops in different directions simultaneously: vertically, in terms of increased hierarchization, and horizontally, in terms of increased number of links or subplans in the plan; with regard to contents, in terms of the meaning elaboration of the problem; and with regard to structure, in terms of the principles used for integrating the different parts of the plan as well as alternate plans.

4. Factor analyses of the general planning skills. Whereas in section III.C.1 we dealt with development in each of the general planning skills separately, in the present section we deal with development in the *interrelations* of these variables. If we treat the 10 variables statistically as items of a scale, the interrelations can be expressed in terms of the coefficients of concordance, which are .51, .63, .69, and .70 (all significant beyond the .001 level) for the four age groups, respectively, or in terms of Cronbach's alpha coefficients, which are .60, .65, .72, and .79 for the four age groups, respectively. These coefficients are fairly high in all age groups and hence indicate that the 10 variables probably belong to one sphere of contents. Because the coefficients increase regularly from one age group to the next, it is plausible to conclude that with age the 10 variables become increasingly interrelated. This tendency reflects an increased uniformity within the sphere of planning and is in accord with the developmentally increasing integration within personality at large.

In order to examine developments in the organization and integration of planning, factor analyses were performed in each age group. The findings show that on all age levels the variables are grouped into three factors (the fourth factor on the level of 5-year olds has a low eigenvalue and thus is unstable but is included because of its developmental importance). The four sets of factors are not identical; yet there are intriguing relations between them, indicative of developmental trends. There seem to be three major elements of planning evident in all age groups in different salience and combinations: (a) Structuring of Plans, reflected in the number of steps the plans include; (b) Information Gathering, reflected in the number of questions asked and items considered; and (c) Information Organization, reflected in the use of references to "general labels" and "domains" that are conceptual units on a higher level of conceptualization. On the level of 5-year olds, Information Gathering is the most salient factor, and it is combined with chronological ordering of plans perhaps because the latter plays a major role in facilitating information generation particularly in young children (see Response No. 13, Table 6.12 and its discussion in section III C.3). However, because chronological ordering also reflects a basic kind of integrative organization in the plan itself, the first factor in 5-year olds appears to be a composite unit including both Organization of Plans and Information Gathering. Hence, this factor may be considered as a General Planning factor, the nuclear matrix out of which planning develops. Structuring of Plans and Organizing of Information appear on the level of 5-year olds but are still very weak factors. The finding that the second factor in this youngest age group concerns the Formation and Elaboration of Alternate Plans indicates that alternate plans are still conceived as constituting a distinct sphere within planning and perhaps as requiring special attention and effort.

On the level of 7-year olds, there are changes in the factorial structure. The General Planning factor, which was the most important one on the level of 5-year olds, does not appear on the level of 7-year olds. Instead, its function is split between two factors: the factor of Structuring of Plans (the first) and the Information factor (the third). It is as if the growing specialization in planning is better served by disbanding the general factor and splitting its functions. This development may be specifically promoted by the fact that 7-year olds do not have to rely so much on chronological sequences for information gathering because they increasingly use for this purpose other and often better principles (Response 14, Table 6.12). Thus, chronological ordering may become limited specifically to its actual function as a plan organizational principle. Accordingly, the factor of Structuring of Plans on the level of 7-year olds includes variables that in 5-year olds were saturated on the General Planning factor and the factor of the Structuring of Plans. This represents a concentration of the plan-structuring variables in one factor, which becomes the most important one. Also the Information factor in 7-year olds represents a concentration of functions that in 5-year olds belonged to separate factors: Information Gathering and Information Organizing. Thus, it seems justified to conclude that in 7-year olds the factorial structure is tighter and more orderly.

Further changes in factorial structure occur in 9-year olds. The most noticeable change is that the factor of the Formation of Alternate Plans does not appear any longer in 9-year olds. The variables that were saturated on it are split between the factor of the Structuring of Plans (Var. 9) and the Information Gathering factor (Var. 1 and Var. 2). Notably, the latter two variables (Var. 1: No. of alternatives; and Var. 2: No. of if–then considerations) seem to have changed their meaning and function, from variables bound with shaping alternative plans to variables subserving the generation of information. Accordingly, in 9-year olds we observe the extension of the factor of Structuring of Plans to both major and alternative plans. The distinction between the latter two kinds of plans is no

Table 6.13. *Factor analyses of the general planning skills in the four age groups*

Age group	First factor	Second factor	Third factor	Fourth factor
5 yr	Items (V. 5) .88 Chronol. (V. 3) .81 Quest. (V. 4) .64 If–then (V. 2) .50	Altern. (V. 1) .95 Steps in alt. plans (V. 9) .84 G. labels (V. 7) .56 If–then (V.2) .55	Steps in all plans (V. 10) .95 Steps in 1st plan (V. 7) .94	Domains (V. 6) .90 G. labels (V. 7) .66
Eigenvalue	4.85	1.87	1.36	.83
Explained Var.	54.5%	21.0%	15.2%	9.3%
Suggested title	Chronological plan ordering & information gathering	Formation of alternate plans	Structuring of plans (major)	Organizing of information
7 yr	Chronol. (V. 3) .87 Steps in 1st plan (V. 8) .52	Steps in alt. plan (V. 9) .96 Altern. (V. 1) .94 If–then (V. 2) .75	Items (V. 5) .90 Quest. (V. 4) .85 Domains (V. 6).77 G. labels (V. 7).50	
Eigenvalue	5.99	3.10	2.01	
Explained Var.	60.8%	26.7%	12.5%	
Suggested title	Structuring of plans (major)	Formation of alternate plans	Information gathering & information organizing	

9 yr

	Factor 1	Factor 2	Factor 3
Steps in all plans (V. 10)	.96		
Steps in alt. plans (V. 9)	.89		
Steps in 1st plan (V. 8)	.81		
Quest. (V. 4)	.52		
Altern. (V. 1)		.92	
If-then (V. 2)		.88	
Items (V. 5)		.77	
Quest. (V. 4)		.75	
G. labels (V. 7)			.85
Domains (V. 6)			.70
Eigenvalue	5.01	3.53	1.44
Explained Var.	49.9%	35.7%	14.4%
Suggested title	Structuring of plans (major & alternate)	Information gathering	Organizing of information

11 yr

	Factor 1	Factor 2	Factor 3
Steps in 1st plan (V. 8)	.95		
Steps in all plans (V. 10)	.94		
Steps in alt. plans (V. 9)	.64		
Domains (V. 6)		.98	
G. labels (V. 7)		.87	
Items (V. 5)		−.68	
Steps in alt. plans (V. 9)		−.70	
ChronoL (V. 3)		−.70	
Altern. (V. 1)			.79
Items (V. 5)			.62
If-then (V. 2)			.60
Quest. (V. 4)			.60
Steps in alt. plans (V. 9)			−.94
Eigenvalue	6.20	2.58	1.52
Explained Var.	60.2%	25.0%	14.8%
Suggested title	Structuring of plans (major & alternate)	Organizing of information	Gathering of information

Note: The table presents the Varimax rotated factor matrix after rotation with Kaiser normalization. For the sake of clarity, only saturations $\geq$ .50 (or −.50) are presented.

longer viable. On the other hand, there is an enhanced distinction between the factors of Information Gathering and Information Organization, which in 7-year olds were still combined.

The factorial structure in 11-year olds is similar to that obtained for 9-year olds. The factors are essentially the same and are only more sharply delineated, as reflected in the negative saturations in the second and third factors. The most salient difference is in the shifted ranks of the two informational factors: In 11-year olds, the Information Organization factor is in the second rank preceding the Information Gathering factor, whereas in 9-year olds the order is reversed. This upward shift of the Information Organizing factor is not surprising in view of the important role of the higher conceptual units in planning itself. It is not unlikely that in older ages there may even be a convergence between the factors of the Structuring of Plans and of Information Organization. But this is merely an hypothesis that remains to be checked.

In sum, the factorial structures in the four age groups are psychologically meaningful. Examining the shifts from one age group to another has provided insight into the emergence of major aspects of planning – that is, structuring of major plans, formation of alternative plans, gathering of information, and organizing of information – and into the developmental stages preceding their grouping into three clear-cut basic factors: Structuring of Plans, Gathering of Information, and Structuring of Information. Notably, these three factors may be assumed to represent three major facets of the cognitive activity of planning, that may be expected to be often manifested as stages in the act of planning.

5. *Factor analyses of the global evaluations of plan adequacy.* The purpose of these analyses was to identify groupings of Planning Situations characteristic for each age group and developmentally meaningful shifts in these groupings. Bearing in mind that the interpretation of factors is highly tentative, especially when it depends so much on the meaning of situations, we focused our attention mainly on factors recurring in different age groups. Information about such factors could shed light on the basic contexts of planning from the viewpoint of children and on their changes with age. It could also provide guidelines for sampling a small number of Planning Situations in future studies.

Table 6.14 shows that the number of relatively stable factors in each age group is three (the fourth factor in 5-year olds and the fourth and fifth factors in 7-year olds are relatively unstable, as indicated by their low eigenvalues and were included because of their importance from a developmental perspective). Summing across all age groups shows that there are the following five groupings of Planning Situations: (a) Interpersonal Relations with Peers; (b) Interpersonal Relations (or Confrontation) with Grown-ups; (c) Roads and Ways; (d) Errands (Including Preparations and Arrangements); and (e) Fantasy Situations. There may be an additional sixth grouping defined by Structural Features of Plans, that is, situations requiring or triggering long and complex plans. In each age group, at least three of these groupings of Planning Situations appear, separately or in combination, but they may differ in the percentage of variance for which they account and even in the variables saturated on them.

The most salient finding on the level of 5-year olds is the distinction between situations focused on interpersonal relations with peers and those focused on relations with adults. The reason for the separation may be that from the viewpoint of children, the former involve mainly social entertainment whereas the latter may often involve confrontation and the need for self-assertion. The separation of the two social factors persists on the level of 7-year olds, but the situations loaded on each factor partly change. Thus, "Confrontation with Grown-ups" includes in both age groups the issue of staying up late (Planning Situation No. 9), but in addition in 7-year olds, it includes realistic situations involving the search for a lost jacket (No. 6) and going on a picnic (No. 4), whereas in 5-year olds, it includes standing up against a giant in symbolic circumstances (No. 5). The same pertains to the factor of Planning Roads and Ways. It appears in both 5- and 7-year olds but is represented by partly different variables (e.g., note the change in the meaning of "going for a visit" of Planning Situation No. 3 which in 5-year olds is saturated only on Roads and Ways, whereas in 7-year olds it is saturated also on Interpersonal Relations with Peers). An interesting finding on the level of 7-year olds is the emergence of two new factors that persist into the next age level: the factor of Fantasy Situations and the still unclear factor of planning in Situations Requiring Preparations.

The factors appearing in 9-year olds have occurred also in 7-year olds but in a different form. In 9-year olds, the factor of Interpersonal Relations includes both the situations emphasizing relations with peers and those emphasizing confrontation with adults. Similarly, in 9-year olds the factor of Errands includes both the situations emphasizing the planning of Roads and Ways and those emphasizing Preparations and Arrangements. These shifts in factorial structure indicate changes in the meaning of problem situations that may be expected in view of the changed life circumstances of 9-year olds. At the age of 9 years, children seem to grasp confrontation with adults more in terms of the interpersonal character of the situation, and planning roads and ways as a special case of managing

Table 6.14. *Factor analyses of the global evaluations of plan adequacy in the 10 planning situations in the four age groups*

Age group	First factor		Second factor		Third factor		Fourth factor		Fifth factor	
5 yr	Sit. 6	.87	Sit. 3	.89	Sit. 9	.83	Sit. 10	.89		
	Sit. 8	.81	Sit. 2	.66	Sit. 5	.78	Sit. 7	.59		
	Sit. 1	.67	Sit. 4	.64						
	Sit. 4	.50								
Eigenvalue	3.98		1.54		1.12		.81			
Explained Var.	53.4%		20.7%		15.0%		10.9%			
Suggested title	Planning interpersonal relations with peers		Planning ways & roads		Planning confrontation with grown-ups		Planning difficult, complex situations			
7 yr	Sit. 3	.94	Sit. 2	.98	Sit. 10	.76	Sit. 6	.88	Sit. 5	.94
	Sit. 8	.75	Sit. 1	.82	Sit. 6	.62	Sit. 4	.55	Sit. 7	.56
	Sit. 4	.50			Sit. 3	.50	Sit. 9	.50		
Eigenvalue	5.08		2.19		1.44		.91		.80	
Explained Var.	52.8%		21.7%		14.0%		6.3%		5.2%	
Suggested title	Planning interpersonal relations with peers		Planning errands: preparations or arrangements		Planning ways & roads		Planning confrontation with grown-ups		Planning a fantasy situation	

9 yr

Sit. 3	.97	Sit. 10	.89	Sit. 5	.90
Sit. 7	.71	Sit. 1	.87	Sit. 4	-.83
Sit. 9	.51	Sit. 2	.76		
Sit. 1	.50	Sit. 6	.50		
Sit. 6	-.50				
Eigenvalue	3.73		2.64		2.20
Explained Var.	43.5%		30.8%		25.7%
Suggested title	Planning interpersonal relations with peers or grown-ups		Planning errands: preparations or arrangements		Planning a fantasy situation

11 yr

Sit. 8	.85	Sit. 2	.89	Sit. 5	.95
Sit. 9	.81	Sit. 10	.89	Sit. 7	.65
Sit. 3	.75	Sit. 6	.82	Sit. 8	.64
Sit. 4	.64			Sit. 10	.50
Sit. 1	.50				
Eigenvalue	5.06		2.40		1.17
Explained Var.	58.5%		27.7%		13.8%
Suggested title	Planning interpersonal relations with peer or grown-ups		Planning errands: preparations or arrangements		Planning long & complex plans

Note: The table presents the Varimax rotated factor matrix after rotation with Kaiser normalization. For the sake of clarity, only saturations $\geq$ .50 (or $-$ .50) are presented. For the description of the variables, see text (III.B.4). For the sake of orientation, here is a brief description of the Situations: (1) Looking for a lost item of a game; (2) Arrival of a new washing machine; (3) Going for a visit, unfamiliar way; (4) Picnic; (5) Jack and the Beanstalk; (6) Search for jacket; (7) Fighting for treasure; (8) Contact with child; (9) Staying up late; (10) A day's errands.

errands. In addition, the factor of planning in Fantasy Situations is greatly strengthened in 9-year olds. This finding corresponds to the characteristic conceptions of children in this age group about domains of planning (see Table 6.2 and section II.C).

On the level of 11-year olds, we find essentially the same first two factors as in 9-year olds, but the third is different and is reminiscent of the fourth factor in 5-year olds. It is possible that difficult planning situations tend to be treated alike regardless of their specific content domain.

In sum, studying the factorial structures of the situational evaluations of planning revealed basic types of planning situations relevant for children in these ages. For younger children, these are situations involving interpersonal relations with peers, situations involving confrontation with adults, situations in which it is necessary to plan roads and ways, and situations involving some preparations; and for older children, these are situations involving interpersonal relations with peers or adults and situations involving errands. For all age groups, the major factor includes interpersonal relations with peers whereas the second factor includes coping with some kind of arrangements in the context of an errand, preparing some future state or action, or simply going to some place. These findings correspond to the domains of action requiring planning indicated by children in the previous study (Table 6.2 and section II.C). Moreover, the findings also show how closely planning is interwoven with the daily life of children. No less important is the evidence that the meaning of planning situations tends to change in different age groups. Hence, a situation that remains objectively the same may not affect in the same way a child who is 7 years old and a child who is 9 years old. This should not be surprising because situations have multiple aspects that may have different appeals and meanings for younger and older children. Thus, the methodological conclusions are that in studying planning in children, several types of Planning Situations should be sampled and special consideration should be directed to the particular meaning of each situation for children at each particular age level.

6. *Variables of planning and IQ.* Table 6.15 presents the correlation coefficients of the general planning skills and the mean of the global evaluations of plan adequacy with the PPVT IQ measure that represents mainly the verbal IQ. The table shows that across age groups, there are three patterns of correlations. The first pattern consists of positive and significant correlations in all age groups. It can be observed in regard to the number of chronological orderings, references to general labels and domains, and essentially also the mean evaluation of plan adequacy

Table 6.15. *Pearson produce–moment correlations of planning variables with IQ*

Planning variables	Age groups				
	5 years	7 years	9 years	11 years	Mean
No. of alternatives	.57***	.93***	.08	−.71***	.33*
No. of if–then considerations	.48***	.68***	.12	−.61***	.20
No. of chronological orderings	.43***	.88***	.43***	.85***	.71***
No. of items	−.58***	.30*	.09	.03	−.06
No. of questions	−.65***	.27*	.12	.17	−.05
No. of domains	.16	.82***	.52***	.63***	.58***
No. of general labels	.61***	.35***	.37***	.53***	.47***
No. of steps in first plans	−.19	.65***	.02	.01	.15
No. of steps in alternate plans	−.23	.60***	.04	.34**	.20
No. of steps in all plans	−.36***	.54***	.20	.63***	.29*
Mean of situational evaluations	.18	.74***	.57***	.44***	.50**
Mean of variables	.03	.67***	.26*	.26*	.33*

Note: The IQ was measured by the Peabody Picture Vocabulary Test. For the description of the planning variables, see text (Section III B.4).
*$p < .05$.
**$p < .01$.
***$p < .001$.

(except in 5-year olds). The second pattern consists of negative correlations in 5-year olds, positive correlations in 7-year olds, and no correlations in the older groups. It can be observed most clearly in regard to the number of items and questions and less clearly in regard to the number of steps in plans (except for the rise in correlations in 11-year olds). The third pattern consists of positive correlations in 5- and 7-year olds, non-significant correlations in 9-year olds, and negative correlations in 11-year olds. It can be observed in regard to the number of alternatives and if–then considerations.

Thus, the findings show that the correlations of planning variables with IQ are irregular both in terms of age groups and in terms of specific variables. From the viewpoint of age groups, the mean correlations show that planning is not correlated with IQ in 5-year olds, is correlated moderately with IQ in 7-year olds, and is correlated lowly with IQ in 9- and 11-year olds. From the viewpoint of planning variables, the mean correlations show that the following variables are correlated moderately with IQ: the number of chronological orderings, probably because in different age groups it promotes information gathering and plan organization (sections

III.C.3 and III.C.4); the overall mean evaluation of plan adequacy, probably because it reflects consideration of multiple aspects and observation of situational constraints; and the numbers of references to general labels and domains, because they are conceptual units on a relatively high cognitive level, enabling progress in the three aspects of planning: information gathering, information organization, and plan structuring (sections III.C.1, III.C.3, and III.C.4). In addition, the following variables were correlated lowly with IQ across age groups: number of alternatives and number of steps in all plans, which reflect mainly structural aspects of plans (section III.C.4). The mean correlations with IQ for the other variables are not significant: Concerning the numbers of items and of questions, the reason may be that, particularly in the 9- and 11-year olds, these variables are replaced by the more powerful conceptual units of general labels and references to domains; concerning the numbers of alternatives and if–then considerations, the reason may be that these variables come to subserve information gathering particularly in older children (section III.C.4).

On the whole, the findings show that the relation of planning to IQ is moderate. The extent of the variance common to planning variables and IQ varies in the range of $-.02\%$ to $+86\%$, but on the whole, across all ages and variables it is merely 11%. Moreover, the relation of planning to IQ is dependent on particular aspects of planning. The relation is clearest in regard to those aspects that reflect the highest conceptual units involved in the organization of information and plans. Accordingly, IQ may account for the general availability of high-level cognitive skills that may be applied also in planning. Moreover, the relation of planning to IQ is relatively highest in 7-year olds, possibly because at this age there is positive motivation for improving mastery over oneself and the environment and there are not yet strong negative conceptions that may reduce the appeal of planning (section II.C). Thus, although planning as a cognitive activity is related to IQ, the observed developments in planning can hardly be attributed mainly to developments in IQ.

IV. An attempt at integration

Like the distinct sections of a plan, the different parts of this chapter need to be combined into a whole. If our work until now were mainly an analysis into increasingly small details or elements, then it would be justified to call the combination a *synthesis;* however, because it resembed rather a presentation of views from different perspectives, what needs to be done is better called *integration.*

In this attempt we will let outselves be guided by two viewpoints: that of planning and that of the planner, not only because these are the major foci of our discussion, but because one can hardly be conceived without the other.

A. *Planning*

Starting from the obvious conception that planning is a cognitive activity, it is only natural that what we learned about planning as an activity is focused on the kind of cognitive processes involved and how they get to function together. We found that children themselves come to conceive of it as a cognitive activity, and the more experienced they are, the more they become aware of its unique character. Children gradually distinguish planning from problem solving, on the one hand, and from fanciful daydreaming, on the other hand. This account is essentially correct, although it needs to be added that nevertheless, planning may include *both* problem solving and daydreaming, as children themselves noted (Table 6.7). Indeed, it includes also further cognitive processes that play a role in other contexts too, for example, hypothesis generation, or data collection. Hence, the specificity of planning does not consist mainly or exclusively in the kind of involved processes, but in their organization, in the way they function together, and in the uses to which it is put. Whereas the manner of functioning is mainly a characteristic of planning, the uses are rather dependent on the planner (see section IV.B).

In order to examine the organization of the cognitive processes that make up planning, it would be best to take the findings of the factor analyses as a starting point (section III.C.4). These findings show that there are three major groupings of processes that gradually emerge as distinct factors from the age of 5 to 11 years: These are the structuring of plans, information gathering, and information organization (regarding their development, see section III.C.4). These factors are defined by the variables we called "cross-situational measures" of aspects of planning. Although the specific variables that are saturated on each factor change to some extent with age, it is possible to identify the major and most characteristic variables. The factor Structuring of Plans is defined mainly by chronological ordering and the number of steps in the major and alternate plans. The factor Information Gathering is defined primarily by number of questions and items but is later reinforced by the number of alternative and if–then considerations. The factor "information organization" is defined all along by the number of general labels and references to domains, which are conceptual units of relatively great power and inclusiveness. It may be recalled (section III.C.1) that the variables defining Structuring of Plans increased only from the age of 5 years to 9 years and then tapered off; the variables defining Information Gathering increased from the age of 5 to 9 years and then declined at 11 years; and the variables defining Information Organization increased linearly from the age of 5 to 11 years.

Earlier (section III.C.1) we suggested that the absence of change in the variables of the Structuring of Plans and the decrease in the frequency of the variables of Information Gathering did not indicate actual freezing in plan structuring or decline in information gathering but rather replacement of the specific assessed cognitive procedures by the powerful cognitive means of general labels and references to domains. These means enable a more concise and economical organization of information and a better integration of the plan itself. The findings concerning the techniques and procedures of planning (section III.C.3) shed light on the dynamics of organization and integration in planning and show how development actually continues across age groups in all spheres of planning: structuring the plan, gathering information, and organizing it.

The study of techniques and procedures of planning revealed some of the major processes involved in the structuring of plans. These include meaning elaboration of the target, which results in identifying the problem and its major themes or aspects; forming hypotheses concerning one (or more) of these themes, so that one shifts away from the original target (detour) yet keeps it always in mind; selecting one (or more) of the hypotheses on the basis of specific criteria and devising a plausible route including specifications of means for its implementation; devising alternate routes to the first planned one, sometimes even alternates within it for the implementation of particular steps it specifies; doing the same concerning other themes or aspects of the problem while keeping the target always in mind; combining the different planned sections according to a set of rules unique for the plan; and reevaluating the original target and redefining it or shifting away from it, in case this proves necessary in view of the contents or structure of planning. Although these processes may seem complex, they have all been observed in the studied children. Moreover, this brief description presents merely the skeletal framework for much finer-grained processes that have been recorded (see section III.C.4). The description clarifies, however, how variegated and multidirectional the development of the structuring of plans actually is. There is development in practically every one of the stages and processes mentioned above: for example, the meaning analysis of the target, the identification of themes, setting up of hypotheses, the criteria for selecting a hypothesis, and so on. It is unlikely that all processes develop simultaneously, at the same rate, and to the same extent in all children. Hence, what one may expect is an increase in individual differences and perhaps an apparent standstill on the overt level of manifestations, while development is proceeding in depth.

What we have learned about the second and third factors leads to similar conclusions. Concerning information gathering, the within-situational responses revealed that there is more to it than merely asking questions and collecting items of information. The study on children's conceptions of planning showed that children consider it difficult to recall all the relevant things and keep them in mind (section II.C). Observation of children's planning, particularly that of the younger children, showed that indeed they are liable to forget relevant things including even the target, may get bogged down in a mass of irrelevant items, sometimes neglect to use a piece of information that was initially presented or for which they asked, and often do not evaluate information adequately, for example, mistaking fantasy for fact, inventing facts, and changing the given constraints of the situation. In addition, they often proceed nonsystematically, jumping from one fact or sphere to another, never being sure whether they have actually recalled, considered, and taken account of everything needed. Naturally all these difficulties are much more frequent in the younger children than the older ones. Our observations reveal that the difficulties are overcome gradually, not necessarily because memory – conceived as a "container" – becomes larger and firmer, but because children learn to apply more powerful conceptual tools. With the introduction of general labels and references to domains, the memory load becomes easier. The child is now able to scan the field more completely and order the labels or domains. Hence, we start observing distinctions between different kinds of information in line with content areas, as well as distinctions between fact and fancy, that are now kept increasingly apart. One of the most important distinctions is that between relevant and irrelevant items. It, too, is enhanced appreciably with age, so that the irrelevant is increasingly sifted out. In the wake of ordering the domains of content, the child discovers other useful principles. Thus we start to observe the systematic scanning of a sphere of a problem in line with different criteria. This procedure not only ensures better and more comprehensive recall but also produces information that is already ordered when it becomes available. Indeed, this successive scanning in line with different principles is a new procedure for the generation of information. In other words, in regard to gathering information and organizing information, development is so multidirectional that what is observed on the surface in terms of global measures reflects only roughly the development in the underlying processes.

Thus, we have studied planning on different levels: first, on the level of the planning skills themselves (e.g., elaborating steps in plans, forming alternate plans); second, on the level of the underlying cognitive dynamics (as reflected in the within-situational responses, e.g. elaborating the meaning of the target, identifying its major themes, and generating hypotheses about each theme are some of the cognitive processes involved in shaping steps in plans); third, on the integrative level on which the cognitive skills are clustered into more stable cognitive structures that form part of the individual's cognitive equipment, constituting his or her style of functioning in the sphere of planning (as reflected in the factors of planning, e.g., gathering of information, structuring of plans); and fourth, on the operative level on which the cognitive skills are activated, leading to the formation of plans, that is, temporary functional combinations in line with the requirements of action in a specific situation (the adequacy of the plans is reflected in the plan evaluations).

As shown, on each level there are different constructs and different problems. Yet they are all interrelated. The shaping of a cognitive skill (on the first level) depends to a large extent on the underlying cognitive dynamics (on the second level) but determines in turn the clustering of the skills into more permanent cognitive structures (on the third level) or less permanent cognitive structures that may function as plans (on the fourth level). In turn, the production of a plan may affect the involved cognitive skills (e.g., if alternative plans proved important and successful in a specific case, the skill of forming alternative plans in general may be strengthened), and so on.

We have shown that from 5 to 11 years, development of planning proceeds on all four levels. However, the development on each level is not regular across ages and is subject to jags, temporary plateaus, and occasional declines when more advanced processes come into play directly or indirectly. Further, development on all four levels is not precisely parallel. For example, from 5 to 7 years, there occurs the relatively largest developmental spurt both in planning skills (first level) and plan formation (fourth level); from 7 to 9 years, however, planning skills develop relatively more than plan formation; and from 9 to 11 years, plan formation develops relatively more than planning skills. There is evidence, however, that with age there are increasing interrelations and thus greater uniformity of the manifestations at least within each level. Thus, as a child grows older, the different aspects of planning – initially distinct and partly autonomous – become more integrated and turn into facets of one sphere: that of planning.

At any rate the sphere of planning and its development are too complex to be accounted for by a single determinant. The moderate relation of cognitive skills and plan formation to IQ suggests that the development of planning may be affected by developmental changes in IQ but cannot be wholly explained in these terms. One reason for this is that cognitive structures and activities like planning surpass in complexity and depth the cognitive aspects assessed by the common IQ measures. Another important reason is that with age, planning on all levels becomes increasingly integrated into the domain of personality at large – its motivations, goals, attitudes, desires, fears, and so on. As the individual grows older, the mere availability of a cognitive skill or structure is less of a reason for applying it. Rather, such skills and structures increasingly become tools for promoting the individual's overall goals in spheres that have initially little to do with planning. Hence, no complete understanding of planning and its development can be reached without studying the planner.

B. The planner

One must never lose sight of the fact that planning exists only as an activity of a planner. Therefore, when we discuss the development of planning, the finding that children increasingly view planning as an activity that also children do is at least as important for understanding the phenomena as the observation that at the age of 9 years children are able to form hierarchical plans. The study on children's conceptions of planning provided some insight into the role and functions of planning in children's lives. From the age of 5 years onward, there is an increasing uniformity in the meaning of planning for different children, particularly concerning the domains of application, causes, purposes, and results of planning. As may be expected, the conceptions of children about these and other aspects of planning do not always conform to those of adults. With age, children become increasingly familiar with the manner in which planning occurs, its time range, frequency, some of its difficulties, and especially its positive and later also its possible negative results. Initially, children conceive of planning as a precursor of any action, particularly a routine recurrent one. With experience they come to regard it as applicable to an increased range of domains in the internal and external spheres, including health and fantasy no less than avoidance of commitments and manipulation of adults. Later they increasingly consider it as bound to actions extraordinary in some respect or performed under extraordinary environmental or psychological circumstances. In terms of contents, the major domains of planning are relations with peers, relations (or confrontation) with adults, preparation of future actions, events or states, managing of errands, and planning of ways and roads. With age, interpersonal relations (with peers or adults) and errands (including preparations or planning of ways, when necessary) emerge as the focal spheres. However, already at the age of 5 years, planning seems to fulfill a psychologically important role in the life of children, mainly in turning recurrent actions into routine automatic actions. There is evidence that after 5 years children increasingly conceive of planning as a means of control over the environment and themselves for the sake of attaining short-range and long-range goals benefiting them both as individuals and as members of society and even humanity. In accordance with children's increased reality-testing, time perspective, and sociability, planning is increasingly applied for the attainment of more important personal and social ends, and is, in turn, itself conceived in more realistic terms. These findings show how deeply planning is involved with the goals, needs, and beliefs of the developing child (see Kreitler & Kreitler, chapter 4, this volume). Thus, whereas planning skills develop as the individual develops, planning itself turns increasingly into a means for promoting the development of the total individual.

Notes

1. None of the children of this sample participated in the study reported in Plans and planning: their motivational and cognitive antecedents (Kreitler & Kreitler, chapter 4, this volume).
2. The complete text of the Planning Situations can be obtained from the authors upon request.

References

Appel, L. F., Cooper, R. G., McCarrell, N., Sims-Knight, J., Yussen, S. R., & Flavell, J. H., (1972). The development of the distinction between perceiving and memorizing. *Child Development, 43*, 1365–1381.

Bjorklund, D. F., Ornstein, P. A., & Haig, J. R. (1977). Developmental differences in organization and recall: Training in the use of organizational techniques. *Developmental Psychology, 13*, 175–183.

Brown, A. L., & Barclay, C. R. (1976). The effect of training specific mnemonics on the metamnemonic efficiency of retarded children. *Child Development, 47*, 71–80.

Brown, A. L., & DeLoache, J. S. (1978). Skills, plans and self-regulation. In R. S. Siegler (Ed.), *Children's thinking: What develops?* Hillsdale, NJ: Erlbaum.

Bühler, K. (1930). *The mental development of the child.* New York: Harcourt, Brace.

Flavell, J. H. (1970). Concept development. In P. H. Mussen (Ed.), *Carmichael's manual of child development* (Vol. 1, 3rd ed). New York: Wiley.

Flavell, J. H., Botkin, P. T., Fry, C. L., Wright, J. W., & Jarvis, P. E., (1975). *The development of role-taking and communication skills in children.* New York: Wiley.

Flavell, J. H., & Wellman, H. M. (1977). Metamemory. In R. V. Kail & J. W. Hagen (Eds.), *Perspectives on the development of memory and cognition.* Hillsdale, NJ: Erlbaum.

Freud, S. (1962). Creative writers and daydreaming. In J. Strachey (Ed.), *The standard edition of the complete psychological works of . . .* (Vol. 9). London: Hogarth.

Freud, S. (1963). Introductory lectures on psycho-analysis. In J. Strachey (Ed.), *The standard edition of the complete psychological works of . . .* (Vols. 15 & 16). London: Hogarth.

Gallistel, C. R. (1980). *The organization of action: A new synthesis.* Hillsdale, NJ: Erlbaum,

Grice, G. R. (1965). Do responses evoke responses? *American Psychologist, 20,* 282–294.

Gunn, B. (1964). Children's conceptions of occupational prestige. *Personnel Guidance Journal, 42,* 558–563.

Hayes-Roth, B., & Hayes-Roth, F. (1979). A cognitive model of planning. *Cognitive Science, 3,* 275–310.

Ingalls, R. P., & Dickerson, D. J. (1969). Development of hypothesis behavior in human concept identification. *Developmental Psychology, 1,* 707–716.

James, W. (1890). *Principles of psychology.* New York: Holt.

Kelly, M., Scholnick, E. K., Travers, S. H., & Johnson, J. W. (1976). Relations among memory, memory appraisal, and memory strategies. *Child Development, 47,* 648–659.

Kreitler, H., & Kreitler, S. (1968). Unhappy memory of the happy past: Studies in cognitive dissonance. *British Journal of Psychology, 59,* 157–166.

Kreitler, H., & Kreitler, S. (1976). *Cognitive orientation and behavior.* New York: Springer Publishing.

Kreitler, H., & Kreitler, S. (1982). The theory of cognitive orientation. Widening the scope of behavior prediction. In B. Maher & W. B. Maher (Eds.), *Progress in experimental personality research* (Vol. 11). New York: Academic Press.

Kreitler, S., & Kreitler, H. (1981). Item contents: Does it matter? *Educational and Psychological Measurement, 41,* 635–641.

Laurendeau, M., & Pinard, A. (1962). *Causal thinking in the child.* New York: International Universities Press.

Leontiev, A. N. (1959). *Problems of the development of the mind.* Moscow: Mysl'. (In Russian)

Lovell, K., & Slater, A. (1960) The growth of the concept of time: A comparative study. *Journal of Child Psychology and Psychiatry, 1,* 179–190.

Luria, A. R. (1960). *The nature of human conflicts or emotions, conflict and will.* New York: Grove Press.

Mandler, G. (1962). From association to structure. *Psychological Review, 69,* 415–427.

Miller, G. A., Galanter, E., & Pribram, K. H. (1960). *Plans and the structure of behavior.* New York: Holt, Rinehart & Winston.

Mischel, W., & Patterson, C. J. (1978). Effective plans for self-control in children. In W. A. Collins (Ed.), *Minnesota symposia on child psychology* (Vol. 11). Hillsdale, NJ: Erlbaum.

Nagy, J. N., & Baird, J. C. (1978). Children as environmental planners. In I. Altman & J. F. Wohlwill (Eds.), *Children and the environment.* New York: Plenum Press.

Paris, S. G. (1978). Coordination of means and goals in the development of mnemonic skills. In P. A. Ornstein (Ed.), *Memory development in children.* Hillsdale, NJ: Erlbaum.

Piaget, J., & Inhelder, B. (1958). *The growth of logical thinking from childhood to adolescence.* London: Routledge & Kegan Paul.

Sacerdoti, E. D. (1977). *A structure for plans and behavior.* New York: Elsevier, 1977.

Salatas, H., & Flavell, J. H. (1976). Behavioral and metamnemonic indicators of strategic behaviors under remembered instructions in first grade. *Child Development, 47,* 81–89.

Schank, R. C., & Abelson, R. P. (1977). *Scripts, plans, goals and understanding.* Hillsdale, NJ: Erlbaum.

Schroder, H. M., Driver, M. J., & Streufert, S. (1967). *Human information processing.* New York: Holt, Rinehart & Winston.

Singer, J. L., & Antrobus, J. S. (1972). Daydreaming, imaginal processes, and personality: A normative study. In P. W. Sheehan (Ed.), *The functions and nature of imagery.* New York: Academic Press.

Urbain, E. S., & Kendall, P. C. (1980). Review of social–cognitive problem-solving interventions with children. *Psychological Bulletin, 88,* 109–143.

Werner, H. (1948). *Comparative psychology of mental development* (rev. ed.). New York: International Universities Press.

Wilkening, F., Becker, J., & Trabasso, T. (Eds.) (1980). *Information integration by children.* Hillsdale, NJ: Erlbaum.

Zaporozhets, A. V. (1960). *The development of voluntary movements.* Moscow: Academy of Pedagogical Sciences. (In Russian)

7   Planning in a chore-scheduling task

Roy D. Pea and Jan Hawkins

I. Introduction

In order to accomplish successfully a coordinated set of activities in the achievement of an overall goal, it is useful to learn skills of planning. A plan is a representation, in some form, of a set of actions designed to produce an intended outcome once put into action. Plans are often never put into action, but their adequacy cannot otherwise be reality tested. Furthermore, a plan can exist at various levels of specificity, and may be designed in different representational forms (e.g., talk, text, images, blueprints).

A general model of planning consists of four components: The planner must (a) construct a representation of the planning situation, including the problem and goal; (b) construct the plan to achieve that goal; (c) execute the plan; and (d) remember the planning process. These four inter-related components of the planning process are discussed in detail elsewhere (Pea, 1982), and each presents major developmental challenges. These model components are frequently discussed as if they take place in sequence, but an important feature of actual planning performances is that any of the components may be thought about, used, or modified any-where in the process of constructing and carrying out a plan. This sort of revision is especially apparent when we examine the planning processes involved in composing a text (e.g., Flower & Hayes, 1981). Thus, for

This research was supported by a grant from the Spencer Foundation. D. Midian Kurland made continuing conceptual and technical contributions to the project. We are particularly grateful to Sally MacKain and Moni Hamolsky for their care-ful work in coding videotapes, datafile work, and help with experimental sessions. Jeff Aron provided assistance with early sessions and videotape analyses. Portions of this paper were presented at the 1983 Biennial Meetings of the Society for Research in Child Development in Detroit.

273

example, attempts to construct a plan may lead to redefining of goals, whereas to execute the plan often results in revisions of the structure of the plan. Planning is thus inherently recursive in nature.

In this paper, we narrow our focus from these multiple complexities to an analysis of the second component of the planning model in a developmental context: the processes and products that emerge when children *construct* a plan. Although our emphasis will be on understanding how children construct plans in a context where the problem situation is defined for them, we recognize in our task design and analyses that the planning model components may have mutually revisionary influences during the course of planning activities.

How do children's planning efforts at different ages relate to these model components for high-level planning skills? We know very little about the development of such high level skills. Therefore, in order to reveal how children are planning, we needed to design a task that would take into account what is known about the features of plan construction, especially information about when planning is likely to be done by children, and that would allow observers to see and analyze the process of plan construction as it occurs.

In developing the planning task for revealing different levels of planning proficiency, five critical aspects of planning were taken into account. These five aspects are discussed in turn.

A.   The need for planning is often not recognized

Planning activities appear to often be tied to specific situations. People learn to apply planning skills in particular situations; it is not necessarily the case that all situations in which planning would be appropriate are recognized as requiring planning efforts. For example, some complex sequences of action are well-practiced routines for individuals, like getting to work in the morning using several modes of public transportation. Conversely, there are nonroutine situations where planning efforts would enhance the quality of outcomes, yet where individuals fail to engage in plan construction. For example, in our previous work interviewing 8- to 12-year old children about planning (Pea, 1982), no children reported that they engaged in planning when doing school work, although they knew what planning was and could describe situations in which plans are important. Thus, a task context was needed where it would be expected that most children would naturally recognize the value of planning.

B. Background knowledge of the situation is necessary for planning

Related to the situational character of planning is the importance of an adequate knowledge base about the planning context so that appropriate moves can be developed, and hypothetically carried out. For example, one might be very hard-pressed to plan an African safari not because of poor planning skills, but because one does not know about key safari activities, probable hardships, the necessary supplies, staff, maps, and the contingencies among events that would constrain the development of such a plan. It is important that the planner have sufficient knowledge about the content of the planning problem. Otherwise the substance of plans is more like fantasy material than a realistic blueprint for action.

C. Planning is more likely when the situation is complex and novel

Planning is most frequently required and best revealed in situations of sufficient complexity and novelty so that the means for achieving a goal are not obvious, and alternative courses of action may be reasonably considered. Effective planners must be able to consider and hypothetically execute different courses of action in order to assess the best means of achieving a goal. As noted above, planners must have a sufficiently rich knowledge base for the domain to anticipate the consequences of "commitments" (Stefik 1981a, 1981b) of specific actions in a plan. For example, doing one action early in a sequence of actions may preclude the possibility of choosing a different desirable action later. Thus we required a situation sufficiently complex, yet well known to children, in order to assess their abilities to experiment with alternatives in the course of planning.

D. Planning is a revisionary process

Planning must be characterized as revisionary. In considering alternatives, effective planners edit and revise their plans. They flexibly use both "top-down" approaches, which proceed from abstract decisions (e.g., to seek a mortgage) to increasingly specific ones (e.g., which bank to seek the mortgage with); and "bottom-up" approaches, which note emergent concrete properties of the plan or the planning environment (e.g., a specific bank is offering very low interest rates); and add data-driven decisions to the plan. Planners might go through several cycles of revision in considering the consequences of differently organized schemes of action. In understanding children's planning, it is important to provide a context where these revisionary efforts can be revealed. Are children able to revise their plans to be more effective on the basis of information gleaned from considering alternative courses of action? How does this ability to incorporate information over the course of planning reveal itself developmentally?

E. Planning decisions are made at different levels of abstraction

Finally, planning decisions can be made at different levels of abstraction. For example, a plan can be generated hierarchically from a consideration of the problem situation as a whole. One may begin very abstractly ("I would like to see a movie tonight with someone"), and proceed by progressively refining or concretizing the plan to a specific alternative ("I will leave with Sam to walk down Broadway toward the Thalia at 95th Street to see 'The Last Metro' at 7:30 p.m. tonight"). Alternatively, planning can occur more concretely as a sequence of local decisions without an overall framework for the situation. Such "planning in action" (Rogoff & Gardner, 1984) is probably more important in everyday activities than preplanning before action. On a comparable note, Scardamalia and Bereiter (1985) describe the efforts of fourth graders at planning to write as more like a "rehearsal" or a first draft of what they will end up with as text rather than like a plan. We were interested in understanding how children come to generate frameworks for the planning situation. The experimental task should be able to reveal different skill levels of children's decision making in their planning efforts.

In sum, it is necessary to consider particular features of the task situation used for assessment in order to reveal abilities of the planner. With respect to the situation, the planning context should be sufficiently complex that alternative courses of action are reasonably available; the situation must be one where it is plausible that children will see planning as appropriate; and it must be a context where children have sufficient knowledge of the domain so that planning is possible. With respect to the planner's abilities, the task should reveal (a) whether alternative plan designs are considered, and whether the planner tries them out and thinks through their consequences; (b) the characteristics of revisions; and (c) the types and levels of abstraction in planning decisions.

We decided that a classroom-chore scheduling situation similar to a task developed by Hayes-Roth and Hayes-Roth (1979) met these requirements for a planning situation. In consultation with teachers of the schoolchildren who participated in our study, we found that all children were required to carry out certain classroom chores on a regular basis. The children were familiar with a list of chores (e.g., washing the blackboards, watering the plants) and the actions involved in doing each one, but the task was made novel by asking children to organize a plan to accomplish the set of chores so that they could be carried out efficiently by one person. Because we wished to see how children engaged in revisions, we utilized a microgenetic method in which they were encouraged to develop and improve upon their plans over the course of an experimental session. The term "microgenesis" (cf. Flavell & Draguns, 1957; Werner, 1956) is derived from the rich but little known developmental studies of the organization of thought processes in the first half of the twentieth century. The term refers to the sequence of cognitive events that unfold over the brief time between initial contact with a stimulus and a relatively stable cognitive response – in our case, the child's final plan. We view the microgenesis of a plan through successive revisions as revealing important features of planning processes that have general developmental significance. This microgenetic method allows us to closely observe the revisionary processes involved in a planning task.

In addition to the analyses of planning processes, we were interested in how certain mental representational abilities may impact on children's approaches to the planning situation. Sophisticated planners must simulate actions mentally, observe their consequences, and consider alternatives. Planning is usually thought about as a fully internalized symbolic process that requires mental, symbolic representation and mental operation upon the symbols. For this reason, we were interested in understanding how individual differences in memory capacity and cognitive style (specifically, field dependence–independence) might contribute to effective plan construction. A successful planning effort for a complex situation is memory-intensive, requiring children to remember complex sequences of actions. Effective planning also requires facility in seeing how potential parts of a plan interrelate with the effectiveness of the plan alternative considered as a whole. We therefore felt it was important to collect information about children's memory capacity and their facility in thinking about part–whole relations. In order to understand how these abilities may relate to planning skills, all children in the study were given a variant of the Wechsler Adult Intelligence Scale (WAIS) Forward Digit Span task (as a measure of memory capacity) and the Wechsler Intelligence Scale for Children (WISC) Block Design Subtest (as a measure of field dependence–independence), as we discuss below.

In constructing our planning situation, we also took into account the *practice* of planning as it occurs in everyday situations. The complex symbolic manipulations involved in planning often necessitates externalizing the representation of the planning space in some way. Planning activities often occur in contexts where the planning process is supported by various sorts of representational "tools" or aids, developed especially to assist in planning for a particular type of activity. Specialized planning tools may be found in a number of professional contexts (e.g., business, education, medicine). For example, designers such as architects and interior designers may construct planning spaces in which they can physically try out alternate arrangements as part of the planning process. And in writing, sophisticated word processors allow for easily created simultaneous comparison of different options for planned text organizational schemas. Likewise, designers may make use of specialized drawing devices and conventions to facilitate both the planning process and its execution, such as computer-aided design and manufacturing systems (CAD/CAM) for computer microcircuits.

These planning supports appear to have at least two functions: (a) to relieve the memory burden required for the representation of complex plans; and (b) to serve as a "symbolic" space in which to try out alternate formulations of a plan before actual execution (e.g., a model for the design of a kitchen). In this sense, "epistemic planning," much like "epistemic writing" (Bereiter, 1980), serves to externalize thought and enable transcendence of human information processing limitations. At these high levels, planning becomes an externalized tool of thought which can be transformed as an object of perception and reflection.

The planning task used in this research takes into account this feature of planning in "real" contexts: A classroom map was designed as an external representational model to support the planning process. This tool enabled children to reveal their planning processes to observers as they constructed their plans.

In the following sections, we present details of the experimental materials used, the task description, experimental procedure, participant characteristics, systems for data analysis, and then the results of our study.

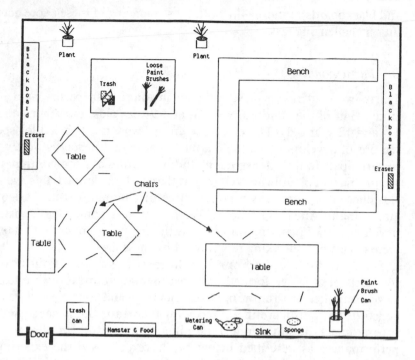

Figure 7.1. Diagram of classroom map.

II. The chore-scheduling task: experimental methods

A. Materials

A transparent Plexiglass map (22 × 30 inches; scale, 1:15 inches) of a
fictitious classroom was developed (see Figure 7.1) for the task.

The *chore list* consisted of six major chores to be done after first entering through the classroom door: (a) watering (2) plants; (b) erasing and
washing (2) blackboards; (c) feeding a hamster; (d) putting (17) chairs
under their adjacent tables; (e) washing (5) tables; and (f) putting away
objects (returning and washing out paintbrushes; disposing of trash
paper) lying on the art table. The final "chore act" was to leave through
the classroom door. These six major chores and their closing act could be
accomplished with a minimum of 39 distinct component chore acts,
some of which were instrumentally necessary to accomplish others (i.e.,
a watercan is needed to water plants; a sponge is necessary to wash tables

and blackboards). Finding the optimal sequencing of these chore acts was thus a challenging task.

B. Participants

Thirty-two students in private school in Manhattan participated in the study. Half of the childrern were 8- and 9-year olds, the other half were 11- and 12-year olds. These two age groups were not selected for specific reasons of developmental theory, but because their teachers were willing to participate in the intensive longitudinal studies of Logo computer programming and planning development that we had planned; this age range was chosen because it is representative of children learning Logo programming in American schools. We nonetheless anticipated substantial development of planning skills across the age period of early to late concrete operational thinking represented by these ages.

The 32 children came from four different classrooms. Four boys and four girls of each age formed an experimental group who were learning Logo computer programming, and four boys and four girls of each age constitued a control group not receiving the treatment. Because the Logo programmers did not significantly differ from controls in their planning performances as described below, we have collapsed the experimental and control groups into a single group for current purposes. The relations between these groupings and planning results are detailed in Pea and Kurland (1984), but will not concern us here. But a year of Logo programming did not help children become more effective planners, at least as indexed in the task described.

Participant selection was not random. For the experimental groups, participants were selected on the basis of two criteria: (a) a large quantity of time spent working at the classroom microcomputers during their first two months of use; and (b) teacher-assessed reflectiveness and talkativeness so that rich, think-aloud protocols during the task might be provided. For the control groups, only the second criterion was used.

Other tasks administered were a digit-span task and the WISC Block Design subtest. The former measure was chosen to assess whether the size of a basic processing capacity affects planning performances during this task. The latter measure was selected as a task for determining an individual's cognitive style in terms of his or her field dependence or field independence. The rationale and procedure for both tasks are discussed in the following sections. Table 7.1 provides a summary of WISC and Digit Span scores for the two age groups.

Table 7.1. *WISC Block Design (BD) and Digit Span scores*

	Digit Span		Standardized WISC BD scores	
Age group	Mean	(SD)	Mean	(SD)
Younger group	5.3	(1.3)	13.4	(2.6)
Older group	6.2	(1.5)	13.3	(2.8)

C. Experimental design

The planning task was administered early in the school year. Between-participant grouping variables for current purposes were: (a) age (younger, older); and (b) sex (male, female). Other between-participant variables were: (c) Wechsler Intelligence Scale for Children (WISC) Block Design Score, and (d) Digit Span. The key within-participant variables were mean scores across all plans, and scores for first and last plans.

D. Procedure

1. Classroom chore-scheduling task. Each child was taken individually from his or her classroom to a filming room, and seated at a table upon which the Plexiglas map stood. The map was oriented upright on an attached stand 6 inches in front of the child, and tilted back 6 degrees from the vertical plane. A videocamera was located approximately 8 feet from the map, and filmed each session through the map.

The experimenter then slowly read the following instructions to the child:

This is a map of a classroom. Today I'd like you to play a game for me. In this game, pretend it is the afternoon, just before school is over. Your classmates have left early, and your job is to make a *plan* to do the classroom chores I will tell you about.

You have to water the PLANTS [point] near the window. You have to erase and wash the two BLACKBOARDS in the room [point]. The HAMSTER in his cage needs to be fed [point to cage and food]. The CHAIRS are out of place around the tables, and each should be put under the tables neatly. All the TABLES in the room also need to be washed [point to each]. There are a few things to do at the ART TABLE [point]. The PAINTBRUSHES there [point] need to be washed, and put in the brush can next to the sink [point]. The TRASHPAPER [point] on the art table should be put in the trashcan [point].

There are a lot of chores to do here. You can plan for as long as you want to do the list of chores [point to child's list of chores] in any order you want. Some ways of doing the chores are ones where you have to walk *farther* to do them. You want to find the *shortest* way of doing the chores. The shortest way is the *best* way. [The experimenter then demonstrated the contrast of shorter versus longer spatial paths by walking straight toward the child (shortest path) versus around the room and then to the child (longer path).]

Now you can practice by trying out different plans until you are ready to show me the *best* plan you can think of. It is real important that you *think out loud* all the time you work on this game. Tell me everything you think about as you are doing it, like if you are making decisions about what to do in your plan. Use the [foot-long wooden] pointer to show the path you would take in your plans to do the chores.

I also have something you can use to *help* you in getting the best plan. There is a pencil and paper for making notes if you want to.

There are a couple of other things. The SPONGE does not need to be rinsed. It is good for all the chores that need to be done. And the WATERCAN has enough water in it for both plants.

After a child completed each plan by moving the pointer to the exit door on the map, the experimenter asked whether he or she had done all the chores they wanted to, in order to prompt the noticing of any omitted chore acts. If the child did not notice chore acts that had been omitted, E asked: "Can you make up a shorter plan?" If the child answered "yes," the session continued with the formulation of another plan; sessions terminated when the child believed he or she had arrived at the shortest plan he or she was able to formulate.

2. Digit Span task. Because the symbolic planning activities that one may use in working on the classroom problem are memory intensive, we utilized a Digit Span measure of short-term memory capacity. As a child planned aloud and constructed a path to achieve the task goal, many different chore acts were named in sequence. It is reasonable to assume that remembering one's plan, so that it may be improved through revisions in a subsequent plan, would be facilitated through greater span capacity.

Within two weeks of the experimental session, the children were individually presented with a variation of the Digits Forward task of the Wechsler Adult Intelligence Scale (WAIS) Digit Span subtest. Numbers were displayed visually[1] by a microcomputer so that the presentation rate could be tightly controlled.

Each number appeared for one second and then vanished as the next digit on the list replaced it. When the presentation of each list was complete, a cursor appeared, instructing the child to start the next list by pressing a specific key. Before pressing the key, children attempted to reproduce orally the numbers in the list in the correct order.

During the task, five lists of each length (from 4 to 11 digits) were given so as to provide reliable measures of span size. Responses were only considered correct if all the numbers in the list were recalled in correct order. Children received lists of increasing length until they reproduced none of the five lists of that length correctly. The cumulative partial scoring method advocated by Brener (1940) and Lyons (1977) was used, according to which one's span size is counted as the sum of (a) the longest list length for which all five lists were recalled correctly; and (b) the proportion of lists reproduced correctly at each of the longer list lengths.

The mean Digit Span for the younger group according to this method was 5.31, for the older group 6.23, but this difference was not significant. However, age was significantly correlated with Digit Span ($r = .35$, $p = .029$).

3. WISC Block Design task. Field dependence–independence is a robust cognitive style variable developed by Witkin and associates (Witkin et al., 1954; Witkin, Dyk, Faterson, Goodenough, & Kark, 1962), and refers to a self-consistent pattern of functioning with respect to separating an item from its background context (field), to confronting a situation analytically, and to preserving an active orientation to the environment. Because planning involves distancing of self from the task, the dimension of field dependence–independence may be linked to planning insofar as planning requires self-task distancing and a corresponding strategy-seeking attitude. A rational analysis of the classroom map problem suggests that it is a task environment in which such distancing from the task is less likely to occur with field dependency than independency. One would thus expect superior performance by individuals who are relatively field independent. Each plan has a large number of components whose interrelationships are important to consider in improving one's plan. Disembedment of proposed plan moves within their field context and reconstruction of move sequences in formulating a new plan should be facilitated by field-independent cognitive style. A related interpretation of direct relevance for the classroom problem is suggested by Case's (1974, p. 549) discussion of this cognitive style variable: "Field dependent subjects are assumed to . . . assign higher weight to perceptual cues than to cues provided by task instructions, in situations where these two sets of cues suggest conflicting executive schemes."

The WISC Block Design task was selected for determining field dependence or field independence because Case and Globerson (1974), among others, found that WISC blocks show a high loading on factors defined by Witkin's Rod and Frame Test for assessing cognitive style. The WISC blocks are also easy to present and score.

The WISC Block Design task is comprised of 11 timed design-reproduction problems, and the score is contingent on the *speed* with which children can copy accurately the examiner's reference design block arrangement with their own set of blocks. The task was administered by a clinical psychologist qualified as a WISC examiner in approximately 10- to 15-minute individual sessions. Scores for this task are given in terms of the national age norms specified in Wechsler (1974).

The mean WISC score for the younger group was 13.4 (*SD*, 2.6); for the older group, 13.3 (*SD*, 2.8). The overall mean for the group of 32 participants was 13.34, well above the national average of 10.

III. Results

Three principal types of analysis were performed. In the first section, we review analyses of plans considered as *products,* with the principal focus on the shortness or efficiency of plans that children produced. In the second section, we consider the types of revisions that children made in their plans. What were the qualitative *features* of plans that contributed to plan improvement? In the third section, we examine planning *processes,* specifically in terms of the types and levels of abstraction of decisions made during the planning process. In addition, we discuss the decision choice flexibility that was revealed in individuals' formulation of plans. In the final section, we integrate findings for these analyses, examining the extent to which a child's processes of plan formulation contribute to the quality of their plans.

A. Product analyses

Data reduction from the videotaped sessions took place in three main phases. Videotapes were carefully transcribed, with sequential notations made of utterances, pointing, and other gesturing. For subsequent analyses of the plans as *products,* the sequence of chore acts (moves) for each plan created was then determined from the transcripts. As in related research by Goldin and Hayes-Roth (1980), we used the final, child-revised version of each plan for our plan distance measurements. We then measured the distances on our map between pairs of chore act locations, and for each plan we calculated the total distance that would be traversed if the plan were to be executed.

Furthermore, a child would sometimes omit a chore act, rendering the plan incomplete. To compare the length of plans for children and groups, we needed a full plan; otherwise plan distance comparisons would be distortive in the sense that they would favor incomplete plans. To make the total distance of each plan comparable from one child to the next, an adjustment method was used to build up each partial plan to a "full plan," that is, one accomplishing every chore act in the task. This conservative adjustment consisted of calculating for each plan for each individual the "median length of moves" (more meaningful than the mean because interchore act distances were sometimes very small or very large). To derive "total plan distance," we then added to the child's partial-plan distance the product of the number of omitted acts and their value for median move length.[2]

The amount of data compiled due to each child's production of multiple plans allowed many comparisons within and between individuals. We analyzed the distances of the individuals' plans, and their *efficiency* relative to the "ideal plan," which would accomplish the chores in the shortest distance. *F* statistics are significant for alpha values less than .01 unless otherwise specified. Several preliminary summary statistics set the stage for plan efficiency result presentations.

1. Number of plans. The mean number of plans per child was 3.94 (*SD*, 1.48), and there were no significant age differences. The number of plans an individual produced was also not related to the efficiency of an individual's best plan.

2. Effects of sex, WISC score, and Digit Span. In general there were few significant relationships between WISC score or Digit Span score and any of the product measures. However, those significant relationships, reported in the relevant sections below, were in the predicted direction, that is, higher WISC scores or higher Digit Span scores were positively correlated with more highly developed planning behaviors. There were no sex differences revealed at all, so in subsequent analyses we will not distinguish boys from girls.

3. Plan efficiency. For each child for each plan, the key variable for efficiency analyses is "plan route efficiency," calculated as a score (Goldin & Hayes-Roth, 1980):

$$\text{Route efficiency} = 100 - \frac{(\text{Total distance}-\text{Optimal distance})}{\text{Optimal distance}} \times 100$$

We believe that this route efficiency score represents the single most straightforward index of the effectiveness of an individuial's planning efforts in this task. Because not all children formulated the same number of plans, we used a child's first and last plan efficiency scores for analyses. Number of plans was not a good index of planning skill because it is possible to make many bad plans, or just a few very good ones.

The efficiency of plans significantly increased with age and from first to last plan. We found that from first to last plan, the mean efficiency score (out of 100 possible) rose significantly from 52.7 to 69.2. A better sense of the improvement of scores may be gleaned from the two-score sequence for each age group from first to last plan. For the young group, we find improvements from 39.5 to 58.4; for the older group, from 65.9 to 88.3. A comparable analysis of the shortest plan overall reveals that the older group produced significantly shorter overall shortest plans, and had shorter overall longest plans.

B.   Qualitative analysis of plan improvements through revisions

We have shown that each age group improves in plan efficiency from first to last plan, but *how* did plan revisions lead to improvements? We would like to know what *kinds* of plan revisions were made; therefore, we need fine-grained observations that point to concrete features that vary across plans, rather than, in the case of strategy analyses, descriptions of general task approaches which may map somewhat indirectly onto concrete plan features. We will refer to this approach as a "featural analysis."

Our aim is not to examine all types of plan revisions, but those accounting for the bulk of progress made across plans. We derived such a set by observing many plans, and noting major changes in plan structure that led to improvements. For the most part, we can characterize the substantive revisions of structure children made in improving their plan as resulting from "seeing" the chores differently over time. These phenomenological shifts, whereby the task and its elements come to be understood differently from plan to plan are characteristic of human problem-solving efforts, and an aspect of problem-solving skill one might expect to be improved by learning to program. The general importance of such "reseeings" in thinking has been extensively documented by Gestalt psychologists (Wertheimer, 1961) and more recent studies of problem solving in cognitive science (e.g., Bamberger & Schon, 1982; DiSessa, 1983; Heller & Greeno, 1979).

More specifically, the initial formulation of our task as the doing of a set of named chores (e.g., clean tables, wash blackboards, push in chairs) is a frame for problem understanding that must be *broken* for the task to be effectively accomplished. Doing each named thing, in whatever order, is not an effective plan. Each chore must be decomposed into its component chore acts, and the parts must be reconstructed and sequenced into an effective whole plan. The child's understanding of part–whole relations for the task is thus transformed during plan revisions. To move toward the optimal solution of this planning problem, a child must *reconfigure* the chore "chunks" in terms of their spatial distribution on the classroom map. Major breakthroughs in plan structuring occur through discovering spatial clusters of chore acts. Progress in plan structure is thus made through restructuring the "chunks" of activities to be accomplished, from a list of named chores to a list of spatial clusters of chore acts.

What kinds of changes children made are better understood in this context. There are two major types of plan features, and we have assigned 1 point for each of 14 plan features present. There are 9 "chore act clusters," and 5 plan features that involve "movables" (such as brushes, watercan, sponge). In all cases, the plan feature eliminates redundancies in travel that arise when an area in the classroom is visited twice to do different chore acts that could be accomplished in one trip. In the following sections we illustrate the types with one example of each; details are provided in Appendix 1. For example, for one "chore act cluster," an improved plan occurred when each of the tables with chairs was visited only once, at which time the table was washed *and* the chairs at that table were pushed in, rather than separate trips being made.

In addition, for one of the cluster types involving "movables," major improvements in plan structure occurred when, in one trip to the sink, *both* instruments (sponge and watercan) that were needed in a sweep around the room were picked up. Likewise, improvement occurred when the sink was returned to, only when all three movable things (sponge, watercan, paintbrushes) were returned simultaneously, i.e., were needed for nothing else.

1. Qualitative featural analysis: first- and last-plan comparisons. Thus, children's plans were analyzed in terms of the way they organized the chore acts into efficient clusters of actions. The mean plan cluster score, with a maximum of 14 points, significantly improved for each of the age groups from first to last plan. For all children combined, the scores for first and last plans were 6.2 and 8.4. The mean score for the younger group improved from 4.8 to 6.6, and for the older children, from 7.6 to 10.2. Thus, children reorganized their plans into more efficient clusters over the course of revising their plans.

What accounted for these improvements? The plan clusters can be divided into two groups: (a) those for which mean scores were relatively high (over 0.5) in children's first plan attempts and therefore accomplished efficiently by the majority of children; and (b) those that less than half the children recognized in their first plan. Of the 14 possible plan clusters, the following five (a–e) had high mean scores for both age groups in the first as well as last plan: (a, b) getting each of two instruments only once; (c, d) doing the erasing and washing together at each blackboard; (e) doing three of the five separate chore acts at the art table (few children received the additional points for doing four or five of these five chores). There were no significant age differences in mean scores for any of these first plan features. In contrast, children received relatively low scores on the remaining nine plan clusters for their first plan.

2. *Improvement in plan feature scores beyond the first plan.* After the experience of creating their first plan in this task environment, children improved significantly in incorporating the remaining nine plan features. For the four table activity clusters, there were significant improvements from first to last plan, and significantly higher feature scores for the older children. For the three activity clusters – one involving getting the sponge and the watercan together, the other involving returning either two or three of the three objects to the sink area in sequence – there were also significant improvements from first to last plan and significantly higher feature scores for the older children. The remaining two clusters involve doing either all five of the five chore acts near the art table in sequence, or four of them. For the former, most efficient cluster, there were significant improvements by plan; on the latter, there were not. There were no age differences for either of these two feature scores. Nonetheless, it is striking that whereas for the first plan nearly none of the young *or* old children recognized the five-act cluster, by the last plan, fully half of the older group, but only one quarter of the younger group, had plans revealing this feature.

These analyses illustrate that children tended to group the chore acts more efficiently after the first plan in terms of spatial arrangements, to "break the set" evident in the first plans of completely carrying out one named chore or repeating the same chore actions successively regardless of spatial location (e.g., getting the watercan, crossing the room to water the plants, and again crossing the room to return the watercan). Overall, children revised their plans into more efficient organizations. This finding corresponds to the general model of planning specifying that the planning process oscillates between constructing plan elements, simulating the plan's execution, and revising it to incorporate improvements that are recognized.

3. Relationships among common kinds of plan features. Another indication of the nature of changes children made when revising their plans is to examine the relationship between plan clusters including similar kinds of actions. Did children's responses indicate that they recognized similarities among chore act groups, and used this knowledge in constructing more effective plans? It would be best to develop a strategy for accomplishing groups of actions efficiently, and then to generalize this strategy to other types of actions in the plan. Such relationships among plan features may be analyzed at two levels of abstraction. For the first, more concrete level, identical chore act sequences such as "clean table – push in its chairs" could be extended to a new location. Feature scores of these four table–chair consolidation clusters were highly correlated: from $r = .67$ to $.85$ for the first plan, and from $r = .75$ to $.88$ for the last plan. For the two blackboard cluster sequences involving consolidating erasing and washing, r values ranged from $.73$ to $.93$ for all plans. Thus, within a plan, children tended to use the same strategy for identical chore act sequences.

For the second type of relationship among plan features, clusters may be grouped according to a more abstract, general principle. Efficient accomplishment of chore groups requires consolidation of actions within a contiguous spatial area. Children have to break their natural tendency or "set," that is, to do all chores of the same kind (such as table washing) at the same time, and instead organize their plan in terms of dissimilar acts that are close to one another spatially. This *general* "principle" of spatial clustering, which crosscuts the two most advanced clusters of the plan feature analysis – the five-chore act group by the art table, and the sequential return of all three sink objects – was not initially apparent for many children, for there was not a significant correlation among scores for these two types of cluster for the first plan. This would have required a more general understanding of efficiency in terms of spatial location. However, for the last plan, children's performance on these major consolidations was significantly related.

Analogously, two other related clusters involved consolidating instrument use, that is, simultaneously picking up all instruments from the origin that would be needed in the chore circuit, and returning them together without separate trips. Children's scores for these two plan features were not significantly related for the first plan, but were for the final plan. At this higher level, children thus evolved "higher-order" strategies of spatial arrangement and instrument consolidation through their revisionary efforts. Children's recognitions of clusters were at first "local" insights, rather than principled groupings of powerful generality, which they came to recognize through revising their plans.

4. Relations between plan feature scores and plan efficiency. An analysis of the relationship between mean cluster scores and the plan efficiency scores discussed earlier determined that the scores were highly and significantly correlated for first plan ($r = .72$) and for last plan ($r = .66$). The qualitative analysis of the plan clusters was thus related to the quantitative analysis of overall plan distance: More efficient organization of chore acts into clusters was highly related to shorter plan distance.

C. Process analyses

Each child's think-aloud protocol was divided into segments of talk assumed to represent individual planning decisions. Each segment was then categorized according to its type and its level of abstraction as specified in the coding system below. The mean number of segments for all plans produced was 44.2, not significantly different for the two age groups (8- to 9-year olds; 11- to 12-year olds), nor for first and last plan.

In discussing the process by which children generated their plans, our central concerns have to do with whether efficient plans are created differently from inefficient plans. The planning studies of Hayes-Roth and colleagues have developed a detailed system for coding the types of planning decisions, and for characterizing the levels of abstractness of planning decisions made by adults as they think aloud while constructing plans to carry out a set of errands in an imaginary small town. Our categories are a subset of those used by Goldin and Hayes-Roth (1980) and Hayes-Roth and Hayes-Roth (1979) in categorizing planning decisions made by adults in this task, supplemented by categories that emerged for this classroom environment. In the final phase of our analyses, we examined the process of plan construction by categorizing each segment of the children's think-aloud protocols in terms of the *type* of planning decision being made and its *level* of abstraction. The aspects of the system germane to our current analytic purposes will now be briefly reviewed.

The "type" categories of analysis specify different conceptual categories of decisions made during the planning process. The first three categories of decisions choose *plan features;* the other two are more "strategic" in nature, determining features of the *planning process.*

1. *Plan.* Represents specific actions the planner intends to take in the world (e.g., "go to wash the art table this way" while tracing out a path)
2. *Plan abstraction.* Involves selecting the desired attributes of potential plan decisions, noting the *kinds* of actions that might be useful without specifying the actual actions (e.g., "Go to closest chore next" or "Organize plan around bunches of chores")

3. *World knowledge.* Involves assessing data (e.g., of chore or instrument locations, distance, or time) concerning relationships in the task environment that might affect the planning process (e.g., "The hamster is next to the door," or "The chores are all in a circle")
4. *Executive.* Involves determining the allotment of cognitive resources during planning, such as what kinds of decisions to make first, or what part of the plan to develop next (e.g., "I'll decide what order to do the chores before figuring out how to walk")
5. *Metaplan.* Reflects the planner's approach to the planning problem, that is, the methods they intend to apply to it, or establishes criteria to be used for making up and evaluating prospective plans.

Planning decisions analyzed according to these five categories, or types of decision making can be further analyzed in terms of the level of abstraction employed within each category. For the "abstractness level" categories of analysis, the general idea is that decisions at each more specific, or concrete level specify a more detailed plan than those at the higher level of abstraction. Levels for all the types except the "metaplan" type are hierarchically organized (see Appendix 2 for details). Goldin and Hayes-Roth (1980) found that good planners in a similar task moved flexibly among both types and levels of abstraction while constructing a plan. Here we present the levels of analysis for the "plan" type described above, moving from abstract to concrete down the list:

Level		Definition
1A:	Outcome	Determine which chores will be accomplished when the plan is executed (e.g., "I'll definitely do the hamster and the plants, because they'll die")
1B:	Design	Determine specific spatiotemporal approach to planned activities (e.g., "I'll do the chores by going in a circle")
1C:	Procedures	Determine specific sequences of gross actions (e.g., "I would do the hamster, and then get the sponge," without noting path)
1D:	Operations	Determine specific sequences of minute actions (e.g., noting the details of the path for a sequence of gross actions in the plan)

The process analysis addresses the question of whether the organization of the planning process in terms of the types and levels of planning decisions made by the children is different for efficient versus inefficient plans.

First we present some general statistics about the process data. We then survey findings on (a) frequencies of different types and levels of planning decisions, (b) decision choice flexibility, (c) relationships between the amount of "executive" and "metaplanning" activity during the planning process and decision choice flexibility, and (d) whether scores on cognitive style and processing capacity measures distinguish different planning process profiles.

1. Frequencies of planning decisions in terms of types.   Five types of planning decisions were distinguished. The first three types: Plan, Plan Abstraction, and World Knowledge, which we will refer to globally as "low-level" types, have to do with the specific details of planning. The latter two, Executive and Metaplan, which we will designate as "high level" types, pertain to higher level executive or metacognitive aspects of planning decision-making.

Most of the planning decisions children made were on the Plan type (95.7%). The overall frequencies of decisions on other types were Plan Abstraction (0.6%), World Knowledge (1.6%), Executive (1.7%), and Metaplan (0.4%). High-level-type planning decisions overall thus constituted only about two percent of all the planning decisions the children expressed. Nonetheless, we find some interesting differences in when and by whom such higher level decisions were made.

As for differences in the types of planning decisions made for first versus last plans by the 32 children, we find that children made significantly more high-level decisions in their first plans than in their last plans (3.5 versus 1.0), and 11- to 12-year olds produced more high-level decisions (3.0) than did 8- to 9-year olds (1.4).

2. Decision choice flexibility.   How flexible was a child's decision making during the planning process? We may address this question from two perspectives (Goldin & Hayes-Roth, 1980). The first looks at the number of transitions a child made between different types of plan decision making while creating a plan, a second involves the number of transitions a child made between levels of plan decision-making irrespective of the type of that decision making. We may note that the mean number of *type* transitions per plan is highly correlated with the mean number of *level* transitions per plan.

The mean number of type transitions for the group of 32 children was 2.8. Although more type transitions were made in the first (3.8) than in the last plan (2.4), this difference was not significant. Age differences in type transitions were striking. Older children made significantly more (4.0) type transitions per plan than did younger (1.5) children.

The mean number of "level" transitions for the group of 32 children was 2.7. As in the case of type transitions, although children made more level transitions in their first than in their last plan (3.1 versus 2.3), this difference was not significant. Older children made significantly more (4.1) level transitions per plan than did younger (1.2) children.

3. High level planning decisions and decision flexibility. Do children who engage in more high-level decision making during planning (i.e., types 4 and 5) also display more *flexible* decision-making by shifting opportunistically between different decision types and levels? We addressed this question by looking at the correlations between frequencies of high-level decision making and both the number of transitions between *types* and *levels* of decision making, and found that high-level decision making during planning was significantly correlated with both the number of type and level transitions overall.

4. High-level planning processes, WISC, and Digit Span. It is of some interest to see whether cognitive style (as indicated by WISC score) and processing capacity (as indicated by Digit Span) are related to the features of high-level planning processes previously defined. We find that Digit Span and WISC scores were not significantly correlated with the frequency of high level (types 4 and 5) planning decisions. And although the mean number of type transitions was significantly correlated with Digit Span, there were nonsignificant correlations of .3 to .4 between Digit Span and mean number of level transitions. WISC score did not significantly correlate with either mean number of type or level transitions per plan.

D. Relating plan as product and as process

How related are the decision-making *processes* that go into the formulation of a plan, to the effectiveness of the plan as a product? We found that, at least for this task, the process and product measures are weakly related. Neither the plan efficiency mean score for all plans produced nor the distance of the shortest plan a child created correlated significantly with *any* of the high-level plan process measures, that is, mean number of type transitions per plan, mean number of level transitions per plan, or frequency of high-level (types 4 and 5) planning decisions.

We also tested for a relationship between the frequency of metaplanning decisions and the mean cluster scores from the feature analysis. Few significant relationships were apparent, indicating that children revise their plans to accomplish the acts more efficiently without necessarily using (verbally explicit) metaplanning resources. Only for the last plan of the younger children are these variables significantly correlated ($r = .65$).

IV. Conclusions

In our study, the development of planning skills was examined in two different ways: by comparing the planning skills displayed by children of two different age groups, and by tracing the development of a plan over the course of its repeated revisions within a planning session. The general model of planning adopted in this work considers planning to be essentially revisionary. Good planners, whether they are adults or children, appear to engage in cycles of plan revision in order to consider different and increasingly efficient plan organizations. They reveal different types and levels of decision making in formulating their plans (Goldin & Hayes-Roth, 1980).

The chore-scheduling task we used was designed to engage children in planning a novel sequence of events within a familiar environment. The task provided an external planning aid, characteristic of many functional planning situations. This classroom map aid also enabled us to observe closely the sequence of children's actions and decisions as they created plans.

In focusing on qualitative aspects of planning processes, we were driven to change traditional experimental methods and modes of interpretation. As noted above, we used a microgenetic method (Flavell & Draguns, 1957) in order to make public and protracted the cycles of revisionary work that characterize highly developed planning. We examined children's abilities to formulate alternative plan organizations by providing them with opportunities for improving the effectiveness of their plans. And unlike the Hayes-Roths' work on planning, we explicitly conveyed to our participants the goal of the task: Children were specifically asked to construct the shortest-distance plan so that the effectiveness of their planning would be assessed relative to that goal. In contrast, developmental comparisons have often ignored the goal-relative nature of the developmental level of a performance in terms of what the person thinks he or she is doing.

Furthermore, in terms of the four components of the planning process described in the introduction, our analyses focused on how children displayed the second component of the planning process, the *construction* of a plan, in a situation in which the goal state, initial state, and operators for transforming the problem space were well defined.

Our findings demonstrate that both older (11- to 12-year old) and younger (8- to 9-year old) children engage in complex revisionary processes over the course of the planning session. Although older children produced significantly better plans than younger children according to a variety of measures, the performance of both groups improved significantly from first to last plans within a session. This improvement can be characterized in several ways. First, plans improved in terms of route efficiency over plan attempts. Children revised their plans to produce shorter, more efficient means of accomplishing the set of chores. Second, children became increasingly sensitive to the constraints of this particular planning situation, and adapted their plans accordingly. In the case of the chore-scheduling task, many children shifted their approach from one in which they performed all chore acts of the same type together (e.g., wash all tables, regardless of where they were located), to one in which they discovered the importance of spatial location and consolidation of actions (e.g., performing all chores in the same area together, regardless of chore category). This major change required a significant reconfiguring of the situation, so that children could incorporate this "reseeing" into the plan construction process.

In terms of cognitive variables related to the character of children's planning, we found only weak relationships between WISC Block Design task performance and effective planning. Because our rational analysis of the cognitive demands of this task leads to a prediction of a strong relationship between these variables, this finding may appear surprising. Nonetheless, we are hesitant to dismiss the field independence/dependence dimension as germane to studies of planning skill because virtually all of the participants in the study scored high on the WISC subtask. Case (1974) classified children who scored one deviation above the mean on national norms as field independent, and those who scored one deviation below the mean on national norms as field dependent. By this criterion, only one of our 32 children is classified as field dependent. In future work, we would recommend that WISC Block Design task scores serve as a grouping variable, with clearly defined field-dependent and field-independent groups for a stronger test of our hypothesis.

We also found only weak relationships between Digit Span and effective planning. Apparently, span size does not figure prominently in distinguishing more effective from less effective planners. One likely reason for this is that children can use visual as well as kinesthetic feedback in remembering their planned route, and do not need to rely entirely upon mental representations of their plan. With versions of the task in which either the visual or kinesthetic feedback could be blocked, we might find Digit Span to play a more significant role in planning performances.

Finally, with respect to the decision-making process, we found that there were differences in types and levels of planning decisions for individual children within planning sessions, and between the two age groups. Both older (11- and 12-year olds) and younger children (8- and 9-year olds) made more high-level and metaplanning decisions in their first plan as compared with their last plan. The older children made more high-level and metaplanning decisions than did younger children. Older children also demonstrated more flexibility in their plan construction process, because they more frequently made type and level transitions than did younger planners. And just as Goldin & Hayes-Roth (1980) found for adults, high-level decision making was associated with planning flexibility.

However, the overall infrequency with which children of any age engaged in executive (1.7%) or metaplanning decisions (0.4%) is noteworthy. Most of their planning decisions concerned concrete-plan-type acts. Further, in their performances of this task, the frequency of such higher-level planning decisions was unrelated to plan efficiency (product) scores. There are several possible reasons for this finding. The first is that children of these ages may, in general, infrequently engage in this form of higher-level decision making in planning situations, preferring to make decisions in terms of specific, concrete actions. A second, alternative reason is that the content of the chore-scheduling task may have influenced the relative frequency of decision types. As noted earlier, in order to focus on developmental processes of plan construction, the chore-scheduling task offered a well-formed planning problem to the children, built around familiar subtasks. The task may be too familiar for the children, and not viewed as challenging enough to require planning, even with the time constraints set out in the task instructions. Perhaps we would find more reflective processing if the planning task exemplified many of the vagaries of everyday planning (Pea, 1982), such as conflicting goals (Wilensky, 1981), absence of prestatable goal criteria (Scriven, 1980), an open rather than closed set of operators for the problem space (Dorner, 1983), and known operators whose consequences of application are unknown (Schutz, 1973).

Although there may be some validity to this second account, independent evidence on planning during the writing process with children in this age range supports the "concreteness" interpretation. Scardamalia & Bereiter (1985) have reviewed findings from various studies that show how composition planning in children starts out like rehearsal (working through a task at about the same concreteness as will be used) and later in development becomes carried out at levels more remote from text production itself. Burtis, Bereiter, Scardamalia, and Tetroe (1983) noted how think-aloud protocols from 11- to 13-year olds start to reveal evidence of a more abstract level of planning than the "rehearsal" of younger children's text production. Our older group of 11- and 12-year olds also began to show higher-level decision making during planning, such as giving verbal accounts of their major reorganizations of action sequences in plans subsequent to their first plan.

It may be that to develop planning skills, children will require instructional support and practice in activities that focus on each component of the planning process. Certainly our planning process results indicate how rarely children engaged in revisions in which they "stepped back" and redefined the planning situation after beginning to construct a plan. The finding that high-level decision making decreased from first to last plan among the children further suggests that children's planning efforts consisted of refining an initial conception, rather than considering top-level reorganization of the plan.

We expect that these results may be useful to educators who wish to promote planning, and to developmental psychologists and cognitive scientists investigating planning processes. Our findings reveal significant capabilities among even 8-year-old children to plan and improve their plans through revisions in a familiar task environment with a clearly defined goal. This finding stands in contrast to young children's revisions in writing tasks, which rarely improve the quality of the written text, a contrast likely due to the difficulty of defining goals in writing. Because even the young children generally improve their chore-scheduling task performance across plans, it appears that it is not that they lack the capability of making progressive revisions in writing, but that the goals are not as apparent in the writing environment as they are in our chore-scheduling task.

Notes

1. Although WAIS subscales are standardized for an auditory–verbal sequence of input–response rather than our visual–verbal, this is not problematic, for two reasons: First, we are not referencing standardized norms from WAIS procedures, but are using the span task as is commonly done in psychological studies as a way of ensuring the comparability of experimental and control groups, and because different span tasks are often used as measures of mental processing capacity, which as Case, Kurland, and Goldberg (1982; also see Hunt, 1978) indicate, relate in theoretically interesting ways to a number of different high-level cognitive tasks. Second, it is well known that memory span values are highly correlated for different modalities of stimulus presentation and recall.
2. Washing the paintbrushes was a chore act forgotten by almost everyone, and many children forgot to erase the blackboards before washing them. Extensive forgetting of chore acts was rare, and there were neither age differences nor group (programming versus non-programming) differences in number of omitted chores. Number of omitted chores was also unrelated to the efficiency of plans.

References

Bamberger, J., & Schon, D. (1982). *Learning as reflective conversation with materials: Notes from work in progress.* (Working Paper No. 17). Massachusetts Institute of Technology, Division for Study and Research in Education, December.

Bereiter, C. (1980). Development in writing. In L. W. Gregg & E. R. Steinberg (Eds.), *Cognitive processes in writing.* Hillsdale, NJ: Erlbaum.

Brener, R. (1940). An experimental investigation of memory span. *Journal of Experimental Psychology, 26,* 467–482.

Burtis, P. J., Bereiter, C., Scardamalia, M., & Tetroe, J. (1983). The development of planning in writing. In C. G. Wells & B. Kroll (Eds.), *Exploration of children's development in writing.* Chicester: John Wiley & Sons.

Case, R. (1974). Structures and strictures: Some functional limitations on the course of cognitive growth. *Cognitive Psychology, 6,* 544–573.

Case, R., & Globerson, T. (1974). Field independence and central computing space. *Child Development, 45,* 772–778.

Case, R., Kurland, D. M., & Goldberg, J. (1982). Operational efficiency and the growth of short-term memory span. *Journal of Experimental Child Psychology, 33,* 386–404.

DiSessa, A. (1983). Phenomenology and the evolution of intuition. In D. Gentner & A. L. Stevens (Eds.), *Mental models.* Hillsdale, NJ: Erlbaum.

Dorner, D. (1983). Heuristics and cognition in complex systems. In R. Groner, M. Groner, & W. F. Bischof (Eds.), *Methods of heuristics.* Hillsdale, NJ: Erlbaum.

Flavell, J., & Draguns, J. (1957). A microgenetic approach to perception and thought. *Psychological Bulletin, 54,* 197–217.

Flower, L., & Hayes, J. R. (1981). A cognitive process theory of writing. *College Composition and Communication, 32,* 365–387.

Goldin, S. E., & Hayes-Roth, B. (1980). *Individual differences in planning processes.* Rand Corporation Note N-1488-ONR, June.

Hayes-Roth, B. (1980). *Estimation of time requirements during planning: The interactions between motivation and cognition.* Rand Corporation Note N-1581-ONR, November.

Hayes-Roth, B., & Hayes-Roth, F. (1979). A cognitive model of planning. *Cognitive Science, 3,* 275–310.

Heller, J., & Greeno, J. G. (1979). Information processing analyses of mathematical problem solving. In Tyler, R. W., & White, S. H. (Eds.), *Testing, teaching and learning.* Washington, DC: National Institute of Education.

Hunt, E. (1978). Mechanics of verbal ability. *Psychology Review, 85,* 109–130.

Lyons, D. R. (1977). Individual differences in immediate serial recall: A matter of mnemonics? *Cognitive Psychology, 9,* 403–411.

Pea, R. D. (1982). What is planning development the development of? In D. Forbes & M. Greenberg (Eds.), *New directions in child development: The development of planful behavior in children.* San Francisco: Jossey-Bass.

Pea, R. D., & Kurland, D. M. (1984). *Logo programming and the development of planning skills.* Technical Report No. 16, Bank Street College, Center for Children and Technology.

Rogoff, B., & Gardner, W. P. (1984). Developing cognitive skills in social interaction. In B. Rogoff & J. Lave (Eds.), *Everyday cognition: Its development in social context.* Cambridge, MA: Harvard University Press.

Scardamalia, M., & Bereiter, C. (1985). Written composition. In M. C. Wittrock (Ed.), *Handbook of research on teaching.*

Schutz, A. (1973). Choosing among projects of action. In *Collected papers: Vol. 1. The problem of social reality*. The Hague, Netherlands: Martinus Nighoff.

Scriven, M. (1980). Perspective and descriptive approaches to problem solving. In D. T. Tuma & F. Reif (Eds.), *Problem solving and education: Issues in teaching and research*. Hillsdale, NJ: Erlbaum.

Stefik, M. (1981a). Planning and constraints (MOLGEN: Part 1). *Artificial Intelligence, 16,* 111–140.

Stefik, M. (1981b). Planning and metaplanning (MOLGEN: Part 2). *Artificial Intelligence, 16,* 141–170.

Wechsler, D. (1974). *Manual for the Wechsler Intelligence Scale for Children*. New York: The Psychology Corporation.

Werner, H. (1956). Microgenesis and aphasia. *Journal of Abnormal and Social Psychology, 52,* 347–353.

Wertheimer, M. (1961). *Productive thinking* (enlarged ed.). London: Tavistock.

Wilensky, R. (1981). Meta-planning: Representing and using knowledge about planning in problem solving and natural language understanding. *Cognitive Science, 5,* 197–233.

Witkin, H. A., Lewis, H. B. Hertzman, M., Machover, K., Meissner, P. B., & Wapner, S. (1954). *Personality through perception*. New York: Harper.

Witkin, H. A., Dyk, R. B., Faterson, H. F., Goodenough, D. R., & Kark, S. A. (1962). *Psychological differentiation*. New York: Wiley.

Appendix 1: scoring system for featural analysis

The 14 plan features were 9 different "chore act clusters," and 5 features involving "movables" (such as brushes, watercan, sponge). For the chore act clusters, improvements in plan structure occurred when:

1. *Clusters 1 to 4.* Each of the four tables with chairs was only visited once, at which time the table was washed *and* the chairs at that table were pushed in.
2. *Clusters 5 to 7.* During the only visit to the art table, five component acts were dealt with in a cluster: The table was washed, the trashpaper and paintbrushes were picked up, and the two nearby plants were watered (Cluster 7). Cluster 6 included any four of these acts; Cluster 5, any three of them.
3. *Clusters 8 to 9.* Each of the two blackboards was visited only once, at which time it was erased and washed (Cluster 8 for one blackboard, Cluster 9 for the other).

For features of plans involving "movables," improvements in plan structure occurred when:

4. *Cluster 10.* Going to the sink, both instruments (sponge, watercan) that would be needed during a sweep around the room were picked up.
5. *Clusters 11 and 12.* The sink was returned to, only when all three movable things that must be returned there (sponge, watercan, paintbrushes) were needed for no other component chore acts (Cluster 12). Cluster 11 was returning any two of these three movables at once.

6. *Clusters 13 and 14.* Instruments at the sink (sponge, watercan) were
    picked up only once, rather than each time they were needed (e.g., getting
    the sponge once to sponge the blackboard, returning it, getting it another
    time to wash the tables). Although not literally a cluster of acts, we des-
    ignate getting the sponge only once as Cluster 13, and getting the water-
    can only once as Cluster 14.

Appendix 2: coding categories and definitions for process analyses

A. Decision-type categories

The coding categories have been slightly modified from Hayes-Roth &
Hayes-Roth (1979) and Goldin & Hayes-Roth (1980), but are comparable
on most points. The type categories of analysis specify different conceptual categories of decisions made during the planning process. The first
three categories of decisions choose *plan features;* the other two are more
"strategic" in nature, determining features of the *planning process.*

1. *Plan.* Represents specific actions the planner intends to take in the world
    (e.g., "Go to wash the art table this way" while tracing out a path)
2. *Plan abstraction.* Involves selecting desired attributes of potential plan
    decisions, noting *kinds* of actions that might be useful without specifying
    the actual actions (e.g., "Go to closest chore next" or "Organize the plan
    around spatial clusters of chores")
3. *World knowledge.* Involves assessing data (e.g., of chore or instrument
    locations, distance, or time) concerning relationships in the task envi-
    ronment that might affect the planning process (e.g., "The hamster is
    next to the door" or "The chores are all in a circle")
4. *Executive.* Involves determining the allotment of cognitive resources
    during planning, such as what kinds of decisions to make first, or what
    part of the plan to develop next (e.g., "I'll decide what order to do the
    chores before figuring out a path")
5. *Metaplan.* Reflects planner's approach to the planning problem, key
    methods they intend to apply to it, or establishes criteria to be used for
    making up and evaluating prospective plans

B. Abstractness-level (within-type) categories

For the abstractness-level categories of analysis, decisions at each more
specific, or concrete level specify a more detailed plan than those at the
higher level of abstraction. Levels for all the types *except* the "metaplan"
type are hierarchically organized. Level stratification moves in the definition charts from abstract to concrete down the list:

1. Plan type

Level		Definition
1A:	Outcome	Determines which chores will be accomplished when plan is executed (e.g., "I'll definitely do the hamster and the plants")
1B:	Design	Determines specific spatiotemporal approach to planned activities (e.g., "I'll do the chores by going in a circle")
1C:	Procedures	Determine specific sequences of gross actions (e.g., "I would do the hamster, and then get the sponge" *without noting path*)
1D:	Operations	Determine specific sequences of minute actions (e.g., noting the details of the path for a sequence of gross actions in the plan)

2. Plan-abstraction type

Level		Definition
2A:	Outcome (intentions)	Determines which *kinds* of chores are desirable to accomplish when plan is executed (e.g., "Do all the important chores")
2B:	Design (scheme)	Determines *kinds* of desirable spatiotemporal organizations of planned activities to achieve outcomes (e.g., "I'll organize a plan around clusters of chores")
2C:	Procedures (strategy)	Determine characteristics of desirable *kinds* of sequencing of gross level individual chore acts (e.g., "I'll do the closest chore next")
2D:	Operations (tactic)	Determine characteristics of desirable kinds of sequencing of the specifics of individual chore acts (e.g., "I'll take the shortest route to the next chore")

3. World-knowledge type

World-knowledge-type decisions suggest decisions at the corresponding plan abstraction level, or instantiate decisions at the corresponding plan level.

Level		Definition
3A:	Outcome (chores)	Notes facts or values regarding specific chores to be accomplished (e.g., "Feeding the hamster is the most important chore," or "Washing blackboards takes a long time")

Level		Definition
3B:	Design (layout)	Notes facts of spatiotemporal organization of a group of planned activities (e.g., "There are a lot of things to do by the sink")
3C:	Procedures (neighbors or instruments)	Note facts regarding the world of the chores relevant to ordering individual chore acts (e.g., "The closest chore to where I am now is watering Plant 1"; "Oh, I have to go get the sponge first")
3D:	Operations (routes or chore act details)	Note facts that relate to the specifics of performing specific chore acts or traveling from one chore act to another (e.g., "Through the benches is the shortest way to get to the blackboard," or "I can hold the watercan in my hand while I'm doing that chore")

4. Executive type

Level		Definition
4A:	Priority	Establishes principles for allocating cognitive resources during the entire planning process (e.g., "I'll decide what to do before deciding when to do things")
4B:	Focus	Indicates what kind of decisions to make at a particular point in the planning process (e.g., "Now I'll figure out the shortest way to get over to the trashcan")
4C:	Scheduling	Resolves any remaining conflicts between competing decisions that have been made, choosing one to execute next in the plan of action

5. Metaplan type

Level		Definition
5A:	Problem definition	Defines the planner's representation of the task and its goals, resources, and constraints
5B:	Problem solving model	Defines the general strategy the planner takes in making up a solution to the planning problem
5C:	Policies	Note a set of global constraints and desirable features for the developing plan
5D:	Evaluation criteria	Define a set of dimensions against which tentative plans may be evaluated

8 The development of children's skills in adjusting plans to circumstances

Barbara Rogoff, Mary Gauvain, and William Gardner

In this chapter we are concerned with children's developing skill in incorporating contextual information in planning. We propose that mature planners are sensitive to the resources and constraints available in a setting that may facilitate or hinder action, and that an important task of development is to increase skill in fitting the action being planned, to the context in which the action will occur. We regard planning as deliberate organization of actions oriented toward reaching a goal. However, plans need not be detailed "mental recipes" for action. The elaborateness and detail of a plan will be adjusted to the circumstances in which planning occurs, the context for carrying out the planned action, the action being planned, and the skill of the planner. We propose that the development of planning skills involves an increase in sensitivity to the contextual features of planning.

The focus of the chapter is the role of the physical and social context in children's planning. First, we discuss approaches to the development of planning skills, contrasting a view of planning that involves tailoring goal-oriented actions to particular problem circumstances with views that propose a general planning ability applicable to problem situations of any sort. We take the approach that the development of planning skills involves originating and tailoring plans in particular problem domains and circumstances. We distinguish planning that is organized during action, from plans devised prior to action ("advance" planning), and suggest that these planning strategies have varying utility according to the task circumstances. We discuss children's adjustment to the circumstances of planning, especially their development of skill in appropriately planning in advance and planning in action, as well as their skills in coor-

We are grateful for the comments of Jamie Germond and Barbara Radziszewska, and of the editors of this volume, as well as the financial support of Grant No. 5R01HD16973-02 from the National Institute of Child Health and Human Development.

303

dinating means with goals. Finally, we suggest that experience in planning collaboratively or under the guidance of others may help children to learn to adapt their planning to the context and to coordinate their actions while keeping the goal in mind.

I. The role of context in planning

Planning is deliberate organization of a sequence of actions oriented toward achieving a specific goal. A planful sequence of actions is observed when:

an individual operates persistently toward achieving an end state, chooses among alternative means and/or routes to achieve that end state, persists in deploying means and corrects the deployment of means to get closer to the end state, and finally ceases the line of activity when specifiable features of the state are achieved. The elements of the cycle, then, comprise aim, option of means, persistence and correction, and a terminal stop order. (Bruner, 1981, p. 41)

This series of actions, as Bruner acknowledges, bears some resemblance to the test–operate–test–exit (TOTE) cycle of planning proposed by Miller, Galanter, and Pribram (1960). Such structuring of action does not necessarily involve conscious intentional focus, but does entail deliberate control of activity.

Determining that a sequence of actions is planful requires consideration simultaneously of the individual's skills and the context in which the sequence of actions is performed. Planfulness cannot be defined simply in terms of achieving a solution to a problem, because a planful solution requires deliberate search for a solution, not just trial-and-error or habitual solutions. For example, Piaget (1969) discusses planfulness in infants as being evidenced by an infant's going around a barrier to retrieve an object. In instrumental action, the infant has distinguished between the end (obtaining the object) and the means (going around the barrier). However, this behavior is likely to be habitual or automatic when performed by an adult. Or, similarly, a 2-year old, trying to manage a dustpan and broom, must plan the coordination of tools. It is not accomplished by trial and error nor is it routine. But for an adult, the task can be achieved in a less deliberate fashion.

It is an important feature of development that skills requiring deliberate attention later become automatized to build larger units, or "chunks." Once an action has become habitual or automatized, it is hardly planful (see Bruner, 1974; Bullinger & Chatillon, 1983; Miller, Galanter, & Pribram, 1960; Reason, 1977; and Sternberg, 1984, for discussions of chunking and automatization). As another example, the process of reading a book may or may not be planful. If a child has acquired expertise in reading, processing of the text proceeds automatically to a high degree. But if the child is reading the book to study for an examination, he or she may be planful in searching through the index and table of contents, and pausing to formulate an answer to a potential test question (Brown & Campione, 1984, discuss planning in studying text).

Thus, the relation of the person's skills to the task characteristics distinguishes planned actions from random ones, on the one hand, or habitual ones, on the other. Planning involves both the context of the task and problem constraints, and the skills and knowledge that the person brings to the situation. We expect the planning of older children to be distinguished from that of younger children in the effectiveness of their adjustment to circumstances, their skill in integrating existing knowledge (as well as the extent of relevant knowledge available), facility in coordinating subgoals to reach goals, and alertness to the utility of planning in the first place.

Our emphasis on the development of context-sensitive planning skills contrasts with approaches assuming that planning is a general ability which children become able to apply with equal facility in any problem domain. For example, in Piaget's stage theory, children's ability to plan undergoes several transformations corresponding to the stages of cognitive development. Children are assumed to plan in the stage-characteristic fashion, regardless of what problem they are trying to solve. In the sensorimotor period, means-to-ends behavior involves disregarding a goal object in the present in order to carry out indirect means to attain it in the future, as when an infant makes a detour to recover a ball which has rolled under a sofa (Fraisse, 1963; Piaget, 1969). In the transition to concrete operational thinking, the child at age 6–7 years begins to anticipate solutions to problems such as classifying objects, rather than using trial-and-error methods (Inhelder & Piaget, 1964; Szeminska, 1965). In the formal operational period, the adolescent becomes able to plan actions systematically based on hypothetical situations (e.g., experimenting on how a chemical solution is made by varying the alternatives according to a systematic plan) rather than planning haphazardly and only with concrete materials. The youth becomes capable of reflective abstraction, to be able to plan planning (Piaget, 1970).

In the literature on memory development, children's planning has also been cast as a general ability, appearing as part of a cognitive executive that assesses a memory problem, determines that the search for a mnemonic mediator is in order, and manages the use of memory strategies and memory knowledge (Brown, 1977; Flavell, 1970; Flavell & Wellman,

1977). In addition, work on children's cognitive style portrays children as reflective (or planful) versus impulsive (Kagan & Kogan, 1970).

Until recently, the cognitive developmental tradition focused on processes assumed to occur solely within the person, and either neglected the importance of context or regarded it as a nuisance. However, observations that children's skills that are assumed to be general or context-free vary across tasks and settings have sparked concern with the role of context in cognitive development (Cole, Hood, & McDermott, 1978; DeLoache & Brown, 1979; Feldman, 1980; Fischer, 1980; Rogoff, 1982; Siegler, 1981). Calling attention to the role of context in the development of children's skills in making plans to remember, Rogoff, Newcombe, and Kagan (1974) emphasized that competences are displayed in specific problem contexts and suggested that statements regarding planning should attend to the task context. "It is likely that most specific competences appear initially in specific contexts and, with development, gradually come to be applied to an increasing number of contexts" (Rogoff et al., 1974, p. 976). Though Rogoff et al.'s findings showed that 8-year-olds but not 4-year-olds were planful in adjusting duration of study to the length of time they would have to remember the information, planfulness has been observed to develop in younger or older children in different tasks (e.g., Brown & DeLoache, 1978; Kagan, 1971; Siegler & Liebert, 1975). But in addition to learning to apply planning skills across a greater number of contexts, we argue here that with development children become more able to discriminate which contexts are appropriate for which planning strategies.

Brown's (1977) characterization of a self-aware mental executive capable of intelligent direction of strategic memory activity can be extended to incorporate skills for using the context: A person needs to learn how to attend to relevant information in the environment, and to know when and how to make use of the problem solving capabilities of others. A person needs to recognize the constellation of internal and external circumstances that constitute an occasion for planning, and to anticipate familiar sequences of environmental cues that provide guidance during problem solving. A person must define the context of the problem so that it attunes him or her to relevant sources of environmental feedback concerning the failure or success of relevant actions.

An adequate conceptual model of planning needs to recognize that planning is not encapsulated within the head of the planner. Even when planning occurs out of the context of action, it often relies upon simulations of aspects of the activity, with maps, lists, or simulations of sequences of events using written, spoken, or drawn symbols as in blueprints, thumbnail sketches, or battle plans. And in planning during action, a planner uses the resources and constraints of the environment in the process of generating and carrying out the plan, again using external aids such as lists, reminders, and the assistance of others. Using the constraints and resources of a particular situation, the planner makes flexible and deliberate use of environmental cues and feedback to "bootstrap" the plan, developing a more successful plan through successive revisions based on information derived from action.

Attention to contextual aspects of planning will further our understanding of the development of planning skills. After elaborating our point that skilled planning involves adjustment to circumstances, we argue that one task of development is for children to learn to incorporate considerations of the circumstances in planning and to learn to fit the means to the goal. Finally we suggest that an important influence on the development of planning skills may be social interaction: Children consider the relation between their plans and those of others in coordinating plans with peers, and they receive guidance by participating in more skilled planning with adults.

II.   Adjustment of planning to circumstances

Although plans may be developed prior to acting in some circumstances, plans may also be developed in the context of action, unrolling in a series of refinements of both goals and means as planners attempt to fit their intents to the circumstances. The planner may begin with an idea of how to work toward the goal and then may refine the plan and the goal opportunistically in accord with constraints and opportunities in the physical and social environment. Such planning involves both thinking and acting, in that planning occurs in the course of carrying out the plan. Perhaps the actor realizes that in such circumstances, the best way to advance one's notion of what to do may simply be to start doing it.

In the service of accomplishing practical goals in particular contexts, planning may proceed in a deliberate but tacit fashion. The planner begins by formulating a first attack on the problem and potentially some secondary options on what to do once that is completed, given feedback on its success. Miller, Galanter, and Pribram (1960) noted that the search for problem solutions is seldom systematic and exhaustive. Rather, it is more efficient to use a heuristic process, generating best guesses. In our view, people work toward goals in a purposeful, flexible way, taking advantage of information from the context to elaborate the means to the goal. In this way, planning utilizes tacit knowledge involving information that is available in the relevant setting (Bransford & McCarrell, 1974; Kuipers, 1979).

In planning during action, some or all of the sequence of action is determined in the course of performing it. A child studying for an examination may begin the sequence of actions with only an understanding of the problem and the relevant materials. It would not, in all likelihood, be efficient for that child to attempt to determine *in advance* how he or she would seek the answers to any particular question: Some answers are directly available in the text; others require a special search. The determination of how a specific question will be answered is a matter of planning during action.

Similarly, in planning a route through familiar terrain, we may not develop a mental map resembling a bird's-eye view of the projected route. We can use event sequences representing relevant parts of a space as we meet the need in navigating the space or imagining our progress to decide on the best route or to give directions. Rather than thinking out the whole route as we begin, we may think of the goal and establish an appropriate intermediate plan, relying on remembering or figuring out the rest of the route as we go (Gauvain & Rogoff, 1983; Klein, 1983).

Karmiloff-Smith and Inhelder (1975) noted the appearance of planning junctures as children tested theories-in-action for balancing blocks: When the child concentrated primarily on actually balancing the blocks, there were few pauses in the action sequence. As the child's attention shifted to understanding how the blocks balance, however, pauses became more frequent. "Only when goal and means are considered simultaneously do pauses *precede* action" (p. 208).

Thus planning may not involve the execution of a well-articulated advance plan, specifying the goal and hierarchical relations between subgoals, prior to initiating action. Specifying the plan in advance is worth doing only when it is desirable to verify that all the components of a plan are in place before acting. We stress that skilled planners adjust their strategy to fit the demands of the situation.

There are some circumstances in which advance planning may be most appropriate. When execution of a plan requires collaboration with other people, formulation of a plan prior to acting may facilitate effective performance. Likewise, when planning involves searching for a unique solution to be reached by specific means ("closed problem systems," Bartlett, 1958), working out a plan in advance may be more profitable than when planning involves "open problem systems" with several loosely defined and possibly inconsistent goals and fluid means to reach them. Another circumstance calling for advance planning is when the problem presents sufficient time to plan but limited time or limited physical or mental resources for carrying out the plan, thus necessitating efficiency in the adopted plan.

However, it is often necessary or more efficient to work opportunistically on whatever aspect of the planning task is easiest to solve or is most in need of solution at a given time (as in Hayes-Roth and Hayes-Roth's Opportunistic Planning Model, 1979). There is a fundamental trade-off between making plans in advance versus planning during action. On the one hand, advance plans may simplify the task by limiting and organizing possible options and promoting more systematic consideration of the relative advantages of the options. On the other hand, because not all of the final outcomes of planning decisions can be foreseen, choosing to leave some decisions open to development during action allows greater flexibility under changing circumstances. It may sometimes be more efficient to plan opportunistically, in order to take advantage of circumstances and to avoid mental effort and delays required to formulate an advance plan, especially when the problem can be adequately handled by a variety of solutions rather than having a unique best solution. Stefik (1981) argued that effective planning requires knowing when to make commitments and when to defer decision making to take advantage of new information. Goldin and Hayes-Roth (1980) suggested that more skilled planners are more flexible in their allocation of attention to decisions at varying levels of abstraction and more sensitive to constraints on particular actions, and that skilled planners make high-level planning decisions guided by attention to pragmatic considerations.

III. Children's adjustment to the circumstances of planning

As we see it, the development of planning skills involves an increase in sensitivity to the characteristics of the problem and to environmental supports and constraints, as well as an increase in skill in developing an advance plan under appropriate conditions. There is evidence that advance planning is more characteristic of older children. Magkaev (1977) found that first and second graders solved number problems resembling the Tower of Hanoi problem by working out the solution step-by-step or with only short-range advance plans, whereas third and fourth graders used at least short-range planning and often planned the entire solution before acting. But we do not expect older children to be more likely to plan ahead before acting across all problems. Their skill involves using advance planning when it is advantageous and planning during action when it is more efficient or less costly to do so. We expect the planning strategies of younger children to be less sensitive to circumstances and less likely ever to involve advance planning. They would be more likely to plan during action, considering only the next few moves, regardless of the characteristics of the problem.

A. Children's adjustment of advance planning or planning in action according to circumstances

Circumstances of task performance determine the degree to which specifiying plans prior to acting is advantageous. With age, children may gain skill in identifying task conditions calling for advance planning or planning in action. Gardner and Rogoff (1985) found that with development, children gain sensitivity to the conditions governing a planning task. In planning routes through mazes varying in structure or circumstances, older children (7½ to 10 years) differentiated their planning strategies according to the conditions of the problem more than younger children (4 to 7½ years) did. When circumstances differed, older children's planning strategies diverged; they did not simply apply a "more sophisticated" planning strategy across all circumstances.

Planning strategies were differentiated in terms of the degree to which children anticipated the routes they would draw on the maze. In advance planning, children determined the entire route through the maze prior to drawing. In planning during action, only a partial route was determined prior to drawing. In trial-and-error planning, children did not look ahead at all, evidencing no planning. Children were presented with a series of mazes along with instructions that emphasized either accuracy or speed and accuracy.

As predicted, 7½- to 10½-year-old children showed greater differences in their planning strategy in the two conditions than did 4- to 7½-year-old children. When accuracy alone was stressed, older children planned more in advance, more frequently determining the entire route through the maze before executing the plan. When speed as well as accuracy was stressed, both younger and older children planned during action, determining the route through only a few choicepoints in the maze prior to beginning to draw the route. Under the speed condition, the older children were actually less likely to make advance plans than the younger children. However, both ages did complete the mazes more quickly in the speed condition, indicating that both groups were responding appropriately to the instructional manipulation.

It is important to note that even the youngest children anticipated the routes they would draw to some degree. Their maze solutions were seldom determined through trial and error, but rather they planned stretches of the route, and sometimes the whole route, before drawing a route. The difference was that the younger children were less likely to discriminate the circumstances of the problem that would call for adjustments in strategy. The younger children did plan in advance at times, but their planning was less tailored to the planning circumstances than that of older children, who demonstrated more systematic use of advance planning and greater consideration of the circumstances in planning during action.

In addition to their adjustment of strategy under speed instructions versus accuracy instructions, the older children also differentiated their strategy according to the characteristics of the maze problems more than the younger children did. With mazes that had long dead ends that could not be seen immediately, older children planned more in advance. With mazes involving short dead ends that could easily be spotted, the older children planned during action. The younger children's planning strategies did not differ as systematically according to the structure of the mazes.

Thus in both types of comparison – speed versus accuracy, and maze structure – the older children's planning strategies were applied more flexibly to fit the problem. Older children do not simply plan *more* than younger children, regardless of the problem. What seems to develop in planning is the ability to adapt planning strategies flexibly to the circumstances of individual problems. Older children adjust planning to circumstances: They are more likely to construct an advance plan *when appropriate* for the circumstances, but can also avoid advance planning if that is more advantageous.

Older children's ability to identify and adjust to task conditions in the course of planning actions may be supported by enhanced skill in coordinating multiple considerations in complex problems. Such functioning entails monitoring the requirements of a cognitive task, as well as organizing appropriate strategic management of problem solving according to task circumstances. The difficulty younger children have in adjusting their planning to circumstances may be due in part to the challenge for young children of coordinating the means and the goal in complex problem solving.

B. Children's coordination of means with goals

When faced with a difficult problem, children may focus their attention on the immediate concrete actions required to make at least superficial progress in the activity, sometimes at the expense of fitting the means appropriately to the goal. This may be the only reasonable way to proceed when the problem is especially challenging. And thus it may be a characteristic not just of young children but of anyone faced with a difficult planning problem. Young children may adjust their planning to the circumstances (e.g., they may construct advance plans when appropriate) when their thinking is not overwhelmed by managing the complexity of the problem. Young children's lesser experience in many domains may frequently make it more difficult for them to adjust their plans. That is, they may not have a general lack of advance planning skill, but may instead have difficulty implementing it appropriately in the many occasions in which the task is hard for them.

To embed lower-level decisions in a higher-level goal structure requires remembering how the means fit together with the goal and keeping track of progress toward the overall goal while focusing on a particular decision. Although chunking actions according to superordinate goals can increase the efficiency of thought, it requires some extra planning to determine the appropriate chunks. In complex problems, this extra effort may exceed children's management skills, and they may focus instead on accomplishing what they can at the level of the next immediate decision. We expect that children's skills in coordinating means and goals would vary according to the complexity of the problem. In simple problems, children may perform similarly to adults planning in complex problems.

Children's difficulty in coordinating means with goals in complex problems may be illustrated by research on children who are planning communication or instruction of other children. With a heavy cognitive load (e.g., in a complex task such as preparing younger children for a memory test on a classification system), children who are planning instruction may lose track of the overall goal of getting the younger child to learn the material. They focus their planning more on the immediate goal of carrying out the specific task they are supposed to be teaching. That is, they may simply classify the objects instead of teaching the other child the rationale organizing the classification system (Ellis & Rogoff, 1986). Heavy demands for managing interaction or for formulating complex ideas may make it more difficult for children to plan their communication (Ochs, 1979). The plans of some 9-year-old children who are instructing other children in a spatial board game focus on the particular path to take without planning instruction to provide an overview of the purpose and rules of the game for the learner (Ellis, in preparation). When the learner appears confused, then the child teacher may backtrack to provide this organizing information. A more planful teacher, on the other hand, plans the instruction so that the rationale introduces the task and covers more detailed information on particular moves when the need arises. Similarly, Pratt, Scribner, and Cole (1977) noted that older children orient listeners to a game with an introductory description of the game materials, whereas preschoolers insert such descriptions haphazardly in the middle or at the end of their explanations, if at all. These studies demonstrate a more skilled focus on the overall goal of achieving listener understanding among older children, contrasting with younger children's exclusive focus on more immediate aspects of the task.

Likewise, Bereiter and Scardamalia (1982) have suggested that children's lack of planning in their written compositions may stem from their difficulty in simply carrying out the lower-level concerns, which must be attended to in order to get anything at all written. The higher-order considerations involved in planning may not appear without a sufficient level of skill in the lower-level content to allow children to focus beyond the immediate next step. Bereiter and Scardamalia claim that children can use more skilled planning when the problem to be solved is structured in a manner that simplifies the cognitive load of managing both immediate lower-level processes and the less immediate processes of planning.

Even when young children manage to keep the goal in mind, they may have difficulty fitting an appropriate plan to the goal. In their inexperience, they may apply a strategy that is not effective for reaching the goal. In a study of memory for spatial layout, 7-year old children exhibited less memory for spatial relationships between rooms in a funhouse when they planned to remember than when they did not expect to remember and were merely involved with the spatial information (Skeen & Rogoff, in press). Apparently, when they planned to remember, they attempted to apply an inappropriate strategy for remembering complex relationships – rehearsing a list of the rooms – which impeded their performance. The performance of 5-year-olds and 10-year-olds was not hurt by planning to remember (within these age groups, performance did not differ across conditions). Presumably the younger children did not differentiate the planning condition from the condition in which they did not expect to be tested. The older children's plans to remember may have been more effective than those of the 7-year-olds, and equally effective as the orienting activity involving children with the space. Effective planning requires flexible and knowledgeable tailoring of the specific means to the goal at hand.

The difficulty young children have in determining the nature of the problem and focusing on the goal is especially apparent when the planning problem is set for children by someone else. In experiments, young children may act on a goal that is at odds with the experimenter's definition of the problem; experience in testing situations appears to aid children in figuring out the experimenter's problem definition (Reese, 1977; Rogoff, 1982). In joint problem-solving of adults and children, one of the primary tasks for the adult is to bring the child's definition of the problem into correspondence with that of the adult (Wertsch, 1984). Whether solving their own problems or those set by others, children make progress in representing problems in a mature fashion (Bereiter & Scardamalia, 1982). (See also Pea, 1982, and Wilensky, 1983, for discussion of the importance of goal detection.)

C.   Learning to adjust plans to circumstances: the role of the social context

In this final section, we speculate that peers and adults may be influential in guiding the development of children's planning skills. We assume that children are motivated to plan in order to solve problems more effectively, and that they learn something about planning through their independent efforts. But we suggest that in addition, children's planning may develop through collaboration with others and through the guidance of those who are more experienced. Much of children's planning occurs in collaboration with peers or under the supervision of adults. People set goals in conjunction with each other, negotiate appropriate means to reach goals, and assist each other in implementing and revising goals as tasks evolve (Cole, Hood, & McDermott, 1978; Rogoff, 1982). Decisions regarding who is to handle what domain of planning are essential to collaborative planning. Making such decisions publicly may make children's planning processes more accessible, encouraging children to learn from their own public attempts to plan and from exposure to the attempts of others.

Individuals who are experienced with a planning activity may support the child's participation in planning by structuring the problem and guiding the child's participation in its solution (Rogoff, 1986; Rogoff, Malkin, & Gilbride, 1984; Saxe, Gearhart, & Guberman, 1984). Adults working with less skilled children appear to take responsibility for keeping track of the primary goal and dividing the problem into subgoals. They give the child increasing responsibility for planning within and then across subgoals, in accord with the child's growing expertise. Eventually the child participates in managing the subgoals and their fit with the primary goal.

Interaction with peers and near-peers provides children with experience coordinating plans that may improve their planning skills (Ellis &

Rogoff, 1986). In coordinating plans, children seem to learn about their own and each other's cognitive activities (Forbes & Lubin, 1979; Gearhart & Newman, 1980; Goldman & Ross, 1978; Lomov, 1978; Lubin & Forbes, 1980). Gearhart (1979) found that even pairs of 3-year-olds publicly prearranged all play episodes in a pretend store situation, but each child's plan lacked a model of the other person's perspective. The younger planner needed her companion in the play, so she told her what to do ahead of time, using her like a tool for the accomplishment of the plan. Gearhart suggested that the fact that the companion does not serve as an effective tool (as he or she generally has a plan of her own) is a condition for learning to coordinate plans. That even the 3-year-olds were learning to plan more effectively was evidenced by their attempts to prearrange elements of the plan that caused difficulty in earlier episodes.

In the process of adjusting plans in collaborative activity, children need to communicate their plans clearly. This may aid in developing skills for defining and articulating goals, determining the specific actions to be carried out, coordinating the specific actions with the goals, and evaluating strategic considerations and success of the plan. Whereas an individual planner may be able to execute a plan devised largely in terms of the next immediate move, collaborative planning may facilitate consideration of the fit of the means with the overall goal, and consideration of environmental circumstances. In order to identify and coordinate the interests and goals of multiple planners, communication regarding the goal and the circumstances may be essential, unless the collaboration is managed by assigning one person the planning task in its entirety, or by taking turns making independent decisions. Coordinating plans in a social context may require all planners to have sufficient information to carry out the plan. Planners who are truly working together need to reach agreement on the goal and problem circumstances in devising operational plans.

A suggestion that coordinating plans with others may encourage advance planning and coordinating means with goals is available in a study of collaborative versus individual planning by 4-year-olds and 8-year-olds asked to plan routes moving a miniature shopper to pick up groceries in a tabletop model of a grocery store (Gauvain & Rogoff, 1985). Both older and younger children planning in teams were more likely to employ strategies to keep track of progress in the task. Teams were more likely to put the item cards constituting the grocery list in the order to be fetched, and they kept better track of the grocery list by deleting grocery items from the list when they were picked up in the store.

More efficient routes were produced by children who used the strategy of locating items in the store before moving the miniature shopper to pick them up. Whether working alone or in teams, older children were likely to use this strategy, surveying the grocery store and locating items before moving the shopper into the store. The younger children working in teams were slightly more likely than those working alone to plan the trip before moving the shopper. The younger children planning alone determined the route largely by browsing through the store. Thus for the younger children it appeared that collaboration with a peer may have enhanced strategies of advance planning.

Similarly, working in teams yielded better problem solving by 8-year olds on a Tower of Hanoi task than did working individually (Glachan & Light, 1982). The Tower of Hanoi problem involves planning an approach to stacking tiles of graded sizes in a particular order on one of several available pegs. An interesting feature of Glachan and Light's procedure was that they enforced collaboration by children working in teams with a rule that they had to pick up the tiles together, using handles on opposite sides of the tiles. When Glachan and Light revised the procedure so that children were not required to move the tiles jointly, peer interaction no longer produced improvement in performance from pretest to posttest. Under these circumstances the children seldom shared responsibility for decision making. Glachan and Light suggested that mutual collaboration is an important feature of the effectiveness of social interaction in affecting learning.

The notion that joint responsibility for planning and problem solving plays a role in the effectiveness of team planning is supported in the grocery store data of Gauvain and Rogoff (1985). The children sometimes divided responsibility for choosing the route through the grocery store by taking turns on the moves. This often meant that decisions were made independently by each team member on successive moves, with little true collaboration. Younger children (4-year olds) working in teams that used this turn-taking strategy indeed produced less efficient routes. The younger children who truly collaborated produced slightly more efficient routes than their agemates who worked alone or who did not collaborate with their partners. Differences were not significant for the older children (aged 8 years), however, perhaps because most of the older pairs worked collaboratively. Thus these data are consistent with Glachan and Light's (1982) suggestion that for social interaction to enhance learning, mutual collaboration may be essential. Simply dividing up the task with another person may not restructure an individual's approach; it may be necessary for both to participate in making planning decisions.

If joint responsibility for decision making is central to learning from social interaction, it will be important in future research to examine the relative participation of children in social interaction, with peers as well as with adults. Both the experience of making planning considerations more explicit to a partner during peer interaction and planning under the guidance of more skilled individuals may contribute to children's increasing skills in adjusting their plans to circumstances and fitting means to goals.

IV. Summary

In this paper, we have suggested that effective planning is accomplished through sensitivity to the constraints and opportunities provided by the task environment and the social context. Under varying planning circumstances, it is appropriate to follow different strategies. A great deal of mature planning is opportunistic, suited to maximizing environmental opportunities to reach a practical goal without expending inordinate effort on organizing the complete series of actions before beginning to execute the plan. It is more appropriate to determine the plan before acting under some circumstances, such as when there is sufficient time to think but limited resources or time for action, or when there is stress on accurate performance.

We suggest that with development, children learn to adjust their planning attempts to the circumstances of the problem, and become more skilled in developing advance plans when it is advantageous to do so. Children become more skilled in considering sequences of actions and their fit with the goal rather than just planning the next action. Older children may plan in advance of acting when the situation favors advance planning (e.g., resources for action are limited) and can plan more opportunistically, relying on use of the context to guide action under other circumstances (e.g., when time for planning is limited, or inefficiencies are not costly). Younger children are more tied to the next immediate planning decision and appear less sensitive to constraints and opportunities in the planning situation. Young children have more difficulty managing the goal and fitting means to it, perhaps because in complex problems it is all they can do to focus on the next action required. However, young children's management of the goal and decisions about the planning process itself may be supported by the social context when a child is planning collaboratively with peers or when a more skilled person assists the child in managing the less immediate decisions involved in planning. We thus emphasize adjustment to the problem context as characteristic of skilled planning, and speculate that planning in social situations may facilitate the development of planning skills.

References

Bartlett, F. C. (1958). *Thinking: An experimental and social study.* New York: Basic Books.

Bereiter, C., & Scardamalia, M. (1982). From conversation to composition: The role of instruction in a developmental process. In R. Glaser (Ed.), *Advances in instructional psychology* (Vol. 2). Hillsdale, NJ: Erlbaum.

Bransford, J. P., & McCarrell, N. S. (1974). A sketch of a cognitive approach to comprehension: Some thoughts about understanding what it means to comprehend. In W. B. Weimer & D. S. Palermo, *Cognition and the symbolic processes.* Hillsdale, NJ: Erlbaum.

Brown, A. L. (1977). Development, schooling, and the acquisition of knowledge. In R. C. Anderson, R. J. Spiro, and W. E. Montague (Eds.), *Schooling and the acquisition of knowledge.* Hillsdale, NJ: Erlbaum.

Brown, A. L., & Campione, J. C. (1984). Three faces of transfer: Implications for early competence, individual differences, and instruction. In M. E. Lamb, A. L. Brown, & B. Rogoff (Eds.), *Advances in developmental psychology* (Vol. 3). Hillsdale, NJ: Erlbaum.

Brown, A. L., & DeLoache, J. S. (1978). Skills, plans, and self-regulation. In R. S. Siegler (Ed.), *Children's thinking: What develops?* Hillsdale, NJ: Erlbaum.

Bruner, J. S. (1974). The organization of early skilled action. In M. P. M. Richards (Ed.), *The integration of a child into a social world.* London: Cambridge University Press.

Bruner, J. S. (1981). Intention in the structure of action and interaction. In L. P. Lipsitt (Ed.), *Advances in infancy research* (Vol. 1, pp. 41–56). Norwood, NJ: Ablex.

Bullinger, A., & Chatillon, J. F. (1983). Recent theory and research of the Genevan school. In J. H. Flavell & E. M. Markman (Eds.), *Cognitive development,* Vol. III of P. H. Mussen's *Handbook of child psychology.* New York: Wiley.

Cole, M., Hood, L., & McDermott, R. P. (1978). Concepts of ecological validity: Their differing implications for comparative cognitive research. *The Quarterly Newsletter of the Institute for Comparative Human Development, 2,* 34–37.

DeLoache, J. S., & Brown, A. L. (1979). Looking for big bird: Studies of memory in very young children. *The Quarterly Newsletter of the Laboratory of Comparative Human Cognition, 1,* 53–57.

Ellis, S. (in preparation). *Impact of collaboration on instructional problem solving.* Ph.D dissertation, University of Utah.

Ellis, S., & Rogoff, B. (1986). Problem solving in children's management of instruction. In E. Mueller & C. Cooper (Eds.), *Process and outcome in peer relationships.* New York: Academic.

Feldman, D. H. (1980). *Beyond universals in cognitive development.* Norwood, NJ: Ablex.

Fischer, K. W. (1980). A theory of cognitive development: The control and construction of hierarchies of skills. *Psychological Review, 87,* 477–531.

Flavell, J. H. (1970). Developmental studies of mediated memory. In H. S. Reese & L. P. Lipsitt (Eds.), *Advances in child development and behavior* (Vol. 5). New York: Academic Press.

Flavell, J. H., & Wellman, H. M. (1977). Metamemory. In R. V. Kail, Jr., & J. W. Hagen (Eds.), *Perspectives on the development of memory and cognition.* Hillsdale, NJ: Erlbaum.

Forbes, D., & Lubin, D. (1979). Reasoning and behavior in children's friendly interactions. Paper presented at the meetings of the American Psychological Association, New York.

Fraisse, P. (1963). *The psychology of time.* New York: Harper & Row.

Gardner, W., & Rogoff, B. (1985, September). Children's improvisational and advance planning. Paper presented at the meetings of the American Psychological Association, Los Angeles.

Gauvain, M., & Rogoff, B. (1983, July). The pragmatic nature of large-scale spatial knowledge. Presented at the XIX Inter-American Congress of Psychology, Quito, Ecuador.

Gauvain, M., & Rogoff, B. (1985, April). The development of planning skills by individuals and dyads. Paper presented at the meetings of the Society for Research in Child Development.

Gearhart, M. (1979). Social planning: Role play in a novel situation. Paper presented at the meetings of the Society for Research in Child Development, San Francisco.

Gearhart, M., & Newman, D. (1980). Learning to draw a picture: The social context of an individual activity. *Discourse Processes, 3,* 169–184.

Glachan, M., & Light, P. (1982). Peer interaction and learning: Can two wrongs make a right? In G. Butterworth & P. Light (Eds.), *Social cognition: Studies of the development of understanding* (pp. 238–262). Chicago: University of Chicago Press.

Goldin, S. E., & Hayes-Roth, B. (1980). Individual differences in planning processes. Rand Note: N-1488-ONR.

Goldman, B. D., & Ross, H. S. (1978). Social skills in action: An analysis of early peer games. In J. Glick & A. K. Clarke-Stewart (Eds.), *The development of social understanding.* New York: Gardner.

Hayes-Roth, B., & Hayes-Roth, F. (1979). A cognitive model of planning. *Cognitive Science, 3,* 275–310.

Inhelder B., & Piaget, J. (1964). *The early growth of logic in the child.* New York: Harper & Row.

Kagan, J. (1971). *Change and continuity in infancy.* New York: Wiley.

Kagan, J., & Kogan, N. (1970). Individuality and cognitive performance. In P. H. Mussen (Ed.), *Carmichael's manual of child psychology* (Vol. 1). New York: Wiley.

Karmiloff-Smith, A., & Inhelder, B. (1975). "If you want to get ahead, get a theory." *Cognition, 3,* 195–212.

Klein, W. (1983). Deixis and spatial orientation in route directions. In H. L. Pick & L. P. Acredolo (Eds.), *Spatial orientation.* New York: Plenum.

Kuipers, B. (1979). On representing common sense knowledge. In N. V. Findler (Ed.), *Associative networks – the representation and use of knowledge in computers.* New York: Academic.

Lomov, B. F. (1978). Psychological processes and communication. *Soviet Psychology, 17,* 3–22.

Lubin, D., & Forbes, D. (1980). Planfulness in children's reasoning and behavior: Interpretive procedures, operative procedures, and children's third party entry behavior. Manuscript, Harvard University.

Magkaev, V. K. (1977). An experimental study of the planning function of thinking in young schoolchildren. In M. Cole (Ed.), *Soviet developmental psychology: An anthology.* White Plains, NY: M. E. Sharpe.

Miller, G. A., Galanter, E., & Pribram, K. H. (1960). *Plans and the structure of behavior.* New York: Holt.

Ochs, E. (1979). Planning and unplanned discourse. *Syntax and Sematics, 12, Discourse and Syntax,* 51–80.

Pea, R. D. (1982). What is planning development the development of? In D. D. Forbes & M. T. Greenberg (Eds.), *Children's planning strategies. New directions for child development* (Vol. 18). San Francisco: Jossey-Bass.

Piaget, J. (1969). *The child's conception of time.* New York: Basic Books.

Piaget, J. (1970). Piaget's theory. In P. H. Mussen (Ed.), *Carmichael's manual of child psychology* (Vol. 1). New York: Wiley.

Pratt, M. W., Scribner, S., & Cole, M. (1977). Children as teachers: Developmental studies of instructional communication. *Child Development, 48,* 1475–1481.

Reason, J. T. (1977). Skill and error in everyday life. In M. Howe (Ed.), *Adult learning* (pp. 21–44). London: Wiley.

Reese, H. W. (1977). Discriminative learning and transfer: Dialectical perspectives. In N. Datan & H. W. Reese (Eds.), *Life-span developmental psychology: Dialectical perspectives on experimental research.* New York: Academic Press.

Rogoff, B. (1982). Integrating context and cognitive development. In M. E. Lamb & A. L. Brown (Eds.), *Advances in developmental psychology* (Vol. 2). Hillsdale, NJ: Erlbaum.

Rogoff, B. (1986). Adult assistance of children's learning. In T. E. Raphael (Ed.), *Contexts of school-based literacy.* New York: Random House.

Rogoff, B., Malkin, C., & Gilbride, K. (1984). Interaction with babies as guidance in development. In B. Rogoff & J. V. Wertsch (Eds.), *Children's learning in the "zone of proximal development."* San Francisco: Jossey-Bass.

Rogoff, B., Newcombe, N., & Kagan, J. (1974). Planfulness and recognition memory. *Child Development, 45,* 972–977.

Saxe, G. B., Gearhart, M., & Guberman, S. R. (1984). The social organization of early number development. In B. Rogoff & J. V. Wertsch (Eds.), *Children's learning in the "zone of proximal development."* San Francisco: Jossey-Bass.

Siegler, R. S. (1981). Developmental sequences within and between concepts. *Monographs of the Society for Research in Child Development, 46* (No. 2, Serial No. 189).

Siegler, R. S., & Liebert, R. M. (1975). Acquisition of formal scientific reasoning by 10- and 13-year-olds: Designing a factorial experiment. *Developmental Psychology, 11,* 401–402.

Skeen, J., & Rogoff, B. (in press). Children's difficulties in deliberate memory for spatial relationships: Misapplication of verbal mnemonic strategies? *Cognitive Development.*

Stefik, M. (1981). Planning and meta-planning. *Artificial Intelligence, 16,* 141–169.

Sternberg, R. J. (1984). Toward a triarchic theory of human intelligence. *Behavioral and Brain Sciences 7,* 269–315.

Szeminska, A. (1965). The evolution of thought: Some applications of research findings to educational practice. In P. H. Mussen (Ed.), *European research in cognitive development, Monographs of the Society for Research in Child Development, 30* (No. 2, whole No. 100, pp. 47–57).

Wertsch, J. V. (1984). The zone of proximal development: Some conceptual issues. In B. Rogoff & J. V. Wertsch (Eds.), *Children's learning in the "zone of proximal development."* San Francisco: Jossey-Bass.

Wilensky, R. (1983). *Planning and understanding.* Reading, MA: Addison-Wesley.

9   Action planning competencies during adolescence and early adulthood

Michael Dreher and Rolf Oerter

I.   Introduction
A.   *Some important aspects of planning*

Planning is an essential part of human life. Although psychological research up to the 1970s did not attend very much to this kind of activity, planning activity now has gained more interest. Some studies deal with planning from the viewpoint of general psychology, including computer simulation (Fahlman, 1974; Hayes-Roth & Hayes-Roth, 1979; Sacerdoti, 1975). Others are more related to planning in working processes (Hacker, 1978; Volpert, 1974). The following contribution incorporates a developmental perspective; that is, we are trying to look for an ongoing improvement of planning strategies and their integration in coping with everyday problems.

In trying to define planning, we may start with the Hayes-Roths' notion of planning "as the predetermination of action aimed at achieving some goal" (Hayes-Roth & Hayes-Roth, 1979, pp. 275–276). A broad range of planning activities is included in this definition: for example, prospective memory (Kreutzer, Leonard, & Flavell, 1975), short-term planning (within minutes and hours), long-term planning (e.g., in economics and politics), and planning of one's own life including personal projects (Little, 1980).

Actually, planning behavior incorporates so many different cognitive activities that it is not useful to begin with a general model of planning. Rather we shall focus on a typical form of everyday planning which represents some essential features of planning in modern culture. Thus, we try to measure planning behavior in a concrete and well-defined situation which represents at the same time important aspects of our culture. The rationale that underlies this procedure is as follows.

321

1. Planning as an essential feature of modern culture. The first reason why we are interested in the development of planning is its importance in modern life. Indeed, planning rules nearly every region of our life. This is especially true in the field of work which is completely governed by planning. The use of the term "planning" in various cultural domains (economics, administration, politics) has led to many different definitions. They can be reduced to the following three main points (Koch, 1961):

1. Planning as projections for the future
2. Planning as the generation of alternative goals and possibilities for realizing them (Decisions must be made then regarding which goals to pursue and which methods to use.)
3. Planning as a system of decisions through which specific responses are determined in advance for all possible circumstances.

Because planning plays such an important role in modern industrial societies, one can assume that essential components of planning are learned in the course of socialization.

When children grow older, they learn to plan more and more effectively and to internalize essential components of planning. In order to understand the development of planning, we must find out which features of the environment are recognized and internalized at each developmental stage. This approach is derived from the notions of Piaget (1977), Kohlberg (1974), and Flavell and Wohlwill (1969), who consider cognitive development as an active process of construction and reconstruction of reality.

2. Restriction of planning to a limited but representative situation. If we want to explore both the development of planning strategies and the construction of reality in relation to planning, we must choose a situation that represents important features of cultural reality and that allows at the same time the observation of planning activities, thus providing the opportunity of inferring planning strategies. A well-defined situation that meets both conditions is the planning and the execution of errands in a given period of time. In an earlier work, several errands for children and young adolescents were selected (e.g., fetching a book from school, going to the playground, returning gloves to an acquaintance). These were presented through a sketch in which the places and distances were drawn (Oerter, Dreher, & Dreher, 1977). The rationale for this method is also used in the study to be presented below. The planning situation was constructed as an everyday situation in which several errands with special planning features have to be completed within given time limits and while considering important values (e.g., cost–benefit relationships).

3. Planning and problem solving. We consider planning as a special case of problem solving. This perspective emphasizes the search for strategies and operations used in solving planning problems. We can assume that during ongoing development, the child will use more and more appropriate and complex strategies in order to cope with planning tasks. The analysis of planning strategies can be better accomplished if a rational model is available that allows us to compare individual planning performance and to assess developmental progress.

B. Planning and action theory

We view planning from the perspective of action theory. Action theory includes a broad variety of quite different approaches ranging from the materialistic notion of activity favored by Soviet psychologists (Leontjev, 1977; Rubinstein, 1977) to "idealistic" approaches of Western philosophy (Lenk, 1978; Thalberg, 1977). Three central ideas that aid in the description of planning can be traced through the different versions of action theory.

1. Goal-directedness and conscious activity of an agent. All action theorists agree with the position that one can speak of an action when an agent is consciously engaged in an activity aimed at reaching a goal. The term "conscious" is problematic. Sometimes it is used as a synonym for goal directed; that is, there is a consciousnes of a goal (Cranach et al., 1980). At other times it is connected with the conception that all action is rational; that is, action is founded on rational and systematic consideration of all possible circumstances. Goal directedness, thus, is always related to an actor who causes or generates the action. Action has to do with the future, with how things might be and should be, and therefore action extends over time. The time period within which action occurs can be divided into phases. These features of action characterize planning processes quite well.

2. Object relatedness. Rubinstein (1977), Leontjev (1977), and others stated that all action is object related. In their opinion it is meaningless to use the term "action" without specifying the object to which it is related. The notion of object relatedness is particularly useful in describing planning activities that are related to errands or tasks that have to be ordered in an effective sequence and that have to be completed reliably. In this case, the objects of planning are the errands themselves, part of the errands, means employed to reach goals, and also superordinate goals like the completion of all errands and/or the construction of an optimal comprehensive plan.

3.   Values and valences.   Action as a goal-directed process includes the evaluation of goals and of activities leading to the goal. We must assume that each errand and each instrumental activity has a valence of its own. The term "valence" was used early by Lewin (1939), who attributed it to regions and objects within the so-called life space, and it was introduced again in action-related research during the 1970s (e.g., Argyle, 1976; Magnusson & Endler, 1977).

Taking planning as a process in which an agent is directed (related) to an object, one can make the following clear-cut distinction: Valence is associated with the concrete *object,* with the object-related action, and with concrete goals. Values, on the other hand, are conceived as general regulating principles associated with the *agent.* A hamburger has a valence for a hungry person. Good nutrition may be a value regulating the behavior of the same person. If that person sees the hamburger as unhealthy, he or she will not buy it despite its valences.

II.   The planning problem

A planning problem was constructed for subjects to solve. They were to explain how they would complete a set of errands in different places within the time allotted. The problem was presented to subjects exactly as follows:

You have arrived home from the office at 4:20 p.m. and still have things to do because you are leaving for a week's camping with friends the next morning.
– You have to change money for the trip (10 minutes time spent). The bank is open until 5:30 p.m. A friend could change the money for you, but you have to call him beforehand. And you would have to be home from 5:00 p.m. until 5:15 p.m. to receive the money and give him back the money he advanced.
– Furthermore, you are supposed to buy 20 cans of food in the supermarket which is open until 6:30 p.m. (time for shopping 6 minutes).
– In the office you have been charged with handing over important business documents to your employer (boss, chief). He will be passing through Augsburg by train (3-minute stop in Augsburg, from 6:08 to 6:11 p.m.) on his way from Munich to Hamburg.

– You really want to meet your boyfriend/girlfriend. The bus which he/she usually takes home leaves at 5:50 p.m. The bus stop has often been your meeting
place.
– You could use your bicycle if you have it repaired. The bicycle-dealer would
repair it immediately – he needs 60 minutes for the repair (5 minutes to be spent
in handing over the bicycle; the shop is open until 6:00 p.m.).
Your task is to make a plan of how you can finish everything in the given time.

You see the map with the different stations:

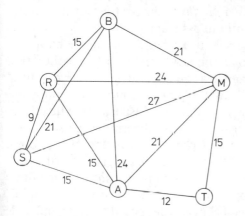

A = Apartment
B = Bank (open until 5:30 p.m.)
M = Meeting place (bus stop)
R = Bicycle repair
S = Supermarket
T = Train station

The minutes given in numbers along the lines (streets) indicate the time needed
for walking the distances. Bicycling the same distance, one third of the walking
time is needed, e.g., 30 minutes of walking = 10 minutes by bicycle. Take into
account that everything should be settled in time. Now think about a solution.

In order to analyze the planning problem, one can take two different
perspectives. Considering nothing but time limits, one can distinguish
only correct and incorrect solutions. There are no better or worse correct
solutions. From this perspective, the planning problem is reduced to a
problem of sequence.

The second perspective also takes the content of the planning problem
into account. In this case, persons, locations, and objects are seen as crucial to the solution of the problem. For example, the problem solver may
complete the bank business first if money is regarded as very important
(high valence of this errand). Now it is important not only to complete
the errands within the time limit, but also to reduce the amount of time
spent on each errand insofar as is possible and to increase as much as
possible the amount of time available for more pleasant activities, for
example, being with girl/boyfriend.

We assume that the problem solver identifies with the agent in the planning problem, applying his or her own values and valences (as defined previously).

The planning problem was designed to incorporate the three aspects of planning described earlier. First, it represents essential features of modern culture. Planning is associated with the completion of everyday errands. Furthermore, the problem deals with the economy of expenditure. Two specific economic features are built in: (a) delegation (of the bank business) and (b) using tools (bicycle). These possibilities introduce a new kind of expenditure, which is *indirect,* in contrast to the *direct* expenditure of doing the errand without assistance.

The planning elements "considering time limits," "using the bicycle," and "delegation" need further explanation. As was described earlier, the planning problem was derived from planning features of everyday life. This procedure is meaningful only if the planning problem represents essential features of the environment. Three main aspects were therefore included: time, machine, and delegation. These determine the structure of modern work. The time schedule of production is one of the most important pressures in economic life. Moreover, the shorter the time for production, the less expensive the goods. The omnipresence of time limits and time pressure can be experienced even in the private domain, where people often plan actions as if they are supposed to be completed within certain time limits even when it is not necessary.

The second feature, using machines, also plays a crucial role in our culture. Not only the production system in economics but also nearly every action in everyday life includes the using of machines. Considering the utility of tools and machines during the planning phase means that expenditure and time are taken into account. Finally delegation of work is a principle that governs not only the distribution of work to different workers but also the coordination of different producers that supply different parts of an object. For a more detailed discussion of the principle of delegation, see E. Dreher (1980). An illustrative example for the effectiveness of time, machine, and delegation is the production of cars. The assembly line guarantees the production of cars within the briefest possible time. The automation of car production has developed to such an extent that manpower can be reduced to a very small number of people. The principle of delegation is realized not only in the construction of the car on the assembly line but also in the delivery of car parts by other firms.

The second aspect, restriction of planning to a limited but representative situation, was taken into account by constructing a specific situation: preparation for a holiday trip.

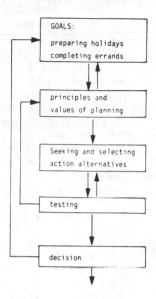

Figure 9.1. Flow chart of the planning process in the planning problem.

The third aspect, planning as a special case of problem solving, is treated in the next section.

III. A model of the planning process

Having described the planning problem in detail, we shall move to a model that describes the strategies necessary for its solution. The process is demonstrated in Figure 9.1. It takes into consideration the three aspects of action theory mentioned in the previous section.

A. *Goals*

The analysis of the problem begins with definition and/or establishment of goals. In the planning problem, the overarching goal is the completion of the errands within the time limits. A second goal is completing preparations for the camping trip. A third is maximizing time spent with boy/girlfriend. The errands become subgoals because they possess valences derived from these more general goals (and the goal of performing one's job well in connection with meeting the boss at the train station). The subject proceeds to solve the planning problem on the basis of a hierarchy

Table 9.1. *Overview of goals and goal valences in the organization task*

Goal	Content	Valence
General goal	Starting the trip successfully	Superordinated goal
Errands	Having repaired the bicycle (R)	Reducing effort: For covering the distances For transportation of cans Reducing time
	Money changing (B)	Most important for and proximate to general goal
	Delegation of money changing (B̶)	Reducing time Reducing effort Raising risk
	Meeting the friend (M)	Personal and sexual attractiveness of the friend
	Train station (T)	Valence of labor and occupation, being prompt
	Supermarket: 20 cans (S)	Most important for and proximate to general goal
Task completion	Being in accordance with the task instruction	Valence of time and time limits

of goals that may be more or less explicit and more or less complete. A list of possible goals, along with their contents and valences, is presented in Table 9.1.

B. Principles and values of planning

This ordering of goals is possible only if the planning agent uses some general principles and values. The planning problem becomes simpler if only one dimension of values is included (e.g., the specific valences of errands) and more difficult if several levels of evaluation are included. At a low level, one principle governing goal analysis might be the execution of errands according to the hierarchy of their valence (e.g., pleasant errands first). The planning agent focuses on the actions necessary for reaching the goals but does not consider time limits. On a higher level, the planning agent may take into account the given time limits, thus regulating the planning process by the general principle of time, which of course can also be seen as a general value stemming from our culture, which emphasizes time and time limits. If solutions are sought that meet time limits only, all other valences of the existing goals are neglected. Indeed, in order to handle the time problem adequately, one must abstract from the meaning or valences of the goals. However, in order to proceed successfully, it is necessary to include again the valences of the single goals. This leads to a higher and more complex level of planning: Completion of errands, considering time limits, and taking into account the rank order of valences of errands entails the coordination of many different operations in order to reach an appropriate solution.

C. Action alternatives

The next step of the planning procedure consists in recognizing alternatives embedded in the instructions that allow choices about (a) using versus not using the bicycle, and (b) delegating versus not delegating money changing. In addition, the subject may reflect on the order in which the tasks will be completed.

D. Testing

In order to make decisions, the subject first must select one or more alternatives for testing. Three main criteria can be used: (a) observing time for errand completion, (b) economizing on time, (c) minimizing expenditure of energy.

E. Decision

Having selected and tested the action alternatives, the subject makes decisions and matches them with the initial goals (feedback loop in Figure 9.1). If the decisions fit the goal, the process of planning stops. If there is no congruence or if the decision is only made for one errand, the process of planning continues, with the subject taking the same steps again.

This model is an idealized one; that is, it describes how strategies of planning would follow in a sequence in order to reach a sufficient solution. It can be used, for instance, for computer simulation of planning behavior. However, if we look at the development of behavior, the ideal sequence of steps will surely not be present in every case. When the capacity for planning is not yet fully realized or developed, people may respond to planning problems irrationally and ineffectively. For instance, an action might follow immediately after the perception of a goal. Principles and values may not govern the planning process, and testing may not be undertaken. Because we are dealing with adolescents and young adults, we can assume that the main links of the flow-chart are in use. But within each step of the process large developmental differences with regard to the level of complexity and generalization may exist. These differences are described in the next section.

Having described the planning model, we note that it includes more general features even though it was primarily developed for the planning problem presented earlier. Among others, those general features are (a) the separation of single steps in order to reach a goal, (b) the arrangement of an efficient sequence of the analyzed steps, (c) evaluating both the goal and the planning steps.

IV. Developmental levels of planning

The planning problem is designed to reveal not only subjects' skill in planning (Can they complete all the errands? How much time do they save to spend with boy/girlfriend?) but also the processes of goal seeking, evaluating, selecting action alternatives, testing, and decision making listed in the boxes of the flow chart.

First, we shall state our assumptions about developmental changes associated with the steps of the planning model. Afterward we shall relate developmental levels to types of solutions.

A.   Assumptions about changes at steps of planning procedure

To start with the analysis of goals, we can assume that at an early stage of planning, errands are considered as discrete goals which have to be completed one after the other. When the completion of a task according to instruction is recognized as an overarching goal, the individual errands are seen as parts of a whole and get related to each other. An even higher level of goal ordering is reached, if (a) time limits, (b) the superordinate goal of preparing for holidays, and (c) the valences of each of the errands are considered altogether. This becomes possible, as was demonstrated earlier, through the regulating activity of the principles and values (see Figure 9.1). Because the essential components of this unit with regard to the planning problem were already described, only some summarizing conclusions will be drawn.

At a low level of planning, the only regulating principle might be the completion of errands, because this is the earliest experience a child has had. The next regulating principle is presumably the observance of time. This is true not only because time is an essential part of the instruction, but also because time is a crucial value in modern culture and regulates most parts of individual and societal life.

The next principle developed by the planning subject is assumed to comprise both the more "formal" aspect of time and the contents of the errands. Considering content in addition to time aspects, the subject needs more complex strategies. He or she must also develop a more general or higher-ordered principle, which was earlier described as a cost–benefit calculation. The valences of each of the errands considered as benefits have to be evaluated from the perspective of costs (expenditure of energy and time) needed for task completion.

We can assume that when time as a regulating principle is established, the only action alternatives that will be taken into account are those that meet the time limits. This means that the choice of action alternatives must focus on the time limits given in the planning problem. If this is not the case, correct sequences of actions can be found only by chance. Hence, meeting time limits becomes a crucial strategy in planning processing. Having reached this level of planning, the agent will be more inclined to use the bicycle. Using machines as an element of planning is a higher level of planning processing, as was demonstrated earlier (Oerter, 1981a; see also the description of the planning problem), because one needs more complex strategies in order to deal with each additional element in the planning problem.

Finally, we would expect, as a last developmental step, that the action alternative of delegating the change of money will be taken into account (see Oerter, 1981b). To delegate an errand seems easy because it saves expenditure. However, to include it in the process of goal-directed and systematic planning means that the subject has to attribute responsibility to another person and has to generate more complex strategies. Therefore, we assume that only older persons would delegate the bank business.

The systematic role of "using machines" and "delegation" was described earlier (see description of the planning problem in Section II).

The sequence of "considering time limits," "using the machine," and "delegating errands" can be interpreted as a developmental order from two perspectives. First, as it was shown through the description of the problem, the successive inclusion of these elements needs new operations and testing strategies which have to be coordinated with the more basic operations, thus leading to a hierarchy of planning operations that is inherent in the structure of the problem itself. Developmental progress consists in the increasing ability to recognize and use the "deeper" and more complex features of the problem. Thus, development is conceived according to Piaget's (1977) approach of gradual (re)construction of reality.

Second, the three components mentioned above represent specific aspects of reality, namely characteristic features of modern culture showing increasing sophistication. The comprehension and use of these components reflect the reconstruction and internalization of cultural reality as a developmental progress. Thus, our planning problem, though constructed as a concrete and restricted everyday situation, incorporates more general aspects of planning, namely with regard to time limits, machines, and delegation – some crucial features of everyday planning. Therefore, it possesses ecological validity (Bronfenbrenner, 1979).

B. Assumptions about developmental changes in task solutions

The device of the planning problem makes it possible for us to infer levels of planning from the type of solution produced by the subject. Table 9.2 depicts all possible solutions. (The possibility of depicting all possible solutions is an advantage of this planning problem as compared with other planning problems, e.g., the one presented by the Hayes-Roths, 1979.)

In the first column of Table 9.2, the different solutions are assembled. They are grouped by the four above-mentioned alternatives. The large bracket over the letters in the Solution column means that the respective paths were traveled with the bicycle. (B) indicates that one had the money brought. For the appraisal of the different paths, the temporal structure of every path is subdivided into the following components:

1. Travel time (column 3).
2. Conveyance time (column 4): time that cans must be carried.
3. Time of arrival and possible stopping time at the meeting place (column 5): If the addition of stopping time does not lead to the arrival time of 5:50 p.m., then this means that the meeting place is reached earlier and left earlier. The given stopping time is the maximum time. The zero (0) means that one must go on without stopping.
4. Extra time (column 6): times resulting from the difference between the time needed for travel and the time when the next errand may be started or completed. The stopping time at the meeting place is included.
5. Total time/end time (column 7): total time that is used (travel time + given time + free stopping time).

"End time" is the time of return to the apartment. One can read the optimal solution with the criteria of the length of time for different set goals of expenditure reduction. For example, which solution (a) requires the least expenditure for the transportation of the cans? (b) allows one to have the most time with one's boyfriend or girlfriend? (c) allows one to have the most available free time?

In Solution No. 1 (Table 9.2), all points of the map are successively linked according to their physical proximity. It is, in a sense, the easiest

Table 9.2. *Overview of correct solutions and their time components*

No.	Solution[a]	Travel time (min)	R	total	Time for can-transport	R	total	Arrival and possible stopping time at M		Extra time[b]	Total and end time
On foot (R)											
1	A S R B M T A	87			72			5:41 p.m.	9	12	
2	A R S B M T A	93			69			5:47 p.m.	3	6	
3	A S B M T A	84			69			5:33 p.m.	17	20	
4	A S B M A T A	102			63			5:33 p.m.	2	2	123 6:23 p.m.
5	A B S M A T A	99			54			5:48 p.m.	2	5	
6	A M B S A T A	102			15			4:41 p.m.	2	2	
With delegating (B)											
7	A S A B M T A	78			15		15	5:36 p.m.	14	21	
Using the bicycle (R)											
8	A R S B R M T A	60	17	77	36	17	53	5:49 p.m.	1	14	115 6:15 p.m.
9	A R S B R M A T A	60	23	83	36	15	51	5:49 p.m.	1	8	
10	A R B S R M T A	60	17	77	9	17	26	5:49 p.m.	1	14	
11	A R B S R M A T A	60	23	83	9	15	24	5:49 p.m.	1	8	
12	A R B R M T S A	45	27	72	—	5	5	5:48 p.m.	2	35	131 6:31 p.m.
13	A R B R M A T S A	45	33	78	—	5	5	5:48 p.m.	2	29	
14	A R B M R T S A	75	23	98	—	5	5	5:26 p.m.	0	9	
15	A R B M R S T A	75	16	91	—	5	5	5:26 p.m.	0	—	
16	A R M B R S T A	75	16	91	—	5	5	5:04 p.m.	0	—	115 6:15 p.m.
17	A R M B R T S A	75	23	98	—	5	5	5:04 p.m.	0	9	131 6:31 p.m.
With delegating (B)											
18	A R A B M R T S A	75	23	98	—	5	5	5:36 p.m.	0	4	115 6:15 p.m.
19	A R A B R M T S A	45	27	72	—	5	5	5:48 p.m.	2	30	
20	A R A B R M A T S A	45	33	78	—	5	8	5:48 p.m.	2	24	131 6:31 p.m.

[a] Legend: A = apartment, B = bank, M = meeting place (friend), R = repair of bicycle, S = supermarket, T = train station (boss).
[b] Time remaining after travel before an errand may be completed.

solution, because the shortest path that can be taken in order to complete the errands coincides with the time demands. Stopping time at the meeting place for the friend is rather long, by chance, but even so it is a poor solution because the cans have to be conveyed on foot for the longest possible time (72 minutes). Solution No. 2 leaves the pure geometrical view but still copes very poorly with the requirement of conveying cans. This is true also for Solution No. 3, but this disadvantage is offset by the maximum time spent with the friend. Thus, if the subject weighed the valence of joining the friend very highly, he or she might prefer this solution, even though it is nearly impossible to carry 20 cans (each about 2 pounds) such a long way.

To simplify the interpretation of our findings, four levels of solution can be postulated as being equivalent both to the level of planning (see Figure 9.1) and to the developmental state of the individual.

Level 1: Solution No. 1 (the geometrical solution).
Level 2: Solution with high expenditure (pure "foot" solution) but with a reduction of the amount of time needed for task completion (e.g., solutions 2, 3, 4, 5).
Level 3: Solutions in which more than one condition is considered and the expenditure of effort and time is reduced (e.g., Solution Nos. 6, 8, 9, 15, 16).
Level 4: Solutions in which the highest possible number of conditions is balanced. Solution No. 7 takes into account the reduction of travel time, conveyance time, delegation of changing money, time for friend, total time. Solutions Nos. 19 and 20 try to balance delegation of changing money, reduction of travel time (using the bicycle), and reduction of expenditure for conveyance of the cans.

Solution Nos. 15 and 16 try to minimize the total amount of time (115 minutes, see last column of Table 9.2). Because they do not include delegation of changing money, time for the friend, and the risk of missing the boss (0 minutes at train station), they were put into Level 3.

The conclusion that subjects' developmental levels are reflected in the overview of possible solutions is misleading with regard to one important condition. Unlike the reader, who is presented with all possible solutions and their systematized components, the subject is given no overveiw. He or she has to find out the essential conditions of the planning problem during the process of problem solving. Thus, being at a disadvantage compared with someone who possesses the ordered information, the subject might produce a relatively low-level solution even though he or she is able to generate appropriate strategies of planning. We would like to point out that knowing what solution a subject has chosen does not tell us the reasons the subject had for making his or her choice or the reasoning processes that led to that choice. Therefore, special data collection and analysis procedures were designed in order to get more information about the process of planning itself. These procedures are described in the following sections.

V. Method

A. Material and procedure

1. Paper–pencil form. The planning problem can be presented as a group experiment for the registration of planning results. The subjects are given the text of the problem with the illustration and are informed about the goal; for the solution of the problem, the planned paths should be written down.

2. Individual run. The subjects in the individual runs sit in front of a map (a green field, exact size of which is 60 cm × 90 cm; the "roads" are marked in red) with two types of *instruction* cards. On each stretch of road, there are travel time cards (yellow, 4 cm × 2.5 cm); on these the time for traveling the respective distances on foot is given. At every location there is a content card (yellow, 3.5 × 13.5 cm); on these the respective errands and the conditions for them are described. The text corresponds to that of the paper–pencil form. All instruction cards are face down on the map. The content cards are marked on the back side with the respective location names (e.g., bank, supermarket).

The subject is then informed about the content of the planning problem and afterward receives instruction on how to handle the cards.

You see here the map with different locations. The time for the respective ways is on the small cards. The times, in minutes, represent the time required for the distance on foot. With the bicycle you need a third of that time; for example, 21 minutes on foot is 7 minutes by bicycle. You may turn every card over as often as you like and read it. Every card must be replaced face down – only one at a time may be face up. Show on the map the way you would take; you don't have to explain it all right away. You should report aloud every thought which occurs to you. You can also ask questions. Now think about a way in which everything can be accomplished in the given time.

The information used for the solution is recorded on special forms made up of a series of maps reduced in size. The chosen instruction cards, the pathway, and the remarks of the subject explaining single steps can be recorded on these.

Table 9.3. *Number of subjects in sample I, divided according to educational system and age*

School type	Average age (years; months)							
	11;6	14;7	15;8	16;1	17;3	18–20	20–24	Older
Hauptschule	225	313	170	—	—	—	—	—
Realschule	—	459	120	35	—	—	—	—
Gymnasium	236	151	—	36	101	—	—	—
Berufsfachschule für Hauswirtschaft	—	—	—	41	38	—	—	—
Fachakademie für Sozialpädagogik	—	—	—	—	—	331	—	—
Fachhochschule (Wirtschaft)	—	—	—	—	—	—	46	—
Universität	—	—	—	—	—	—	110	—
Abendrealschule	—	—	—	—	—	—	—	18

Definition of school types:

Hauptschule: Grades 5–9. Compulsory for those who do not qualify for one of the following two forms of secondary schooling. Usually followed by vocational training.

Realschule: Grades 7–10. Technical secondary school leading to vocational training and/or higher technical education in fields such as management, engineering, accounting.

Gymnasium: Grades 5–13. Preuniversity secondary school with predominantly arts and sciences curriculum.

Berufsfachschule für Hauswirtschaft: Post-secondary school training for housekeepers, cooks, and institutional kitchen directors.

Fachakademie für Sozialpädagogik: Post-secondary school training for child care workers and nursery school teachers.

Fachhochschule (Wirtschaft): Post-secondary school for applied business training.

Universität: Higher education in arts and sciences and the professions. Different from U. S. universities in beginning later (see *Gymnasium,* above) and excluding most applied fields.

Abendrealschule: Evening school for adults who have completed only *Hauptschule* and wish to qualify for entry into higher education.

3. Group discussion. First subjects solve the task individually; then they discuss their solutions in a group of three or four members in the following manner. Each member presents his or her solution and reasoning. Next, the pros and cons of each alternative are weighed, and finally the group decides on a common solution. This solution can be one of those given, or it can be a new solution. The materials of the individual runs are available during the discussion. The discussion is recorded on videotape.

B. Subjects

The experiment was completed by two groups. Sample I was given the paper–pencil form of the planning problem. This group consisted of pupils or students from various levels of the West German educational system. The planning problem was administered as a group test during school hours. Table 9.3 gives an overview of the composition of Group I.

Sample II was given the task as individual runs which were followed by group discussions. The indiviudal runs and the videotaping took place in rooms at the university where the technical facilities for recording were available. The subjects in Sample II were volunteers who were to sign up for the experiment in groups of three or four persons. The selection of such "natural" groups (Kruse, 1972) or "groups with history" (Sader, 1976) has the advantage that the discussions are conducted among people who already know each other and for whom the discussion will be no particular burden. The assumption may be made, then, that the interaction pattern shown in the experimental situation does not vary greatly from that found in everyday interaction. Labov (1970) pointed out that it is precisely adolescents in their peer groups who interact uninfluenced in the experimental observational situations. This is indicated, among other ways, by the continued use of their colloquial language and by their informal behavior style. Sample II consisted of 24 subjects from *Hauptschule* (average age, 15.3 years), 26 subjects from *Fachakademie* (average age, 18.7 years), and 24 subjects from the university (average age, 21.5 years).

VI. Results

The results are described in the following sequence: (a) results of the paper–pencil conditions; (b) results of the individual-run conditions; and (c) some results of the group discussion.

A. Results of the paper-and-pencil test

1. Conditions of observing time and reducing expenditure. One way to analyze the developmental progress of planning is to look at the criterion of time limits. As is shown in Table 9.4, a gradual increase of solutions that meet time limits occurs with increasing age. Nonetheless, more than 10% of the university students failed to give "correct" solutions. On the

Table 9.4. *Percentage of solutions in which the time limits were met (Sample I)*

School type	11	14	15	16	17	18–20	20–24	Older
				Age in years				
Hauptschule	39	55	55	—	—	—	—	—
Realschule	—	60	84	73	—	—	—	—
Gymnasium	49	81	—	67	81	—	—	—
Berufsfachschule für Hauswirtschaft	—	—	—	60	79	—	—	—
Fachakademie für Sozialpädagogik	—	—	—	—	—	83	—	—
Fachhochschule (Wirtschaft)	—	—	—	—	—	—	91	—
Universität	—	—	—	—	—	—	89	—
Abendrealschule	—	—	—	—	—	—	—	89
Mean	45	63	70	67	80	83	90	89

whole, the observance of time limits turned out to be a clear indicator of improvement in planning behavior with regard to the given problem.

As shown earlier, the planning problem includes more features of everyday planning than the observance of time limits. We expected that "using the bicycle" and "delegating the bank business" as elements of the task would be taken into account only by older subjects. Table 9.5 shows the proportion of subjects who produced solutions with the three alternatives: (a) correct solution, "on foot"; (b) correct solution, "using the bicycle"; and (c) correct solution, "delegating" (with or without using the bicycle).

Up to the age of the university students, there is an increase in solutions in which the bicycle was used and a slight increase in delegating the bank business. Two groups do not fit this picture. The students in the *Berufsfachschule* produced a higher rate of bicycle solutions and delegation solutions than was expected. This group, consisting of females only, may have been best acquainted with everyday errands.

Organizing errands and buying food are part of the curriculum as well as of the subjects' everyday experience. This may have made this group more sensitive to the reduction of physical effort than the other groups. Students of the *Abendrealschule* produced unexpectedly low percentages of bicycle solutions and delegation solutions. On the other hand, this

Table 9.5. *Percentage of solutions according to the solution alternatives*[a]

School type		Age in years							
		11	14	15	16	17	18–20	20–24	Older
Hauptschule	(a)	68	67	54	—	—	—	—	—
	(b)	29	30	32	—	—	—	—	—
	(c)	3	3	11	—	—	—	—	—
Realschule	(a)	—	64	41	20	—	—	—	—
	(b)	—	30	51	63	—	—	—	—
	(c)	—	4	6	17	—	—	—	—
Gymnasium	(a)	55	58	—	36	50	—	—	—
	(b)	36	31	—	44	41	—	—	—
	(c)	5	10	—	11	7	—	—	—
Berufsfachschule	(a)	—	—	—	29	26	—	—	—
	(b)	—	—	—	61	50	—	—	—
	(c)	—	—	—	10	24	—	—	—
Fachakademie für Sozialpädagogik	(a)	—	—	—	—	—	42	—	—
	(b)	—	—	—	—	—	45	—	—
	(c)	—	—	—	—	—	9	—	—
Fachhochschule (Wirtschaft)	(a)	—	—	—	—	—	—	46	—
	(b)	—	—	—	—	—	—	41	—
	(c)	—	—	—	—	—	—	13	—
Universität	(a)	—	—	—	—	—	—	40	—
	(b)	—	—	—	—	—	—	44	—
	(c)	—	—	—	—	—	—	15	—
Abendrealschule	(a)	—	—	—	—	—	—	—	67
	(b)	—	—	—	—	—	—	—	28
	(c)	—	—	—	—	—	—	—	6

[a]Solution alternatives: (a) on foot (R̸B); (b) using the bicycle (R/B); (c) with delegating (R̸B and R/B̸).

group presented the highest percentage of correct solutions. Because the total number of subjects is low (18), an interpretation of this result would be speculative.

The overall percentage of delegating the bank errand is rather low. This striking result might be attributed to the risk inherent in delegating an errand which is closely related to the main goal of starting a trip the next day.

Table 9.6. *Distribution of correct solution types[a] among four age and/or educational levels (in percentages)*

School type (and age)[b]	Sample (n)	On foot/without delegating							Using the bicycle/without delegating											Delegating				
		1	2	3	4	5	6	Total	8	9	10	11	12	13	14	15	16	17	Total	7	18	19	20	Total
Hauptschule and *Gymnasium* (age 11)	177	11	1	24	—	36	1	73	6	—	11	2	1	—	1	2	—	—	23	3	—	1	—	4
Hauptschule, Realschule, Gymnasium (age 14)	538	7	2	24	—	40	—	73	5	—	11	1	4	—	1	1	—	—	23	2	—	2	—	4
Fachakademie (age 13–20)	247	3	—	22	—	20	—	45	5	—	27	1	11	—	2	—	—	—	46	8	—	1	—	9
Universität (age 20–24)	91	1	1	23	—	19	—	44	7	—	16	—	13	—	2	—	—	—	38	11	—	7	—	18

[a]See Table 9.2.
[b]For an explanation of school type, see Table 9.3.

2. Solution types and developmental levels of planning. In Table 9.2 we presented a list of correct solutions and suggested a developmental sequence of increasingly complex solutions. Table 9.6 shows the percentages for each of 20 possible types of correct solutions. There is a higher proportion of younger subjects giving lower-complexity solutions (e.g., No. 1, Table 9.2). More subjects of the older age group, especially university students, showed higher-order solutions (e.g., Nos. 7 and 19). On the other hand, many university students produced solutions at a rather low level (e.g., Nos. 3 and 5). Some solution types were not chosen at all, probably because they are not very sensible compared with other solutions of the same level. Solution No. 2, for example, does not make very much sense except for the fact that it is correct. If one takes into consideration that the subjects did not have an overview over all possible solutions, the results in Table 9.6 are not surprising. However, the tendency of older and/or higher educated subjects to give higher-order solutions is evidence of a developmental sequence. Of course, this statement implies that experience and school education are necessary conditions for development. Actually, human development depends on the directed influence of the environment toward adaptation and integration into society. This point will be discussed further in section VII. Actually, developmental progress could be proved only by longitudinal studies.

Besides this general information about developmental progress in planning, the results presented so far provide some hints for the first and second processing step in our planning model. (See the first two boxes in Figure 9.1.) The observance of time limits refers to both the goal of completing errands in time (Step 1) and the more general value of time, which becomes more and more important as a regulating principle for planning (Step 2). The developmental progress can be seen under the general regulating principle of cost–benefit calculation (Step 2) in the use of time as a general value or regulating principle, respectively, in recognizing and integrating more aspects (valences, Step 1) of the problem.

B. Results of the individual-run condition

The observed differences regarding the reduction of effort clearly refer to Step 2 of the planning model (see Figure 9.1), showing that a more general principle of cost–benefit analysis is used unexpectedly more by students of a moderate educational level, whose education and experience may be particularly well suited to the task. Thus, experience may guide development in a specific direction such that we have to take into account differential development during adolescence. We return to this point again in section VII. In the following, we try to analyze results with regard to the next steps of planning behavior (Figure 9.1).

1. Seeking and selecting action alternatives. As shown earlier, the action alternatives are given through the structure of the planning problem and consist of (a) the number of combinations of errands; (b) using versus not using the bicycle; (c) delegating versus not delegating the bank business. In the individual-run condition, the subjects had to turn over the "content cards" (containing information about errands) and the "travel-time cards" (containing information about times between two positions). This procedure allows us to draw conclusions about the number of action alternatives taken into account. Three measures are available: (a) the number of content cards used; (b) the number of travel-time cards used; and (c) the number of decisions.

The last point needs further explication. Decision is operationalized through the following criteria: (a) the number of chosen points, which includes repeated and/or corrected choices; (b) the chosen alternatives among "using the bicycle," "on foot," and "delegation," each alternative counted separately. Notice that all chosen alternatives during the solution process are included, resulting in a number of alternatives that can be much higher than the number of steps and alternatives represented by the final solution.

Table 9.7 presents, in the first column, the number of content cards used by three selected samples. The subjects from the *Hauptschule* (15 years old) used the lowest number of content cards, followed by the subjects from the *Fachakademie für Sozialpädagogik* (18–20 years old); the highest number of cards was used by the university students. Obviously, the last group more frequently used the information available for choosing action alternatives.

Similar results were obtained with regard to the number of travel-time cards. As may be seen in the second column of Table 9.7, there is a significant increase in the number of travel-time cards used with increasing age and/or educational level.

Although the data shown in Table 9.7 only suggest, but do not prove, an increasing consideration of action alternatives, a combined measure provides clear evidence for the number of alternatives taken into account. If we compare the number of decisions with the number of travel-time cards used, we get information about whether the subejct has considered more alternatives than the number of final decisions. A quotient of the number of travel-time cards used, divided by the number of

Table 9.7. *Number of content cards used, travel cards used, and testing indices (quotient of travel time cards and decisions)*

Group	No. of content cards used[a]	No. of travel cards used	No. of decisions made[a]	Travel cards/ decisions ratio
Hauptschule	7.7	4.2	6.46	.64
Fachakademie	9.1	7.0	7.16	.99
Universität	9.3	8.6	6.71	1.22

Note: Group differences were significant ($p < .05$) for the number of travel-time cards used and the ratio of travel time cards to decisions ($F = 3.7$ and 4.3, respectively).
[a]Group differences are not significant.

decisions, was calculated for each subject. Results for three selected groups are presented in the last column of Table 9.7.

Scores higher than 1.00 indicate that more alternatives were considered than were brought into the final solution, that is, the number of actual decisions. As is shown in Table 9.7, the sample from the *Hauptschule* lies far below the value of 1.00, indicating that these subjects, on average, neglected at least some possible action alternatives. The university students, on the other hand, show a mean considerably higher than 1.00, and actually examined more alternatives before they made decisions. Of course, this measure does not include alternatives that are not indicated by the use of travel-time cards. But even so, the testing index is not very high, which leads us to the conclusion that by no means all alternatives had been considered by any of the samples. This is in accordance with the finding described earlier that the subjects were not able to get an overview of all possible solutions and of all action alternatives (see Table 9.2).

Because the planning process becomes more difficult as more alternatives are perceived, one may assume that solutions using the bicycle and/ or delegating the bank errand are checked with regard to the time limits less often than solutions on foot. Table 9.8, in which two samples are compared, reveals that the sample of the *Fachakademie für Sozialpädagogik* reaches a mean coefficient of 1.11 with solutions on foot, whereas solutions using the bicycle and delegating the bank errand show a mean coefficient below 1.00. On the other hand, the university sample showed the highest mean testing index with the bicycle solutions. This demonstrates that university students were able to cope with a more complex level of problem solving. Again, a different kind of experience, academic

Table 9.8. *Testing indices of two samples according to type of solution*

Sample	Type of solution	Mean	Variance	t^a	p
Fachakademie	On foot	1.11	0.43		
	Using the bicycle	0.88	0.07		
	Delegating	0.82	0.09		
				4.54	.01
Universität	On foot	1.06	0.19		
	Using the bicycle	1.41	0.05		
	Delegating	1.11	0.27		

[a]Student's *t*-test.

education, might be responsible for this result. University students seem to use a different action structure of planning, which shows that one has to consider differential development, as was mentioned earlier.

2. Testing and decision. The last two steps of planning are separated in the flow chart of Figure 9.1. Actually, in the individual-run condition the use of content cards and travel-time cards serves both the exploration of action alternatives and the testing of choices. Before the subject chooses the next errand to be completed, he or she has to check the time limits. Thus, an increasing use of the cards indicates also an increase in testing choices. The testing indices can also be referred to the decisions. Indices lower than 1.00 show that not all decisions could have been tested. Indices of about 1.00 indicate a sufficient testing of the decisions, because on the average each decision is counterbalanced with a testing action. Indices above 1.00 must be attributed to the consideration of further alternatives.

Thus, results presented in Tables 9.7 and 9.8 demonstrate also an increase of testing activity with increasing age and/or education. The visualization of the testing procedure provides additional information. It turned out that some subjects did not test at all, others tested after having made their decision, and others tested before the decision. On the whole, three main developmental levels were found (Figure 9.2). At the first level, the problem solver picks up a content card (sometimes also a travel-time card) and makes a decision without considering the time needed for reaching the chosen point. At Level 2, the subject makes a decision which is followed by his or her turning over a content card and the associated travel-time card. At Level 3, testing precedes the decision, thus following our model of planning processing (see Figure 9.1). At this

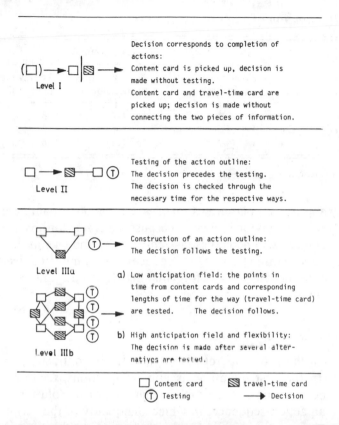

Figure 9.2. Operationalization of planning levels.

level, subjects may represent a low "anticipation field" and test only one step, or they may have a high "anticipation field" and make the decision after having tested several alternatives.

In Table 9.9, the three main levels are represented for three selected groups. As can be seen, the *Universität* sample shows the highest level of testing, followed by the *Fachakademie für Sozialpädagogik* sample, and by the students of the *Hauptschule,* who even show a substantial proportion at the lowest level.

Finally, we should examine briefly the number of decisions made by the subjects (see Table 9.7, column 3). As mentioned, the number of decisions is defined by the steps the subject takes from errand to errand during completion of the planning problem. If the subject does not observe time limits, he or she needs to make only a few decisions. The number of decisions rises as the complexity of the task is perceived but cannot be

Table 9.9. *Distribution of levels of control*

| | | Levels of testing | | |
Sample	*n*	No adequate testing of decision	Testing follows the decision	Testing precedes the decision
Hauptschule	24	7 (29)[a]	14 (58)	3 (13)
Fachakademie	26	1 (4)	12 (46)	13 (50)
Universität	24	1 (4)	5 (21)	18 (75)

[a]Percentages are given in parentheses.

mastered by appropriate planning strategies. On the other hand, the flexibility of planning behavior increases because several solutions are considered. The subject who perceives task complexity and uses at the same time appropriate planning strategies, reduces the number of decisions again because he or she tests before making decisions, thus avoiding wrong decisions.

C. Analysis of the group discussion

The analysis of the protocols results in two clearly contrasting conceptualizations. In the first, planning is aimed at action execution. This means that the meaning of the problem planning or its solution is seen in designing an action sequence, in which the quality of the action is in the foreground. Essential criteria for the evaluation and legitimation are execution-oriented components, such as realization probability, practicality, and plausibility. The representation of the agent's situation or identification with the agent, plays an important role in this. This level is called "execution-oriented planning." Contrasted with this level is the second level, where construction is the central idea, with an abstraction from concrete action execution. The main construction criterion is "time" as objective control-specific, and instance- and errand-specific dimensions – for example, keeping to allotted times, and calculation of expenditure. At this level, the information can be reduced to the dimensions implied in the problem, so that, as principles or values, they are included in the planning. This level we call "conceptual planning." Considering a possible identification of the planning level as a cognitive level, parallels to Piaget's levels of concrete and formal operations can be seen. Execution of action-oriented planning means that the concrete carrying through of action, which is directly subject to the alleged reality, is anticipated. Within the frame of the conceptual planning, however, hypothetical solution-constructs are possible (cf. Flavell, 1977); they are oriented toward formal criteria and are first subjected to a reality test in the light of examining the action quality.

During the phase of the group discussion in which subjects presented their solutions and reasoning, the characteristics of such levels are recognizable. As already mentioned, structural characteristics are especially emphasized in the aspect of the communication of planning intention. It is clear that the two levels are to be understood as ideal types. There is an area of overlap in which elements from both levels are to be found.

An attempt at clarification of the levels is made by the following examples of individual solution conceptions:

1. *Execution-oriented planning* (Hauptschule; *Group 2-7*).

B: Yes, hm. So now my solution. I just came home, well, and then I thought I'm not that stupid and specially go have my bike fixed.

A: But you said that already.

B: Let me finish talking, okay? I didn't go to the bike repairman, otherwise it'd take eternally long till I get my bike back again and fixed my bike right away myself, I quickly cycled to the supermarket, brought the cans, and then I put my bag on the carrier, yes.

D: But, now, I only want to ask, how long did you take till you had fixed your bike? What kind of damage was it? We don't know that.

B: How long could I have taken?

D: But surely longer than the bicycle repairman, because the bicycle repairman can do it better than you.

A: He's a pro.

D: Much longer.

B: But why? He had to fix another bike, then he said he needs an hour for it, because I changed a wheel, changed tires.

D: So, what did you do, put a tube in or what?

A: Probably the tire was worn out.

D: Or put a new tire on.

B: Yes, yes, put a new tire on.

D: Yes, that takes about 15 minutes.

B: In any case, I took that long. Then I cycled to the supermarket and then to the bank. I had my bag on the carrier and then I also had the side bags, I also put all the stuff in there. Then I went to the bank, fetched the money, and then to my meeting point; there I had a little chat with my girlfriend, and then I said, "Well, now I have to go," cycled to the train station, gave the papers to my boss. Then I was a bit out of breath and slowly cycled back to my apartment.

As the example shows, the representation of the action orientation is placed in the foreground; we are informed in detail what was done, what was thought and what was said while doing it.

2. Conceptual planning (Universität; *Group 16*). When subjects who used conceptual planning described their solutions in the group discussion, they reported the sequence of their route, pointing out single steps, but also explained the reasoning behind their overall plan.

In the following example (*Universität,* Group 16), the subject validates his or her solution by demonstrating that it matches the imposed conditions.

> A: Okay now. From the apartment the exact time was 4:20 p.m. and then I start from the bicycle repairman – the bicycle takes 60 minutes. And after I had looked at these 60 minutes and only 5 minutes to stay, I thought to myself, it seemed all too lengthy to me. That's why I immediately thought, I didn't calculate it, but I thought that I won't even go to the bicycle repairman, because I don't even have that much time. If I go there from 4:20 p.m. until 6:00 p.m., so that's why I immediately went to the supermarket in the first place, because – this with the bike. Then I have 15 minutes, yes? And then, I'm 21, 15 minutes, makes 35, plus 6 minutes, 4:41 p.m. And I didn't go to the bank but did that by phone. So, I called beforehand and must be home again from 5:00 until 5:15 p.m. yes? So this is the hint with the bank. So I·go back again – 4:41 p.m. we said – again 15 minutes add up to 4:56 p.m., so I'm there at 5:00 p.m. (A) and I'm in the apartment until 5:15 p.m.. From 5:15 p.m. onward, I can go to the meeting point, yes? There are 21 minutes, 5:35 p.m., :36, so I'm at the meeting point at 5:36 p.m., and wait – so I saw to it that I'll be with my girlfriend or boyfriend early (laughter). That means from 5 – when did we say?
>
> All: 5:36 p.m.
>
> A: 5:36 p.m. to 5:50 p.m. So, I thought to myself that due to the course that I don't do the bank and also skip the bicycle repairman, I'm here earlier and have more time here – till 5:50 p.m., and then from 5:50 p.m. onward I'll easily make it to the station – 15 minutes, that makes it 6:05. That's okay, the boss only arrives at 6:08 p.m. And then I go back, yes? So this was my way. I avoided the bicycle shop because it seemed such a long way to me and then I saw to it that I'd be at the meeting point as soon as possible. That's it.

If one inspects the phase of the group discussion in which the members of a group are supposed to agree upon a commonly acceptable solution, it can be seen that discussion partners who are at the conceptual level are better able to reach an optimal solution. They do not ignore concrete content, but treat it as less important than the formal structure of the problem. In contrast to those employing execution-oriented planning, they considered more aspects simultaneously, exchanged more points of view, and produced more integration of dimensions. Connected with this is the possibility of oscillation between the concrete representations and abstraction, that is, one can consider concrete actions and things but also see them abstractly as "time" or "expenditure."

We found more clear-cut cases of conception-oriented planning among subjects with increasing age or education and, conversely, more clear-cut cases of execution-oriented planning among younger subjects and those with less education (fewer years in school as well as less academically oriented education).

VII. Discussion

First, we have to check whether the results really show evidence of developmental progress. Because higher levels of planning are combined with age and/or education, one may argue that the observed differences are due only to experience factors. In order to resolve this dilemma, one must have in mind that the developmental argument is based on the developmental logic that underlies the different levels of problem solving in the planning problem. Each lower level is the necessary (but not sufficient) condition for the level above it. The task analysis of the planning problem revcaled that higher levels can be characterized through a higher number of single operations together with a higher grade of coordination of those operations. Therefore, a higher developmental level of planning can be attributed to a subject's performance at a higher strategy and/or solution level. Needless to say, experience and age are conditions for this kind of development. Results show different courses of development. University students seem to produce better strategies of planning, that is, "conceptual planning." Subjects of the post-secondary school that trains housekeepers tend to produce solutions with low effort, which use the bicycle (see Table 9.5). Thus, in contrast to a one-directional developmental approach, a multidirectional description of development of planning seems to be more appropriate. Socialization through education and vocational training channels individual development toward specific outcomes. Qualitatively different courses and results of development remain, even with the general view of cognitive development as restructuring and coordination of operations (Flavell & Wohlwill, 1969; Piaget, 1977).

As was stated in the introduction, the planning process cannot be analyzed at a "molecular" level. On the other hand, the "molar" level of planning according to the steps of the flow chart can be sufficiently inferred from the data presented in the previous section. A computer simulation might be useful only if it contains some essential features of human planning. Our results provide an empirical basis for computer simulation.

The results also show some evidence for another phenomenon which was brought to attention only recently. Problem solving and intellectual capacity seem to be associated with the structure of knowledge (Chi, 1984; Chi, Feltovich, & Glaser, 1981; Keil, 1979). More sophisticated knowledge includes also more effective strategies of problem solving. For example, an individual with detailed knowledge and experience in planning and execution of everyday errands may consider cost–benefit calculation, whereas an individual with little knowledge and experience may neglect important features of planning and use simpler strategies. Actually, we found a rather high level of solutions in individuals having a low level of education, namely, in the home economics group. They took into consideration the weight of the cans to be carried and chose more often than other groups the shortest possible distance.

On the other hand, university students showed the highest level of planning strategies. Thus, they might have been more sophisticated at the stages of seeking and selecting alternatives and testing, whereas the samples from the *Berufsfachschule* and *Fachakademie für Sozialpädagogik* (vocational schools) showed more sophistication at Stage 1 and 2 (goal determination and regulating the planning procedure by the general principle of cost–benefit calculation).

Another comment refers to the relation between models of planning processing and actual planning behavior. Our model, following the tradition of psychological research on thinking, is based on the conception of a rational problem solver who proceeds more or less in a logically consistent manner step by step. However, we have to take into account that during the planning process the individual may switch from a high-level strategy to a low-level strategy or may make incidental decisions that cannot be traced back to a planning rationale. Our model also suggests a top-down process of planning rather than a bottom-up process; that is, the model assumes that the problem solver proceeds logically from prior and more general steps to subsequent ones. The Hayes-Roths (1979) emphasize a multidirectional process of planning that includes both top-down and bottom-up processing. However, although our model is preliminarily conceived as a top-down process in the flow chart (see Figure 9.1), it also includes bottom-up processing; for example, beginning with decisions, which are tested subsequently, followed by considering other action alternatives, which in turn may lead to new goals. Again, we have to keep in mind that we can draw conclusions only at a molar level rather than at a molecular level.

The most appropriate procedure for observing multidirectional planning is the group-discussion condition. Actually, this condition revealed processing in both the bottom-up and top-down directions as well as "incremental" planning (Hayes-Roth & Hayes-Roth, 1979), the latter referring to the fact that individuals rarely produce complete plans but rather show incremental steps of planning, which finally may or may not lead to a complete plan.

As a further point, we have to consider the relationship between planning behavior and executive behavior. The execution entailing monitoring and guiding the single steps of a plan is not taken into account in our study. In everyday life, there usually are continuous interactions between planning behavior and executive behavior. For example, in many cases during task completion, unexpected obstacles arise that force the individual to change his or her plans. Thus, once again the question arises whether the planning problem has ecological validity (Bronfenbrenner, 1979). If we look only at overt behavior in real-life situations, our results might be misleading, because they do not include the phase of execution. On the other hand, results provide evidence for the process of internalization of important features in our culture, for example, using tools, delegating errands, and considering time limits. Furthermore, the results provide evidence for anticipatory cognitive activity, which is indeed an essential part of human behavior.

Further studies should examine the interaction between planning processes and the execution of planning. One approach, we would emphasize in this context, is the notion of two components of behavior (better: "activity") advocated by Galperin (1957), Luria (1979), and Vygotsky (1978). These authors distinguished between orienting actions and executive actions; both are involved in any human activity and alternate with each other.

An appropriate design may consist in presenting a planning problem in real-life situations or under role-playing conditions where the subjects not only have to plan the single steps but also have to complete the errands by overt action. Obstacles can be introduced under controlled conditions and adaptive planning behavior can be recorded.

Last but not least, some interventional aspects should be discussed. If one holds the position that planning activity is an essential part of human life, the improvement of planning also incorporates better coping styles. The anticipation and organization of future events enables the individual to cope more effectively with the environment.

Practice in planning can be realized in two main ways. First, the individual can gain knowledge about planning. For example, the individual may learn several solutions and strategies for organizing and completing everyday tasks. Second, the individual can be trained with concrete tasks of planning execution. He or she can be exposed to projects that have to be planned and realized afterwards. Shared planning and executive activity within a group appears to be an effective and ecologically valid method of training.

VIII. Conclusions

The study described in this chapter focused on planning activities in everyday life situations. A planning problem was constructed which represents both essential features of modern culture and important segments of the adolescent environment.

The advantage of this method seems to be that it realizes the notion of Cole (1982) and Whiting (1980) of development as being context- or setting-related. Thus, our procedure fits well into a "cultural practice theory" (Cole, 1982), resisting the separation of the individuals from the environment. It also was shown that this kind of proceeding does not necessarily mean a loss of experimental control or of "hard data." We were able to follow the individual's information processing and to test special hypotheses.

Although the specifity of the planning problem presented in this chapter was accentuated, it is obvious that the planning performance obtained by our method has much to do with planning in general, especially with planning in everyday life. General features of the obtained planning behavior are:

1. Division of a means – end sequence into single steps
2. Arrangement of an optimal sequence of the analyzed steps
3. Evaluation processes of both the goal and the steps of planning
4. Inclusion of essential aspects of everyday planning, such as the completion of errands, using machines, and delegating errands

Therefore, it can be claimed that the results presented in this chapter may show to some extent both external validity and, to use an expression of Bronfenbrenner (1979), ecological validity, if we consider point (4).

If we summarize the three aspects of action theory chosen as one basis of our research, planning seems to be an excellent example for proving the usefulness of this approach. The first aspect, *goal directedness and conscious activity of an agent,* is the basic condition of planning. Actually, it is defined through anticipation of actions and sequences of action which may lead to a certain goal. In the previous study, the goal was clearly defined by instruction. Conscious activity could be inferred from the individual-run condition and from the group discussion conditions.

The second aspect, *object relatedness,* was operationalized through the main goal and the subgoal of the planning problem. The errands, as well as the bicycle condition, represent objects toward which activity is related.

The third aspect, *values and valences,* is included in both the task conditions and the model of planning processing. In the latter, values refer to superordinate principles and orientations such as cost–benefit calculation and consideration of time limits, whereas valences refer to objects in the planning task such as the errands. The action approach to planning is even more interesting for long-term processes that play an essential role in the individual's own engagement in his or her development. From this point of view, individuals become directors of their own development (Lerner, 1982; Lerner & Busch-Rossnagel, 1981; Mischel, 1977).

It is our impression that long-term planning activity might be quite different from that kind of activity we investigated through the planning problem. Studies about developmental tasks, especially the investigation of the conception of adulthood, show that other cognitive activities are involved than those found in everyday planning behavior (Dreher & Oerter, 1986).

References

Argyle, M. (1976). Predictive and generative rules models of P × S interactions. In D. Magnusson & N. S. Endler (Eds.), *Personality at the crossroads: Current issues in interactional psychology.* Hillsdale, NJ: Erlbaum.

Bronfenbrenner, U. (1979). *The ecology of human development.* Cambridge, MA: Harvard University Press.

Chi, M. T. H. (1984). Interactive roles of knowledge and strategies in development. In S. Chipman, J. Segal, & R. Glaser (Eds.), *Thinking and learning skills: Current research and open questions* (Vol. 2). Hillsdale, NJ: Erlbaum.

Chi, M. T. H., Feltovich, P. J., & Glaser, R. (1981). Categorization and representation of physics problems by experts and novices. *Cognitive Science, 5,* 121–152.

Cole, M. (1983). Culture and cognitive development. In W. Kessen (Ed.), *Handbook of child psychology: History, theory and methods.* New York: Wiley.

Cranach, M. V., Kalbermatten, U., Indermühle, K., & Gugler, B. (1980). *Zielgerichtetes Handeln.* Bern: Hans Huber.

Dreher, E. (1980). *Handlungsplanung als Komponente kognitiver Sozialisation.* Dissertation, Augsburg.

Dreher, E., & Oerter, R. (1986). Children's and adolescents' conceptions of adulthood: The changing view of a crucial developmental task. In R. K. Silbereisen, K. Eyferth, & G. Rudinger (Eds.), *Development as action in context.* Berlin: Springer.

Fahlmann, S. E. (1974). A planning system for robot construction tasks. *Artificial Intelligence, 5,* 1–49.

Flavell, J. H., & Wohlwill, J. F. (1969). Formal and functional aspects of cognitive development. In D. Elkind & J. H. Flavell (Eds.), *Studies in cognitive development.* New York: Oxford University Press.

Galperin, P. (1957). Dependence of the motor habit on the type of orientation toward a task. Presentations of APN RSTSR, No. 2.

Hacker, W. (1978). *Allgemeine Arbeits- und Ingenieurpsychologie* (2nd ed.). Stuttgart: Huber.

Hayes-Roth, B., & Hayes-Roth, F. (1979). A cognitive model of planning. *Cognitive Science, 3,* 275–310.

Keil, F. C. (1979). *Semantic and conceptual development: An ontological perspective.* Cambridge, MA: Harvard University Press.

Koch, H. (1961). *Betriebliche Planung.* Wiesbaden: Betriebswirtschaftlicher Verlag.

Kohlberg, L. (1974). *Zur Kognitiven Entwicklung des Kindes.* Frankfurt: Suhrkamp.

Kreutzer, M. A., Leonard, C., & Flavell, J. H. (1975). An interview study of children's knowledge about memory. *Monographs of the Society for Research in Child Development, 40* (serial No. 159).

Kruse, L. (1972). Gruppen und Gruppenzugehörigkeit. In C. F. Graumann (Ed.), *Handbuch der Psychologie* (Bd. 7, pp. 1539–1593). Göttingen: Hogrefe.

Labov, W. (1970). The study of language in its social context. *Studium Generale, 23,* 30–87.

Lenk, H. (1978). Handlung als Interpretationskonstrukt. In H. Lenk, (Ed.), *Handlungstheorien interdisziplinär* (Bd. 2). München: W. Fink.

Leontjev, A. N. (1977). *Tätigkeit, BewuBtsein, Persönlichkeit.* Stuttgart: Klett.

Lerner, R. M. (1982). Children and adolescents as producers of their own development. *Developmental Review, 2,* 342–370.

Lerner, R. M., & Busch-Rossnagel, N. A. (1981). Individuals as producers of their development: Conceptual and empirical basis. In R. M. Lerner & N. A. Busch-Rossnagel, (Eds.), *Individuals as producers of their development: A life-span perspective.* New York: Academic Press.

Lewin, K. (1939). Field theory and experiment in social psychology. *American Journal of Sociology, 44,* 868–897.

Little, B. R. (1980). Personal projects: A rationale and method for investigation. Department of Psychology, Carlton University, Ottawa/Ontario, Canada. Unpublished manuscript.

Luria, A. R. (1979). *The making of mind.* Edited by M. Cole & S. Cole. Cambridge, MA: Harvard University Press.

Magnusson, D., & Endler, N. S. (Eds.) (1977). *Personality at the crossroads: Current issues in interactional psychology.* Hillsdale, NJ: Erlbaum.

Mischel, W. (1977). On the future of personality measurement. *American Psychologist, 32,* 246–254.

Oerter, R., Dreher, E., & Dreher, M. (1977). *Kognitive Sozialisation und subjektive Struktur.* München: Oldenbourg.

Oerter, R. (1981a). Cognitive socialization during adolescence. *International Journal of Behavioral Development, 4,* 61–76.

Oerter, R. (1981b). Development of the structure of action during late childhood and adolescence: An application of action theory. Paper presented at the Sixth Biennial Meeting of the International Society for the Study of Behavioral Development in Toronto, Canada, August.

Piaget, J. (1977). *The development of thought: Equilibration of cognitive structures.* New York: Viking.

Rubinstein, S. L. (1977). *Sein und BewuBtsein. Die Stellung des Psychischen im allgemeinen Zusammenhang der Erscheinungen in der materiellen Welt.* Berlin/DDR: Akademie Verlag.

Sacerdoti, E. D. (1975). A structure for plans and behavior. Technical Note 109, Stanford Research Insitute, Menlo Park, CA, August.

Sader, M. (1976). *Psychologie der Gruppe.* München: Juventa.

Thalberg, I. (1977). *Perception, emotion and action: A component approach.* Oxford: Oxford Univ. Press.

Volpert, W. (1974). *Handlungsstrukturanalyse als Beitrag zur Qualifikationsforschung.* Köln: Pahl-Rugenstein.

Vygotsky, L. S. (1978). *Mind in society: The development of higher psychological processes.* Edited and translated by M. Cole, V. John-Steiner, S. Scribner, & E. Souberman. Cambridge, MA: Harvard University Press.

Whiting, B. B. (1980). Culture and social behavior: A model for the development of social behavior. *Ethos, 8,* 95–116.

10 Cognitive and social variables in the plan of action

Louis Oppenheimer

I. Introduction

In the previous chapters of this volume, an outline has been presented of theoretical views on the development of planning competencies. The aims of this chapter are, after a short discussion of several action theoretical concepts, to present a theoretical model for plans placed within a developmental framework, and to describe a number of studies that were based on action theory thinking and the model.

A. Definitions and basic concepts

The concept of planning presupposes directionality: Plans are functional only if they have a purpose. This rather simple and straightforward assumption is derived from a large body of literature from various fields including philosophy, economics, sociology, and psychology. The integration of elements from these writings in the mid-1970s resulted in a revival of action theoretical thinking in Western, Continental Europe. On the one hand, attempts were made to formulate theoretical models (Dreher & Oerter, chapter 9, this volume; Oppenheimer, 1979) and, on the other hand, models of analysis were developed that predominantly center on concrete actions representing the "interactions (i.e., *Verknüpfungen*) between environment and individual" (Eckensberger & Silbereisen, 1980, p. 39). The latter definition of an action introduces the whole scale of psychological phenomena because actions *deal with* individuals, occur in space and time, and are *executed by* individuals. From a theo-

The ideas presented in this chapter are the result of the discussions with many bright and enthusiastic students of which I want to thank Loes van der Griend, Jan Heller, Jet van Santen, Hanneke Veerman, and Roderik van der Wilk. Also thanks are due to Sarah Friedman, Ellin Scholnick, and Rod Cocking, who with unbelievable patience succeeded in creating order where chaos was.

retical point of view, actions represent the interactions between the *external* social world and the *internal,* or perceived social world in which subjects are seen as active constructors of their own social knowledge (Oppenheimer, 1979).

The feature of directionality in planning implies a relationship between planning and goals. This contingency becomes more apparent if the more operational definitions of actions within the action theory context are considered: Actions are thought to be "future-oriented, purposeful, and goal-directed" and are "potentially, fully conscious" for the actor (cf. Hollis, 1977; Kreitler & Kreitler, chapter 4, this volume). Hence, goals are placed in the future and, consequently, pull actions rather than push them from behind as causes do (Hollis, 1977). This teleological relationship between goals and actions is one of the salient characteristics of the action theory approach. Because we tend to attach affective values to future goals, we are "motivated" to attain these goals: We are prepared to spend energy and time to reach these goals. It is assumed that the mental goal-representation and the related motivation to reach it prompt planning, leading to the intent to act (Oppenheimer & Heller, 1984). The latter implies an almost exclusive emphasis on *intentional* actions. The often raised criticism addressing the problem of the existence of apparently many nonintentional actions is, among others, addressed by Enç. (1975). Enç suggests distinguishing between "reason actions" (i.e., actions directed toward a goal) and "non-reason actions" in order to interpret actions as complexes consisting of more fundamental and/or simple actions that are related to each other by a reason action.

From this definition of actions as intentional (i.e., fully conscious) and goal directed, it can be postulated that the grounds on which an intention can be assigned to individuals are the "intensity or elaboration of *planning,* which appears to have an action of a certain sort as a consequence" (Louche, 1966, p. 116; author's italics). Planning, then, refers to the intermediate stage between the *motivation to act* and the *intent to act* and is referred to by most action theorists as the *plan of action* (henceforth, the plan). In other words, the constituting factor of an action is not the real implementation of the action, acting itself, but the *conscious anticipation* of the action in a plan, that is, the final relation of a positively evaluated goal of action with possible methods to reach it and their causally determined effects (Reinshagen, 1977). As such, planning exceeds simple anticipatory infant responses, and research in problem solving and related planning (cf. Klahr & Robinson, 1981; Shure & Spivack, 1972) become pragmatic instances of goal-directed and intentional planning.

A plan can also be regarded as a regulatory principle referring to three different stages inherent in action: (a) the beginning or triggering of output programming, (b) the course of action, or the regulation of the successive steps present in the plan, and (c) the end-stage, that is, the attainment of the goal, or the completion of an action (Boesch, 1976; Kreitler & Kreitler, 1976).

In the literature dealing with planning abilities of children and adults, an imbalance can be observed between studies directed at these planning abilities and those directed at plan execution skills. Questions pertaining to these latter skills refer to how a plan is monitored and controlled, and how errors in planning are corrected, or, as Pea (1982) has noted, to "how planners integrate the processes of plan construction and execution" (p. 13).

1. The plan. The description of a plan, including the final relationship between a goal and the methods to reach it, as well as the anticipated effects of the methods, possible obstacles, and alternative courses of action, is schematically represented in Figure 10.1. The arrows in the model refer to relationships among the various elements. Thus the relation between the methods and the goal is final or "teleonomic," that is, the goal pulls the actions: The goal determines the amount of energy (i.e., motivation) an individual is willing to exert in order to reach the goal. The methods, however, cause either intended or nonintended effects, which will be intentional or functional with respect to the goal or the methods, respectively.

From the model it can be derived that the degree of sophistication or elaboration of planning will depend on various abilities of the planner. According to Pea (1982; see also Pea & Hawkins, chapter 7, this volume) "planning is a complex form of symbolic action that consists of consciously preconceiving a sequence of actions that will be sufficient for achieving a goal" (p. 6). From a structural developmental point of view such an assumption implies that the planner (a) has to possess a symbolic system enabling him or her to mentally construe plans; (b) should be able to order sequences of events temporally, hence (c) will have to evidence a certain level of cause–consequence and consequence–cause thinking, that is, causal thinking; (d) has to be able to evaluate the effectiveness of the successive steps in the plan; (e) should be aware of the prevailing norms or rules in the society or social environment in which the plan will be executed, and (f) should possess evaluative abilities with respect to the situation (cf. Shure & Spivack, 1972). The first three of these requirements are thought to be fundamental to and necessary for planning as a separate ability. The final three requirements concern the effectiveness,

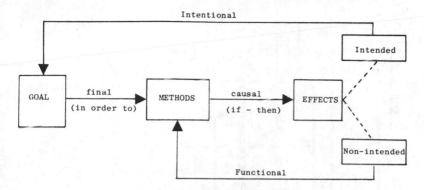

Figure 10.1. A schematic representation of the plan with the different types of relationships among the various components (see also Eckensberger & Silbereisen, 1980).

moral acceptability, and feasibility of the plan, respectively, and contribute to the sophisication of the plan. In order to regulate plan execution, the plan has to be flexible and accessible to changes. The assumption that the plan should be open to accommodation and assimilation (Kreitler & Kreitler, 1976) places the plan in direct relation with the intellectual (i.e., operational) system (Lidz & Lidz, 1976).

Equally important within this context is the assumption that each act within the sequence of actions leading to goal attainment will change the environment in which the act occurs; at least it will have certain effects as a consequence (Von Wright, 1976). If everything goes well, no need for modifications in the overall plan will be necessary and the goal will be attained without any direct problems for the actor. The processes taking place can be described as matching procedures between the real events and the anticipated events in the plan based on feedback processes (Miller, Galanter, & Pribram, 1960). If, however, effects or events occur that were not anticipated or taken account of (i.e., nonpredicted effects which can be either intended, or nonintended), the plan will have to be changed. Such unanticipated effects may be the source of conflicts whenever they prevent goal attainment.

B. A developmental perspective

The model presented in Figure 10.1 offers a schematic outline of theoretical relationships and their types among the various components inherent in planning. Although a number of tentative entries for the exploration

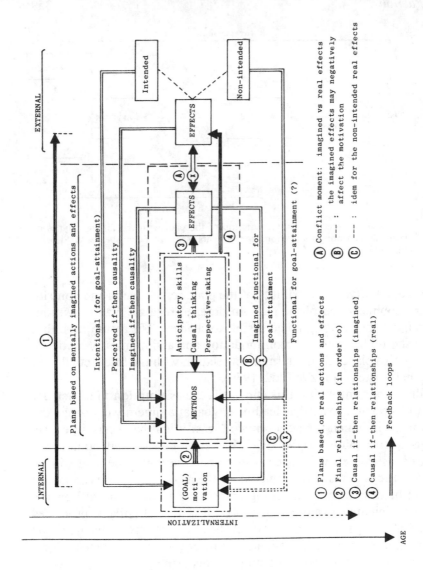

Figure 10.2. A schematic representation of the plan within a developmental framework, including internal and external aspects of the plan, types of relationships among the various components, as well as the feedback loops and the possible conflict moments.

of the elaboration or sophistication of plans have been mentioned, the model presented needs to be specified further and placed within a developmental context (see Figure 10.2).

The first component subject to developmental changes and mentioned in the previous section is that of symbolic representation. Without the ability of mentally representing sequences of events or actions, planning as a mental competence is difficult to conceive. Planning requires "an all-embracing representation," which is possible only if the various events can be simultaneously represented and are released from the temporal and spatial characteristics of the concrete action. Accordingly, Piaget (1950) noted that with sensorimotor intelligence "actions thus involve only very short distances between subject and object . . . it never concerns anything but responses actually carried out and real objects" (p. 121). Conceptual and symbolic thinking enables the child to go beyond these short distances and physical pathways and opens ways to reflective thinking. Three conditions are assumed to be essential in order to make this transition from sensorimotor to reflective thinking:

Firstly an increase in speed allowing the knowledge of the successive phases of an action to be moulded into one simultaneous whole. Next, an awareness, not simply of the desired results of an action, but its actual mechanisms, thus enabling the search for the solution to be combined with a consciousness of its nature. Finally, an increase in distances, enabling actions affecting real entities to be extended by symbolic actions affecting symbolic representations and thus going beyond the limits of near space and time. (Piaget, 1950, p. 121)

These assumptions imply that goal-directed actions of young children will be predominantly unreflected and direct one-step actions; the outcomes of such actions will determine the nature of the next step. In the course of development, such actions will become symbolically represented and included in larger integrated complexes of actions, the plan. Hence, a child who shouts at another child in order to get a turn on a tricycle demonstrates such a direct and concrete action. Depending on whether such an action is successful, alternative actions could be to (a) try to hit the other child, (b) pull him off the tricycle, or (c) get mother. The availability of these actions in a repertoire of actions is thought to be the result of internalization by imitation. These actions, then, are symbolically represented in the child. Additional cognitive abilities are also necessary: "The construction of transitive, associative and reversible operations . . . a conversion of . . . egocentricity into a system of relations and classes that are decentralised with respect to the self" will make reflective thinking (i.e., planning) possible. This decentralization process is assumed to occupy the whole of early childhood (i.e., approximately until the age of six years; Piaget, 1950, pp. 122–123).

In this chapter, therefore, planning is assumed to develop from the inability to plan mentally, to make plans based on mental considerations and evaluations, consisting of progessively more subgoals and concerning longer periods of time.

Besides including the essential conditions necessary for planning, plans should be functional in relation to goal attainment. The functionality or effectiveness of a plan or its separate actions can be assessed only if the plan can be mentally simulated (Pea, 1982). In other words, reflection on a plan will require the mental execution of that plan. Such execution or simulation skills are assumed to be based on progressing competencies in anticipatory movements, their end states and their inverses (Piaget & Inhelder, 1971). The progressive flexibility of these anticipatory skills will be reflected in the incorporation of possible obstacles in the plan which could hinder or prevent goal attainment, and in countermeasures to remove, bypass, or prevent these obstacles (i.e., alternative courses of action).

In Figure 10.2, the plan is placed in a developmental framework, by which distinctions are made among (a) internal mental planning and external, real effects; (b) the types of relationships and feedback loops among the various components, both internal and external; and (c) internal and external conflict moments (i.e., A, B, and C in Figure 10.2) which may affect the motivation to reach the goal.

A second component subject to developmental processes refers to competencies in the understanding of causal relationships. The more accurate the imagined "if–then" thinking, the smaller the possible conflict between the imagined and perceived effects of particular actions intended for goal attainment. This conflict moment (i.e., A in Figure 10.2) is characteristic for the Piagetian internal–external conflict as a fundamental source for cognitive development. This conflict moment represents the discrepancy between imagined effects of accommodative operational structures and the real effects of manipulative actions on the environment (Furth, 1981), which may result in progressive structural accommodations, that is, operational development. Similarly, within the social or action domain, discrepancies between expected or imagined and real effects of one's actions may result in the development of new actions or methods, which may also evidence a progressive level of effectiveness. Thus a child may develop the method to share the tricycle by turns after the experience of failure by the method of pulling or hitting.

Despite the above, it should be evident that discrepancies between expected and real outcomes of methods to reach a goal may have far-reaching consequences for (a) the motivation to reach a particular goal, or (b) the plan and its included methods. Nonintended effects may be either positive or negative with respect to goal attainment. In the former case, no modifications of the plan will be required, whereas the motivation to reach the goal, that is, to further implement the planned sequence of actions or events, may increase. In the latter case, however, the negative nonintended effects may reduce the motivation for goal attainment, that is, may diminish the attractiveness of the goal, or may lead to a complete reconsideration of the initial plan (see also the beginning of this section).

In addition to this understanding of the meaning of feedback related to the effects of one's actions, the nature of the methods to attain a goal will also depend on the level of knowledge about the social and nonsocial environment. The perspective-taking ability, that is, the ability to place oneself in the position of another individual and infer his or her view, perspective, or attitude toward particular events, is here taken as illustrative of such social-cognitive knowledge. The ability to evaluate the opportunities to act offered by the nonsocial environment can be considered an example of such cognitive knowledge.

On the basis of the preceding account, it is possible to discern two separate but interrelated research questions concerning plans and planning. The first concerns the processes by which such plans are generated and elaborated. The second deals with the ways in which goals (and plans intended to reach them) are integrated with alternative plans of one's own or of others. Each of these issues will be taken up in turn in the sections that follow.

II. Planning and plans: study 1

Planning is considered to be goal directed and to occur in the intermediate stage between the motivation to act and the intent to act. Although planning refers to a mental activity, it was assumed (a) to be potentially fully conscious to the actor, and (b) to result in a plan including the various relationships between a goal, methods to attain this goal, the (mentally) anticipated effects of these methods, possible obstacles that may prevent goal attainment, and subsequent alternative courses of action (i.e., methods). These different characteristics refer to distinct components or ability-complexes of a plan. The first component that can be dis-

cerned alludes to the competence in generating methods with, as quali-
fying features, their levels of effectiveness or complexity. The second
component is thought to concern the ability to evaluate mentally the
effectiveness of methods. The latter skill is assumed to codetermine
which method will be employed to attain the goal. Earlier (Section I.B),
I noted that the ability to evaluate the effectiveness or "functionality" of
a plan and/or its methods depends on anticipatory competencies. These
anticipatory competencies are expected to be reflected by the "ease" with
which children are able to offer alternative courses of action if the first
method cannot be realized after the occurrence of either a physical or
social obstacle. In other words, the selection of a particular sequence of
actions based on the evaluated effectiveness of the method presupposes
a close relation among the method-generation component and the evaluative component. Finally, the choice of a method for goal attainment
will be affected by knowledge about the goals of other individuals. Competencies in inferring the goals of *others* should not necessarily form an
integral part of the plan itself, but they may be related to the general ability to plan.

In a study by Oppenheimer and Veerman (1980), which was primarily
descriptive rather than predictive and sought only to develop a means of
documentation rather then to assess the behavioral consequences of
plans, these aspects of planning in social contexts were explored. The
methodology adopted in this study roughly corresponded to that
employed by Shure and Spivack (1972), who also stressed method–goal
thinking. According to these authors, the development of a plan can be
defined as "an ability to carefully plan, step by step, means to reach a
stated goal" (Shure & Spivack, 1972, p. 348), and includes reference to
the forethought which is required to forestall and develop alternative
routes that circumvent potential obstacles to one's goal.

A.   Methods

In order to gain insight into ways in which children develop and employ
plans, six short social episodes were developed, illustrated by pictures
that depicted events in which the story characters were required to reach
a goal (see Table 10.1 for a short description of the six events).

These stories were presented to 30 first, third, and fifth graders in a
pilot study in which they were required to describe ways in which the
respective goals could be attained. After an answer was obtained a second
solution was asked for. These methods were then judged by 10 independent adult raters for the degree of plan effectiveness. Consequently, effec-

Table 10.1. *A short description of the six events employed by Oppenheimer and Veerman (1980).*

1. Recently, Marjolein moved with her parents to a new neighborhood. She very much wants to make friends with the children in the neighborhood.
2. At a birthday party, three children take away all the cakes, and the other children get nothing although they very much want to have some.
3. Rob is busy collecting hay; he is not yet finished. Dark clouds appear in the sky, and he is afraid it will rain. He wants to bring the hay as quickly as possible to the barn.
4. Two children want to take some apples from the apple tree. However, the farmer whose tree it is, is looking at them.
5. Marja wants to buy a present for her mother whose birthday is tomorrow. However, she has no money.
6. Two children travel to some place by bus. As they arrive, however, they realize that they have left their bag in the bus.

tive and ineffective methods were obtained for each event. For the first story, the most effective method was: "She should go outside to the playing children, tell them her name, and ask whether she might join the play." The method judged to be the most ineffective was: "She should go outside and sit in front of the house." Two methods somewhere in between these two extremes were: "She should ask her mother to go outside with her to the playing children and ask whether she might play with them" (i.e., moderately effective), and "She should make friends at school" (i.e., barely effective). Based on these methods and their classification in terms of effectiveness, obstacles were developed that would prevent the implementation of proposed methods with the purpose of eliciting alternative methods. Such obstacles were: "She is afraid to ask the children," "Her mother is not at home," and "Her school is not in the neighborhood" for the effective, moderately, and barely effective methods, respectively.

On the basis of this information the stories were also reconstructed so that four different questions could be asked for each social event referring to (a) the preferred methods for reaching the stated goal and an alternative method after the introduction of the obstacle, (b) the effectiveness and (c) the ineffectiveness of the methods, and (d) the goals of the story characters depicted in the episode after the presentation of a sequence of actions derived from the most effective method.

In the main study, 105 children from the first, third, and fifth grades (mean ages 6;8, 9;0, and 11;1 years, respectively) were presented with the episodes and corresponding questions. Because the four types of questions were dependent, a Latin square design was employed, such that each child was presented with all six stories, but each with a different question. This design made it possible to analyze the relation between method generation, the ability to infer the goals of others, and the judgments of the effectiveness and ineffectiveness of the methods within each age group. A comparison over age groups in regard to developmental differences was also possible through such a design.

B. Results

The data of this study indicated that at the age of 9 years children are able to generate methods for reaching goals that adults judge to be effective. The major developmental difference was found to lie between the 7- and 9-year olds. The alternative methods that were offered after an obstacle to the first method was introduced showed an identical pattern, although the level of effectiveness of the second answer was significantly lower among the first- and third-grade children. The fifth graders were able to offer almost equally effective methods before and after the obstacle. The fact that older children can plan more than one possible effective course of action for reaching a goal may be the result of a capacity to anticipate possible events that may prevent the implementation of the first course of action they think of. That is, the obstacles presented in this study may have been a priori present in the generation of the first method, requiring the instantaneous availability of alternative courses of action.

Additional analyses of the methods demonstrated that with progressing age, the complexity of the methods, in terms of the number of actions (i.e., subgoals) within one method, increased. This was most evident with methods based on one action, such as: "She should ask the children whether she might join the game" (a predominant type of method for all studied age groups); and methods based on two or more actions such as: "She should go outside – go to the children – tell them her name – and ask whether. . . ." (The respective frequencies of occurrence for this latter type of method were 5, 6, and 18 for the first, third, and fifth grade, respectively.) This finding may be related to the increasing competence to oversee and temporally order events into the future (cf. Oppenheimer & Van der Lee, 1983). Finally, indications were found that use would be made of other persons not present in the described situation in order to reach the goal whenever the situation required or enabled such and that the use of another person tended to increase rather than decrease with age.

The ability to infer the goal of another person, referring to the questions "why did that person do what he just did . . . what motive or goal, if any prompted it?" (Flavell, 1977, p. 134), was found to be age related. The data indicated a linear increase in the ability to infer accurately the goal underlying a particular sequence of actions.

Children were also asked to evaluate the ineffective and effective methods we proposed. They were asked whether or not they themselves would have selected particular methods. A major finding was the difference between the evaluation of effective and ineffective methods. The majority of children participating in this study indeed judged the ineffective methods to be ineffective for reaching the goals. No age effect could be demonstrated. No such unequivocal data were found for the effectiveness judgments. The results suggest that the judgment of the effectiveness of methods is differentially related to age. In a replication study conducted in 1978, in which children of different ages and adults were required to judge the same methods for degree of effectiveness, a U-curve developmental course became evident, showing a greater correspondence between the ratings of the first graders and adults than between the former groups and the third and fifth graders. Children appear to have more difficulties in judging the effectiveness (i.e., "goodness"), than the ineffectiveness (i.e., "badness") of a method, which may be related to the phenomenon that "children acquire the concept of bad before the concept of good" (Keasey, 1978). Although "right" and "wrong" are dichotomous, "right" has many ways of being achieved, and this is where styles, values, and other personal qualities that develop with time and experience enter into the equation.

The final analysis of the data dealt with an examination of the relationships among the explored components of plans. In the beginning of section II, I hypothesized that a close relation should exist between the components of method generation and method evaluation, and that competence in inferring the goals of others was not necessarily expected to form an integral part of the plan but might be related to the general ability to plan.

A first calculation of Pearson product–moment correlation coefficients among the variables demonstrated that all studied abilities were related to each other (with coefficients ranging from .39 to .91). With the exception of the ability to judge the ineffectiveness of the methods, all abilities were also highly related to age. A subsequent partialing out of the effect of age revealed that the correlation coefficients between method generation and the effectiveness and ineffectiveness judgments increased to almost 1.0 (i.e., from .89 to .98), whereas none of the relations between the ability to infer the goal of others and the former abilities remained significant.

Similarly, with the effects of age present, a principal-component analysis resulted in a one-factor structure (eigenvalue 2.9, and an explained variance of 100%). This factor was interpreted as representing the "plan," the intermediate stage between the motive and the intent to act, that is, the competence and planning aspect of actions. The same analysis with the effects of age partialed out resulted in a two-factor model. The first factor, consisting of the competencies of method-generation and effectiveness judgment, was interpreted as the method aspect of the plan (eigenvalue, 2.8; explained variance, 72%). The second factor, a specific factor, representing the ability to infer the goal of others, was interpreted as a social cognitive dimension. The first factor, then, represents the ability to develop effective and functional methods to reach goals; the second factor, knowledge about the social environment and the abilities to deal with it. Both competencies appear to function independently. Nevertheless, the exceptionally prominent one-factor model, resulting from the principal-component analysis with the effects of age present, may imply that with progressing age the effectiveness of the developed methods is increasingly more put to the test in relation to the available knowledge about the social environment. Conversely, the knowledge of the social environment may be increasingly more involved in the production of methods whose effectiveness still has to be determined.

C. Discussion

Within the context of a competence approach, this study centered upon children's growing abilities to plan. Older children were found to be better and more effective planners than young children: Their plans reflected higher levels of complexity in terms of the number of subgoals or separate actions, and they were able to produce equally effective alternative plans when their first plan could not be implemented as a result of the introduction of an obstacle. In short, at the age of approximately 11 years, children can be considered competent planners when required to reach simple social goals.

The results of this study also provided information about the status of the construct "plan." The competencies to produce methods (i.e., the more specific actions to reach a goal), and to evaluate their effectiveness were found to form part of one principal component with and without the effects of age being partialed out. The ability to infer the goals of others, as an ability representing a more general repertoire of social cognitive competencies, was found to function independently from the former abilities thought to be involved in planning. Nevertheless, the data warrant the assumption that with progressing age the influence of social cognition and its abilities on the production and effectiveness of methods will increase.

III. Further contributions from action theory

A. Determinants of action

The previous study was primarily descriptive. The children were not required to carry out their plans, and no attempts were made to measure actual behaviors. In addition, it is evident that the most important explanatory variable employed in this study was age: The older child is the better planner. A remedy for such a restricted approach is to embed planning in a wider context of cognitive or operational development (cf. Chapman & Skinner, 1984; Piaget, 1950), or social and cognitive development (cf. Eckensberger & Silbereisen, 1980; Keller & Reuss, 1984; Silbereisen, 1984).

Besides the almost exclusive emphasis on the "action" as the most important psychological unit of analysis, the approaches cited do not significantly differ from the existing ones dealing with planning and problem solving. These studies, like the one described, merely focus on the rational and cognitive characteristics of planning. These studies provide strategies and procedures to give detailed descriptive accounts of single actions or complexes of actions.

In other words, one may conclude from the preceding discussion of plans and planning that planning is still considered to be a particular skill functioning in an apparent contextual vacuum. However, actions as central units of analysis were considered to reflect the interaction between an individual's cognition, emotional makeup, and the social and physical environment. Consequently, Hollis (1977) assumed that if action is the rational expression of intentions within rules, it should have determinants of its right interpretation. The inner determinants are defined by the "interests" of the actor. Hollis, however, did not further elaborate the concept of inner determinants nor its defining concept of "interests." As a result, external determinants of action, which are characterized by symbolic challenges like verbal orders or requests, are not discussed, and a more detailed examination of the nature of these inner determinants is lacking. This neglect was addressed by Von Wright (1976), who characterized the inner determinants by intentions or mental states (i.e., "epistemic attitudes"). The intention, that is, the motive for pursuing a particular goal, is formed by either *wants* or *duties*. "Wants" refer to the intrinsic values of actions, whereas "duties" refer to explicit and implicit rules set by the social role of the actor (i.e., "role-holder duties," Von Wright, 1976, p. 249). In an attempt to answer the question "Why ... people have the intentions (i.e., motives) they have" (p. 427), Von Wright referred to (a) determinants totally within the social environment (i.e., the symbolic challenges), (b) determinants that are codefined by the social environment with respect to particular roles, but internalized by the subject (i.e., the role-holder duties), and (c) determinants that originate from within the subjects (i.e., the wants).

These three different kinds of determinants can be placed either alongside each other and treated as equals, or in some hierarchical order by which the determinants originating from within the subject are fundamental to (a) the internalization of role-holder duties, and, prior to this internalization, the selection of (social) roles, and (b) the responses to symbolic challenges. Hence, it is assumed that the grounding determinants of action are the "wants" of the individual, or as Hollis (1977) defined them, the "interests" of the actor.

From a completely different perspective, Frijda (1980) concluded, on the basis of a functional analysis of emotions, that emotions represent the "values" or "interests" of the system and are signals to indicate that such a value or interest is at stake. Emotions, then, have two fundamental functions: (a) to protect, and (b) to promote the individual's interests. Threats to, or violations of these interests will result in "*e(nd)*-motions," that is, stagnation of ongoing activities. However, if such threats are absent or removed "*e*-motions" will be the result, that is, the continuation of existing, or initiation of new activities (Frijda, 1980). Combining these ideas with the earlier discussion of the determinants of action leads to the assumption that even if an individual is ordered to act, he or she will act only if, or will act in such a way that, no value or interest will be threatened or violated ("wants," "interests," and "values" are here used as synonyms). In other words, it is postulated that "human action will always be in accordance with, and based upon, the values or interests of the individual."

In addition, contemporary theories of emotion (cf. Plutchik & Kellerman, 1980) indicate that there is evidence for the existence of interests, instincts, needs, values, ways of life, attitudes, etc. (cf. Shank & Abelson, 1977), which are fundamental (Heise, 1979), general (Scott, 1980), or life themes (Shank & Abelson, 1977), but which may also be transient (Heise, 1979) or temporal. Furthermore, a number of these fundamental interests or values may be unconscious, not known to the reflective, active organism, whereas the "conscious" interests will be based on or derived from these more fundamental ones in the form of rationalizations in terms of beliefs (Kreitler & Kreitler, 1976).

Hence, in order to answer the question "Why do people act as they do," knowledge about the interests or values of the individual will be necessary. These interests (a) represent the inner determinants of all intentional and goal-directed actions; (b) determine when activities will be initiated, continued, or stagnated; (c) determine to which goals (high) positive affective loadings will be attached; (d) codetermine the subjective "best" methods or strategies to attain these goals; and (e) may completely overrule rule-governed action, resulting in (ir)rational action. An extreme, but possible implication of this line of thinking is that human action could be totally unrelated to human competencies such as cognitive or social cognitive abilities (Keller, 1980).

B. Research Proposals

Based on the distinct points of emphasis dealing with the interests or values of the individual, an encompassing research program can be designed in which each point mentioned represents a topic of study, in this particular instance, of a developmental psychological nature.

Hence, interests or goals of children should be studied, not only in the academic context (cf. Larcebeau, 1982) but foremost in the social domain. In a current study (Oppenheimer & Van der Wilk, 1984), children were interviewed about their interests and goals in the near and far future. Preliminary results indicate a shift from concrete material interests related to the "here and now" or very near future in children of 4–6 years of age, to goals and interests of a more philosophical nature, that is, in terms of life themes or ways of life in adolescents (i.e., 14–16 years of age). This parallels cognitive development from concrete to abstract, operational thinking.

Interesting with this context is Serafica's (1982) discussion of the activating conditions of friendships. Departing from Bowlby's (1969) assumption that attachment behavior and the maintenance of proximity can be conceptualized as a "goal in the earliest form of an interpersonal relationship" (p. 124), Serafica pointed to empirical data demonstrating that proximity behavior and the "experience of the other's presence" (i.e., contact) are also goals in peer relationships and friendships at later ages.

Attachment behavior is not always manifested but activated only under certain subjective and objective conditions. It is also assumed that "discrepancies between the goal and actuality will activate specific . . . interaction patterns designed to restore the desired goal between the partners" (p. 125). Proximity and contact are examples of what was been discussed previously as interests or values of the system. Hence, because it is essential for survival among infants and for the social well-being among children, adolescents, and adults, particular individuals become targets or goals to which the attachment behaviors are directed, such that they become close as caretaker(s), friends(s), or partner(s).

A different approach would be to set goals for children and to examine the ways children of different ages cope with problems in attaining these goals. For instance, goals can be created that are unattainable or conflicting. On the basis of the results from the first study, it can be assumed that children will use particular methods to attain these goals and that with progressing age these methods will become increasingly more sophisticated. Futhermore, it can be expected that the developed methods and their modes of implementation will be affected by the opportunities provided by the situation (Von Wright, 1976). Finally, if the assumption is correct that plans are subject to the intellectual system (Lidz & Lidz, 1976), then the developed methods are expected to be related to cognitive abilities required by, or inherent in, the particular problems.

IV. A shortage of resources: study 2

A. Introduction

In a study attempting to assess children's level of decentration, we unintentionally discovered the initial plans of children to solve a primarily cognitive problem. "Decentration" refers to the developing ability to consider more than one salient aspect of a problem in order to solve it. The cognitive problem was as follows: A child is confronted with a model tower of Lego blocks with a height of 20 blocks, and a width of 2 blocks (in total consisting of 40 blocks) and is given 20 Lego blocks with the request to build a tower "as high as" the model tower. In order to achieve this goal, the child will have to compensate the height of the tower by its width and build the tower using only a single row of blocks in order to attain a tower that is 20 blocks high. This solution requires the simultaneous consideration of both height and width.

In a pilot study, children from a kindergarten, and a first and third grade of an elementary school were presented with this task. Although compensatory abilities as described previously were expected to be present around the ages of 6–7 years (Piaget, 1950), all children without exception started to build a tower with a base of two blocks, leading to a tower of a double row of blocks. Somewhere along this course of action, they discovered that the resources would not suffice to attain an identical height, as represented by the model tower.

These findings suggest that children base their initial plan to attain the stated goal on the erroneous assumptions that "as high as" means "identical to" and that the available pile of blocks will suffice to build an "identical" tower to the model tower. Irrespective of the exact origin and nature of the latter error, all children encountered the problem described as "a shortage of resources," preventing the completion of the originally selected plan.

When the child is required to solve this problem individually, only one possible solution is evident, which is based on the cognitive compensatory abilities. The latter solution will be referred to as the *individual method*. An analogous problem situation was developed for a dyadic condition, in which 40 blocks were available to two children, in which each child separately received the instruction to build a tower as high as the model tower. Hence, each child could make use of the *individual method* and use the 20 blocks to achieve this goal.

However, it was expected that the children in the dyadic condition could make use of alternative methods other than the *individual method*. They could also make use of two interactional methods based on either cooperation or competition. In the former method, children could change the initial goal (i.e., instruction) from "to build individually a tower as high as," to "to build together a tower as high as (i.e., identical to) the model tower" (henceforth, the *cooperative method*). In the *competitive method,* the children may decide to take away the blocks from one another. It should be noted here, in order to prevent any misunderstanding, that the individual, cooperative, and competitive methods are not goals themselves. Although it is common from a "socialization perspective" to consider cooperative behavior as a socially appropriate goal, in this case it is considered as a particular method by which a goal can be attained.

1. Cognitive and social-cognitive variables. The methods that children could develop to achieve the stated goal are theoretically contingent upon the development of various cognitive and social cognitive skills. The individual method, as already mentioned, would require compensatory abilities inherent in the conservation ability (Piaget, 1950). Although the relationships between social-cognitive abilities and cooperative behavior (here defined as sharing resources to reach identical goals) are unclear (cf. Light, 1979; Shantz, 1975), it was assumed that affective, and conceptual perspective-taking (i.e., role-taking) would be related to the cooperative method (Hartup, 1970). With respect to the competitive method, a negative relation between levels of perspective taking and this method was expected (Chandler, 1973, 1977; Light, 1979; Neale, 1966). In order to explore further the relationship among children's planning abilities and cognitive and social-cognitive skills, assessment instruments for conservation and affective and conceptual perspective-taking were included as covariables in this study (Oppenheimer, 1978: adapted from Urberg & Docherty, 1976).

2. Autonomy. The shortage of resources and consequent changes in plans can be considered from a personality point of view, in addition to the cognitive and social–cognitive perspective. Such a point of view regards the shortage of resources as the experience of an "object obstacle," in the individual condition, and a "subject obstacle" in the dyadic condition. In the former case, the obstacle arresting the implementation of the initial plan is defined by the resources. In the latter, the thwarting entity is another person, hence the second child who makes use of the resources of the first child and vice versa. A transformation of these experiences into measures of self-reliance with regard to object and subject (i.e., peers or parents) obstacles was accomplished by Shouval, Zakay, and Halfon (1977). These authors described an instrument to assess the child's level of self-reliance (i.e., autonomous activity) if confronted with problems resulting from objects or peers.

If we assume that actions, that is, the implementation of plans and ability to adapt plans to changing circumstances, are related to self-reliance, then we expected that high levels of autonomy with regard to objects and peers would result in strong relationships with the cognitive and interactional methods, respectively. For this purpose, the scales measuring autonomy with regard to objects and peers were translated into Dutch, adapted and validated for a younger age group (i.e., from approximately 5 to 10 years of age), and included as independent variables in this study.

3. Behavioral categories. Whereas age and condition were considered the major independent variables and the method (selected after the children encountered the shortage of resources) the dependent variable, a second set of dependent variables was included which centered on the resolution of the shortage of resources. More specifically, we were interested in (a) the moment children would discover (i.e., anticipate) that the resources would not suffice, (b) whether they verbally or nonverbally expressed this realization, (c) whether they would continue to search for another method, (d) directly or after some experimentation would develop such an alternative method, (e) request help from each other, and (f) would check their progress with the model tower. For this purpose, an observation system was constructed including the above behavioral categories as dichotomous variables.

Finally, after the completion of the tower task, a number of questions pertaining to the explanation of the shortage, remembrance of the original instructions (i.e., goal), and the extent of the application of the latter instructions during their course of activities were presented to the children as a short questionnaire.

B. Methods

In order to test this interrelated set of hypotheses, the tasks and instruments were administered to 72 children from three age groups (mean ages 5.7, 7.3, and 9.1 for the kindergartners, and first and third graders, respectively). Within each age group of 24 children, 8 children were randomly assigned to the individual condition, whereas the remaining children were assigned to the dyadic condition (i.e., eight dyads). In all dyads, the children knew each other but were not direct friends. No restrictions were made in regard to gender, although there were approximately equal numbers of boys and girls within each age group and condition.

The instruments and tasks were administered in two sessions separated from each other by an interval of 1 week. The order of the tasks for cognitive, social-cognitive, and personality variables, in the first session, was systematically counterbalanced. In the second session, the tower task was always presented prior to the questionnaire.

C. Results

One of the most striking results of the present study was that in none of the dyadic groups, at any age, was there any evidence that subjects adopted the competitive method. Either the cognitive or the cooperative method was chosen. This was most likely the result of the task demands of the experimental situation.

In the individual condition, adoption of the cognitive method increased with age. In addition, the abilities of conservation, affective perspective-taking, and autonomy with regard to objects were found to be related to this method. The finding that the development of the conservation ability is related to the cognitive method confirmed the expectation that the latter method, representing a typical cognitive prob-

Table 10.2. *The frequency and types of methods selected by the three age groups in the individual and dyadic conditions*

	Individual condition		Dyadic condition			
	n	Cognitive	*n*	Cognitive	Cooperative	Total
Kindergarten	8	1	8	0	3	3
First grade	8	2	8	1	3	4
Third grade	8	7	8	2	5	7
Total		$10^{a,b}$		$3^{b,c}$	11^{c}	14^{a}

[a]Age: $F(2,42) = 6.62$; $p < .05$; no effect for conditions.
[b]Age: $F(2,42) = 8.13$; $p < .01$; condition: $F(1,42) = 7.85$; $p < .01$.
[c]No effect for age; types of solution: $F(1,21) = 4.96$; $p < .05$.

lem-solving strategy, would be contingent on the development of the compensatory ability as assessed by competencies in conservation. Similarly, the relationship between autonomy with regard to object obstacles and this method supported the expectation that children who are highly reliant when faced with obstacles produced by objects would more easily reach adequate solutions to this type of problem. In Table 10.2, the main results with regard to the types of methods selected by the children are given.

Contrary to the above results, no age-related development could be demonstrated for either the individual or the cooperative method in the dyadic condition, whereas the overall number of instances leading to goal attainment was found to increase with age. The children in the dyadic condition chose the cooperative method significantly more than the individual method. Again, contrary to the findings in the individual condition, none of the independent variables was related to either method, i.e., conservation, affective and conceptual perspective-taking, and the measures of autonomy with regard to object- and peer-obstacles.

A more detailed examination of these results revealed that the relationship between conservation, affective perspective-taking, and autonomy with regard to objects and the individual method in the individual condition disappeared when the effects of age were partialed out. This finding substantiates and elaborates the conclusion drawn from the first study, in which it was suggested that cognitive and social–cognitive variables as well as personality characteristics function independently from the method-generation abilities (see section II.B). In addition, this finding again suggests that with progressing age the use and influence of social-cognitive, cognitive, and personality variables will increase on the production and effectiveness of methods. This conclusion, however, applies only to the individual condition. In the dyadic condition, no such effects could be demonstrated: Irrespective of whether or not the effects of age are present, no relationships whatsoever between the cognitive, social-cognitive, and personality variables and any of the methods were demonstrated.

After these initial analyses, attention focused on the six behavioral categories of the observation measure. The data showed these categories to be age related, implying that with increasing age, children (a) improved in anticipating the shortage of resources before it was actually encountered; (b) more often either verbally or nonverbally expressed this realization of the shortage; (c) became more tenacious of goal attainment, that is, less often developed an alternative method directly after the realization of the shortage; (e) more often requested help from one another; and (f) more often compared their progress with the model tower during their course of action.

In the individual condition, the behavioral categories (with the exception of the categories pertaining to the expressive reactions to the shortage of the resources and requests for help, which did not apply in this condition) were all related to the individual method and to the cognitive and social-cognitive abilities. In the dyadic condition, however, almost none of the behavioral categories was related to either the cognitive or the cooperative method. The behavioral category assessing the children's ability to anticipate the shortage of resources was found to be related to the competencies in conservation and perspective-taking. Because the latter abilities are indices of decentration, within the Piagetian tradition, this finding is in agreement with Piaget's (1950) assumption that decentration is a necessary but not sufficient prerequisite for the development of anticipatory abilities. Whereas, with the effects of age partialed out, the interrelationships among conservation and emotional and conceptual perspective-taking remained very strong (i.e., with coefficients ranging from .55 to .88), the relation between these competencies and the behavioral category of anticipation disappeared (cf. also Oppenheimer & Van der Lee, 1983).

These cognitive and social-cognitive abilities were also related to, first, the requests for help (also after the effects of age were partialed out), and second, the ad hoc explanation of the shortage (as assessed by the questionnaire). The first relationship suggests that the ability to convey a message of distress may depend on social-cognitive abilities, as, in all likelihood, does the interpretation of such a message and the subsequent altruistic or helping behavior (Oppenheimer & Heller, 1984). The relationship between the social–cognitive abilities and the explanation of the shortage of resources can be understood in terms of the types of explanation children used. Instead of basing the shortage of the resources on the realization that "as high as" does not mean "identical to," the shortage was explained by the fact that two children were working simultaneously with only one pile of blocks: If they had been working alone (as in the individual condition), no shortage would have occurred. In other words, the physical obstacle became a source of an interpersonal conflict in which the obstacle was the other child. The additional relationship between the explanation of the shortage and autonomy with regard to object-obstacles further corroborates this assumption, because it illustrates the children's realization that the shortage could have been solved if they had been working alone.

In both conditions, the data indicated that higher levels of control over the object environment (i.e., autonomy with regard to object obstacles) resulted in higher levels of tenacity of goal attainment; in addition, this tenacity was found to be related to the direct development of a new method in the individual condition. Autonomy with respect to peer obstacles played a role only in the dyadic condition and was negatively related to the expressive reaction to the shortage and requests for help. These results suggest that the higher the level of social autonomy with peers, the lower the amount of overt reactions or expressions and requests for help.

D.   Discussion

The guiding assumption of the present study was that children's goals and methods of goal attainment promote the utilization of the resources provided by the situation. The manipulation of resources led to a conflict between the anticipated effects of a selected method and the real effects, the shortage of resources (see also Figure 10.2: conflict moment A).

The development of a new method in order to overcome the shortage of resources and reach the stated goal was naturally situation dependent. If no choice was present between methods, then the children evidenced an age-related increase in the development of a suitable method to reach their goal (i.e., the individual method). In addition, only in the restricted choice situation was the development of this latter method found to be related to cognitive and social-cognitive variables. If, however, the child was given a free choice to select a method, cooperative, individual, or competitive, quite a different picture emerged. Although the children appeared to be quite able to make use of the individual method (see the individual condition, Table 10.2), they rarely employed this method in the dyadic condition. Instead they preferred to change their original goal (i.e., "to build individually") and adopt an analogous, but not identical cooperative goal (i.e., "to build together").

In a chapter on interpersonal problem solving, Myrna Shure (1982) noted that higher social-cognitive abilities may enable the child to "better evaluate possible solutions because of his/her greater sensitivity of how his/her actions might affect others" (p. 158). The complete absence of the competitive method may underscore this assumption. In addition, Shure's remark very closely resembles earlier notions related to the observed increase in the application of cognitive and social-cognitive abilities in the development and effectiveness judgments of methods to reach particular goals (see sections II.B and IV.C), whereas no direct relation between these methods and the cognitive and social-cognitive abilities was demonstrated.

From a developmental perspective *with* the effects of age present, the results of both studies described suggest that the presence and strength of the relationship between cognitive and social-cognitive abilities and the methods may be a function of the number of possible alternative methods present to reach a particular goal. If only one solution or method is available, the relationship will be present and strong; if, however, more alternative methods are present and the child is allowed to freely select any of them, no relationship will be evident. Hence, it is argued here that cognitive and social-cognitive skills are necessary but not sufficient prerequisites for planning in restricted choice situations, and that they are enhancing antecedents for planning in free-choice situations.

The latter may be illustrated by the children's behavior before, during, and after the encounter with a shortage of resources and the necessity of abandoning the initial plan and developing a new one. Already in the first study, a link was made between the older children's developing anticipatory competencies and availability of more than one effective alternative method. These anticipatory abilities were thought to be directed to possible obstacles that could prevent the implementation of the initially developed method. In the present study, such an obstacle was experimentally induced. It was demonstrated that the older children anticipated or foresaw the shortage of resources earlier than did the younger children, were more tenacious, but also evidenced a more immediate change of their course of action to either the individual or the cooperative method.

Despite the conceptual relationship among these competencies, there were no statistically significant interrelationships among them: Each competence functioned independently.

Perhaps the competitive method, as a suitable alternative, was ruled out at the moment of realization of the shortage or even before this moment. We conclude this because, if the latter method were discarded on the grounds of developing social-cognitive competencies, it should have occurred in the younger age groups, which was not the case.

These apparent contradictions and inconsistencies would indicate that we should focus our attention elsewhere when searching for variables affecting the selection of methods and the development of specific plans. In a later section, we will return to this issue.

In summary, the results of the present study confirm those of the first: The older children possess greater anticipatory competencies and have more direct asccess to alternative methods. The relationship between social-cognitive skills and planning, however, remains unclear.

V.   Conflicting goals: study 3

In contrast to the previous study in which children were presented with identical instructions (i.e., to reach identical goals), a task was developed in which two conflicting goals or instructions were presented. This task, the tower-box task, required one child to build a tower from a pile of Lego blocks, and the other child to put the same pile of blocks into a box. Each instruction was presented either to one child (i.e., the individual condition) or to two children (i.e, the dyadic condition) by two experimenters. In the dyadic condition, the instructions were given individually, but simultaneously; in the individual condition, the instructions were given sequentially and in a counterbalanced order.

Furthermore, the way in which children would succeed in solving this goal conflict was studied in a condition in which children were promised an incentive (i.e., candies) and in a condition in which no such incentive was offered. Again the relationships between cognitive (i.e., conservation) and social-cognitive (i.e., affective perspective-taking) competencies and the way children would handle the conflict (i.e., the method selected to solve the conflict) were examined (Van der Griend, 1982; Van Santen, 1982).

The underlying idea for this study is based on Miller et al.'s (1960) assumption that resolving conflicting goals will require a great amount of intelligence. In other words, if the cognitive and social-cognitive abilities, as assessed by competencies in conservation and affective perspective-

Table 10.3. *Different types of methods that could be employed to solve the goal conflict for the individual and dyadic conditions, and their respective scores*

	Dyadic condition			Individual condition	
No.	Method	Score	No.	Method	Score
1.	No activity – passivity.	1	1.	No activity – passivity.	1
2.	Not coordinated; competitive: Each child attempts to attain his/her own goal.	2	2.	Not applicable.	
3.	Partially coordinated I: One goal is attained by cooperative activity.	3	3.	Partially integrated I: One goal is attained.	3
4.	Partially coordinated II: Both goals are attained sequentially.	4	4.	Partially integrated II: Both goals are attained sequentially.	4
5.	Completely coordinated: The tower in the box.	5	5.	Completely integrated: The tower in the box.	5

taking represent indices of intellectual functioning, then it is expected that with progressing social-cognitive development, children will be able to handle an *intra*personal, as well as an *inter*personal, goal conflict in qualitatively better ways: Their methods, based on plans to reach the given goals, should become more adequate in dealing with the conflict as the children grow older.

In a pilot study, it was found that the individual and dyadic conditions enabled similar ways to solve the conflict, but that they should be interpreted and scored differently (see Table 10.3). From Table 10.3, the reader can observe that individual activities of the children in the dyadic condition based on the realization of separate and individual goals is the only solution not present in the individual condition. The latter method was characterized as competitive because each child would attempt to reach the individual, stated goal as efficiently as possible. In agreement with the previous study, it was expected that this method would show a negative relation with social-cognitive competencies (Chandler, 1973). The alternative methods of building the tower and putting the blocks into the box were thought to be based on the selection of the most preferred goal and were considered to reflect a basic form of cooperative behavior, requiring social-cognitive competencies, but characterized by the absence of any *coordination* of goals. The method of first building the tower and then putting the blocks into the box (or in the reversed order) was thought to represent a higher-order form of cooperative behavior interpreted as a compromise, or the *partial coordination* of the two goals. The final method, by which the tower was built in the box, was consequently regarded as reflecting a *complete coordination* of both goals and, hence, a real cooperative method which required both cognitive and social–cognitive skills (cf. Hartup, 1970).

For the individual condition, the methods were characterized as representing different extents, not of goal coordination, but rather, of *goal integration*. Consequently, the last two methods in Table 10.3 represent a *partial* and a *complete* integration of both goals, respectively.

The introduction of an incentive was thought to increase the respective importance of goal attainment and, consequently, would promote more individual behavior (i.e., competitive methods) in the dyadic condition and possibly might increase the intensity of the conflict and lead to stagnation of activity in the individual condition.

A. Methods

One hundred forty-four children participated in both the incentive and nonincentive conditions, divided over three age groups (mean ages 7;1, 8;10, and 11;4 years in the nonincentive condition, and 7;2, 9;6, and 11;4 years in the incentive condition, for the first, third, and fifth graders, respectively). The children in each age group in each condition ($n = 24$) were assigned at random to the individual ($n = 8$) and the dyadic condition ($n = 16$: eight dyads). Again, in all dyads the children knew each other but were not direct friends; no restrictions were made in regard to gender and there were approximately equal numbers of same-sex and mixed-sex dyads. All children were tested in two sessions separated by an interval of approximately three weeks. In the first session, the tower-box task, and in the second, the conservation and perspective-taking tasks were presented.

Because of the exploratory nature of the present study, the procedure was interrupted after 10–30 seconds when it was clear (by verbal interaction of the children or by the manual activities of the individual child) what the initial course of action would be. After the interruption, a short interview was introduced in which the children were asked to explain what they were planning to do in order to verify the observation of their plans (the reliability of the observations reached .96). The procedure of terminating the children's activity was followed because it was not certain what emotional effects the induced conflict would cause.

Table 10.4. *The frequencies for the types of methods employed by the individual children and the dyads, for each age group, in the nonincentive and the incentive conditions*

	7 yr Incentive		9 yr Incentive		11 yr Incentive		Total Incentive	
Type of solution	−	+	−	+	−	+	−	+
Individual condition								
1. Passivity	0	0	0	0	1	0	1	0
2. —	—	—	—	—	—	—	—	—
3. Partial integration I: one goal	6	6	4	8	6	4	16	18
4. Partial integration II: both goals, sequentially	2	2	4	0	1	4	7	6
5. Complete integration: tower in box	0	0	0	0	0	0	0	0
Total (*n* and total *N*)	8	8	8	8	8	8	24	24
Dyadic condition								
1. Passivity	0	0	0	0	0	0	0	0
2. Not coordinated: Each child has his/her own goal	0	1	1	1	3	2	4	4
3. Partial coordination I: one goal together	7	6	6	4	5	4	18	14
4. Partial coordination II: both goals, sequentially	1	0	0	2	0	0	1	2
5. Complete coordination: tower in box	0	1	1	1	0	2	1	4
Total (*n* and total *N*)[a]	8	8	8	8	8	8	24	24

[a] *n* = 8 refers to the number of dyads and not to the total number of subjects.

Before comparisons between the individual and dyadic conditions, and the nonincentive versus incentive conditions were made, it was ascertained that the subjects in the respective conditions did not differ in their cognitive, and social–cognitive development.

B. Results

Table 10.4 shows the frequencies for the types of methods in the individual and dyadic conditions, for each age group and incentive condition. In the individual condition, no differences could be demonstrated in the types of methods used by the three age groups, or in the incentive conditions. In general, the results for the individual condition indicate that children between the ages of 7 and 11 years preferred first, either to build the tower or to put the blocks into the box ($n = 34$), and second, to attempt to attain both goals by sequentially carrying out the two goals ($n = 13$). None of the children in the individual condition gave evidence of considering the highest-order integrative method of building the tower in the box. In addition, no effect on the type of method was present as a result of the introduction of an incentive. Also no relation could be demonstrated between the employed methods and the cognitive and social-cognitive variables.

In the dyadic, nonincentive condition, the effect of age tended toward significance ($F(2,24) = 3. 10$; $p < .10$), revealing, contrary to expectation, that the older children (i.e., the 11-year olds) selected the noncooperative, individual method more than the younger children. In this condition, it was one dyad of the 9-year olds who developed the method of building the tower in the box.

In the dyadic, incentive condition, no effects for age were evident. An ad hoc analysis also did not reveal any gender differences nor Age × Gender interactions. Although no significant effect for the introduction of an incentive on the cooperative types of method was found ($\chi^2 = 1.4$, $p = .12$), the data suggest that the incentive promoted coordinated, cooperative methods, rather than competitive methods. That is, the methods of building the tower and then putting the blocks into the box or vice versa (i.e., the partial coordination of goals) and building the tower in the box (i.e., the complete coordination of goals) occurred more often in the incentive (i.e., 12.5%) than in the nonincentive condition (i.e., 4.14%; Fisher Exact Probability Test: $p < .03$).

An examination of the methods for the individual and dyadic conditions representing partial and complete goal integration and coordination, respectively, indicated that in the individual condition, significantly more *partially integrated* methods were selected (i.e., 27.1%) than *partially coordinated* methods in the dyadic condition (i.e., 6.25%), whereas in the dyadic condition, more *completely coordinated* methods (i.e., 10%) were used than *completely integrated* methods in the individual condition (i.e., none; Fisher Exact Probability Test: $p < .03$).

Again no relationship could be demonstrated between the cognitive and social-cognitive variables and any of the methods selected by the children in the dyadic condition. As can be observed from Table 10.4, with the exception of one 11-year-old in the individual, nonincentive condition, no problems as a result of the induced conflict were encountered.

Because of the short procedure employed in the present study (i.e., from 10 to 30 seconds), no valid analyses of the behavior of the children could be made.

C. Discussion

The purpose of the study described in the previous section was to obtain information on how children of different ages handle conflicting goals and to verify whether progressing age and subsequent social-cognitive development would be reflected by the developed methods.

In the second study (see sections IV.A through D) concerning the shortage of resources the initial plans of the children who were requested to build a tower "as high as" a model tower, were deduced from the first steps in the building process, that is, by the base of two blocks. This deduction resulted in children's assumption that "as high as" meant "identical to," and therefore, they set out to build a tower "as high as" *and* "identical to" the model tower. In the present study, the plans to solve the goal conflict were obtained by (a) observation of the children's behavior, and (b) an interview after the interruption of the task. Whereas these plans accurately reflected the possible methods formulated on the grounds of the pilot study (see section IV.A), the almost perfect relationship between the inferred plans from the observations and the obtained plans as reflected by the interviews indicated a close correspondence between the plan and the concrete actions. The various methods that would lead to conflict reduction or a solution for the goal-conflict were thought to represent qualitatively different forms of cooperative action defined by the level of goal coordination in the interpersonal, dyadic condition, and goal integration in the intrapersonal, individual condition.

In the present study, no relationship among the various levels of coordination and integration and levels of cognitive and social-cognitive development could be demonstrated. In addition, no age-related shift from noncoordinated and nonintegrated methods to methods representing higher levels of goal coordination and integration was evident. These findings confirm the results of the second study (see section IV), which also failed to demonstrate an age-related development for cooperative action, and question earlier assumptions about the prerequisite nature of social role-taking competencies for cooperative behavior (Hartup, 1970).

IV. Discussion and conclusions

About a decade ago, Shantz (1975) concluded that the "hypothesis of substantial relationship between role-taking and social behavior has not been strongly supported to date, but neither, certainly, has it been refuted" (p. 308). A similar lack of correspondence between social thought and action has been observed within the domain of moral development. As Flavell (1977) noted, despite considerable research efforts devoted to the problem, we are still quite unsure what the relation is – if any exists – "between a person's assessed moral reasoning stage and his level of moral behavior in real situations" (p. 143). In other words, it remains unclear what relation exists between assessed competencies and observed performance.

None of the three presented studies in this chapter had as its purpose to answer these questions unequivocally. Nevertheless, each study provided information, albeit contrary to almost all expectations, about relationships among cognitive, social-cognitive, and planning competencies and between the latter and the actual methods employed to attain goals. Within the action-theory approach, planning and plans are thought to refer to the intermediate stage between the motive and the intention to act in order to attain a goal. That is, planning reflects children's abilities to plan and execute plans mentally.

The action theory approach to actions, however, adds an additional dimension to the examination of the relation between these competencies, resulting plans, and behavior in real situations. According to Von Wright (1976) and Hollis (1977), human action is too complex to warrant the postulation of a direct link between the intention to act, that is, the underlying plan regulating actions, and the resulting real action. As Hollis remarks:

A causal law is a contingent connection between contingent events (or facts). [However,] firstly, . . . the *explanans* (i.e., the intention) is not a distinct antecedent; secondly, it not contingently connected to the *explanandum* (i.e., the action); thirdly, since the agent knows what he is doing without having to know that he is an instance of a class, the connection is not general. (p. 115)

In other words, "to talk of intentions is . . . to answer the question *what* and *why*" (Louche, 1966, p. 106). Such a perspective rejects a priori the assumption that knowledge of plans or levels of planning ability will predict what an individual will *do* in an everyday situation. Conversely, however, a particular action or sequence of actions enables us to infer the intent or plan behind the observed behavior. It is exactly this point of departure that focuses attention on real actions as a central unit of psychological analysis instead of on particular competencies.

The third study in this chapter, in which children were confronted with a goal conflict, illustrates this point. In this study, we were able to hypothesize an order of progressively more sophisticated methods to cope with the conflict in either an individual or a dyadic situation. The plans of the children inferred from brief observations of their actual behavior corresponded almost perfectly with the plans reported by the children themselves after the interruption of the tasks. These plans, in turn, corresponded to the hypothesized methods, although the expected shift to higher-order plans as a function of age and/or social-cognitive development (i.e., decentration) could not be demonstrated. In the second study, in which the manipulation of resources enabled the observation of how children adapt their initial plans in order to attain their goals and build a tower as high as a model tower, also no age effects in the employed methods were evident in the interpersonal, dyadic condition.

Although both studies offer information about the plans children employed (but not about their planning abilities) and about how they were able to modify these plans at the moment of a real encounter of an obstacle, we did not obtain any information on the *why* of these plans. Theoretically and traditionally, the *why* is defined by cognitive and social-cognitive abilities, as well as by personality characteristics, which set the limits for the level of sophistication for planning, plans, and resulting actions (cf. Piaget, 1950). Neither the results of the first study, characterizing a competence approach, nor those of the second and third studies, representing performance approaches, warrant the assumption that planning and real actions are determined and/or limited by intellectual competencies like conservation and perspective taking. These abilities were found to enhance rather than determine or limit planning, plans, and actions.

Within the context of a competence approach, the first study centered upon children's growing abilities to plan. Underlying the operationalization for this study was the model presented in Figure 10.2 (see section I.B). Although the model refers to the double function of a plan as a blueprint for action and as an action-regulating principle, only the first aspect was studied. Older children were found to be better and more efficient planners than younger children: Their plans reflected higher levels of complexity in terms of the number of subgoals or separate actions, and they were able to produce equally effective alternative plans when their first plan could not be implemented as the result of the introduction of an obstacle. In short, at the age of approximately 11 years, children can be considered competent planners when required to reach simple social goals. The results of this study also provided information about the status of the construct "plan." From a developmental point of view with the effects of age present, the competencies (a) to produce methods (i.e., the more specific actions to reach a goal), (b) to evaluate their effectiveness, and (c) to infer the goals of others were found to form part of one principal component interpreted as the "plan." If the effects of age are partialed out, the ability to infer the goals of others, although related, was found not to form an integral part of the "plan." More precisely, the method aspect of the plan, consisting of method generation and evaluation, was found to function independently from the ability to infer the goals of others. This result gave a first indication that the methods to attain a particular goal are developed independently from knowledge about other people's goals or the ability to infer these goals.

In the following two studies, emphasis was placed on the performance dimension of planning, that is, the real behavior of children when confronted with inter- and intrapersonal conflicts concerning (a) a mismatch between the expected and real effects of their plans, and (b) the incompatibility of the two goals.

The results of these studies reveal patterns that, although consistent, do not correspond to assumptions based on the literature, concerning the development of particular types of social behavior (e.g., cooperation) and the relations among these behaviors and cognitive and social-cognitive skills. The most striking finding of these studies is the absence of any age-related development for cooperative actions. In the reported studies, cooperative actions were defined by the coordination of methods to attain identical goals and the coordination of two incompatible goals. It is stressed (see section IV.A) that cooperation per se is not considered to be goal setting but only a method to attain a particular goal. The task situations were structures in such a way that if cooperative actions of the above types did occur, the children would be required to be engaged with one another and be involved in a common goal. In addition, the task situation could be characterized as neutral with respect to the encounter of both children (i.e., they knew each other but were not direct friends), and as enabling other than cooperative actions. These characteristics of the task situation and the resulting cooperative actions closely corresponded to those given by Eckerman and Stein (1982) for cooperative play. Although an increase in the successful implementation of the cooperative method in the second study can be observed, the absence of a clear age effect may indicate the presence of at least a cooperative motive for the youngest age group (i.e., the 5- to 6-year olds). The results of the third study, and those for the incentive condition in particular, support this assumption. No shift to higher forms of cooperative behavior as a function of age could be demonstrated. In the condition in which no incentive was offered, the opposite developmental trend was found. That is, the older children preferred noncooperative, individual to cooperative methods more than the younger children did. Contrary to expectation, the introduction of an incentive for attaining individually the stated goals results in higher levels of cooperative behavior. The exploratory nature of this study, however, commands caution in interpreting these results.

A second interesting result concerns the contextualization of social-cognitive development, referring to the relation between certain cognitive and social-cognitive skills and actual social behavior (Shantz, 1982). In none of the interpersonal conditions was any relationship evident between the assessed cognitive and social–cognitive competencies and the methods developed to attain the given goals. The relationships that could be demonstrated among these competencies and social behaviors before, during, and after the encounter of the shortage of resources, in the second study, are too few to allow any unequivocal conclusions. Only if the task situation allowed for only one possible method to resolve the conflict or to attain the given goal (i.e., in the individual condition in the second study) was an exception to the earlier findings found: In this condition, the expected relationships between the assessed competencies in conservation and perspective taking and the development of this method were evident (see section IV).

In the competence approach to planning (see the first study), the partialing out of the effects for age also resulted in an absence of any relation between plan-generation abilities and the ability to infer the goals of others as an index of social cognition. These results point to the possibility that if a child is free to choose from various alternative methods to reach a goal, the cognitive and social-cognitive skills may enhance the quality of planning and plan-execution skills rather than being necessary prerequisites for them. The latter appears evident in resolving problem situations in which only one method is the correct one. That is, although children approximately 11 years old evidence qualitatively well-developed planning competencies, they were found to express these abilities only when no choices were available

The finding that children become more sophisticated planners as a function of age (see the first study) and also the absence of any age-related development in the application (i.e., development) of qualitatively higher-order plans in real situations illustrate again the often observed discrepancy between competencies and performance. Whereas in a study exploring children's plans for the present and future, Martorano (1980) concluded that understanding of operational abilities does not necessarily guarantee that children will apply this knowledge in the planning phase, the results reported here question the assumption that method-goal thinking, planning, or plans are predominantly based on cognitive abilities.

It is doubtful whether the actual methods children and adults choose and apply to reach goals should be placed within a cognitive or social-cognitive developmental context. Abilities derived from the latter context may enhance planning and plan execution but appear not to determine the methods that are finally applied. In natural social situations in which various alternative ways to attain goals are often present, the variables affecting the development of a particular plan are predominantly related to subjective interests, such as emotional well-being, in addition to or rather than, well-considered intellectual reasoning.

In conclusion, it is evident from the results of the presented studies that additional research is necessary to reach a proper understanding of planning processes and their relationship with actual behavior. Neither asking children to verbalize their plans for reaching particular goals nor observing how children cope with obstacles preventing goal attainment is sufficient to form a clear idea about planning and its application in real situations. Knowledge about the subjective interests of children in addition to the discrepancies between verbalized plans, as an index for planning competencies, and the way children attempt to reach goals on which these plans are based, in real situations, may offer the information necessary for developing a detailed picture concerning which variables at which moments are prerequisite and essential for, or enhance, planning and plan-execution processes.

References

Boesch, E. E. (1976). *Psychopathologie des Alltags*. Bern: Huber.

Bowlby, J. (1969). *Attachment and loss* (Vol. 1). New York: Basic Books.

Chandler, M. J. (1973). Egocentrism and antisocial behavior: The assessment and training of social perspective-taking skills. *Developmental Psychology, 9,* 326–332.

Chandler, M. J. (1977). Social cognition: A selective review of current research. In W. F. Overton & J. McCarthy (Eds.), *Knowledge and development* (Vol. 1). New York: Plenum.

Chapman, M., & Skinner, E. A. (1984). Action in development/development in action. In M. Frese & J. Sabini (Eds.), *Goal directed behavior: Psychological theory and research on action*. Hillsdale, NJ: Erlbaum.

Eckensberger, L. H., & Silbereisen, R. K. (1980). Einleitung: Handlungstheoretische Perspektiven für die Entwicklungspychologie Sozialer Kognitionen. In L. H. Eckensberger & R. K. Silbereisen (Eds.), *Entwicklung sozialer Kognitionen*, Stuttgart: Klett-Cotta.

Eckerman, C. O., & Stein, M. R. (1982). The toddler's emerging interactive skills. In K. H. Rubin & H. S. Ross (Eds.), *Peer relationships and social skills in childhood*. New York: Springer.

Enç, B. (1975). On the theory of action. *Journal for the Theory of Social Behavior, 5,* 145–167.

Flavell, J. H. (1977). *Cognitive development*. Englewood Cliffs, NJ: Prentice-Hall.

Frijda, N. (1980). *Kunnen computers voelen?*. Paper presented to the Royal Dutch Academy of Science, The Hague, August.

Furth, H. G. (1981). *Piaget and knowledge* (2nd ed.). Chicago: University of Chicago Press.

Hartup, W. W. (1970). Peer interaction and social organization. In P. Mussen (Ed.), *Carmichael's manual of child psychology* (Vol. 2). New York: Wiley.

Heise, D. R. (1979). *Understanding events: Affects and the construction of social action.* Cambridge: Cambridge University Press.

Hollis, M. (1977). *Models of man: Philosophical thoughts on social action.* Cambridge: Cambridge University Press.

Keasey, C. B. (1978). Children's developing awareness and usage of intentionality and motives. In C. B. Keasey (Ed.), *Nebraska Symposium on Motivation* (Vol. 25). Lincoln, NE: University of Nebraska Press.

Keller, M. (1980). Entwicklungspyschologie sozial-kognitiver Prozesse. In M. Waller (Ed.), *Jahrbuch für Entwicklungspsychologie: Vol. 2 Soziale Entwicklung im Kindesalter.* Stuttgart: Klett-Cotta.

Keller, M., & Reuss, S. (1984). An action-theoretical reconstruction of the development of social-cognitive competence. *Human Development, 27,* 211–220.

Klahr, D., & Robinson, M. (1981). Formal assessment of problem-solving and planning processes in preschool children. *Cognitive Psychology, 13,* 113–148.

Kreitler, H., & Kreitler, Sh. (1976). *Cognitive orientation and behavior.* New York: Springer-Verlag.

Larcebeau, S. (1982). Intérêts, valeurs et choix professionels [Interests, values and vocational choice]. *Orientation Scolaire et Professionelle, 11,* 341–354.

Lidz, C. W., & Lidz, V. M. (1976). Piaget's psychology of intelligence and the theory of action. In J. J. Loubser, R. C. Baum, E. Effrat, & V. M. Lidz (Eds.), *Explorations in general theory in social science.* New York: The Free Press.

Light, P. (1979). *The development of social sensitivity.* Cambridge: Cambridge University Press.

Louche, A. R. (1966). *Explanation and human action.* Berkeley: University of California Press.

Martorano, S. H. (1980). *Children's plans for the present and future.* Paper presented at the Tenth Annual Symposium of the Jean Piaget Society, Philadelphia.

Miller, G. A., Gallanter, E., & Pribam, K. H. (1960). *Plans and the structure of behavior.* New York: Holt.

Neale, J. (1966). Egocentrism in institutionalized and non-institutionalized children. *Child Development, 37,* 97–101.

Oppenheimer, L. (1978). *Social cognitive development.* PhD dissertation, University of Nijmegen.

Oppenheimer, L. (1979). *On action.* Unpublished manuscript, University of Nijmegen.

Oppenheimer, L., & Heller, J. (1984). Development of cooperative and help-seeking activities: An action theoretical approach. In E. Staub, D. Bar-Tal, J, Karylowski, and J. Reykowski (Eds.), *Development and maintenance of prosocial behavior: International perspectives.* New York: Plenum.

Oppenheimer, L., & Van der Lee, H. (1983). Social perspective-taking and event sequences: A developmental study. *Psychological Reports, 53,* 683–690.

Oppenheimer, L., & Van der Wilk, R. (1984). Interests and goals and how to achieve them: Development and gender differences. *De Psycholoog, 19,* 642.

Oppenheimer, L., & Veerman, H. (1980). The plan-of-action: Explorations of several of its components. *Newsletter Soziale Kognition, 3,* 53–71.

Pea, R. D. (1982). What is planning development the development of? In D. L. Forbes & M. T. Greenberg (Eds.), *New directions for child development: Children's planning strategies* (No. 18). San Francisco: Jossey-Bass.

Piaget, J. (1950). *The psychology of intelligence.* London: Routledge.

Piaget, J., & Inhelder, B. (1971). *Mental imagery in the child.* London: Routledge.

Plutchik, R., & Kellerman, H. (Eds.). (1980). *Emotion: Theory, research, and experience* (Vol. 1). New York: Academic Press.

Reinshagen, H. (1977). Handlungsvorstellungen als konstituierende Kategorie sozial-kognitiver Prozesse. *Newsletter Soziale Kognition, 1,* C128–142.

Scott, J. P. (1980). The function of emotions in behavioral systems: A system theory analysis. In R. Plutchik & H. Kellerman (Eds.), *Emotion: theory, research, and experience* (Vol. 1). New York: Academic Press.

Serafica, F. C. (1982). Conceptions of friendship and interaction between friends: an organismic–developmental perspective. In S. F. Serafica (Ed.), *Social cognitive development in context.* New York: Guilford Press.

Shank, R. C., & Abelson, R. P. (1977). *Scripts, plans, goals and understanding.* Hillsdale, NJ: Erlbaum.

Shantz, C. U. (1975). The development of social cognition. In E. M. Hetherington (Ed.), *Review of child development research* (Vol. 5). Chicago: University of Chicago Press.

Shantz, C. U. (1982). Children's understanding of social rules and the social context. In F. C. Serafica (Ed.), *Social cognitive development in context.* New York: Guilford Press.

Shouval, R., Zakay, D., & Halfon, Y. (1977). Autonomy or the autonomies? Trait consistency and situation specificity. *Multivariate Behavioral Reserach, 12,* 143–158.

Shure, M. B. (1982). Interpersonal problem solving: A cog in the wheel of social cognition. In F. C. Serafica (Ed.), *Social cognitive development in context.* New York: Guilford Press.

Shure, M. B., & Spivack, G. (1972). Means–end thinking, adjustment and social class among elementary-school-aged children. *Journal of Consulting and Clinical Psychology, 38,* 348–353.

Silbereisen, R. K. (1984). Action theory perspective in research on social cognition. In M. Frese & J. Sabini (Eds.), *Goal directed behavior: Psychological theory and research on action.* Hillsdale, NJ: Erlbaum.

Urberg, K. A., & Docherty, E. M. (1976). Development of role-taking skills in young children. *Developmental Psychology, 12,* 198–203.

Van der Griend, L. (1982). *Handelingsplannen voor het oplossen van tegenstrijdige doelen onder beloningskondities: Een ontwikkelingsstudie.* Unpublished M.A. thesis, University of Amsterdam.

Van Santen, J. (1982). *Handelingsplannen voor het oplossen van tegenstrijdige doelen: Een ontwikkelingsstudie.* Unpublished M.A. thesis, University of Amsterdam.

Von Wright, G. H. (1976). Determinism and the study of man. In J. Manninen & R. Tuomela (Eds.), *Essays on explanation and understanding.* Dordrecht: Reidel.

Part IV

Influences on planning

11   Familial influences on planning

*Ann V. McGillicuddy-De Lisi, Richard De Lisi, Janice Flaugher,
and Irving E. Sigel*

I. Introduction

Susan and her mother were going through a story about a child who had found a
rock. Susan's mother said, "Susan, what would you do with a rock if you found
one?" Susan answered that she would pretend that the rock was a turtle. Mother
asked how she would do that. Susan said, "I'd put the turtle in the water and
pretend it was sleeping." They turned the page, and Mother said, "I wonder what
the boy is going to do with it." Susan stated that he would probably throw the
rock at someone. But the story told of the boy's painting the rock, and Mother
said, "Remember when you made a paperweight for Daddy's desk? Tell me how
you made that rock into a paperweight."

A. *Parental influences on children's representational abilities:
distancing*

Nearly every model of planning assumes that planning is dependent on
a subset of cognitive abilities that change with development, and that
environmental factors may interact with developmental cognitive processes to produce changes in these abilities involved in children's planning. Although there are no studies that deal explicity with familial influences on children's planning abilities, the literature has established that
relationships do exist between parents' child-rearing practices and many
aspects of children's cognitive development.

The vignette above provides several examples of a parental child-rearing dimension that has been linked theoretically to children's representational abilities. Representational ability is one aspect of cognitive functioning that is likely to be included in that subset of cognitive abilities

Research reported in this paper was partially supported by NIH Grant No.
R01MH32301 and Office of Education Grant No. G007902000 to the first and
fourth authors and by a New Jersey Research Development Award to the first
author. Special thanks go to all the children and parents who participated in these
projects.

395

that affect children's planning, for the child must represent possible outcomes to strategies in planning. When Mother talks to Susan about what Susan would do with the rock, what the boy might do with the rock, and how Susan once made a paperweight, the discussion focuses on topics that are not concrete or observable in the present activity. Some type of internal representation is called for when Susan proposes a hypothetical activity, anticipates a possible behavior in the story theme, and recalls a past activity involving a rock. Although the mother is not focusing on acts of planning in a functional sense, her behaviors do serve to encourage Susan to engage in representational thinking, that is, to anticipate an outcome, propose alternatives, and reconstruct prior similar experiences and outcomes, which are all involved in planning activities. Sigel (1979) proposed that all children have the potential to develop representational abilities, which he defines as abilities to anticipate outcomes, reconstruct events, and interpret transformations of objects.

Although all children have the potential to develop representational abilities, certain instructional techniques used by parents and teachers are assumed to enhance the development of such potential. Sigel termed these techniques or teaching strategies "distancing behaviors" on the assumption that the adult behavior encourages the child to engage in mental activities that are psychologically removed or distant from the concrete observable object or event confronting the child. Parental behaviors can be conceptualized along a continuous dimension of distancing, ranging from those that encourage minimal representation on the part of a child (e.g., encourage the child to label), to those that require much more complex representations (e.g., synthesize information or concepts). The optimal point along this continuum for an individual parent's behavior is that point that challenges the developing representational capabilities of the child. For example, a focus on getting the child to label objects/colors/events is appropriate and challenging to the representational ability level of a 2-year old, but would be below the level of Susan's abilities in the vignette above. Research on parents' distancing behaviors has focused largely on preschool and young school-age children. Adult behaviors that encourage minimal representation are called "low level" distancing behaviors when used with children this age because they focus on representational abilities that have already been developed. For example, parental utterances such as "What is that?" "Look at that model over there!" and "This is a point over here, right?" focus the child on labeling, observing, and describing, which are not likely to challenge the developing representational abilities of a 5- or 6-year old. Messages that focus the child on anticipating, proposing alternatives, evaluating outcomes, and so on, are considered high-level distancing behaviors because they are likely to challenge the representational abilities of the child, as the mother in the vignette encouraged Susan to represent possibilities related to the story theme.

When teachers were trained to use high-level distancing behaviors often with preschool children, the children performed significantly better than a contrast group on assessments of language, memory, and antici-patory abilities (Cocking, 1979). Parents who were observed to use high-level distancing more often than other parents when teaching their preschool-age children, had children who outperformed their peers on anticipatory and memory tasks (Sigel, 1982). These findings provide sup-port for the hypothesis that when children's representational abilities are challenged and encouraged by adults' use of high-level distancing, the development of such abilities is enhanced.

Although it should be clear that Sigel's distancing theory was not for-mulated to address the nature of the development of children's planning, it does address the nature of familial influences on the development of children's representational abilities, abilities upon which planning activ-ities rest. If parents encourage their children to use their representational abilities, the children should become more adept with such skills. The children of parents who do not encourage representation through the challenge of high-level distancing behaviors in the course of day-to-day interactions are likely to be at a disadvantage in representational ability as compared to other children. In a later section of this chapter, we will see the extent to which this is true, as we investigate the relationships between parents' distancing behaviors and children's anticipatory and memory abilities.

Up to now, we have considered only representational abilities that are components of planning abilities. Let us now turn to Mark and David, who are engaged in functional aspects of planning, that is, behaviors that are designed to attain a goal.

B.   Children's planning behaviors during interpersonal interactions: Vygotsky

Mark and David are brothers who are trying to build a house by stacking blocks. They are having trouble putting a large roof on the stacks of blocks, when sud-denly Mark stands up and says: "We can't do it this way. Every time we get the roof on this side, the blocks at that corner fall. Let's get this side on, and you hold the roof up while I build the corner under it on that side." David agrees, but he moves slightly while holding the roof, tumbling the blocks that were holding up the roof on the other side. Both boys sigh loudly and David says, "Mark, I think your plan stinks. *You* hold up this end."

In a chapter reviewing the psychological literature pertaining to planning, Friedman, Scholnick, and Cocking (this volume, chapter 14) have indicated that planning involves setting a goal and coming up with and implementing strategies to reach that goal. As the vignette above shows, this use of planning is very different from Mother's encouragement of Susan's anticipatory and memory skills in the previous vignette. In the present vignette, Mark and David really have a problem that they want to solve. They have set a goal. They have to figure out how they can reach their shared goal of putting the roof on four stacks of rickety blocks, that is, come up with a strategy to reach that goal. Discussions of what a boy with a rock in a story might do will seem very irrelevant to Mark and David now. Mark does appear to have devised a strategy to reach the goal, but upon implementing this strategy, David concludes that it was a poor strategy, and he proposes a modification of Mark's strategy.

As Mark and David interact with one another, play with one another, and solve problems together in their daily interactions, they are likely to engage in planning actions. Their experiences of planning with one another could lead to many outcomes that might affect future planning behaviors of each sibling. For example, David might comply with Mark's plan merely because David has seen that some of Mark's previous plans have led to fun (after countless rounds of "What do you wanna do?" "I dunno. What do you wanna do?"). Or, David might comply because some of Mark's plans have succeeded in solving problems in play when more random, trial-and-error behavior did not succeed. Thus, we could propose that children develop the ability to plan through observation, imitation, and interactions with other family members. Although children might indeed learn of the importance of plans and some strategies through observation and imitation, recognizing the need for a plan and becoming systematic in devising ways to reach a goal are unlikely to be attained through simple observation/imitation. It is likely that young children at first behave within the context of a plan laid out by some other family member more competent than the child, much as David complies with Mark's plan at the beginning of the vignette. Vygotsky (1978), one of the first developmental theoreticians to refer to children's planning, stated that parents are responsible for recognizing the need of a plan, formulating a plan, and implementing the plan when the planning capacities of their preschool-age children are inadequate for the task at hand. Vygotsky conceptualized the source of the child's planning functions as within social interactions with other people, especially parents, who are more competent than the child. (The following section will elaborate on Vygotsky's definition of areas of competence.) These planning functions only gradually shift from being imposed by others to the control or self-regulation of the child. Eventually the child comes to regulate her or his own behavior and is able to formulate and implement plans without other people serving as the monitor of the planful behavior. Wertsch (1985) has pointed out that young children probably do not understand the goals and plans imposed upon them by parents or more competent siblings in the same way that an adult would understand them. He has found, however, that young children seem to learn that planning is important, and that mothers' guiding or monitoring behaviors can facilitate the shift to the child's self-imposed planful behavior.

Thus, Vygotsky proposed that planning functions will gradually shift from being imposed by more competent others (like from Mark to David) to the control or self-regulation of the child. Vygotsky (1962, 1978) was explicit in stating that children become able to plan, order, and control their behavior, as well as other people's behavior, through speech. The next section explores the importance of speech in the development of children's planning abilities and its possible effects on interactions within the family that are assumed to affect the cognitive abilities involved in planning.

C. Speech and planning

Ben and his father tried to make a whale by folding paper, following a model of the steps involved. Father said, "We're supposed to make a whale like that, Benjamin. How do you think we should start?" Ben said, "Oh, like this," and folded a piece of paper through the first three steps. Then he stopped and studied the model while Father watched him. Ben said, "I have to turn the paper over to make those flippers, I think." Father said, "Let's see."

Meanwhile, in another room John and his father were involved in the same task. The following is an account of how they approached the task.

As John entered the room, Father took him by the arm and guided him to a chair, saying, "Sit here, John. Look at the board, John. (John looks but turns away.) It's a whale. Look at the board, John." John looks, and Father puts a piece of paper in his hands and helps him fold it in half, saying, "Can we fold it like that one, John?" John creases the fold, looks at the board, but then sees a Muppet puppet left in the room to divert children. He gets up and brings the puppet back to the table, makes it kiss Father and says, "Bert." Father says, "Very good, John. That is Bert. Can Bert help us make this whale?" John laughs and says, "No." Father says, "See the next step? Now we have to fold it here, right?" John nods, makes a fold and then another, which his father praises.

John and Ben are the same age, and assessments show that John's and Ben's intelligence were within the normal range. John, however, is classified as communication handicapped, and he is currently in speech therapy. He has trouble communicating orally with others, his father tells us, so he has to encourage John to try to speak. John gets along well with other 5- to 6-year olds although he seems easily distracted, the father says. Within Vygotsky's developmental framework, we would expect that John would not be able to plan or control his own or his siblings' behavior as well as Ben could. For Vygotsky, children initially use social speech, which serves the function of communicating to others. As the child develops competency in this area, however, speech becomes differentiated to serve two functions: the initial communicative, social function; and a new self-regulatory function. This latter function, often referred to as "inner speech," is intrapsychological functioning because it does not involve other people as communicative speech does. It results in an increasing ability to direct and control one's own behavior. John, with his communication handicap, has not yet mastered the initial function of social speech. As a result, it is likely that the development of inner speech has been delayed, and John's ability to direct and control his own behavior would be deficient within Vygotsky's theory. John and Ben differ from one another in their approaches to the task. In addition, John's father differs from Ben's father in that John's father directs and guides John's behavior through his verbalizations more than Ben's father does.

To summarize thus far, a communication handicap is likely to inhibit the development of functional planning because speech has not developed to the point where it regulates social communication or thinking. Planning processes cannot be internalized by the communication-handicapped (CH) child through the course of dialogic speaking and reasoning interactions with more competent others to the extent that this occurs with nonhandicapped (NH) children.

There is an additional problem, however, that could even further exacerbate the CH child's problems with respect to planning abilities. Recall that the initial portion of this paper dealt with representational abilities that comprise skills involved in planning, and the likelihood that parents' behaviors influence the development of such abilities in children. We know that parents do not behave in a vacuum, nor in a random fashion. One factor that is likely to influence their behavior is the ability level or behavior of their own child. That is, parents might take into account the handicap of their child during interactions. Perhaps they encourage speech in the child, or perhaps they avoid behaviors that require spoken responses to avoid frustrating the child. If they do not receive information about the ability level of their child through the child's verbal responses, perhaps it is too difficult for them to find that optimal level of distancing that challenges developing representational abilities. Within the context of distancing theory, this creates further problems for the child because representational skills involved in planning, such as anticipation and memory, will therefore also suffer.

As a result of the unique roles attributed to speech, that is, to serve a communicative and a self-regulatory function, a handicap in this area could affect planning skills in at least two ways. First, intrapsychological functioning is not likely without mastery of communicative speech, leaving the CH child's functional planning within the regulation of other people during social interactions. Second, parents may respond to the communication problems of their child in such a way that the representational skills involved in planning do not develop to their full potential. We will be able to explore some of these problems in later sections as we analyze interactions between parents and CH children and between CH children and their siblings. Some data on CH children's anticipatory and memory abilities will be looked at in relation to their parents' behaviors during parent–child interactions, but it was not possible to determine if relationships were due to parents' influence on children or to children's effects on parental behavior. The next section explores one method of determining if parents were reacting to the communication handicap in a way that might affect their behaviors and thereby influence children's planning.

D. Parental beliefs about the development of planning

Previous research has indicated that some relationships exist between the way parents think children develop abilities and the way parents teach their children (McGillicuddy-De Lisi, 1984). Furthermore, there is some evidence that beliefs and expectations about children are affected by the parents' life experiences, for example, the ability level of their own child, sociocultural factors, and so on (Goodnow, 1984; McGillicuddy-De Lisi, 1982; Sutherland, 1983). We therefore hypothesized that parents' beliefs about how children become able to plan would be affected by the communication limitation of their child. That is, we expected that parents with a child who had a communication handicap would have had different child-rearing experiences with that child (as opposed to parents of a NH child) and that these experiences would lead to differences in how parents thought children develop planning abilities. Therefore, these parents would interact differently with their CH child than parents of NH children. If parents of CH children differ from other parents in the ways they think children develop abilities to plan, we would at least know that some differences in behaviors were probably due to the child's effects on the parents' beliefs.

E. Types of familial influences

It is probably apparent that we think all family members influence each other in such numerous and complex ways that it is difficult to discuss them, let alone test such possibilities. Nevertheless, we will attempt to provide some information about family processes that could affect children's planning. It will be useful to recall that at least two aspects of planning are probably influenced by social interactions within the family. First, representational abilities necessary for planning may be influenced by parents' use of distancing behaviors by enhancing the development of such abilities in planning. Second, functions of planning, that is, actually devising, implementing, and evaluating strategies necessary to achieve a goal, may develop from the course of social interactions with competent others as the child moves from interpsychological to intrapsychological functioning.

Both of these aspects of planning may be affected by the communication abilities of the child. It is unclear, as of now, if CH children show a deficit or delay in functional aspects of planning. If Vygotsky is correct in the functions he has assigned to speech, we would expect CH children to evidence interpsychological functioning during social interactions with siblings, whereas NH peers evidence intrapsychological functioning. This would suggest that CH children need others who are more competent than themselves to monitor and guide the activities of the handicapped child. In the family environment, this function is likely to be filled by parents, but may also be filled by siblings who are more capable of intrapsychological functioning than the child with problems in communicative speech.

In addition, we do not yet know if representational abilities that are involved in planning (e.g., anticipation, memory, etc.) are also related to the communication handicap and to parents' distancing behaviors. These relationships should be examined because if the CH child evidences poor representational ability, the development of planning abilities may be hindered in two ways. That is, the representational abilities, such as anticipation or memory, that are involved in planning, as well as speech abilities necessary for self-regulation, may each need remediation efforts in order to enhance the CH child's planning abilities. Finally, we should ask if parents' beliefs about children's planning are affected by their child's communication handicap. This could provide some clues about the cycle between parent and child that are discussed as reciprocal family influences. We investigated these questions with two samples of families with children diagnosed as communication handicapped and two samples with children who have no known handicaps. We asked all of the parents about their beliefs concerning children's planning and observed all of the parents interacting with their child on two teaching tasks. In addition, the anticipatory and memory abilities of younger preschool-age subjects were assessed. These representational abilities were looked at in relation to parental distancing behaviors, as well as compared across CH versus NH groups. Finally, the samples of older school-age children were observed interacting with their siblings during problem-solving tasks so that the functional planning of CH and NH children could be compared.

II. The samples of families and procedures

A. *Participant families*[1]

Data from two different research projects were analyzed to obtain information concerning familial influences on the development of planning skills. One-hundred and twenty families participated in the first study, which was a project funded by The National Institute of Mental Health (NIMH) to investigate the effects of a child evidencing atypical development on family interaction patterns. Each family had a child aged 5½ to 7½ years old (mean = 76.53 months, SD = 7.61). In half of these families, this target child had been diagnosed as communication handicapped by service personnel in the community. The remaining 60 families had children with no known disabilities or handicaps. Families in the CH group and in the NH group were matched to one another on the basis of target child sex, age, and ordinal position, and of parents' educational levels. For the most part, the sample was white and middle-class and consisted of male target children who were middle children in a three-child family constellation.

All mothers and fathers were individually interviewed to obtain information about how they thought children develop planning abilities. Each parent was also observed interacting with his or her child on two teaching tasks. Finally, 86 of the target children were observed interacting with their sibling on two problem-solving tasks. In addition, all target children and their siblings who were over 3 years old were administered standard ability tests that assess verbal and performance aspects of intelligence.

The CH and NH target children performed within the normal range on the Raven's Progressive Matrices Test (Raven, 1956), a performance-based test of intelligence [mean total scores (and SD) = 17.35 (6.99) and 19.92 (4.62) for the CH and NH groups; mean level scores = 4.43 (1.92) and 5.20 (1.19), respectively]. The CH and NH groups did not differ significantly from one another, although the difference approached significance [$F(1/115) = 3.61$; $p = .06$], with mothers' and fathers' education and mothers' age used as covariates. As expected, the CH children performed at significantly lower levels than the NH children on the Crichton Productive Vocabulary Test (Raven, 1977) [mean (and SD) total scores = 17.82 (12.35) and 27.70 (8.52), respectively; mean level scores = 3.63 (2.64) and 6.12 (1.65), respectively; total score $F(1/114 = 21.28$; $p < .01$, with mothers' and fathers' age, fathers' education, and amount of the child's preschool experience as covariates]. The CH children were also less successful than the NH children on the Peabody Picture Vocabulary Test (PPVT; receptive vocabulary test developed by Dunn, 1954), although the difference was not as large as that obtained on the Crichton Test [mean (and SD) raw scores = 60.72 (16.48) and 67.38 (7.26); PPVT IQ scores = 106.37 (29.18) and 118.30 (13.57); raw score $F(1/117) = 7.53$; $p < .01$, with fathers' education as a covariate].

To summarize thus far, one sample of participants consisted of 120 families with a young school-age child. Half of these target children were diagnosed as communication handicapped. Their performances on both performance-based and receptive vocabulary intelligence tests were within normal bounds, though lower than that of their NH peers. All parents in this sample reported their beliefs concerning the development of planning abilities in children, and were observed interacting with their children. Finally, the children were observed interacting with siblings on two problem-solving tasks.

The second sample of families also consisted of 120 families, half with a CH child and half with an NH child. This project was funded by the Office of Education, and focused on the parents' role in the development of preschool-age children's representational abilities. The target children were 3½ to 5½ years old in this sample (mean = 53.25 months; SD = 7.13). Again, families with CH and NH children were matched to one another on demographic characteristics. The two samples of differing age groups resembled one another in most categories except for age of the target child.

As a result of the different goals of the two original projects, some of the data differed for each sample. The parents of the preschool-age children were interviewed about beliefs and observed interacting with their child as the parents of the school-age children had been. However, no observations of sibling interactions were conducted with the younger sample of children. The younger children were administered several representational tasks. Their performance on an anticipatory task and on a memory task will be presented in this paper. In addition, the preschool-age target children in this study were administered the Wechsler Preschool Primary Scale of Intelligence (Wechsler, 1976). The mean (and *SD*) verbal IQ score of the CH group was 95.60 (22.27), whereas the verbal score of the NH group was 116.42 (13.96). Performance IQ scores were 98.47 (24.82) and 116.25 (15.28) for the CH and NH groups, respectively. Although the CH children performed at a significantly lower level than their NH peers, both the performance and verbal scores of the CH children were within normal range [analyses of covariance (ANCOVAs) following a multivariate analysis of covariance (MANCOVA), $F(1/111)$ = 21.83; $p < .01$ for performance scores and $F(1/111)$ = 39.43; $p < .01$ for verbal scores; child's age, child's birth order, number of children in the family, mothers' education, and fathers' income were covariates].

Thus, in both the preschool- and school-age samples, the CH and NH groups differed from one another, but both groups were within normal ranges of intelligence. Furthermore, the most consistent and significant difference between the CH and NH groups was in verbal ability scores, in spite of the fact that even the "performance" measures required an understanding of verbal instructions.

Although the inclusion of the CH children in these two samples was originally based on an effort to compare family interaction processes to those of families with normally developing children, analyses relative to children's planning skills for this paper included comparisons of CH and NH children for an additional reason. Special education and speech and language professionals view communication handicaps as deficits in the ability to use speech effectively (either productively, i.e., speaking, or receptively, i.e., understanding speech) although intelligence is within the normal range. The CH samples in these studies performed within normal ranges on intellectual ability tests, although they had communication problems. The performance of the CH children in the present study can provide information about the role of communicative or speech abilities in school-age children's planning activities during the interactions with their siblings, in preschool-age children's anticipatory and memory abilities, and in children's interactions with their parents.

III. Assessments and results

A. Parents' ideas about the development of children's planning abilities

Previous research indicates that parents differ from one another in how they think children develop, and that such differences are often related to how parents interact with their children (McGillicuddy-De Lisi, 1982). Parents' ideas about how children develop planning abilities might also vary across parents and be related to parents' behaviors that focus on the development of such skills. For example, parents of preschool-age children might believe that maturation and readiness are very salient factors in children's planning abilities. Parents who think that 3- to 5-year-old children are not ready to plan, and place great importance on readiness, are not likely to encourage planful behaviors during interactions with their child. Parents of older children, however, might believe that parents *should* encourage their children to plan, or perhaps these parents would set up situations that require the child to plan. Similarly, parents of a child with a communication handicap might feel that direct instruction from adults is necessary for the child to develop planning skills. Parents of a child without such handicaps might see the child's planning ability as a result of the child's own experimentation and feedback from the world. We would expect differences in parents' beliefs to result in different parental behaviors that might affect the development of their child's planning abilities. Therefore, we asked parents about the development of children's planning abilities, and then compared groups of parents to see if parents differed from one another in their beliefs about their ability to influence children's planning skills.

An interview was used to assess parents' beliefs about a variety of issues with respect to their child's development. During this interview, parents in each study were asked individually how they thought children eventually become able to plan. Parents' responses were taped on a cassette recorder, and their verbalizations were subsequently coded for references to learning and developmental processes such as maturation, imitation, exposure to role models, abstraction, negative or positive feedback, practice, experimentation, direct instruction from adults, and so on. Nine of the tapes were coded by four scorers acting independently, and 81.11% agreement resulted across the entire instrument. Various pairs of scorers coded an additional ten interviews, yielding an average agreement of 81.17%.

There were no significant differences between mothers versus fathers, parents of CH versus NH children, or parents of preschool-age versus school-age children (ANOVA). Parents most often referred to direct instruction from adults as the means through which children develop planning abilities (48%). Some parents thought that children learn planning through seeing others plan for themselves (21%), and an additional 9% of the parents referred to imitation as a source of children's planning. Eighteen percent of the parents' verbalizations indicated that planning is the result of an accumulation of skills that evolve through practice. References to the child's own experimentation, to discovery, or to stages in the development of planning were very infrequent.

These results indicate that a consensus exists among parents that children will not develop planning skills on their own, but they must be tutored or specifically taught such skills. Within our coding system, direct instruction was defined as verbal presentation of information by adults, indicating that a great proportion of parents believed that parents and/or teachers must tell children from 3½ to 7½ years how to plan in a direct, straightforward manner. Children learning to plan through observing the example of others was the next most often cited developmental process, though it occurred with less than half the frequency of direct verbal instruction.

B. Parental distancing behaviors during interactions with children

Each parent performed a storytelling task and a paper-folding task (e.g., making a boat by folding paper following a model of the steps involved) with their child. Parents were observed interacting with their child on two tasks for several reasons. First, we hypothesized that the parents of CH children would evidence low-level distancing behaviors more often than the parents of nonhandicapped children. Low-level distancing by parents tends to require simple associative responses from the child, responses that are more likely to be within the verbal competency of the CH child (e.g., "What color is it?" "See the boat!" "Tell me what it is," etc.). Second, we wanted to compare the behaviors of parents across the two tasks. The storytelling task was more verbal than the paper task and as such, mothers might be more comfortable with this task than fathers, who might be more at ease with the paper-folding task. This could result in greater use of high-level distancing by mothers on the story task, and by fathers on the paper task. Similarly, the differences in task demands might lead parents of CH children to evidence a higher level of distancing during the paper task than during the more verbal story task. The third reason for observing parents' teaching behaviors on two tasks was to assess the relationship between parents' use of distancing during these tasks and preschool-age children's anticipation and memory abilities.

The interactions of parent and child during the story and paper tasks were videotaped through a one-way mirror. The initial 2 minutes, final 2 minutes, and 1 minute at the midpoint of the interaction were coded for frequencies of behavioral categories. This sampling of behaviors was used to ensure that data were obtained concerning how the parent introduced the task and concluded the task. The mean (and SD) length of time used to complete the paper-folding product and to go through the storybook once was 361.58 (SD = 127.41) and 527.97 (SD = 199.59) seconds, respectively. Videotaping of the parent–child interaction continued for 5 minutes when the task was completed in less than that amount of time. There were no significant differences between groups in length of time spent on each task.

Only categories of parental behaviors related to distancing were analyzed for the present study. Therefore, the frequencies of high-level distancing demands and of low-level distancing demands were coded. Examples of high-level distancing demands include requiring the child to propose alternatives, plan, recall sequences, and so on, whereas low-level distancing demands include requiring the child to label, describe, observe the parent and so on. Ninety-six of the videotapes were scored by four pairs of coders working independently of one another. Agreement ranged from 63.5% to100% (mean = 91.55%).

1. Comparison of parental distancing behaviors between groups. Parents' use of low-level and high-level distancing behaviors during the paper task were related to their distancing behaviors during the story task. In addition, low-level distancing was related to high-level distancing during each task, and to several demographic characteristics. A $2 \times 2 \times 2 \times 2$ MANCOVA (CH vs. NH groups, mothers vs. fathers, paper vs. story tasks, younger- vs. older-child age group; N = 960; mothers' and fathers' educational and age levels used as covariates) was therefore conducted on frequencies of low- and of high-level distancing behaviors. The means (and SD) of both levels of distancing are presented in Table 11.1 by CH–NH group, parent sex, task, and age of child group.

Parents' use of distancing strategies depended upon whether the child was communication handicapped or not, upon whether the task involved storytelling or paper folding, and upon the age of the child [F's(2/950) =

Table 11.1. *Mean (and SD) number of low- and high-level distancing behaviors evidenced by mothers and fathers of pre-school- and school-age children on two tasks*

Task and distancing	Mothers				Fathers			
	CH		NH		CH		NH	
	P	S	P	S	P	S	P	S
Paper								
Low	20.43 (8.68)	29.30 (11.14)	17.78 (6.57)	26.35 (9.02)	19.35 (9.02)	27.60 (11.06)	17.50 (7.10)	25.37 (7.27)
High	19.32 (8.38)	17.75 (7.10)	18.80 (6.58)	17.78 (7.78)	17.87 (8.69)	19.33 (8.42)	20.02 (6.99)	17.67 (6.41)
Story								
Low	31.18 (14.33)	23.37 (13.78)	22.28 (8.15)	19.63 (9.28)	33.05 (15.13)	26.75 (15.87)	24.47 (10.47)	22.48 (10.67)
High	16.95 (7.73)	13.13 (6.17)	18.02 (6.46)	12.63 (6.82)	16.63 (7.67)	13.72 (6.41)	18.83 (8.13)	12.58 (7.03)

Note: CH = communication handicapped; NH = nonhandicapped; P = preschool-age child; S = school-age child.

18.11, 33.00, and 17.44, respectively; p's $< .01$]. In addition, these interactions were significant: CH–NH groups and tasks [$F(2/944) = 4.29$; p
$< .01$]; CH–NH groups and child age groups [$F(2/944) = 4.19$, $p < .05$];
child age groups and tasks [$F(2/944) = 47.64$; $p < .01$]; and parent gender and tasks [$F(2/944) = 3.34$; $p < .05$].

Inspection of the follow-up ANCOVAs and means for each group clar-
ified these results. Because each of the factors was involved in a significant interaction effect, the focus will be upon the interactions. The interaction between CH–NH groups and tasks was due to the use of low-level
distancing behaviors by parents of CH children more often while performing the story task than the paper task [$F(1/945) = 7.97$, $p < .01$,
means (and SD) $= 28.59$ (14.78) for the story and 24.17 (9.98) for the
paper]. Parents of nonhandicapped children did not differ across tasks in
their use of low-level distancing [means (and SD) $= 21.75$ (7.49) for
paper and 22.22 (9.64) for story].

The story task was more verbal in nature, and the parent of a CH child
could be expected to encourage oral communication through low-level
distancing demands such as labeling rather than using high-level
demands that require the child to anticipate outcomes, to recall related
events, or to employ other representational skills. The paper task, on the
other hand, involved a visual display of steps involved in the child's
active construction of an object. Parents of CH children did encourage
lower-level representational processes of their children during the paper
task. They used both low- and high-level distancing behaviors during the
paper task and to the same extent as parents of NH children. Thus, parents of CH and NH children behave similarly when they interact with
their children on a task that is conducive to planning strategies, but they
differ from one another when the interaction occurs around a story.

The interaction between CH–NH groups and age of child was due to
differences in parents' use of high-level distancing behaviors [$F(1/945) =$
4.73, $p < .05$]. Parents of the younger and of the older CH children differed very little from one another in their use of high-level distancing
[means (and SD) $= 17.69$ (8.12) and 15.98 (7.03), respectively]. In the
NH group, parents of younger children used high-level distancing strategies more often than parents of older children [means (and SD) $= 18.92$
(7.04) and 15.17 (7.01) for parents of younger and older children,
respectively]. Parents' use of high distancing more often with younger
NH children than with older NH children is consistent with findings
reported by Wertsch, McNamee, McLane, and Budwig (1980). In a study
of adult–child problem-solving dyads, these authors found that adults'
communications to younger preschool-age children serve a regulative

function more often than communications to older preschool-age children, who in turn evidence more self-regulated behaviors. In the present study, parents of younger preschool-age, NH children appear to use high-level distancing, which serves the function of encouraging and guiding representational skills involved in solving the problem. Parents of the older school-age, NH children did not evidence such encouragements and guidance as often, allowing the children to proceed with their own plans. The lack of a difference between parents of preschool- and of school-age children in the CH group could be attributed to the handicap. That is, regardless of the age of the CH child, parents perceive the need to encourage anticipation, memory, and thinking about transformation in guiding the child's behavior and planning.

The differences in parental behaviors that occurred with the age of the child support Vygotsky's notion that adults initially guide children's behaviors during interpersonal interactions, and are the source of the child's planning activities at younger ages. As the child with social communication mastery develops and internalizes planning strategies, parents may see less of a need to engage in high-level distancing, and thus allow children to proceed with their own plans. If the child fails to evidence this mastery, as in the case of the CH child, the parent continues to act as a guide for the child's planning behavior into the later school-age years.

The interaction between task and age group occurred for both high- and low-level distancing behaviors of parents [F's$(1/945)$ = 15.63 and 87.33, p's < .01, respectively]. Parents of older children used fewer high-level distancing behaviors during the story task than all other groups (mean = 13.02 versus 17.61, 18.13, and 19.00). Inspection of the videotapes revealed that these children tried to read the story themselves, and parents tended to encourage this reading activity, rather than focusing on the content of the story. Parents of the younger, 3½- to 5½-year-old children approached the task as storytelling, rather than as a reading task. The former approach is more likely to include high-level distancing behaviors on the parents' part as they discuss what has happened and what might happen.

With respect to low-level distancing, parents of the younger children were less likely to use such behaviors during the paper task than during the story task [means (and SD) = 18.77 (7.84) and 27.75 (12.02), respectively], whereas parents of the older children did not show such a difference with task [means (and SD) = 23.06 (12.40) for story and 27.16 (9.62) for paper]. The paper task, consisting of a sequence of steps to produce a specific outcome, requires somewhat more planning than the story task. This interaction effect suggests that parents of younger children were more reluctant than parents of older children to focus on low-level representational skills during the task that requires more planning skills. Again, the age and task effect provides support for Vygotsky's proposal that a shift from dependence on parents to self-regulatory processes occurs. That is, parents of older children might be more likely than parents of younger children to make comments concerning observations and descriptions (low-level distancing) because children can do much of the anticipation, remembering, sequencing, and planning on their own during this task. The parents, sensitive to the ability of their children, do not need to encourage such activities through high-level distancing. Parents of younger children, on the other hand, may have evidenced fewer of these low-level distancing behaviors during the paper task because these younger children do not evidence such planning abilities on their own when the parents use low-level distancing behaviors.

The final interaction effect of parent gender and task was due to a greater use of low-level distancing behaviors by fathers than by mothers during the story task [$F(1/945) = 6.56, p < .01$; means (and SD) = 26.69 (13.04) for fathers and 24.12 (11.39) for mothers]. During the paper task, mothers and fathers used low-level distancing behaviors with equal frequency [means (and SD) = 23.47 (8.85) and 22.46 (8.61), respectively].

C. Children's representational abilities

The preschool-age children were administered tasks designed to assess anticipatory and memory-and-sequencing abilities. The first task was adapted from Piaget and Inhelder's (1971) anticipatory imagery task of a snail crawling around a window frame and frames of various other shapes. The child's task is to anticipate where the snail will sit (e.g., on the lower inside or upper outside surface of the frame) and which direction the snail will face as it crawls around to different positions on the window frame. Piaget and Inhelder proposed that children use anticipation in imagining the outcome of the snail's movement about the frame.

To minimize the effects of ability to comprehend verbal instructions, children were first trained through demonstration and correction to make a magnetic animal crawl along a straight metal, horizontal track to various locations whenever a light was turned on at that location. This training apparatus was turned upside down as part of the training so the child could see that the animal would not fall off the track. For testing, an hourglass-shaped apparatus with six lights was presented. The child was shown that the animal traversed the inner perimeter of the apparatus, and then each of the six lights was turned on in a specified order. After performing the six trials, children were allowed to run the animal around the track themselves, and the six trials were presented again. Although all children succeeded in placing the animal in the correct track area indicated by the light, they often placed the animal on the top of the track, behaviors that have been termed "transposition" errors by Piaget and Inhelder (1971). The number of correct placements was recorded for the first six and the last six trials. Because scores for the two phases were highly related (r's = .69 and .73 for the two groups, p's < .01), these were collapsed to make a total of 12 trials.

The second task was designed to assess children's memory-and-sequencing abilities. This involved presentation of cards with pictures on them, in succession. The child's task was to order the cards in the sequence that they were presented. As with the anticipatory ability task, a brief training session was introduced first, to minimize effects of verbal instructions. Training was done with two-card sets. Demonstration and correction were used only during training.

Two sets of picture cards were used for testing. One set depicted pictures of familiar objects, such as a cup or hat, whereas the other set consisted of unfamiliar geometric forms. The first presentation involved several trials of three cards presented in succession, then four cards, then five, for a total of 20 test trials. Children's ordering of the cards in a row after they had been presented sequentially was scored for placement of each card in its correct place in the arrangement (e.g., first, second, third, etc.) and for correct placement relative to another card (e.g., hat after cup). Because these two scores were highly correlated for both groups (r's = .90 and .96 for the two groups, p's < .01), only scores for correct placement in the arrangement were analyzed.

The order of the familiar objects and unfamiliar geometric form sets was counterbalanced across families. Additionally, half the parents were observed interacting with their child before each parent was interviewed and the child assessed, and the other half performed the tasks in the reverse order.

The CH children were less successful than the NH children in both correctly anticipating the toy animal locations [result of 2 × 2 (CH vs. NH × child gender) MANCOVA, $F(8/104) = 4.90$; $p < .01$; followed by ANCOVA $F(1/111) = 8.97$; $p < .01$], and in remembering sequences of familiar items [ANCOVA $F(1/111) = 16.50$; $p < .01$] and unfamiliar items [ANCOVA $F(1/111) = 13.30$; $p < .01$]. On the anticipatory task, CH children positioned the animal correctly 7.98 (3.89) mean (and SD)

times out of 12 trials. The nonhandicapped children were correct 9.78 (2.55) mean (and *SD*) times. The CH children performed at much lower levels than the NH children on the familiar items of the memory-and-sequencing task [means (and *SD*) = 23.68 (13.85) and 32.12 (12.82), respectively]. The difference in performance levels of the CH and NH groups was not quite so striking for the unfamiliar geometric form items, but the difference was significant [means (and *SD*) = 16.70 (11.61) and 22.72 (9.95) for the CH and NH groups, respectively]. As the means indicate, both the CH and NH children performed at higher levels when they were asked to reconstruct a sequence of pictures of familiar objects rather than a sequence of unfamiliar items.

This latter finding for both CH and NH children violated our original hypotheses regarding performance on the memory task. We expected NH children to have an advantage in that they might encode familiar items verbally, whereas CH children would be less likely to use verbal encoding. Both the CH and NH children were expected to have approximately equal difficulty encoding the unfamiliar forms verbally, because no labels were readily available. It is possible that the NH children did have a verbal advantage with the unfamiliar items as well as with the familiar objects, although to a somewhat lesser degree than they had with the familiar, easily labeled items. On the other hand, it is also possible that processes not involving verbal ability contributed to performance on the memory task. If this is the case, it is likely that problems in communicative speech exist in parallel with a disruption of those nonverbal processes involved in reconstruction of sequential information.

Although the CH children were less successful than their NH peers in both the anticipatory and memory-for-sequences tasks, we did not find that CH children completely lack or show extreme deficiencies in these areas necessary for planning. For both the anticipatory and the memory tasks, CH children were performing above the chance level, indicating that they do have some ability in these areas, albeit less than NH children.

At this point we analyzed the relationship between parents' distancing behaviors during the two observation tasks and the preschool children's performance on these tasks in an effort to find relationships between parental practices and the development of these representational skills in both CH and NH children.

1. Relationships between parents' distancing behaviors and children's representational abilities. In accordance with the distancing hypotheses, we expected that parents who tend to require planning, anticipation, and reconstruction of events (high-level distancing behaviors) from their child more often than other parents, would have children who have developed more anticipatory and memory skills. However, we were hesitant to make such predictions in the case of the CH child. It is possible that the child's verbal ability is so salient in the development of these skills that it overrides the impact of environmental factors such as parental teaching strategies. Furthermore, it seemed likely that the parents of CH children might focus on the development of communication skills during interactions with their child, rather than cognitive processes such as anticipation and memory, leaving us with a low frequency of high-level distancing behaviors. It is always difficult to determine if parents are affecting children's development or reacting to the child's ability level that changes with development. Even with predictions based on distancing theory, it seems logical to assume that parents *do* react to atypical communicative ability in their children, and this must account for at least some of the statistical relationship found. As a result of these considerations, all analyses of relationships between parents' teaching behaviors and children's anticipation and memory abilities were conducted separately for the CH and NH samples.

Correlations between frequencies of parental use of high- and low-level distancing behaviors on each task and children's scores on the anticipation and memory-and-sequencing tasks are presented in Table 11.2.

There are three areas of interest in Table 11.2. The first two issues involve predictions derived from the distancing framework. First, do parents' high-level distancing behaviors correlate positively with children's anticipatory and memory performance? Second, do parents' low-level distancing behaviors correlate negatively with children's anticipatory and memory performance? Distancing theory (Sigel, 1982) proposes that parents who tend to use high-level distancing during interactions with their children have provided encouragement for the development of representational abilities such as anticipation and memory. The converse is also predicted within the distancing framework. That is, parents' use of low-level distancing strategies encourages children to give associative responses and think in concrete terms, in essence discouraging the development of representational abilities. As a result, relationships between parents' use of high- and low-level distancing strategies and children's anticipation and memory scores would provide support for the predictions that parents can enhance or diminish the development of children's representational abilities that are involved in planning.

The third area of interest in Table 11.2 involved a comparison of the correlations obtained for the CH and for the NH children. Is the pattern

Table 11.2. *Correlations of children's anticipation and memory-and-sequencing scores with frequencies of parental distancing behaviors*

Distancing behaviors, parent sex, and task	Children's scores					
	Anticipation		Familiar memory-and-sequencing		Unfamiliar memory-and-sequencing	
	CH	NH	CH	NH	CH	NH
Low level						
Mothers						
Paper	−.31*	−.27*	−.35*	−.08	−.30*	−.16
Story	−.51*	.11	−.54*	−.36*	−.44*	−.30*
Fathers						
Paper	−.09	−.05	−.25	−.12	−.20	−.07
Story	−.34*	−.02	−.40*	−.30*	−.29*	−.24
High level						
Mothers						
Paper	.30*	.01	.01	−.08	.01	−.05
Story	.30*	.06	−.01	.08	−.01	.06
Father						
Paper	.17	.32*	.08	.18	.05	.18
Story	.37*	.10	.19	.13	.03	.18

*$p < .05$

of relationships between parental distancing and children's representational abilities similar for CH and NH children? If not, this would suggest that the processes responsible for establishing the relationship between parental behavior and child ability are affected when the communicative abilities of the child are considered. Each of these three areas will be discussed below.

Inspection of the correlations for high-level distancing (lower half of Table 11.2) reveals that parents' use of high-level distancing was related only to children's scores on the anticipatory task, and not to children's performance on the memory-and-sequencing task. The positive relationship between high-level distancing by parents and children's anticipatory ability is consistent with distancing theory. Predictions based on distancing theory include, however, a positive relationship between high-level distancing by parents and children's memory for sequences.

Parents' use of low-level distancing was negatively related to both anticipatory and memory performance of the children. As the upper portion of Table 11.2 indicates, mothers who frequently used low-level demands had children who obtained lower scores on both representational ability tasks. Fathers who used low-level distancing often during the storytelling task also had children who were less successful on the anticipatory and memory tasks.

The relationships reported between parental distancing behaviors and children's representational abilities were obtained for both the CH and NH groups. However, these relationships were more consistent and slightly stronger for the CH group than for the NH group. For example, six of the eight possible parental factors did relate to CH children's anticipatory scores, but only two parental behavior factors were related to NH children's performance in this area. In addition, parents' use of low-level distancing was related to CH children's lower memory scores in all cases except fathers' behavior during the story task, whereas only mothers' low-level distancing during the story task was consistently related to NH children's memory performance.

To summarize thus far, high-level distancing was positively related to children's anticipation scores, but not to children's memory scores. Low-level distancing was negatively related to both anticipation and memory scores of children. Although the relationship between low-level distancing and children's scores is completely concordant with distancing theory, and may suggest that low-level demands hinder the development of anticipatory and memory abilities, the fact that the pattern of relationships is stronger for CH children, coupled with the group comparison results reported in the previous section, suggests that these relationships may be due to parents' accommodations to the ability level of their child. That is, parents may be reacting to the lower anticipatory and memory abilities of the child by *not* placing many high-level demands upon them, whereas children who have higher levels of ability in these areas are exposed to greater numbers of high-level distancing behaviors as their parents repond to their high level of ability.

We are attempting to tease apart statistically this bidirectional relationship to determine how much parents might affect children's ability levels through distancing and to what degree the relationship is due to parents' adapting their strategies to match the child's level of ability. To return to results that are available, there was a significant negative relationship between children's anticipation scores, memory scores, and their parents' use of low-level distancing. The lower the performance of children during the anticipation and memory tasks, the more often their parents used low-level distancing behaviors during the parent–child interactions. This relationship was consistently stronger, though not statistically higher for the CH group than for the NH group. In addition, correlations between children's representational ability scores and parents' usc of high-level distancing indicated that the higher the child's anticipatory ability, the more often his or her parent used high-level distancing behaviors during the parent–child interactions. The children's scores on the memory-and-sequencing task were not related to the frequency of parents' use of high-level distancing strategies. This could occur for several reasons. For example, high-level distancing includes many more anticipatory categories (e.g., plan, propose alternatives, etc.) than behavioral categories that focus on memory. Or parents of preschool-age children might be more likely to focus on anticipatory skills when distancing, whereas parents of older children might focus on memory abilities with high-level distancing.

D.   Sibling interactions

Most studies of family influences on children's development focus on the parent–child relationship, neglecting the role of siblings in the family (Lamb, 1982). Yet siblings are likely to play, plan, and problem-solve with one another at least as often as they do with their parents. The school-age children were therefore observed interacting with one another on two problem-solving tasks.

Eighty-six of the 120 children aged 5½ to 7½ years old had siblings over 3 years old. These 86 sibling dyads were administered two tasks designed by Paulson, Whittemore, McDonald, Hirschon, and Tripplet (1971). One task involved building a tower taller than the shorter child out of blocks. The other was to build a house with blocks and a large roof that was difficult to maneuver. Each interaction was videotaped through a one-way mirror for 5 minutes. For 23 of the 86 dyads, the target child was older than the sibling, and for 63 of the dyads, the target child was younger than his or her sibling. The sex of the children was not considered in analyses because there were only 5 first-born female and 13 later-born female children in each group, and some with brothers, others with sisters. Previous studies of sibling interaction have reported that the sex of the children does not seem to be a salient factor at young ages (Lamb & Sutton-Smith, 1982).

Although the sibling interactions were initially scored according to the Paulson et al. system, each child's behavior was also scored in a manner designed to assess planful behaviors during sibling interactions. Specifically, the *frequency* of three categories of planning activities was scored: (a) plans proposed by each child, (b) compliance with plans proposed by the other child, and (c) responses of alternative proposals or suggestions. Eighteen of the sibling interactions were scored by two coders acting independently, resulting in 87.50% average agreement for this scoring system. Because children's behaviors on the two tasks were significantly correlated for both the CH and NH groups (range $= .57$ to $.70$; all p's $< .01$), scores were summed across the house and tower tasks for subsequent analyses.

The target children's initial proposals of plans were negatively related to their compliance of plans proposed by the sibling (r's $= -.80$ and $-.53$ for the NH and CH groups, respectively; p's $< .01$). Therefore a 2 $\times$ 2 MANCOVA (CH vs. NH groups $\times$ Older vs. Younger child in the dyad) was conducted on the frequency scores for the three categories of planning behaviors (sibling age and father income as covariates). The CH children and NH children differed significantly from one another, $F(3/79) = 5.26$; $p < .01$. Follow-up ANCOVAs indicted that CH target children differed from NH target children in frequency of initial proposals of plans to the siblings [$F(1/81) = 4.96$, $p < .05$], in their compliance and acceptance of plans proposed by the sibling [$F(1/81) = 4.09$, $p < .05$], and in proposing alternative plans in response to the sibling's plan [$F(1/81) = 7.37$, $p < .01$]. Communication-handicapped children proposed fewer initial plans than NH children [means (and SD) $= 32.91$ (12.85) and 39.81 (14.48), respectively], and CH children complied and accepted plans proposed by the sibling more often than NH children [means (and SD) $= 31.48$ (13.57) and 26.02 (12.93), respectively]. The CH children were not simply taking directions from their siblings, however. Communication-handicapped children were more likely than NH children to propose alternative plans after the sibling presented initial plans [means (and SD) $= 15.18$ (9.04) and 11.21 (6.10) for CH and NH groups, respectively]. This pattern of findings suggests that siblings of CH children are most likely to suggest the initial plans in tackling each step of the building projects, but CH children responded with new suggestions and plans in addition to accepting and carrying out plans proposed by their siblings. Communication-handicapped children seem to be able to understand, and in fact, evaluate and introduce modifications of plans, although they are less likely to communicate plans at the outset of each step or problem than their NH peers.

The findings that CH children proposed fewer initial plans in approaching each step of the tasks, coupled with their acceptance and compliance of siblings' plans, suggests that these children were guided by others more than their NH peers. The deficit in social communicative speech appears to be related to planning activities (in accordance with

Table 11.3. *Correlations between target children's planning behaviors and targets'/siblings' raw scores on standard tests*

Target child's planning behavior	Target children[a]			Siblings[a]		
	PPVT	Raven's	Crichton	PPVT	Raven's	Crichton
Proposes an initial plan	.20[c]	.23*	.35*	−.27*	−.29*	−.22*
Complies and carries out siblings' plan[b]	−.08	.03	.09	.34*	.38*	.32*
Proposes alternative plan/ modifies sib's plan[b]	−.01	.04	.14	−.05	−.13	.02

[a]Total sample (CH and NH).
[b]In proportion to the number of plans proposed by the sibling.
[c]Test scores.
*$p < .05$.

Vygotsky's view). In addition, the sibling can apparently take the teaching/guiding role of "the more competent other," who acts as a monitor of planning activities during interpersonal interactions.

In order to assess the relationship between competency of the members of the dyad and the target child's planning behaviors, correlations of both targets' and siblings' Peabody Picture Vocabulary Test raw scores (PPVT), Crichton Vocabulary raw scores, and Raven's Progressive Matrices raw scores with the three categories of planning activities were computed for the whole sample (groups based on birth order and CH–NH status were too small to be reliable). Because the findings suggest that the siblings controlled or guided much of the interaction with the target children, the frequency of the target children's compliance and modification of siblings' plans was divided by the number of times the sibling proposed an initial plan. In this manner, the degree of opportunity to comply and to propose modifications to siblings' plans was equated across all target children. Results are reported in Table 11.3.

Inspection of Table 11.3 indicates low but significant relationships between target children's raw scores on the performance-based intelligence test (Raven's), and the productive vocabulary test (Crichton), and the children's tendency to propose initial plans to their sibling. The relationship between target children's receptive vocabulary (PPVT) and proposals of initial plans failed to reach significance. There were no relationships between the target children's standard ability scores and their tendency to comply with or modify plans proposed by siblings.

Siblings' competencies were also related to the target child's planning behaviors. Low but significant relationships for the siblings' PPVT, Raven's, and Crichton scores with target children's proposals of initial plans indicate that the more competent the sibling, the fewer initial plans proposed by the target child. In addition, relationships between siblings' competencies and the target children's compliance with plans suggest that more competent siblings were guiding and controlling the interaction more than less competent siblings. Even with the number of initial plans proposed by siblings controlled across subjects, those siblings with higher ability levels managed to get their target child dyad partner to comply with their proposed plans. The target children's modifications of siblings' plans were not related to either their own or their siblings' competencies when opportunity to modify plans was held constant.

In summary, the siblings tended to control the course of interactions with the target children. The "smarter" the sibling, the less the target child proposed plans, and the more the target child carried out plans of the sibling. The smarter the target child, the more she/he proposed initial plans her/himself. Although these relationships might seem intuitive (e.g., "bigger, smarter kids boss other kids"), there is some support for Vygotsky's contention that more competent others act as planning monitors for children, that is, the less competent children functioned on an interpsychological plane. When the target children were more competent, they proposed their own plans, indicating intrapsychological functioning. When the sibling was more competent, the target child carried out the sibling's proposed plans more often. There is, however, little support for Vygotsky's proposal concerning the role of speech in the development of planning abilities. The target children's Raven's scores, a performance measure of intelligence, were related to their proposals of plans. This suggests that general competency, rather than verbal ability alone, might be related to children's planning abilities, and to siblings' tendency to act as the monitor of plans, proposing initial plans and convincing the target child to carry out the plan.

IV. Summary and conclusions

The theoretical frameworks that are able to address the issue of familial influences on planning each propose a relationship between how adults behave during interactions with children and the development of abilities children need in order to plan. An assumption is shared by Vygotsky, distancing theory, and most of the parents in the two studies, which is that parents must somehow teach their children to plan. Sigel's distancing framework focuses on a specific class of behaviors that will help the child develop repesentational skills that are likely to be necessary, though not sufficient, for the development of planning abilities. Vygotsky focuses upon the regulation of the child's behavior by others, that is, parents and siblings within the family, until the child becomes able to regulate his or her own activities.

Each of these approaches is unidirectional, assuming that other people, notably parents, influence the development of the child's planning abilities. If this is the case, the results presented are easy to interpret. Relationships between parents' use of distancing strategies and children's anticipation and memory scores can be seen as a result of parental enhancement of children's representational abilities through distancing during the history of parent–child interactions that have occurred throughout the child's life. Differences in relationships for groups of children who varied in communicative competency or age, and relationships between a sibling's competency and the target child's planful behavior during interaction with that sibling are more difficult to interpret with the use of models that assume unidirectional effects of others on the child.

It is not entirely fair to characterize these approaches as necessarily unidirectional, however, although it is not clear how the child affects others within either approach. Both distancing and Vygotsky's frameworks assume that the development of abilities necessary for planning occur within the context of social experiences, which must include some degree of reciprocal influence between parties involved in interaction with one another. For example, Sigel's distancing behaviors are teaching strategies that adults use during interactions with children in order to encourage representational thinking on the child's part. The parent as teacher must be assumed to be responsive to the ability level of the child during these social interactions so that developing abilities can be challenged and exercised. Similarly, Wertsch interprets the Vygotsky approach as:

. . . predicated on the fact that children do not exist in a social vacuum during the early part of their lives and then abruptly begin to function as independent problem-solvers, memorizers, etc. Rather, in those skill areas where a child will eventually be required to solve problems by herself/himself, such independent functioning follows a period during which he/she engages in activities in collaboration with an adult or other relatively experienced member of his/her culture (Wertsch, 1979, p. 2)

Thus, simply by virtue of the fact that planning abilities are viewed as developing within the context of social interaction, some effect of the child on the family members who influence the child's development can be inferred.

This reciprocal or bidirectional nature of influence complicates the question of familial influences on children's planning to some degree, but such an approach is consistent with both the two theoretical models and the empirical results obtained. The distancing framework and Vygotsky's framework are developmental approaches, which means the child changes and grows as a result of biological maturation and experience. Given such a developmental basis, it is unlikely that a straightforward model of familial influences on children's planning would be possible. On one hand, the representational abilities that parents' distancing strategies are aimed at are assumed to change with the growth of the child and with experiences in activities and with both physical objects and social beings. As the child's abilities change, so do his or her interactions with the parent, and hopefully the parent's teaching strategies are modified in response to the child. Similarly, the child's communicative abilities change as the child matures and benefits from experience, leading to more potential for Vygotsky's developmental shift to intrapsychological functioning. Again, the parent (or sibling) must be sensitive to the child's abilities and respond by increasing or decreasing the type or degree of guidance over the child's behavior.

As a result of assumptions that children's planning abilities occur within a social context, the family can be viewed as the crucible for the onset and development of planning abilities. The family provides the most intensive milieu for an array of interpersonal experiences that lay the groundwork for subsequent social and individual activity. However, the influences of the family are also viewed as in a constant state of change, as dynamic as the development of each family member. The results of the present studies must therefore be viewed as only a moment in the family life, frozen in time during the process of change.

Because the child changes, and because of the importance of the social context, different aspects of the child's planning abilities are likely to be influenced in a variety of ways. For example, the child's social communication abilities could affect the development of the child's planning abilities in at least two ways, in addition to the impact Vygotsky posits as due to the link between speech and self-regulation. First, the development of representational skills that are involved in planning, such as anticipation and memory, may be delayed or deficient when social communication ability is low. In the extreme case of children with communicative abilities so poor that they are labeled communication handicapped, this was the case. The success rate of CH children was lower than that of NH children on anticipation and memory tasks. This lesser representational ability may be due to a general physiological problem that

affects many forms of representation, or to the different experiential base
CH children have as a result of limited ability to use social communicative speech.

The second manner in which a child's social communicative abilities
could affect the development of planning is due to reciprocal influences
assumed to operate during parent–child interactions. The child's own
behaviors have the capacity to evoke greater or lesser degrees of control
or guidance, greater or lesser degrees of organization and monitoring, and
greater or lesser use of low- or high-level distancing behaviors from other
people. Both the child's communicative ability and his or her representational thinking ability are likely to influence the behaviors of others that
are directed at the child and influence subsequent development of planning abilities in the child. Thus, the relationships obtained between parents' use of low- and high-level distancing and children's anticipation and
memory scores most likely reflect the parents' ability to match their
teaching strategy to the child's ability level, as well as the parents' influence on the development of representational skills through encouragement of such thinking by the child.

The strength of the relationship between the child's representational
ability and the parents' behaviors seemed to be affected by the communicative ability of the child. At first glance, it seemed this could be due to
greater difficulty in being responsive to the CH than the NH children's
representational abilities due to the problem in social communication.
But, in fact, the relationships between parents' behaviors and children's
anticipation and memory scores were stronger for CH than NH children.
This suggests that the parent's role in the development of representational abilities may be even more important when a child has problems
with communicative speech. Perhaps the parent of the CH child is more
vigilant in constantly assessing abilities more precisely than parents of
NH children, who may be viewed as less in need of adult guidance and
challenges by the parent. Or perhaps the parents of CH children have
included low-level distancing more often during their history of interactions with the child, encouraging verbalizations such as labels and
descriptions to increase the quantity of simple speech from the child. As
a result of exposure to these low-level distancing behaviors, the development of children's representational abilities may have been hindered.
Perhaps the parent's role as planning monitor is necessarily prolonged
until the child has mastered social speech and developed intrapsychological self-regulation. It would be important to conduct similar research
longitudinally in order to investigate whether parents constrain the representational development of their CH children by failing to decrease the

frequency of low-level distancing as the child matures, or if the parent responds to subsequent child growth in a manner that indicates sensitivity and responsiveness to the child's changing abilities.

The planning activities during interactions between target children and their siblings were related to the ability levels of both target children and their siblings, indicating that developmental status (i.e., intellectual competency) and interpersonal experiences are interdependent. Each of these factors alone and in combination is likely to be related to the development of planning abilities. Specifically, the smarter the sibling, the more often the target child carried out the sibling's plans and the less often the target child proposed his or her own plans. The smarter the target child, the more plans he or she proposed to the sibling. It is not how smart the child is when it comes to planning, it is how smart the child is in relation to the other person. The more competent child in the dyad takes control of the interaction, in essence determining the planful activities of both children. The importance of considering developmental status (or competency) and interpersonal experiences was evident in these findings. Thus, the developmental status of both participants, and the experiences of proposing plans and carrying out others' plans that stem from that status, are each likely to influence the course of development of the child's planning abilities.

The communicative ability of the target children was also a factor in the sibling interactions. When target children evidenced communication handicaps, fewer initial plans were proposed to siblings, and they carried out siblings' plans more often than when the target children were non-handicapped. It is likely that the communicative ability of the target child affected the nature of the social interaction with the sibling such that siblings of CH children took control of the interaction. More attention to sibling interactions could reveal whether NH siblings prevent intrapsychological functioning or enhance its development in CH children as they control the interaction through proposed plans that the CH child carries out under the sibling's guidance.

In summary, the developmental theories that can address the issue of familial influences on children's planning are clear in proposing that interactions with family members should influence the course of the child's developing planning abilities. Data from the present studies, as well as consideration of the importance of social interaction and developmental status of the child at any one point in time, suggest a complex and dynamic nature to familial influences on children's planning. The child's age and representational abilities in areas such as anticipation and memory most likely influence how parents interact with their child. The child's social communicative ability is related to how well parents monitor their child's progress, in all likelihood, and to how siblings interact with the child during cooperative problem-solving activities. The child's developmental status in these areas is important in determining the nature of the child's social experiences within the family environment. Given the child's current developmental status, these social experiences are seen as the major source of influence on both the representational skills and the planning behaviors that the child will develop. Change, or development, in the child's planning, must come about as the child's ability level (e.g., in representational or communicative speech) changes, as a result of maturational growth or social experiences, or when the nature of the social experience of the child changes, as when a sibling shows an increase in competence due to his or her own growth or experience thereby altering the nature of sibling interactions. Thus, familial influences on children's planning reside in social interactions, but these social interactions are continuously changing as individual family members grow, exercise their competencies during interactions with others, and respond to the abilities that are evidenced by the other family members.

Notes

1. All families with CH children were recruited through hospitals, pediatricians, private speech therapists, and university programs in the area. The families in the NH groups were recruited through public and private schools and newspaper advertising. Data collection occurred at the laboratories of Educational Testing Service in Princeton, New Jersey. All families were paid for their participation.

References

Cocking, R. R. (1979). *Influences of distancing behaviors on language and cognition of pre-schoolers.* Paper presented at the Fifth Biennial International Symposium of the Society for the Study of Behavioral Development, Lund, Sweden.

Dunn, L. M. (1954). *Peabody Picture Vocabulary Test.* Minneapolis, MN: American Guidance Service.

Goodnow, J. J. (1984). Change and variation in ideas about childhood and parenting. In I. E. Sigel (Ed.), *Parental belief systems: The psychological consequences for children* (pp. 235–270). Hillsdale, NJ: Erlbaum.

Lamb, M. E. (Ed.). (1982). *Nontraditional families: Parenting and child development.* Hillsdale, NJ: Erlbaum.

Lamb, M. E., & Sutton-Smith, B. (Eds.). (1982). *Sibling relationships: Their nature and significance across the life span.* Hillsdale, NJ: Erlbaum.

McGillicuddy-De Lisi, A. V. (1982). The relationship between parents' beliefs about development and family constellation, socioeconomic status, and parents' teaching strategies. In L. M. Laosa & I. E. Sigel (Eds.), *Families as learning environments for children* (pp. 261–299). New York: Plenum.

McGillicuddy-De Lisi, A. V. (1984). The relationship between parental beliefs and children's cognitive level. In I. E. Sigel (Ed.), *Parental belief systems: The psychological consequences for children* (pp. 7–24). Hillsdale, NJ: Erlbaum.

Paulson, F. L., Whittemore, S. L., McDonald, D. L., Hirshon, S., & Tripplet, T. A. (1971). *Manual for the Oregon Preschool Test of Interpersonal Cooperation.* Monmouth, OR: Testing Research.

Piaget, J., & Inhelder, B. (1971). *Mental imagery in the child: A study of imaginal representation.* New York: Basic Books.

Raven, J. C. (1956). *Coloured progressive matrices* (rev. ed.). London: Lewis. Distributed by the Psychological Corporation, New York.

Raven, J. C. (1977). *The Crichton Vocabulary Scale* (rev. ed.). London: Lewis. Distributed by the Psychological Corporation, New York.

Sigel, I. E. (1979). Consciousness raising of individual competence in problem solving. In M. W. Kent & J. E. Rolf (Eds.), *Primary prevention of psychopathology: Social competence in children* (Vol. 3, pp. 75–96). Hanover, NH: University Press of New England.

Sigel, I. E. (1982). The relationship between parental distancing strategies and the child's cognitive behavior. In L. M. Laosa & I. E. Sigel (Eds.), *Families as learning environments for children* (pp. 47–86). New York: Plenum.

Sutherland, K. (1983). Parents' beliefs about child socialization. In I. E. Sigel & L. M. Laosa (Eds.), *Changing families* (pp. 137–166). New York: Plenum.

Vygotsky, L. S. (1962). *Thought and language.* Cambridge, MA: MIT Press.

Vygotsky, L. S. (1978). *Mind in society: The development of higher psychological processes.* Cambridge, MA: Harvard University Press.

Wechsler, D. (1976). *Wechsler Preschool and Primary Scale of Intelligence* (rev. ed.). New York: The Psychological Corporation.

Wertsch, J. V. (1979, March). *Functioning on Vygotsky's interpsychological plane: The social origins of strategic self-regulation.* Paper presented at the Biennial Meeting of the Society for Research in Child Development, San Francisco, CA.

Wertsch, J. V. (1985). Adult–child interaction as a source of self-regulation in children. In S. R. Yussen (Ed.), *The growth of reflection in children* (pp. 69–97). New York: Academic Press.

Wertsch, J. V., McNamee, G. D., McLane, J. B., & Budwig, N. A. (1980). The adult–child dyad as a problem-solving system. *Child Development, 51,* 1215–1221.

12 Social influences on representational awareness: plans for representing and plans as representation

Rodney R. Cocking and Carol E. Copple

I. Introduction: planning as cognition

Without the ability to form mental representations, we would be unable to plan. Planning how to arrange the livingroom furniture, how to drive to the new shopping mall, and how to approach our boss for a raise involve the formation of mental representations of spatial arrangements, object transformations, potential verbal exchanges, and so on. Essential to planning is the ability to anticipate the outcomes of actions. Without this representational capacity, we could not make the simplest plan. This does not mean that successful action sequences, even complex ones, do not take place without planning. In the anthill or beehive, for instance, elaborate sequences of actions are carried out through instinctual patterns. But unless actions or goals are to some degree formulated in advance, planning is not said to have taken place. In order to do this, we must be able to anticipate the outcomes of actions.

At the root of planning, then, is the ability to think about future goals and the actions needed for achieving them. Such thinking about events, object transformations, and spatial arrangements that have not yet occurred may be termed "anticipatory." Planning also depends on the ability to draw on previous learning, which again involves mental representation. Thus, representational abilities are necessary, though not sufficient, for planning to take place.

Metacognitive development would appear to be closely related to the development of planning skills. Both metacognition and planning involve representation; both imply a degree of reflectiveness and distance from the immediate action. The metacognition involved in knowing what one does and does not know how to do, for instance, is relevant to

The research reported in this paper was funded under two grants from NIH Biomedical Research Support Grants No. 5-S07 RR05729-3, S. Messick, Program Director, R. R. Cocking & C. E. Copple, Principal Investigators.

428

planning how to approach or carry out a given task. Even judging the difficulty of a task and how much planning it requires is a metacognitive activity.

Figure 12.1 shows our view of the relationship of planning and metacognitive skills to mental representation. Representation is necessary for planning and for metacognition. Metacognition and planning involve some of the same abilities and processes and are frequently mingled.

In developmental research, there is evidence that metacognitive capacities and tendencies increase over time (e.g., Flavell, 1968), as do planning skills (e.g., Kreitler & Kreitler, chapter 6, this volume). Children increasingly become more purposeful and reflective in approaching activities; with age they engage in more self-regulation and self-interrogation. For the child who has learned to survey the available materials before beginning to build a block structure, it would be difficult to disentangle metacognition from planning and determine where one ends and the other begins. In the acquisition of this survey strategy, both metacognition and planning are involved and are closely related.

One implication of this discussion is that it may be useful to study metacognition as we study planning. To get a clearer understanding of children as planners, we need to find out what kinds of metacognitive activities they are engaging in.

Another implication is that the study of planning should include a concern for some of its more rudimentary manifestations, such as the child's envisaging or thinking about a product before making it. Little research has been done on the development of such fundamental aspects of planning; for example, to what extent and in what ways young children think about final products or outcomes they want to create *before* they act and as they engage in the task. For investigating such questions, methodologies on the naturalistic end of the continuum may be more appropriate than the kinds of experimental paradigms frequently used in planning research. By contrast, planning research often has specific task demands associated with it, such as the time or sequence demands of doing errands or planning a party. For example, when a child draws a picture, it is necessary to break down the subject content into basic components and to think about their spatial arrangements or crayon color options. However, there is no demand implied in the task for one aspect to be produced prior to any other, for one color to be chosen over another, or for the task to occur in any particular sequence or time frame. We thought it useful to consider behaviors in a paradigm where task demands are not influencing or directing the child.

Our intention in this chapter is, first, to review a selection of the rele-

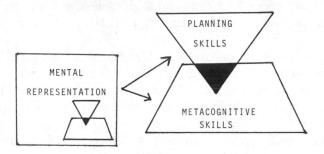

Figure 12.1. The relationship of mental representation, planning, and meta-cognition.

vant literature and focus on studies that examine children's early planning or organizing behaviors. We will then turn to two of our own research endeavors that shed some light on metacognitive and planning activity in two of young children's favorite pastimes, drawing and make-believe play.

II. The emergence of planning skills

Memory, communication, mental systematization of diverse experiences, and thinking about nonpresent events are all dependent upon the development of concepts and representational skills. Object permanence is one example of the infant's abilities to think representationally about nonpresent events. This type of thinking gives our world stability, as well as providing vehicles for going beyond perceptual information as we make inferences, in essence, as we think. Over the years, psychology has focused a great deal of attention on conceptual learning and concept formation. No theory of learning challenges the central role of this kind of representational activity in accounting for intellectual growth. All investigators on the subject (e.g., Smith & Medin, 1981) point out that mental life would be chaotic if there were not some way to give organization and structure to experiences. Looking both forward and backward depends upon the organizational skills of representation.

When do we begin to see evidence of children's early organizational abilities and early planning behaviors? One approach to this question has been to ask when children begin to take an ordered approach to tasks. The research conclusions, unfortunately, are not unanimous in their interpretations. For example, in a review by Spungen and Goodman (1983), several studies were cited that suggest children under 3 years of age are incapable of ordering the environment in any useful way (Elkind, Koegler, & Go, 1964; Elkind & Weiss, 1967; Goodman, 1979, 1981; Gottschalk, Bryden, & Rabinovitch, 1964; Wellman, Somerville, & Haake, 1979), whereas others claim that evidence of organized actions in children have been obscured by the research tasks (Gelman, 1979; Gelman & Gallistel, 1978; Keil, 1979; Mehler & Bever, 1967; Pottery & Levy, 1968; Ricciuti, 1965; Schaeffer, Eggleston, & Scott, 1974). The large literature on children's language and conceptual growth by such researchers as Nelson (e.g., 1974, 1977, 1978, 1979, 1982, and 1983) suggest that concept formation is an organization function that begins to emerge well before the age of three.

Recent work (e.g., Bertenthal & Fischer, in press) with children as young as 12–24 months has demonstrated that children employ systematic search strategies. Spungen and Goodman (1983) also found evidence for the early emergence of organizing abilities, which developed gradually and continuously in children 18–24 months of age. These studies suggest that goal-oriented, sequentially organized actions begin to emerge in the early months of life; these actions may be viewed as early signs of planful behavior. The argument is that organization is critical to planful behavior and that there is a great deal of evidence of early organizational behavior. Numerous studies by Piaget, Bruner, and Sigel have all been directed toward understanding the growth of representational skills during early childhood. The question is whether or not this capability for organization that grows out of conceptual development actually aids in planning behavior. Are the concepts driving behavior in "planned" and "planful" directions? For example, if a child wants a particular type of object to serve as a part of a pretend play sequence, are there criteria for choosing objects that are selected and rejected? Does the child's concept of an object direct the search behavior? Are the children deliberating, reflecting, and anticipating about their activities even before they begin? Do object classes ("This will serve my needs") and anticipated needs ("What I need now is . . . ") evolve after the fact?

III. Object choices in symbolic play

When children are engaging in pretend play, they will often take up an object of some kind to serve as a prop in performing an action in the play sequence. We were interested in the extent to which the child's object choices were careful selections based on representational criteria. We wondered whether children reflected before making choices, projecting ahead in terms of how they would use the object in the make-believe play sequence.

Answers to these questions would furnish additional insight into the nature of children's planning and representational processes and the metacognition accompanying make-believe play. We felt that children's play behaviors would reflect what they held as concepts of particular objects, their criteria for classifying objects, and their applications of these criteria as they searched for play objects.

To study these behaviors, we involved children in dramatic play situations in which they played along with an adult experimenter who was well-known to them. A wide range of objects from which to choose as they played was available. As the experimenter and the child played store or house, the experimenter suggested at intervals the need for an object to perform a certain function in the ongoing play scenario, for example: "We'll need a spoon for scooping out some ice cream."

We were interested in whether children who were choosing a spoon to scoop and those choosing a spoon to stir make different selections from objects that, at best, share only some of the features of spoons. From their selections, we sought to determine how much influence specific antici-pated uses have on object choices. By noting the children's behaviors and verbalizations, we hoped to gain insight into the metacognitive aspects of this representational activity and the planning that accompany make-believe play.

The results confirmed the hypothesis that children would make differ-ent object choices, depending on the function the object was to serve in the make-believe play scenario. We also found, as expected, that children exhibited their sensitivity to the anticipated function through their ver-balizations and actions. In general, the amount of spontaneous verbali-zation about object choices was high. The verbalizations provided a wealth of useful information about the level and nature of children's "representational awareness," specifically their metacognition and reflec-tiveness in finding make-believe representations for real objects.

A.   Children's verbal reflections on making object substitutions

Children freely commented on their object choices. They spoke of the appropriateness of objects for the intended use, of problems with the objects as substitutes, of the lack of satisfactory choices, and of the diffi-culty in making up their minds. Such commentary, as a whole, reflects the fact that choosing objects for use in pretending is not an automatic process. Instead, selecting props for play is a reflective process in which the play participant maintains a self-awareness regarding his or her sym-bolic play activity. It is true that the tendency to ponder choices is probably heightened by the experimental setting, in spite of our efforts to provide a casual, make-believe framework. However, comments indicative of reflection and self-awareness have been noted to occur in the course of interactive free play as well (e.g., Matthews, 1978). It seems likely that covert verbalization would be more characteristic of solitary play, whereas overt verbalizations would arise more frequently in play with others.

The types of things children say when making object substitutions, we suggest, reflect the nature of the cognitive activity underlying their choices as well as the extent of the children's reflectiveness about their representational efforts. The principal types of verbalizations of this sort that we identified are listed, along with examples, in Table 12.1.

Comments of the types described are of considerable interest for what they tell us about preschool children's use of objects in pretend play. First, it is clear from these spontaneous remarks that the children have standards about what constitutes a suitable substitute object in a given situation and that the children make their choices after considerable thought. A request by an adult for an object in make-believe was readily accepted by all the children, and they did not seem to think that any object would do equally well. The children went through an evaluation process, sometimes very explicit, considering the available alternatives with respect to the criteria they were seeking to meet.

Second, the children's comments included thoughts about *why* a given object was a good choice, *why* a rejected object was not desirable, and what was less than ideal about a chosen object though it might be the best available. Sometimes children talked about how difficult it was to decide between one object and another or expressed their dissatisfaction with all the available choices. On occasion we heard them ask themselves aloud whether or not a given object would do. In some of these remarks, the children showed an awareness of their own evaluation processes or of the representational task. These are particularly interesting as evidence of metacognition. But to the point of the present volume, standards of evaluation, comparisons among skills and products, and statements of planning all reflected various aspects of planned, organized thinking.

In many of the remarks, we see the child doing what might be thought of as transforming the object and imposing a new identity upon it, a sort of planning-in-action. At the least, children showed a tendency to see verbalization as a bridge for the gap between the object as it was and as it should be for the play episode. They knew if the item met the specifications or if they could supplement, verbally or gesturally, for any shortcomings. This was a kind of monitoring by the children, in that they were

Table 12.1. *Principal types of verbalizations reflecting the cognitive and metacognitive activity accompanying object choices*

A. Verbalizing satisfaction with object
    1. Conveys satisfaction in finding an appropriate object *without commenting on why it is suitable*

        Examples:

        "Ah, *there* is an envelope."
        "I found the bowl that would be good."
        "That's not a spoon, but it could be a spoon."
        "That's what I could find that looks most like a shoe."
    2. Conveys satisfaction in finding appropriate object, *commenting on why it is suitable*

        Examples:

        "This has shoelaces."
        "I think this is a shoe. You know why? [Demonstrates that it can be worn] That is why."
        "This is a shoe because it's got string."
B. Verbalizing what is wrong with object(s) chosen
    1. Conveys dissatisfaction with object(s) rejected *without commenting on what's wrong*

        Examples:

        "There's no shoe."
        "Too silly. This can't be a shoe. No."
        "Not this one. This can't be good . . . not this, not this, not that, not that, and not this [about each object but the chosen one]"
        "This is not a shoe [laughing]."
        "Is this the telephone? No, probably not."
    2. Conveys dissatisfaction with object(s) rejected, *commenting on what's wrong*

        Examples:

        [Looking for shoe for tying] "It doesn't have any string."

        [Looking for pitcher for pouring] "This one doesn't have a handle [pointing to the spout on other pitcher; confused about the word]. Needs to have a handle."

        [Looking for bowl for fish] "I know which one that would not be a good one. This one [colander] would not because it has holes in it. The water can get out."
C. Verbalizing dissatisfaction with object chosen
    1. Conveys some dissatisfaction with object chosen by *commenting on what's wrong*

        Examples:

        "Maybe this into a – . I know how to make one of these into a telephone [holds object to ear]."
        "This would be better with a handle [referring to pitcher with spout, selected for pouring water]."
    2. Conveys some dissatisfaction with object chosen by *modifying it* (and commenting on modification)

        Examples:

        "Here's one part [bone for telephone receiver]. I can't find the other part in here [finally adds dial]."

Table 12.1 *(cont.)*

"This one [milk carton 'shoe'] doesn't have one [a shoelace]. Poke a hole in it and we could take this [lace from peg board 'shoe']. Get this for a shoelace."

"We need to put this [picks up 'scooping spoon,' mumbling, then 'stirring spoon']. Hm-m-m, you have to put that together somehow [puts scoop at end of stirrer; finally, puts scoop back). I'm pretending something's right here."

D. Pondering choices verbally
   1. Verbalizes that more than one object has appeal

     Examples:

     "This or that?"
     "Let's see; which pitcher should I take?"
     "I can't find the goodest one."
     "Could this be a phone . . .? (Experimenter: "Could it be?") . . . I don't know."
     "Is this it? No. This? No. This could be it."

   2. Talks while choosing, "thinking aloud."

     Examples:

     "Envelope? [Looks at object] Yes."
     "Look in there and see what would be good for a shoe [looking in drawer]. Good for a shoe, good for a shoe. Is this? [puts shoe on foot]. It probably will."
     "Where is the telephone anyway? Is this the telephone? No, probably not."

---

checking against some standard at various junctures during the activity. Similar verbalizations have been observed in other activities where children are representing something in the world. Investigators have found that in drawing (as we will discuss in the next section), children frequently make spontaneous comments to supplement their drawings or clay constructions (Cocking & Copple, 1979; Copple, Cocking, & Waxman, 1980; Golomb, 1974). Children often perceive a discrepancy between what they are trying to represent and what they are able to achieve (in the case of their own creations) or select (in the case of object choices). In these instances, investigators have found that children are not automatically satisfied. Alongside their imaginative abilities, the children manifest their active use of standards or criteria of representation.

Children engage in a different type of monitoring when they check a product to determine if they have succeeded in what they attempted. Whereas the former type of checking along the way involves monitoring and editing, this latter type is evaluative for judging whether one has been successful in what one has intended to achieve.

The value of verbal data for understanding children's thinking has been cited in the cognitive literature and the literature on metacognition for some time. Vygotsky deserves credit for bringing children's language to the foreground of cognitive data. With respect to planning, Vygotsky's

writings argue for verbal data as primary sources for understanding planning-in-action, and the function of langauge in organizing activities (see
Vygotsky, 1978).

As we began our program of research on children's drawing skills, we
were struck by the collateral role language played in the child's graphic
representations of the world. The child's "story" was not a pictorial essay,
nor was it a narrative account. Rather, words and graphic displays were
combined, but not necessarily coordinated, into the objectifications of
their experiences and the events they knew about. Thus, as we set about
to study representational thinking, we collected audio, observational, and
graphic protocols of children's drawing activities. We will discuss how the
verbal data eventually told us about the children's problem-solving strategies and, specifically, how they reflect both planning-in-action and
planned actions.

IV. Planning and representational awareness in children's drawings

Drawing is one of the representational modalities that undergo rapid
development during the preschool years, a time during which children
show a great deal of interest in the activity itself. The significance of children's art as a cognitive phenomenon has been recognized by numerous
investigators in the past (e.g., Arnheim, 1967; Goodenough, 1926; Harris,
1963; Piaget, 1969). Goodnow (1977) has emphasized the problem-solving aspect of children's attempts to draw representationally. One dimension that is important to the developmental psychologist or educator who
is charting the emergence of a basic representational system is the child's
own understanding of the system or mode of representing. What does the
child understand about the representation? How consciously does the
child invent solutions of representational problems? Does the child have
standards and goals that he or she struggles to attain in the drawings?
Does the child think of how the drawing will be seen by others and plan
accordingly? Does the child anticipate problems in spatial arrangement
and other aspects of the drawing and reflect on how to solve them? Do
the verbal comments tell us anything about how the child uses criteria
and standards for monitoring representational activities?

These cognitive and metacognitive questions have not thus far been
much investigated, partly because the focus of past research has generally
been what the children drew rather than what they said as they drew.
Drawings were often collected in situations that were not conducive to
children's talking as they drew; in fact, verbalizations were rarely

recorded. As investigations began to take place more often in naturalistic settings, such as the home (e.g., Fenson, 1977), and as there was more interaction between experimenter and the children, investigators began to notice that children said interesting things as they drew. The monitoring activities of children also have not been studied in any great detail. These monitoring processes are ongoing activities in which the child holds the product in mind in relation to some standard. Eventually, at the conclusion of the activity, the child once again has to take stock of the whole endeavor and determine if he or she achieved what was intended. Thus, the metacognitive activity of monitoring may occur as an editing process or an evaluation of the finished product. Verbal comments of children as they perform tasks can potentially tell us about this type of "thinking about thinking" by children.

A. What the social context elicits

Over the course of our research project, we tapped into children's verbalizations about their drawings in a variety of settings. The data we will be looking at closely here are from ten sessions spaced approximately two weeks apart over the course of a school year. Sessions 4 through 10 were observed for study, with Sessions 1–3 dropped to reduce novelty effects being reflected in the data. Twenty-one boys and thirteen girls from a predominantly middle-class preschool participated. Half of the chidren were between 3;5 and 4;1, and half were between 4;3 and 4;10 years of age at the beginning of data collection.

An experimenter familiar to the children provided them with magic markers and paper and described a topic which she requested the children to draw. The topics were generally based on the children's recent experiences (e.g., a field trip) or events that occurred regularly (e.g., snack time). If the children's drawings were unrelated to the topic, the experimenter gently reminded them of the initial suggestion. However, if the children did not want to draw anything related to the suggested topic, they were left to proceed as they wished.

To assure that the commentary in these small-group sessions was not a function of implicit task demands, data were also gathered in the classroom context by placing a microphone on a table where the same drawing materials were available to the children during free-play times. Data from the classroom and nonclassroom settings were sufficiently similar to permit the assumption that commentary in the small group sessions was typical of spontaneous conversations when children were together in larger groups. Classroom data revealed two general aspects of young children's speech: (a) Frequencies of responses were lower in the larger classroom context; and (b) language used in both contexts was similar and of comparable complexity. Thus, the data indicate the strong influence of an adult for evoking verbalizations, as well as the child's own development as a factor regulating the complexity of verbal behaviors. Though the context may have influenced the volume of verbal output, the complexity of the verbalization was not a function of the context.

From the total set of coded response categories, the following subset was examined for this investigation:

1. *Naming* or labeling of picture elements ("This is my dad"; "Look at the grass")
2. *Description* of the appearance or location of picture elements ("The snowman's hat is black"; "Car on the road")
3. *Planning* of subject, technique, or sequence ("I'm gonna draw my daddy," "I'll draw the table first")
4. *Evaluation of peer picture/skill* ("That's not a boy – you drew a dress!"; "If that's a table, how come it has six things for legs?")
5. *Evaluation of own picture/skill* ("I made a good space ship")

Results indicated that planning and evaluation were collateral behaviors as hypothesized: On the whole, children showed either both or neither of these verbalization types. Both age groups used many labeling and descriptive statements in reference to their drawings, but it was only the older children who showed a significant level of planning, self-evaluative, or peer-evaluative statements.

These categories reflect the child's organization of experiences. The verbal expression of the organization does something else, however. These verbalizations objectify the experience. The child can once again become an actor on his or her object of reconstruction or anticipation. Hence, explicit verbalizations allow children to engage in objectified planning, sequencing, evaluation, and other commentary about a world that is known to them but which is no longer physically present. The effect is feedback, in the cybernetic sense of the term, where feedback serves as a reality check for reconstructions and as hypothesis-testing for anticipations and as such constitutes a type of behavior that might be termed "planning-in-action" (Cocking, 1982; Cocking & Copple, 1979a, 1979b).

B. Construct validity

An important question is whether or not these data relate to representational thinking in any general sense, or merely reflect descriptive commentary on representations.

Table 12.2. *Verbal data from children's drawings: analyses of variance using percentage data*

Source	SS	df	MS	F	p
Naming (Own Drawing)					
Treatment[a]	.17	1	.17	15.64	.0005
Planning (Own Drawing)					
Sex	.14	1	.14	6.5	.02
Treatment	.08	1	.08	3.7	.06
Sex × Age	.12	1	.12	6.65	.02
Naming (by Peer)					
Sex	.002	1	.002	3.01	.09
Sex × Age	.002	1	.002	3.43	.08
Describing (by Peer)					
Sex × Age	.001	1	.001	4.42	.05
Sum: Naming & Describing					
Treatment	.15	1	.15	7.25	.01
Sum: Evaluation & Planning					
Sex	.07	1	.07	2.88	.10
Treatment	.09	1	.09	3.58	.07
Sex × Age	.10	1	.10	4.53	.04
Total					
Between					
Sex	.005	1	.005	3.75	.06
Within					
Sex × Task	.29	9	.03	2.7	.005
Treatment × Task	.51	9	.06	4.7	.000
Sex × Age × Task	.30	9	.03	2.89	.003

[a]Treatment: type of nursery school program.

The children who were the subjects in the pilot work came from two nursery school programs: One was traditional in its curriculum and approach to teaching; the other was a cognitive-based curriculum which utilized an inquiry-teaching strategy. The second program was clearly one that focused upon reflectiveness, planning, and *representational thinking.* No teaching was geared to drawing skills (Copple, Sigel, & Saunders, 1984); however, a program comparison was made which produced the treatment effects reported in Table 12.2.

The children, taken from both nursery school programs to participate in the study, were randomly assigned to the various small drawing groups. All the children had been evaluated on language measures for determining preschool program impact, so we knew that the children had comparable linguistic skills. The language indices were the following: *receptive vocabulary,* as measured by the Peabody Picture Vocabulary

Test (PPVT; Dunn, 1959); *receptive syntax,* as measured by the Bellugi-Klima Comprehension Test (Bellugi-Klima, 1971); and *productive language,* as measured by a modified version of the Potts Test of Syntactic Structures (Potts, 1973). The effects reported in Table 12.2, in favor of the program emphasizing categories related to representational thinking, were particularly interesting and could not be accounted for by differences in language usage, because our pretest measures had already established no language differences prior to the study. Thus, whereas verbal skills were comparable across two different preschool programs, the effect of the cognitive program that was geared toward representational thinking was evidenced by the strong treatment effect in the analysis of variance. It should be noted also that the ANOVAs were run with percentage data rather than raw data from the coded drawing protocols, so as to minimize individual differences among children in the *amount* they talked. That is, task-relevant categories from the coded protocols were adjusted by each child's own overall total amount of verbalization. Thus, sheer amount of talking, which might have differed in the two programs, was not an influencing factor. These results, then, speak to the validity of verbal data for detecting verbal planning that relates to representational thought.

Representational competence is, in part, the skill of bringing previous experiences to bear upon present circumstances. Naming events, labeling them, planning and sequencing one's activities, and the like are behaviors that are employed in this reconstructive process. The verbal categories that were significantly different for children from the two preschool programs were those that would be expected from such a view of representational competence (see Table 12.2).

This initial study was the beginning of an extensive research program. We will now examine the variety of data from this research in terms of three strands of results: (a) developmental and age trends; (b) audience awareness; and (c) event categories in the social context.

In Vygotsky's (1978) account, speech has a second function in children's thinking, in addition to the organizing role. This function, which emerges after the initial stages of language growth, is that of mediation. Mediation can occur at both the individual level and at the social level. The important feature is that when processes are mediated, they are also changed: " . . . [W]hen a process becomes mediated this does not mean that the same mental or practical process is carried out more efficiently or faster; rather it means that this process is restructured into something qualitatively different" (Levina, 1968). Thus, explaining, justifying, or simply planning aloud in the presence of others qualitatively changes the planning. We decided to have a look at this feature of representational thinking in the social context, and to ask how planning and evaluating were influenced by socially mediated speech. Thus, although the meta-cognitive processes of representational thought were the focus of our research, the context in which we collected the data had an additional payoff. Many of children's monitoring and editing activities are more likely to be verbalized in the company of others.

1. Developmental and age trends. As we point out, the more advanced categories of Planning and Evaluation were found to be more character-istic of the older children from 3 to 5. One crucial support to this bridge between speech and organized representational thought may be the social context itself and the child's sensitivity to social input. In the peer draw-ing sessions, there was not only a greater quantity of verbalization about the drawing, but a wider range or commentary as well. Whereas children drawing alone primarily named parts of their drawings or told stories about them, in group sessions children planned aloud, evaluated their own and each others' drawings, and explained or justified the way they had drawn things. Such verbalizations suggest that even 4-year olds are beginning to be more deliberate in their approach to drawing. In the older children, particularly the girls, there was a greater tendency to engage in such reflective behaviors as explicitly planning the picture and judging the success of their own or others' representational efforts. Children began noting problems and discrepancies in the likeness to the real thing, as well as expressing pleasure when they saw representational attempts as successful.

These developmental changes were not an artifact of the fact that the older children talked more as they drew. Developmental changes were investigated by performing all analyses not only with the raw data but with percentage data as well (the ratio of number of verbalizations in each category to the total number of task-related verbalizations).

In summary, evidence was found that children's approach to drawing is increasingly reflective with age, even within the narrow age range of 3 to 5.

This developing "metapictorial" capacity would seem to be related to other reflective behaviors that emerge at about this age, such as metalin-guistic awareness (e.g., Cazden, 1972). The major shifts that occur in such representation involve critically selecting and evaluating what is neces-sary for verisimilitude. That is, planning and categorical thinking that reflect planned actions are important developments that can be seen in children's drawing behaviors.

2. *Audience awareness.* Though interesting developmental and age trends emerged in the analyses described in the previous section, it seemed that other intriguing developmental changes and achievements were being obscured by the use of broad coding categories. In subsequent work, we undertook far more fine-grained and qualitative examinations of those comments that reflected children's awareness of the nature of pictorial representation and of their own problem-solving struggles. From among the numerous aspects of such awareness which were identified in our data, we have chosen two to discuss.

The first of these is an aspect of the child's conception of the nature of representation, that is, awareness of the "audience," either a specific person or the generalized other, who will potentially view the drawing. The second aspect of representational awareness to be discussed lies within the problem-solving domain, that is, children's consciousness of their handling of space and sequence in their drawings. With respect to planning, the former is an issue of social perspective: planning so that others will understand. The latter (consciousness of space and sequence) is planning as an ancillary executive aid.

  a. Representational awareness: drawing as communication. In some of the children's commentaries we can see an awareness of the fact that drawings can convey information to other persons. We divided awareness of the "audience" or viewer of the picture into several preliminary categories.

One type of comment (Table 12.3) appears to reflect children's knowledge that drawings can show what things look like to someone who is not familiar with the referent, and they can permit the viewer to identify familiar objects or persons. A comment such as "I'm gonna show you where they make the Egg McMuffins" indicates that this child knows he can communicate spatial information through the drawing, that he can inform someone who is in the dark about where Egg McMuffins are made. Similar comments can be seen in this set of examples (A.1, A.3, A.4). Comments of this kind were more common where the referent, setting, or event was one the adult was *unfamiliar* with, particularly when it was emphasized at the start of the drawing session that the adult did not know what the place or event was like.

These are interesting verbalizations from the point of view of perspective taking. What kinds of inferences is the child making? Is he or she taking the perspective of the other person who does not know what X looks like? As Flavell and colleagues (1968) have noted, there are various components of fully developed perspective taking. The kinds of statements we see here do not require all of the abilities Flavell et al. describe. For example, we do not know if the children are considering what features the viewer unfamiliar with the referent would find most informative, which Flavell et al. would call "prediction."

Flavell and associates describe another component ability, "need," which refers to the child's ability to perceive that a particular situation is one that calls for perspective taking. As Flavell et al. noted, whether the child realizes this about a particular situation at a given development level is a function of how salient it is that the need exists in that situation. In some of the cases we observed, the adult mentioned explicitly to the child that she did not know what X looked like. With this type of flag to the children, we see what they appear to know: that when someone does not know what something looks like, you can help that person by drawing it. Beyond this, the verbalizations in this set do not tell us much about the children's knowledge about drawings with respect to the anticipated viewers. Some of the other sets of comments fill in the picture a bit more.

In the next group of comments of Table 12.3 (Group B), we see indications of the concept that the more complete or detailed a picture is, the easier it is for someone to figure out what it depicts. Again, this is a fairly global idea – that the more you draw, the more the viewer can tell – the limits of which could be readily tested by experimental studies. For example, we could investigate whether children always judge "more" to be "better" for making predictions about picture interpretability; or whether they recognize that some features are likely to be more informative than others. Parallel studies have appeared in the literature on communication in the verbal domain (e.g., Gibson, 1969; Glucksburg, Krauss, & Higgins, 1975). Here we simply see evidence of the notion that the more one puts into the drawing, or the more complete it is, the easier it will be for the viewer to interpret it correctly.

There is a notion that implicitly accompanies the aspects we have thus far examined: that the viewer can *misidentify* a picture. There are some comments, examples of which are listed in part C of Table 12.3, that show an understanding that it might not be immediately obvious to everyone what the picture depicts. For example, one child commented, "This is not a church. Our house is this huge." This seems to be an idea that involves some perspective taking ("You might think this is a church because it's so big, but we have a very big house").

As an extreme interpretation, one could argue that whenever children name an object – for example, "This is a tree," "This is my dad" – they are showing they think that the object might not be identified unless it is labeled. But this is far too broad an interpretation. Children do lots of

Table 12.3. *Representational awareness: audience*

A. *Drawing can show what things look like to someone who doesn't know.*

1. H: That's to show you where the plant at McDonald's is.

2. J: I'm gonna show you where they make the Egg McMuffins. And this is what you call an egg ring.

3. R: I'm gonna draw a house – to show you how the McDonald's looked.

4. L: I'm gonna put my house on it so Colleen can know what my house looks like.

5. C: I'm gonna put some hair on him so nobody will know who it is, not even Colleen [plans to disguise his person because otherwise he can be identified by audience].

B. *The more you add to your drawing, the likelier the other is to identify it correctly.*

1. C: [To adult] What do you think I'm going to make?
   E: Oh, let's see. It has two eyes. Gee, Let's see. Mike, do you have an idea what it could be? [Mike doesn't respond.]
   C: Adding something else.

2.   [After peers have guessed incorrectly what his drawing is, adds more]
   M: *Now* guess what it is.

3. D: [To S] What are you making?
   S: You'll see when I'm done.
   D: Is it a train with all these wheels?
   S: No, it couldn't be that. You'll see. Just wait. You'll see.
   S: It looks like a train, on a track.
   S: See? Now it doesn't look like a train.

4. S: What do you suppose this is?
   D: A gate?
   S: Guess again.
   D: I don't know what it is. I give up.
   S: It's a pencil.
   D: It doesn't look like a pencil.
   S: It will! It will!

5. T: [After some guesses of whom he is drawing] No, try to guess again. Not now, when I'm done.
   C: It will be easier.

C. *Drawings can fail to convey information accurately; can be misinterpreted.*

1. T: This is not a church. Our house is this huge.

2. J: These are not the eyes [on Halloween mask in drawing]. These are the puffs.

3. K: I'm going to put an "M" so they'll know it's McDonald's.

4. C: And this is supposed to be a squirrel sticking his head out here.

D. *The particular viewer makes a difference in feasibility of identification of drawing.*
   (Corollary: You draw differently depending on the viewer.)

1. C: I don't know if it looks too much like a bunny to my Dad, but I do know if it looks too much like a bunny to Jude [peer who was present during the drawing of the bunny].

Table 12.3. *(cont.)*

2. H: [Drawing a car for a puppet who doesn't know what cars look like] Here, I'll show you how it looks different from a bus. It's longer.

E. *Interactive episodes with salient audience reaction.*

1. A: [To T about her drawing] Oh, that ball doesn't look very good in drawing it.
   T: So, it could be a ball.
   A: Well, it doesn't look rounded up.
   T: No, this is an egg I'm making. An egg, that is the shape of an egg.

2. M: I'm making you, Kay. Thea, I'm making Kay.
   D: That isn't Kay. It looks like a boy.
   M: It's Kay because you notice the brown hair.

3. T: Your "goon" is lying down.
   M: Nope, standing up. That's how a goon looks like. Its legs are crossing that way.

4. M: [About T's drawing] I think it's a spider.
   T: Your're right!
   M: I knew it was a spider!
   F: What about it made you think it was a spider?
   M: The legs . . . all the legs.

naming, particularly in this setting where the adult encourages them to tell her about their pictures. However, it might be interesting in a free-play art situation to observe what things children spontaneously label, and perhaps how this varies as a function of who is listening and viewing the picture. Does the child realize that others will have a more difficult time telling Dad from Uncle Bill than Dad from Mom or Dad from baby brother? What identifying attributes are necessary? A counterpart in children's play is to allow them to use clown makeup to disguise themselves. Here the problem is to identify which features are critical to conceal so that one cannot be recognized.

These are questions that tap perspective-taking abilities and representational awareness or knowledge about the possibilties and limitations of pictorial representation. In our observations, we found frequent labeling of persons and of things that seemed hard to draw, such as (a) actions; (b) details that required skills beyond the child's level; and (c) referents that are inherently difficult to draw, like the wind.

One caveat in interpreting these remarks: We must recall Vygotsky's (1978) assertion that the organizing function of speech is initially for the self and only later serves social functions. Children may often be labeling their drawings for themselves rather than for others. The function of an utterance may be for the self, to establish that this bunch of lines really *is* a walkie-talkie whether it looks like one or not. Such labeling seems to occur also in symbolic object play; it is probably operating to some extent in children's comments about drawings. Experimental studies would be useful in disentangling the communicative function from the for-the-self function.

We have been looking at comments that reveal an awareness that the viewer might not be able to identify one's drawing. The next set of examples in Table 12.3.D may be seen as a special case of these, an awareness that a particular audience might have trouble interpreting the drawing; for example: "Dad might not know this is a bunny because he didn't see me draw it," the child seems to be saying. Another child mentioned that the kids in the morning preschool groups might not know what he had drawn because they had not gone to McDonald's. The second example listed in this set is a somewhat different situation taken from a classroom interaction in which a puppet named Mr. Forgetful did not know what a car looked like. The children spontaneously suggested drawing the car for the puppet instead of trying to describe it in words.

An awareness of the particular viewer's experience base, or other viewer characteristics, would be a further differentiation within the perspective-taking dimension seen in the earlier sets of comments. This might be a promising aspect to follow developmentally, perhaps by having children make predictions about who could interpret which pictures.

Along with those utterances in which children seemed to show that they realized others could fail to identify their drawings correctly, there were instances of the opposite situation, in which children realized they themselves might not be able to read others' drawings correctly. Children frequently were found to ask their peers what they were drawing. In other instances, they made guesses about what was being drawn and asked the peer who drew it if they were right. There were instances in which the child perseverated in his or her own identification of a drawing despite the claims of the artist herself, but the behavior of turning to the artist as the one who knew what he or she was drawing was quite common. There were numerous instances in which the child found identification to be ambiguous and requested information from the individual who drew it. It seems quite plausible that this experience of confusion over another's drawing plays some role in the child's coming to know that his or her own drawings may not be clear. Trying to predict these ambiguities and trying to avoid viewer confusion may figure into the development of early planning behaviors.

Perhaps more directly, we would hypothesize that children's developing awareness of possible misinterpretation of their drawings is related to the experience of having someone else actually misinterpret or criticize something they draw. Children frequently did question each others' drawings, and those who drew the pictures reacted in a variety of ways. Sometimes they defended their pictures, explaining why they drew them as they did. Sometimes they modified their labels to correspond with the peer suggestion, as in the first example under the interactive episodes sections of Table 12.3.E. Often they made changes or additions in the drawing itself. But in a large proportion of the cases in which a peer questioned or criticized a drawing, the child made some active response. The extent to which children then begin to anticipate others' reactions as they draw cannot be judged from the current data. However, it seems reasonable to suggest that children do develop more awareness of how others will react to their drawings partly through their experiences with others' reactions.

One could speculate on how children who never heard comments on their drawings would differ in their reflectiveness about audience reactions and so forth. This is related to a major question in the area of verbal communication: That is, how children's awareness of listener needs is affected by listener questions, misinterpretations, and other feedback. The answer to this question would also relate to subsequent behaviors of anticipation and preplanning needs and strategies.

    b. Summary. It was found that comments showing an "audience awareness" were more common when the experience of the anticipated viewer was manifestly different from that of the child. For example, in some cases the experimenter had not been with the children on a field trip, or the child was drawing the picture to show to a parent who was not familiar with the classroom routine. In such situations, children were more likely to verbalize an awareness of the fact that the viewer might not be able to interpret the drawing; for example: "My dad might not know this is a rabbit."

Another type of audience awareness comment shows a consciousness that the success with which a picture conveys information to the viewer depends on how it is drawn or on what is included in the drawing. For example, one child said, "I'm gonna draw my house so that Colleen can see what it looks like." Another child, possibly doubtful of the accuracy of her rendition of a well-known landmark, said, "I'm gonna put an 'M' so they'll know it's McDonald's."

These higher levels of audience awareness in the preschool child are particularly interesting and theoretically important, but it will also be useful to examine related categories of verbalizations that come earlier. Gopnik (1982), for example, has identified classes of verbal behaviors that are indices of early planning in both problem-solving contexts and representational thinking. She has charted those associated with 12-month and 18-month milestones of development. Tracing the link between these early behaviors of planning and speech-mediated planning is the next step.

    c. Representational awareness: drawing as problem solving. Numerous developmental and cognitive psychologists of diverse theoretical orientations have been attracted to children's drawings and paintings as sources of study. Some of the researchers have concerned themselves primarily with the developmental changes of a qualitative nature that occur in the ostensive features of the art productions. For example, Fenson (1977), Golomb (1974), Goodnow (1977), and Peck (1976) studied features that change with development. The focus of these investigations ranged from Peck's interest in correlations between picture parts and Piagetian operations, to Fenson's study of conservative reapplications of certain drawing routines and subroutines throughout the development of artistic skills. Other researchers have concerned themselves primarily with individual differences in intelligence or cognitive style as witnessed in the drawings, notably Goodenough (1926) and Harris (1963).

Reference to children's drawings has cropped up in Piaget's writings at various points. In discussing general intellectual development, Piaget's theory supported the research efforts that relate children's drawings to cognitive functioning. It was his contention that the structuration of space and the child's drawings progress through the same stages of development. In discussions of play behavior and in his treatment of mental imagery, Piaget pointed to examples of children's graphic productions. He noted that for children, drawings have attributes of play: They are pleasurable and they are self-directed activities. Drawings also have an important feature in common with the mental image, in that there is some attempt to represent reality. Thus, Piaget concluded that drawing is " . . . a form of the semiotic function which should be considered as being halfway between symbolic play and the mental image" (1969, p. 63). Children's copies of reality, or visual realism, are not done with great skill at age 4 or 5. Their drawings, however, reflect what they *know* about reality and as such are based more on conception than upon perception.

Goodnow (1977) reported developmental changes in children's handling of problems of sequence and space in drawing. By examining the verbal data that accompany the drawing process, we can see not only how the children actually deal with these problems but also what they think. We can get clues about the extent to which children are reflective in their approach to the solving of various organizational problems and in planning their productions. In children's verbalizations we find a reflection of their awareness of their own problem-solving processes in the representational realm. Several steps in planning and dealing with space were identified in our research:

1. *After the fact*
   Description of one's spatial or sequential dilemmas after the fact ("There's not enough room for a house"; "I need to turn the page to draw a horse – it's too crowded here.")
2. *Articulating plan sequence: what? where?*
   a. One-step-ahead articulation of a plan for drawing sequence and/or spatial arrangement ("I'm gonna make the mother next to the daddy;" "I'll need blue to make the sky.")
   b. Planning one's drawing sequence and/or use of space two or more steps ahead, but with no references to the reasons for such plans ("First I'll make his head, then his hair.")
3. *Articulating spatial arrangements or strategy*
   Planning one's solution or articulation of one's strategy for dealing with a stated spatial or sequential problem ("I got it. I got it . . . I have to put him (puppet) down here (bottom of page) for his feet so I can put the string all the way up here.")

In summary, in dissecting statements that reflect the planning children put into their work, one needs to consider that many different kinds and levels of planning may be in evidence. Planning may involve statements of *intention*, statements of identifying *what* will be drawn, *how* one will proceed, the sequence or sequences that may follow, after-the-fact reflection on what has been done and what needs to follow, and comments on progress and completion. These all reflect different kinds of knowing what one intends to do, how one intends to accomplish a goal, and when one has achieved a goal.

Our description of the audience-awareness and metaorganizational comments represent only two aspects of the data on children's representational awareness. We chose these two for discussion in order to exemplify the way in which spontaneous commentary during the drawing process sheds lights on what drawing is to the child and how it involves planning by the child. The major limitation of verbal data, however, is that they do not convey "levels" of the planning process. Verbal data give substantiation of planning, but they are not very useful for telling us how much in advance (number of steps) or how long a time frame ahead the child plans. The verbal comments reflect steps and sequences in planning and reflective assessment, and through such comments we get an idea of what the child understands about the nature of pictorial representation, as well as what that child is aware of in his or her own mental and motor efforts to depict and organize things in the world. By examining a large body of data gathered in a setting conducive to spontaneous verbalizations, we were able to see that children have higher levels of such awareness than has been imagined previously. There were numerous comments that showed a metacognitive dimension in young children's artistic endeavors. More notable is the fact that the children's comments reflected a degree of perspective taking, an awareness of how their drawings would be interpreted by others. These comments helped organize their thoughts about what would have to go into the drawings, and thus reflected their planning for their pictures and how they would be seen and understood by others.

3. *Event categories in a social context.* For any domain of metacognition, one question of interest is how the capacity develops and what role, if any, the environment plays. Accordingly, we looked at the social context of our drawing studies. In our research, we noted that children did a substantial amount of borrowing, copying, and incorporating drawing routines from peers. Others have also noticed these behaviors (Fenson, 1977; Gardner, 1980; Gearhart & Newman, 1980). The question here is whether peer interaction can be hypothesized to play a role in the development of representational awareness.

As we began investigating the nature of peer interactions during drawing, we found three types of feedback operating at the control of the social participants. In a social setting, the child was often in a position of having to justify or explain to others who were reacting to his or her depicted reconstructions. These reactions might have been instigated by others who shared the knowledge of the depicted event and who elaborated or questioned the child's renderings. Others who were not party to the events being drawn might have had questions concerning the meaning of the graphic displays. Thus, some peer verbalizations contained challenges about the accuracy or organization of the drawing, whereas others were questions about meaning. The artist could choose to ignore or to reject others' comments; she could justify or further elaborate her constructions for omissions or ambiguities that had been pointed out through peer inquiry; she could even modify her notions of events, objects, or spatial arrangements because of someone else's differing account of a shared experience. In this sense, the feedback to the child came from others and served an accommodative function.

The kinds of feedback we looked at in our studies included: (a) self-monitoring, in which verbalizations were mainly about one's own reconstructions (primarily an assimilative function); (b) social comparisons of

Table 12.4. *Verbalization indicating interaction*

A. Reactions
    Reacts to peer comments
    Explains, justifies, or answers
    Agrees or repeats
    Rejects verbally (without justification/explanation)
    Ignores label or aspect of story in response to peer comment
B. Influence
    Verbalizations indicating "borrowing" or other influence of peer drawing
      Borrowing of subject
        Part
        Whole item/object
      Borrowing of technique
        Color
        Any aspect of technique except color
      Response to peer verbalizations about peer's own picture

---

others' productions and accounts of events in light of one's own reconstruction (self-directed); and (c) social regulation, in which the verbalizations from someone else about one's work became part of the reconstruction, either graphically or cognitively (primarily accommodative in
function). Table 12.4 is a scheme for looking at social feedback (types b
and c).

To provide a description of the context for children's developing representational awareness, we sorted intereactions into major event types.
Five typical event categories emerged from our data:

1. A hears B comment on a representational problem or solution.
2. A hears B comment on an aspect of the nature of drawing or on the
    drawing process.
3. A hears B ask how to draw something or find fault with his or her own
    drawing.
4. A identifies B's drawing differently from the way B does.
5. A is confronted by a question or critique from B.

Table 12.5 presents some examples of the interchanges of these types.
Although these categories are not exhaustive, they reflect the major types
of interactions we identified in our data and provide insight into the
social aspects of learning to organize and execute (e.g., planning *for* and
planning *to do*) a representational task (Copple, Waxman, & Cocking,
1981).

Gearhart and Newman (1980), among others, discussed the benefits of
social interactions during problem-solving tasks such as drawing. These

Table 12.5. *Categories of peer interaction*

I. *Child₁ questions or criticizes drawing of Child₂*

    1. A: Oh, that ball doesn't look very good in drawing it [T's drawing].
        T: So, it *could* be a ball.
        A: Well, it doesn't look rounded up.
        T: No, this is an egg I'm making. An egg, that is the shape of an egg.

    2. D: Why all the colors purple?
        T: 'Cause.
        D: 'Cause why? 'Cause why?
        T: 'Cause – that's right. A person is not all colors. A person is only white.

    3. J: I'm putting my purple eggs.
        C: They are not supposed to be colored purple. They could be either brown or
            white. Those are the only colors they could be.
        J: There's some yellow eggs.
        C: Yellow eggs. Hey, they could be your white eggs, Jennifer.

    4. B: It's red – that's a Phillies jacket, all right.
        C: That doesn't look like a Phillies jacket.
        B: Wowee. Well, it is red and it has a little white patch on it.

    5. M: [To C about his duck] That looks like a worm, Courtney. The one flying up
            in the air looks like a worm, Courtney.

    6. S: [To C about her picture] You can hardly see yourself.
        C: Well, you can see me.
        S: Hardly.
        C: You can see the grass behind me.
        S: Hardly, hardly.

II. *Child₁ and Child₂ identify the same picture differently*

    1. C: Oh, you drew a sun.
        S: It's a flower.

    2. M: Now guess what it is.
        D: Looks like a kangaroo. It has big ears.
        M: But it's not a kangaroo.

    3. S: What do you suppose this is?
        D: A gate.
        S: ... It's a pencil.
        D: It doesn't look like a pencil.
        S: It will. It will!
        D: That is not a pencil. A pencil has a straight line. There's a line and a point
            like this.

    4. T: Your goon is lying down. [The children are drawing "goons" from a
            favorite song].
        M: Nope, standing up. That's how a goon looks like. Its legs are crossing that
            way.

    5. D: What are you making?
        S: You'll see when I'm done.

Table 12.5 *(cont.)*

D: Is it a train with all these wheels?
S: No, it couldn't be that. You'll see. Just wait. You'll see.
D: It looks like a train. On a track.
S: See, now it doesn't look like a trian.

III. *Child₁ hears Child₂ asking how to draw something or finding fault with his/her own drawing*

1. J: [To E] Does the trees – don't trees have bottoms like that?
2. M: [To E] Are mustaches up here or down there?
3. S: I made the arms too long.
4. C: I made a kitten that looks like a mouse.
5. L: I don't remember how her tail is.
6. C: I just did a mistake. He's [the duck] looking away from here. He's supposed to look that way but he's looking *that* way.
7. T: I don't know how to make a duck.
    L: So there. It's two lines, a line across, and two lines, a line across, and a head and a beak.
    T: I still don't know how to make a duck.
    L: Try all that and then you'll do it.

IV. *Child₁ hears Child₂'s comment expressing an aspect of the nature of drawing or the drawing process*

See Table 12.1 for numerous examples. Some additional examples:

[Verbalizing about one's planning, reflecting, or problem solving]

1. K: I have to think what it looked like.
2. C: I'm making the body first so I'll have room for it all.
3. K: Here, I have to try it on this paper [a trial page] 'cause I did it wrong. In case I did it wrong, I try it on this paper.
4. M: First I'm gonna make the head and then the body.
5. J: See him? He's talking with his mouth open, with an "O" in this mouth, with pink.
6. L: I'm making his arm crooked 'cause he's throwing.
7. T: I got it. I got it . . . I have to put him [a puppet] down here [bottom of page] for his feet so I can put the strings all the way up here. I put the handle right here. I put the strings all the way up to here.

[Verbalizing about one's drawing schemes]

8. H: I'm making a circle for the face.
9. M: A dot for the raindrop. A big dot for the snow.
10. L: It's two lines, a line across and two lines, a line across, and a head and a beak.

researchers, using Vygotsky's (1978) concept, posited a "scaffolding" effect due to the social exchanges. "Scaffolding," in Gearhart and Newman's discussion, was used to describe the teacher's support for a child's organization of a task, but the implication of such a concept is that any social network can potentially provide a foundation for the child's constructive endeavors. Ways in which peers influence representational awareness is our next topic, building on the notion of scaffolding: Peer inquiry helps build a stronger structure to support the child's constructive and reconstructive thinking.

V. Hypotheses about peer influences on representational awareness

Piagetian theory contains a number of formulations about the role of experience in conceptual development. One central notion is that of reflective abstraction; that is, the process through which one derives information from one's own actions – putting them into correspondence, linking them, ordering them, and so on. Reflexive abstraction provides the links between and among experiences. It has two aspects: (a) projection of knowledge from a lower to a higher level; and (b) reorganization or reconstruction of knowledge at a higher level (Gallagher & Reid, 1981; Piaget, 1977).

The impetus for reflexive abstraction is in activity, but this does not necessarily mean the manipulation of objects. Activity also refers to a mental process, which can be triggered through social interchanges and verbal input as well as physical experience. Purely verbal input can provoke reflexive abstraction by disturbing an existing construct or by requiring the child to bring implicit or practical knowledge to a conceptual level. We will see this mechanism as we examine the data.

One point before we proceed: We are not suggesting that peer interactions are *necessary causes* of the emergence of representational awareness. A variety of factors surely operate in this development, factors in the child's emerging capacities and in his or her interactions with the world of pictures and people. Interactions with adults no doubt play a role, and encounters with older siblings have been noted by Fenson (1977) and Gardner (1980). Our observations allow us to consider one part of the social context of drawing: the interactions that take place when children draw in the company of peers, as often happens in the preschool and school settings. These observations and drawing data, along with the verbal protocols, were gathered using three groups of children: 76 preschool children, 18 kindergarten children, and 20 first graders. The procedures were the same as those described previously.

A. Evidence of representational awareness in young children

In addition to the verbal categories we have discussed, such as possibilities and limitations for conveying information, difficulties in conveying concepts, and so on, we found some additional categories that were *relatively rare* in children under 6 years of age. Thus, the findings have developmental implications.

The children in the study had quite a lot to say about their drawings, so we will begin this discussion with a brief overview of children's knowledge of the nature of drawing and then turn to the interpersonal events hypothesized to play a role in the development of representational awareness.

1. Children's understanding of the nature of drawing: six categories. Of the six categories listed in Table 12.6, the first (Possibility/Need for Likeness) shows an awareness that the drawing is supposed to look like its referent. The child knows that there are standards of resemblance and that one can succeed or fail to varying degrees in achieving a good likeness.

The next set of comments reveal an awareness that drawings can or should convey information to those who view them (Possibility/Limitation in Conveying Information). The child knows that a drawing can depict a referent such that a viewer is able to identify it, and he or she also knows that viewer misinterpretation is a possibility, as well.

The third category of comments shows an awareness of the Possibility of Exercising Selection/Discretion in Drawing. The child expresses the idea that there are different ways of drawing the same referent or the notion that one can select from all the possible parts or features that could be included. A related type of comment shows an awareness of the Possibility of Altering Reality in Drawing. The child has the idea that one can play with the elements of drawing: One can make McDonald's purple or draw bald boys, even though one knows that is not the way things usually are in reality.

In the next category of utterances listed in Table 12.6, the child displays the knowledge that a referent can be drawn in various transformations: happy versus sad, light rain versus heavy rain, etc. The child may not be able to achieve distinctive depictions of the state, expression, or position

Table 12.6. *The child's understanding of the nature of drawing*

Possibility/Need for Likeness
1. "Hey, you have to do hands like that. Look, I'll show you." (Instructing peer on achieving a likeness)
2. "That's not how big airplanes are [to peer]. They're bigger than that. I'm making mine bigger than you." (Critiquing peer likeness)
3. "Are mustaches up here or down there [above or below the mouth; asking E]. (Soliciting information in order to achieve likeness)
4. "I'm not finished with mine yet. What did I forget? The body and the neck." (Reflecting on completeness/accuracy of likeness)
5. "I know how to make kids but not a playground." ('Knowledge of not knowing' how to create the likeness)
6. "It's going to be hard to draw my dress." (Knowledge of the difficulty of creating the likeness)

Possibility/Limitation of Drawings in Conveying Information
1. "Guess what this is?" (Recognizing the possibility of conveying information)
2. "I'm gonna draw a house to show you how the McDonald's looked."
3. "I'm gonna put my house on it so Colleen will know how my house looks."
4. "This is not a church. Our house is this huge." (Recognizing the possibility of misinterpretation)
5. "These are not the eyes [in the picture of Halloween mask] These are the puffs." (Recognizing the possibility of misinterpretation)
6. "I'm gonna put an 'M' so they'll know it's McDonald's." (Recognizing the possibility of misinterpretation)

Possibility of Exercising Selection/Discretion in Drawing
1. "Now I'm making a real bad storm, but I'm not going to do it like Henry's." (Recognizing that there are different ways of drawing X)
2. "You don't have to make everything." (Recognizing the possibility of selection in drawing)
3. "I'm not gonna make all the rugs. I'm just gonna make some of it." (Recognizing the possibility of selections discretion)
4. "I think I'll get a darker color for my dress." (Recognizing the possibility of selection/discretion)

Possibility of Altering Reality in Drawing
1. [In response to peer suggestion of making her McDonald's purple] "It's not funny. You can do that. It doesn't matter what colors you make it."
2. "I'm going to make the elevator. There's no elevator there, but I want to make one."
3. "That's black 'cause that's how I want McDonald's to look."
4. "Now I'm going to make a black boy. Guess what? Girls have hair and boys have hair, but I'm making a boy that's bald. No hair at all, but a little, I guess."

Possibility of Drawing Objects or Events in Various States, Forms, and Positions
1. "That's when the snow is just falling. So we'll put a little grass in 'cause that's when the snow is just falling."
2. "Now, I'm going to make Kathy. She's going to be happy in this one."
3. "No, I'm making that kind of duck [duck in the air]. I'm making a *mad* duck."
4. [In reaction to peer saying he was drawing a rain storm] "I'm gonna make mine only be sprinkling."

Table 12.6 *(cont.)*

Difficulty of Conveying a Certain Aspect in Drawing

1. [Child draws on the back of his page the mirror image of the pig he has drawn on the front] "Here's the mouth. The other part is in the back. I did the other part in the back."
2. "You can only see two wheels [of a car]. The other two are on the other side."

---

of the referent, but the intention is there and is evident in the verbalizations (see examples for Possibility of Drawing Objects or Events in Various States, Forms, or Positions).

The last set of comments in Table 12.6 (Difficulty of Conveying Certain Aspects in Drawing) is relatively rare in children under 6 years, at least in the situation we were using. A few remarks appeared in our protocols that dealt with a problem or limit imposed by the pictorial modality: for example, some children wanted to draw both sides of an object or tried to show motion.

B. Peer interactions and the development of representational awareness

Because this was a naturalistic investigation, we cannot make causal statements with authority. We can only state what sorts of behaviors occur and suggest the mechanisms through which a given type of event may play a role in provoking representational awareness. We will begin with the events in which there is the strongest suggestion of impact, those in which there is a direct confrontation by one child and an overt response from another. We will return to Table 12.5 for examples.

Children often looked at each other's drawings and questioned or criticized what they saw. In some cases these comments probably had little effect. In other cases, it was evident that a question or critique produced a conflict in the child about the drawing. Under Section I of Table 12.5, Anna's critique of Tanya's ball is first met with a rather vague defense ("So it *could* be a ball"). When Anna further specifies her misgivings ("Well, it doesn't look rounded up"), Tanya changes the referent to an egg. She has used one possible strategy for resolving the conflict precipitated by Anna's comment. If her creation is not round enough to be a satisfactory ball, how about changing it to an egg? Tanya used this strategy in a later session, again in drawing balls (apparently her *bête noire*). On the second occasion, she relabeled her oddly shaped balls as lightbulbs.

The second example in this category is another instance of a child's reexamining her drawing in the light of a peer question. Until Dara's challenge, Thea has shown no sign of being dissatisfied with her multi-colored person. When confronted with a question from her friend, she was able to reflect on the issue of the color a person should be.

Events such as these may increase the child's awareness of certain aspects of drawing, for example, shape or color. More broadly, it is hypothesized that by provoking the child to stand back from her drawing, peer critiques promote the tendency to take a reflective stance in relation to one's drawing.

Another type of discrepancy children encounter when they draw in a group can be seen in the second set of examples. $Child_1$ labels his drawing as a chicken; $Child_2$ looks at this friend's page and sees a four-legged creature that to his eye is not very chickenlike. Or a child looks at her friend's picture, remarking that it looks like a sun, and is informed that it is a flower. In these events a conflict is potentially generated by the discrepancy – whether one is the artist or the viewer. The artist is pulled into the role of viewer by confronting someone else's perception of what he has drawn. The viewer is confronted by the disparity between her own impressions and what the artist states as his intended referent. In both cases, a distance is created from the immediate action or perception.

A third event type that may be hypothesized to play a role in provoking or consolidating representational awareness may be seen in the examples of section III of Table 12.5. Here a child hears a peer expressing uncertainty or dissatisfaction with his or her own drawing. In some instances, as in the first six examples, the child is simply witness to a question or self-appraisal. The actual effect on the child hearing such verbalization is unknown, but our data suggest that it depends on a number of factors.

One factor that influences the child's response is the degree of interest he has in what his peer is inquiring or fretting about. She may be drawing something similar, a frequent state of affairs in our sessions, which undoubtedly increased verbal exchanges. Or the child may be particularly interested in the topic of the peer's drawing or the type of problem she is describing. Peers are also likelier to give each other advice when they are drawing the same thing, as in Lee's assistance to Tanya in example 7 of category III:

T: I don't know how to make a duck.
L: So there. It's two lines, a line across and two lines, a line across, and ahead and a beak.
T: I still don't know how to draw a duck.
L: Try all that, and then you'll do it.

Clearly, Lee sees that he has given Tanya a plan, and all she needs to do is to follow it!

At this point, we digress briefly to mention a set of variables that cut across all the kinds of peer interactions we have observed. Children differ in their status within the group for a variety of reasons: age, ability, personality, and so on. Higher-status children on the whole have more impact than lower-status children, at least to the point of having their remarks taken more seriously. There are also special friends who seem to pay more attention to each other's remarks than to those of other children. Individual differences in personality can be observed in response to peer comments. One child may consistently take criticism to heart, whereas another barely hears it. We have only informal impressions on the effect of these factors, but it seems reasonable to assume that the effect of a given comment varies with the individual children involved and with their relationship to each other.

The final category of events to be considered are the occasions when a child hears a peer comment that conveys knowledge or reflection about drawing. Examples can be seen under category IV of Table 12.5. The peer remark may be about a representational problem or solution, that is, a comment made at the same time the peer is attempting to draw something. The comment may show an awareness of some aspect of the possibilities or limitations of drawing, such as the demands of drawing so that a viewer can interpret correctly. The examples listed in Table 12.5 are representative of the category we refer to and are relatively high-level comments of representational awareness that other children hear a peer make. Additional instances are listed; in some of these cases, the original comment was followed by some verbalization indicating that a child had responded to it. Sometimes children reacted by looking at the speaker or his paper. We can often do no more than infer that a response has registered with a child. Even greater inference is required to assert that comments of any of the types discussed definitely have an impact on children's development. What we can state with certainty at this point is that events and interactions of the kinds discussed are commonplace when children draw in the company of peers.

It should be noted that some of the kinds of events discussed in this last section can occur with adults or older siblings as well as with peers. For instance, an older sibling may ask, "What's that – a flower?" when the child has tried to produce a tree. Or an adult may make a comment that communicates some aspect of the nature of the drawing, for example: "I can tell that's you because of the blonde pigtails." These events can be assumed to have effects that are not dissimilar from those that operate with peers. On the other hand, adults generally are less likely to criticize a child's drawing. Children also react differently to a given comment, depending on its source. When a peer makes a comment, a child is likelier to offer a rebuttal or justification than if the comment were made by an adult or older sibling. For a variety of reasons the kinds of events observed in this investigation are more characteristic of peer situations while drawing than of other social situations children have.

VI. Some final comments

Having examined some of the predominant types of interactions during peer drawing sessions, let us return to the notion of reflexive abstraction. To reiterate, reflexive abstraction has two essential aspects: projection of knowledge from a lower to a higher level, and reorganization or reconstruction of knowledge at a higher level. At the risk of oversimplifying these notions, we will conclude by a return to several examples and look at how these two aspects operate in peer drawing experiences.

In the dialogue between Lee and Tanya, Lee had finished his duck when Tanya expressed her uncertainty as to how a duck should be drawn. Lee had performed the activity of drawing a duck, but it is probable that he had not reflected on his activity. Tanya's question was apparently the impetus for Lee's analysis of his drawing in terms of its component parts and their relation to each other. This is one type of exchange that provokes the projection of an action scheme from a lower to a higher level of knowing.

In other instances, the child is pulled toward a higher level of knowing by an encounter in which he tries to explain what is unsatisfactory about a drawing, as in Anna and Tanya's dialogue. Anna has practical knowledge of the roundness of balls before this encounter. She may or may not have this knowledge at a conceptual level. Anna's desire to instruct Tanya as to what is wrong with Tanya's drawing may play a role in triggering a more representational level of understanding for Anna. The common point in these instances is a situation in which there is a need or reasons for articulating what has formerly been implicit or practical knowledge.

The second aspect of reflexive abstraction, the restructuring or reconstruction of knowledge, is typically provoked by a conflict of some kind. We have given numerous examples where it appers that a mental conflict is precipitated by peer criticism or by a discrepancy between one's own and another's perception of a drawing.

A discrepancy can also arise through hearing someone express an idea about drawing that differs from one's own conception or an idea that is at a higher level of knowledge. Even without a child being personally involved in an interaction, a peer comment can create a conflict that leads to a change in the child's awareness or understanding.

The reader, by now, has discerned the constant interplay among meaning, experience, and organization of experience in the development of planning tools. Two processes of abstraction play critical roles in the development of planning. Although meaning and information can be drawn from external sources, such as the feedback gained by experimenting with shapes and colors on the drawing surface, as well as others' reactions to those shapes and colors, there is another level of mental activity that "goes beyond the information given" (Bruner, 1973). This process is the mental restructuring that results from engaging in a task, thinking about the task, and thinking about doing the task. For example, the child may recognize and be capable of producing triangular and square shapes with a magic marker, and complain about not being able to draw a house. However, witnessing a peer placing a triangle atop a square, that same child may spontaneously label the result a house. This meaning, gained through reflexive abstraction, is internal to the individual, though perhaps provoked by physical or social agents.

Clearly, both types of abstraction operate in the development of planning. The child gets some external feedback by experimenting and talking through his drawing problem, sometimes verbalizing his "a-ha" experiences and sometimes hearing others having such insights; development can occur from exposure to others' problem solving and verbalized metacognitions. Piaget pointed out, with respect to the two types of abstraction, that "reflexive does not replace empirical but frames it . . . and goes infinitely beyond it . . ." (1974). This interplay between empirical abstraction and reflexive abstraction is the heart of the *meaning* of the activity in the learning that occurs (Gallagher & Reid, 1981). Alongside organization and abstracted meaning, much of it gained through social supports, the child begins to explore the "possibilities" of representational thinking that we have discussed and categorized. These categories of possibilities and limitations of the specific representational modality reflect the child's planning, and it is at these stages of representational thinking that one also sees the emergence of what might be considered "personal style." Gardner (1973), in discussing children's storytelling, noted that organizational aspects with reference to affect accompany *planning* and the beginnings of personal style as well.

We have pointed to the internal processes of reflexive abstraction that regulate the growth of planning skills, and we have suggested ways in which the social context may play a role in communicating and organizing, and therefore, in planning. The social setting creates an environment in which anticipating what others will ask presses one to plan ahead or to plan "en route." From another perspective, being asked how to do something forces one to articulate one's own formula or plan for accomplishing a task, as Lee did for Tanya. In the former sense, the social context requires the child to articulate plans for representing experience. The latter is a case of the plan itself being a representation.

As the child acquires a more conscious and explicit awareness of the important dimensions of any activity, for example, drawing pictures, working puzzles, or writing stories, we might surmise that he or she would engage in different kinds of planning, and perhaps do more planning than before attaining this awareness.

Likewise, as children come to better understand how their own minds function and what kinds of task performers they are, in a given domain and in general, we would expect them to be more accurate in foreseeing their own planning needs and more effective in developing their own planning styles. More empirical evidence on these changes is needed. Our findings provide a starting point for this undertaking. The data on children's object choices in make-believe play and on their drawings indicate that young children have already developed representational criteria and considerable knowledge of the "rules of the game" in these activities. Furthermore, they spontaneously engage in processes of planning, self-interrogation, self-monitoring, and evaluation. Children's growing knowledge of the nature of pictorial and object representation and their ability to anticipate how others will see their representational efforts shape the planning and editing they do in drawing and in choosing objects in pretend play. It will be the task of others to see whether the child who evidences planning in a familiar and explicitly representational domain shows comparable behavior in domains that are less familiar and less explicitly representational.

Notes

1. A complete description of materials, procedures, and results is reported in C. Copple and R. Cocking (1984).

References

Arnheim, R. (1967). *Visual thinking*. Berkeley, CA: University of California Press.
Bellugi-Klima, U. (1971). Some language comprehension tests. In C. B. Lavatelli (Ed.), *Language training in early childhood education*. Urbana, IL: University of Illinois Press.

Berenthal, B., & Fischer, K. (in press). Toward an understanding of early representation. In *Proceedings of the 9th annual conference on Piagetian theory and the helping professions*. Los Angeles: University of Southern California Press.

Bruner, J. S. (1973). *Beyond the information given: Studies in the psychology of knowing*. New York: Norton.

Cazden, C. (1972). *Child language and education*. New York: Holt, Rinehart, & Winston.

Cocking, R. (1982). Social facilitation of representational awareness. American Educational Research Association meetings, New York.

Cocking, R., & Copple, C. (1979a). Children's commentary while drawing in small groups: The growth of reflective and critical tendencies. In M. Poulson & G. Lubin (Eds.), *Piagetian theory and the helping professions*. Los Angeles: University of Southern California Press.

Cocking, R., & Copple, C. (1979b). Change through exposure to others: A study of children's verbalizations as they draw. In M. Poulson & G. Lubin (Eds.), *Piagetian theory and the helping professions*. Los Angeles: University of Southern California Press.

Copple, C., & Cocking, R. (1984). Objects, symbols, & substitutes: The nature of the cognitive activity during symbolic play. In T. Yawkey & A. Pellegrini (Eds.), *Child's play: Developmental and applied*. Hillsdale, NJ: Erlbaum.

Copple, C., Cocking, R., & Waxman, B. (1980). *The emergence of representational awareness: An examination of children's comments as they draw*. Southeastern Conference on Human Development, Alexandria, VA.

Copple, C., Sigel, I., & Saunders, R. (1984). *Educating the young thinker*. New York: Van Nostrand, 1979; reprinted by Erlbaum.

Copple, C., Waxman, B., & Cocking, R. (1981). *Children's interactions as they draw: Hypotheses about peer influences on representational awareness*. The 11th Annual Symposium of the Jean Piaget Society, Philadelphia, PA.

Dunn, L. (1959). *Peabody Picture Vocabulary Test*. Minneapolis, MN: American Guidance Service.

Elkind, D., Koegler, R., & Go, E. (1964). Studies in perceptual development: II. Part–whole perception. *Child Development, 35*, 81–90.

Elkind, D., & Weiss, J. (1967). Studies in perceptual development: III. Perceptual exploration. *Child Development, 38*, 553–561.

Fenson, L. (1977). *The structure of one child's art from ages three to four*. Unpublished manuscript, San Diego State University.

Flavell, J., Botkin, P., Fry, C., Wright, J., & Jarvis, P. (1968). *The development of role taking and communication skills in children*. New York: Wiley.

Gallagher, J., & Reid, D. (1981). *The learning theory of Piaget and Inhelder*. Monterey, CA: Brooks-Cole.

Gardner, H. (1973). *The arts and human development*. New York: Wiley.

Gardner, H. (1980). *Artful scribbles*. New York: Basic Books.

Gearhart, M., & Newman, D. (1980). Learning to draw a picture: The social context of an individual activity. *Discourse Processes, 3*, 169–184.

Gelman, R. (1979). Preschool thought. *American Psychologist, 34*, 900–905.

Gelman, R., & Gallistel, C. (1978). *The child's understanding of number*. Cambridge, MA: Harvard University Press.

Gibson, E. (1969). *Principles of perceptual learning and development*. New York: Appleton-Century-Crofts.

Glucksberg, S., Krauss, R., & Higgins, T. (1975). The development of communication skills in children. In F. Horowitz (Ed.), *Review of child development research* (Vol. 4). Chicago: University of Chicago Press.

Golomb, C. (1974). *Young children's sculpture and drawing*. Cambridge, MA: Harvard University Press.

Goodman, J. (1979). The lock box: An instrument to evaluate mental organization in preschool children. *Journal of Child Psychology and Psychiatry, 20,* 313–324.

Goodman, J. (1981). *The Goodman lock box.* Chicago: Stoelting.

Goodenough, F. (1926). *Measurement of intelligence by drawings.* New York: Harcourt, Brace, & World.

Goodnow, J. (1977). *Children drawing.* Cambridge, MA: Harvard University Press.

Gopnik, A. (1982). Words and plans: Early language and the development of intelligent action. *Journal of Child Language, 9,* 303–318.

Gottschalk, J., Bryden, M., & Rabinovitch, M. (1964). Spatial organization of children's responses to a pictorial display. *Child Development, 35,* 811–815.

Harris, D. (1963). *Children's drawings as measures of intellectual maturity.* New York: Harcourt, Brace & World.

Keil, F. (1979). The development of the young child's ability to anticipate the outcomes of simple causal events. *Child Development, 50,* 455–462.

Levina, R. (1968). L. S. Vygotsky's idea about the function of speech in children. *Voprosy psikhologii, 4,* 105–115.

Matthews, W. (1978). *The notion of equivalence in children's representation activity.* Unpublished manuscript, Harvard University.

Meher, J., & Bever, T. (1967). Cognitive capacity of very young children. *Science, 158,* 141–142.

Nelson, K. (1974). Concept, word, and sentence: Interactions in acquisition and development. *Psychological Review, 81,* 267–285.

Nelson, K. (1977). The syntagmatic–paradigmatic shift revisited: A review of research and theory. *Psychological Bulletin, 84,* 93–116.

Nelson, K. (1978). How children represent knowledge of their world in and out of language: A preliminary report. In R. S. Siegler (Ed.), *Children's thinking: What develops?* Hillsdale, NJ: Erlbaum.

Nelson, K. (1979). Explorations in the development of a functional semantic system. In W. A. Collins (Ed.), *Children's language and communication.* Hillsdale, NJ: Erlbaum.

Nelson, K. (1982). The syntagmatics and paradigmatics of conceptual representation. In S. Kuczaj, II (Ed.), *Language, thought, and culture.* Hillsdale, NJ: Erlbaum.

Nelson, K. (1983). The derivation of concepts and categories from event representation. In E. Scholnick (Ed.), *New trends in conceptual representation.* Hillsdale, NJ: Erlbaum.

Peck, J. (1976). *Relationships between the spatial structure of children's free drawings and logical operations.* Unpublished manuscript, Kent State University.

Piaget, J. (1969). *Science of education and the psychology of the child.* New York: Orion.

Piaget, J. (1974). *Adaptation vitale et psychologie de l'intelligence: Sélection organique et phenocopie.* Paris: Hermann.

Piaget, J. (1977). The role of action in the development of thinking. In W. Overton & J. Gallagher (Eds.), *Knowledge and development: Vol. 1. Advances in research and theory.* New York: Plenum.

Potter, M., & Levy, E. (1968). Spatial enumeration without counting. *Child Development, 39,* 265–272.

Potts, M. (1973). A technique for measuring language production in three, four, and five year olds. In *Proceedings of the 80th Annual Convention of the American Psychological Association* (Vol. 9, pp. 11–13).

Ricciuti, H. (1965). Object grouping and selective ordering behavior in infants 12–24 months old. *Merrill–Palmer Quarterly, 11,* 129–148.

Schaeffer, B., Eggleston, V., & Scott, J. (1974). Number development in young children. *Cognitive Psychology, 6,* 357–379.

Smith, E., & Medin, D. (1981). *Categories and concepts.* Cambridge, MA: Harvard University Press.

Spungen, L., & Goodman, J. (1983). Organizing strategies in children 18–24 months: Limitations imposed by task complexity. *Journal of Applied Developmental Psychology, 4* (2), 109–124.

Vygotsky, L. (1978). *Mind in society: The development of higher psychological processes.* Cambridge, MA: Harvard University Press.

Wellman, H., Somerville, S., & Haake, R. (1979). Development of search procedures in real-life spatial environments. *Developmental Psychology, 15,* 530–542.

Part V

Instruction of planning

13 Instruction in problem solving and planning

Martin V. Covington

I. Introduction

Perhaps nowhere has the time-honored dictum, "The whole is greater than its parts," been portrayed more dramatically than in Theordore Sturgeon's award-winning science fiction novel *More Than Human* (1953). Sturgeon describes a new breed of human being, the next step in an ongoing psychic revolution, *homo gestalt*. This paragon of thinking efficiency is but a single identity; yet it is built from the assorted scraps and leavings of humanity, a complex information-processing organism composed variously of an idiot savant (computer), a sickly pair of twins with a telepathic gift (information sensors) and an adolescent sociopath (central ganglion). Alone, each component would surely die, but together they created a series of unparalleled scientific innovations. Sturgeon contended that, in reality, *homo gestalt* has been with us since the dawn of human experience – a universal analogy to the act of creative discovery.

Social scientists have been quick to grasp this essential point about the nature of creative thinking, namely that creative individuals possess an extraordinary ability to capitalize on a unique combination of gifts. They balance and manage many conflicting tendencies and opposing functions in the pursuit of excellence. For one thing, productive thinkers are passionately involved in and dominated by the challenge at hand; yet they must also remain analytic and aloof in order to gain the larger perspective. For another thing, they remain open to experience and to their own playful fantasies; yet they also stand ready to foreclose further search and play in the interests of decisiveness. In short, the productive thinker is at once new and old, open and closed, child and adult (not surprisingly, Sturgeon's entourage included identities of all ages). But the point goes deeper still. These creative tendencies are not merely blended. Rather it appears that they are kept in a dynamic tension so that each can contribute uniquely to problem resolution (Barron, 1965; MacKinnon, 1962).

469

For example, the productive individual must determine at a given point in his or her work on a problem whether it would be more fruitful to suspend critical judgment and give free rein to speculation in search of entirely new ideas, or whether, by contrast, it would be more helpful to examine systematically the ideas he or she already has. Moreover, that person must decide when it is time to abandon one direction of thought and embark on another. It is this overall managerial capacity – viewing the whole problem, not just its parts – that represents the essence of the creative act, and which forms the focus of this chapter on enhancing planful behavior. Our purpose is to review the evidence that school-based instruction in problem-solving skills can promote such a managerial capacity among children and to consider various conceptual and practical issues that relate to the development of new generations of even more effective cognitive instruction for planning.

Despite the recent upsurge of interest in managerial and planning processes, relatively little is known about them, and about their relationship to successful problem solving, and even less about how to encourage such planfulness through direct instruction. Yet there can be little doubt about the pressing need for such instruction, given the pervasive evidence of planning deficits at all age levels. Several examples serve to illustrate the dimensions of the problem. First, consider the question of what young students know about the nature of problem-solving resources and how they enter into effective thinking and self-management in school. Evidence on this point comes from my laboratory (The Berkeley Productive Thinking Project) and confirms the presence of strategic deficiencies (Schnur, 1981). Junior high school pupils were asked to judge the likelihood that hypothetical students would experience success on an upcoming social studies test, given various combinations of achievement factors: amount of time allocated for study (sufficient/insufficient), intensity of study effort (high/low), test difficulty (easy/hard), and student aptitude (high/low). Most pupils could readily distinguish between the single combination in which all factors augered well for test success (i.e., High ability × Sufficient study × Easy test) and the opposite combination that militated fully against success. Otherwise, however, student estimates of test outcome were far from sensitive. For example, knowing only that a test was difficult or easy or that the hypothetical pupil had little or much time to prepare made little difference in student predictions. It would seem reasonable for teachers to expect that students should know that a combination of high effort and easy task presents a greater likelihood of success than does either high effort or easy task alone, or that individuals need study less if the test is easy than if it is hard. But this research, corroborated by other investigations (Nicholls, 1978, 1980), indicates that such teacher expectations are unrealistically high off the mark. Additionally, advice was sought from these same students about how hypothetical achievers might improve their chances of doing better on the test or how they might proceed if forced by circumstances to change their study plans. Given the saliency of effort as a perceived cause of achievement success in early adolescence (Weiner & Peter, 1973), it was not surprising to find that most students simply advised expending more energy (e.g., study longer, harder). Such advice reveals a singular lack of appreciation of *how* best to work harder. At a time (junior high school) when children stand on the threshold of truly independent learning, they appear altogether naïve regarding the rudiments of achievement planning and especially deficient in their ability to distinguish between *quality* and *quantity* of effort.

Research on adults is no more reassuring. After investigating how adults formulate and conduct plans of action for solving mundane, everyday tasks (e.g., completing a series of shopping errands), Hayes-Roth (1980) concluded that her subjects were uniformly unrealistic. They consistently overestimated what they believed they could accomplish in the time available. Moreover, as the difficulty of achieving their announced goals increased, these same persons became increasingly unrealistic about how much could be accomplished. Finally, when they were required to modify their overblown expectations, they focused on the least important goals! In effect, these subjects sacrificed both quality and quantity as the planning task became more difficult.

The mere recognition of such planning deficiencies carries us only a short distance toward realizing the goals of this chapter. The effective translation of such an obvious educational need into viable educational solutions is a highly complex process, and is further complicated by our imperfect understanding of planning behavior. For this reason, this chapter is not intended primarily as a compilation of previous research on problem planning, nor only as a review of existing school-based instruction to foster such planning, but most important, it involves a critique and proposal regarding the lines of research that should next be followed to enhance our understanding of planning behavior as it relates to broader educational objectives. The chapter is divided into two main sections. In Section II, we will consider a working taxonomy of problem tasks that will hopefully prove serviceable as a blueprint for the development of comprehensive planning instruction in problem solving. Both educational and psychological issues will be considered. Educationally, little attention has been given to taxonomies that describe those school-related tasks that presently confront children, and which in altered and more complex forms may continue to confront them as adults as well. At the same time, psychologically, there has been an insufficient appreciation of the fact that different types of problems require different forms and varieties of planning. For example, depending on the nature of the problem, plans of action can be simple or complex, brief or protracted, and open to objective verification or largely idiosyncratic and subjective in nature. It will be argued that a taxonomic matrix formed on the one dimension by type of tasks, and on the other dimension by different plans of action, is the proper focus and guide for the development of omnibus curricula designed to enhance problem-planning behavior. In Section III, we will locate several school-based training programs within this matrix and review the evidence that broad-gauged instruction in thinking skills can foster the kinds of planful behavior necessary to effective school achievement. To anticipate, we will find that contrary to various optimistic reports that thinking can be trained (Torrance, 1972), such conclusions are somewhat premature. This is not to suggest that there is no cause for optimism but only that it must for the moment remain guarded. Substantial gaps in our knowledge must first be closed, and various criticisms must be addressed before the prospects brighten for the development of truly comprehensive and effective instruction in planning behavior.

A. Defining terms

Before proceeding, some basic definitions are in order:

1. Problems. First, consider the term "problem." There is general agreement in the psychological literature that a problem refers to any situation in which persons encounter a task never before seen in precisely that same form, and for which the information necessary for a solution is insufficient (Resnick & Glaser, 1976). This definition reflects two fundamental aspects of any problem state: first, the element of transfer – the need to apply old, familiar strategies in new ways, or to invent entirely new approaches; and second, the need to go beyond the information given (Bruner, 1973). This definition also permits the maintenance of an important distinction between "presented" problems and "discovered" problems (Getzels, 1976). In the case of presented problems, the solution and the procedures for its attainment are already known to the presenter (teacher) and must be worked out by the learner (student); whereas, in the case of discovered problems, the difficulty arises precisely because there are no known or preset solutions. This is the domain of the truly creative product – a scientific discovery, a painting that forces the viewer to see the world in novel ways, or an idea for a new effective social organization. The validity of the planning processes through which the novice goes to solve a presented problem is not diminished owing to the humbleness of the activity, nor are the kinds of thinking employed in solving a discovered problem necessarily exalted because of the nobility of the task. The process by which Liebnitz created the calculus shares more in common with the struggle of the school child to understand it than was once suspected. In short, the capacity for productive thinking is to be found in every individual, not merely among a chosen few.

It should also be made clear that the term "problem" is meant broadly, and pertains to all kinds of subject matter in all domains of human activity. Both simple and highly complex problems are included, as well as precisely stated, well-structured problems, in contrast to those that are loosely defined and weakly structured. Moreover, to be educationally meaningful, the spectrum of problem types must also include the briefest task, lasting a few seconds, and also those problems that stretch out over prolonged periods of time with many sessions of work required by an individual or by a group. Furthermore, problems may not only be fixed and static in nature, but may also undergo constant changes in structure as they are worked on. Also, from an educational perspective, problems include those for which there are unique solutions as well as those for which there are multiple solutions, and partial solutions as well as complete definitive answers. Problems also differ in the type of solution sought. Some pertain to the achievement of an understanding, as in the assimilation of new information; others pertain to creating explanations, as in accounting for a puzzling phenomenon in science; still others pertain to the creation of innovative plans for accomplishing a worthwhile end, such as resolving a conflict of human relations.

2. Planning and monitoring. Next, consider the meaning of the terms "planning" and "monitoring." These processes are the basic elements of all effective problem solving and enter into every variety of problem type mentioned above. Planning involves the initial development of a course of action to achieve a desired goal. As a concept, planning has been used in a variety of ways, depending on the focus of the particular investigator (for a review, see Scholnick & Friedman, chapter 1, this volume). Planning has been treated from at least two frameworks. In one approach, that often favored by cognitive scientists, planning is viewed as an information-processing phenomenon in which the thinker organizes a series of

individual cognitive operations and skills – question asking, idea generation, and information retrieval strategies – in a simultaneous, planful
fashion. Here the focus of planning is on the "metacognitive" aspects of
thinking, that is, the purposeful assembly of individual cognitive processes. It is this effective orchestration of a variety of separate component
skills, content-specific rules, and affective dispositions that epitomizes the
essence of planning for many observers, a theoretical position anticipated
over 30 years ago by Sturgeon's fictional device, *homo gestalt*. Researchers in this tradition emphasize an executive or managerial role in problem solving around such concepts as "learning hierarchies" (Gagne,
1977), "higher-order rules" (Scandura, 1974, 1977), "master-thinking
skill" (Crutchfield, 1961; Kahn, 1981), and an "executive mechanism"
(Butterfield & Belmont, 1977).

A second broad approach emphasizes the general structure of planning
and the procedures by which individuals translate an abstract representation of the problem environment into specific functional steps consistent with prevailing local circumstances. For example, according to the
elaborated model proposed by Hayes-Roth (1980), this progression from
abstract to functional involves an interaction between five frames of reference which variously include abstract knowledge about the essentials of
planning, a concern for priorities, goal selection and cost effectiveness,
and knowledge about specific problem content.

Despite such differences in emphasis, however, most researchers consider planning behavior to involve a purposeful, goal-directed formation
of organizing strategies whether they be viewed in terms of underlying
cognitive processes or as functional plans of action.

"Monitoring" refers to the process by which the plan, once it is initially
established, is guided toward a successful conclusion. This control function involves the ability to recognize and deal with the strategic implications of new, unexpected events – unforeseen obstacles or potential
windfalls – that can change the character of a problem in unexpected
ways because a plan of action that is effective at one point can quickly
become inappropriate or even counterproductive as circumstances
change.

Given the broad purposes of this chapter, we will entertain all of the
conceptual aspects of planning encompassed in the preceding remarks.
At an abstract/functional level, we will examine the evidence that instruction can enhance the child's ability to identify good, poor, or indifferent
plans of action, and to generate their own plans as well. At a cognitive
assembly level, we will consider evidence that instruction can change how
individuals process problem information, and whether or not such
changes enhance a higher-order integration and timely application of var-

ious components skills. Finally, in this latter connection, we will also explore the possibility that instruction can strengthen individual component skills per se. For example, we will inquire as to whether or not ideational fluency can be enhanced by providing students with planful heuristics for the systematic search of an "idea-space."

II. A proposed problem/planning taxonomy

The heterogeneity of problem characteristics described above implies a variety of problem-solving plans. But how can we represent this plethora of cognitive events, and in educationally meaningful ways? At present, there is no generally accepted taxonomy of school-relevant problem tasks nor of the metacognitive skills and plans necessary to their solution (for a review, see Gagne & Briggs, 1974; Thomas, 1972). This not only limits our ability to evaluate the comprehensiveness of existing cognitive training programs, but also handicaps the development of new generations of instructional procedures. Central here, as we shall see, is the question of what specific planning and allied thinking strategies should be included in a complete course on learning to solve problems. The following taxonomy is intended as a first step toward a formal set of notions regarding the nature of problem solving, which can eventually act as a touchstone for guiding systematic instruction in planning behavior. Such a model must be flexible enough to accommodate our previous observations regarding the diversity of problem types as well as to provide a practically oriented schema within which we can prioritize the demands of schools. In short, such a taxonomy must be both functional and visionary: functional, in that it should reflect events that are meaningful to the classroom teacher; and visionary, in that it should stimulate teachers to view thinking and planfulness as trainable educational objectives.

To these ends, consider the taxonomy of problem domains and thinking processes reflected in Table 13.1. The basic elements of this taxonomy draw heavily on an earlier proposal by Getzels (1976) and is expanded here for our purposes (for a general consideration of problem taxonomies, see Greeno, 1973). Presented at its simplest, the problem-planning process consists, first, of a problem-finding or formulation stage, and second, an implementation stage in which various problem-solving methods, strategies, and skills are brought into play, eventually leading to the third and final stage of solution attainment (Polya, 1957; Thomas, 1977). What differentiates this functional description into meaningful problem types is whether each stage is either well specified (+), or vague and indeterminant (−). This known/unknown distinction applies equally to both

Table 13.1. *Proposed problem-solving taxonomy*

	Problem specified	Plan of action	Solution
Reproductive thinking	+	+	−
	+	+	+
Productive thinking	+	−	−
Strategic thinking	−	−	−
	+	−	+

Source: After Getzels (1976).

presented and discovered problems. The important point is not whether others are in possession of an answer, but rather what makes the situation difficult for the potential problem solver. The various combinations of known and unknown stages create a clustering of tasks around three problem modes, each of which requires qualitatively different kinds of planning and which draws on substantially different component skills: reproductive, productive, and strategic problems.

A. Reproductive problems

According to Table 13.1, reproductive problems are well specified in advance with plans of action that are clear and straightforward; only the solution is unknown (+ + −). The task is simply to reproduce known procedures in a static fashion (Greeno, 1973). Typically, the problem-formulation stage is either short-circuited or completely omitted, with problems presented in a neatly packaged form. The relevant terms and conditions of the problem are clearly and specifically stated, and the question to be answered is explicitly put. Likewise, the solution plan is well rehearsed, if not overlearned, and is invoked by the learner in an automatic, "script-like" fashion (e.g., Schank & Abelson, 1977). Actually, according to our earlier definition of a problem state, some reproductive tasks may not involve a problem at all; that is, individuals may simply reproduce well-known plans of action in an invariate fashion across highly similar tasks. Such problems are heavily represented in schools in most content domains as when, for example, the learner must apply a known arithmetic formula (plan) in a mechanical, unswerving manner in order to solve a simple word problem. Moreover, in some cases (as reflected in Table 13.1) *all* the problem elements may be known to the learner, even the solution itself $(+ \; + \; +)$. This would occur when the answers to the odd- or even-numbered mathematics problems in an assignment are presented in the back of the textbook.

Reproductive thinking also dominates procedures for assessing what students know or have learned. The most ubiquitous example is the use of testing in a rote mode. Here the problem solver attempts to reproduce or recognize the correct facts, dates, or associations from memory storage in a form that is little altered from the way it was first rehearsed. Thus the key cognitive elements in reproductive plans of action are memory and retrieval strategies, and consequently the preferred methods for enhancing reproductive thinking are the repetition of information, the proper distribution of practice, and the use of various external incentives such as gold stars or grades.

Obviously, this description of reproductive thinking is highly simplified. Although, on the whole, it is not a bad approximation to the majority of student learning experiences, this presentation is not intended to imply that the acquisition and use of unmodified information *must* proceed in a rote fashion. When most properly viewed, the *acquisition* process in school should be thought of as a process of *assimilation* in which incoming information must be operated on by the individual, restructured, and transformed and fitted meaningfully into his or her own conceptual world. In effect, when taught creatively, content acquisition (and the dominant reproductive mode) gives way to productive and strategic modes of thought. For example, even in the simplest acquisition task, it is well known that good students spontaneously reorganize their learning to fit the demands of future recall (Cromer & Wiener, 1966; Frase, 1968, 1970; Steiner, Wiener, & Cromer, 1971), seek out information that limits task difficulty (Miller & Parlett, 1974), as well as arrange their study in ways that reduce heavy demands on memory load (Gray, 1982). In contrast, poor learners tend to proceed by rote overlearning, irrespective of task demands (Covington, 1985b). Thus any general problem-solving program should seek to ensure that even the simplest learning tasks be viewed as an occasion for the application of higher-order organizing and planning strategies, a point to be amplified later.

B. *Productive problems*

Productive thinking invokes the true meaning of a problem as defined in the previous section. Irrespective of task content, the individual must go beyond the information given, to seek and implement strategies for a solution, and in situations that often differ substantially from one's prior experience (+ − −). Productive thinking tasks are legion, and many school-relevant examples can be cited: the discovery and testing of hypotheses to explain the puzzling result of a science experiment, proposing alternative interpretations for a poem, or tracing the numerous implications of an event in history. In such problems, the individual cannot rely solely on the retrieval of unaltered information, but must proceed by reason and analysis (and sometimes by trial and error). It is this unknown, initially ill-structured aspect of plans for action that differentiates reproductive and productive thinking. Yet these two problem models also share much in common. For one thing, productive problems can quickly become reproductive in nature once the creative insight necessary for their solution has become internalized and made automatic. Sternberg (1979) offers a neat demonstration of this dynamic. By mastering a simple relational rule (which takes only a few moments) individuals can short-cut all of the complex reasoning involved in solving "transitive-inference" problems (e.g., John is not as tall as Pete; Bill is not as short as Pete. Who is tallest?), and thereby transform this sometimes challenging task into a rote exercise. For another thing, the facts, data, and subject-matter information that form the context in which most productive-thinking problems occur are typically acquired through the reproductive processes described above. This observation underscores the critical relationship between memory, retrieval, and effective high-level cognitive functioning. The creation and monitoring of plans of action depend on one's ability to retrieve both content knowledge and procedural knowledge from working memory (Feigenbaum, 1970; Greeno, 1973).

1. Problem formulation. We have classified both productive and reproductive tasks as "problem well-formulated." This was done largely for expository purposes to underscore the other and most fundamental source of difference between these two modes: the presence or absence of a clear plan for achieving a solution. In actuality, however, many productive-thinking dilemmas do not present themselves initially in a form that is easily amenable to solution. It is only through the proper formulation of such problems, and identification of the difficulties that created them that they can be sensibly contemplated. Thus a critical aspect of productive planning is to gauge the problem correctly. The importance of this problem-formulation stage is indicated by the disproportionate amount of time initially devoted by experts to an understanding of the elements of a problem as compared to the attention given these issues by the novice (Crutchfield, 1961; Sternberg, 1979). Moreover, the fact that solutions often follow spontaneously upon the reformulation of problems in a new way underscores the importance of this problem-solving stage. The most familiar and convincing example of this dynamic is Wertheimer's (1959) classic experiment in which an initially unfamiliar task, calculating the area of a parallelogram, was suddenly transformed into a routine exercise in reproductive thinking when youngsters were coached to view the parallelogram as a kind of rectangle. We are also reminded of the literature on functional fixity in which a rigidity of perceptual set precludes the elements of a situation from being seen as part of the solution rather than as only part of the problem (Duncker, 1945; Luchins, 1942).

2. Ideational search and evaluation. Once the problem is properly defined, the individual must come up with possibilities for solution, directions to be explored, or hypotheses to be tested; and in turn he or she must evaluate these possibilities against various criteria. In the case of productive thinking, researchers have tended to emphasize either idea-generation strategies or idea-evaluation strategies, depending on whether their focus is on *divergent* or *convergent* tasks, respectively. Convergent tasks stress the individual's capacity to eliminate a number of possibilities progressively, so as to converge on the few ideas that best fit the constraints of the problem. Here investigators emphasize instruction in techniques for evaluating ideas for goodness of fit, and for how intially inadequate ideas can be modified or elaborated to better satisfy a problem. The classic laboratory example of convergent tasks is Duncker's x-ray problem (1945), in which the problem solver must propose ways to kill a malignant tumor deep inside the human body using x-rays without harming the surrounding healthy tissue. In contrast, divergent tasks are intended to stimulate a rich variety of possible mental products (e.g., "think of all the consequences of everyone in the world being blind"; "list various novel ways to use tin cans"), and for this reason are widely regarded as a simple analogue to creative thinking (Torrance, 1972; Treffinger, 1971). Divergent skill training emphasizes ideational flexibility, fluency, and defining an ideational search space as broadly as possible by the systematic listing of product attributes (Gordon, 1961; Parnes, 1967).

In summary, the key to successful productive thinking is not only the possession of individual cognitive components such as ideational fluency and elaboration, but also a sense of timing as to when to evoke these component operations via the problem-formulation stage. Herein lies the greatest potential source of planning deficiency. For example, Hayes-Roth (1980) found that the mere possession of various subroutines for setting up a series of shopping errands (e.g., spatial clustering of errands) was not sufficient to optimize subject behavior. Individuals tended to use procedures with which they were most familiar, irrespective of their appropriateness to variations in the task including the amount of shopping time available, and the number and importance of the errands. Only after direct practice in how plans must reflect prevailing circumstances were most subjects able to make the proper choice between different courses of action. Thus any comprehensive planning instruction should include direct, systematic practice in the timely orchestration of various cognitive skills within the context of changing perceptions of the problem itself (Brown, Palincsar, & Armbruster, 1983; Forrest-Pressley & Giles, 1983; Peterson & Swing, 1983).

C. Strategic problems

Finally, we turn to those tasks that exemplify a strategic thinking mode. Both reproductive and productive problems depend on the creation of plans of actions for their solution; in effect, plans are in the service of a solution. By contrast, in strategic problems, typically the solution *is* the plan.

1. Problem finding.   Table 13.1 suggests two prototypic forms of strategic problems. First, consider those situations in which there is, in reality, no problem at all, or at least not yet; nor, as a consequence, is there even the glimmer of a solution, and of course, no known steps to be taken (− − −). To Getzels (1976), the epitome of this problem type reduces to the admonition: "Pose an important problem and then solve it!" Such demands arise in schools whenever students grope for term paper topics, search for worthwhile science fair projects, or engage in any form of individually devised, self-directed learning assignments. The essence of this form of strategic task is *problem finding* or *detection* (Doner, 1978), in which the individual expresses a continual readiness to find problems everywhere, to be puzzled by the obvious, and to see the extraordinary in the ordinary. As Wertheimer (1959) put it: "The function of thinking is not just to solve an actual problem but discovering, envisioning, going into deeper questions. Envisioning, putting the productive question is often more important, often a greater achievement than the solution of a set question." One component of this discovery process involves the ability to detect inconsistencies, incongruities, or something odd that violates the expected. Thus general problem-solving instruction should include training in such sensitivities as well as the capacity to encourage an expectation that as the student works on a problem, wholly *new* problems may arise unexpectedly that lead in entirely new directions. Likewise, solutions to unforeseen problems can occur in the same way, if the thinker is but sensitive to them. The classic example here is Alexander Fleming's discovery of penicillin through his sudden realization that this substance could solve a far more profound problem (the control of bacterial infections) than the one that initially engaged his attention, namely his search for the troublesome agent that was spoiling his experiments.

Once an individual becomes aware of a problem – either through recognizing a potential dilemma or puzzle that already exists, or by creating a novel problem out of one's own experiences – then the problem-formulation stage can proceed as described above, with the result that a solution may simply follow in a routine fashion according to the principles of reproductive thinking.

2. *Strategic means–ends analysis.* The essence of the second type of strategic planning is reflected in the person's capacity to represent a problem both in its present state and as a desired end state along with a sensitivity for what broad problem-solving steps or moves are necessary to reduce and eventually eliminate these differences between present reality and future hope. This metacognitive capacity is well described by Simon's (1972, 1973) concept of means–ends analysis in which the problem solver isolates certain goals to be achieved and then searches for the best method to achieve each specific goal. Typically, the current problem state, whether it be a deficiency, a puzzle, or a misunderstanding, can be reasonably well defined as can the final desired end state, that is, the absence of the deficiency, the puzzle understood, or the misunderstanding corrected $(+ - +)$. The significant task is to create a plan of action that progressively reduces the differences between the undesirable and desired state of affairs. Such problems are generally protracted in nature and typically involve the management of one's own personal resources as well as the resources and cooperation of other individuals. Research on human problem-solving and on artificial intelligence has shown that such search processes are used in a variety of task environments by both human and artificial problem-solvers (Polson & Jeffries, 1985). In its broadest formulation, means–ends analysis also implies a constant vigilance regarding changing priorities and unexpected events because, as already noted, an earlier problem statement may no longer serve to represent present circumstances realistically. Concrete examples of such strategic manipulation include the intention of a football coach to turn a previously losing season into a winning one, a hostess's efforts to coordinate a variety of culinary steps in the proper temporal sequence so as to fulfill her vision of the perfect dinner party, and the signing of a new union contract before the old contract lapses.

In the school context, strategic planning of this second type is central to effective study and test preparation. Successful academic achievement requires the organization of one's time, energy, and ability in responding to the demands of acquiring and recalling subject-matter material. In terms of our taxonomy, effective study involves both reproductive thinking with its emphasis on memorizing and information retrieval, and the strategic capacity to orchestrate and direct subject-matter rehearsal. Of course, all students can envisage the desired goal – a satisfactory grade, or its negative counterpart, the desire to avoid failure. The basic problem, however, is to bring the task into a meaningful focus in the absence of complete information. Knowledgeable students seek out information about the test to determine the kinds of demands it will place on them, by inquiring, variously: "What must I remember?" "Must I remember it again later?" "What kind of test?" "What aspects of the assignment will be most emphasized?" (Bransford, Nitsch, & Franks, 1977). Effective recall occurs when learners anticipate correctly the form in which the information will later be tested, and study accordingly (Postman, 1975; Tulving & Thompson, 1973). If the test is an exercise in rote recall, then rehearsing the material originally as isolated, unconnected events may be sufficient (reproductive thinking), but if the test demands reordering of the material or its productive application to new situations, then rote overlearning will be inadequate (Covington, 1985b). If we are to judge from the previously described findings of Schnur (1981), most students are singularly deficient at recognizing the implications of different tasks' demands for their choice of study strategies. Moreover, planning for effective study is made more difficult by the fact that students typically possess a highly inaccurate picture of their own learning capacities, limitations, and idiosyncrasies. Astute problem solvers can estimate with some accuracy the amount of time needed to learn something (Neimark, Slotnick, & Ulrich, 1971), and when they know something well enough for the task at hand, and when they do not (Brown, 1978). Yet the current evidence indicates a wide range of individual differences in these capacities, with generally depressed levels of average performance (Denhiere, 1974).

Several additional heuristics not yet discussed are uniquely suited to the planning demands of all strategic thinking: Realistic goal setting and task division.

3. Goal setting. A desired end state is rarely attained in every particular. Problem solving involves a process of compromise, negotiation, and transaction with those factors that caused the problem initially. In the example of the labor contract, the final solution requires concessions by both sides so that only a mutually satisfactory, not a perfect, resolution can be obtained. Realism in goal setting (defining the parameters of the desired goal) may be present from the beginning of problem planning, or it may be interjected periodically as events force a change of plan or require successive retreats from an initially unrealistic position. Sometimes, of course, individuals become less, not more, realistic as events unfold. In this regard, we have already noted the conclusions of Hayes-Roth (1980) that individuals consistently overestimate what they can accomplish in the time available, and that when the difficulty of achieving their plans becomes apparent, they often become increasingly unrealistic regarding substitute actions. From this we can conclude that skill training is needed not only in initial goal setting, but also in recognizing when changes in circumstances require a reconsideration of goals as well as practice at recapturing as much of one's potential losses as possible. Several findings suggest fruitful directions for such goal-setting instruction. First, the higher the level of planning abstraction, the more that individuals tend to overestimate what can be accomplished (Hayes-Roth, 1980). By dealing solely in generalities, individuals often fail to consider all the time-consuming details of planning actions. Thus despite the demonstrated advantages of taking a hierarchical approach to planning, in which the general features of a plan are devised before worrying about details, an exclusive preoccupation with abstract representations can also do a disservice. A balance between abstract and practical concerns must be sought through training. Second, poor planning also occurs when individuals set unrealistic goals because of a desire for the approval of others. For example, Sears (1940) discovered that children who enjoyed a history of success in their classroom work set realistic academic goals, whereas students who experienced continual failure set their aspirations without regard for present performance levels. They often overestimated how well they would perform on various arithmetic and reading tasks. Sears proposed that such maladaptive planning is caused by an intense, unfulfilled desire for approval in which the mere statement of a worthy goal, and not its attainment, becomes the source of gratification (also, see Covington & Beery, 1976). For this reason, instruction in realistic planning should also involve the strengthening of alternative criteria for judging excellence such as encouraging a personal sense of accomplishment beyond the typically prevailing standards in schools that appeal to external authority, whether it be the standards of a teacher or the often intimidating performance of fellow students.

4. Task division.   Another technique critical to strategic problem planning and monitoring involves the division of seemingly insoluble tasks into more manageable subtasks. Obviously, this technique requires both effective problem formulation and prioritizing skills as well as effective goal setting. Solving one part of a larger problem at a time may increase the prospects that the remaining issues will thereby be rendered more amenable to solution. For example, the veteran labor negotiator who scores an initial success by getting agreement on one key point of the contract may be in a better position to conclude the entire task successfully than another negotiator who works on all points of conflict simultaneously. The important point is that problems that appear beyond one's resources initially may nonetheless be solved without reducing one's goal aspirations or giving up.

D. Summary and questions

In section II, we have considered a working taxonomy of three generic problem-solving types, and have identified various plans of action and the allied skills necessary to their solution. In the case of reproductive tasks, planning demands are typically at a minimum, with the problem solver following well-specified, preordained steps necessary to reproduce information in the same form in which it was encoded. As to productive tasks, an effective search for answers requires going beyond the information given with plans of action featuring a balance of problem formulation, ideational fluency, and evaluation skills. In the case of strategic problems, plans of action are epitomized by a means–end analysis, in which the differences between present realities (the problem) and a desired future state (solution) are reduced by invoking such techniques as progressive goal setting and task simplification. The essential point is that different kinds of problem solving require different plans for their solution, depending on whether or not solution states can be specified in advance, or whether the initial problem statement is ill-defined or explicitly stated.

From an educational perspective, this presentation suggests that any comprehensive instruction intended to enhance problem-solving planning should focus simultaneously on three objectives: (a) strengthening those specific prerequisite cognitive skills necessary for planning (e.g., realistic goal setting); (b) increasing the individual's capacity to assemble these cognitive skills in a manner that reflects ongoing changes in the problem itself; and (c) aiding recognition of whether problems are essentially reproductive, productive, or strategic in nature, thereby dictating which broad plans of action to invoke. These observations raise several basic issues regarding the development and implementation of school-based curricula intended to promote planfulness in problem solving.

1. Instructional effectiveness. The first issue concerns the nature and number of planning strategies to be taught, and their relationship to sub-ject-matter knowledge. Obviously, the kinds of skills and strategies dis-cussed above are quite general in nature (e.g., "Solve the problem one part at a time"; "Set realistic goals"; "Think of many ideas"). These con-cepts are not unreasonable, but they are abstract and potentially difficult to grasp and to apply. This suggests a dilemma for advocates of general problem-planning instruction. The more broadly applicable training strategies become, the more likely they are to appear platitudinous and far removed from the demands of the specific situation. For this reason, Newell (1980; Newell & Simon, 1972) described such strategies as inher-ently weak because they trade power for generality. In contrast, strong heuristics designed to deal with specific content-bound problems in, say, physics, chemistry, or English composition are likely to lack generality but possess immediate applicability. The debate over the question of which instructional strategy to adopt – either a weak/general or a strong/ specific approach – is of long standing (see Baron, 1985; Perkins, 1985; Sternberg, 1985) and difficult to resolve precisely because these general techniques are themselves not well understood, nor do we fully appreci-ate how they combine and interact with subject-matter knowledge in the course of problem solving. Consequently, it remains largely a matter of speculation as to which broad organizing and planning techniques, and how many, are fundamental to each of the three general problem types presented in Table 13.1.

We do know, however, that the issue of generality versus power is not essentially a question of the importance of subject-matter content. Evi-dence on this point is uncontestable. No problem can be solved unless the individual possesses or has access to the necessary subject-matter knowledge. Research on tasks as diverse as physics problems (Larkin, 1977), algebra word problems (Paige & Simon, 1966), and engineering thermodynamics (Bhaskar & Simon, 1977) strongly indicate that expert problem-solving behavior is mediated by a combination of specific (power-oriented) subject-matter heuristics and content knowledge. More-over, artificial intelligence research indicates that programs that perform tasks like medical diagnoses must incorporate a large amount of content knowledge about a specific domain. Complex problems cannot be solved by the planful application of general search-and-evaluation strategies alone. This means that children must acquire subject-matter knowledge simultaneously with instruction in procedural or planning knowledge. But, again, should this metaknowledge be strong/specific or weak/general? Fundamentally, this question reduces to the issue of the transferability of general planning strategies (e.g., "get the facts of the problem well in mind"), and whether or not there are circumstances under which they will facilitate the use and manipulation of specific subject-matter material.

2. *Conditions of instruction.* A second question concerns instructional delivery, and whether or not the teaching of general problem-planning skills can be achieved by the same instructional means that have proven effective for other complex learning objectives. For example, should the acquisition of planning techniques be treated as an exercise in complex concept formation? If so, the most effective instruction would call for the orderly presentation of repeated examples of the application of these skills in a variety of problem-solving contexts, and with clear relationships established between successive illustrations (Neves, 1978; Winston, 1970). Moreover, should such instructional sessions provide distributed or massed practice? And how much training is needed? Answers to such questions depend in great measure on the nature of the training effect itself and on whether instruction merely sensitizes students to problem-solving capacities they already possess; or, conversely, whether instruction must first build in capabilities where none existed before, thereby likely requiring far more extensive, protracted instruction.

3. *Learner differences and instruction.* A third question involves the matter of learner differences. It is well documented that the quality of problem solving depends on variations in intelligence (Covington & Crutchfield, 1965), differences in cognitive styles such as reflectivity versus impulsiveness (Greer & Blank, 1977), and on variations in anxiety proneness (Covington, 1985a). To what extent, then, can all children profit from cognitive skill training in planning, irrespective of such learner differences? A related question is how, if at all, will such instruction alter the relationship between learner differences and the quality of thinking? For instance, will instruction act to strengthen the dependency of performance on ability, as in the case of bright, trained students who may become even more proficient relative to the thinking gains enjoyed by less-bright instructed students? Or, conversely, will instruction act to eliminate the influence of ability on performance?

As a group, these comments lead to a series of questions around which we will organize our review of the existing literature on school-based instruction in problem-solving planning.

1. Can general problem-planning skills, especially those germane to productive thinking and strategic thinking, be taught to school children? Does such instruction transfer to and aid in the solution of problems of clear curriculum relevance?
2. What are the most effective conditions of instruction for these general problem-solving and planning strategies?
3. Can general planning skills be acquired by children differing in various learner characteristics including variations in ability? What is the impact of cognitive instruction on the relationship between such individual learner variations and planning strategies?

III. Research findings

Only a fraction of the voluminous literature on the teaching of children's thinking forms the basis for addressing the three questions posed above. The relevant research is drastically limited by the fact that most published sources provide little more than anecdotal information regarding the efficacy of cognitive instruction. Moreover, of the relatively few research-based studies available, many are either improperly or inadequately evaluated, and are often subject to various methodological and procedural shortcomings (for a critique, see Mansfield, Busse, & Krepelka, 1978). For our purposes, the main source of evidence comes from applied field research in school settings on a few instructional programs of sufficient scope to qualify as general cognitive skill training, and with enough research evidence gathered under sufficiently rigorous conditions to permit us to draw reliable conclusions. The main focus of this review is on the evidence generated by the Productive Thinking Program (Covington, Crutchfield, Davies, & Olton, 1965, 1967, 1972, 1974) because of its primary focus on the training of cognitive assembly and planning mechanisms, and because of the relatively large body of research that has accumulated around this program over the past two decades. Several other instructional programs, and their allied research findings, will also be introduced and reviewed as they become appropriate to the questions posed above. We begin with a brief description of the Productive Thinking Program and of the key studies that form the core of this review.

A. The Productive Thinking Program

The Productive Thinking Program (PTP) was designed as a research instrument by the Berkeley Thinking Project to study the nature and facilitation of children's problem solving at the upper elementary school

Table 13.2. *The thinking guides from the productive thinking program*

1. Take time to reflect on a problem before you begin work. Decide exactly what the problem is that you are trying to solve.
2. Get all the facts of the problem clearly in mind.
3. Work on the problem in a planful way.
4. Keep an open mind. Don't jump to conclusions about the answer to a problem.
5. Think of many ideas for solving a problem. Don't stop with just a few.
6. Try to think of unusual ideas.
7. As a way of getting ideas, pick out all the important objects and persons in the problem and think carefully about each one.
8. Think of several general possibilities for a solution and then figure out many particular ideas for each possibility.
9. As you search for ideas, let your mind freely explore things around you. Almost anything can suggest ideas for a solution.
10. Always check each idea with the facts to decide how likely the idea is.
11. If you get stuck on a problem, keep thinking. Don't be discouraged or give up.
12. When you run out of ideas, try looking at the problem in a new and different way.
13.. Go back and review all the facts of the problem to make sure you have not missed something important.
14. Start with an unlikely idea. Just suppose that it is possible, and then figure out how it could be.
15. Be on the lookout for odd or puzzling facts in a problem. Explaining them can lead you to new ideas for a solution.
16. When there are several different puzzling things in a problem, try to explain them with a single idea that will connect them all together.

level and emphasizes student understanding of how convergent and divergent skills are coordinated in an overall, planful attack on a problem. The main teaching component of the PTP consists of a series of 16 self-instructional lessons, each centering on a complex detective-type mystery problem. As a problem unfolds, page by page, students are required to perform various problem-solving operations: writing down ideas, determining what new information is needed, or formulating the problem in their own words. On successive pages, students receive immediate feedback on their efforts in the form of a range of responses (e.g., possible questions or ideas that would be appropriate at that point in the problem). Through such guided practice in a variety of problem contexts, the student is led to understand what constitutes relevant and original ideas, how to proceed when faced with a difficult problem, and what strategies to employ whenever they encounter difficulties. This practice/feedback mechanism is built around a set of 16 thinking guides listed in Table 13.2. The planning and control schema taught by this program is an elementary one: Whenever students work on a problem, especially if they become stuck, they should examine the list of thinking guides for ideas about how to proceed. This procedure embodies a highly simplified version of Simon's means–ends analysis (1980), in which students are encouraged to review periodically what problem they are working on, to consider if the problem has changed, to judge what has been accomplished toward a solution, and to decide what more information or steps are now needed to achieve a solution. In addition to these strategic objectives, systematic instruction is also provided for various component skills with special attention to idea generation. One such ideational strategy (guide No. 8; Table 13.2) involves the systematic search for all possible solution ideas through the orderly, planful exploration of "idea-trees." Here the student proceeds from the enumeration of general possibilities to the spelling out of all specific ideas within each general solution category (Crutchfield, 1961; Resnick & Glaser, 1976). Further practice on the thinking guides and their orchestration is provided through a series of supplementary exercises that follow each of the basic lessons. These additional exercises feature curriculum-relevant problems in science, the arts, and the humanities in order to facilitate planning transfer beyond the core detective format.

Three PTP evaluation studies will be reported in detail because they provide some of the most rigorous field evidence to date on the questions before us (for a critique, see Mansfield, Busse, & Krepelka, 1978; Polson & Jeffries, 1985). Moreover, as a group, these studies were designed to chart the instructional conditions under which general problem-solving instruction would be most effective for students of widely varying ability levels. A brief description of each study follows.

1. The Racine study. The purpose of the Racine Study (Olton et al., 1967; Wardrop, et al., 1969) was to explore the impact of cognitive instruction under the least advantageous classroom conditions – in effect, to establish the lower limits of effectiveness of the PTP. The basic lessons were administered with no supplemental practice exercises and at a compressed rate of presentation, one lesson per school day, thereby permitting only the briefest opportunity for consolidation of skill practice. Additionally, the PTP was administered on a purely self-instructional basis with no teacher participation or encouragement. The entire project was treated simply as a series of extra assignments to be completed by students on their own. This large-scale study involved all 47 fifth-grade classrooms in the Racine, Wisconsin, public school system, totaling some 1300 students who represented a wide range of abilities and backgrounds typically found in such an urban system. Students in all classrooms were administered a 4-hour pretest criterion battery of productive thinking, planning, and related measures. Classrooms were then randomly assigned either to an instructed or a control condition. At the end of the training period, another criterion battery, similar in composition to the pretest, was administered in all classrooms.

2. *The Berkeley studies.* In contrast to the Racine study, two subsequent PTP studies conducted in the Berkeley, California, public schools were designed to establish the upper limits of instructional effectiveness. The PTP was administered in its entirety, including the supplementary practice exercises – a total of some 32 hours of classroom instruction. Moreover, the rate of presentation of the basic lessons was reduced to two per week, thus distributing skill practice. Finally, teachers participated by conducting a brief classroom discussion following each lesson designed to reiterate the thinking guides.

In the study conducted at the Cragmont Elementary School, some 280 students from six fifth-grade and six sixth-grade classrooms were involved (Olton & Crutchfield, 1969). All classes at each grade level were split on a random basis so that half of each class was combined into an instructed group, and the other half into a control group that did not receive the instructional materials, but which was comparable in all other ways. Whereas students in the instructed group met together for the administration of the PTP and for group discussion, control students met in other nearby rooms to participate in an activities program of stories, movies, and group projects chosen to interest the students. In the study conducted at Hillside Elementary School, students in four intact classrooms – two at the fifth-grade level and two at the sixth-grade level – were randomly divided into instructed and control groups and treated in a manner similar to that at Cragmont School.

Given this description of the PTP, and the studies on which much of the following review is based, we now turn to a consideration of the various organizing questions listed earlier.

B. Instructional effectiveness

Can school children be taught to be more planful in their approach to problem solving, especially in the case of productive and strategic tasks? Does such instruction transfer to and aid in the solution of problems of clear curriculum relevance?

Given our imprecise understanding of how individuals marshal their problem-solving resources, how can investigators determine whether or not a purposeful orchestration of cognitive skills has occurred, let alone measure the degree to which such planfulness might be enhanced by educational intervention? Two approaches are open to us, one dealing primarily with productive thinking tasks and the other more germane to strategic thinking tasks. The first line of inquiry suggests that effective planning is reflected indirectly in the quality of the productive-thinking solutions generated (Covington, 1966b). Productive-thinking tasks typically require the coordinated and parsimonious explanation of several disparate puzzles, contradictions, or inconsistencies. Therefore, in order to achieve "best fit" solutions, ideational search strategies must of necessity be tempered by quality control and comprehension monitoring. It will be recalled that this implied orchestration of cognitive functions epitomizes the planning process, when viewed as an information-processing phenomenon. Evidence for such a purposeful integration of cognitive functions, as reflected in the quality of solutions, is presented below.

A second source of evidence for enhanced planning behavior involves the direct observation of an individual's proposed plan of attack on strategic problems, not as the plan develops covertly, but rather as it is created in advance as part of the problem-formulation stage. Here the quality of planning and its improvement can be reflected in several ways. First, at the simplest level, instruction may merely increase the individual's ability to identify good, poor, or indifferent plans of action. This tells us about the individual's capacity to *recognize* planning issues, but little more. Second, at a more profound level, instruction can alter the capacity of individuals to *produce* their own plans of action, either spontaneously or when directed to do so.

1. Problem resolution. If we accept the argument that problem resolution is a key behavioral marker of effective cognitive assembly, then the quality, frequency, and timing of solution ideas following instruction becomes a critical part of the answer to the question of whether or not planfulness can be enhanced. Much of the evidence on this point relates to convergent thinking tasks.

a. Convergent thinking problems. Several convergent problems were developed to assess the efficacy of the PTP. Each problem required the discovery of a single idea that best fit various problem constraints. (For a psychometric discussion of these measures, see Covington, 1966a, 1966b, 1970, 1984b.) These tasks are representative of problems currently facing scientists and scholars in various subject-matter fields: medical science, anthropology, biology, and history. For instance, in the Ancient City Problem students formulated the best explanation as to why an apparently thriving civilization came to an abrupt end, given a variety of seemingly unrelated pieces of physical evidence. In general, the accumulated findings suggest that cognitive instruction is effective at enhancing the likelihood of "best fit" convergent solutions. By way of specific illustration, in one other problem, students were provided with data describing the flight pattern of a flock of birds migrating to their summer feeding grounds. Embedded unobtrusively in the text were three puzzling findings. In the Cragmont study, control students satisfactorily accounted for an average of 1.08 of the facts, whereas instructed students were able to explain an average of 1.90, almost twice as many. Moreover, nearly 38% of the instructed students explained all three facts with their best solution, whereas only 12% of the control students were able to do so. Furthermore, the fact that the bird migration problem was administered four months after training in the Cragmont study attests to the longevity of instructional effects. This overall pattern of solution superiority favoring instructed students has been corroborated by other investigators using the PTP with similar test problems and employing similar research designs (Ripple & Darcey, 1967; Treffinger, 1971; Treffinger & Ripple, 1970). As to the question of transfer of instruction, these findings suggest that children can successfully apply the same strategies learned in one context (a detective format) to a wide range of school-related contexts for which the particular subject-matter content is unfamiliar, as in the bird migration example.

There is also evidence that general problem-solving instruction increases proficiency on the individual convergent skills that support solution assembly. The PTP evaluation problems described previously are so designed that evidence for the effective operation of component skills (e.g., idea generation) can also be gathered as work toward a solution proceeds. In each of three PTP studies described earlier and in other studies (e.g., Covington & Crutchfield, 1965), instructed students also demonstrated superiority over control students on a wide array of component skills including ideational fluency, sensitivity to puzzling phenomena, and the number and quality of questions asked.

Similar findings regarding the trainability of component convergent skills come from the research on the teacher-led Philosophy for Children Program (Lipman, 1976; Lipman, Sharp, & Oscanyan, 1977) which focuses primarily on enhancing the formalistic, logical aspects of thinking (e.g., drawing syllogistic inferences). A review of some half-dozen field-based evaluation studies employing upper-elementary school children provides convincing evidence that instruction promotes substantial increases in the child's capacity to provide reasons for puzzling events, to discover alternative interpretations of data, and to identify fallacies (Lipman, 1985). Moreover, these cognitive gains were accompanied by significant improvement in teacher ratings of student academic readiness, as well as gains in reading and math skills as measured by standardized achievement tests.

b. Divergent thinking problems. Parallel evidence indicates that originality of divergent thinking can also be enhanced via cognitive training. Here cognitive assembly mechanisms involve a combination of various ideational search strategies and the continuous monitoring of ideas against a criterion of novelty (i.e., statistical infrequency). Research on the Purdue Creative Thinking Program is most germane (Feldhusen, Speedie, & Treffinger, 1971). This program consists of several dozen audio tapes with accompanying printed exercise material, each of which provides practice on various divergent ideational techniques. To date, the accumulated evidence of five studies employing the Purdue Program with middle- and upper-elementary school children suggests that such divergent search strategies are responsive to training (for a review, see Mansfield, Busse, & Krepelka, 1978). For example, in one representative study (Feldhusen, Treffinger, & Bahlke, 1970), 54 fourth-, fifth-, and sixth-grade classrooms were administered the Purdue Program at a rate of two lessons per week for 14 weeks. Seven different instructional conditions involved the presentation of various components of the program both singly and in combination. In general, all instructed groups tended to outperform a control group that received only a posttest battery. However, this generally favorable evidence must be qualified by the consideration that the Purdue Program involves practice on divergent tasks quite similar to those employed in the posttest evaluation batteries (Torrance Tests of Creative Thinking, 1972). Perhaps the most convincing evidence for divergent transfer of training comes from gains on the Torrence Tests following instruction with the PTP (Covington & Crutchfield, 1965; Moreno & Hogan, 1976; Shively, Feldhusen, & Treffinger, 1972; Treffinger, 1971). As will be recalled, PTP instruction focuses primarily on the strategic assembly and monitoring of various processes with little direct instruction on divergent production per se.

2. Strategic plans of action. The second source of evidence regarding the efficacy of planning instruction involves measurement of the child's ability to recognize effective plans of actions as well as to produce such plans on his or her own. As to the recognition mode, a special test was constructed by the Berkeley staff. Students were presented with a complex, extended task in a sequential fashion. At various choice points throughout the program, students were required to select the best next planning step from among a list of several alternative courses of action. Naturally, the specific content of these alternatives changed as the problem unfolded depending on previous events, as did the arguments for the soundness of each choice. Each list contained a "best" course of action; a second "best" action (reasonable, though not as effective as the first); a "contrary fact" course of action (one that ignored or violated an already established fact); an appealing but irrelevant action (one that was attractive but would not aid in solving the problem), and finally, a course of action that would force a premature conclusion to the problem. This test was administered as part of the posttest battery employed in the Racine study. Following PTP instruction, trained students were better able than control students to trace the best strategic course of action from problem presentation to its solution. Instructed students were also less attracted to "appealing but irrelevant" actions, less likely to be seduced by "contrary fact" actions, and more often selected the "best" over the "next best" action.

A second line of evidence bears on the increased capacity of trained students to produce plans of action on their own. Data on this point are provided by two additional PTP studies. As part of a follow-up test given four months after the completion of PTP training, students in the Cragmont study were asked to outline several possible steps that scientists might take to establish the identity of a recently unearthed mummy that had deteriorated beyond recognition. Students were provided with supplementary information indicating the dates that various Egyptian royalty were known to have lived and those individuals whose burial locations had already been established. Student protocols were scored for the presence or absence of various elements of a simple elimination strategy (e.g., "draw up a list of yet-to-be-discovered kings or queens"). A single global rating reflecting an overall sense of planfulness was also made by judges. On each of these various measures of effective planning, instructed students outperformed their control counterparts to a significant degree. The fact that instructed students received no specific training in such progressive elimination strategies provides additional, tentative evidence for the transfer of general cognitive instruction; and the fact that the training/test interval was four months in duration further underscores the reasonably robust nature of this effect.

A second study involved the work of Cox and Swain on instruction in strategic planning (Cox & Swain, 1981; Cox, Swain, & Hartsough, 1982).

Some 1,000 third-, fourth-, fifth-, and sixth-grade students from seven school sites in Sonoma County, California, were assigned randomly on an intact classroom basis to either an instructed or a control condition. Instructed students received the PTP over the course of a school year supplemented by materials developed in teacher workshops designed to reinforce the means–ends analysis component of the PTP. Criterion tasks were developed especially to assess how students would manage a variety of school-related, independent learning tasks. In one problem, students assisted a hypothetical classmate to set up and carry out a plan for writing a school report; in another problem, plans were developed for a science fair exhibit; and yet another task involved raising money for a school carnival. Written protocols were scored for evidence of students' ability (a) to ask strategic questions that delineated the scope, form, and timing of the task; (b) to outline a sequential plan of action; (c) to revise plans in the face of unforeseen events (e.g., changes in the due date of the school report); and (d) to invoke various criteria for evaluating the success of completed plans.

After controlling for initial pretest performance by means of covariance, Cox and Swain found reliable posttest differences favoring instructed groups, with the gains being most consistent at the fifth- and sixth-grade levels, and on those measures concerned with strategic questioning and product evaluation.

With regard to question asking, instructed students made more inquiries than did control students about broad planning issues concerning the timing and execution of various subtasks within the larger project. It appears that such strategic questioning is quite amenable to training at least at this age. For example, Greer and Blank (1977) reported that following PTP instruction fifth-grade students asked more fact-seeking and constraint-seeking questions than did matched controls. Similar findings were also obtained using a preliminary, exploratory version of the PTP (Blank & Covington, 1965). Unfortunately, however, as yet there is no evidence as to the durability of such effects nor much information about whether these increased skill levels translate spontaneously into a heightened willingness on the part of the student to ask questions in meaningful ways when not required to do so.

With regard to product evaluation, instructed students in the Cox and Swain study were more likely to judge the success of their plans in terms of intrinsic criteria (e.g., how much they learned from their report apart from any grade) as compared to their almost exclusive reliance on external sources of authority (teacher, peer opinion) prior to instruction. In light of earlier comments about the need for self-defined successes in personal planning and goal setting, these findings are especially gratifying. In contrast, evidence was marginal for student gains in a strategic sense for modifying plans as circumstances changed. Both instructed and control students persisted in the same disheartening tendency described previously (Schnur, 1981), in which any interruption of an existing plan is met with the simple panacea of working harder, faster, or longer. This failure of instruction is likely due in part to the fact that the perceived saliency of sheer effort as a cause of academic success reaches its maximum in the upper-elementary years (Harari & Covington, 1981; Weiner & Peter, 1973). This is but one more instance of the need to accommodate instructional strategies to prevailing developmental trends.

Perhaps the most significant implication of the Cox and Swain study was the demonstration that systematic instruction in planning can set in motion broad-gauged changes in the way students approach their school work as reflected by improved teacher ratings of student classroom performance. This point is further underscored by the work of deCharms on origin training (deCharms, 1968). "Origin" refers to individuals who are in control of their own achievement chiefly through the exercise of skillful goal setting, planfulness, and a readiness to accept personal responsibility for their actions. Origin training consists of a series of exercises designed (a) to encourage teachers to treat their students as if they were self-starters, that is, establishing a classroom climate conducive to student self-management; and (b) to provide students themselves with some of the managerial skills necessary to self-responsibility. These skills included realistic goal setting, problem analysis, and the specification of concrete steps necessary to reach goals as well as learning to detect whether or not progress is being made toward these goals. The results of several evaluation studies are promising. In one study (deCharms, 1968), several dozen junior high school teachers were found to be significantly more "origin"-like in their treatment of students some two years after teacher training was completed, as compared to the behavior of a group of matched control teachers. As to the effectiveness of the student training component, research has been concentrated largely on inner-city minority children (deCharms, 1972). For example, origin training was administered by regular classroom teachers to black ghetto children over a two-year period beginning in the sixth grade. By the end of the seventh grade, instructed youngsters, as compared to matched control children, expressed more confidence in their ability to manage their own learning, acted in a more positive goal-directed fashion, and posted substantial increases in their academic accomplishments as reflected on standardized achievement tests.

Several additional studies suggest that these positive academic effects are likely achieved through improved students' capacity to set personal learning goals that are consistent with their present ability to achieve them (Hill, 1974; Kolb, 1965; Shea, 1969). When students overestimate what they can accomplish, failure is the likely result; but when students establish a match between current skill levels and task difficulty, achievement increases for students at all ability levels (Woodson, 1975). Given these dynamics, it is gratifying to note that systematic instruction in goal setting not only reduces the tendency for unrealistic self-appraisal (Ryals, 1969; Shea, 1969), but also seems to have its greatest impact on those failure-prone children whom Sears (1940) described as driven to overestimate their ability through an unfulfilled desire for approval.

C. Conditions of instruction

What are the most effective conditions of instruction for general problem-solving and planning strategies?

The generally positive findings cited in the previous section, regarding gains in convergent-problem solution following PTP intervention need be qualified. The magnitude of these training effects is related to the conditions of instruction. For example, for the Racine study, in which the PTP was deliberately administered under disadvantageous conditions, the margin of solution superiority for instructed students was minimal. By contrast, when instructional conditions were maximized in the Cragmont and Hillside studies, the results were far more impressive. Likewise, instructional increases in the component skills necessary to cognitive assembly also depended on these same variations, with the smallest gains associated with the Racine study, and the largest gains with the Cragmont and Hillside studies. These findings suggest that training in problem-solving planning depends on the same kinds of instructional delivery variables that dictate the effectiveness of most educational programs. Teacher participation seems especially critical. Moreover, prevailing classroom atmosphere also appears to play a discernable role, as indicated by further results from the Racine study. Prior to the administration of the PTP, all 22 instructed classrooms were evaluated by district supervisors regarding the degree to which the overall classroom atmosphere (including teachers) tended to facilitate or inhibit the development of thinking skills. Although the magnitude of various Atmosphere × Performance interactions were modest, when they did occur the greatest programmatic changes in problem solving were associated with those classrooms that offered the least facilitative environments. Cognitive skill instruction may have its greatest impact as a compensatory agent by offsetting negative environmental conditions, rather than by enriching those environments that are already facilitative.

One additional, subsidiary study (Covington & Crutchfield, 1965) sheds further light on the nature of the instructional effects. Some 300 fifth-grade and sixth-grade students were assigned to several treatment groups. One group was administered the PTP in a manner similar to that employed in the Racine study. A second group simply viewed the PTP lessons vicariously with no requirement that they think on their own. A third group received an abridged summary of the PTP thinking guides in didactic form just prior to working on the posttest criterion battery, whereas a control group receiving no form of instruction completed the design. Various pairwise comparisons among the first two instructed groups indicated that solution gains occurred equally whether students actively solved the practice problems or merely passively observed the application of the guides. In contrast, the mere possession of the guides without practice in some form made little impact on subsequent solution performance. Therefore, although the type of practice may not be critical (active or passive), exposure to the use of these guides via repeated example seems essential. Finally, other evidence from the same study indicated that instructional effects may be achieved after only a few lessons. Such rapid gains in problem-solving efficiency after only modest amounts of practice suggest that instruction may act primarily to sensitize children to the use of capacities they already possess.

D. Learner differences and instruction

Can the instructional benefits described in previous sections be enjoyed by children of widely different learning characteristics including variations in intelligence? What is the impact of cognitive instruction on the relationship between individual learner variations and planful behavior?

Based on the results of the previously cited PTP studies, it is clear that gains in thinking effectiveness occur for youngsters across a wide range of intellectual capacity, regardless of initial level of thinking performance. Table 13.3 illustrates this point. These data represent a composite of results from six different PTP studies and display the average percentage of solutions achieved across several convergent-test problems for children of high, middle, and low IQ. Not surprisingly, the higher the IQ level, the more likely either the instructed or the control group was to solve the problems. However, despite this substantial dependency of performance on ability, the absolute level of thinking proficiency was increased for all instructed students, irrespective of their initial IQ level.

Table 13.3. *Average percentage solutions of convergent problems following cognitive instruction by IQ level*

IQ level	Control subjects (%)	Instructed subjects (%)
Below 100	5	30
100–115	13	46
Above 115	25	53

Moreover, the magnitude of these instructional gains was not necessarily related to IQ. In this particular case, instruction produced relatively equal gains at all IQ levels. However, it is unlikely that cognitive instruction will reduce the wide range of individual differences in thinking proficiency or will alter the relative standing of groups within a school population because of the substantial dependency of performance on initial ability status.

These findings take on considerable significance in light of speculation that links intellectual capacity to the quality and speed of cognitive assembly (Butterfield & Belmont, 1971, 1977; Sternberg, 1979). Specifically, it has been suggested that intelligence represents the ability to think strategically, that is, the capacity to plan for and to make the most of one's personal resources as the situation demands (Covington, 1983b, 1984c). However, if intelligent behavior depended on the capacity to plan and act strategically, then in what sense does such a strategic capacity emerge through instruction? Several additional studies conducted by members of the Berkeley Productive Thinking Project illustrate how cognitive training can moderate the relationship between basic abilities, cognitive heuristics, and problem-solving performance, and therefore bear directly on the matter of the strategic integration and balancing of newly acquired thinking skills.

In one study (Covington & Fedan, 1978), two separate regression analyses were performed on the data from the Hillside study, one for those students who had received the PTP and the other for the untrained, control students. The quality of the single best solution idea produced by each student on a given problem was the criterion variable of interest. Various predictor variables were employed, including the child's verbal IQ as well as measures of individual cognitive skills such as number of ideas generated (fluency) in the course of working on a problem, the number of questions asked, and sensitivity to the puzzling features of the problem. We knew from previous experience that these latter measures were highly sensitive to PTP training, and therefore could act as markers of enhanced component skills. A revealing instructional pattern emerged. Among untrained children, the quality of solution ideas depended heavily on variations in intelligence. By contrast, training attenuated this dependency for instructed students so that the quality of solution ideas now came to depend to a greater degree on a combination of cognitive skills trained for in the PTP. Moreover, the composition of these skills changed, depending on problem type. For example, ideational fluency components were most important in the solution of divergent tasks, whereas sensitivity to problem constraints and idea-evaluation skills emerged as the more important components of convergent solutions. Thus the presence of newly acquired heuristics, and not intelligence per se, became the more important factor in the quality of problem-solving performance, a situation that especially compensated the less bright, instructed students so that they now performed at a level equal to that of high IQ control students. By comparison, less bright control students who possessed neither the trained strategies nor the native capacity to generate them spontaneously performed at a far poorer level than did either of these other two groups. Most important to the present discussion, however, was the fact that these trainable heuristics operated in combination, and that their composition changed depending on the character of the problem, suggesting the emergence of a higher-order assembly process brought under cognitive control via instruction. This interpretation is consistent with an information-processing view of the nature of planfulness in problem solving.

Further light is shed on these organizational functions through an additional regression analysis of the same data base (Covington, 1984a), but this time exploring affective, emotionally linked predictor variables (anxiety level). It has long been known that anxiety interferes with effective thinking (e.g., Yerkes & Dodson, 1908), but only in recent times has the complexity of this seemingly simple relationship been fully appreciated (see Covington, 1985a; von der Ploeg, Schwarzer, & Spielberger, 1984). For example, research indicates that although anxiety actually enhances the sheer frequency of ideas generated by raising drive level, it also acts simultaneously to suppress the quality of these ideas (Covington, 1983a), thereby causing a net loss in problem-solving effectiveness. An examination of the performance differences between instructed and control subjects from the Hillside study indicated a significant improvement in the quality of ideational output among highly anxious children following PTP instruction. This training effect was achieved not by a direct reduction in anxiety level per se, but rather by a complicated dynamic in which cognitive instruction suspended the debilitating influence of anxiety on quality control so that the surfeit of ideas normally generated by anxious children were of higher quality.

The results of these several studies hold two noteworthy educational implications. First, they provide a fine-grained analysis as to why general cognitive skill training is effective. Instruction does not simply override factors inimical to effective planning such as low ability or anxiety, but rather appear to stimulate a higher-order, more harmonious integration of existing processes that tends to operate in compensatory ways. This implies that through cognitive instruction, teachers can increase that which according to Alfred Binet constitutes intelligence: "Comprehension, planfulness, invention and judgment – in these four words lies the essence of intelligence" (1909, p. 54). Thus in the school context, intelligence (i.e., planning and monitoring) means being able to recognize when one does not understand a concept, having the capacity to reevaluate homework assignments in light of changing circumstances, and knowing what to do – or whom to see – when previously successful learning strategies are no longer effective. Second, the efficacy of cognitive training depends to a great extent on differing task demands. For example, although teaching idea-production strategies facilitated the performance of less able students on divergent-thinking tasks, such heuristics appeared insufficient in themselves to promote the discovery of more elegant, constraint-bound solutions demanded by convergent problems. These results raise again the all-important issue of the generality of transfer of general cognitive skill training and just how "problem-specific" such cognitive training should be.

IV. Remaining issues

This review has revealed both problems and promises for planning research as it relates to broad educational goals. As to the promising developments, three observations seem in order. First, a substantial body of evidence suggests that effective problem-solving planning can be enhanced by direct, systematic, school-based instruction. Moreover, at least some of these instructional effects appear capable of persisting for relatively prolonged periods. Second, the magnitude of these cognitive gains are lawfully related to the conditions of instruction. Thus they can be brought under the control of well-understood instructional delivery variables, and as a consequence, can be reliably reproduced. Third, youngsters of widely varying ability levels can profit from cognitive instruction, even though initial levels of thinking proficiency depend heavily on ability status. This finding strengthens the growing belief that intelligent *behavior* (planning, in Binet's terms) – as distinct from intelligence as a psychometric concept – can be enhanced, irrespective of ability level. Overall, then, considerable strides have been made in creating a solid empirical and theoretical case for the efficacy and desirability of problem-solving instruction as well as an enhanced understanding of the instructional conditions that constrain and promote problem-planning behavior.

On the problematic side of the ledger, the problems alluded to above arise largely out of the failure of researchers to pursue with equal vigor several of the main issues identified earlier as pertinent to effective curriculum development and innovation. These issues concern questions about the ontogenetic development of planful behavior and transfer of training.

A. Developmental considerations

A major unanswered question concerns issues related to cognitive development, and specifically which general planning strategies should or can be promoted at any given age. If it is true that in order to be most effective, cognitive skill training must proceed over a period of years – embodied as a kind of life-course cognitive curriculum – then the matter of timing and staging of such instruction becomes critical (Covington, 1969). A developmental perspective is important not only because instruction may actually hasten the *onset* of various planning capacities, but also because properly staged intervention may increase the readiness of children to use already existing capacities to their fullest at *any* developmental level. This latter educational objective seeks not to accelerate growth as much as to reduce the gap between one's potential for thought and actual performance throughout the developmental span. In either case, we are essentially uninformed about what broad planning heuristics and rules represent the true precursors of later adultlike strategic thought. For example, it is by no means clear that those cognitive skills associated with childhood creativity such as ideational fluency (Torrance, 1962) are synonymous with or even similar to the cognitive functions responsible for creative expression in adulthood (Nicholls, 1972). Thus, it is entirely possible that instruction in a set of skills appropriate to planning at one developmental level may add little to, or conceivably even interfere with, planning behavior at a later age.

Most cognitive training programs, including those reviewed in this chapter, are targeted at a relatively narrow age range without sufficient concern for the larger developmental span within which the specific training is focused. Yet, we know that the quality of planning behavior follows a developmental course. Some of the best evidence on this point comes from the work of Scardamalia and Bereiter (1985), which tracks agewise changes in the heuristics and rules that control plans for expository writing in young children. However, this research is an exception. If educators envision truly comprehensive planning instruction over prolonged periods of time – not just weeks (as is typically the case at present), nor even months, but years – then we must identify and build on those broad intellectual skills that are the true precursors of later adultlike, strategic thinking.

B.   Limits of transfer

As to the second issue, transfer of training is central to any vision of general problem-solving instruction. Yet here, too, virtually nothing is known systematically about the robustness and the limits of the potential transfer mechanisms involved, nor about the instructional factors that likely control them. On the whole, the evidence reviewed here merely strengthens the vague impression that children are capable of generalizing problem-planning instruction, and that they will do so on occasion, even spontaneously. The most encouraging note in this regard is the recurring evidence of enhanced subject-matter acquisition following cognitive instruction as reflected on standardized achievement tests and by teacher ratings of improved student academic readiness. Unfortunately, however, the transfer mechanisms by which such gains occur following cognitive instruction remain unclear. Naturally, such imprecision can scarcely serve educational planners, especially in light of the accumulating laboratory evidence that some kinds of problem transfer may be highly specific and sharply restricted by instructional circumstances (e.g., Posner, 1967).

Of all the planning skills that might qualify as the most generalizable, *goal setting* appears to be a prime candidate. Goal setting enters into virtually all aspects of thinking, particularly strategic thinking; and, given the evidence reviewed here, goal setting has the most consistent record of responsiveness to instruction both among children and adults (see Locke, 1968; Locke & Latham, 1984). Another possible candidate is *problem formulation*. Numerous investigators have remarked on the centrality of this skill cluster for all thinking and planning; but, once again, its instructional promise is at present more assumed than demonstrated. In short, we lack even the most rudimentary empirical basis for deciding what skills are most central to overall planning behavior by reason of their robustness for transfer.

In closing, we can entertain several potential lines of inquiry for future research on transfer as it relates to planning instruction. The first focus concerns the unreliability of transfer as noted above. Especially worrisome is the frequent failure of learners to apply well-rehearsed, cognitive strategies to problems similar to those that were successfully solved only a short time before.

The question is *why* students fail to employ strategies known to be in their repertoire and in situations familiar to them. Eventually we will likely find that the most satisfying explanations can be stated in motivational as well as cognitive terms. Trainees are unlikely to use newly acquired skills reliably, especially when not directed explicitly to do so, if they lack confidence in their own thought processes and in their ability to make sound judgments. Motivational dispositions such as a *willingness* to be planful, or the inclination to risk failure in the pursuit of a deeper, more profound understanding of a problem would appear to be especially vulnerable to negative emotional factors (Covington & Beery, 1976; Covington & Omelich, 1979). For example, it is well known that a lack of self confidence and a fear of failure result in inaction and indifference (Covington & Omelich, 1984). Interestingly, the available evidence suggests that dispositions such as a willingness to risk failure are in themselves modifiable via problem-solving instruction. In several of the PTP studies described earlier, instructed students showed an increased willingness to undertake problems that required complex monitoring and planful deliberation when given a free choice of tasks ranging from rote, reproductive problems to complex, strategic ones (Olton & Crutchfield, 1969). In yet another instance (Allen & Levine, 1967), PTP students demonstrated an increased reliance on their own judgments to the extent that they were better able than control youngsters to withstand the conformity pressure of peers when they believed their ideas to be correct. Research that focuses on the interface between training for cognitive skill acquisition, the planful application of such skills, and the motivations that drive, divert, or suppress such purposeful actions should pay dividends in our understanding of the unreliability of transfer mechanisms.

A second potentially fruitful focus for research regarding transfer concerns the question of the dimensions along which transfer should properly proceed. Consider the proposal that for transfer to be educationally meaningful, it must extend in two directions simultaneously. First, in terms of our taxonomy, transfer mechanisms should extend *top down,* hierarchically speaking, proceeding from the application of planning techniques to ill-defined, multifaceted, *strategic* problems (e.g., eliminating environmental pollution) to highly defined, *reproductive* problems controlled by clear subject-matter constraints (e.g., solving algebraic word problems). The evidence for cognitive transfer at various points along this continuum (from underdetermined to overdetermined problems), although somewhat favorable, is spotty and unsystematic in the extreme. We can deduce from our review only that general cognitive instruction facilitates planning and monitoring in the middle range of this continuum which reflects reasonably well-defined *productive-thinking* problems (particularly convergent tasks), the specific content of which was previously unfamiliar to children. However, at either end of this continuum, evidence on the question of transfer is largely nonexistent. For example, there is little evidence, one way or the other, that cognitive instruction can manifest itself in the spontaneous reorganization of vague indeterminate, real-life problems outside the narrow demands of the academic context (e.g., selecting a career). Nor, at the same time, is there much direct evidence that the possession of general problem-solving skills aids thinking about specific, well-defined subject-bound problems. In this connection, it may be that general planning instruction reaches its effective lower limits of transfer at the juncture between reproductive and productive problem modes, so that the most efficient use of instructional time for subject-matter acquisition per se (and for reproductive thinking) would be to teach specific power-oriented strategies around particular subject domains. Naturally, it is also possible that a combination of instruction in both general planning strategies (e.g., goal setting) and specific procedural knowledge (e.g., "how to write an English composition") will prove the most effective means for turning the process of rote subject-matter *acquisition* into one of creative *assimilation*. In any event, it seems clear from the broader perspective championed here that general instruction in problem-planning behavior will always be justified in its own right, if for no other reason than its apparent suitability for mediating gains in productive and strategic thinking domains, a point that brings us to the second dimension of transfer alluded to above.

Transfer of cognitive training must also extend *outward* (in time) from the reasonably well-articulated academic problems that currently confront young people in school today to those problems of a largely unknown nature that will confront the individual and society as well in the midst of the 21st century. The consequences of some of these future problems can already be dimly perceived (e.g., the ability to change mankind's very nature through biochemical techniques). The resolution of such problems will likely require entirely new ways of thinking, which in turn must await further developments in scientific technology and bioethics. Other predictable future problems are as old as mankind but must be resolved anew and in different ways by each generation (e.g., how to replace war as the habitual method for achieving peace). Finally, entirely unforeseen problems will be created out of our efforts to solve existing ones. Here society's goal must be to implement only those solutions that are likely to alleviate more problems than they create. According to our schema of problem-solving types, such future-oriented problems seem predominantly strategic in nature and call for the creation of plans of action in the face of dramatically changing events and insufficient information. It would seem reasonable to expect that research within the present problem-solving taxonomy with special attention given to questions of how the growing child creates and executes strategic plans of action in ill-defined circumstances would pay dividends for our eventual understanding of future-oriented transfer.

In the end, Theodore Sturgeon's *homo gestalt* also turned to the future and to concerns for its responsibility to upcoming generations. In part, this process was epitomized by *homo gestalt's* struggle to achieve higher levels of self-consciousness (metacognitive sophistication) and increased self-respect so that its future actions would not only be productive but also sound. Herein lies the greatest of all educational challenges: to encourage in children the wisdom and daring to plan well.

References

Allen, V. L., & Levine, J. M. (1967). *Creativity and conformity.* Technical Report No. 33. Madison, WI: University of Wisconsin Research and Development Center for Cognitive Learning.

Baron, J. (1985). What kinds of intelligence components are fundamental? In J. Segal, S. Chrysman, & R. Glasen (Eds.), *Thinking and learning skills: Relating instruction to basic research.* Hillsdale, NJ: Erlbaum.

Barron, F. (1965). The psychology of creativity. In F. Barron, W. C. Dement, W. Edwards, H. Lindman, L. D. Phillips, J. Olds, & Marianne Olds (Eds.), *New Directions in Psychology* (Vol. II). New York: Holt, Rinehart & Winston.

Binet, A. (1909). Les idées modernes sur les enfants. Paris: Ernest Flamarion.

Bhaskar, R., & Simon, H. A. (1977). Problem solving in semantically rich domains: An example from engineering thermodynamics. *Cognitive Science, 1,* 193–215.

Blank, S. S., & Covington, M. V. (1965). Inducing children to ask questions in solving problems. *Journal of Educational Research, 59,* 21–27.

Bransford, J. D., Nitsch, K. E., & Franks, J. J. (1977). The facilitation of knowing. In R. C. Anderson, R. J. Spiro, & W. E. Montague (Eds.), *Schooling and the acquisition of knowledge.* Hillsdale, NJ: Erlbaum.

Brown, A. L. (1978). Knowing when, where, and how to remember: A problem of metacognition. In R. Glaser (Ed.), *Advances in instructional psychology.* Hillsdale, NJ: Erlbaum.

Brown, A. L., Palincsar, A. S., & Armbruster, B. B. (1983). Instructing comprehension-fostering activities in interactive learning situations. In H. Mandl, N. Stein, & T. Trabasso (Eds.), *Learning and comprehension of text.* Hillsdale, NJ: Erlbaum.

Bruner, J. S. (1973). *Beyond the information given: Studies in the psychology of knowing.* New York: Norton.

Butterfield, E. C., & Belmont, J. M. (1971). Relations of storage and retrieval strategies as short-term memory processes. *Journal of Experimental Psychology, 89,* 319–328.

Butterfield, E. C., & Belmont, J. M. (1977). Assessing and improving the executive cognitive functions of mentally retarded people. In I. Bialer & M. Sternlicht (Eds.), *Psychological issues in mental retardation.* New York: Psychological Dimensions.

Covington, M. V. (1966a). A childhood attitude inventory for problem solving. *Journal of Educational Measurement, 3,* 234.

Covington, M. V. (1966b). *Programmed instruction and the intellectually gifted: Experiments in productive thinking.* Invited paper presented at Symposium on Programmed Instruction and the Gifted, International Convention of the Council for Exceptional Children, Toronto.

Covington, M. V. (1969). A cognitive curriculum: A process-oriented approach to education. In J. Hellmuth (Ed.), *Cognitive studies* (Vol. 1). Seattle: Special Child Publications.

Covington, M. V. (1970). Issues in the assessment of productive thinking potential by means of sequential problem solving techniques. Paper presented at Symposium on Issues in the Assessment of Sequential Problem Solving. American Psychological Association, Miami.

Covington, M. V. (1983a). Anxiety, task difficulty and childhood problem solving: A self-worth interpretation. In H. M. van der Ploeg, R. Schwarzer, & C. D. Spielberger (Eds.), *Advances in test anxiety research* (Vol. 2). Hillsdale, NJ: Erlbaum.

Covington, M. V. (1983b). Motivated cognitions. In S. G. Paris, G. M. Olson, & H. W. Stevenson (Eds.), *Learning and motivation in the classroom.* Hillsdale, NJ: Erlbaum.

Covington, M. V. (1984a). Anxiety management via problem-solving instruction. In H. van der Ploeg, R. Schwarzer, & C. Spielberger (Eds.), *Advances in test anxiety research* (Vol. 3). Hillsdale, NJ: Erlbaum.

Covington, M. V. (1984b). Strategic thinking and the fear of failure. In J. Segal, S. Chipman, & R. Glaser (Eds.), *Thinking and learning skills: Relating instruction to basic research.* Hillsdale, NJ: Erlbaum.

Covington, M. V. (1984c). The motive for self-worth. In R. Ames & C. Ames (Eds.), *Research on motivation in education.* New York: Academic Press.

Covington, M. V. (1985a). Anatomy of failure-induced anxiety: The role of cognitive mediators. In R. Schwarzer (Ed.), *Self-related cognitions in anxiety and motivation.* New York: Erlbaum.

Covington, M. V. (1985b). The effects of multiple-testing opportunities on rote and conceptual learning and retention. *Human Learning, 4,* 57–72.

Covington, M. V., & Beery, R. (1976). *Self-worth and school learning.* New York: Holt, Rinehart & Winston.

Covington, M. V., & Crutchfield, R. S. (1965). Experiments in the use of programmed instruction for the facilitation of creative problem solving. *Programmed Instruction, 4,* 3–5, 10.

Covington, M. V., Crutchfield, R. S., Davies, L. B., & Olton, R. M. (1965, 1967, 1972, 1974). *The Productive Thinking Program: A course in learning to think.* Columbus, OH: Merrill.

Covington, M. V., & Fedan, N. (1978). Metastrategies in productive thinking. Unpublished manuscript, Department of Psychology, University of California, Berkeley.

Covington, M. V., & Omelich, C. L. (1979). Effort: The double-edged sword in school achievement. *Journal of Educational Psychology, 71,* 169–182.

Covington, M. V., & Omelich, C. L. (1984). Controversies or consistencies? A reply to Brown and Weiner. *Journal of Educational Psychology, 76,* 159–168.

Cox, H., & Swain, C. (1981). *Student success in school: A lesson guide for problem solving.* Sonoma County Office of Education, California.

Cox, H., Swain, C., & Hartsough, C. S. (1982). *Student success in school.* Final report: Elementary and Secondary Educational Act IV-C, Sonomo County Office of Education, California.

Cromer, W., & Wiener, M. (1966). Idiosyncratic response patterns among good and poor readers. *Journal of Consulting Psychology, 30,* 1–10.

Crutchfield, R. S. (1961). The creative process. Paper presented at the Conference on the Creative Person, University of California Alumni Center, Lake Tahoe, California.

deCharms, Richard. (1968). *Personal causation: The internal affective determinants of behavior.* New York: Academic Press.

deCharms, R. (1972). Personal causation training in the schools. *Journal of Applied Social Psychology, 2,* 95–113.

Denhiere, G. (1974). Apprentissages intentionnels à allure libre: Etude comparative d'enfants normaux et debilés mentaux. *Enfance, 3–5,* 149–174.

Dorner, D. (1978). Theoretical advances of cognitive psychology relevant to instruction. In A. M. Legold, J. W. Pellegrino, S. D. Fokkema, & R. Glaser (Eds.), *Cognitive psychology and instruction.* New York: Plenum Press.

Duncker, K. (1945). On problem solving, *Psychological Monographs, 58,* No. 270.

Feigenbaum, E. A. (1970). Information processing and memory. In D. A. Norman (Ed.), *Models of human memory.* New York: Academic Press.

Feldhusen, J. F., Treffinger, D. J., & Bahlke, S. J. (1970). Developing creative thinking: The Purdue creativity program. *Journal of Creative Behavior, 4,* 85–90.

Feldhusen, J. F., Speedie, S. M., & Treffinger, D. J. (1971). The Purdue Creative Thinking Program: Research and evaluation. *NSPI Journal, 10*(3), 5–9.

Flavell, J. H. (1973). Metacognitive aspects of problem solving. In L. B. Resnick (Ed.), *The nature of intelligence.* Hillsdale, NJ: Erlbaum.

Flavell, J. A. (1976). Metacognitive aspects of problem solving. In L. B. Resnick (Ed.), *The nature of intelligence.* Hillsdale, NJ: Erlbaum.

Forrest-Pressley, D. L., & Giles, L. A. (1983). Children's flexible use of strategies during reading. In M. Pressley & J. R. Levin (Eds.), *Cognitive strategy research: Educational applications.* New York: Springer-Verlag.

Frase, L. T. (1968). Effect of question location, pacing, and mode upon retention of prose material. *Journal of Educational Psychology, 59,* 244–249.

Frase, L. T. (1970). Boundary condition for mathemagenic behaviors. *Review of Educational Research, 40,* 337–347.

Gagne, R. M. (1977). *Essentials of learning instruction.* New York: Holt, Rinehart & Winston.

Gagne, R. M., & Briggs, L. J. (1974). *Principles of instructional design.* New York: Holt, Rinehart & Winston.

Getzels, J. W. (1976). Problem-finding and the inventiveness of solutions. *Journal of Creative Behavior, 9,* 12–18.

Getzels, J. W. (1976). Problem-finding and the inventions of solutions. *Journal of Creative Behavior, 9,* 12–18.

Gordon, W. J. (1961). *Syntectics.* New York: Harper & Brothers.

Gray, L. E. (1982). Aptitude constructs, learning processes, and achievement. Unpublished doctoral dissertation. Stanford, CA: Stanford University.

Greeno, J. G. (1973). The structure of memory and the process of solving problems. In R. L. Solso (Ed.), *Contemporary issues in cognitive psychology.* Washington, DC: Winston.

Greer, M. R., & Blank, S. S. (1977). Cognitive style, conceptual tempo and problem solving: Modification through programmed instruction. *American Educational Research Journal, 45,* 295–315.

Harari, O., & Covington, M. V. (1981). Reactions to achievement behavior from a teacher and student perspective: A developmental analysis. *American Educational Research Journal, 18,* 15–28.

Hayes-Roth, B. (1980). Human planning processes. Rand Publications Series (R-2670-ONR), Santa Monica, CA.

Hill, R. A. (1974). *Achievement competency training: A final report.* Philadelphia: Research for Better Schools, Inc.

Kahn, T. (1981). An analysis of strategic thinking using a computer-based game. Unpublished Ph.D. dissertation, University of California, Berkeley.

Kolb, D. A. (1965). Achievement motivation training for under-achieving high school boys. *Journal of Personality and Social Psychology, 2,* 783–792.

Larkin, J. H. (1977). Skilled problem solving in physics: A hierarchical planning model. Unpublished manuscript, Group in Science and Mathematics Education, University of California, Berkeley.

Lipman, M. (1976). Philosophy for children. *Metaphilosophy, 7.*

Lipman, M. (1985). Thinking skills fostered by the middle-school Philosophy for Children Program. In J. Segal, S. Chipman, & R. Glaser (Eds.), *Thinking and learning skills: Relating instruction to basic research.* Hillsdale, NJ: Erlbaum.

Lipman, M., Sharp, A. M., & Oscanyan, F. S. (1977). *Ethical inquiry: Instructional manual to accompany Lisa.* Upper Montclair, NJ: IAPC.

Locke, E. A. (1968). Toward a theory of task motivation and incentives. *Organizational Behavior and Human Performance, 3,* 157–189.

Locke, E. A., & Latham, G. P. (1984). *Goal setting: A motivational technique that works.* Englewood Cliffs, NJ: Prentice-Hall.

Luchins, A. S. (1942). Mechanization in problem-solving. *Psychological Monographs, 54* (No. 6), 384.

Luchins, A. S. (1977). *Wertheimer's seminar recorded: Problem solving and thinking.* Albany, NY: SUNY Student Faculty Evaluation.

MacKinnon, D. W. (1962). The nature and nurture of creative talent. *American Psychologist, 17,* 484–495.

Mansfield, R. S., Busse, T. V., & Krepelka, E. J. (1978). The effectiveness of creativity training. *Review of Educational Research, 48,* 517–536.

Miller, C. M. L., & Parlett, M. R. (1974). *Up to the mark: A study of the examination game.* London: Society for Research into Higher Education.

Moreno, J. M., & Hogan, J. D. (1976). The influence of race and social-class level on the training of creative thinking and problem-solving abilities. *Journal of Educational Research, 70,* 91–95.

Neimark, E., Slotnick, N. S., & Ulrich, T. (1971). The development of memorization strategies. *Developmental Psychology, 5,* 427–432.

Neves, D. M. (1978). A computer program that learns algebraic procedures by examining examples and by working problems in a text book. *Proceedings of the Second National Conference of the Canadian Society for Computational Studies of Intelligence.*

Newell, A. (1980). One final word. In D. Tuma & F. Reif (Eds.), *Problem solving and education.* Hillsdale, NJ: Erlbaum.

Newell, A., & Simon, H. A. (1972). *Human problem solving.* Englewood Cliffs, NJ: Prentice-Hall.

Nicholls, J. G. (1972). Creativity in the person who will never produce anything original or useful: The concept of creativity as a normally distributed trait. *American Psychologist 27,* 717–727.

Nicholls, J. G. (1978). The development of the concepts of effort and ability, perception of academic attainment, and the understanding that difficult tasks require more ability. *Child Development, 49,* 800–814.

Nicholls, J. G. (1980). The development of the concept of difficulty. *Merrill-Palmer Quarterly, 26,* 271–281.

Olton, R. M., & Crutchfield, R. S. (1969). Developing the skills of productive thinking. In P. Mussen, J. Langer, & M. V. Covington (Eds.), *Trends and issues in developmental psychology.* New York: Holt, Rinehart & Winston.

Olton, R. M., Wardrop, J. L., Covington, M. V., Goodwin, W. L., Crutchfield, R. S., Klausmeier, H. J., & Ronda, T. (1967). *The development of productive thinking skills in fifth-grade children.* Technical Report, Research and Development Center for Cognitive Learning. Madison, WI: The University of Wisconsin.

Paige, J. M., & Simon, H. A. (1966). Cognitive processes in solving algebra word problems. In B. Kleinmuntz (Ed.), *Problem solving: Research, method, and theory.* New York: Wiley.

Parnes, S. J. (1967). *Creative behavior guidebook.* New York: Scribner's.

Perkins, D. N. (1985). General cognitive skills: Why not? In S. Chipman, J. Segal, & R. Glaser (Eds.), *Thinking and learning skills: Current research and open questions.* Hillsdale, NJ: Erlbaum.

Peterson, P. L., & Swing, S. R. (1983). Problems in classroom implementation of cognitive strategy instruction. In M. Pressley & J. R. Levin (Eds.), *Cognitive strategy research: Educational applications.* New York: Springer-Verlag.

Polson, P. G., & Jeffries, R. (1985). Instruction in general problem-solving skills: An evaluation. In J. Segal, S. Chipman, & R. Glaser (Eds.), *Thinking and learning skills: Relating instruction to basic research.* Hillsdale, NJ: Erlbaum.

Polya, G. (1957). *How to solve it* (2nd ed.). Garden City, NJ: Doubleday.

Posner, M. I. (1967). *Human performance.* Belmont, CA: Brooks/Cole.

Postman, L. (1975). Test of the generality of the principle of encoding specificity. *Memory and Cognition, 6,* 663–672.

Resnick, L. B., & Glaser, R. (1976). Problem solving and intelligence. In L. B. Resnick (Ed.), *The nature of intelligence.* Hillsdale, NJ: Erlbaum.

Ripple, R. E., & Darcey, J. (1967). The facilitation of problem solving and verbal creativity by exposure to programmed instruction. *Psychology in the Schools, 4,* 240–245.

Ryals, K. R. (1969). An experimental study of achievement motivation training as a function of the moral maturity of trainees. Unpublished Ph.D. dissertation, Washington University, St. Louis, MO.

Scandura, J. M. (1974). Role of higher order rules in problem solving. *Journal of Experimental Psychology, 102,* 984–991.

Scandura, J. M. (1977). *Problem solving.* New York: Academic Press.

Scardamalia, M., & Bereiter, C. (1985). Fostering the development of self-regulation in children's knowledge processing. In J. Segal, S. Chrysman, & R. Glaser (Eds.), *Thinking and learning skills: Relating instruction to basic research.* Hillsdale, NJ: Erlbaum.

Schank, R. C., & Abelson, R. P. (1977). *Scripts, plans, goals, and understanding.* Hillsdale, NJ: Erlbaum.

Schnur, A. E. (1981). The assessment of academic self-management skills in adolescents. Unpublished Ph.D. dissertation, University of California, Berkeley.

Sears, P. S. (1940). Levels of aspiration in academically successful and unsuccessful children. *Journal of Abnormal and Social Psychology, 35,* 498–536.

Shea, D. J. (1969). The effects of achievement motivation training on motivational and behavior variables. Unpublished Ph.D. dissertation, Washington University.

Shively, J. E., Feldhusen, J. F., & Treffinger, D. J. (1972). Developing creativity and related attitudes. *Journal of Experimental Education, 41,* 63–69.

Simon, H. A. (1972). The heuristic compiler. In H. A. Simon & L. Siklossy (Eds.), *Representation and meaning.* Englewood Cliffs, NJ: Prentice-Hall.

Simon, H. A. (1973). The structure of ill-structured problems. *Artificial Intelligence, 4,* 181–202.

Simon, H. A. (1980). Problem solving and education. In D. T. Tuma & F. Feif (Eds.), *Problem solving and education.* Hillsdale, NJ: Erlbaum.

Steiner, R., Wiener, M., & Cromer, W. (1971). Comprehension training and identification for poor and good readers. *Journal of Educational Psychology, 62,* 506–513.

Sternberg, R. J. (1979). Stalking the IQ quark. *Psychology Today, 13,* 44–54.

Sternberg, R. J. (1985). Instrumental and componential approaches to the nature and training of intelligence. In S. Chipman, J. Segal, & R. Glaser (Eds.), *Thinking and learning skills: Current research and open questions.* Hillsdale, NJ: Erlbaum.

Sturgeon, T. (1953). *More than human.* New York: Ballantine Books.

Thomas, J. W. (1972). *Taxonomies and models of the intellect.* Philadelphia: Research for Better Schools, Inc.

Thomas, J. W. (1977). *Inventive problem solving and future studies.* Philadelphia: Research for Better Schools, Inc.

Torrance, E. P. (1962). *Guiding creative talent.* Englewood Cliffs, NJ: Prentice-Hall.

Torrance, E. P. (1972). Can we teach children to think creatively? *Journal of Creative Behavior, 6,* 114–143.

Treffinger, D. J. (1971). *Improving children's creative problem solving ability: Effects of distribution of training, teacher involvement, and teacher's divergent thinking ability on instruction* (Final Report, Office of Education, Bureau Number BR-8-A-042, Grant Number OEG-5-70-0029(509)). West Lafayette, IN: Purdue University. (ERIC Document Reproduction Service No. ED 063 268)

Treffinger, D. J., & Ripple, R. E. (1970). Programmed instruction in creative problem solving: An interpretation of recent research findings. Mimeographed. Lafayette, IN: Purdue University.

Tulving, E., & Thomson, D. M. (1973). Encoding specificity and retrieval processes in episodic memory. *Psychological Review, 80,* 352–373.

von der Ploeg, H. M., Schwarzer, R., & Spielberger, C. D. (1984). *Advances in test anxiety research* (Vol. 3). New York: Erlbaum.

Wardrop, J. L., Olton, R. M., Goodwin, W. L., Covington, M. V., Klausmeier, H. J., Crutchfield, R. S., & Teckla, R. (1969). The development of productive thinking skills in fifth-grade children. *Journal of Experimental Education, 37* (No. 4).

Wardrop, J. L., Olton, R. M., Goodwin, W. L., Covington, M. V., Klausmeier, H. J., Crutchfield, R. S., & Ronda, T. (1979). The development of productive thinking skills in fifth-grade children. *Journal of Experimental Education, 37,* 67–77.

Weiner, B., & Peter, N. (1973). A cognitive–developmental analysis of achievement and moral judgments. *Developmental Psychology, 9,* 290–309.

Wertheimer, M. (1959). *Productive thinking.* New York: Harper & Row.

Winston, P. H. (1970). Learning structual descriptions from examples. Artificial Intelligence Laboratory, A1 TR-231. Cambridge, MA: MIT.

Woodson, C. E. (1975). Motivational effects of two-stage testing. Unpublished manuscript, Institute of Human Learning, University of California, Berkeley.

Yerkes, R. M., & Dodson, J. D. (1908). The relation of strength of stimulus to rapidity of habit formation. *Journal of Comparative Neurology, 18,* 459–482.

Part VI

Conclusion

14 Reflections on reflections: what planning is and how it develops

Sarah L. Friedman, Ellin Kofsky Scholnick,
and Rodney R. Cocking

In 1981, the National Institute of Education issued a Request for Proposals for a 3-year project on the development of planning as a basic cognitive skill. The project was to have three components:

First it calls for the formulation of a theory of planning specifying what is developed and when planning occurs. The model may be extrapolated from existing models of planning and problem solving in adults and from theories of cognitive development. Second, observational and experimental work will be conducted to validate selected aspects of the theory as it applies to planning in the out-of-school environment. Third, experimental research will explore children's planning skills as these are applied to school work (academic tasks). (NIE-R-81-0008)

At the time that the call for proposals was issued, the field of cognitive psychology had drawn increasing attention to the concept of plans in order to explain text comprehension and problem solving, but very little theoretical or empirical work (with the exception of Klahr, 1978) dealt with the development of planning skills. Although the development of planning was invoked to explain changes in a large variety of behaviors, there were few explanations of the development of planning itself. This is, to a large extent, true today. None of the excellent proposals that were submitted to the National Institute of Education was funded. The Institute's priorities were shifting from basic to more applied research, and the money allocated to fund research on planning was diverted to other projects. The volume *Blueprints for Thinking* is a statement by its editors who developed the original Request for Proposals and the authors, some of whom submitted replies, that the topic of the development of planning deserves the attention of cognitive developmental psychologists.

Dr. Friedman's work was supported by the National Institute of Mental Health, Bethesda, Maryland and by the John D. and Catherine T. MacArthur Foundation Research Network Award on the Transition from Infancy to Early Childhood, Chicago, Illinois.

515

When planning this volume, the editors invited authors to write about (a) the prevalence of planning, (b) models and conceptions of planning, (c) the development of planning, and (d) social and instructional influences on planning. Although we categorized each chapter into one of those four topics, most of the chapters address several of these issues. Thus we will draw upon all of the pertinent information in summarizing how the authors dealt with each topic and in suggesting issues that still need to be resolved or addressed.

I. The prevalence of planning

A.   The prevalence of planning in the psychological literature

Until recently, the psychological analysis of planning was mainly the province of cognitive psychologists. In the cognitive psychology literature, planning has been described in three ways: (a) as a general model for executive control of strategic, problem-solving behavior (Hayes-Roth & Hayes-Roth, 1979; Miller, Galanter, & Pribram, 1960); (b) as a specific component of problem solving (e.g., Newell & Simon, 1972); and (c) as a schema for understanding goal-directed behavior (e.g., Schank & Abelson, 1977). Because many goal-directed behaviors are planned, analyses of planning began to be offered by those interested in motivation, particularly European Action Theorists such as Von Cranach, Kalbermatten, Indermuhle, and Gulger (1982), in their volume on *Goal-Directed Behavior,* and Nuttin (1984) in his book, *Motivation, Planning and Action.* Similarly, the motivation to plan is part of the Kreitlers' (1976) model of cognitive orientation.

There have been some recent books and chapters on the development of planning skills (e.g., Forbes & Greenberg, 1982; Klahr, 1978; Wellman, Fabricius, & Sophian, 1985). Those analyses interpreted plans as strategies or as schemas for social understanding. However, the chapter by Scholnick and Friedman (this volume) shows that even within the psychological literature that is not explicitly addressed to planning, there is much information that is very pertinent to the topic of planning and its development but which has been neglected by psychologists who wrote about planning. The same chapter also indicates that there is as yet no generally accepted model of the developmental components and prerequisites for planning although De Lisi and the Kreitlers (this volume) offer some analyses of what those developmental components might be.

B.   The prevalence of planning in human behavior

The planning literature reveals a controversy about the prevalence of planning in human behavior because of different definitions of planning. When planning is characterized as a set of complex cognitive skills, it is assumed that people do not engage in much planning unless confronted with dire problems and that those skills must be acquired through instruction and consolidated through extensive practice. The National Institute of Education Request for Proposals takes this approach to planning, noting that for many students, the transition to an open admissions college or junior college presents a crisis because of drastically increased demands on their capacities to plan and manage their own planning activities. Consequently, higher educational institutions throughout the nation are developing programs to assist students in developing the basic cognitive skills they need in order to function successfully at the college level. Such programs typically emphasize the reduction of impulsive reactions to school tasks and the development of planning skills (e.g., Feuerstein, Hoffman, & Miller, 1980; Whimbey & Lockhead, 1980). Covington's chapter in this volume also stresses the need to instruct productive-thinking skills. He claims that school-age children have difficulty in identifying good plans and in generating their own plans in school-related, problem-solving situations.

From the chapters in this volume by Covington, De Lisi, Dreher and Oerter, Oppenheimer, Pea and Hawkins, and Scholnick and Friedman, the reader learns about the many cognitive and executive skills that must be orchestrated in order for successful planning to occur. For example, Scholnick and Friedman identify the following components that have been mentioned in the problem-solving and planning literature: representation, choosing a goal, deciding to plan, knowing when to plan, formulating a plan, executing and monitoring plans, and learning from plans. Some of these components are subdivided further. For example, "choosing a goal" is divided into detection, selection, monitoring, and evaluation. Such a listing of the components of planning is overwhelming and implies that planning cannot possibly permeate too much of human activity, or otherwise people would, like Hamlet, be lost in thought. These componential descriptions of planning seem to support the notion that many individuals, especially children, are not good planners and must acquire planning skills through special instruction.

Not everybody agrees with this account. Instead they equate planning with goal-directed behavior and propose that planning permeates human action. Von Cranach (Von Cranach et al., 1982) suggests that everyday activities such as preparing breakfast or driving to the office are goal directed and involve "the consciousness of setting a goal, of planning and control and of purpose" (p. 6). Not every plan has to be constructed de novo, and planning is not always conscious throughout action. In that sense, Von Cranach's approach resembles Randall's (this volume) conception of planning. Randall describes planning as the flexible use of routines. He illustrates how Philippine scad fishermen choose and adjust their fishing strategies to different circumstances. The fishermen know and use ready-made fishing plans. Yet, they do not use them blindly. Their use of acquired routines is continually evaluated and modified when the fishing conditions are better or worse than expected. These routines are typical of all fishermen and there is no report of their being beyond the capability of most adults. Joseph Nuttin (1984), another European psychologist, also claimed that planning is central to human action: "The fact that humans set goals for themselves and make plans which they try to carry out is, indeed, one of the most striking characteristics of their behavior" (p. vii).

In our volume, the planning situations that the authors choose to discuss or investigate reveal their view of the prevalence of planning. The majority of contributors assume that planning occurs frequently in the lives of children and adults. The Kreitlers asked children to name the situations they thought called for planning, and they later constructed hypothetical situations that were based on what their informants told them. The situations were quite mundane. For example, "R's mother notices that R came back from school without his jacket. She wants to go and look for it. What should she ask R in order to be able to look for the jacket?" Goodnow's examples of situations in which one plans are also drawn from daily life: planning the use of time during a vacation, planning children's participation in housekeeping chores, planning one's education when trying to combine a career with marriage to an executive who is likely to make many moves. Dreher and Oerter devised an errand-running task, and Cocking and Copple studied children's conversations while they planned and executed drawings and when they engaged in play behaviors. Each of these authors implicitly or explicitly suggests that planning is a common activity and makes it clear that persons can engage in planning well before they are proficient in it. Plans do not have to be as well differentiated as the models of problem solving that have been proposed (De Lisi, this volume). Because some planners also collaborate with more expert individuals (McGillicuddy-De Lisi et al., this volume;

Vygotsky, 1978), planning is more prevalent than if it were an activity solely performed by high-powered thinkers.

The distinction between planning as a very high-level family of cognitive and executive skills that many people are not good at, and planning as a set of behaviors that people engage in most of the time is due to different emphases in the conceptualization of planning. Those who have tried to build cognitive models of planning during problem solving based them on the optimally efficient behavior of an individual who works alone. It is unrealistic to expect this rarefied type of cognition to occur frequently in the daily life of social beings. Psychologists who are interested in the development of cognition throughout the life-span or in social behavior are more likely to construct models of human cognitive and executive functioning that allow less than optimally efficient or differentiated behavior to be considered a manifestation of planning, and they are more likely to include collaborative planning and examples from common behaviors.

II. Models and conceptions of planning

Blueprints for Thinking provides information about opportunistic planning and anticipatory planning; about short-term and long-term plans, about plans that are simple or very elaborate; about the cognitive components of plans and their motivational aspects; about planning in the laboratory and in daily life; and about the cultural, social, developmental, and personality variables that produce variations in planning. There is so much variation in the format and setting for plans and influences on them that the question of definition arises.

We confront once again the issues that arose in discussing the prevalence of planning. There are two general approaches to the field of planning. Much of the interest in research on planning developed from investigations of solutions to intellectual problems. In that literature, planning is either a part of problem solving or synonymous with the whole problem-solving sequence. As a result, it is often difficult to distinguish between planning and problem solving. However, some cognitive psychologists (including contributors to this volume) have been concerned with planning as a component of goal-directed behaviors that are not confined to intellectual puzzles. The choice of definition determines answers to questions about the prevalence of planning, its development, the influences upon it, and the nature of individual variations in planning skill.

We will first describe the view that equates planning partly or fully with problem solving, and then we will discuss limitations of that view.

A. Planning as problem solving

Glass and Holyoak (1986) offer a description of problem solving which typifies current textbooks in the field:

The term *problem* is typically reserved for situations in which the goal is not achieved by an automatic process of perception or recognition. Rather problems are cases in which some obstacle initially blocks achievement of the goal. The four major steps in the process are (1) forming an initial representation of the problem [in terms of goals, objects, operations, and constraints]; (2) using problem-solving methods to plan a potential solution; (3) if necessary, reformulating the problem; and (4) executing a procedure to carry out a plan and checking the results. A plan is a procedure for a sequence of actions that implicitly makes a prediction. If I take the following actions, then I will achieve a solution. One of the most basic aspects of problem solving is that a plan is often created and then mentally tested before overt actions are taken. This step is important because many problems are unforgiving of errors. (pp. 366–367)

Because planning is, from this framework, seen as part of problem solving, it often leads to a confusion of the part with the whole. Many of the conceptions and theories cited by Scholnick and Friedman (this volume) lose the distinction between planning and problem solving, and the headings and subheadings in that chapter may also lead the reader to think that planning and problem solving are equivalent. The research by Dreher and Oerter and by Oppenheimer (both this volume) also defines planning as problem solving. Unlike most authors in this area of investigation, Goodnow and the Kreitlers (this volume) explicitly distinguish between planning and problem solving. For example, the Kreitlers argue that

planning differs from problem solving as commonly conceived, in three major respects: First, planning is a cognitive construction of one or more steps to be undertaken, whereas problem solving is a cognitive execution of plans, evaluation of their adequacy, and sometimes even a mere motor manipulation. Second, planning refers to a future action, whereas problem solving may deal with issues that are unrelated to action or the future. Third, planning is focused specifically on *how* to do or attain something (e.g., how to get to a certain location, how to manage with limited resources, etc.), whereas problem solving may deal with other issues, too, for instance, *why* something exists or acts the way it does, what are the *results* of some object or event, what is the *purpose* of a given occurrence, and so forth. (p. 208)

B. Planning as an aspect of goal-directed behavior

There are several objections to the view that plans are a part of problem solving. One objection is that researchers are not sure which part is planning. In the Scholnick and Friedman chapter (this volume), we have elaborated on this observation, showing that different psychologists refer to different sets of behavior or of skill when they discuss planning. Our own view agrees with Anderson (1983) that planning is generating a set of anticipatory strategies.

A litmus test for planning [is as follows]: The system sets forth a sequence of intended actions, notes a conflict in the sequence and reorganizes it. If it can be shown that a system reorders a preferred sequence of actions in anticipation of a goal conflict, then that system is engaged in planning. . . .
Two demands are placed on the system to permit successful planning. First is the architectural feature of being able to spin forth a goal structure without acting upon it. Second, working memory has to be able to maintain the goal structure for operation [while planning]. (Anderson, 1983, p. 167)

A second objection is that the domain of planning is broader than the solution of intellectual problems. The literature on problem solving usually describes mind twisters such as the following:

You are given four separate pieces of chain that are each three links in length. It costs two cents to open a link and three cents to close a link. All links are closed at the beginning of a problem. Your goal is to join all 12 links into a single circle at a cost of no more than 15 cents. (Silveira, 1971; cited in Anderson, 1980, p. 289)

These are puzzles that intelligent people find challenging and many of them have only one correct solution. Often cognitive psychologists have stayed away from "ill-defined" problems or problems that exist outside the laboratory or those that involve group efforts. Consequently, discussions of planning as part of problem solving have frequently dealt with intellectual problems as the context for or content of planning. In contrast, Von Cranach and his colleagues (1982) have taken a broader approach.

Our key concept is that of "action." By that we mean a type of behavior that is (in part, at least) conscious, directed toward a goal, planned and intentional or willed. (p. 16)
Goals, plans and intentions characterize the building of a house, the preparation of a dissertation, a government decree, or Caesar's Gallic Wars. On theoretical, methodological and practical grounds, we must confine ourselves to simple actions, similar to the everyday ones described above. (p. 19)

The writers of this volume use the broader definition of planning. They present to children problems taken from everyday life that can be solved at different levels of efficiency (Dreher & Oerter; Pea & Hawkins, this volume) or complexity (De Lisi, this volume). The problems are not mind benders but are mostly problems of resources or social interactions. They are the kind of problems that people frequently collaborate on (Goodnow; McGillicuddy-De Lisi et al., both this volume) or delegate responsibilities for (Dreher & Oerter, this volume). Because the problems are familiar and often embedded in daily routines, there is often much contextual support for their solution. Schank and Abelson (1977) have suggested that in the course of developing scripts for behavior in familiar situations, we amass a set of cognitive routines that enable us to overcome errors and obstacles, and that form the basis for planning. Consequently, it is easy to assemble a strategy and evaluate it in advance for its fit to the problem at hand when there is much contextual support. This difference between the content of the problems that the problem-solving literature describes and those described by some contributors to this volume has led to considerations of *aspects* and *levels* of planning absent in the problem-solving literature.

Third, *Blueprints for Thinking* contains a different approach to the components of problem solving, reflecting a developmental perspective. The traditional cognitive psychologist's view of problem solving has focused primarily on adult cognition, and there has been little interest in problem solving that falls short of the adult ideal. Many of the contributors to our volume, in contrast, are interested in cognitive development. Children's cognitive skills change considerably between infancy and late adolescence owing to improvements in knowledge representation, increasing skill in knowledge acquisition, perception, and reasoning. These changes reflect maturation of component processes, exposure to schooling, and more experience with different domains. Reflections on the nature of cognitive development lead to interesting questions regarding the appropriate model of planning. In the problem-solving literature, changes in the adequacy of planning are described as changes in expertise, growing awareness of a domain, and practice in problem solving in it. When a novice plans, all of the components of planning are present, but there are faulty, incomplete, or unintegrated representations, inadequate attempts at monitoring, etc. An alternative model is presented by De Lisi (this volume), who suggests that some components are absent in the planning of young children. Skills in reasoning and representation must develop before they can be recruited for planning.

Fourth, a broader outlook on problem solving and planning also results from the cross-cultural perspective of the contributors to this volume. The cognitive scientist's conceptualization of problem solving appears to be culture-free and free of social considerations. If there is a problem to solve, one automatically applies universal rules or strategies for planning and reaches the solution. But some of our contributors have lived in different cultures, and they are aware of the differences in cognitive performance that are due to the value that different cultures and social orders place on problem solving and planning, and the different ways of achieving a solution. Hence these authors focus their attention on aspects of planning that cognitive scientists working in the realm of problem solving have often ignored, particularly the motivation to plan in the service of problem solving and in other situations.

Those who first included the word "planning" in the titles of their publications may have had nothing in mind except drawing attention to their work on problem solving. However, the term "planning" does have connotations different from the term "problem solving" and may therefore lead to novel twists in conceptualization and research on cognitive development. "Problem solving" connotes difficult or urgent situations, in which we must quickly figure out how to restore the situation to normal, to the way we know it has been or could be, given our knowledge of similar situations. The word "planning" reminds us of dreams and aspirations (i.e., fantasies) that we strive to turn into reality. Frequently, we do not feel that same sense of urgency regarding "planning," or we feel that we have the luxury to play with different possible ways to materialize our dreams.

Some other connotations that come to mind have to do with time orientation. We plan in order to make the unknown future more familiar when we reach it; we problem-solve in order to correct something that went wrong in the past or is going wrong right now. It is true that the strategies we use for planning and for problem solving may be the same. Yet in terms of the scholarly and scientific elaboration of all the considerations that are brought to play at each turning point in the process of planning, the different connotations of "planning" and "problem solving" may make a difference.

The emphasis, the content, and the scope of our volume reflect a conceptualization of planning that overlaps with the field of problem solving but is not interchangeable with it. The conceptualization of planning that emerges from *Blueprints for Thinking* and from other publications about planning highlights the interplay of at least six factors, only some of which are addressed in the cognitive science literature on problem solving. These factors are: (a) motivation to set new goals and to implement ideas about ways to reach goals (Nuttin, 1984); (b) culturally prescribed notions as to the need to plan, the domains of life in which planfulness is valued, and the conditions under which planning is appropriate within a given domain (Randall; Goodnow, both in this volume); (c) individual differences in such areas as cognitive maturity (e.g., De Lisi; McGillicuddy-De Lisi et al.; Kreitler & Kreitler; Pea & Hawkins; Scholnick & Friedman, all this volume), beliefs about the importance of planning (Kreitler & Kreitler, this volume), and a sense of agency as opposed to helplessness (Breznitz, in press; Chapman, 1984); (d) differences due to specific domains of planning such as science or art, mathematics or biology, sculpture or playwriting (e.g., Covington; Goodnow; Rogoff et al.; all in this volume); (e) the nature of the planner, who may be an individual acting alone without consulting others (Dreher & Oerter, this volume) or working collaboratively in teams (Cocking & Copple; Goodnow; McGillicuddy-De Lisi et al.; Oppenheimer, all in this volume) which may sometimes consist of individuals at different levels of expertise (McGillicuddy-De Lisi et al., this volume); (f) the constituents of planning, when applied to a present- or future-oriented goal (reviewed by Scholnick & Friedman; De Lisi; Dreher & Oerter; Pea & Hawkins, all in this volume). The above factors are believed to interact in every planning situation and to influence the quality of the plan and its execution.

In summary, the conceptions of planning presented in *Blueprints for Thinking* both narrow and broaden the topic as construed by the cognitive psychology literature. They narrow the topic by claiming that the key element in planning is deliberate and anticipatory choice of a strategy that may be executed or held in abeyance. Those strategies as they are represented in plans may be very simple and require minimal representational skill, or they may be very complex. The conceptions of planning presented in this volume broaden the topic by arguing that planning can occur even when there is no immediate problem to be solved or when the immediate problem is not an intellectual one.

III. Children's skills in planning: research findings

A. *Do children know about plans and engage in planning?*

The chapters of *Blueprints for Thinking* show that young children have conceptions of when it is appropriate to plan, and that they plan spontaneously as well as at the experimenter's request.

When the Kreitlers interviewed 200 5- to 12-year-olds, they discovered that these children "knew" what needed to be planned, when one plans, and who usually plans, as well as the frequency and purpose of planning, the results, the feelings accompanying the planning process, the importance of planning, the difficulties one encounters in planning, and the relative ease of planning tasks.

But do children put their knowledge of the utility of planning into practice? In an even younger population, Cocking and Copple noted that children ranging in age from 41 to 58 months spontaneously planned their drawings so that others would be able to understand them. McGillicuddy-De Lisi and her colleagues described the spontaneous planning behavior of 5½- to 7½-year-olds with their siblings when the children were asked to build a tower that was taller than the shorter child and a house with a large roof that was difficult to maneuver.

In a still older population, Oppenheimer observed the problem solving of 5-, 7-, and 9-year-olds in a task that required management of apparently insufficient resources. In another study, he gave 7-, 9-, and 11-year-olds the problem of coping with conflicting goals. Like McGillicuddy-De Lisi, Oppenheimer found that the children were able to devise effective strategies for planning and problem solving.

The 5- to 12-year-olds whom the Kreitlers studied were presented with stories of real-life situations that call for anticipatory thinking. Even though the children's planning responses improved with age, at every age children came up with reasonable suggestions for handling each situation. Similarly, Oppenheimer asked 5- to 9-year-olds what a child who just moved into a neighborhood should do in order to become friends with new neighbors, and he, too, found that the children had good ideas about how to reach the goal.

When Pea and Hawkins asked 8- to 12-year-olds "to make a *plan* to do classroom chores," they found that children plan and that it is possible to evaluate their planning in the same terms that adult plans are evaluated: efficiency, improvement with revisions, and flexibility of decision making. The children's plans were much like those of adults, except that the children did not articulate as much their overall strategies for planning.

That young children can plan is in itself interesting because it contradicts some beliefs about children. Consider the following statement by the Kreitlers (p. 205):

Planning is based on dealing with the hypothetical, with what is not yet present physically. This requires hypotheticodeductive reasoning abilities which do not appear before the age of 11–12 years (Piaget & Inhelder, 1958). Thus, when analyzed from the viewpoint of adult cognition, it may seem that planning may not be expected to start developing before adolescence.

But the observation of children's behavior during play and during problem solving suggests that children do engage in planning well before adolescence. They may do so when the planning tasks are not complex, and when the tasks are drawn from domains that are so familiar to children that they can give rise to anticipatory plans. Under such circumstances, the child can represent the situation and use the representation to map strategies.

B. What develops?

Because contributors to this volume assumed that children can plan, their research and writing addressed questions about the features of children's plans and planning, the development of planning skills, and the extent to which planning is related to other cognitive and noncognitive characteristics of children.

There seem to be two implicit developmental models of planning: The expertise model assumes that all planners possess all the components of planning, but with increased experience, these components are elaborated and executed more efficiently and flexibly. The "classic" developmental model assumes that some components are absent from the repertoire of young children and must be assembled before they are recruited for planning. Many chapters in this volume do not explicitly ascribe to one viewpoint and frequently report data that could support both. The reported research indicates that there are both qualitative and quantitative age-related changes in the development of knowledge about planning and of planning skill.

Although Rogoff, Gauvain, and Gardner do not present an explicit model of planning, their findings seem to support the expertise model. They studied children's adjustment of their planning strategies (advance planning versus planning in action) according to the circumstances (mazes with long or short dead ends; task requirements for speed or accuracy) and found that 4- to 7½-year-olds do little adjustment of their strategies to different task circumstances whereas older children tend to be more flexible. Children's repertoires of strategies that could be used to solve problems expand, and the children learn to match the strategy to the situation and to decide how much planning to do.

Pea and Hawkins discuss a different kind of flexibility, but the developmental parameters they address are still within the model of increases in expertise. Children received a list of chores which they were to execute in the shortest time. The children were to practice aloud by trying out different plans until they hit upon the best one they could think of. The investigators found no age difference in the number of plans attempted. But 11- and 12-year-olds devised more efficient plans than 8- and 9-year-olds, and the older children made more high-level and metaplanning decisions. They also demonstrated more flexibility in their planning in shifting from concrete details to consideration of long-range goals. This research suggests that the growth of planning involves greater evaluation of projected schemes and more ability to shift attentional focus from long-range goals to concrete obstacles and problem constraints.

Dreher and Oerter suggest that there are quantitative and qualitative differences in the planning behaviors of their research subjects, who ranged in age from 11 to young adulthood and in education from elementary school to college. The subjects were asked to schedule errands around town while observing time constraints. The planners could take advantage of a bicycle or could delegate responsibilities to a friend, but they were not required to do so. As in the research we have just cited, planning efficiency increased. The percentage of solutions that conformed to the time constraints increased with age. Up to college age, the number of efficient solutions increased, that is, those involving use of a vehicle and delegation of responsibilities. It was rare for the youngest children to use either aid, whereas older subjects devised more plans that involved instruments and other social agents. In Dreher and Oerter's framework, the older planner used the cultural tools and social relations available. Hence their plans were more reflective of their social and societal awareness. They were operating in a different "problem space."

The Kreitlers' study of 5- to 11-year-olds showed age improvements in the knowledge of the situations that call for planning, in understanding the purpose and consequences of planning, and in many of what the Kreitlers considered to be the cognitive building blocks for planning. These include consideration of alternative strategies, chronological ordering of events, larger number of planning steps, and use of conditional reasoning.

In summary, there are expected quantitative, age-related differences in planning. Klahr (1978) described them in terms of the number of schemes available to the planner and the ability to integrate those schemes into a hierarchy of subgoals. This would imply that improved planning ability simply reflects memory capacity, representational skills, and growth in knowledge of particular domains. With development, planning also appears to become more carefully attuned to contextual situations such as shifting task demands.

But there are also qualitative differences. More mature plans seem to be evaluated by abstract considerations. There is a shift from asking whether a plan will work, to asking whether the plan is the best plan. Older individuals generate more than one plan before choosing a course of action. Planning may be done for the sake of planning (see De Lisi, this volume) or for problems that do not immediately confront the individual. The Kreitlers and De Lisi also claim that the structure of the causal framework that generates plans may change with development to include temporal, causal, conditional, and spatial constraints.

But what governs these developmental changes? There are at least three candidates: cognitive maturity, increasing familiarity with an area, and increased motivation to recruit cognitive skills in the service of planning. With the exception of the Kreitlers, most of the researchers have chosen only a single explanation, usually linking the growth of planning skills to changes in the cognitive status of children.

One way to investigate the link between cognition and planning is to define cognition in terms of individual differences in some global intellectual measure, for example, IQ. Are more intelligent people better planners? In some situations, this is the case. Covington, who studied the relationship between IQ and percentage of solutions on problems that called for convergent thinking, found a marked relationship between the two variables. However, his planning problems were actually problem-solving tasks, and thus he may simply be reporting the correlation between problem solving and IQ. McGillicuddy-De Lisi and her colleagues, who studied the planning behaviors of siblings in two collaborative planning tasks, found low but significant correlations between the child's frequency of proposing initial plans and scores on Raven's Progressive Matrices Test and on the Crichton Productive Vocabulary Test. Oppenheimer used conservation task performance as a measure of cognitive maturity. When conservation scores were correlated with the child's solitary performance on a task where there was a shortage of resources, there was a significant relation, but there was no relation between conservation performance and collaborative planning when the children could pool their talents.

When the Kreitlers correlated their subjects' performance on the Peabody IQ test with their scores on a task of planning how to handle everyday situations, the correlations of planning variables with IQ within age groups and across each planning variable were irregular. This may reflect the fact that the planning tasks seemed to call on diverse strategies and abilities. A factor analysis of the tasks did not reveal a single planning variable. IQ tests themselves often measure multiple abilities so that IQ per se and planning per se might consist of families of skills, some of which are interrelated and some of which are not. The Kreitlers argued that IQ is not a homogeneous entity, and that certain intellectual abilities might be more conducive to planning than others. For example, vocabulary scores might not be the best indicators of solutions on an errand-planning task. They also noted that there is a difference between skill and use of that skill. A child who could plan well might not be motivated to plan certain situations. Dreher and Oerter also found that less intelligent students whose schooling involved running errands similar to those in the experimental task, did better on the errand-running task than more intelligent students, again showing that intelligence is not the only factor affecting planning.

Because a global intelligence score might not be the best indicator of the child's planning skills, the Kreitlers examined the child's proclivity to use certain dimensions of experience to structure events ("meaning variables") and found some strong relations between these "meaning variables" and planning performance. When they analyzed the connection between "meaning variables" that reflect those cognitive processes considered to be essential to planning such as conditional thinking, and planning scores, the relations were indeed significant. Children who thought that events should be understood in terms of temporal connections and antecedents and consequences were also skilled planners. But this is inevitable because the "meaning" categories and the scoring of planning contents measured related psychological features. If one defines a plan as a sequence of behaviors designed to meet a goal, we would expect temporal thinking and antecedent–consequent thinking to correlate with planning. Moreover, the Kreitlers used a measure of cognition, "meaning," which combines salience and competence. That is, a person who construes events in temporal terms must first possess skill in temporal ordering and think that ordering is important. So the Kreitlers were actually measuring motivational and intellectual issues. This may be the appropriate course to take, but it suggests that planning is dependent on more than intellectual processes.

Pea and Hawkins predicted that memory and field independence would affect performance on a chore-planning task. It was assumed that more field-independent children would be more flexible in their problem representations and that a larger working memory would be conducive to developing more elaborated and efficient plans. They measured memory by the Digit Span task of the Weschsler Adult Intelligence Scale and cognitive style with the Wechsler Intelligence Scale for Children Block Design. But there were few significant relations between Digit Span or Block Design scores and planning, although the correlations were in the predicted direction. Higher scores were positively correlated with more mature planning. The authors attributed their failure to find a relationship to the homogeneity of their sample with respect to cognitive style and to other factors aside from verbal memory (such as kinesthetic and visual memory), which may affect planning.

There is, it seems, a great gap in the literature. Although the view exists that planning is a cognitive skill that relies on many components, there is so far little evidence that skill in representation, knowledge acquisition, and reasoning are sufficient to produce expert planning. In fact, possession of those skills may not be enough to harness appropriately one's cognitive repertoire to the task of planning. The Kreitlers bring to our attention the importance of metaplanning knowledge (e.g., when, why) and beliefs about the value of planning as components of the planning equation. Those components are particularly important as we move out of the laboratory to study daily planning tasks and as we use subjects other than volunteers recruited from college psychology classes. Moreover, it may be unreasonable to expect that IQ or tests of particular reasoning skills will be equally predictive of all planning domains. We may also need to take other cognitive factors into account. Thus expertise in a given area surely affects planning skill. McGillicuddy-De Lisi et al. and Covington argue that instruction and practice may greatly influence children's performance.

C. Directions of influence

The discussions of the relationship of planning and cognitive development in this volume have all focused on the claim that cognitive development influences the acquisition of planning skills and did not entertain the possibility that planning influences cognitive development. However, we would like to suggest that a cultural emphasis on the importance of planning in daily life and the consequent familial and school pressure on children to behave in a planful manner, lead to exercise and improvement of specific cognitive skills. This possibility can be tested by comparing the cognitive performance of children whose environments vary in the value placed on planning in general and on planning by children in particular. In addition, one could study the effects of interventions emphasizing planning on gains in cognitive performance. Perhaps experience in planning improves the child's ability to think sequentially or in terms of cause and effect. As a result of such practice, the child's reasoning may improve. Nelson (1983) has argued that children learn conditional and temporal relations from scripts. If the child is exposed to planning scripts for bedtime, mealtime, and bathtime routines, then the child learns not only the steps in the script, but also the notions of order and contingent relations that underlie plans. Planning requires the elaboration of representations. The components of the plan need to be spelled out, and possible barriers to reach the goal need to be considered. Therefore, exercising planning skills may induce the person to produce elaborate and complex representations, with many paths to goals, even when not planning. Because planning involves hypothetical thinking often in the service of problem solving, it may help the child to enjoy and exercise the powers of imagination even when there is no pressing problem.

In summary, the volume presents data about children's ability to plan in domains that are familiar to them. Those skills are shown to improve with age; yet we need to know more how this change in planning is related to other aspects of cognitive development or to intelligence. The role of children's planning skills in the development of other aspects of their cognition or of their intelligence is therefore a promising area for future research.

IV. Social and instructional influences on planning

Blueprints for Thinking provides us with a description of planning as a set of skills that can be and is shaped by social interactions and by instruction. It also describes planning as a process that takes into account culturally and socially prescribed standards or limitations. Whereas Piaget contended that planning emerges as the child develops a representation of problem-solving efforts, which then is used inevitably to anticipate strategies, few of the writers in this volume think that the ability to plan develops independently in the child. Rather the child learns to plan from others and gains skill by practice.

When McGillicuddy-De Lisi and her colleagues asked parents how they thought children acquire planning skills, they found that parents deem social influences to be paramount in planning, thereby supporting Vygotsky's notions about the importance of skilled partners for the cognitive development of children.

Parents seem to provide children with many opportunities to learn when and how to plan. They also insist that children practice their planning and problem-solving skills. In a study planned by Friedman and Sherman (1985), mother–toddler interactions in a homelike environment were videotaped. The mother's language and behavior were coded for instances in which the mother engaged in planning and problem solving or involved the child in such behavior. Mothers' statements that generated a situation that calls for planning or problem solving included open-ended questions such as "What would you do if you had a snake?" Mothers' questions such as "Would you like to watch TV?" were coded as decision-making questions pertaining to planning and problem solving. In addition, instances in which the mother asked the child to engage in a plan she had made were noted. Frequently mothers exemplified planning by saying "I am going to go to the bathroom for a minute" or "When we leave here, we will stop at the market first, then we will pick up your sister, and then we will all go to visit Grandma." Preliminary results show that out of a mean of 54 messages from mother to child that conveyed "cognitive contents," 21 conveyed information pertaining to planning/problem solving, and 80% of these involved the child in planning.

The fact that parents believe that children learn planning skills from their interaction with adults and the fact that parents exemplify planning and engage their children in planning do not prove that children's planning skills indeed improve due to interaction with adults or due to instruction by adults. The question is, How is that influence exerted? McGillicuddy-De Lisi and her co-workers hypothesized that parents who tend to require planning, anticipation, and reconstruction of events from their child more than other parents would have children who have developed more of the representational skills that are required for planning. Their data, however, did not support their expectations. Perhaps their results would be different if they were experimental, not correlational. There is a need for studies investigating the question of whether children who begin with the same planning skill but who are exposed to different amounts of practice and instruction vary in their acquisition and retention of planning skills.

A volume edited by Segal, Chipman, and Glaser (1985) and a review by Friedman and Cocking (1986) present evidence that instruction and practice have an impact on the development of higher-order cognitive skills such as planning. Covington provides data in his chapter showing that participation in programs that are designed to enhance problem solving improves both the problem-solving and planning skills of the learner. Improvement is notable in the solving of problems that call for convergent or divergent thinking and in the learner's ability to recognize and generate better strategic plans. Covington reports that children benefit regardless of their IQ (below 100, 100–115, and above 115) and that more intensive instruction is most conducive to cognitive gains, as we would expect. There is no evidence that there is a set of cognitive prerequisites that must be possessed before planning can be taught successfully. However, we need to know much more about how to teach planning because there are several approaches that could be taken. One could simply teach the child where planning is necessary; alternatively, one could teach specific plans or teach broader cognitive skills including the components of strategies such as determining goals, generating and evaluating alternatives, and so on. Certain situations or children might require different kinds of instruction. These are important issues to consider because it is not clear whether planning is a single skill or a family of skills and whether planning skill or skills are general in nature or situation specific. Resolution of these issues will affect instructional design and theoretical models of planning and its development.

Up to this point, we discussed social and instructional influences on the acquisition of planning. The chapters by Goodnow, Randall, Cocking and Copple, and the Kreitlers indicate that cultural and social considerations influence the decision to plan and the process of planning. Goodnow, in particular, emphasizes social constraints on planning. Clearly, beliefs about the appropriateness of planning vary considerably among the population, depending on the situation encountered.

V. Summary

Our reflections on planning lead us to several conclusions. Whether one takes the view that planning is a component of problem solving, the equivalent of problem solving, or a part of goal-directed action, planning is a central facet of human behavior. It is no accident that in the problem-solving literature it is claimed that experts devote more time to planning than to strategy execution. It is no accident that we equate higher-order animal behavior with the acquisition of planning skill. In each domain, planning is a central executive function, yet, as a topic of scientific investigation, planning has been very elusive. The reasons for this elusiveness are multiple: Planning has many components; its evocation and application are influenced by cognitive, affective, and social factors and its content differs widely across domains. Consequently, we are at the beginning of our search for information about the development of planning skills, its prerequisites, and consequences. The authors of chapters in this volume have shaped the initial understanding of planning, its development, and the role of social, motivational, and instructional influences on the acquisition and execution of plans.

References

Anderson, J. R. (1980). *Cognitive psychology and its implications.* San Francisco: W. H. Freeman.

Anderson, J. R. (1983). *The architecture of cognition.* Cambridge, MA: Harvard University Press.

Breznitz, S. (in press). The effect of hope on coping with stress. In M. Appley & R. Trumbull (Eds.), *Dynamics of stress.* New York: Plenum Press.

Chapman, M. (1984). Intentional action as a paradigm for developmental psychology: A symposium. *Human Development, 27,* 113–114.

Feuerstein, R., Hoffman, R., & Miller, R. (1980). *Instrumental enrichment: An intervention program for cognitive modifiability.* Baltimore: University Park Press.

Forbes, D. L., & Greenberg, M. T. (1982). *Children's planning strategies: New directions for child development* (Vol. 18). San Francisco: Jossey-Bass.

Friedman, S. L., & Cocking, R. R. (1986). Instructional influences on cognition and on the brain. In S. L. Friedman, K. A. Klivington, & R. W. Peterson (Eds.), *The brain, cognition and education.* New York: Academic Press.

Friedman, S. L., & Sherman, T. L. (1985). Mothers as mediators of their 2- to 4-year olds' cognitive development. Paper presented at a symposium of the Society for Research in Child Development, Toronto, Canada, April.

Glass, A. L., & Holyoak, K. J. (1986). *Cognition* (2nd ed.). New York: Random House.

Hayes-Roth, B., & Hayes-Roth, F. (1979). A cognitive model of planning. *Cognitive Science, 3,* 275–310.

Klahr, D. (1978). Goal formation, planning and learning by preschool children or "My socks are in the dryer." In R. S. Siegler (Ed.), *Children's thinking: What develops?* (pp. 181–212). Hillsdale, NJ: Erlbaum.

Kreitler, H., & Kreitler, S. (1976). *Cognitive orientation and behavior.* New York: Springer.

Miller, G. A., Galanter, E., & Pribram, K. (1960). *Plans and the structure of behavior.* New York: Holt, Rinehart & Winston.

Nelson, K. (1983). The derivation of concepts and categories from event representations. In E. K. Scholnick (Ed.), *New trends in conceptual representation: Challenges to Piaget's theory?* (pp. 129–149). Hillsdale, NJ: Erlbaum.

Newell, A., & Simon, H. (1972). *Human problem solving.* Englewood Cliffs, NJ: Prentice-Hall.

Nuttin, J. (1984). *Motivation, planning and action: A relational theory of behavior dynamics.* Hillsdale, NJ: Erlbaum.

Piaget, J., & Inhelder, B. (1958). *The growth of logical thinking from childhood to adolescence.* New York: Basic Books.

Schank, R. C., & Abelson, R. (1977). *Scripts, plans, goals and understanding.* Hillsdale, NJ: Erlbaum.

Segal, J. W., Chipman, S. F., & Glaser, R. (1985). *Thinking and learning skills: Relating instruction to basic research.* Hillsdale, NJ: Erlbaum.

Silveira, J. (1971). *Incubation: The effect of interruption, timing and length on problem solution and quality of problem processing.* Unpublished Ph.D. dissertation, University of Oregon.

Von Cranach, M., Kalbermatten, V., Indermuhle, K., & Gulger, B. (1982). *Goal-directed action.* New York: Academic Press.

Vygotsky, L. S. (1978). *Mind in society: The development of higher psychological processes.* Cambridge, MA: Harvard University Press.

Wellman, H. M., Fabricius, W. V., & Sophian, C. (1985). The early development of planning. In H. M. Wellman (Ed.), *Children's searching.* Hillsdale, NJ: Erlbaum.

Whimbey, A., & Lockhead, J. (1980). *Problem solving and comprehension: A short course in analytical reasoning.* Philadelphia: Franklin Institute Press.

Name index

Abelson, Robert P., 3, 6–7, 11, 12, 29, 43, 56, 57, 58, 63, 70, 71, 80, 110, 206, 476, 516, 522
Adams, J. A., 93
Agar, Michael, 40, 52, 55
Allen, V. L., 504
Allport, D. A., 110
Anderson, J. R., 10, 12, 21, 80, 521
Antrobus, J. S., 217
Anzai, Y., 9, 68, 69
Appel, L. F., 209
Ardener, S., 195
Argyle, M., 324
Armbruster, B. B., 480
Arnheim, R., 436
Asarnow, J., 15, 28

Bahlke, S. J., 493
Baird, J. C., 206
Baker, L., 27
Bamberger, J., 286
Bandura, A., 14
Bar-El, Z., 113, 115, 120, 176
Barclay, C. R., 26, 210
Baron, J., 485
Barron, F., 469
Bartlett, F. C., 110, 308
Baszormeny-Nagy, I., 193
Becker, J., 207
Beeghly, M., 106
Beery, R., 483, 504
Bellugi-Klima, U., 440
Belmont, J. M., 474, 499
Bereiter, C., 27, 28, 276, 278, 296, 313, 314, 503
Berger, P. L., 198
Berger, R., 198
Berger, R. M., 161
Bertenthal, B., 431
Bever, T., 431
Bhaskar, R., 485
Binet, Alfred, 501, 502
Bjorklund, D. F., 223–4
Blank, S. S., 486, 495
Boden, M. A., 80–1, 84

Boesch, E. E., 358
Borkowski, J. G., 14
Borys, S. V., 80, 89
Botkin, P. T., 206, 442–3
Bowlby, John, 8, 32, 371
Bransford, J. D., 3, 26, 92, 308, 482
Bretherton, I., 106
Breznitz, S., 425
Briggs, L. J., 475
Bronfenbrenner, U., 332, 351, 352
Brown, A. L., 3, 26, 28, 92, 97, 98, 99, 101, 206, 210, 305, 306, 480, 482
Brown, J. S., 7, 9, 11
Bruce, B. C., 7, 10
Bruner, J. S., 24, 95, 188, 304, 431, 461, 472
Bryden, M., 431
Budwig, N. A., 410
Bühler, K., 205
Bullinger, A., 304
Bullock, D., 187
Burland, S., 15
Burns, A., 181, 183, 198
Burtis, P. J., 27, 296
Busch-Rossnagel, N. A., 353
Busse, T. V., 487, 489, 493
Butler, John, 42
Butterfield, E. C., 474, 499
Byrne, R., 19, 33, 102, 126

Callan, H., 195
Cameron, R., 15
Cammarata, S., 23
Campione, J. C., 3, 26, 92, 305
Carter, D. B., 17, 18
Case, R., 80, 99, 283, 295
Cashmore, J., 181
Cazden, C., 441
Chandler, M. J., 374, 381
Chapman, M., 5, 13, 14, 369, 524
Chatillon, J. F., 304
Chi, M. T. H., 102, 350
Chipman, S. F., 532
Chomsky, Noam, 63
Christensen, P. R., 161

535

Subject index

abstraction, 29, 162, 174, 348, 461; degree of, 25–6; and goal setting, 483; in higher-level planning, 527; progression to functional, 474; types/levels of, in planning decisions, 276, 277, 284, 289, 290–3, 294, 295–6; *see also* reflexive abstraction

academic achievement, 482, 496–7; effort in, 470–1, 496

academic goals, 483

acculturation, 31

achievement planning, 470–1

achievement tests, 493, 503

action, 31, 32, 370, 371; defined, 356–7; determinants of, 369–71; distinct from planning, 208; non-reason, 357; social thought and, 385; stages in, 358; as unit of psychological analysis, 386

action alternatives, 329, 330, 331; seeking and selecting, 342–4, 350

action clusters, 287–8, 289

action rules, 43

action theory, 356–7, 386, 516, 521; determinants of action, 369–71; planning in, 323–4, 352–3; research proposals, 371–2

activity, 454

activity selection, 58, 62, 63

address term(s): marked/unmarked, 47; plans for selecting, 41–2, 65–8, 69

adjustment of plans to circumstances, 303–20

adolescence, 371, 372, 471; planning competencies during, 321–55

adult-child interactions: adult guidance in, 410–11, 421–2; *see also* parents

adultomorphism, 81

adults, 24, 26, 411; and acquisition of planfulness, 16; directing problem-solving behavior of children, 106; evoking verbalizations in children, 438; guiding children in planning, 307, 314–17; joint problem-solving with children, 313–14

advance planning, 303, 307, 308–10, 317; adjustment to circumstances, 310–11, 312; collaborative planning and, 315; *see also* preplanning

affective tone, 226, 242–3

age: and content of plans, 7; and distancing behaviors, 408–12; and plan of action, 366, 367, 368, 369, 372, 376–7, 378–80, 384, 385, 387, 388, 389; and plan types, 98; and planfulness, 106; and representational thinking in children, 440, 441; *see also* development

agency, 14, 524

agriculture, primitive, 40

algorithms, 19

alternative actions, 58, 163, 174, 275, 361, 362, 364; planning as one of, 180, 182, 185–6

alternative methods, 379, 380; plan of action, 365, 366

alternative plans, 140, 211, 387; in children's planning, 252, 253, 254, 255, 258, 264, 265, 276–7, 294; developmental aspects in, 368; goals integrated with, 322, 363, 372–80

ambiguity: and development of children's planning, 446–7; intolerance of, 120

analyses of planning, 4, 516

animals, 80–1, 82, 84

antecedents of planning, 9, 219–21, 227, 229

anthropomorphism, 81

anticipation, 95, 101, 397, 401, 402, 403; capacity for, 366; development of, 423, 438; of outcomes, 396, 428; parental encouragement of, 411

anticipatory abilities, skills, 362, 377, 379–80, 397; preschool children, 405, 408, 412–18, 422, 424

anticipatory cognitive activity, 351

anticipatory competencies, 364

anticipatory goal response, xi

anticipatory movements, 362

543